SOME
CONNECTICUT NUTMEGGERS
WHO MIGRATED

Compiled By

Grace Louise Knox and Barbara B. Ferris

HERITAGE BOOKS, INC.

Published 1988 By

HERITAGE BOOKS, INC.
1540E Pointer Ridge Place, Bowie, Maryland 20716
(301)-390-7709

ISBN 1-55613-162-3

A Complete Catalog Listing Hundreds Of Titles On
Genealogy, History, And Americana
Available Free Upon Request

TABLE OF CONTENTS

COVER ILLUSTRATION

Drawn by Steven M. Phillips
Adapted from sketch by Dorothy J. Many

INTRODUCTION

As any "Would Be Genealogist" knows, it is not long before a member of the family being searched, suddenly shows up in another state. For some reason he decided to migrate whether it was with a feeling of restlessness or curiosity, or the opportunity to find better land and purchase it or take a grant for service he has performed in the military. He has undoubtedly heard the glowing accounts of those who have moved as the idea spread like the fever. For some of the same reasons it was not unusual for him to move, not once, but several times.

In our quest for these elusive migrants, it meant searching state and town records, genealogies, biographies, histories, cemetery records, Barbour Collection of Vital Records of Connecticut, and other volumes. Some of these accounts were better than others but it soon became fascinating to connect one surname with another, to find where the family had come from, where its members had settled and died, and how a living had been made for the growing family.

After years of amassing facts, we decided to record them so others could share the excitement and perhaps find some long lost family member. As a caution, it should be remembered that these have been taken from many and varied sourcse of information and should be used as clues to further verification.

-/-/-/-/-

According to Webster's International Dictionary – "Connecticut; – Nutmeg State is defined as the nickname alluding to the accusation, jocosely made, that in that State wooden nutmegs are manufactured and palmed off on purchasers as genuine."

v

ABBEY

Abel – b 8/8/1792 in Mansfield, CT, s/o **Gideon** and **Sybil (Campbell)**; Abel d 9/12/1867 age 74 in Middlebury, VT. He m 6/24/1818 **Lydia Abbey**, b 3/25/1801 in Bradford, NH, d 3/31/1869 age 70 in Middlebury, VT, d/o **Solomon** and **Susan (Gile) Abbey**. (*Abbe-Abbey Genealogy*, p. 145)

Solomon Jr. – b 2/9/1774 in Mansfield, CT, s/o **Solomon** and **Lucy (Johnson)**; Solomon Jr. d in Hinesburg, VT, 4/24/1859 at age 85. He m 9/5/1800 **Susan Gile**, b 6/18f/1780, d/o **Noah** and **Elizabeth (Howe) Gile**. (*Abbe-Abbey Genealogy*, p. 146-7)

ABBOTT

Ebenezer – b 3/31/1792 in Hampton, CT, s/o **Benjamin Jr.** and **Lucy (Flint)**; Ebenezer d 7/15/1867 at age 73-3-15 in Braintree, VT. He m 5/9/1815 **Sally Flint**, bc1796, d 7/23/1887 at age 91-3-4. (*History of Braintree*, VT, p. 109)

Walter – b 7/10/1796, d 1/2/1879 at age 82-6 in Brookfield, VT. He m 12/2/1819 **Sarah Amidon**, bc1801, d 3/31/1873 at age 72-1. (*Brookfield V. Rec. - 1850 Orange Co. Census-Brookfield*)

Urial – b 1/17/1780, s/o **Henry** and **Sarah (Greenslit)**; Urial d 7/23/1857 at age77 in Williamstown, VT. He m (1) **Polly ----**, d 4/14/1806 at age 24 in E. Brookfield, VT, and m (2) **Pamelia ----**, d 1/19/1854 at age 64 in Williamstown, VT. (*Cemetery Records of Williamstown, VT*)

Ensign William – b 10/7/1745 in Pomfret, CT, s/o **Caleb** and **Elizabeth**; Ensign William d 7/25/1832 at age 87 in Clinton, NY. He m (1) **Mary Coy**, and m (2) **Esther Green** of Willington, CT, b 12/31/1753 in Killingly, CT, d 12/23/1839 in Clinton, NY, at age 86. (*Clinton Memorial-Kirtland Ave. Cemetery*, p. 11)

ABELL

Isaiah – b 7/24/1738 in Norwich, CT, s/o **Benjamin** and **Mary (Hazen)**; Isaiah d 8/10/1813 age 75 in Orwell, VT, buried in Mt. View Cemetery. He m 11/5/1762 **Rhoda Pettis**, d 3/13/1813 in Orwell, VT, d/o **Joshua** and **Elizabeth (Crocker) Pettis**. (*Abell Fam.*, p. 84, 110, 120 - *Gazeteer of Addison Co., VT*, p. 187)

Thomas – b 10/9/1749 in Norwich, CT, s/o **Simon** and **Parnel**; Thomas d 10/10/1814 in Fredonia, NY. He m1771 **Eunice Griswold** b 4/20/1752 in Norwich, CT, d 2/21/1841 in Fredonia, NY, d/o **Ebenezer** and **Hannah (Merrill) Griswold**. (*Abell Fam.*, p. 103, 134-7 - *Soldiers of Am. Rev., Chautauqua Co., NY*)

1

William - b 8/14/1778 in Norwich, CT, s/o **Thomas** and **Zerviah (Hyde)**. He m **Mehitable Meach**, d 6/8/1852 in Columbus, NY. (*Abell Fam.*, p. 80. 100 - *1850 Census Chanango Co., NY*)

ADAMS

A b n e r - b 11/5/1735 in Windham Co., CT; Abner d 8/5/1825 at age 89 in Hartwick, NY. He m **Abigail Hubbard**, d 12/10/1816 at age 84 in Hartwick, NY. (*DAR Magazine* v. 107, p. 417 - *DAR Patriot Index*, p. 3.)

Abraham - b 3/2/1769, s/o **Samuel** and **Dorcas**; Abraham m **Lovica** ---- b in NY. (In Benson, VT, in *1850 Rutland Co. Census*)

Allen - b 11/1/1762 in Hartford, CT, d 3/7/1854 age 91 in Ferrisburgh, VT. Allen m 5/11/1785 **Alice Adams**, d 4/11/1820 in Ferrisburgh, VT. (*Genealogy of Henry Adams*, p. 598-9 - *Gazeteer Addison, VT*, p. 108)

Anson - b 4/20/1788 in Canterbury, CT, s/o **Roswell** and **Eunice (Davenport)**; Anson d 1/17/1864 age 76 in Northfield, VT. He m 12/5/1811 **Susan Gold**, d 1/14/1877 age 86 in Northfield, VT, d/o **Joseph** and **Patience (Goodnuff)**. (*Genealogical Hist. of Henry Adams*, p. 128-9, 172 and *1850 Census Washington Co., VT*)

Arunah - b 3/15/1768 in Canterbury, CT, s/o **Samuel** and **Phebe (Pellet)**; Arunah d 4/13/1850 age 82 in Royalton, VT. Arunah m 2/7/1793 **Patience Rix**, b 8/7/1767 in Preston, CT,d 9/14/1857 age 90 in Royalton, VT, d/o **Thomas** and **Eunice**. (*Genealogical Hist. of Henry Adams*, p. 543, 603 and *Hist. of Royalton, VT*, p. 249)

David - b 8/24/1772 in Canterbury, CT, s/o **Lt. Samuel** and **Phebe (Pellet)**; David d 11/12/1854 age 82-2-12. David m 11/9/1796 (or 11/9/1797) **Clarissa Pendleton**, b in RI, d 4/1854 age 74 in Royalton, VT. (*Genealogical Hist. of Henry Adams*, p. 543, 603-4 and *Hist. of Royalton*, p. 651-2)

Elijah - b 12/17/1783 in Canterbury, CT, s/o **Samuel** and **Betty (Littlefield)**; Elijah d 1/17/1857 in Malone, NY. He m **Eunice Kendall**, bc1786 prob. in NH, d 6/1857 in Malone, NY. (*1850 Orange Co. Census of Williamstown, VT*)

Elisha - b 9/28/1732 in Colchester, CT, s/o **Thomas**; Elisha d 5/8/1823 age 91 in Pittsford, VT. He m **Sarah Taylor**, bc1740, d 3/14/1814 age 74 in Pittsford, VT. (*Hist. of Pittsford, VT*, p. 203)

J o h n   C a l v i n - b 5/1/1793 in New London, CT; John Calvin d 7/25/1847 in Franklin Mills, OH. John Calvin m 1/1/1817 in Chatham, NY, **Hepzibah Chadwick**, b 3/18/1787 in Lyme, CT, d 1/14/1853 in Franklin Mills, OH. (*Hist. of the Original Town of Concord, NY*, p. 892-3)

Richard Saxton - b 3/16/1734 in Simsbury, CT, s/o of **Daniel**. Richard Saxton m 12/23/1762 at Simsbury, CT, **Lucy Matson**. Went to Pittsford, VT, then moved to Bastard, Canada. (*History of Pittsford, VT*, p. 63)

Roswell - b 6/13/1753 in Canterbury, CT, s/o **Elihu** and **Jerusha (Adams)**. Roswell m 3/6/1753 in Canterbury, CT, **Eunice Davenport**. Resided in Canterbury, CT, and E. Roxbury, VT. (*Gen. Hist. of Henry Adams*, p. 128-9)

Rufus - b 2/17/1788 in Hampton, CT, s/o **Lt. Thomas** and **Mary**; Rufus d 6/24/1859 age 91. He m (1) 3/23/1815 **Nancy Morgan**, d

2

5/1/1839 age 50 in Randolph, VT, and m (2) 11/17/1840 **Lydia Bigelow**, bc1795 (Randolph Center Cem. gravestone). (*Gen. Hist. of Henry Adams*, p. 133, 179 and *1850 Census of Orange Co, VT*)

Samuel - b 9/4/1736 in Suffield, CT, s/o **Abraham** and **Anne**; Samuel d 3/24/1811 in W. Haven, VT. He m (1) 11/19/1767 in Suffield, CT, **Dorcas Frost**, d 1/26/1778, and m (2) 2/18/1779 at Suffield, CT, **Elizabeth Purchase**, d 9/27/1820 in W. Haven, VT. (*Des. of Robert Adams*, p. 46 and *Rutland Co. Gazeteer*, p. 256)

Simeon - b 1/8/1776 in Suffield, CT, s/o Capt. **Simeon** and **Susanna (Underwood)**; Simeon d 12/13/1846 in Marlboro, VT. He m 8/1797 **Lucy Mather**, b 2/26/1780, d 3/31/1860, d/o Maj. **Timothy**. (*Des. of Robert Adams*, p. 47-8, 100.)

Thomas - b 11/8/1770, s/o **Elisha**; Thomas d 1/20/1852 age 82 in Pittsford, VT. He m **Polly Cole**, d 1/25/1853 age 77 in Pittsford, VT. (Gravestone Inscription at Pittsford, VT)

AGARD

Joseph - b 8/17/1746 in Litchfield, CT, s/o **John** and **Mary (Mason)**; Joseph d 8/25/1836 in Smithville Flats, NY. He m **Tabitha Leach** of Wenham, MA, bc1749, d1818, d/o **Richard Jr.** and **Rebecca (Bigelow)**. (*Agards in America*, p. 19-24 - *DAR Patriot Index*, p. 6 - French's *Historical Gazeteer*, p. 230)

Joshua - b 4/16/1789 in Stafford, CT, s/o **Joshua** and **Ruth (Needham)**; Joshua d 9/18/1860 in Concord, NY. He m (1) 3/1814 **Lucy Sibley**, b 6/18/1792, d 6/9/1831, and m (2) 11/15/1831 Mrs. **Electa Canfield**. (*Hist. of Original Town of Concord, NY*, p. 273)

ALEXANDER

Henry Augustus - b 3/28/1791 in Voluntown, CT, s/o **James** and **Mary (Babcock)**; Henry Augustus dc1856 in Winfield, NY. He m 1/23/1817 at Voluntown, CT, **Elizabeth Gallup**, d1842, d/o **Nathaniel**. (*Hist. of Herkimer Co., NY*, by Hardin p. 467-8)

ALGER

John - b 3/19/1739, s/o **John** and 2nd w **Mary (Roger)** at Lyme, CT; John (the younger) d 8/13/1829 in Conesus, Livingston Co., NY. He m (1) 12/25/1760 at Lyme, CT, **Mary Wade**, d/o **George Jr.** and **Hannah**, and m (2) 4/15/1782 at Strafford, VT, **Elizabeth (Pennock) Baldwin**. *Hartford Times* Query.

Col. **Silas** - b 8/13/1742 in Lyme, CT, s/o **John** and 2nd w **Mary - - - -**; Col. Silas d 11/26/1811 age 40 in Strafford, VT. He m 12/11/1766 in Kent, CT, **Elizabeth Brown**, d 5/11/1822, age 48 in Strafford, VT (gravestone). (Kibling Cemetery Inscriptions, Strafford, VT)

ALLEN

Abel - b 8/14/1733 in Windsor, CT, d 8/18/1808 in Surry, NY. He m1756 **Elizabeth Chapin**, b1736 in CT, d 11/13/1820 in Surry, NH, d/o **Ebenezer** and **Elizabeth (Pease)**. (*DAR Patriot Index*, p. 9 - *Town of Gilsum, NH*, p. 254-5)

Ethan - b 1/10/1737/8 in Litchfield, CT, s/o **Joseph**; Ethan d 2/12/1789 in VT (possibly in Colchester). He m (1) 6/23/1762

Mary Bronson of Woodbury, CT, and m (2) Mrs. **Frances (Brush)**
Buchanan. (*Des. of Samuel Allen*, p. 49)
Heber - b 10/4/1743 in Woodbury, CT (or Cornwall, CT), d 4/10/1782
in Putney, VT. He m 3/17/1768 in Salisbury, CT, **Sarah Owen**.
(*DAR Patriot Index*, p. 9 - The *Nutmegger* 6/1981 p. 74)
Heman - b 10/15/1740 in Cornwall, CT, s/o **Joseph** and **Mary**
(Baker); Heman d 4/14/1778 in Goshen, CT. He m 2/18/1773 at
Salisbury, CT, **Abigail Beebe**, who m (2) 4/1780 **Solomon**
Wadhams. (*Descendants of Samuel Allen*, p. 50 - *History of Col-
chester*, VT, p. 22-30)
Ira - b 4/12/1751 in Cornwall, CT, s/o **Joseph** and **Mary**; Ira d
1/7/1814 in Philadelphia, PA. He m **Jerusha Hayden Enos**, b
2/6/1764, d 5/16/1838, d/o Gen. **Roger** of Colchester, VT. (*Des. of*
Samuel Allen, p. 54-5 - also *History of Colchester, VT*, p. 22-30)
Jedediah Sabin - b 8/21/1795 in Killingly, CT, s/o **Nathan**; Jedediah
Sabin d 4/15/1876 age 81-7-25 in E. Brookfield, VT. He m **Celia**
---- bc1798 in NH, d 3/3/1876 (according to gravestone at E.
Brookfield, VT). (*1850 Orange Co., VT Census-Brookfield* - grave-
stones)
Dr. Silas - b 2/9/1754 in Canterbury, CT, s/o **Barnabus** and **Elizabeth**
(Fuller); Dr. Silas d 9/7/1825 at Royalton, VT. He m 5/16/1776
Mary Cleveland, b 2/12/1754, d 10/7/1843 in Royalton, VT, d/o
Samuel and **Ruth (Darbe)**. (*Hist. of Royalton, VT*, v. 2 p. 655)
Sluman - b 10/24/1760 in Norwich, CT, s/o **Isaac** and **Sarah (French)**;
Sluman d 4/15/1834 age 73 in Chelsea, VT. He m **Hannah ----**,
bc1765, d 6/3/1858 age 92-11-21. (Chelsea, VT, Old Cemetery in-
scriptions)

ALVORD
Phineas - b 8/7/1763 in Middletown, CT, s/o **Phineas** and **Phebe**
(Hedges); Phineas d 5/14/1836 in Rochester, VT. He m (1) ----,
and m (2) **Nancy Wood**, bc1769, d 10/8/1852 in Rochester, VT, d/o
----, a sea captain from CT. (*Alvord Gen.*, p. 143, 256-7 - *1850*
Census of Windsor Co., VT)

AMBLER
Rev. **Silas** - b 3/12/1798 in Danbury, CT, d 11/22/1857 in Stanford,
NY. He m 8/29/1822 **Eunice Olmstead**, b 10/28/1800 in Wilton,
CT, d 10/3/1892 in Stanford, NY. (*Com. Biog. Rec. Dutchess Co.,*
NY, p. 399)

AMES
Abner - b 12/16/1766 in Mansfield, CT, s/o **Joseph** and **Elizabeth**
(Parker); Abner d 9/17/1833 in Shoreham, VT. He m (1) **Mary**
Johnson, b in CT, d in VT, and m (2) 11/8/1804 in Orwell, VT,
Chloe Gillett. (*Ames Family of Bruton, Somerset, England*, p. 59-66)
Joseph - b 6/10/1738 in Mansfield, CT, dc1831 in S. Shaftsbury, VT.
Joseph m 5/11/1761 in Mansfield, CT, **Elizabeth Parker** of Brim-
field, MA. (*Ames Fam. of Bruton, Somerset, England*, p. 57)

ANDERSON

Lemuel - b 8/5/1764 in Mansfield, CT, s/o **George** and **Abigail (Brown)**; Lemuel d 2/16/1845 age 80 in Otego, NY. He m 2/1/1787 in Mansfield, CT, **Rachel Hall**, d/o **Gershom**. (*DAR Patriot Index*, p. 14 - *Biog. Rec. of Otsego Co., NY*, p. 273-4)

ANDREWS

Rev. **Elisha** - b 2/18/1783 in Southington, CT, s/o **Jonathan** and **Ruth (Deming)**; Rev. Elisha d 1/12/1852 in Armada, MI. He m 9/13/1808 **Betsey Lathrop**, b 7/28/1788 in W. Springfield, MA, d 6/5/1859 in Armada, MI, d/o **Seth** and **Anne (Abbott)**. (*Andrews Memorial*, p. 271-2 - d *VT History Magazine* v. 5)

John - b 10/15/1758 in Glastonbury, CT, d 10/15/1841 in Salem, PA. John m (1) **Lucy Eddy**, and m (2) **Sarah Fox Brown**. (*Rev. Soldiers Buried in Wayne Co., PA*)

Laban - b 4/25/1728 in Wallingford, CT, s/o **Samuel** and **Abigail (Tyler)**; Laban d 1/24/1813 age 85. He m1758 **Prudence Stanley**. (*DAR Patriot Index*, p. 16 - *History of Greene Co., NY*, p. 448 and *New Haven, CT, Families*, p. 50)

Moses - b 4/7/1755 in New Britain, CT, d 7/20/1848 age 93 in Montague, MA. Moses m1779 **Elizabeth Clark** who d 12/8/1840, age 82. (*DAR Patriot Index*, p. 16 and *American Monthly* v. 40)

Samuel - b 1/21/1800 in Berlin, CT, d 6/16/1890 in W. Bloomfield, Oakland Co., MI. Samuel m (1) **Annie Marskley**, dc1833, and m (2) 1834 **Susan P. Cullen**. (Reference not given)

ANTISEL

Silas - b 9/13/1749 in Norwich, CT, s/o **Lawrence** and **Mary (Armstrong)**; Silas d 9/3/1817 in Madison, OH. He m 5/4/1775 in Willington, CT, **Maria Bethiah Curtis**, bc1751 in Marblehead, MA, d 9/18/1824 in Madison, OH. (*Rev. Soldiers Buried in Lake Co., OH*, p. 8 - *Gen of Des. of Lawrence and Mary Antisell*, p. 28-30)

ARCHER

Obadiah - b1760 in Hebron, CT, d 4/8/1852 in Marion, Wayne Co., NY. Obadiah m **Elizabeth Fitch**, d 4/4/1852 (4 months before him). (*American Monthly* v. 36 p. 537)

ARMSTRONG

Jonathan - b 2/10/1743 in Norwich, CT, s/o **William** and **Mary (Pitcher)**; Jonathan d 12/27/1826 in Dorset, VT. He m **Abigail Haynes**. (*Bennington Co., VT*, v. 1, p. 187 - *DAR Patriot Index*)

ARNOLD

Jonathan - b 10/7/1758 in Guilford, CT, d in Dyberry Twp., Wayne Co., PA, (or Granville, NY ?). Jonathan m **Mary P. Lester**. (*Rev. Soldiers Buried in Wayne Co., PA* - *Hist. of Wayne Co.*, p. 298)

ASPINWALL

Asa - b 7/10/1739 in Woodstock, CT, s/o **Nathaniel** and **Mary (Derby)**; Asa d 6/14/1789 in W. Fairlee, VT. He m (1) **Anna Adams**, b1738 (or b1745) in Canterbury, CT, d 7/21/1768, and m (2)

1/22/1773 **Hannah Bennett** of Hampton, CT, b 9/11/1746, d
6/21/1793. (Bowen's *Woodstock Families*, p. 267-8)

ATWATER

Amos – b 1/3/1787 in New Haven, CT, s/o **Joshua** and **Betsey**
(Goodyear); Amos d 5/7/1849 in Beardstown, IL. He m (1)
2/10/1813 **Mary B. Woodside**, b 7/22/1791, d 2/9/1833, and m (2)
2/12/1839 **Abigail Hull**. (*Atwater Gen.*, p. 74, 116 – *Anc. Families
of New Haven*, p. 80 – *Chautauqua Co., NY*, p. 593)

Caleb – b 12/28/1759 in New Haven, CT, s/o **Samuel** and **Sarah**
(Bell); Caleb d 9/20/1817 in Genoa, NY. He m **Thankful Cotter**, b
11/3/1761, d 12/29/1820, d/o **John** and **Thankful (Goodyear)**.
(*Atwater Gen.*, p. 66, 101-2 – *History of Cayuga Co., NY*, p. 493)

Joshua – b 5/13/1753 in New Haven, CT, s/o **David** and **Elizabeth**
(Bassett); Joshua d 7/31/1814 in Homer, NY. He m (1) 1/20/1778
in New Haven, CT, **Betsey Goodyear**, b 1/2/1756, d 12/22/1808,
d/o **Asa** and **Mehitable (Sackett)**, and m (2) **Esther Hull**, d
10/17/1849 age 76. (*Atwater Gen.*, p. 48, 37 – *Chautaugua Co. NY*,
p. 593 – *Ancient New Haven Families*, p. 80)

AUGUR

Peter Jr. – b 11/27/1876 in Branford, CT, s/o **Peter** and **Chlorama**
(Blakeslee); Peter Jr. d 3/10/1864 in Hartwick, NY. He m (1) **Ruth**
Rogers, b 11/31/1788, d 8/1808, d/o **Ebenezer** and **Ruth**, and m (2)
Mattie Lattin, bc1785, d 8/29/1860 in Hartwick, NY. (*Auger Fam.*,
p. 49-50, 74-5, 125-6 – *Biog. Rec. of Otsego Co.*, p. 626)

AUSTIN

Abial – b 10/15/1774 in Salisbury, CT, s/o Col. **Seth** and **Hannah**
(Smith); Abial d 9/13/1862 at Bethel, VT. He m 1/22/1804 in
Bethel, VT, **Anna Stone**, d 3/25/1873, Bethel, VT, d/o **David** and
Anny (Moffit). (*Gen. of Des. of Richard Austin*, p. 88, 175 – *1850
Census of Windsor Co., VT*)

Hon. **Apollas** – b 3/31/1762 in Suffield, CT, s/o **Caleb** and **Phebe**
(King); Hon. Apollas d 12/20/1842 age 80 in Orwell, VT. He m
4/18/1793 **Sarah Leonard**, b 1/20/1776 in Shaftsbury, VT, d
4/23/1861 in Orwell, VT, d/o **David** and **Hannah (Whipple)**. (*Gen
of Des. of Richard Austin*, p. 69-70 – *Hist. of Orwell, VT*, p. 30)

Daniel – b 4/28/1720 in Suffield, CT, s/o **Nathaniel** and **Abigail**
(Hovey); Daniel d 6/24/1804 in Wilmington, VT. He m 12/21/1749
in Suffield, CT, **Abigail Phelps**, b 11/22/1731, d 1/1816, d/o Capt.
Timothy and **Abigail (Merrick)**. (*Gen. and Des. of Richard Austin*,
p. 37)

David – b 7/5/1734 in Mansfield, CT, s/o **David** and **Mary (Harmon)**;
David d 7/7/1814 in Springfield, NY. He m 11/25/1760 in
Mansfield, CT, **Mary Harmon**, b 8/10/1737 in Suffield, CT, d
11/22/1810 in Waterbury, VT. (*Gen. and Des. of Richard Austin*, p.
80)

Eli – b 9/28/1778 in Salisbury, CT, s/o **Seth** and **Hannah (Smith)**; Eli
d 7/11/1857 age 78 in Tunbridge, VT (gravestone). He m 1/2/1803
Tunbridge, VT, **Sally Allen**, bc1781, CT, d 8/31/1871, age 91

(gravestone). (*Gen. and Des. of Richard Austin*, p. 176 and *1850 Census of Orange Co., VT*, for Tunbridge)

Rev. Linus - b 9/15/1773 in Suffield, CT, s/o **Daniel** and **Abigail (Phelps)**; Rev. Linus d1853. He m (1) 11/20/1803 in Wilmington, VT, **Mary (Polly) Hudson**, bc1779, d 7/2/1805 age 25-11, in Wilmington, VT and m (2) 12/5/1805 in Wilmington, VT, **Temperance Parmele**, bc1777, dc1848. (*Gen. and Des. of Richard Austin*, p. 98)

Samuel, b 2/7/1773 in Salisbury, CT, s/o **Seth** and **Hannah (Smith)**; Samuel d 3/17/1859 age 86 in Tunbridge, VT. He m (1) 8/1/1793, in Tunbridge, VT, **Chloe Cowdrey**, b 2/15/1776, d 1/19/1800, d/o **John** and **Ruth** and m (2) 1/23/1820 in Tunbridge, VT, **Electa Durkee**, d/o **Andrew**. (*Gen. and Des. of Richard Austin*, p. 175 – *1850 Census of Orange Co., VT*, for Tunbridge.)

Col. Seth - b 9/13/1748 in Salisbury, CT, s/o **Thomas** and **Hannah (Hale)**; Col. Seth d 7/23/1819 in Tunbridge, VT. He m 4/26/1770 in Salisbury, CT, **Hannah Smith**, b 6/19/1753 in Salisbury, CT, d 2/19/1848 age 94-9 in Tunbridge, VT, (Buzzell Cemetery). (*Gen. of Des. of Richard Austin*, p. 88-9 – *On the Beginning of Tunbridge, VT* (small book)

AVERY

Asahel - b 10/15/1793 in Tolland, CT, s/o **Asahel** and **Clarissa (Hartshorn)**; Asahel d 4/17/1872 age 78 in Morris, NY. He m 11/15/1815 in Great Bend, PA, **Nabby Buck** b 10/11/1793 Great Bend, PA, d 12/9/1832, d/o Rev. **Daniel** and **Olive (Stevens)**. (*Groton Avery Clan*, p. 527, 848, 1189 – *Biog. Rec. of Otsego Co., NY*, p. 664)

Asahel - b 5/6/1765 in Coventry, CT, s/o **Amos**; Asahel d 2/1813 in Great Bend, PA. He m 12/17/1789 in Tolland, CT, **Clarissa Hartshorn**, b 7/6/1765 in Norwich, CT, d 6/6/1848 in Montrose, PA, d/o **Col. Ebenezer** and **Abigail (Barstow)**. (*Groton Avery Clan*, p. 527, 848 – *Biog Rec. of Otsego Co.*, p. 664)

Benjamin - b 3/4/1758 in Preston, CT, s/o **Benjamin** and **Elizabeth ----**; Benjamin (the younger) d 5/4/1843 in Lyon, NY. He m (1) **Anna Foote**, b 10/15/1757, d/o **Samuel** and **Mary (Lyon)** and m (2) **Lucy Dickinson**. (*Groton Avery Clan*, p. 298, 455 – *DAR Patriot Index*, p. 23 v. 36 – *American Monthly*, p. 537)

Christopher - b 10/15/1773 (possibly in Groton, CT), s/o **Andrew**; Christopher d 3/30/1843 in Corinth, VT. He m (1) 12/15/1794 in Meriden, CT, **Sally Jones**, b 1/20/1776, d 7/15/1819 in Corinth, VT and m (2) 4/4/1820 at Corinth, VT, **Sophia Lund**, b 8/15/1790, d 11/1872, d/o **Noah** and **Betsey (Hale)**. (*Groton Avery Clan*, v. 1 p. 543 – *Hist. of Corinth, VT*, p. 307-310 and 339-40 – *Gazeteer of Orange Co., VT*, p. 251)

David - b 5/8/1779 in Groton, CT, s/o **Benjamin**; David d 11/27/1866 in Scipio (now Venia), NY. He m 2/25/1808 in Groton, CT, **Fanny Avery**, b 4/22/1788 in Groton, CT, d 3/30/1869, d/o **Ebenezer** and **Hannah (Morgan)**. (*Groton Avery Clan*, p. 299-300 – *Hist. of Cayuga, NY*, p. 433)

Ebenezer P. - b 5/21/1765 in Groton, CT, d 9/10/1840 in Pompey, NY. Ebenezer m1787 **Lovina Barnes**, b 3/10/1767 in Great Barrington, MA, d 3/10/1767 in Pompey, NY, d/o **Phineas** and **Phebe**

7

(Bement). (*Groton Avery Clan*, p. 360, 601-4 – *DAR Patriot Index* p. 23 – *Reunion of Old Town of Pompey, NY*, p. 254-5)

George Dolbeare – b 8/19/1763 in Groton, CT, s/o **William** and **Mary**; George Dolbeare d 4/16/1860 in Oxford, NY. He m (1) 4/1/1790 in New London, CT, **Mary ----**, b 12/3/1752, d 1/28/1799, wid/o Capt. **Lodowick Champlain,** d/o **Guy** and **Elizabeth (Harris) Richards,** and m (2) 6/26/1800 in Newport, RI, **Mary Hurlburt,** b 3/2/1772. (*Groton Avery Clan*, p. 353)

Nathan – b 3/31/1759 in Groton, CT, d 1/16/1841 in Newbury, VT, at over 81 years of age. He m 2/20/1782 in Hebron, CT, **Anna Ayers,** b 3/31/1758, d 5/22/1840. (*Groton Avery Clan*, p. 270-1 – *DAR Patriot Index*, p. 23 – *American Monthly*, v. 36 p. 537 – *Hist. of Newbury, VT*, p. 431)

Capt. Samuel – b 11/7/1742 in Pomfret, CT, s/o Rev. **Ephraim** and **Deborah (Lathrop);** Capt. Samuel d 1/30/1836 in Horton, Nova Scotia. He m 9/27/1784 in Halifax, Nova Scotia, Mrs. **Mary Roah (Fillis),** b 3/27/1760, d 8/25/1848 age 88 in Horton, Nova Scotia, wid/o **John Ackencloss,** d/o **John Fillis.** (*Kings Co., Nova Scotia*, p. 547-9)

Simeon – b 9/17/1759 in Norwich, CT, s/o **Charles** and **Abigail (Post);** Simeon d 1/16/1803 in Rutland Co., VT. He m **Sarah Bump,** d/o **Levi** and **Patience** of Norwich, CT. (*Groton Avery Clan*, p. 201, 317-18 – *Hist. of Rutland Co., VT*, p. 480-1)

BABCOCK

Elias – b 2/24/1765 in Stonington, CT, s/o **Elijah** and Sarah **(Brown);** Elias d1836 in Poultney, VT. He m **Hannah Barber.** (*Babcock Gen.*, p. 182-3 – *Hist. of Rutland Co., VT*, p. 773)

Frederick – b 6/16/1782 in Stonington, CT, d 8/17/1861 in Clarkson Twp., Monroe Co., NY. He m **Fanny Gallup,** b 3/24/1780 in Stonington, CT, d 12/28/1862. (Tombstone Record – Clarkson Twp., NY)

Jonathan – b 12/8/1762 in Stonington, CT, d 5/16/1842 age 79-5, buried in Bemis Pt. Cem., Ellery, NY. Jonathan m **Rebecca Cutler,** d 7/5/1841 age 78 in Ellery, NY. (*DAR Patriot Index*, p. 25 – *Soldiers of the Am. Rev. in Chautauqua Co., NY*, p. 23-4)

BACON

Abner – b 8/15/1768 in Brooklyn, CT, s/o **Nehemiah** and **Ruth (Adams);** Abner d 5/16/1864 age 95-9 in Putney, VT. He m 9/6/1795 in Putney, VT, **Katherine Read,** b 3/6/1773 in Dunstable, MA, d 9/26/1861 age 88-6 in Putney, VT. (*Gen. of Woodstock Families* by Bowen v. 2 p. 292-3 – *Gazetteer of Windham Co., VT*, p. 279)

Henry – b 2/16/1802 in Litchfield, CT, s/o **Caleb** and **Caty (Peck);** Henry d 10/25/1881 age 74 in Camden, NY. He m (1) 5/20/1829 in New Haven, CT, **Sally M. Edwards,** d 8/1832, and m (2) 1/29/1834 **Betsey Jones** of New Haven, CT. (*Pioneer History of Camden, Oneida Co., NY*, p. 355-6)

John – bc1781, d 11/30/1863 age 82-5 in Strafford, VT, s/o **Levi** and **Esther.** He m **Betsey West,** d 9/6/1871 (or 9/6/1874) age 88 in

Strafford, VT. (Gravestones in Clough Cem. - *Gazetteer of Orange Co., VT*, p. 409)

Nehemiah - b 9/6/1736 in Pomfret, CT, s/o **Henry** and **Sarah (Holland)**; Nehemiah d 11/6/1832 age 96 in Gustavus, OH. He m 12/28/1756 in Brooklyn, CT, **Ruth Adams**, bc1736, d 6/28/1825 in Palmyra, OH, d/o **Joseph** and **Mary (Davenport)**. (Reference not given)

BACKUS

Elijah - b 3/14/1726/7 in New London Co., CT, s/o **Samuel**; Elijah d in New London, CT, but at least one son, Elijah, went to OH. Elijah m (1) 1/8/1753, **Lucy Griswold**, b 7/6/1726, d 12/16/1795 age 69, and m (2) **Margaret Grant**, wid/o **Jared Tracy**. (*OH's Deep Roots in CT*, p. 75)

John - b 4/11/1781 in Norwich, CT, d 3/17/1842 in Oxford, NY. John m (1) ----, and m (2) **Abigail Glover** of Oxford, NY, bc1790, dc1872 in Oxford, NY. (*Annals of Oxford, NY - 1850 Census Chenango Co., NY*)

Stephen - b 11/27/1759 in Plainfield, CT, s/o **Andrew** and **Lois (Pierce)**; Stephen d 8/31/1845 age 86 in Royalton, VT. He m 9/29/1782, **Polly Shepard**, b 4/5/1760, d 3/11/1843 age 83, d/o **Simon** and **Rachel (Spaulding)** of Plainfield, CT, (gravestone). (*Hist. of Royalton, VT*, p. 664-5 - *New Eng. Anc. of Dana Convers Backus*, p. 32, 42-44)

BAILEY

Amos - b 1/1777 in Groton, CT, s/o **Obadiah Jr.** and **Esther (Wilham)**; Amos d 11/9/1865 in 89th year in Brooklyn, PA. He m 2/1801 in Groton, CT, **Prudence Geer**, bc1768, d 7/15/1854, age 85-9. (*Hist. of Susquehanna, PA*, p. 123-5, 653 by Blackman)

Dan - bc1806 in Groton, CT, d 9/20/1890 age 84 in Parma Twp., Monroe Co., NY. Dan m 11/28/1833 in Groton, CT, Mrs. **Wealthy Ann Rathburn**. (Tombstone Rec., Parma Twp., Monroe Co., NY)

Col. Frederick - b Groton, CT, s/o **Obadiah Jr.** and **Esther (Williams)**; Col. Frederick d1851 in Brooklyn, Susquehanna Co, PA. He m (1) 1806 **Polly Witter**, bc1789, d1828, and m (2) **Lucinda Morgan**, bc1780, d1869. (*Hist. of Susquehanna Co., PA* by Stocker p. 655)

Joshua - b1800 in East Hampton, CT, d 1/21/1875 in Waterford, NY. Joshua m **Almira Miller**, b 2/20/1804 in Glastonbury, CT, dc1862, d/o **William** and **Esther (Kilborn) Miller**. (*Hist. of Saratoga Co., NY*, p. 337)

Lodowick - bc1785, s/o **Obadiah Jr.** and **Esther Williams Bailey**; Lodowich dc1873 in Brooklyn, PA. He m1813 **Hannah Avery** of Groton, CT, bc1789, d1860. (*Hist. of Susquehanna Co., PA* by Stocker p. 655-6)

Philander - b 5/7/1824 in CT, d 9/30/1890 in Cavendish, VT. Philander m **Hapilona Stoddard**, b 2/22/1813 in CT, d 11/13/1901 in Cavendish, VT (Hillcrest Cemetery). (*1850 Windsor Co., VT, Census* - Cemetery Stone at Cavendish)

BAKER

Lot - b 5/17/1780 in Ellington, CT, d 6/18/1856 age 76 in S. Royalton, VT. Lot m 12/31/1801 **Polly Shepard**, b 2/28/1782. (*History of Royalton, VT*, p. 667-8 by Lovejoy - gravestone.)

Remember - b 6/26/1737 in Woodbury, CT, d 8/22/1775 age 35 in Colchester, VT. Remember m **Desire Hurlburt**. (*Hist. of Town of Colchester, VT* by Wright - *New England Quarterly*, v. 10 #4 - *VT Hist. Magazine*, v. 1 p. 765-76)

BALDWIN

Benjamin Jr. - b 12/9/1733 in Norwich, CT, s/o **Benjamin** and **Elizabeth**; Benjamin (the younger) d 2/12/1818 age 85 in Bradford, VT. He m 11/25/1761 in Hebron, CT, **Lydia Peters**, b Hebron, CT, d 9/3/1825 in Bradford, Orange Co., VT, d/o **John Jr.** (*Baldwin Gen.*, p. 630-1 - *A Hist. of Bradford, VT*, p. 141-157)

David - b 3/23/1779 in Milford, CT, s/o **Richard**; d/9/10/1857 in Forest Lake Center, PA. David m 1/1/1807, **Ruth Stanley**, b 9/19/1784, d 1/2/1869, d/o **Elijah** and **Elizabeth (Peck)**. (*Baldwin Gen.*, p. 143, 195-6.)

Israel - b 3/19/1736 (or 3/19/1737) in New Milford, CT, s/o **Theophilus**; d 3/16/1778 in Hinesburgh, VT. Israel m 2/25/1761 **Elizabeth Warner**, d 3/13/1811 age 73 in Hinesburgh, VT. (*Baldwin Gen.*, p. 103-4, 122)

Nathan G. - b 4/27/1767 in New Milford, CT, s/o **Isaac** and **Hannah (Davis)**; Nathan G. d 8/30/1820 in Monckton, VT. He m ---- **Chamberlain**. (*Baldwin Gen.*, p. 120, 158 - *Gazetteer of Addison Co., VT*)

Nathaniel - b 7/20/1761 in Goshen, CT, d 8/30/1840 in Rochester, Oakland Co., MI. Nathaniel m **Susannah Sherman** (niece of **Roger Sherman**), b1765, d1839. (*CT Soldiers Buried in MI* - typed DAR.)

Noah - b 4/13/1745 in Saybrook, CT, s/o **Moses** and **Abigail (Royce)**; d 1/19/1818 (or 1/19/1827) in Bridgewater, PA. Noah m 12/5/1776 **Sarah Scott**, b1756, d1842. (*Baldwin Gen.*, p. 516, 546-7 - *Hist. of Susquehanna Co., PA*, p. 337)

Samuel - b 5/25/1755 in CT, d 6/6/1838 in Lexington, Greene Co., NY. Samuel m **Lucina Hill**, b1757 (or b1767) in CT, d1838 in Lexington, NY. (*DAR Patriot Index*, p. 31 - *Car-Del Scribe* Query 7/1977 p. 30)

Thomas - bc1774 in Mansfield, CT, s/o **Joseph**; Thomas d 7/4/1854 age 80 in Dorset, VT. He m (1) 4/14/1807 **Polly** or **Mary Sanfrere**, b in CT. (*Baldwin Gen.*, p. 702-13 - *1850 Bennington, VT, Census*)

BARBER

David - b 3/15/1770 in Simsbury, CT, s/o **David** and **Sarah (Lawrence)**; David (the younger) d 6/11/1860 in Hubbardton, VT. He m (1) 1792 **Clarissa Whelpley**, dc1825, and m (2) **Phoebe** ----, wid/o **Judge Rich** of Shoreham, VT. (*Barber Gen.*, p. 84-5, 139 - 1850 Rutland Co. Census - *VT Historical Magazine*, v. 4 p. 1174)

Elihu - b 3/17/1768 in Hebron, CT, s/o **David** and **Abigail (Newcomb)**. Elihu d 3/27/1848 age 80 in Delphi Falls, NY. He m 1/25/1791 **Hannah Gott**, d 4/1/1858 age over 88 years. (Pompey, NY). (*Onondaga Co.*, p. 283-6)

Elisha - b 8/21/1742 in Simsbury, CT, s/o Lt. **Thomas** and **Mary** (**C a s e**); Elisha d 11/29/1806 age 64 in Fairfield, VT. He m 6/3/1764 at Simsbury, CT, **Elizabeth Adams**, d 12/20/1833 in her 89th year in Fairfield, VT. (*Hist. and Tales of Hinesburgh, VT*, p. 37 - *Barber Gen.*)

BARKER

Eliasaph - b 1/4/1779 in Watertown, CT, s/o **Eliasaph** and **Mabel** (**Sanford**); Eliasaph (the younger) d 10/16/1857 in Camden, Oneida Co., NY. He m1805 **Clarissa Parks**, d 7/15/1857, d/o **Daniel**. (*Pioneer Hist. of Camden, NY*)

John - b 12/18/1755 in Pomfret, CT, s/o **Ephraim** and **Hannah** (**Grow**); John d 3/15/1834 in Stoddard, NH. He m (1) 7/9/1786 **Esther Richardson**; and m (2) Mrs. **Sally Guild Warren**. (*DAR Patriot Index*, p. 35 - *Town of Gilsum, NH*, p. 260)

John A. - b1787 in Norwalk, CT, d1858 in Chautauqua Co., NY. John A. m1810 in Chenango Forks (Broome Co., NY), **Phebe Ogden**, b1787 in Elizabethtown, NJ, and d1860. (*Chautauqua Co., NY*, p. 480)

Leverett - b 5/6/1787 in Branford, CT, s/o **Russell**; Leverett's d date unknown. He m 3/3/1811 **D e s i r e   B a r k e r**, d/o **H e z e k i a h**. (*Chautauqua Co., NY*, p. 379-80)

Levi - b 3/11/1761 in Westbury, CT, d 6/19/1835 age 72-10. Levi m **Lydia Benton**, b 5/4/1771 in Barkhamsted, CT, d 5/9/1838 age 67 in Clinton, NY, d/o **B a r n a b u s**. (*DAR Patriot Index*, p. 36 - *Kirkland Ave. Cem., Clinton, NY*, p. 11 - Clinton Memorial NSDAR - DAR Lineage #43993 and #48733)

BARNES

Asahel Sr. - b 9/21/1777 in Bristol, CT, d 6/17/1859 in New Haven, VT. Asahel m **Keturah** ----, bc1777, d 9/29/1840 age 63. (*Addison Co., VT*)

D a n i e l - b 12/4/1762 in Waterbury, VT, d1854 in Portland, NY. Daniel m1783 **Lucinda King**, d1854. (*Soldiers of Am. Revolution - Chautauqua Co., NY*, p. 13-14.)

Elijah - b 8/8/1810 in Washington, CT, s/o **Caleb** and **Jane**; Elijah d 1/2/1888, buried in W. Hill Cem., Chelsea, VT. He m **S a r ah Rogers**, b 12/17/1814 in VT, d 10/23/1904 in Chelsea, VT. (*1850 Orange Co. Census* - Gravestone West Hill Cem., Chelsea, VT)

I s a a c - bc1793 in CT, d 10/7/1871 age 78 in Sweden Twp., Monroe Co., NY. Isaac m 5/17/1826 **Lydia** ----, b in CT, d 3/24/1881 age 76. (*Hist. of Monroe Co., NY*, p. 160, 242, 276 - Tombstone Rec. of Brockport Cem.)

Ithiel - b 4/27/1763 in New Fairfield, CT, s/o **James** and **Experience** (**Wise**); Ithiel d 4/23/1840 age 77, in Pittsford, VT. He m1784 **Grizzel Hunt**, b 12/10/1765 in New Milford, CT, d 9/5/1845 age 80, Old Cong. Cem., Pittsford, VT. (*Hist. of Pittsford, VT*, p. 227-8)

J a c o b - bc1743 in Woodbury, CT, d 1/27/1821 age 76 at Fair Haven, VT. Jacob m in Milford, CT, **Rebecca Crowell**, d1822 age 77 in Fair Haven, VT. (*Hist. of Fair Haven, VT*, p. 307)

11

James - bc1742 in New Fairfield, CT, d 2/11/1809 in 69th year in Pittsford, VT. James m **Experience Wise** of Cape Cod, d 11/12/1825 age 82. (*Hist. of Pittsford, VT*, p. 277)

John - b 3/13/1756 in New Fairfield, CT, s/o **John**; John (the younger) d 1/2/1820 in Pittsford, VT. John m 9/1785 **Saloma Howard** b 3/5/1768 in Bennington, VT, d 9/26/1825. (*Hist. of Pittsford, VT*, p. 59, 375-6)

Jonathan - b 3/2/1760 in Waterbury, CT, d 6/1845 in Camden, NY. Jonathan m 11/22/1781 **Sybil Bartholomew**. (*DAR Patriot Index*, p. 37 - *Pioneer Hist. of Camden, NY*)

Tillotson - b1784(or b1785) in Watertown, CT, s/o **Isaac** and **Lucy**; Tillotson d 2/1836 in Camden, NY. He m 5/13/1813 **Clarissa Byington**, b in CT, d/o **Heman**. (*Pioneer Hist of Camden, NY*, p. 228-232)

Timothy - b 4/19/1741 in Hartford, CT, d 11/1825 in Clinton, NY. Timothy m 10/28/1772 **Eunice Munson**, b 11/19/1754 in Wallingford, CT. (*Clinton Memorial Kirtland Ave. Cem.*, p. 12 - *CT in the Rev. and 1812*, p. 470)

Zophar - b1759 in Plymouth, CT, d1842 in Camden, NY. Zophar m **Mary E. Barnes** of Plymouth, CT, d1820. (*Pioneer Hist. of Camden, NY*, p. 56-7)

BARNEY

Luther - b 3/4/1757 in Norwich, CT, s/o **John**; Luther d 9/30/1844 in Ellery, NY. He m (1) **Abigail Windhip**, d1799 in Genoa, NY, and m (2) c1800 **Ruth Garrison**, b 1/24/1777 in MD, d 10/16/1848. (Bemis Pt. Cemetery). (*DAR Patriot Index*, p. 38 - *Soldiers of Am. Rev., Chautauqua Co., NY*, p. 24-5)

BARNUM

Thomas B. - b 9/20/1800 in Danbury, CT, s/o **Asher** and **Rhoda (Burt)**; Thomas d 7/3/1887 in LeRoy, NY. He m 9/24/1824 **Harriet Rose**. (*Pioneer Collections of MI*, v. 13 p. 138-9)

BARRETT

Benjamin - b 5/6/1728 in Killingly, CT, s/o **Benjamin** and **Mary**; Benjamin d 5/6/1813 age 84 in Strafford, VT. He m (1) **Thankful** ----; and m (2) **Sarah** ----. (Gravestone - *Woodstock Families* by Bowen v. 2 p. 392, 393)

Ezra Lathrop - b 9/27/1775 in Norwich, CT, s/o **Ezekiel** and **Sarah (Lathrop)**; Ezra Lathrop d1857 in Northeast, NY. He m **Rhoda Dakin**, d1860, d/o **Caleb**. (*Commemorative Biog. Rec. - Dutchess Co., NY*, p. 487)

James - b 2/17/1761 in Killingly, CT, d 5/21/1813 age 53. James m **Elizabeth Hibbard**, b 5/6/1760, d 5/8/1854 age 94 in Strafford, VT. (Gravestones in Kibling Cem., Strafford, VT)

Thomas M. - b 3/20/1777 in Woodstock, CT, d 9/1844 in Concord, NY. Thomas M. m in Otsego, NY, **Hannah Chase**, dc1867 (or dc1868). (*Hist. of Original Town of Concord, NY*, p. 277-8)

BARROWS

Rev. Eleazer – b 1/18/1790 in Mansfield, CT, s/o **Eleazer** and **Mary** **(Hall)**; Rev. Eleazer d 7/28/1847 age 57 in Utica, NY. He m 5/7/1822 **Catherine Fuller**, d/o Dr. **Thomas** of Cooperstown, NY. (*Reunion of Old Town of Pompey, NY*, p. 258-9)

BARTHOLOMEW

Elisha – b 10/17/1772 in Woodstock, CT, s/o **John** and **Candace** **(Ainsworth)**; Elisha d1843 in Hiram, OH, at age 41. He m 11/23/1795 in Woodstock, CT, **Lovica Hall**. (*Rec. of the Bartholomew Family*, p. 224 – *Hist. of Royalton, VT*, p. 671.)

Erastus – b1783 in Goshen, CT, d 9/28/1860 age 77. Erastus m (1) 1/25/1800 **Sally Bartlett**, d 8/8/1813 in Chelsea, VT, and m (2) 10/8/1819 Mrs. **Elizabeth (Haywood) Coburn** of Boston, MA, d 4/27/1876 age 83-7 in Post Mills, VT. (*Bartholomew Family* 173-177, 274-6, – *Cemetery Post Mills*)

Luther – b 2/18/1758 in Washington, CT, s/o **Noah**; Luther d 5/5/1839 age 81 (Christian Street Cem. stone). He m **Azubah Farnum** of Litchfield, CT, d 9/18/1827 age 60 in Hartford, VT, (Christian St. Cemetery). (*Bartholomew Family* p. 149-151 – *Hist. of Hartford, VT* p. 409-10)

Luther Jr. – b 8/25/1789 in Litchfield, CT, s/o **Luther** and **Azubah** **(Farnum)**; Luther Jr. d 5/28/1880 age 90 in Hartford, VT. He m 7/22/1815 **Fannie Fox** of Hartford, VT, b 7/17/1799 in Hanover, NH, d 8/21/1881 age 82 in Hartford, VT. (*Bartholomew Family* p. 241-3 – *Hist. of Hartford, VT* p. 410)

Noah – b1732 (or b1733) in Branford, CT, s/o **William**; Noah d 2/16/1813 age 82 in Hartford, VT (Christian St. Cem.). He m **Mabel Parmely**, d 2/23/1813 (7 days after Noah), d/o **Thomas**. (*Bartholomew Fam.* 99-101 – *Hist. of Hartford, VT*)

Sheldon – b 9/23/1787 in Litchfield, CT, d 8/28/1868 age 80 in Norwich, VT. He m 8/28/1811 **Anna Chapman**, b 8/28/1793 in VT, d 9/4/1867 age 74. (*Bartholomew Fam.* p. 240-1, 365 – *1850 Census Windsor Co.*)

Timothy – b 8/11/1745 in Wallingford, CT, s/o **Timothy** and **Abigail** **(Phelps)**; Timothy d 2/20/1831 in Thetford, VT (gravestone). He m 12/23/1773 **Esther Grant** of Lyme, CT, b 9/25/1745, d 6/29/1824 age 78. (*Bartholomew Fam.* p. 126)

William – b 1/16/1788 in Waterbury, CT, s/o **Abiel** and **Mary**; William d1868 age 80 in Vienna, OH. He m 2/25/1813 in Vienna, OH, **Mary Boyd**, b 5/9/1791, d 8/10/1859. (*Bartholomew Fam.* p. 286 – War of 1812)

BARTLETT

Christopher – b 2/26/1767 in Stafford, CT, s/o **Samuel** and **Rachel**; Christopher d 12/27/1842 in Morgan, VT. He m 11/16/1786 in Somers, CT, **Anna Buck**, b 8/4/1765 in Somers, CT. (*Orleans Co., VT, Gazetteer*, p. 288)

BARTRAM

Daniel – b 10/23/1745 in Fairfield, CT, d 5/17/1817 in Madison, OH. Daniel m 10/10/1769 in Redding, CT, **Ann Merchant**, d/o **Gurdon**.

13

(*History and Gen. of Old Fairfield*, p. 70-71 - *Revolutionary Soldiers in Lake Co., OH*, p. 9)

BASS

Joel - b 3/4/1774 in Windham, CT, s/o **Ebenezer** and **Ruth (Waldo)**; Joel d 10/15/1871 age 97-7-11 in Williamstown, VT. He m (1) 12/22/1796 in Windham, CT, **Polly Martin** who d 12/14/1849 age 72, Williamstown, VT, (East Hill Cem.) and m (2) **Sarah C.** ---- who d 12/17/1867 age 88-5 in Williamstown, VT. (*1850 Orange Co. Census* - East Hill Cem. gravestones)

Joseph - b 4/17/1772 in Windham, CT, s/o **Ebenezer** and **Ruth (Waldo)**. Joseph m 12/30/1795 in Windham, CT, **Lucy Gager**, d/o **Jason** and **Lucy (Peck)**, b 1/31/1774. Joseph and Lucy lived in Lebanon, Wayne Co., PA. (*Hist. of Wayne Co., PA*, p. 148)

Dr. Zaccheus - b 2/18/1791 in Windham, CT, d 2/16/1881 in Middlebury, VT. Dr. Zaccheus m **Susan Dorrance** b 1/29/1798 in Windham, CT, d 4/2/1876. (Middlebury, VT, Cemetery gravestone)

BATES

Samuel - b 8/9/1760 in Haddam, CT, d 8/21/1822 in Kendall, NY. He m **Abigail Willard**. Samuel and Abigail lived after war in Randolph, VT, then Kendall, NY. (*Pioneer Hist. of Orleans Co., VT*, p. 284-5 - *DAR Patriot Index*, p. 44)

BATTELL

Philip - b1807 in Norfolk, CT, d 12/3/1897 in Middlebury, VT. Philip m **Emma Hart Seymour** b1808, d 11/3/1841, d/o **Horatio**. (Middlebury, VT, Cem. gravestone)

BEACH

Asa - b 8/1/1759 in Wallingford, CT, d 9/27/1832 in Whitney Point, NY. Asa m 2/1/1781 **Elizabeth Benham** b 8/21/1765, d/o **Shadrack** and **Elizabeth (Austin)**. (*Yankee Magazine* 4/1977 - French's *Historical Gazetteer of New York*, p. 181 - *Families of Ancient New Haven*, p. 197)

Daniel - b 3/16/1785 in Warren, CT, s/o **Reuben** and **Hannah (Kimball)**; Daniel d 5/21/1862 in Huron Co., OH. He m (1) 1/1/1810 **Lorinda Sacket** who d 11/16/1856; m (2) Mrs. **Frances Peck**, wid/o **Taylor Peck**. Drafted in War of 1812 in Summit Co., OH. (Typed List - Huron, OH)

Jonathan - b 10/2/1761 in Goshen, CT, d1850 in Genessee Co., MI. Jonathan m **Lucy Baldwin** (Mt. Morris Cem.). (*Conn. Revolutionary Soldiers Buried in Michigan*)

Orrin - b in CT, s/o **John**; Orrin d 5/26/1856 age 62 in Oneonta, NY. He m **Annie Choate** who d 1/18/1843 age 52, d/o **William** and **Annie**. (*Biog. Rec. of Otsego Co., NY*, p. 764)

Stephen - bc1775 in Trumbull, CT, d 2/11/1859 in Ferrisburgh, VT. Stephen m **Ann** ---- who d 10/28/1847. (*Gazeteer of Addison Co., VT*, p. 105)

BEADLE

Benjamin - b 12/18/1741 in Wethersfield, CT, s/o **David** and **Abigail**; Benjamin d 6/24/1810 in Sherburne, Chenango Co., NY. He m (1) 2/6/1766 in Colchester, CT, **Mary Munn**, b 1/27/1741 in Colchester, CT, d 9/9/1781 in Colchester, CT, d/o **James Jr.** and **Martha Smith**; m (2) 10/21/1781 in Colchester, CT, **Sybel Gillett**, b 10/4/1753 in Colchester, CT, d 1/11/1789 in Colchester, CT, d/o **Israel** and **Mary**; m (3) **Rhoda Hinckley** who d 12/21/1841 in Columbus, PA. (*Samuel Beadle Fam.*, p. 703, 707 - *Biog. Review Otsego Co.*, p. 95)

Flavel - b 3/18/1788 in Colchester, CT, s/o **Benj.** and 2nd w **Sibyl (Gillett)**; Flavel d 8/1/1854 in Cooperstown, NY. He m **Polly Tuller**, b 10/11/1787 in Stockbridge, MA, d age 77 in Franklin, Delaware Co., NY. (*Biog. Review Otsego Co.*, p. 95 - *Samuel Beadle Fam.*, p. 708, 775-6)

BEAMAN

Capt. Elijah - b in CT, d 12/3/1833 age 90 in Strafford, VT, (Kibling Cem.). Capt. Elijah m **Patience** ---- (possibly **Hatch**) who d 11/19/1830 age 81. (Gravestone Kibling Cem. Strafford, VT)

BEARDSLEY

Andrew - bc1744 in Stratford, CT, d before 9/27/1796 probably in Wyoming Co., NY. Andrew m **Elizabeth** ----. (*Beardsley Fam.*, p. 74, 159 - *History of Wells, VT*, p. 40.) He was Orig. Settler at Wells, VT, and went to Wyoming Co., NY, ca. 1790.

Benjamin - b 1/30/1754 in Stratford, CT, s/o **Benjamin**; Benjamin (the younger) d 6/6/1837 in East Venice, NY. He m 9/2/1785 **Amelia Stevens** who d 6/14/1849. (*Beardsley Gen.*, p. 58 - *DAR Patriot Index*, p. 47)

Ephraim - b 3/30/1773 in Kent, CT, s/o **Ephraim**; Ephraim (the younger) d 3/9/1878 in St. Albans, VT. He m (1) **Hannah Berry** and m (2) 1/8/1818 in So. Hero, VT, **Sally Adams**, b1789, d 6/29/1834 in St. Albans, VT, d/o **Joseph** and **Abiah (Edgerton)**. (*Beardsley Gen.*, p. 89)

Ezra - b 10/17/1781 in New Fairfield, CT, d 12/12/1849 in Racine Co., WI. Ezra m (1) **Nancy Brush** b Delhi Co., NY, d1818 Clark Co., OH and m (2) **Mary (Chatfield) Niblach** b 6/1785 in RI, d 10/5/1862 in Racine, WI. (*Nutmegger* Query June 1981 p. 83)

Herman - b 7/21/1800 in Kent, CT, s/o **Ephraim** and **Hannah (Berry)**; Herman d 3/9/1878 in St. Albans, VT. He m **Abigail** ----. (*Beardsley Gen.*, p. 89 - *History of Vermont* v. 5 by Crockett)

Israel - b 3/13/1721 in Stratford, CT, s/o **Josiah** and **Mary (Whittemore)**. Israel m **Elizabeth French** b 7/31/1726 in Stratford, CT, d/o **Samuel** and **Mary (Price)**. Israel lived at both Dorset and Manchester, VT. (*Beardsley Gen.*, p. 26, 57)

James B. - b 5/28/1811 in New Preston, CT, s/o **Philo**, d 2/14/1884. James B. m (1) 3/23/1826 **Laura M. Platt** who d 7/1837 and m (2) in 1837 **Prudence Barrass** from Saratoga Co. In 1835 James B. and Laura M. moved to Farm Ridge, LaSalle Co., IL, and later Vermilion, OH. (*Beardsley Gen.*, p. 226 - *History of LaSalle Co., IL*, p. 383)

15

Capt. **Jehiel** - b 1/9/1733/4 in Stratford, CT, s/o **John** and **Keziah (Wheeler)**; Capt. Jehiel d1846 age 112 in Peru, NY. He m **Hannah Gifford** of Middletown, VT. (*Beardsley Gen.*, p. 51, 105 - *Hist. of Town of Wells, VT*, p. 40)

John Jr. BEARDSLEE - b 11/1759 in Sharon, CT, s/o **John** and **Deborah (Knickerbacker)**; John Jr. d 10/3/1825 in Manheim, NY. He m1795 **Lavinia Pardee** of Sharon who d1854 age 85. (*History of Herkimer Co., NY*, p. 435-6)

Josiah - b 2/6/1756 in CT, d 8/6/1842 in Butternuts, NY, (Prentiss Cem.). Josiah m **Abigail Bulkely**. (*DAR Patriot Index*, p. 47 - *DAR Magazine* 1977 p. 914)

Price - b 5/19/1761 in Newtown, CT, s/o **Israel**, d1838 in Dorset, VT. Price m **Freelove French**, d/o **Samuel** and **Elizabeth (Loring)**, b 4/29/1759 in Manchester, VT. (*Beardsley Gen.*, p. 57)

Whitmore - b1759 in Huntington, CT, s/o **Benjamin**; Whitmore d 2/8/1833 in 74th year in Fairfield, VT. He m 3/2/1780 in Huntington, CT, **Dolly Beard**, d Fairfield, VT, d/o **Nathan** and **Sarah (Smith)**. (*Beardsley Gen.*, p. 59, 123-4)

BECKLEY

Zebedee - b 12/31/1763 in Wethersfield, CT, s/o **Zebedee** and **Hannah**; Zebedee d 2/5/1851 in Barre, VT. He m 2/8/1789 **Elizabeth Belding** of Farmington, CT_, b1769, d 8/25/1856 in Barre, VT. (*Washington Co. Gazetteer*, p. 160 - *Hist. of Wethersfield, CT*, p. 64 - *DAR Patriot Index*, p. 49)

BECKWITH

Andrew - bp 6/26/1743 in Lyme, CT. Andrew m 4/20/1775 **Lois Copp**, d/o **Samuel**. Andrew and Lois had children who were born in Horton, King's Co., Nova Scotia. (*Kings Co., Nova Scotia*, p. 555-562)

Benjamin Jr. - b 7/22/1739 in Lyme, CT, s/o **Benj. Sr.** and **Patience (Eden)**. Benjamin Jr. m (1) 2/18/1766 **Hopestill Beckwith** and m (2) 7/3/1783 **Lydia Babcock** of Cornwallis, NS, d/o **John** and **Jane (Worden)**. (*King's Co., Cornwallis, Nova Scotia*, p. 555-562)

John - b 10/10/1713 in Lyme, CT, d 4/18/1810 in Cornwallis, Nova Scotia. John m 4/20/1727 in Norwich, CT, **Jane Worden** prob. b Stonington, CT. (*King's Co., NS*, p. 555-562)

John Jr. - b 3/16/1738 in Norwich, CT, s/o **John**; John Jr. d 12/15/1816 either in Horton or Aylesford, NS. He m in Cornwallis, NS, **Jane Allen Chipman**, b 11/11/1746, d 6/21/1812, d/o **Handly** and **Jane**. (*King's Co., NS, Family Sketches*, p. 557-8)

Samuel - b 5/24/1709 in Lyme, CT, s/o **James** and **Sarah**. Samuel m **Miriam Marvin** bc1720, d/o **Reynold** and **Martha (Waterman)**. In 1761 Samuel and Miriam went to Cornwallis, Nova Scotia. (*King's Co., Nova Scotia*, p. 555-562)

Zachariah - bc1800 in Bristol, CT, d 3/15/1862 age 62 in Middlebury, VT (gravestone). Zachariah m **Julia Smith** bc1800, d 9/22/1886 age 86. (Gravestones in Middlebury Cem.)

BEEBE

Azariah - b 3/28/1783 in Lyme, CT, s/o **Azariah** and **Diodamy (Marvin)**, d 12/22/1834 in Sandusky, OH. Azariah m in New London, CT, **Mary Ryon** d 12/11/1864. (Typed List - Huron, OH)

John - b 12/5/1727 in Colchester, CT, s/o **John**; John (the younger) d 9/18/1786 age 59 at Chatham, NY. He m **Cynthia** ---- who d 5/29/1799 age 25-6. (French's *Historical NY Gazetteer*, p. 244 - *Columbia Co., NY, Cemetery Inscriptions*, v. 1 p. 5)

Jonathan - b 9/24/1745 in Waterbury, CT, s/o Lt. **Jonathan**. Jonathan (the younger) m 8/25/1767 in Waterbury, CT, **Azubal Warner**, d/o **Abraham**. Jonathan and Azubal lived in Pomfret, VT. (*Pomfret, VT*, p. 439)

Sgt. Robert - b 5/8/1747 in East Haddam, CT, s/o **Cabot** and **Phebe (Buckingham)**; Sgt. Robert d1813 in Wells, VT. He m1772/3 **Abigail Martin**. (*Branches and Twigs*, v. 1 #4 p. 60 - *History of Wells, VT*, p. 40)

Timothy - b1768 in Litchfield Co., CT, d1844 in Windsor, NY. Timothy m **Sally Lovridge**, b1768 in CT, d1831. (*Hist. of Susquehanna Co., PA*, p. 559)

BEERS

Daniel - b1757 in Stratford, CT, d1839 in Tompkins Co., NY. Daniel m **Elizabeth Dykeman**, b1762, d1830. (*Yesteryears* - Spring 1976 p. 111)

Zachariah - b 6/3/1758 in Woodbury, CT, s/o **Daniel** and **Phebe (Walker)**; Zachariah d 2/3/1842 probably in Onondaga Co., NY. He m **Mary Hurd**. (*DAR Patriot Index*, p. 50 - *Onondaga Hist. Soc. of 1914*, p. 191)

BELKNAP

Moses - b 9/1/1754 in Ellington, CT, d 9/2/1836 in East Randolph, VT, s/o **Simon** and **Elizabeth**. Moses m1775 **Sarah Kibbe**, d/o **Daniel** and **Mary (Pratt) Kibbee**. He lived in Royalton, VT. (*Royalton, VT* by Nash p. 198)

BELL

Jesse - b 3/6/1745/6 in Darien, CT, s/o **James** and **Sarah**; Jesse d 10/20/1834 in Milton, Saratoga Co., NY. He m (1) 11/8/1767 in Stamford, CT, **Comfort Garnsey** or **Guernsey** who d 3/3/1772 in Stamford, CT, and m (2) 1/25/1773 **Mary Scofield**, d/o **Joseph** and **Mary (Hait)** and m (3) **Sarah** ----. After Revolution moved to Dutchess Co., NY. (*DAR Patriot Index*, p. 51 - *Yesteryears*, Summer 1956)

BELSHAW

David - b 6/26/1777 near Hartford, CT, s/o **Thomas** and **Elizabeth**; David d 11/6/1868 in Herkimer Co., NY, possibly in Warren or Hardin. He m (1) 2/1801 **Lydia Isham**, b in CT, d 3/26/1831, d/o **Zebulon** and **Rose (Ellis)** and m (2) **Betsey Bennett**, d1872 age 81. (*Hist. of Herkimer Co.*, p. 137)

17

BENEDICT

Asa – b 7/7/1781 in Norwalk, CT, s/o **Nathaniel** and **Anna (Raymond)**; Asa d 2/15/1850 in Brockport, Monroe Co., NY. He m (1) 1/5/1804 **Hannah Reed**, d 11/11/1830 and m (2) 12/19/1830 Widow **Ruth Hanford**, d 12/2/1857. (Tombstone Records for Brockport Cem., NY)

Elijah – b 1/1741 in New Milford, CT, s/o **Gideon** and **Dorothy (Botsford)**; Elijah d 1/1811 in Peru, VT. Elijah m in New Milford, CT, **Mabel Hurlburt**, d1814 in Peru, VT. (*Des. of John Benedict*, p. 134, 81, 62 – *Chittenden Gazeteer*, p. 256)

Ezra – b 1/15/1780 in CT, s/o **Samuel**; Ezra d 3/23/1854 in Malone, NY. He m 8/1802 **Sally Stockwell**, b1779, d 10/24/1850, d/o **Moses**. (*Benedict Gen.*, p. 273-5 – *Gazeteer of Orange County, VT*, p. 532)

John – b 2/17/1785 in New Milford, CT, d1873 in Cornwall, VT, age 87. John m 5/1807 **Laurie Smith** of Monckton, VT, b 5/22/1788, d/o **Hezekiah** and **Sarah (Willoughby)**. (*Benedict Gen.*, p. 413-414 – *Gazetteer of Addison Co., VT*, p. 72)

John Thomas – b 11/26/1773 in Norwalk, CT, s/o **John** and **Elizabeth**; John Thomas d 3/7/1845 near Dansville, NY. He m 2/7/1795 **Betsey Bart**, d 2/5/1838, d/o **Nathan** of Boston. (*Benedict Gen.*, p. 163 – *1812 Index*)

Julius – b 11/3/1818 in Sharon, CT, s/o **Abel** and **Wealthy (Wheeler)**; Julius d probably in NY City. He m 1/5/1846 **Maria Canfield** d/o **Lee** of Falls Village, CT. (*Benedict Gen.*, p. 279 – *Comm. Biog. Rec. of Dutchess Co., NY*, p. 396)

Levi – b 9/23/1761 in CT, s/o **Bushnell**; Levi d 5/18/1839 and is buried in Briggs Cem., Ballston, Saratoga Co., NY. He m **Elizabeth Davis**, b 5/9/1772, d 8/20/1854, d/o **Jabez** and **Sarah**. (*DAR Magazine* 1977 p. 914 – *Benedict Gen.*, p. 212-213)

Michael – b 2/14/1787 in Danbury, CT, s/o **Daniel** and **Rebecca (Meeker)**; Michael d 12/22/1862 in Preston, Wayne Co., PA. He m 2/23/1808 **Clarissa Hurlburt** of Wilton, CT, b 2/7/1787, d 8/25/1860. (*Benedict Gen.*, p. 361, 325 – *Biog. Rec. of Otsego Co., NY*, p. 475)

Uriah – b 2/15/1745 in CT, d 2/25/1800 in Ballston, Saratoga Co., NY. Uriah m **Mary Howes**. (*DAR Patriot Index*, p. 53 – *Hist. of Saratoga Co.*, p. 249)

BENNETT

Elder **Alfred** – b 9/26/1780 in Mansfield, CT, d 5/10/1851 in Homer, Cortland Co., NY. He m1802 in Hampton, CT, **Rhoda Grow**. (*Pioneer Hist. of Cortland Co., NY*, p. 364-5)

Dudley – b 6/8/1797 in Stonington, CT, s/o **Aaron** and **Abigail (Smith)**; Dudley d 4/23/1887 age 90-7-8. He m **Phebe ----**, b in NY, d 2/19/1887 age 87-10-20. (*Cemeteries Sherburne, Chenango Co., NY*, p. 196 – *1850 Census Chinango Co., NY*)

Jared – b 8/23/1768 in Windham, CT, s/o **Isaac** and **Sarah**; Jared d 4/28/1845 age 81 in Smyrna, NY. He m **Parthena ----**, b 11/10/1859 age 89-5-25 in Saybrook, CT. (*Smyrna, NY* by Munson p. 56-8 – *1850 Census Chenango Co.* – Cemetery)

18

Joseph - b 10/5/1779 in New Milford, CT, s/o **Edward** and **Rhoda**; Joseph d 3/27/1853 age 74 in Lebanon, PA. He m **Elizabeth** ----. (*Wayne Co., PA*)

Stephen - b 5/28/1761 in CT, d 10/21/1831 and was buried in Paupack Cem. Palmyra, PA. He m 4/27/1785 in Canterbury, CT, **Mary Gates**, d/o **Nathaniel** and **Deborah**. (*Rev. Soldiers Buried in Wayne Co., PA*)

BENTON

Medad - b 3/19/1733 in Tolland, CT, s/o **Jonathan**; Medad d 9/10/1810 in South Royalton, VT. He m **Abigail** ----, b1735, d 2/9/1820 age 85 in South Royalton, VT. (*History of Royalton, VT,* p. 678)

Samuel Slade - b 4/27/1777 in Harwinton, CT, s/o **Jacob** and **Hannah** (**Slade**); Samuel Slade d 12/15/1857 in Newbury, VT. He m 2/7/1802 **Esther Prouty**, b 4/23/1782 in Charlestown, NH, d 3/14/1860 age 78 at daughter's in Waterford, VT. (*Samuel Slade Benton His Anc. and Des. - 1850 Census Orange Co., VT* - Newbury)

BERRY

Lyman - bc1798 in CT, d 6/9/1869 age 72 in Post Mills, Thetford, VT. He m **Abigail N.** ----, bc1807 in VT, d 3/22/1882 age 76 in Thetford, VT. (*1850 Orange Co. Census of VT*)

BETTS

Isaiah - b 1/1758 in CT, d 6/30/1843 in Broadalbin, Fulton Co, NY. Isaiah m **Hannah Thacher**. (*DAR Magazine*, v. 40 p. 246 - *DAR Patriot Index*)

BICKNELL

Hezekiah - b 3/9/1785 in Killingly, CT, s/o **Peter** and **Hannah** (**Kent**); Hezekiah d 2/19/1876 age 90-11-10 in Tunbridge, VT. He m 12/3/1812 **Hannah Carpenter**, b 1/24/1787, d 12/28/1841 age 54-11-4. (*Bicknell Gen.*, p. 42, 85, 185 - *1850 Orange County, VT, Census*)

BIDWELL

Birdsey J. - b 9/14/1810 in Colebrook, CT, s/o **Asa** and **Eunice**; Birdsey d 5/17/1892 in Tecumpseh, Lenawee Co., PA. He m 2/1842 **Elizabeth A. Cushing** of Tecumpseh, Lenawee Co., PA. (*Bidwell Gen.*, v. 1 p. 78, 168)

Ephraim - b1781 in Glastonbury, CT, d 7/23/1830 and buried So. Sterling Cem., Wayne Co., PA. Ephraim m **Dorcas Andrews**. (*Rev. Soldiers Buried in Wayne Co., PA*)

George - b 10/7/1756 in Hartford, CT, s/o **Amos** and **Phebe** (**Williams**); George d 4/17/1840 in Middlebury, Addison Co., VT. He m 9/15/1781 **Sarah Sedgwick**. (*Gazetteer of Addison Co., VT* - *DAR Patriot Index*, p. 58)

BIGELOW

Addi - b 10/18/1752 in Colchester, CT, s/o **Isaac** and **Abigail** (**Skinner**). Addi m 7/29/1804 in Barre, VT, **Zelinda Ingalls**. Many years in Barre, VT, and then probably went to OH. (*Bigelow Family*, p. 122)

David - b 6/6/1776 in CT, d 8/1839 in Sardinia, NY. David m **Anna Cone**, b1781 in CT, d 5/2/1857. (*Hist. of Original Town of Concord, NY*, p. 854-5)

Eli - b 5/29/1756 in Colchester, CT, s/o **Amasa** and **Jemima** **(Strong)**; Eli dc1830/1835. He m 9/10/1778 in Brookfield, VT, **Annie Freeman**. (*DAR Patriot Index*, p. 58)

Elisha - b 1/17/1752 in Colchester, CT, s/o **Elisha** and **Mary** **(Kilborn)**; Elisha (the younger) d 11/15/1826 in Reading, Windsor Co., VT. He m (1) 12/16/1773 in Colchester, CT, **Wealtha Gorton**, b 2/26/1753, d 3/11/1813 in Reading, VT, and m (2) **Susanna Townsend**. (*Bigelow Family*, p. 122)

George - b 9/30/1801 in CT, s/o **David**; George d 4/28/1875 in Concord, Erie Co., NY. He m 8/13/1826 **Martha Titus**, b 3/16/1809 in VT. (*Hist. of Original Town of Concord, NY*, p. 855-6)

Marcelion - b 2/22/1843 in Colchester, CT, d 9/15/1929 in Royalton, VT. Marcelion m (1) **Mary Shattuck Foote**, and m (2) 3/16/1886 **Mary MacDonald**. (*Royalton, VT*, p. 200)

Noah - b 2/7/1759 in Colchester, CT, s/o **Elisha** and **Mary (Kilborn)**; Noah d 5/20/1883 in Reading, VT. He m 2/25/1788 **Sarah Soule**. (*The Bigelow Family*, p. 123)

Seth - b 7/5/1777 in Colchester, CT, s/o **Amasa** and **Jemima** **(Strong)**; Seth d 4/21/1852 age 74 in Brookfield, VT (gravestone). He m 12/26/1808 **Lucy Wheatley**, b 6/16/1788 in Lebanon, NH, d 11/21/1833 age 45-7 in Brookfield, VT. (*Hist. of Waitsfield, VT*, p. 234 - *1850 Orange Co., VT, Census*)

BILL

Dr. Eliphalet M. - b 9/6/1775 in Lebanon, CT, s/o **Eliphalet** and **Dorothy (Mason)**; Eliphalet M. d 9/21/1854 in West Topsham, VT. He m1803 **Rhoda Pitkin** in Hartford, VT, b 10/26/1774 in Bolton, CT, d/o **Thomas** and **Rhoda (Marsh)**. (*Bill Family Memoir*, p. 207 - *1850 Orange Co. Census, VT*)

Elipalet - b 8/25/1750 in Lebanon Crank, CT, s/o **Benajah** and **Mary**; Elipalet d 9/1825 age 75 in Cabot, VT. He mc1772 **Dorothy Marsh**, b 4/20/1752, d 3/1835 age 83 in Orange VT, d/o **Joseph** and **Mary (Bill)**. (*Bill Family Memoir*, p. 162)

Samuel - b 9/25/1719 in Groton, CT, d 5/8/1800 in Gilsum, NH. Samuel m 9/16/1742 in Hebron, CT, **Sarah Bond**, b 5/28/1719 in Hebron, CT, d 2/22/1796. (*Town of Gilsum, NH*, p. 265)

BILLINGS

Benjamin - b 9/23/1753 in Preston, CT, d 1/13/1838 age 85 in Macedon, Wayne Co., NY. Benjamin m (1) 3/18/1781 **Martha Hewitt**, b Groton, CT, and m (2) 4/27/1794 in Preston **Eunice Tracy**, and m (3) **Wealthea Allyn**. (*American Monthly*, v. 36 p. 537 - *DAR Patriot Index*, p. 59)

John - b 11/10/1751 in Montville, CT, s/o **Samuel** and **Grace** **(Minor)**; John d 8/22/1832 in Royalton, VT. He m 10/10/1772 **Olive Noble**, b1754, d 5/14/1843, d/o **James**. (*Hist. of Royalton, VT* - *Genealogy of Des. of William Billings*, p. 11-12)

Joseph W. - b 3/21/1773 in Somers CT, s/o **John** and **Eunice (Cooley)**; Joseph W. d 5/18/1847 age 74 in Smyrna, Chenango Co., NY. He m **Abi Pomeroy**, b Somers, d 9/1/1851 age 84 in Smyrna, NY. (*Smyrna, NY*, p. 13-14 - Cemeteries - *Sherburne, Chenango Co., NY*, p. 196 - *1850 Census Chenango Co., NY*)

BINGHAM

Abiel - b 1/3/1780 in Bozrah, CT, s/o **Nathan**; Abiel d 9/14/1842 age 70 in Canajoharie, NY. He m (1) **Sarah Fowler** of Lebanon and m (2) **Susan Lathrop Stark** and m (3) **Adoshe Williams**. (*Bingham Gen.*, v. 2, p. 79 - *Biog. Rec. of Otsego Co., NY*, p. 822)

Capt. Elias Jr. - b 7/22/1779 in Windham, CT, d 6/28/1859 age 80 in Fletcher, LaMoille Co., VT. Capt. Elias Jr. m (1) 2/27/1803 **Betsey Hutchins**, d 9/10/1803 age 19 and m (2) 12/28/1803 **Abigail Hutchins**, d 9/14/1804 age 24 and m (3) 4/12/1805 **Martha Robinson**, b1789, d 3/20/1860 age 71. (*Hist. of Stowe, VT*, p. 184 - *Bingham Gen.*, v. 2, p. 103)

Hezekiah - b 8/7/1737, s/o **Thomas** and **Sarah (Huntington)**; Hezekiah d1811 in Paupac, Pike Co., PA. He m 12/23/1762 **Phoebe Boynton** of Coventry, CT. (*Bingham Gen.*, v. 1, p. 237, 313-314 - *Wayne, Pike, and Monroe Co., PA*, p. 69)

Jeremiah - b 6/26/1748 in Norwich, CT, s/o **Joseph** and **Ruth (Post)**; Jeremiah d 1/24/1842 in Cornwall, VT. He m (1) 5/4/1771/2 Widow **Abigail Hawks**, d 5/17/1817 and m (2) Widow **Abigail Smith** of West Haven, VT, d1852. (*Bingham Family of U.S.*, v. 1, p. 27 - *Gen. of Bingham Family*, p. 82-7 - *VT Historical Magazine*, v. 1)

John - b 12/22/1737 in Windham, CT, d 12/18/1815 in Gilsum, NH. John m **Sibyl Wright** of Windham, CT, d 12/25/1815 in Gilsum, NH. (*Town of Gilsum, NH*, p. 266 - *Bingham Gen.*, v. 1, p. 353)

Johnson - b 3/22/1764 in Canterbury, CT, s/o **Gideon** and 2nd w **Abigail Baker**; Johnson d 6/8/1843 in Solon, Cortland Co., NY. He m 12/22/1791 **Anna Johnson**, b 12/9/1763, d 1/4/1865 in Solon, NY. (*DAR Patriot Index*, p. 60 - French's *Historical Gazetteer*, p. 254 - *Bingham Gen.*, v. 1, p. 413)

Samuel - b 3/24/1753 in Scotland, CT, d 9/8/1845 age 92 in Clinton, Oneida Co., NY. Samuel m 1/1/1778 **Alithea Hebard/Hibbard**, b 10/5/1754 in Windham, CT, d 8/12/1822 age 68, d/o **Nathan** and **Zipporah (Bushnell)**. (*Clinton Memorial-Kirtland Ave, Cem.*, p. 12 - *Bingham Genealogy*, p. 393 - *Conn. Hist. Soc. Collection*, v. XII, p. 128)

Thomas - b 7/3/1742 in Windham, CT, s/o **Gideon** and **Mary (Carey)**; Thomas d 9/23/1823 age 82 in Royalton, VT. He m (1) 1766 **Marcy House** of Lebanon, CT, d 9/10/1812 and m (2) Widow **House Wilson** (sister of 1st wife - possibly named **Lovica**). (*History of Royalton, VT*, p. 682-6 - *Gen. of Bingham Family*, p. 36, 405 - *DAR Patriot Index*, p. 60)

BIRCHARD

Jesse - b 12/14/1770 in Norwich, CT, s/o **Jesse** and **Lydia (Backus)**; Jesse (the younger) d 5/20/1840 in 70th year in Forest Lake, Susquehanna Co., PA. He m **Harriet Tracy**, b 11/15/1773, d

5/13/1859 (gr-d/o **Winslow Tracy** – perhaps her name not Tracy). (*Hist. of Susquehanna Co., PA*, p. 480-1)

BIRD

Col. **Nathaniel** – b 5/17/1763 in Salisbury, CT, s/o **Joseph** and **Huldah (Sprague)**; Col. Nathaniel d 1/12/1847 in 80th year at son-in-law's, **Joseph Foster**. Nathaniel m 11/8/1787 in New Marlborough, MA, **Hannah Bullard**. (*Soldiers of American Revolution – Chautauqua Co., NY*, p. 594)

BIRDSEYE

Victory – b 12/25/1782 in Cornwall, CT, s/o **Ebenezer** and **Eunice (Tomlinson)**; Victory d 9/16/1853 in Pompey, Onondaga Co., NY. He m 10/14/1813 in Onondaga Hill, **Electa Beebe**, bc1793, d 10/5/1860, d/o Capt. **James**. (*Pompey, NY*, p. 273-83)

BIRGE

Elijah Jr. – bc1756 in Watertown, CT, s/o **Elijah** and **Lydia (Hill)**; Elijah Jr. d 10/11/1829 age 73 in New Haven, Addison Co., VT. He m 9/28/1783 at Watertown, CT, **Abigail Peck**, d in 87th year. (*Gazeteer of Addison Co., VT*, p. 181)

BISHOP

Joel – b 10/2/1759 in CT, d 4/17/1839 age 80 in Havana, OH. Joel m1789 **Phebe Avery**. (*American Monthly*, v. 36 p. 537 – *DAR Patriot Index*, p. 61)

John – b1709 in New London, CT, s/o **Eleazer** and **Sarah (Dart)**; John d 10/28/1785 in Greenwich, Horton, Nova Scotia. He m (1) 5/20/1731 **Rebecca Whipple**, d 10/17/1751 and m (2) Mrs. **Hannah (Allen) Comstock**, b1712, d/o **Samuel** and **Lydia (Hastings) Allen** and widow of **Gideon Comstock** of Montville, CT. (*Kings Co. – Family Sketches*, p. 570-1)

Joy Jr. – b 10/11/1745 in Fairhaven CT, d 6/1837 in Readsboro, Bennington Co., VT. Joy Jr. m **Abigail Tuttle**. (*Bennington Gazeteer – DAR Patriot Index*, p. 61)

Samuel – b 2/21/1765 in Lisbon, CT, s/o **Ebenezer** and **Tabitha**; d 11/17/1850 in Rochester, Monroe Co., NY. He m **Rebecca ----**, b1795 in Norwich, CT, d1879. (Tombstone Records – Mt. Hope Cem. – *History of Monroe Co., NY*, p. 154-5)

BISSELL

Asahel – b 2/18/1761/2 in Windsor, CT, s/o **Jerijah** and **Lydia (Bartlett)**; Asahel d 9/3/1852 in Wilmington, Windham, Co., VT. He m 11/28/1799 **Polly Caulkins**, b 5/6/1778 in MA, d 1/7/1861. (*1850 Census Windham Co., VT – Des. of John Bissell of Windsor*, p. 105)

Austin – b 9/26/1787 in Vernon, CT, s/o Capt. **Ozias** and **Elizabeth (Kilborn)**; Austin d 3/6/1873 age 85-5 in Vershire, Orange Co., VT. He m **Clarissa Story**, b 12/8/1793, d 9/21/1879 age 74-3. (*Des. of John Bissell*, v. 2 p. 234-5 – Vershire Cem. stone)

Benjamin – b 3/30/1761 in Lebanon, CT, s/o **Joseph** and **Hannah (Partridge)**; Benjamin d 10/1/1841 in Painesville, OH. He m1784 in Lebanon, CT, **Elizabeth Heath**, d 2/24/1851 age 89. (*Rev. Soldiers Buried in Lake Co., OH*)

Benjamin – b 7/6/1765 in Bolton, CT, s/o **Elisha** and **Sarah (Thomas)**; Benjamin d 12/8/1850 in Shoreham, Addison Co., VT. He m **Triphena Little**, b1773, d 5/6/1830. (*DAR Patriot Index*, p. 61 – *Des. of John Bissell*, p. 72, 136-7)

Chauncey – b 9/17/1782, s/o **Daniel** and **Beulah (Rockwell)**; Chauncey d 3/31/1853 age 71 in Dover, Windham, Co., VT. He m (1) 1811 **Philena Cone** of Brattleboro, VT, b 2/23/1789, d 6/29/1818 and m (2) 6/30/1819 **Mary Hatch**, b1783 in CT, d 8/16/1858 age 75. (*1850 Census of Windham Co. – Gen and Des. of John Bissell*)

Harvey – b 12/6/1786 in CT, s/o **Isaac** and **Amelia (Leavitt)**; Harvey d 12/26/1850 in Hartford, Windsor Co., VT. He m 1/23/1816 **Arabella Leavitt**, b 7/15/1793 in NH, d 12/1/1868, d/o **Freegrace** and **Jerusha (Loomis)**. (*Des. of John Bissell of Windsor*, p. 168)

Thomas – b 3/5/1772 in Bolton, CT, s/o **Elisha** and **Sarah (Thomas)**; Thomas d 5/19/1854 in Shoreham, Addison Co., VT. He m (1) **Polly Rockwell**, d 5/13/1816 age 39 and m (2) **Sally Peck** of Cornwall, VT and m (3) **Mehitabel (Darte) Newell** of Shoreham. (*Des. of John Bissell of Windsor*, p. 72, 137-8)

BIXBY

Archelaus – b 12/21/1784 in Thompson, CT, s/o **Daniel**; Archelaus d 11/7/1869 age 67 in Townshend, VT (buried in Wiswell Cem.). He m (1) 9/21/1807 **Parmelia Blandin** of Brookline, VT, b 2/19/1789, d 2/2/1841 age 52 and m (2) 4/4/1841 **Susan Dunton**, d 7/27/1856 age 62. (*Des. of Joseph Bixby*, p. 309 – *Gazetteer of VT*, p. 304 – *1850 Census of Windham Co., VT*)

Ebenezer – b 6/16/1782 near Stafford, CT, d 4/17/1868 in Williamstown, Orange Co., VT. He m1807 in Randolph, VT, **Hannah Tracy Flint**, b 7/24/1784 in Randolph, VT, d 7/13/1863 in Williamstown, VT, d/o **James** and **Jerusha (Lillie)**. (*Bixby Gen.*, p. 303-4, 632-3)

Ichabod – b 1/9/1757 in Killingly, CT, s/o **Solomon**; Ichabod d 1/12/1824 age 67 in Chelsea, Orange Co., VT. He m 3/8/1781 in Stafford, CT, **Lydia**, b 4/15/1756, d 6/14/1820 in 64th year in Chelsea, VT, d/o **Daniel** and **Lydia (Cushman) Orcutt**. (*Bixby Gen.*, p. 632-638, 303-4)

Samuel – b 5/5/1767 in Thompson, CT, s/o **Jacob** and **Sarah (Younglove)**; Samuel d 10/11/1849 in Bridport, Addison Co., VT. He m 2/28/1788 in Thompson, CT, **Esther Elithorpe**, b 9/21/1765, d 9/25/1831, d/o **Nathaniel** and **Jemima (Younglove)**. (*Gazetteer of Addison Co. VT*, p. 80 – *Des. of Joseph Bixby*, p. 311-12)

BLAKELY

David – b 7/25/1749 in Woodbury, CT, d 7/10/1821 age 72 in Pawlet, Rutland Co., VT. He m **Phoebe Hall**, d1831 age 85. (*Rutland Co. Gazetteer*, p. 171)

BLAKESLEE

Enos – b1756 in Harwinton, CT, d 8/1842 age 86 in Camden, Oneida Co., NY. Enos m1785 in Harwinton, CT, **Sara Northrop**, b1762 in

Harwinton, CT, d 8/1848 age 86. (*Pioneer Hist. of Camden, NY*, p. 146-8 - *DAR Patriot Index*, p. 64)

BLISS

Amos - b 1/10/1774 in Lebanon, CT, s/o **Timothy** and **Zerviah (Williams)**; Amos d 2/18/1857 in Essex, Chittenden Co., VT. He m1796 **Hannah Clark** of Lebanon, CT, b 11/1769 d 10/23/1836. (*Bliss Fam. Gen.*, p. 169, 316, 492-3 - *1850 Census Chittenden Co., VT*)

David - b 6/17/1763 in Hebron, CT, s/o **Ellis** and **Tamar (Dewey)**; David d 3/18/1835 in Springwater, NY. He m (1) 4/8/1784 in Hebron, CT, **Bathsheba Cole** of Lebanon, b 4/22/1762, d 11/23/1790, d/o **Ebenezer** and **Abigail (Wise)** and m (2) **Jane McDuffee** of Bradford, b 2/1/1768. (*Bliss Fam.*, p. 119 - *DAR Patriot Index*, p. 66)

Ellis - b 4/6/1759 in Hebron, CT, s/o **Ellis** and **Tamar (Dewey)**; Ellis (the younger) d 8/22/1829 in Bradford, VT. He m **Abigail Taylor** of Hebron, CT, b 4/6/1757, d 2/13/1799. (*Bliss Fam. Gen.*, p. 119-120 - *A Hist. of Bradford, VT*, p. 223-9 - *DAR Patriot Index*, p. 66)

Jonathan Jr. - b 2/4/1711/12 in Windsor, CT, s/o **Jonathan** and **Sarah (Eggleston)**; Jonathan Jr. d 4/1799 in Gilsum, NH. He m **Sibbel Fox**, d 6/2/1789 in Gilsum, NH. (*Bliss Gen.*, p. 55, 86 - *Town of Gilsum, NH*, p. 270-1 - *DAR Patriot Index*, p. 66)

Peletiah Jr. - b 4/3/1749 in Lebanon, CT, s/o **Peletiah** and **Hepzibah (Goodwin)**; Peletiah Jr d 1797/8 in Newbury, Orange Co., VT. He m 8/22/1772 in Newbury, VT, **Ruth Lowell**, d/o **George**. (*Bliss Fam. Gen.*, p. 170, 317-18 - *DAR Patriot Index*, p. 66 - *History of Newbury, VT*, p. 466)

Zenas - b 5/11/1767 in Lebanon, CT, s/o Deacon **Henry** and **Sarah (Woodward)**; Zenas d 1/26/1861 in Leroy, Bradford Co., PA. He m 10/22/1789 in Lebanon, CT, **Polly Wright**, b 9/3/1767, d 4/24/1845, d/o **Charles** of Columbia, CT. (*Hist. of Susquehanna Co., PA*, p. 500 - *Bliss Fam. Gen.*, p. 171-2)

BLISH

Benjamin - b 2/11/1753 in Colchester, CT, s/o **Benjamin** and **Mary (Adams)**; Benjamin (the younger) d 3/11/1825 age 72 in West Painesville, OH. He m1774 **Phebe Skinner**, d 10/5/1844 age 91. (*Rev. Soldiers Buried in Lake Co., OH*, p. 11-12)

BLODGETT

Asael or **Asa** - b1720, bap. 12/5/1736 in Suffield, CT, s/o **Asa** or **Henry**; Asael or Asa d1806 in Cornwall, VT. He m 12/7/1750 in Salisbury, VT, **Irene Owen**, b1730 in Lebanon, CT, d1812 in Cornwall, VT, d/o **Joseph** and **Ruth (Woodward)**. (*DAR Patriot Index*, p. 67)

Luther - b 11/7/1784 in Stafford, CT, s/o **Benjamin** and **Mary Ann (Riddle)**; Luther d 11/1842 in Trenton, OH. He m 4/4/1808 **Elizabeth Starkweather**, b1788 in Norwich, CT, d 12/21/1864 in Oshkosh, WI, d/o **Amos** and **Jemima (Bates)**. (*Blodgett Gen.*, v. 2 typescript p. 287)

Nathan - b CT, d 3/17/1843 in Tunbridge/E. Randolph, VT (gravestone). Nathan m **Sarah** ----, d 11/12/1847 age 47 (gravestone). (Kelsey Mt. Cem., hilltop between Tunbridge/E. Randolph, VT - *Branches and Twigs*, v. 6 #2)

Reuben - b 11/30/1771 in CT, d 1/19/1847 age 72 in Jericho, Chittenden Co., VT. Reuben m **Clara Kellogg**, b 5/2/1786 in Pittsford, VT, d1860 in Jericho, Chittenden Co., VT. (*Des. of Thomas Blodgett*, v. 1 p. 141)

Samuel - b 5/26/1751 in Salisbury, CT, s/o Asa and **Irene (Owen)**; Samuel d 8/5/1838 age 87 in Cornwall, Addison Co., VT. He m (1) **Mary Palmer**, d 9/6/1803 in Cornwall, VT, and m (2) **Mrs. Dickenson**. (*History of Cornwall, VT*, p. 50 - *Des. of Thomas Blodgett*, v. 2 p. 264 - *DAR Patriot Index*, p. 67)

Sylvanus - b 1/10/1765 in Stafford, CT, s/o **Seth** and **Susanna (Orcutt)**; Sylvanus d 8/1853 in Randolph, VT. He m 9/4/1788 in Stafford, CT, **Relief Edson**, b 3/16/1765 in Stafford, CT, d 8/22/1823 in Randolph, VT, d/o **Timothy** and **Lydia (Joy)**. (*Blodgett Gen.* typescript v. 2 p. 276)

William P. - b 9/18/1767 in Stafford, CT, s/o **Nathan** and **Abigail (Cushman)**; William P. d 2/25/1855 in Tunbridge, VT. He m 10/19/1797 in Randolph, VT, **Jerusha Flint**, b 8/4/1775 in Williamstown, VT, d 3/14/1855 in Tunbridge, VT. (*Des. of Thomas Blodgett*, v. 2 p. 273)

BOARDMAN

Amos - b 11/17/1764 in E. Middletown (now Portland), CT, s/o **Samuel**; Amos d 7/31/1854 age 88-9 in Corinth, Orange Co., VT. He m 2/4/1789 **Prudence Chapman**, b 3/3/1768, d 7/21/1851 age 83-4. (*Boardman Gen.*, p. 394 - *DAR Patriot Index*, p. 68)

Joel - b 7/11/1766 in E. Middletown, CT, s/o **Samuel**; Joel d 7/31/1863 age 97 in Middlebury, Addison Co., VT. He m (1) 6/18/1795 **Esther Turner**, b 7/9/1763, d 12/7/1803 and m (2) 9/12/1804 **Rebecca Selleck** b 6/28/1772, d 1/16/1864. Both wives were from Salisbury, CT. (*Boardman Gen.*, p. 394-5)

Moses - b1763 in E. MIddletown, CT, s/o **Samuel**; Moses d 2/29/1816 (or 9/29/1816) in Middlebury, Addison Co., VT. He m **Abigail Mead**, d 2/1/1820 age 51. (*Boardman Gen.*, p. 390 - *DAR Patriot Index*, p. 68)

Dr. Nathaniel - b 10/20/1759 in Bolton, CT, s/o Capt. **Nathaniel** and **Esther (Carver)**; Dr. Nathaniel d 3/17/1843 age 84 (gravestone) in Norwich, Windsor Co., VT. He m 9/9/1790 in Bethel, VT, **Philomela Huntington**, d 2/12/1837 age 63 (gravestone), d/o **Jabez** and **Judith (Elderkin)**. (*A History of Norwich, VT*, p. 166-7 - *Boardman Gen.*, p. 387-8)

Capt. Nathaniel - b 3/14/1731/2 in E. Middletown, CT, s/o **Stephen** and **Abigail (Savage)**; Capt. Nathaniel d 11/11/1814 age 82 in Norwich, Windsor Co., VT. He m 5/29/1758 **Esther Carver**, b 3/26/1738, d 12/19/1834 age 96. (*Boardman Gen.*, p. 313-14 - *DAR Patriot Index* p. 68)

Ozias Jr. - b 1/4/1774 in Canaan, CT, s/o **Ozias** and **Lydia (Hinsdale)**; Ozias (the younger) d 9/10/1843 in 69th year in Morristown, VT. He m1802 in Morristown, VT, **Lydia Whitney**, b1783, d/o **Eliphalet** and **Lois (Holton)** of Marlboro and Morristown, VT. (*Boardman Gen.*, p. 337-8, 418-19)

Samuel Allen - b 3/9/1751/2 in Middletown, CT, s/o **Moses**; Samuel Allen d 9/24/1780 while in Service. He m 3/31/1774 **Katherine Thorp** of Farmington, CT. (*Boardman Gen. - DAR Patriot Index*, p. 68 - *Hist. of Norwich, VT*, p. 165-6)

Stephen - bap. 5/3/1772 in Bolton, CT, d 9/3/1801 in Chelsea, VT. Stephen m **Sarah Sargeant**, d/o **Dr.** Sargeant of Norwich, VT. (*Boardman Gen.*, p. 390)

Timothy - b 1/20/1754, s/o **Timothy** and **Jemima (Johnson)**; Timothy (the younger) d 4/3/1839 age 86 in Rutland, VT. He m 9/28/1783 **Mary Ward**, b 10/21/1753, d 12/1836 in Rutland, VT. (*Boardman Gen.*, p. 352-4 - *Hist. of Pittsford, VT*, p. 376 - *Rutland Co. Gazetteer*, p. 216)

BOGUE

Ebenezer - b 1/28/1779 in Farmington, CT, s/o **Oliver** and **Lucy (Darrin)**; Ebenezer d 3/13/1857 in Enosburg, Franklin Co., VT. He m1803 in Georgia, VT, **Roxana Loomis**, b1783, d 6/18/1856. (*Bogue and Allied Families*, p. 59-60)

Harris - b 5/27/1783 in Farmington, CT, s/o **Oliver** and **Lucy (Darrin)**; Harris d 12/9/1856 in Waterloo, IN. He m 2/18/1819 in Pittsford, VT, **Laura Hubbell**. (*Bogue and Allied Families*, p. 40, 60-1)

Jeffrey Amherst - b 8/21/1759 in Farmington, CT, s/o Rev. **Ebenezer**; Jeffrey Amherst d 8/31/1828 in Pittsford, Rutland Co., VT. He m **Freedom Barnard** of Coventry, CT, b 3/21/1773, d 8/31/1850 in Pittsford, VT. (*Hist. of Pittsford*, p. 371-2 - *Bogue and Allied Fam.*, p. 42, 63, 175 - *DAR Patriot Index*, p. 69)

Oliver - b 4/13/1757 in Farmington, CT, s/o **Ebenezer** and **Demaris (Cook)**; Oliver d 2/2/1828 or 2/22/1828 in 71st year in Pittsford, VT. He m **Lucy Darrin**, b 2/15/1762, in Guildford, CT, d 10/16/1850 age 80. (*Hist. of Pittsford, VT*, p. 693, 333, 204 - *Bogue and Allied Families*, p. 40-41 - *1850 Rutland Co. Census* for Pittsford)

Publius Virgilius - b 3/30/1764 in Avon, CT, d 8/28/1836 age 73 in Clinton, NY. Publius Virgilius m **Catherine Robinson**. (*DAR Patriot Index*, p. 69 - *Clinton Memorial - Kirtland Ave. Cem.*, p. 14)

BOHONON

Major **Ananiah** - b 4/6/1765 in CT, s/o **Andrew** and **Susanna (Webster)**; Major Ananiah d 9/7/1853 age 88-5 in Chelsea, Orange Co., VT. He m 6/16/1795 in Salisbury, NH, **Sarah Cushing**, b 12/26/1771, d 8/12/1850 in Chelsea, VT. (*Hist. of Salisbury, NH*, p. 490, 493 - Old Cem., Chelsea, VT)

BOLLES

Robinson - b 1/25/1766 in Groton, CT, s/o **Amos** and **Abigail (Smith)**; Robinson d 1/28/1842 age 76. He m 11/26/1789 **Hannah Stoddard**, b 6/26/1768 in Groton, CT, d 11/22/1852 in Jessup, PA, d/o

Elkanah and Esther (Gallup). (*Hist. of Susquehanna Co.*, p. 359 - *Bolles Gen.*, p. 87, 155)

BOOGE
Rev. Ebenezer - b Farmington, CT, d 2/2/1767 age nearly 51 years in Pittsford, Rutland Co., VT. He m 12/19/1750 in Wallingford, CT, Damaris Cook, d/o Samuel. (*Hist. of Pittsford, VT*, p. 370-1)

BOOTH
Benjamin - b 5/17/1768 in Union, CT, s/o Isaac and Rebecca; Benjamin d 1/18/1839 in Pittsford, Rutland Co., VT. He m1800 Anna Needham of Brimfield, MA, d 5/1839. (*History of Pittsford, VT*, p. 312)

Elam - b 5/1801 in Tolland Co., CT, d 11/2/1882 age 81-5-8 in Concord, Erie Co., NY. Elam m Sibyl Ingalls. (*Hist. of Original Town of Concord, NY*, p. 285-6)

Elisha - bap. 12/18/1755 in Woodbury, CT, s/o Gideon and Ann (Hawley); Elisha d 2/24/1830 age 73 in So. Hinesburg, Chittenden Co., VT. He m 12/23/1783 in New Milford, CT, Elizabeth Clark, bap 5/8/1768 in Milford, CT, d after 3/22/1830 in So. Hinesburg, VT. (*Ezra Thompson Clark's Anc. and Des.*, p. 83)

BOSTWICK
Arthur - b 6/28/1729 in New Milford, CT, d 1/10/1802 in Jericho, Chittenden Co., VT. He m 7/1/1752 in New Milford, CT, Eunice Warriner, b 6/3/1729 in Brimfield, MA, d 5/26/1801 in Jericho, VT, d/o William and Sarah. (*Gen. of Bostwick*, p. 143-4 - *Gazetteer of Chittenden Co.*, p. 231 - *DAR Patriot Index*, p. 73)

Austin - b 11/1/1766 in New Milford, CT, s/o Joseph and Mary (Roberts); Austin d 5/5/1844 in Fairfield, Franklin Co., VT. He m 1/13/1791 in New Milford, CT, Mary Sturdevant. (*Bostwick Gen.*, p. 221)

Ebenezer - b 6/22/1751 in New Milford, CT, s/o Edmund and Mercy; Ebenezer d 3/16/1840 in Rootstown, OH. He m 6/10/1777 in New Milford, CT, Rebecca Northrup, d1803. (*DAR Patriot Index*, p. 73 - *Bostwick Gen.*, p. 187-8 - *History and Tales of Hinesburgh, VT*, p. 14)

Edmund - b 9/13/1732 in New Milford, CT, d 2/20/1826 age 94-2-5 in Rootstown, OH. Edmund m 9/3/1754 in New Milford, CT, Mercy Ruggles, d 1/21/1822 in Rootstown, OH, d/o Capt. Joseph and Rachel (Tolls). (*Bostwick Gen.*, p. 139-140 - *DAR Patriot Index*, p. 73 - *Hist. and Tales of Hinesburgh, VT*)

Erastus - b 8/31/1767 in New Milford, CT, s/o Jonathan and Rebecca (Bronson); Erastus d 3/3/1864 in Hinesburgh, Chittenden Co., VT. He m 2/10/1795 in Hinesburgh, VT, Sally T. Welch, d 4/19/1842 in Hinesburg, VT, d/o Rev. Whitman Welch. (*Bostwick Gen.*, p. 229-30, 383)

Isaac - b 9/6/1730 in New Milford, CT, d 4/21/1808 age 78 in Hinesburgh, Chittenden Co., VT. Isaac m 11/27/1754 in New Milford, CT, Prudence Warner, b 12/3/1733 in New Milford, CT, d 10/4/1801 age 71 in Hinesburgh, VT, d/o John and Mary (Curtis).

(*Hist. and Tales of Hinesburgh, VT*, p. 25 – *DAR Patriot Index*, p. 73 – *Bostwick Gen.*, p. 153-6)

Lemuel – b 12/27/1758 in New Milford, CT, s/o **Isaac** and **Prudence** (**W a r n e r**); Lemuel d 10/17/1819 possibly in NY state. He m 6/27/1784 in New Milford, CT, **Polly Trail** b 7/10/1764. (*Bostwick Gen.*, p. 211-12, 349)

BOTSFORD

Dr. Amos – b 2/13/1780 in Newtown, CT, s/o **Gideon**; Dr. Amos d 8/16/1864 in Greenville, Greene Co., NY. He m 9/20/1801 **Elizabeth Clark**, d/o **Joseph** of Washington, CT. (*Hist. of Greene Co.*, p. 311)

BOTTOM/BOTTUM

Elijah Bottum – bc1724 in Norwich, CT, d 3/4/1809 in 86th yr. in Shaftsbury, Bennington Co., VT. Elijah m **Dorothy Williams**, d 6/18/1809 in 83rd yr. in Shaftsbury, VT. (*Bennington Co. Gazetteer*, p. 197)

Jesse Bottom – d 7/11/1762 in Norwich, CT, s/o **David** and **Lucy** (**R e e d**); Jesse d 7/29/1847 in Orwell, Addison Co., VT. He m 2/7/1784 **Betsey Bennett** of Norwich, CT. (*Gen. of Longbottom-Bottum Families*, p. 26A)

Simon Bottum – b 8/23/1759 in Norwich, CT, s/o **Elijah** and **Dorothy** (**Williams**); Simon d 2/7/1822 in Shaftsbury, Bennington Co., Vt. He m 5/13/1790 in Shaftsbury, VT, **Elizabeth Huntington**, b1767 in Norwich, CT, d 3/12/1848 age 80, d/o **Nathan**. (*Bottom–Longbottom Families*, p. 46-7, 60 – *Gazetteer*, p. 198)

BOWEN

Gen. Daniel – b 7/20/1783 in W. Woodstock, CT, s/o **Henry**; Gen. Daniel d 9/3/1859 in Weathersfield, Windsor Co., VT. He m (1) 2/8/1809 **Lucy North**, b Farmington, CT, and m (2) 8/11/1818 **Sylvia North**, b 1/2/1778, d 9/8/1868, d/o **Samuel** and **Lucy** (**Deming**). (Both wives were sisters.) (*1850 Census of Windsor Co., VT* – Bowen's *Woodstock Families*)

Elisha – b 2/20/1779 in W. Woodstock, CT, s/o of **Henry**; Elisha d 6/8/1853 in Weathersfield, Windsor Co., VT. He m 10/20/1806 in S. Wilbraham, MA, **Fanny Chandler Morris**, b 4/27/1787 in MA, d 11/23/1863 in Ascutneyville, VT, d/o **D a r i u s** and **R e b e c c a** (**Chandler**). (*1850 Census of Windsor, VT* – *Woodstock Families*, p. 345-6, 530)

Silas – b 9/6/1774 in Woodstock, CT, s/o **Henry** and **Lydia**; Silas d 9/16/1857 in Kearney or Nebraska City, NE. He m 9/11/1803 **Polly Chandler**, b1786 in Alstead, NH, d 4/9/1853 in Clarendon, VT, d/o **Capt. Jonathan**. (*Hist. of Rutland Co., VT*, p. 571 – *Genealogies of Woodstock Fam.*, p. 529)

BOYD

Pierce – b 12/1/1798 in CT, s/o **Robert**; d 8/15/1878 in VT. Pierce m 10/1/1829 **Lucy Whitman**, d/o **Charles**. (*Pomfret, VT*, v. 2, p. 441 – *Hist. of Royalton, VT*, p. 701)

BRACE

Hon. **Jonathan** - b 11/12/1754 in Harwinton, CT, s/o **Jonathan**; Hon.
Jonathan (the younger) d 10/26/1837 in Pawlet, Rutland Co., VT.
He m 4/15/1778 Mrs. **Ann Kimberly** of Glastonbury, CT, wid/o
Thomas Kimberly. (*Hist. of Rutland Co.*, p. 701 - *Brace Lineage*,
p. 89-90)

BRADLEY

Andrew - b 1/13/1754 in Fairfield, CT, s/o **Gershom** and **Jane
(Dimon)**; Andrew d 6/2/1832 in 79th yr. in Fairfield, Franklin Co.,
VT. He m (1) **Ruth Wakeman**, d 5/26/1793, d/o **Wm.** and **Sarah
(Hull)**, and m (2) Mrs. **Jane (Dimon) Fanton**, d 10/23/1823 in 66th
yr. and m (3) Mrs. **Orissa (Wilmarth) Barlow.** (*Some Early Rec. of
Fairfield, VT*, p. 8, 15)

Justus - b 11/6/1782 in Cheshire, CT, s/o **Oliver** and **Deborah**; Justus d 9/1829 in Tallmadge, OH. He m **L a u r a   E l y**, b1786 in Troy,
NY. (1972 Spring Issue of *OH Gen. Soc.*, p. 35)

L e m u e l - b 2/26/1750 in Guilford, CT, d 12/11/1800 in 50th yr. in
Sunderland, Bennington Co., VT. He m (1) **Lucy Baker**, and m (2)
Mercy Washburn. (*Bennington Co., VT, Gazetteer*, p. 208 -
gravestone, Sunderland Cem.)

L e n t - b 6/14/1751 in New Haven, CT, d 12/20/1840 age 89 in
Westfield, Chautauqua Co., NY. Lent m (1) **Ann Bristol**, and m (2)
Roxana Collins of Ripley d 5/17/1854, age 80. (*Soldiers of Am.
Rev. Chautauqua Co., NY - DAR Patriot Index*, p. 80)

Phillip - b 9/7/1770 in Ridgefield, CT, s/o **Philip** and **Molly**; Phillip
(the younger) d 9/1861 age 83 in Whitehall, NY. He m **Eleanor** (or
Ellen) Meeker, b CT, d 12/13/1875 age 96. (*1850 Rutland Co.
Census - VT Hist. Mag.*, v. 4, p. 1176-7)

BRAINERD

A n s e l - b 5/4/1765 in Chatham, CT, d 6/12/1855 in OH. Ansel
m1785 **Mary Warren**, b 7/19/1767 in NY, d 9/5/1859. (*DAR
Patriot Index*, p. 80 - *Brainerd Gen.*, p. 56, 96)

Asahel - b 10/7/1771 in Haddam, CT, s/o **Elijah** and **Lucy (Smith)**;
Asahel d 3/22/1865 age 94-5-17 in Randolph, Orange Co., VT. He
m 11/25/1796 **Lydia Loveland**, bc1770 in CT, d 4/2/1858, d/o
Titus and **Lydia (Chapman).** (*Brainerd Gen.*, v. 2, p. 67-8 - *Gazetteer of Orange Co., VT*, p. 354)

D a v i d - b 11/27/1748 in CT, d1828 in French Grant, Lawrence Co.,
OH. David m 1/2/1772 **Hannah Willard**, b 6/13/1750 in Saybrook,
CT, d1840 age 90 in OH, d/o **George** and **Hannah (Merrill).**
(*Brainerd Gen.*, p. 82 - *DAR Patriot Index*, p. 80)

Isaac - b 10/26/1763 in Haddam, CT, s/o **Benjamin** and **Mary (Colt)**;
Isaac d 8/24/1825 in Westmoreland, NY, but buried Randolph, VT.
He m 6/25/1784 **Alice Brainerd**, d 12/24/1850 age 85-9-6, d/o
Elijah. (*Brainerd Gen.*, p. 67)

Israel - b 2/10/1748/9 in Haddam, CT, s/o **Josiah** and **Hannah
(S p e n c e r)**; Israel d1818/1819 in Danville, VT. He m widow
Deborah (Willey) Hoyt, bap. 6/25/1747 in Middle Haddam, CT, d/o
Abel and **Mary (Holman) Willey**, wid/o **Benjamin Hoyt.** (*Brainerd

Gen., p. 53-4, 73-6 - *DAR Patriot Index*, p. 80 - *Caledonia, VT, Gazetteer*, p. 331-2)

Hon. **Lawrence** - b 3/16/1794 in E. Hartford, CT, s/o **Ezra** and **Mabel (Porter)**; Hon. Lawrence d 5/9/1870 age 79-1-23 in St. Albans, VT. He m 1/16/1819 **Fidelia Barnett Gadcomb**, b 3/31/1793 in Gloucester, RI, d 10/18/1852 age 59-6, d/o **William** and **Amy (Owen)**. (*Brainerd Gen.*, p. 67-8 - *Franklin, VT, Gazetteer*, p. 185)

Loudon - b 1/19/1791 in Haddam, CT, s/o **Isaac** and **Alice (Brainerd) Brainerd**; Loudon d 1/16/1865 (or 1/18/1865) age 74 yr. in Westmoreland, NY. He m 2/21/1821 in Westmoreland, NY, **Betty Hunt**, b 4/13/1801 d 4/9/1890 age 89. (*Brainerd Genealogy*, p. 128-9, 239)

Ozias - b 4/23/1771 in Chatham, CT, s/o **Ozias** and **Elizabeth**; Ozias d 3/2/1858 in Brooklyn, OH. He m 4/12/1796 **Mary Strong**, d 12/6/1864, d/o **Jabin** and **Betsey**. (*Hist. of Cuyahoga Co., OH*)

BRANCH

Francis - b 6/5/1812 in Middle Haddam, s/o **Seth** and **Rachel (Hard)**; Francis d 11/4/1877 in Brooklyn Heights, OH. He m 10/21/1837 **Sarah Slaght**, d/o **Abraham**. (*History of Cuyahoga Co., OH*, p. 334)

Samuel - b 5/7/1768 in Norwich, CT, d 1/21/1843 in NY (possibly Genoa). He m1794 **Ruth Chidsey**, d/o **Augustus** of Aurora. (*Patriot Index*, p. 81 - *Hist. of Cayuga Co., NY*, p. 397)

William - b 9/3/1760 in Preston, CT, s/o **William** and **Hannah**; William (the younger) d 4/13/1849 in Madison, OH. He m **Lucretia Tracy**. (*DAR Patriot Index*, p. 81 - *Rev. Soldiers Buried in Lake Co., OH*, p. 13)

BREED

Caleb - bc1762 in Stonington, CT, d 9/14/1828 in Pharsalia, Chenango Co., NY. He m **Rhody ----**, d 12/9/1827 age 60 in Pharsalia, NY. (*Hist. of Chenango Co.*, p. 423)

Stephen - b 7/4/1786 in Stonington, CT, d 3/9/1852 in Brooklyn, Susquehanna Co., PA. He m1811 **Sophia Gere**, b 6/12/1786, d 3/30/1882, d/o **Robert** of Poquanoc, CT. (*Hist. of Susquehanna Co., PA*, p. 661 - *Breed Fam. Assoc.*, p. 260, 280)

BREWSTER

Anson Alvord - b 11/28/1807 in Bolton, CT, s/o **Anson** and **Aurelia (Alvord)**; Anson Alvord d 1/1864 in Hudson, OH. He m **Sarah Porter White**, d/o **Dr. Israel**. (*Reminiscences of Hudson, OH*, p. 34-5)

Elisha - b1790 in Norwich, CT, d 7/12/1838 in Middlebury, Addison Co., VT. Elisha m 9/28/1812 **Rebecca Fish**, d 12/26/1867 in Aurora, IL, d/o **Miller** and **Huldah (Corning)**. (*Brewster Gen.*, p. v. 1, p. 424-5 - *Gazetteer of Addison Co., VT*)

Ephraim - b 8/20/1731 in Preston, CT, s/o **Jonathan**; Ephraim d 5/10/1810 age 79 in Woodstock, Windsor Co., VT. He m **Margery Parks**, d 2/1841 age 88, d/o **Paul** of Preston, CT. (*Hist. of Woodstock, VT*, p. 108-11 - *Brewster Gen.*, p. 122-3 - *DAR Patriot Index*, p. 84)

Israel – b CT, d 9/3/1823 age 87 in Pittsford, VT (gravestone, Old
Cong. Cem.). Israel m **Abigail** ----, d 3/7/1823 age 86 (gravestone
Old Cong. Cem.). (Gravestones in Pittsford, VT, Cem.)
Sanford – b 3/3/1788 in Preston, CT, s/o **Judah** and **Lucy**; Sanford d
4/26/1857 in Huron, OH. He m (1) 9/10/1809 in Preston, CT, **Lucy
Avery**, b 12/20/1787, d 3/18/1838, and m (2) **Mrs. Jackson**, and m
(3) in 1847, **Emily Hutchins**, b 3/30/1814 in Strafford, VT, d
2/22/1859 in Sandusky, OH. (*Brewster Genealogy*, p. 160, 337 –
War of 1812)

BRIDGMAN

John – b 7/30/1769 in Coventry, CT, s/o **John**; John (the younger) d
6/7/1857 in Hardwick, Caledonia Co., VT. He m 11/21/1793 in
Hanover, NH, **Lydia Hall**, b 1/15/1773 in Lebanon, CT, d
4/30/1863. (*Gen. of the Bridgman Fam.*, p. 52-3, 5, 64-6)

BRIGHAM

Paul W. – b 10/26/1776 in Coventry, CT, s/o **Paul** and **Lydia
(Sawyer)**; Paul W. d 1/3/1865 age 89 in Norwich, Windsor Co., VT.
He m 2/22/1801 **Mary Ayers** of Haverhill, MA, b 3/16/1782, d
9/28/1869. (*History of Brigham Fam.*, p. 280-1 – *1850 Windsor Co.,
VT, Census*)
Dr. Thomas – b 3/23/1769 in Coventry, CT, s/o **Paul** and **Lydia
(Sawyer)**; Dr. Thomas d in Norwich, Windsor Co., VT, (no stone).
He m **Polly Dana**, d 4/30/1853 age 84 (gravestone), d/o Gen.
James. (*History of Brigham Fam.*, p. 277-8 – *A History of Norwich,
VT*, p. 186-7)

BRISTOL

Moses – b 2/11/1716 in New Haven, CT, s/o **Eliphalet** and **Esther
(Peck)**; Moses d 5/1802 in Clinton, Oneida Co., NY. He m **Rachel
Trowbridge**, b 11/18/1719 in Stratford, CT, d/o **Isaac** and **Ruth
(Perry)**. (*Clinton Memorial-Kirtland Ave. Cem.*, p. 14 – *Trowbridge
Gen.*, p. 129 – *CT Men in the Revolution*, p. 467)

BROCK

John – b 4/13/1755 in Woodstock, CT, s/o **John** and **Sarah
(Southwick)**; John (the younger) d 3/26/1830 age 75 in Dorset, VT.
He m 2/10/1785 in Danby, VT, **Hannah Tabor** of Danby, b1763, d
6/30/1843 age 79. (*Gen. of Woodstock Fam.*, v. 2, p. 652-5 – *History of Danby, VT*, p. 117 – *DAR Patriot Index*, p. 87)

BROCKWAY

John – b 11/29/1766 in Hartford, CT, s/o **Edward** and **Mary (Ely)**;
John d 10/28/1842. He m **Hannah Simonds**, d1855. (*Pomfret, VT*,
v. 2, p. 442-3)
Jonathan – b 2/25/1766 in Lyme, CT, s/o **Jonathan** and **Phebe
(Smith)**; Jonathan (the younger) d 5/1847 in Rockingham, Windham
Co., VT. He m 2/24/1789 **Mary Proctor** of E. Washington, NH, d
3/7/1872 age 101-11-23. (*Hist. of Rockingham*, p. 605-6)
Walston/Woolston – b 12/25/1711 in Lyme, CT, d 10/3/1789 in Gilsum, NH. Walston/Woolston m (1) 9/30/1736 **Anna** (or **Mary**)

Brook of New London, and m (2) 8/24/1760 **Esther** ---- of Lyme, d 12/1797 age 74. (*Town of Gilsum, NH*, p. 175, 277 - *DAR Patriot Index*, p. 88)

BROMLEY
Bethuel - b 12/22/1737 in Preston, CT, d1808 age 70 in Danby, Rutland Co., VT. He m (1) **Arabella Herrick**, and m (2) **Susanna Weller** (separated), and m (3) **Lydia McCleveland**. (*Hist. of Danby, VT*, p. 114 - *DAR Patriot Index*, p. 88)

BRONSON
Roswell - b 9/9/1751 in Waterbury, CT, s/o **James**; Roswell d 2/1836 in Clinton, NY. He m **Susannah Adams**. (*DAR Patriot Index*, p. 88 - *Clinton Memorial, Kirtland Ave. Cem.*, p. 14 - *CT State Lib. Rev. War Archives*, v. 21 246a, 256 - *Hist. of Waterbury, CT*, p. 349)

BROOKS
Willard Lyman - b 7/20/1808 near Bristol, CT, s/o **Solomon** and **Hannah (Benham)**; Willard Lyman d 12/5/1883 in Portland, Ionia Co., MI. He m (1) 7/24/1834 in Harwinton, CT, **Lucina Sanford**, and m (2) 8/26/1844 in Portland, MI, **Nancy Reed**, b 11/19/1823 in Rehoboth, MA, d 2/28/1907 in Portland, MI. (*Detroit Society Gen. Res.*, Winter 1970 p. 74)

John - b 2/7/1753 in Ashford, CT, s/o **John** and **Abial (Wright)**; John (the younger) d 2/8/1820 in Winhall, Bennington Co., VT. He m **Rachel Taylor** of Montague, MA. (*VT Hist. Mag.* v. 1, p. 246-7 - *DAR Patriot Index*, p. 89)

John - b 4/20/1790 in CT, s/o **Nathaniel** and **Lucy (Richards)**; John d 6/7/1858 in Colden, Erie Co., NY. He m 3/21/1816 **Lydia Booth**, d 4/10/1870 in Wales Center, NY, d/o **Isaac** and **Elizabeth**. (*Hist. of Orig. Town of Concord, NY*, p. 893-4)

Samuel Lewis - b1750 in CT, d 1/23/1846 in Penfield, Monroe Co., NY, and is buried in Penfield Cem. Samuel Lewis m **Phebe Beers**. (*DAR Patriot Index*, p. 89 - *DAR Mag.*, p. 914, 1977 issue)

Thomas - b 11/22/1763 in CT, d 5/24/1835 in Penfield, Monroe Co., NY, and is buried in Penfield Cem. Thomas m **Esther Beers**. (*DAR Mag.*, 1977 - *DAR Patriot Index*, p. 89)

BROWN
Benjamin - b 12/25/1778 in Stonington, CT, s/o **Ichabod** and **Thankful (Baldwin)**; Benjamin d 2/1/1857 age 78 in Pharsalia, Chenango Co., NY. He m in Stonington, CT, **Phoebe Brown**, d 1/26/1856 age 79. (*Hist. of Chenango Co.*, p. 424)

Ebenezer - bc1763 in Canterbury, CT, s/o **Shubael** and **Edith (Bradford)**; Ebenezer d 9/25/1822 age 59 (gravestone). He m (1) 1/13/1793 **Anna Murdock**, d 11/13/1802 age 32 (gravestone), d/o Hon. **Thomas**, and m (2) 1/12/1814 **Mary Dana**, d/o Rev. **Josiah** of Barre, MA. (*A History of Norwich, VT*, p. 168)

Elijah Jr. - b 3/28/1756 in Coventry, CT, s/o **Elijah** and **Lydia (Gary)**; Elijah Jr. d1800 in Pittsford, Rutland Co., VT. He m **Sarah Adams** of Coventry, CT. (*Hist. of Pittsford, VT*, p. 201, 693 - *DAR Patriot Index*, p. 91)

Joseph - bc1784 in Thompson, CT, d 3/7/1877 age 93 in Henrietta. Twp, Monroe Co., NY. Joseph m **Abby** ---- of Douglas, MA. (*Hist. of Monroe Co.*, p. 250, 252, 313)

Nathan - b 11/1/1779 in Stonington, CT, s/o **Nathan** and **Mercy** (**Babcock**); Nathan (the younger) d1871 age 92 in Otsego Co., NY. He m **Lydia Burdick** of Brookfield, NY, d1862 age 80. (*Biog. Rec. of Otsego Co., NY*, p. 473)

Capt. Nathan - b 6/18/1765 in Stonington, CT, s/o **Nathan** and **Lydia** (**Dewey**); Capt. Nathan d 6/2/1847 age 82 in Pharsalia, Chenango Co., NY. He m **Eunice Brown**, d 9/28/1826 age 59, d/o **Ichabod**. (*Hist. of Chenango Co., NY*, p. 425)

Nehemiah - b 7/11/1740 in Stonington, CT, s/o **Daniel** and **Mary** (**Breed**); Nehemiah d 12/15/1824 age 84 in Pharsalia, Chenango Co., NY. He m **Rebecca Lewis**, b Westerly, RI, d 12/5/1831 age 84. (*Hist. of Stonington, CT*, p. 261-3 - *Hist. of Chenango Co., NY*, p. 423)

Oliver - b 2/9/1760 in Stonington, CT, s/o **Zebulon** and **Anne**; Oliver d 6/5/1845 in Concord, OH. He m (1) 1780 Mrs. **Gracie Welch**, d1832, and m (2) **Mrs. Beardsley**, d1840, and m (3) Mrs. **Hannah Perkins** (possibly). (*Rev. Soldiers Buried in Lake Co., OH - DAR Patriot Index*, p. 93)

Owen - b 2/15/1771 in West Simsbury, CT; Owen d 5/8/1856 age 85. He m (1) 2/11/1793 **Ruth Mills** of Simsbury, d 12/10/1808, and m (2) 11/8/1810 **Sallie Root**, and m (3) 8/1841 Mrs. **Lucy D. Hinsdale**. (*Reminiscences of Hudson, OH*, p. 47-9)

BRUNSON

James - b 10/22/1727 in Waterbury, CT, d 7/16/1810 in Cinton, NY, and buried in Sunset Hill Cem. James m 8/22/1750 Sarah Brockett, d/o **Josiah** and **Deborah** (**Abbot**). (*Clinton Memorial*, p. 39 - *DAR Patriot Index*, p. 88)

BRUSH

Jonas - b 4/20/1755 in Litchfield Co., CT, d 1/30/1831 in E. Bridgewater, PA. Jonas m **Tamar Ann Ruggles**, d1837 in E. Bridgewater, PA. (*Hist. of Susquehanna Co., PA*, p. 564 - *DAR Patriot Index*, p. 95)

Stephen - b1796 in Fairfield Co., CT, d 1/14/1860 in Honesdale, PA. Stephen m **Dianthe** ----. (*First Presbyterian Soc. of Honesdale, PA*, p. 81)

BRYAN

John - b1755 in Watertown, CT, d 11/24/1858 in Clinton, NY. John m (1) ----, and m (2) **Mehitable Alcott Bradley**. (*Pioneer Hist. of Camden, NY - Hist. of Oneida Co.*, p. 433)

BRYANT

Daniel Damon - b 11/24/1755 in E. Hartford, CT, d 8/27/1805 age 49 in Thetford, VT. Daniel Damon m **Bethia Newton**, b 8/17/1765 in Colchester, CT, d 9/25/1852 age 87 in Thetford, VT, d/o **Asahel**. (*1850 Orange Co., VT, Census* for Thetford - *DAR Patriot Index*, p. 96)

BUCK

Hon. **Daniel** – b 11/9/1753 in Hebron, CT, s/o **Thos. Jr.** and **Jane**; Hon. Daniel d 8/16/1816 age 62 in Chelsea, Orange Co., VT, and is buried in Old Cem., Chelsea, VT. He m 9/22/1786 **Content Ashley**, d 1/11/1850 age 78. (*DAR Patriot Index*, p. 97 – *A Hist. of Norwich, VT*, p. 171-5)

Capt. **Ichabod** – b 11/25/1757, s/o Rev. **Daniel** and **Ann (Denton)**; Capt. Ichabod d 3/19/1849 in Franklin, PA. He m (1) **Lucy Boardman**, and m (2) **Sybil Dayton**. (*DAR Patriot Index*, p. 97 – *Hist. of Susquehanna, PA*, p. 60)

Isaac – b 3/29/1729/30 in New Milford, CT, s/o **Joseph** and **Ann (Gould)**; Isaac d 1/20/1776 age 71 in Pittsford, VT. He mc1757 **Elizabeth Waters**. (*DAR Patriot Index*, p. 97 – *History of Pittsford, VT*, p. 35)

Lemuel – b 9/6/1732 in New Milford, CT, d1790 in Arlington, Bennington Co., VT. Lemuel m **Bertha McEwen**. (*DAR Patriot Index*, p. 97 – *Bennington Co. Gazetteer*, p. 78)

BUCKINGHAM

Charles J. – b 7/7/1810 in Columbia, CT, s/o **Stephen** and **Polly (Brewster)**; Charles J. d 10/2/1889 in Poughkeepsie, NY. He m 10/16/1839 in Poughkeepsie, NY, **Emily Williams** of NY City, d 1/26/1848 in Poughkeepsie, NY. (*Comm. Biog. Rec. of Dutchess Co., NY*, p. 394)

Hon. **Jedediah** – b 4/7/1758 in CT, s/o **Jedediah** and **Martha (Clark)**; Hon. Jedediah d 9/27/1840 age 83 in E. Thetford, VT. He m (1) 5/6/1787 in Hebron, CT, **Nancy Cook** of Newburyport, MA, d 7/18/1835 age 75 in E. Thetford, VT, and m (2) 9/20/1835 **Mirabah F. Springer**, b 9/30/1794, d 10/11/1883. (*Gazeteer of Orange Co., VT*, p. 43-4 – *Chapman-Buckingham*, p. 173)

BUCKLAND

William – b1727 in Hartford, CT, d 3/11/1795 in Poultney, VT. William m **Margaret Barret**, b1735, d/o **John**. (*Branches and Twigs*, Winter 1976, p. 26 – *Hist. of Rutland Co., VT*)

BUEL/BUELL

Ashbel Buell – b 1/12/1765 in Litchfield, CT, s/o Capt. **Archelaus** and **Mary (Landon)**; Ashbel d 11/3/1853 age nearly 89 in West Newbury, VT. He m 11/1/1787 in Litchfield, CT, **Huldah Webster**, b 2/22/1767, d 10/10/1856 age 89, d/o **Timothy** of Litchfield, CT. (*Hist. of Newbury, VT*, p. 480 – *Buell Gen.*, p. 196-8 – *Gazetteer of Orange Co., VT*, p. 305-6)

Major **Elias Buel** – b 10/8/1737 in Coventry, CT, s/o Capt. **Peter**; Major Elias d 5/17/1824 in Albany, NY. He m 8/6/1758 in Coventry, CT, **Sarah Turner**, b 9/25/1738, d 4/4/1824. (*Buel Fam.*, p. 63-4 – *A Hist. of Coventry, Orleans Co., VT*, p. 6)

Ephraim Buel – b 8/21/1742 in Hebron, CT, s/o **Samuel**; Ephraim d 1/4/1820 in Crosby, OH. He m 2/22/1764 in Kent, CT, **Priscilla Holmes** of Litchfield, CT, b1745, d 1/5/1820. (*DAR Patriot Index*, p. 98 – *Hist. of Rutland Co.*, p. 519 – *Buell Fam.*, p. 98-9)

Miner Buell - b 12/28/1788 in Lebanon, CT, s/o **Isaac** and **Prudence** (**Sprague**); Miner d 1/15/1863 age 75 in Camden, NY. He m **Melinda** ----, dc1869 age 84. (*Pioneer Hist. of Camden, Oneida Co., NY*)

Roswell Buell - b 8/27/1772, at Killingworth, CT, s/o **David**; Roswell d1812/1813 age 40 (probably in Fairfield, Herkimer Co., NY). He m1795 **Sarah Griswold**, b Killingworth, CT, d/o **Daniel**. (*Hist. of Herkimer Co.*, p. 295-8 by Benton - *Hist. of Herkimer Co.* by Hardin p. 468-70)

Solomon Buell - b 4/12/1760 in Coventry, CT, s/o **Elias** and **Sarah** (**Turner**); Solomon d 10/18/1837 in Coventry, Orleans Co., VT. He mc1789 in Coventry, CT, **Sophia Root**, bc1764, d 7/27/1845 age 55, d/o Judge **Jesse**. (*DAR Patriot Index*, p. 98 - *Hist. of Coventry VT - Buell Fam.*, p. 116)

Timothy Buell - b 5/3/1757 in CT, d 1/26/1849 in E. Bloomfield, Ontario Co., NY, and is buried in Rice Cem., Bloomfield, Ontario Co., NY. Timothy m **Olive Norton**. (*DAR Mag.*, 1977 p. 914 - *DAR Patriot Index*, p. 98)

BUGBEE

Abiel - b 2/27/1746 in Woodstock, CT, s/o **Jesse** and **Experience** (**Peake**); Abiel d 1/17/1824 in Pomfret, Windsor Co., VT. He m 11/15/1770 **Hannah Harwood** of Sutton, MA, b 7/21/1751, d 10/17/1836, d/o **David** and **Elizabeth**. (*Pomfret, VT*, v. 2, p. 446-7 - *DAR Patriot Index*, p. 98 - *Woodstock Families*, v. 3, p. 23-4, 37-9)

Abial - b 1/2/1774 in Ashford, CT, s/o **Abial** and **Hannah**; Abial (the younger) d 4/18/1829 in Pomfret, VT. He m1797 **Mary Hewitt**, d 11/16/1829 in Pomfret, VT, d/o **Increase**. (*Pomfret, VT*, v. 2 p. 447-8 - *Woodstock Families*, v. 3 p. 23-4)

Adin - b 3/18/1778 in Ashford, CT, s/o **Abial** and **Hannah**; Adin d 3/12/1839 (or 1849) in Pomfret, VT. He m (1) 3/3/1805 **Sophie Peabody**, d 8/7/1808, and m (2) 1/30/1810 **Hannah Sessions**, d 1/3/1876, d/o **Resolved**. (*Gen. of Woodstock Families*, v. 3 p. 38-9 - *Pomfret, VT*, v. 2)

Benjamin - b 5/19/1765 in Ashford, CT, s/o **Nathaniel** and **Sarah**; Benjamin d 4/22/1849 in Hartford, Windsor Co., VT. He m (1) c1784 **Esther Colton**, b 9/9/1765, d 3/4/1793, and m (2) **Betsey Colton**, b 1/8/1768, d 11/17/1835, and m (3) 3/10/1836 Mrs. **Mabel** (**Colton**) **Guild**, d 4/15/1860. (*Hist. of Hartford, VT*, p. 411 - *Woodstock Families*, v. 3 p. 28, 46)

Benjamin - b 12/5/1729 in Woodstock, CT, s/o **Benjamin** and **Elizabeth**; Benjamin (the younger) dc1790. He m 1/18/1753 **Susannah Morse**, b 8/24/1734 in Woodstock, CT, d/o **John** and **Sarah** (**Peake**). (*Pomfret, VT*, v. 2 p. 445-6 - *Woodstock Fam.*, v. 3 p. 15-16)

Capt. Calvin - b 4/19/1780 in Ashford, CT. Capt. Calvin m (1) 12/6/1804 **Fanny Sessions** of Pomfret, VT, b 2/21/1782, d 11/8/1818, and m (2) 3/14/1819 **Mary Bullard Chandler**, b 11/19/1788 in Goffstown, VT, d 4/10/1867 in Hyde Park, VT. (*Gen. of Woodstock Fam.*, v. 3 p. 39 - War of 1812)

David - b 2/2/1776 in Ashford, CT, s/o **Abial** and **Hannah**; David d
1/3/1821. He m 1/7/1808 **Rebecca Swift**, b 2/9/1786, d 12/6/1858,
d/o **Thomas** and **Margaret (Aiken)**. (*Pomfret, VT*, v. 2 p. 448-9 -
Woodstock Fam., v. 3 p. 38)

Elisha - b 11/2/1771 in Ashford, CT, s/o **Abiel** and **Hannah**
(Harwood); Elisha d 10/21/1863 age 91-11-18 in Morristown, VT.
He m 10/29/1795 **Elizabeth Hewitt**, b 7/16/1776 in Brooklyn, CT, d
10/20/1858, d/o **Increase** and **Elizabeth (Tyler)**. (*Pomfret, VT*, v.
2 p. 447 - *Woodstock Fam.*, v. 3 p. 37)

Jesse - b 3/10/1711 in Woodstock, CT, s/o **Samuel** and **Dorothy**
(Carpenter); Jesse d1756 in Pomfret, Windsor Co., VT. He m
3/14/1734 **Experience Peake**, b 2/15/1716 in Woodstock, CT, d
1/6/1797 in Pomfret, VT, d/o **Christopher** and **Mary (Stratton)**.
(*Gen. of Woodstock Fam.*, v. 3 p. 11)

Jonathan - b 1/26/1795 in CT, s/o **Benjamin** and **Lucy (Colton)**;
Jonathan d 10/4/1851 in Hartford, Windsor Co., VT. He m
5/31/1821 **Cynthia Pease**, b 5/27/1799 in Enfield, CT, d 2/4/1868.
(*Hist. of Hartford, VT*, p. 411 - *1850 Census of Windsor Co., VT* -
Woodstock Fam., v. 3 p. 47)

Jonathan - b 7/2/1749 in Woodstock, CT, s/o **Jonathan**; Jonathan (the
younger) d 7/30/1820 in Stockton, NY. He m **Mary Dean**, b1751 or
1756 in Ashford, CT, d 6/1829 age 69 in Ellington, CT (at son's
home), d/o **Zephaniah** and **Hannah (Howard)**. (*Woodstock Fam.*, v.
3 p. 26 - *Chautauqua Co., NY*, p. 558-9)

Jonathan Jr. - b 5/11/1789 in Woodstock, CT, s/o **Jonathan** and
Mary (Dean); Jonathan Jr. d 10/19/1829 in Stockton, NY. He m
2/14/1813 **Harriet Putnam**, b 10/28/1792 in Greenfield, MA, d
10/7/1880 in London, NH, d/o Capt. **Andrew** and **Azuba (Stanhope)**.
(*Woodstock Families*, v. 3 p. 43-4 - *Chautauqua Co., NY*, p. 558-9)

Nathaniel - b 4/5/1721 in Ashford, CT, s/o **Josiah** and **Sarah**
(Hubbard); Nathaniel d 7/23/1808 age 86 in Hartford, VT. He m
1/22/1746 **Sarah Johnson**, b1722 in Ashford, CT, d 3/18/1815 age
93 in Hartford, VT. (*Hist. of Hartford, VT* - *Woodstock Fam.*, v. 3
p. 14-15)

Peletiah - b 2/17/1775 in Enfield, CT, s/o **Nathaniel**; Peletiah d
5/2/1827 age 53 in Chelsea, VT (gravestone), and is buried in Old
Cem., Chelsea, VT. He m **Sally Cook**, b1781, d 4/3/1846 age 65
(Old Cem., Chelsea, VT). (*Woodstock Families*, p. 28-9, 46-9 -
Gravestones, Old Cem., Chelsea, VT.)

Dr. Ralph - b 2/9/1796 in Ashford, CT, s/o **Amos** and **Martha**; Dr.
Ralph d 1/11/1881 age 85 in Waterford, Caledonia Co., VT. He m
10/5/1820 in Waterford, VT, **Irene Goss**, b 8/16/1798 in Waterford,
VT, d 7/21/1887 in Littleton, NH, d/o **Abel** and **Irene (Sprague)**.
(*Gen. of Woodstock Fam.*, v. 3 p. 45)

BULKELEY

Isaac Newton - b 8/2/1781 in Colchester, CT, s/o **Peter**; Isaac Newton d probably in VT. He m (1) 7/11/1802 in Montpelier, VT, **Betsey Darling**, bc1785, d 6/6/1813 in Cambridge, VT, and m (2)
Susan W. ----. (*Des. of Rev. Peter Bulkeley*, p. 301)

BULKLEY

Roger Griswold - b 5/6/1786 in Colchester, CT, d 2/21/1872 in Moretown, VT (gravestone). He m1809 in Berlin, VT, **Sally Taylor**, d 2/19/1871 in Moretown, VT (gravestone), d/o **Daniel**. (*Bulkley Gen.*, p. 735-6 - *Gazeteer of Orange Co., VT*, p. 160-1)

BUNDY

Solomon - bc1774 in Huntington, CT, d 2/24/1851 in Oxford, Chenango Co., NY. Solomon m **Jane Fraser** b Huntington, CT, d 8/22/1846 age 70 (possibly in NY). (*Annals of Oxford, NY*, p. 477-80 - *1850 Census Chenango Co.*)

BURDICK

Elijah - bc1758 in Stonington, CT, d 12/17/1833 age 75 in Pharsalia, Chenango Co, NY. He m **Avis Robinson** d 2/18/1836 age 75. (*DAR Patriot Index*, p. 101 - *Hist. of Chenango Co.*, p. 425)

Ezra - b in Stonington, CT, s/o **Elijah**; Ezra d 7/3/1859 age 75 in McDonough (or Pharsalia) NY. He m (1) **Martha Fish**, d 4/11/1827 age 41, and m (2) **Mary Hart**, d 5/17/1858 age 69. (*Hist. of Chenango Co., NY*, p. 425)

BURNELL

Samuel - b 10/4/1758 in Woodstock, CT, probably s/o **Samuel** and **Mary (Allard)**; Samuel (the younger) d 7/5/1838 age 80 in Brandon, VT. He m 2/2/1780 **Mary Tucker**, d 3/16/1760 in Woodstock, CT, d 5/23/1849 age 89 in Brandon, VT, d/o Capt. **Stephen** and **Lois (Lyon)**. (*DAR Patriot Index*, p. 102 - *Gen. of Woodstock Fam.*, v. 3 p. 133)

BURNHAM

Augustus - b 8/4/1751 in Hartford, CT, d 8/27/1823 in Laona, Chautauqua Co., NY. Augustus m1771 **Mary Stedman**. (*DAR Patriot Index*, p. 102 - *Soldiers of American Rev. - Chautauqua Co.*, p. 14)

Enoch - b 6/17/1776 in CT, s/o **Andrew** and **Jane (Bennett)**; Enoch d 2/18/1856 in Williamstown, VT. He m 12/6/1796 **Eunice Martin**, b 3/2/1774 in Windham, CT, d 2/12/1853 in Williamstown, VT. (*1850 Orange Co., VT, Census - Gazetteer of Orange Co.*, p. 528)

Thomas - b 11/25/1788 in Lisbon, CT, s/o **Jedediah** and **Lydia (Kent)**; Thomas d 5/1845 in LaSalle Co., IL. He m **Climena Clark** of Granby, MA. (*History of LaSalle Co., IL*, p. 464)

BURR

Jabez - b 8/20/1752 in Redding, CT, s/o **Jabez** and **Elizabeth (Hull)**; Jabez (the younger) d 6/28/1825 age 72-10-8 in Fairfield, Franklin Co., VT. He m 2/12/1778 in Redding, CT, **Mary Bartram**, d 2/18/1842 age 80-9, d/o **Paul** and **Mary (Hawley)**. (*DAR Patriot Index*, p. 103 - *Some Early Records of Fairfield, VT*, p. 18)

Oliver - b CT, s/o **Ebenezer** and **Elizabeth (Dorchester)**; Oliver d 6/30/1844 age 63 in Thetford, VT. He m **Celinda Stowell** of Grantham, NH, b 6/6/1787 in Grantham, NH, d 11/12/1864 age 77 in

Thetford, VT, buried in Old. Cem. (*The Burr Family*, p. 322 –
Gazetteer of Orange Co., VT, p. 443-4)

BURRITT

Andrew – b 5/28/1741 in Newtown, CT, or New Milford, CT, s/o
Stephen and **Anne (Sherman)**; Andrew d 8/5/1836 age 96-3 in
Hinesburgh, Chittenden Co., VT. He m 1/27/1763 **Eunice Welles**,
b 7/1739, d 3/15/1835 age 96-8. (*Burritt Fam.*, p. 18, 30, – *DAR
Patriot Index*, p. 104 – *1861 History – Tales of Hinesburgh*).
Capt. **Peleg** – b1721 in Stratford, CT, s/o **Peleg**; Capt. Peleg d1789 in
Hanover, PA. He m (1) **Elizabeth Blackleach**, and m (2) **Deborah
Beardsley**. (*Hist. of Hanover Township, PA*, p. 397)
Tille – b 6/24/1776 in Newtown, CT, s/o **Andrew** and **Eunice (Wells)**;
Tille d 6/2/1870 in Hinesburgh, Chittenden Co., VT. He m in
Hinesburgh, VT, **Hannah Davis**. (*Burritt Fam.*, p. 44, 75-6)

BURROUGHS

John Jr. – b 4/16/1711 (?) in Enfield, CT, d 2/21/1798 in Gilsum,
NH. John Jr. m 1/9/1739 **Sarah Abbey** at Enfield, CT. (*DAR
Patriot Index*, p. 104 – *Town of Gilsum, NH*, p. 279-80)

BURTON

Jacob – b 9/14/1715 in Preston, CT, d 6/12/1798 in Norwich, VT
(gravestone). Jacob m (1) **Rachel Benton**, d 11/1779 age 52
(gravestone), and m (2) **Elizabeth ----**. (*DAR Patriot Index*, p. 105
– *A History of Norwich, VT*, p. 168-9)

BUSHNELL

Abisha – b1752 in Norwich, CT, d1841 in 89th yr. in Otsego Co., NY.
Abisha m ---- **Griswold**, d1834 age 79. (*Biog. Rec. of Otsego Co.,
NY*, p. 762)
Alvah – b1796 in Litchfield Co., CT, d 11/16/1865 in Dutchess Co.,
NY. Alvah m **Melinda Lapham**, d 10/28/1861. (*Comm. Biog. Rec.
of Dutchess Co., NY*, p. 773)
Benajah – b 3/21/1743 (or 1744) Norwich, CT, d 10/19/1814 in
Pawlet, Rutland Co., VT. Benajah m in Norwich, CT, **Lucy Abell**,
d/o **Noah** and **Ann (Marshall)**, b 3/23/1743 in Norwich, CT, dc1814
in Pawlet, VT. (*DAR Patriot Index*, p. 105)
Rev. **Jedediah** – b 11/26/1769 in Saybrook, CT, d 8/20/1846 in
Cornwall, Addison Co., VT. Rev. Jedediah m **Elizabeth Smith**, d
3/26/1847 in Cornwall, VT, age 68, d/o **Ezra** of Richmond, VT.
(*Hist. of Cornwall, VT*, p. 165-179)
Hon. **Pope** – b 2/11/1789 in Salisbury, CT, s/o **Gideon**; Hon. Pope d
12/17/1839 age over 92, in Dyberry, Wayne Co., PA. He m
1/3/1812 ---- **Hurlburt**, b 3/26/1788 in Goshen, CT, d 1/11/1883,
d/o **Gideon** and **Anna (Beach)**. (*Bushnell Fam.*, p. 313 – *Hist. of
Wayne Co., PA*, p. 295-6)

BUTLER

Benjamin – b 1/30/1764 in Norwich, CT, s/o Dr. **Benjamin** and
Diadama (Hyde); Benjamin d 1/15/1839 in Oxford, Chenango Co.,

NY. He m **Hannah Avery** of Groton, CT, d 8/1/1829 age 58. (*Annals of Oxford, Chenango Co., NY*, p. 422-4)

Ebenezer - b 12/1/1733/4 (or 12/19/1733/4) in Branford, CT, s/o **Isaiah** and **Martha**; Ebenezer d1829 age 96 in Pompey Hill, NY. He m 3/30/1757 **Desire Barns** of New Haven, CT. (*DAR Patriot Index*, p. 106 - *Onondaga Hist. Soc. of 1914*, p. 192)

Ebenezer Jr. - b 6/29/1760 in Harwinton, CT, s/o **Ebenezer** and **Desire (Barns)**; Ebenezer Jr. d 9/1829 age 68 in OH. He m after the Rev., **Rebecca Davis**, d at Pompey Hill, NY. (*DAR Patriot Index*, p. 106 - *Onondaga Hist. Soc. of 1914*, p. 166)

Eli - b 1/26/1740 in Middletown, CT, d 4/19/1802 age 61 in New Hartford, Oneida Co., NY. Eli m **Rachel Stocking**. (*DAR Patriot Index*, p. 106 - *History of Oneida Co.*, p. 489 - *Oneida, Our Country and Its People*, p. 484)

Isaac - b 6/15/1752 in Windsor, CT, s/o **Samuel** and **Mary (Goodwin)**; Isaac d 6/16/1833 in 81st yr. in Fairfield, Franklin Co., VT. He m **Hannah Hull**, d 2/22/1819 age 65 in Fairfield, VT, d/o **Jehiel** and **Ruth (Phelps)**. (*DAR Patriot Index*, p. 106)

John - b 11/1804 in Waterford, CT, s/o **L. Nathan** and **Eunice (Moore)**; John d 11/2/1888 in Unadilla, Otsego Co., NY. He m **Abigail Reed**. (*Biog. Rec. of Otsego Co., NY*, p. 204)

Riley - b Harwinton, CT, s/o **Jesse** and **Louise (Soper)**; Riley d1869 in MI. He m1811 **Rachel Frisbee** of Harwinton, CT, d Albion, NY. (*Pompey Reunion*, p. 405-9)

Salmon - b 3/5/1761 in Branford, CT, s/o **Nathan** and **Rebecca (Rogers)**; Salmon d 8/15/1836 age 75 in Clinton, Oneida Co., NY. He m **Anna** ---- d 6/10/1839 age 78. (*Clinton Memorial-Kirtland Ave. Cem.*, p. 15)

BUTTON

Joseph Jr. - b 7/13/1782 in CT, d1859 age 79 in Harmony, NY. Joseph Jr. m **Polly Gifford**, d1867 age 84 Wells, VT. (*Hist. of Wells, VT*, p. 69)

Joseph - b 1/16/1753 in Canterbury CT, s/o **Matthias** and **Phebe (Butt)**; Joseph d 10/30/1826 age 73 in Wells, VT. He m (1) 5/2/1773 **Sarah Glass**, d1821, and m (2) **Betsey** ----, wid/o **Simeon Parks**. (*Hist. of Wells, VT*, p. 68 - *DAR Patriot Index*, p. 107)

Capt. Mathias - b 4/22/1732 in Norwich, CT, s/o **Matthias**; Capt. Mathias d1811 age 79 in Wells, VT. He m (1) 1753 **Phoebe Butts**, and m (2) 1765 **Elizabeth Butts**, (sister of Phoebe). (*Hist. of the Town of Wells, VT*, p. 43 by Grace Woods)

Thomas Welch - b 1/1777 in CT, d 3/11/1859 in Tunbridge, Orange Co., VT. He m **Hannah** ----, bc1782 in MA, d 5/31/1852 age 70 in Tunbridge, VT. (*Button Fam. of America*, p. 761-2 - *1850 Orange Co., VT, Census* of Tunbridge - Button Hill Cemetery in Tunbridge, VT)

BUTTS

Ebenezer - b 9/13/1747 in Canterbury, CT, s/o **Josiah** and **Elizabeth**; Ebenezer dc1825 in Wells, VT. He m 1/4/1769 in Canterbury, CT, **Prudence Glass**, d/o **Antony** and **Eunice (Bennett)**. (*Hist. of Wells, VT* by Wood p. 44 - *Hist. of Wells* by Parks p. 70)

John - b 5/7/1795 in CT, d 12/10/1861 in Langford's Creek, Chenango Co., NY. John m **Nancy Barker**, b 3/9/1802 in NY, d 10/30/1875 in Elmira, NY. (*Detroit Soc. Gen. Research*, v. 38 #3, 1975 p. 161)

M a r b l e - bc1803 in CT, dc1872 in Otsego Co, NY. Marble m **L u c y Fitch** of New Lisbon, NY, bc1804, d1873. (*Biog. Rec. of Otsego Co., NY*, p. 532)

BYINGTON

D a n i e l - b1772 in Wolcott, CT, d 8/20/1843 age 71 in Camden, Oneida Co., NY. Daniel m (1) **Hannah Alcott (or Alcox)**, b1772 in Wolcott, CT, d 12/3/1835, and m (2) **Huldah Norton**, and m (3) **Huldah Wakefield**. (*Pioneer Hist. of Camden, NY*, p. 249)

H e m a n - bc1771 in Wolcott, CT, d 9/7/1831 age 60 in Camden, Oneida Co., NY. Heman m **Patience Peck**, d 6/7/1844 age 70. (*Pioneer Hist. of Camden, NY*, p. 215)

CADWELL

Lt. Moses - b 4/3/1728 in Farmington, CT, s/o **Moses**; Lt. Moses d 3/14/1807 age 79 in E. Thetford. He m **Hannah ----**, d 9/28/1807 age 74 in E. Thetford, VT (gravestone). (East Thetford Cemetery)

Sheldon - bc1793 in Middletown, CT, d1853 age 60 in LaSalle Co., IL (possibly Vermillionville). Sheldon m **Alphia Van Valkenburgh** from Greene Co., NY, bc1795, d1876 age 81. (*History of LaSalle County, IL*, p. 337)

CADY

Deacon **Calvin** - b 4/20/1786 in Pomfret, CT, s/o **Calvin** and **Abigail (Simmons)**; Deacon Calvin d1867 in Northfield, Washington Co., VT. He m 5/18/1809 **Betsey Merrill**, b 6/30/1785, d 10/11/1858. (*Des. of Nicholas Cady*, p. 151-2 - *Early Settlers of Northfield, VT*)

J o h n - b 11/28/1736 in Killingly, CT, s/o **B e n j a m i n**; John d 2/25/1824 in Westport, NY. He m **Hannah (Miller or Miles)**, b 6/17/1736, d 12/25/1823. (*Des. of Nicholas Cady*, p. 72-3 - *DAR Patriot Index*, p. 109)

L e w i s - b 2/20/1794 in Killingly, VT, s/o **D a v i d** and **N a n c y (Waterman)**; Lewis d 9/27/1864 in Bennington, VT. He m (1) **Sally S m i t h**, b 9/20/1798, d 11/1814, and m (2) **L u c y V a u g h n**, b 1/10/1806, d 4/14/1873. (*Cady Gen.*, p. 278-9, 149-50 - *1850 Bennington Co., VT, Census*)

Nebadiah - b 12/7/1751 in Killingly, CT, d 3/26/1838 in Reading, Windsor Co., VT. Nebadiah m (1) 5/1/1780 **M a r y Buck**, b 9/28/1760, d 8/17/1798, d/o **Samuel** and **Martha (Boss)**, and m (2) 11/4/1799 **Sarah Washburn** b 1/13/1766. (*Des. of Nicholas Cady*, p. 75 - *DAR Patriot Index*, p. 109 - *Hist. of Reading, VT*, p. 197)

Stephen - b 9/12/1750 in Plainfield, CT, s/o **Abijah**; Stephen d 7/31/1829 in Windsor, VT. He m (1) 4/22/1773 **Jane Patrick**, b1751, d 2/6/1794, and m (2) 9/23/1794 **Esther Parker** b1752, d 3/29/1834. (*Des. of Nicholas Cady*, p. 112 - *History of Cornish, NH*, p. 48-9)

CALKIN

Ezekiel – b 11/11/1728 in Lebanon, CT, s/o **John**; Ezekiel d probably in Cornwallis, King's Co., Nova Scotia. He m 12/22/1748 at Lebanon, CT, **Anna Dewey**, b 10/23/1727. (*King's Co. - Family Sketches - Cornwallis, NS*)

CALKINS

Frederick – b 11/14/1748 in CT, s/o **William** and **Mary (Prentiss)**; Frederick d 11/21/1815 age 61 in Chelsea, VT (gravestone). He m 12/2/1772 at Norwich, CT, **Annis Huntington** of Norwich, CT. (*DAR Patriot Index*, p. 110 – Chelsea Old Cemetery gravestones – *Calkin Family Lines in U.S. and Canada*, p. 42, 47)

Capt. **S t e p h e n** – b 3/13/1731 in Lyme, CT, d1814 age 83 in Danby, Rutland Co., VT. Capt. Stephen m **Rebecca Rowland**, d1813 age 73. (*Hist. of Rutland Co. - DAR Patriot Index*, p. 110 – *History of Danby*, p. 121–2)

CAMP

A b i a l – bc1782 in CT, d 1/19/1860 in Chelsea, Orange Co., VT (gravestone). Abial m **Sally ----**, b in CT, d 1/10/1872 age 82 (gravestone). (*1850 Orange Co. Census, Chelsea, VT* – gravestones)

Talcott – b 3/4/1762 in Durham, CT, s/o **Elnathan** and **Eunice (Talcott)**; Talcott d 9/25/1832 in Oneida Co., NY (possibly Old Schuyler). He m1785 in Glastonbury, CT, **Nancy Hale**. (*DAR Patriot Index*, p. 111 – *Hist. of Oneida Co., NY*, p. 267)

CANFIELD

Andrew – b 2/3/1760 (or 1761) in Litchfield, CT, d 6/13/1843 age 85 in Rush, Susquehanna Co., PA. He m (probably) **Eunice Fairchild**. (*DAR Patriot Index*, p. 112 – *Hist. of Susquehanna Co., PA*, p. 438)

Israel – b 3/13/1733 in New Millford, CT, s/o **Azariah** and **Mary**; Israel d 3/20/1818 in Arlington, Bennington Co., VT. He m **Mary Sackett**, d 6/28/1818 in Arlington, VT. (*DAR Patriot Index*, p. 112 – *Bennington Co. Gazeteer*, p. 77–78 – *VT Hist. Soc. Magazine* v. 1 by Hemingway)

Nathan – b 7/28/1739 in New Milford, CT, s/o **Zerubbal** and **Mary (Bostwick)**; Nathan d 4/16/1809 age 69 in Arlington, Bennington Co., VT. He m (1) 11/14/1765 at New Milford, CT, **Lois Hard**, d/o Capt. **James**, and m (2) **Betsey Burton**. (*Bennington Gazette*, p. 77–78 – *VT Hist. Soc.* v. 1 p. 136)

CARLTON

Peter – b 6/13/1786 in Stafford, CT, s/o **Caleb** and **Margaret**; Peter d1861 in Portage Co., OH. He m 11/29/1810 **Clarissa Ladd**, b 2/25/1779, d/o **Daniel** and **Persis (Davis)**. (*Portage County, OH*, p. 755)

CARPENTER

Asa – b 12/18/1739 in Coventry, CT, s/o **Ebenezer** and **Eunice (Thompson)**; Asa d 7/10/1801 in Sharon, Windsor Co., VT. He m (1) **Patience Dunham**, and m (2) **Eunice Parker**. (*Carpenter Memorial*, p. 98)

Rev. **Asa** - b 10/10/1770 in Pomfret, CT, s/o **Jonah** and **Zeriuah** (Whitmore); Rev. Asa d 9/10/1826. He m 7/4/1798 **Erepta Grow**, b 1/8/1780, d 12/12/1842 in Reading, MI, d/o **John**. (*Carpenter Memorial*, p. 203 - *Waterford, A Vermont Village*)

Cephas - b 7/8/1770 in Coventry, CT, s/o **James** and **Irene** (Ladd); Cephas d 4/1/1859 in Moretown, Washington Co., VT. He m (1) **Anne Benton**, b 8/9/1773, d 3/23/1845 age 71, and m (2) Mrs. **Mary Day**. (*Carpenter Memorial - Rehoboth Fam.*, p. 184 - *1850 Washington Co., VT, Census*)

Elias - b 10/7/1761 in Woodstock, CT, s/o **Ephraim** and **Tabitha** (Chaffee); Elias d 2/16/1851 age 90 in Strafford, Orange Co., VT. He m 12/6/1798 **Sarah Prescott**, b 8/6/1779 in Deerfield, NH, d 8/6/1837 age 58 in Strafford, VT, d/o **James** and **Jesse** (Hilliard). (*Woodstock Fam.*, v. 3, p. 166 - *1850 Orange Co., VT, Census*)

Ephraim - b 6/7/1780 in Woodstock, CT, s/o **Ephraim** and **Tabitha** (Chaffee); Ephraim (the younger) d 6/11/1863 in Strafford, Orange Co., VT. He m (1) 6/30/1802 **Elizabeth Prescott**, d 1/18/1841, and m (2) 10/21/1841 **Sally N. King**, b 12/8/1799 in Tunbridge, VT, d 1/18/1868. (*Woodstock Families*, v. 3, p. 167 - *Carpenter Memorial*, p. 290)

Isaiah - b 6/29/1783 in CT, s/o **Jonah**; Isaiah d 7/6/1871 age 88 in Waterford, Caledonia Co., VT. He m 4/21/1808 **Caroline Bugbee**, b 12/27/1785, d 8/2/1865, d/o **Amos** of Ashford, CT. (*Carpenter Memorial*, p. 203-4)

James - b 4/4/1741 in Coventry, CT, s/o **Ebenezer** and **Eunice** (Thompson); James d 11/4/1813 age 72 in Sharon, Windsor Co., VT. He m 4/5/1761 **Irene Ladd**, b 5/30/1744, d 6/19/1817 age 73. (*DAR Patriot Index*, p. 115 - *Carpenter Memorial*, p. 98 - *Middlesex Gazette*, 2/17/1814)

Jason - b 8/15/1772 in Coventry, CT, s/o **James** and **Irene** (Ladd); Jason d 10/1/1845 in Waitsfield, Washington Co., Vt. He m **Betsey Ingraham**. (*1850 Washington Co., VT, Census - Carpenter Genealogy*, p. 310)

Jonah, Jr. - b 10/4/1777 in Pomfret, CT, d 8/1867 age 80 in Waterford, Caledonia Co., VT. Jonah, Jr. m **Hannah Rice** d1865 age 86, d/o **Obadiah**. (*A Vermont Village - Waterford*, p. 75-6)

Willard - b 4/3/1767 in Woodstock, CT s/o **Ephraim** and **Sarah** (Prescott); Willard d 11/14/1854 in Strafford, Orange Co., VT. He m 2/23/1791 **Polly Bacon**, b 3/15/1769, d 3/4/1860 age 91, d/o **Oliver**. (*Carpenter Memorial*, p. 290 - *Gazeteer of Orange Co.*, p. 409 - *Woodstock Families*, v. 3, p. 173 - *1850 Orange Co., VT, Census*)

CARR

Capt. **Robert** - b 5/23/1742 in Norwich, CT, d 10/20/1823 in Otsego Co., NY. Capt. Robert m 12/31/1765 in Plainfield, CT, **Prudence Wheeler**. (*DAR Patriot Index*, p. 116 - *Biog. Rev. of Otsego Co., NY*, p. 151)

CARRIER
John - bc1764 in either Colchester or Haddam, CT, d before 9/6/1834 in Vershire, VT (?). John m **Jerusha** ----, d 9/8/1820 age 55 in Vershire, VT. (P. 102 of booklet on Carrier)

CARY
Anson - b 3/15/1762 in Windham, CT, d 5/3/1842 age 80 in Oxford, Chenango Co., NY. Anson m 3/4/1784 **Hannah Carew**, d 7/9/1842 age in the 70's. (*Annals of Oxford, NY*, p. 88-9 - *DAR Patriot Index*, p. 118 - *Hist. of Chenango Co., NY*, p. 258)

CASE
Isaac P. - b1772 in Simsbury, CT, d1851 in Huron Co., OH. Isaac P. m1789 in Cooperstown, NY, **Eunice Tracy** b1775 and d1855, d/o **Bachaus**. (Typed List - Huron Co., OH)

Jonathan - b 3/27/1779 in Willington, CT, s/o **Bernard** and **Phebe (Goodell)**; Jonathan d 7/17/1860 in Ypsilanti, Washtenaw Co., MI. He m prob. 1813 in Washington, Oneida Co., NY, **Ruth Harrison**, bc1794, d before 1860 in Ypsilanti, Washtenaw Co., MI. (*Detroit Soc. Gen. Research*, Summer 1973)

CASTLE
David - b Dec. 1725 in Woodbury, CT, d1823 age 97 in Wells, Chittenden Co., VT. David m 11/29/1747 **Phebe Sanford**. (*Chittenden Gazeteer*, p. 235 - *History of Town of Wells, VT*, p. 45 - *DAR Patriot Index*, p. 120)

Eric - bc1779 in Plymouth, CT, d 7/15/1842 age 63 in Camden, NY (?). Eric m **Polly Ford**, d1815. (*Pioneer History of Camden, NY*, p. 41)

Samuel - b 8/16/1782 in Roxbury, CT, s/o **Abraham**; Samuel d 3/16/1874 age 92 in Monroe Co, NY, (prob. Parma). He m1809 **Ruby Seely**, dc1871. (*History of Monroe County, NY*, p. 179, 173, 174, 176)

CHAFFEE
James Stuart - b 10/3/1846 in Sharon, CT, s/o **Jerome** and **Aritta L. (Stuart)**; James Stuart d prob. in Dutchess Co., NY. He m 9/17/1872 in Kent, CT, **Lydia A. Judd**, b 12/16/1850 in Kent, d/o **Edward M.** and **Laura (Cartwright)**. (*Chaffee Gen.*, p. 505-6 - *Comm. Biog. Rec. Dutchess Co, NY*, p. 171)

Jerome Seymour - b 12/14/1814 in Ellsworth, (Sharon), CT, s/o **Joshua**; Jerome Seymour d prob. in Amenia, NY. He m (1) 10/24/1839 in Kent, CT, **Aritta Stuart**, b 12/15/1812 in Kent, CT, d 11/26/1872 in Amenia, NY, d/o **James** and **Melina (Berry)**, and m (2) 6/8/1876 **Adelia E. Fuller**, b 3/13/1841 in Sharon, CT, d/o **Cyrus** and **Harriet (Skiff)**. (*Chaffee Gen.*, p. 348-9 - *Comm. Biog. Rec. Dutchess Co., NY*, p. 171)

Rufus - b 3/2/1769 in Woodstock, CT, s/o **Ezra** and **Jerusha (Hurlburt)**; Rufus d 4/12/1857 in Athens VT. He m1792 in Athens, VT, **Elizabeth Stickney**, b in MA, d 7/27/1860, buried Lyndon, VT. (*1850 Census Windham Co., VT* - *Chaffee Gen.*, p. 117, 196-7 - *Gen. of Woodstock Families*, v. 3, p. 237)

43

CHAMBERLAIN

Aaron - b 1/19/1758 in Colchester, CT, s/o **Job** and **Deidamia (Dunham)**; Aaron d 8/25/1825 in Franklin, Delaware Co., NY. He m (1) **Catherine Waters**, d1786, and m (2) 1787 **Wealthy Root**, d/o **Ebenezer**. (*Chamberlain Fam. of New England and NY*, p. 88 - *DAR Patriot Index*, p. 122)

Abner - b 10/4/1745 in Hebron, CT, s/o **John** and **Mehitable (Fuller)**; Abner d 8/1832 in Scipio, NY. He m (1) **Lucretia Strong**, and m (2) 1805 **Mary Seaver**, wid/o ---- **Seaver**. (*Chamberlain Families of Early New England and NY*, p. 92 - *DAR Patriot Index*, p. 122)

Amasa - bc1748 (bp 6/5/1748) in Colchester, CT, s/o **William** and **Jael (Davis)**; Amasa d 4/8/1826 age 78 in Strafford, VT. He m1772 **Molly Briscoe**, d 1/20/1824 (or 6/20/1826), d/o **William**. (*DAR Patriot Index*, p. 122 - Strafford Kibling Cem. - *Chamberlain Families of Early New England and NY*, p. 92)

Amos - b 1/3/1748 (or 1749) in Hebron, CT, s/o **John**; Amos d1796 in Thetford, Orange Co., VT. He m (1) by 1770 **Martha** ----, and m (2) **Anne Alger**. (*DAR Patriot Index*, p. 122 - *Chamberlain Families of Early New England and NY*, p. 92)

Asahel - bp. 5/4/1755 in Colchester, CT, s/o **William** and **Jael (Davis)**; Asahel d 2/3/1833 in Strafford, Orange Co., VT (gravestone). He m (1) 1/30/1770 in Lebanon, CT, **Lucy Briscoe**, b 1/30/1770 in Lebanon, CT, and m (2) **Abigail Root**, d 11/23/1814 age 60 in Strafford, Orange Co., VT, (Kibling Cem. gravestone), d/o **Wm.** of Hebron. (Kibling Cem. Strafford - *Chamberlain Families of Early New England and NY*, p. 92)

Asher - b1751 in Litchfield, CT, s/o **Moses** and **Jemima (Wright)**; Asher d in Troy, VT. He m (1) 1773 in Haverhill, NH, **Olive Russell**, and m (2) **Hannah Child**, d/o **Jonathan**. (*Chamberlain Families of Early New England and NY*, p. 92)

Benjamin - b 10/5/1742 in Hebron, CT, s/o **John, Jr.** and **Mehitable (Fuller)**; Benjamin d 3/7/1810 in Thetford, Orange Co., VT. He m 1/7/1761 in Hebron, CT, **Jerusha Green** (his step-sister), b 8/5/1742, d1812. (*DAR Patriot Index*, p. 122 - *Chamberlain Families of Early New England and NY*, p. 9 - *Genealogy of Chamberlain-Curtis and Allied Families*, p. 4, 47)

Charles - bp1759 in Colchester, CT, s/o **Wm.** and **Jael (Davis)**; Charles d 1/14/1835 age 76 in Livonia, NY. He m **Mary** ----, d 4/1/1831 age 69. (*Chamberlain Families of Early New England and NY*, p. 93)

Colby - b 12/13/1739 in Tolland, CT, s/o **Joseph** and **Mary (Johnson)**; Colby d 9/1/1796 age 58 in Amenia, NY. He m1765 in Amenia, NY, **Catherine Winegar**, d 5/26/1808 age 59, d/o **Conradt**. (*DAR Patriot Index*, p. 122 - *Chamberlain Families of Early New England and NY*, p.48)

Elias - b 7/25/1753 in Colchester or Hebron, CT, s/o **Wm.** and **Jael (Davis)**; Elias d 12/27/1838 in Livonia, NY. He m (1) 1777 **Betsey Gillett**, d 3/31/1806 age 43. He was said to have also m (2) **Anna**, and m (3) **Eunice Ursley**. (*DAR Patriot Index*, p. 122 - *Chamberlain Families of Early New England and NY*, p. 93)

Gurdon - b 1/27/1755 in Colchester, CT, s/o **Jehu** and **Sarah (Day)**; Gurdon d 12/10/1810. He m **Hannah Lawrence**, b1758, d1851. (*Chamberlain Families of Early New England and NY*, p. 52 - *DAR Patriot Index*, p. 122)

Isaac - bp. 6/14/1752 in Colchester, CT, s/o **Wm.** and **Jael (Davis)**; Isaac d 4/28/1822 age 70 in Strafford, Orange Co., VT. He m **Lucy Powell**. (Strafford-Kibling Cem. stones - *Chamberlain Families of Early New England and NY*, p. 94)

Jonathan - b 2/15/1747 in Colchester, CT, s/o **Peleg** and **Experience (Bartlett)**; Jonathan d 9/12/1823 in his 77th year in Austerlitz, NY. He m1769 **Rachel Ford**, d 3/26/1847 in her 90th year. (*Hist. of Columbia Co., NY*, p. 389 - *DAR Patriot Index*, p. 122 - *Chamberlain Families of Early New England and NY*, p. 54)

Judah - b1761 in Colchester, CT, s/o **John** and **Sarah (Day)**; Judah d 5/29/1847 prob. in Harmony, Clark Co., OH. He m (1) **Diademia Howard**, d 8/14/1795 age 23 in Amenia, NY, and m (2) 1801 in Chenango Co., NY, **Phebe Mead**. (*Chamberlain Families of Early New England and NY*, p. 53, 55)

Laban - b 4/21/1781 in Woodstock, CT, s/o **Ezra** and **Huldah (P e r i n)**; Laban d 7/25/1865 in Pomfret, Windsor Co., VT. He m (1) 1806 **Abigail Melina**, b 3/27/1783 in Sutton, MA, d 6/20/1833, d/o **John** and **Sarah (Eddy)**, and m (2) **Annis Orr Chandler**, b 2/3/1795 in VT, d 9/1/1865, d/o **Josiah** and **Margaret**. (*Pomfret, VT*, v. 2, p. 457 - *Windsor Co., VT, Census*)

Moses - b 12/21/1749 in Litchfield, CT, s/o **Moses** and **Jemima (Wright)**; d 2/14/1832 poss. in Newbury, Orange Co., VT. He m 5/1779 **Abigail Stevens**, d/o **Simeon**. (*DAR Patriot Index*, p. 122 - *Chamberlain Families of Early New England and NY*, p. 58)

Remembrance - b 12/19/1747 in Litchfield, CT, s/o **Moses** and **Jemima (Wright)**; Remembrance d 1/10/1813 poss. in Newbury, Orange Co., VT. He m **Elizabeth (Elliott) Johnson**. (*Chamberlain Fam. of Early New Eng. & NY*, p. ? - *DAR Patriot Index*, p. 122)

Swift - b 11/25/1764 in Kent, CT, s/o **Peleg** and **Abigail (Swift)**; Swift d 11/25/1828 in Monkton, Addison Co., VT. He m (1) 3/24/1791 in New Milford, CT, **S a r a h   S h e r w o o d**, d 9/16/1793, and m (2) 3/8/1795 in Bristol, VT, **Mary Tuttle**, b1779, d 1/20/1853 in 80th year in Monkton, VT, d/o **Thomas**. (*DAR Patriot Index*, p. 122 - *A Chamberlain Gen. Rec./Chamberlain Assoc.*, p.62)

William - b 1/25/1745 in Tolland, CT, s/o **Joseph** and **Mary (Johnson)**; William d 11/27/1810 age 65 in Amenia, NY. He m1767 in Amenia, NY, **Abigail Hatch** of Kent, CT, d 4/4/1812 age 60. (*DAR Patriot Index*, p. 123 - *Chamberlain Families of Early New England and NY*, p. 63)

Wyatt - b1758 in Colchester, CT, s/o **Jehu** and **Sarah (Day)**; Wyatt d prob. Guilford, Chenango Co., NY. He m1787 **Dinah Taylor**, b1761. (*Chamberlain Families of Early New England and NY*, p. 64)

CHAMPION

John - b 12/12/1792 in S. Lyme, CT, s/o **Ezra**; John d 10/27/1879 in Hartford, VT. He m 6/20/1816 **Harriet Abbot**, b 4/12/1786 in Concord, NH, d 4/1/1862 in Hartford, VT, d/o **E z r a** and **B e t t y (Andrews)**. (*Champion Genealogy*, p. 143, 172-3)

CHAPIN
Justus - b 1/30/1753 in Somers, CT, s/o **Aaron**; Justus d 7/15/1825
poss. in Gilsum, NH. He m (1) 2/29/1776 **Johannah Fuller**, b
6/9/1757 in CT, d 1/15/1779 in Surry, NH, d/o **Joshua**, and m (2)
5/19/1785 **Martha Taylor**, b 9/15/1764 in Bolton, CT, d
6/12/1839. (*Hist. of Town of Gilsum, NH*, p. 284-5)

CHANDLER
Andrew - b 10/30/1762 in Woodstock, CT, s/o **Seth** and **Eunice**
(Durkee); Andrew d 1/11/1802 in Strafford, Orange Co., VT. He m
11/13/1784 **Relief Haven** of Strafford, VT, d 10/6/1846 age 40 in
Sharon, VT, d/o **Abram**. (*Des. of William and Annis Chandler*, p.
517-18 - *Gazeteer of Orange Co., VT*, p. 407)

Rev. **Augustus** - b 12/1/1830 in Woodstock, CT, s/o **John** and
Deborah; Rev. Augustus d 3/26/1880 in Strafford, Orange Co., VT.
He m 9/4/1860 **Lucy Lord** of Norwich, VT, b 4/21/1832, d/o **John**
and **Lucy (Bliss)**. (*Gen. of Woodstock Fam.*, v. 3, p. 392)

Cyril - b 7/16/1776 in Woodstock, CT, s/o **Seth** and **Eunice (Durkee)**;
Cyril d after 1850 in Strafford, Orange Co., VT. He m1800 in
Hanover, NH, **Abigail Carpenter**, b 8/15/1781 in Hanover, NH, d
4/16/1849 in Strafford, VT. (*1850 Orange County Census - Chandler*
Fam., p. 523-4)

Daniel - b 1/21/1784 in Pomfret, CT, s/o **Daniel** and **Mary (Galucia)**;
Daniel (the younger) d 10/3/1860 at nearly 82 years in Berlin,
Washington Co., VT. He m **Hannah Sloan**, b 12/14/1787, d
2/5/1850 in Berlin, VT, d/o **Joseph** and **Temperance (Waterman)**.
(*Chandler Fam.*, p. 539 - *Washington Co. Gazeteer*, p. 196 - *1850*
Washington Co., VT, Census)

John - b 12/26/1727 in Enfield, CT, s/o **Henry** and **Hannah (Foster)**;
John d 4/25/1800 in 74th year in Wilmington, Windham Co., VT.
He m **Elizabeth Wells**, b 5/4/1740 in Colchester, CT, d 3/25/1832.
(*Chandler Family*, p. 77, 172-3, 364-7 - *DAR Patriot Index*, p. 123)

Rufus - b 1/6/1785 in Woodstock, CT, s/o **Andrew** and **Relief**
(Haven); Rufus d 1/27/1866 age 85 in Strafford, Orange Co., VT. He
m 4/28/1805 in Chelsea, VT, **Clarissa Tucker**, b 3/20/1784 in
Woodstock, VT, d 4/11/1871, d/o **Zephaniah** and **Hulday (Holmes)**.
(*Chandler Fam.*, p. 517-18 - *1850 Orange Co. Census*)

Samuel - b 4/16/1781 in Pomfret, CT, s/o **Silas** and **Grace (Fascit)**;
Samuel d 7/5/1861 in 81st year poss. in Peacham, Caledonia Co.,
VT. He m 3/31/1808 **Mehitable Blake**, b 11/12/1785 in Hopkinton,
NH, d 5/14/1870, d/o Major **Henry**. (*Chandler Fam.*, p. 542, 939-
42 - *Caledonia Gazeteer*, p. 277)

William Brown - b1792 in Pomfret, CT, s/o **Henry** and **Martha**
(Brown); William Brown d 5/10/1881 age 89 in Brooklyn, NY. He m
11/7/1816 **Electa Owen**, b 4/17/1796 in Northumberland, NH, d
6/6/1866 age 70, d/o **Joel** and **Mary (Gillett)**. (*Des. of Wm. and*
Annis Chandler, p. 867 - *Gazetteer of Orange Co., VT*, p. 366 - *His-*
torical Souvenir of Randolph, VT, p. 91)

CHEDELL

John - b 8/26/1732 in Ashford, CT, s/o **George** and **Martha (Burge)**; John d 10/1/1805 in Pomfret, VT. He m (1) 11/5/1761 in Ashford, CT, **Mary Bosworth**, and m (2) 5/11/1768 in Ashford, CT, **Rachel Allen**, b 7/21/1746, d 1/18/1791. (*Pomfret, Vermont*, p. 460 - *DAR Patriot Index*, p. 127)

Gen. **John Hatch** - b 4/24/1806 in Coventry, CT, d 6/19/1875 age 69 in Auburn, Cayuga Co., NY. Gen. John Hatch m 1/1828 **Melita Cook**, d/o **Philip** of Steuben Co., NY. (*History of Cayuga County, NY*, p. 223)

CHENEY

Abial - b 8/14/1773 in Ashford, CT, s/o **Benjamin** of Ashford; Abial d 9/16/1841 in Waterford, Caledonia Co., VT. He m 5/11/1797 **Alathea Carpenter**, b 9/19/1772 in Ashford, CT, d 5/13/1866 in Waterford, VT, d/o **Jonah**. (*Cheney Gen.*, p. 111-12 - *Carpenter Memorial*, p. 203)

CHESTER

Joseph - b 10/13/1815 in Colchester, CT, d in Logansport, IN. Joseph m 5/14/1838 in Cincinnati, OH, **Hannah T. McMasters**. (*Hist. of Cuyahoga Co., OH*, p. 160)

CHILD

Abner - b 4/13/1772 in Thompson, CT, s/o **Elijah** and **Rachel (Palmer)**; Abner d 6/8/1859 in Moretown, Washington Co., VT. He m (1) 1/23/1800 **Achsah Carpenter**, b 8/16/1780 in Coventry, CT, d 4/9/1823, and m (2) **Dolly Franklin**, d 8/1/1860. (*Child Gen.*, p. 460-1 - *Washington Co. Gazeteer*, p. 403)

Darius - b 12/26/1777 in N. Woodstock, CT, s/o **Alpha** and **Molly (May)**; Darius d 12/10/1862 age 85 in Fairlee, Orange Co., VT. He m 2/2/1802 **Letitia Morris**, b 10/2/1780 in Woodstock, CT, d 11/17/1859 in Fairlee, VT, d/o **William** and **Sarah (Bowman)**. (*Child Gen.*, p. 253 - *Gazetteer of Orange Co., VT*, p. 267 - *Woodstock Families*, v. 3, p. 512, 540-1)

Capt. David - b 7/25/1764 in Thompson, CT, s/o **Elijah** and **Rachel (Palmer)**; Capt. David d 7/22/1824 (drowned) in Pomfret, Windsor Co., VT. He m (1) c1782 **Ruth Brown**, and m (2) **Mrs. Billingly**. (*Child Gen.*, p. 445 - *Pomfret, VT*, v. 2, p. 464)

Henry - b 1/3/1780 in Woodstock, CT, s/o **Willard** and **Lydia (Morse)**; Henry d 4/8/1861 age 72 in West Fairlee, Orange Co., VT. He m (1) **Lucretia Child**, b 4/12/1791, d 4/3/1816, d/o **Nehemiah** and **Eliza (Shipman)**, and m (2) 4/3/1818 **Henrietta May**, b 11/18/1791, d 1/28/1822, d/o **Ephraim** and **Abigail (Chandler)**, and m (3) 11/10/1823 **Lucy May**, b 9/4/1797 in West Fairlee, VT, d 3/20/1843, d/o **Asa** and **Anna (Fillebrowne)**, and m (4) 4/28/1845 **Betsey Buel** of Newport, NH, d 6/18/1877. (*Gazetteer of Orange Co., VT*, p. 508 - *Gen. of Child-Childs*, p. 185-6 - *Woodstock Families*, v. 3, p. 534-5, 559-60)

Col. Jonathan - b 12/17/1731 in Woodstock, CT, s/o **Wm.** and **Deborah (Goddard)**; Col. Jonathan d 4/5/1814 age 83 in E. Thetford, Orange Co., VT. He m 6/12/1755 **Dinah Bacon**, b 5/2/1735 in

Woodstock, CT, d 1/3/1814 age 79 in E. Thetford, VT, d/o Thomas. (*DAR Patriot Index*, p. 129 - *Gen. of Child/Childs*, p. 325 - *Gazetteer of Orange Co., VT*, p. 435)

Rev. **Willard** - b 11/14/1796 in Woodstock, CT, s/o **Willard** and **Sylvia (Child)**; Rev. Willard d 11/13/1877 in Moores, NY. He m 9/13/1827 **Katherine Griswold Kent**, b 2/7/1805 in Benson, VT, d 2/25/1851, d/o Rev. **Dan** and **Betsey (Griswold)**. (*Gen. of the Woodstock Families - Child Gen.*, p. 190-5)

William - b 12/10/1757 in CT, s/o Col. **Jonathan** and **Dinah (Bacon)**; William d 8/27/1843 age 86 in E. Thetford, Orange Co., VT. He m 9/28/1780 **Mary Heaton**, b 10/14/1756 in Swansea, NH, d 12/23/1836 age 80 in E. Thetford, VT. (*Genealogies of Woodstock Families*, v. 3, p. 514 - *DAR Patriot Index*, p. 129 - *Gen. of Child/Childs*, p. 325)

CHIPMAN

Ammi - b 2/7/1764 in Salisbury, CT, s/o **Amos** and **Sarah (Daggett)**; Ammi d 12/10/1808 in Harlem, Ontario, Canada. He m1785 **Sarah Evarts**, b 12/8/1764, d1828. (*A Chipman Genealogy*, p. 50-1, 101-2 - *DAR Patriot Index*, p. 129)

Amos - bc1727 in Groton, CT, s/o **Thomas** and **Abigail (Lothrop)**; Amos dc1790 in Sunderland, Bennington Co., VT. He m (1) 10/18/1749 **Sarah Daggett** of Lebanon, CT, b 4/12/1728, and m (2) 4/27/1772 **Sarah Boardman**, b 1/31/1755, d1820, wid/o ---- Boardman. (*A Chipman Genealogy*, p. 23-4, 48-51 - *DAR Patriot Index*, p. 129)

Barnabus Lothrop - b 11/5/1762 in Salisbury, CT, s/o **Amos** and **Sarah (Daggett)**; Barnabus Lothrop d1847 in Malone, NY. He m 8/18/1788 **Beulah Evarts**, b 3/28/1761 in Sunderland, VT, d/o **Abner** and **Susannah (Scoville)**. (*DAR Patriot Index*, p. 129 - *A Chipman Gen.*, p. 49-50, 99-101)

Dr. **Cyrus** - b 12/3/1761 in Salisbury, CT, s/o **Samuel** and **Hannah (Austin)**; Dr. Cyrus d 12/3/1840 in Pawlet, VT (or Pittsdown, NY). He m 10/3/1787 **Anna Fitch**, b 12/28/1772. (*A Chipman Gen.*, p. 45-6, 91-3 - *DAR Patriot Index*, p. 129)

Daniel - b 10/22/1765 in Salisbury, CT, s/o **Samuel** and **Hannah (Austin)**; Daniel d 4/23/1850 in 85th year in Ripton, Addison Co., VT. He m1796 **Elutheria Hedge**, b 2/23/1776, d/o Rev. **Samuel** of Warwick, MA. (*A Chipman Genealogy*, p. 46-7, 94-5 - *History of Vermont*, v. 5, p. 195-6)

Darius - b 8/17/1756 in Salisbury, CT, s/o **Samuel** and **Hannah (Austin)**; Darius d 4/23/1832 (or 3/22/1832). He m (1) 1782 **Lydia Dickenson**, and m (2) **Hannah Mead**, d/o Capt. **William** of West Rutland, CT. (*DAR Patriot Index*, p. 129 - *A Chipman Gen.*, p. 44-5, 90-1 - *Am. Monthly*, p. 41)

Jesse - b 2/2/1755 in Salisbury, CT, s/o **Amos** and **Sarah (Daggett)**; Jesse d 6/4/1841 in Malone, NY. He m1779 **Mary White** of Salisbury, CT, b 6/22/1758, d/o **William**. (*A Chipman Gen.*, p. 49, 97-99 - *DAR Patriot Index*, p. 129)

Jonathan - b 10/24/1729 in Groton, CT, s/o **Thomas** and **Abigail (Lothrop)**; Jonathan d1820 in Essex, VT. He m 10/5/1756

Catherine Reed of Stamford, CT. (*A Chipman Gen.*, p. 24-5, 51-2 - *DAR Patriot Index*, p. 129)

Joseph - b 8/5/1761 in Salisbury, CT, s/o **Jonathan** and **Catherine** (**Reed**); Joseph d 3/25/1826 in Granville, OH. He m1789 **Amy Reed**, b1766 in Salisbury, CT. (*A Chipman Gen.*, p. 51, 102-5 - *DAR Patriot Index*, p. 129)

Lemuel - b 7/25/1754 in Salisbury, CT, s/o **Samuel** and **Hannah** (**Austin**); Lemuel d poss. 4/28/1831 in Pittstown, NY. He m1780 **Asenath Fitch**, d/o **William** and **Althea**. (*A Chipman Gen.*, p. 44, 88-90 - *DAR Patriot Index*, p. 129)

Nathaniel - b 11/15/1752 in Salisbury, CT, s/o **Samuel**; Nathaniel d 2/15/1842 age 91 in Tinmouth, VT. He m 9/13/1781 **Sarah Hill** of Tinmouth, VT, b 3/20/1762, d1831. (*A Chipman Genealogy*, p. 42-3 - *Hist. of Vermont*, v. 5, p. 30-32 - *DAR Patriot Index*, p. 129)

Samuel - b 3/7/1772 in Middletown, CT, s/o **Ebenezer**; Samuel d 3/21/1860 in Westminister, Windham Co., VT. He m 7/2/1794 **Anna Frazier**, b 9/12/1772 in VT, d 4/18/1845, d/o **Simon**. (*1850 Census Windam Co., VT - Windham Co. Gazetteer*, p. 304 - *A Chipman Gen.*, p. 112-114, 56)

Samuel - b 3/22/1721 in Groton, CT, s/o **Thomas** and **Abigail** (**Lothrop**); Samuel d1812 in Tinmouth, Rutland Co., VT. He m (1) 1/23/1749 **Hannah Austin** of Suffield, CT, b 6/5/1725, d/o Dr. **Nathaniel**, and m (2) a widow. (*A Chipman Gen.*, p. 23, 42-3, 86-88 - *Hist. of Rutland Co., VT*, p. 823 - *DAR Patriot Index*, p. 130)

Samuel - b 12/10/1763 in Salisbury, CT, s/o **Samuel** and **Hannah** (**Austin**); Samuel (the younger) d 3/24/1839 in Madrid, NY. He m 11/10/1785 **Hannah Spofford**, b 2/16/1765. (*A Chipman Genealogy*, p. 46, 93-4 - *DAR Patriot Index*, p. 129)

CHITTENDEN

Jared - b 5/3/1756 in CT, d 4/2/1828 prob. in Westmoreland, Oneida Co., NY. Jared m (1) **Elizabeth Lusk**, b 10/5/1803, and m (2) **Asena Douglas**, b 9/19/1783, d 12/30/1851 age 68. (*Oneida, Our County and Its People*, p. 608 - *DAR Patriot Index*, p. 130 - *Gen. of Chittenden Family*, p. 63-4, 112)

Thomas - b 1/6/1730 in E. Guilford, CT, s/o **Ebenezer** and **Mary** (- - - -); Thomas d 8/25/1797 age 67 in Williston, Chittenden Co., VT. He m 10/1749 **Elizabeth Meigs**, b 10/7/1731, d/o **Janna** and **Elizabeth** (**Dudley**). (*DAR Patriot Index*, p. 130 - *VT Hist. Magazine*, v. 1, p. 905-29 - *Chittenden Fam.*, p. 33-5)

CHOLLAR

Deacon **Thomas** - b 10/24/1778 in Pomfret, CT, d 8/6/1855 in Homer, Cortland Co., NY. Deacon Thomas m 3/5/1805 **Sally B. Dresser**. (*Pioneer Hist. of Cortland Co., NY*, p. 358)

CHURCH

Charles - b 11/14/1797 in E. Hartford, CT, d 8/18/1830 in Rochester, Monroe Co., NY, buried in Hope Cemetery. Charles m **Amanda Jewett**, b 11/6/1796 in E. Haddam, CT, d 4/2/1832. (*Hist. of Monroe Co., NY*, p. 181-2, 184 - Tombstone Rec. Mt. Hope Cem.)

Isaac - b 1/31/1742 in Killingly, CT, d 5/5/1836 in Vershire, Orange
Co., VT. He m 9/5/1765 **Eleanor Daniels**, b 11/20/1749 in
Pomfret, CT, d/o **Nathaniel, Sr.** and **Ann (Grosvenor)**. (*DAR
Patriot Index*, p. 131 - *Daniels Family Notes*, 5/1959 #2)
Ozias - b 1/31/1785 in Windham, CT, d 12/10/1863 in Barre, Orleans
Co., NY. Ozias m 10/13/1809 **Parmelia Palmer**, b 10/3/1786 in
Windham, CT, d 12/7/1861. (*Pioneer History of Orleans County,
NY*, p. 114)
Deacon **Perley** - b 5/7/1764 in Mansfield, CT, d 4/5/1853 in Water-
ford, Caledonia Co., VT. He m (1) **Zerviah Jacobs**, and m (2) 1829
Lucinda Felch. (*DAR Patriot Index*, p. 131 - *Caledonia Gazetteer*,
p. 371 - *Richard Church of Plymouth*, p. 317)

CLAPP
Major **Stephen** - b 8/10/1752 in CT, d 5/3/1829 age 77 in Salem,
Washington Co., NY. Major Stephen m **Katherine Wheeler**, b
6/12/1762, d 9/8/1813. (*DAR Patriot Index*, p. 132 - *Hist. of
Washington Co. Rev. War Cem.*)

CLARK
Andrew - b 3/22/1750 in Wallingford, CT, s/o **Andrew** and **Mehitable**
(**Tuttle**); Andrew (the younger) d 4/7/1819 age 64 in Wells, VT. He
m 11/24/1774 **Mary Robinson**, b 8/8/1755, d1841 age 87, d/o **John**
and **Lois (Sanford)**. (*Hist. of the Town of Wells, VT - Families of
Anc. New Haven*, p. 416 - *DAR Patriot Index*, p. 133)
Asa - b in Colchester, CT, d 5/19/1819 in Cornwallis, King's Co.,
Nova Scotia. Asa m **Sarah Hopson** of Colchester, CT, d1823, d/o
Capt. **John** and **India (Kellogg)**. (*Kings County - Family Sketches*, p.
605)
Beebe - b 5/10/1797 in New Milford, CT, s/o **Edmond** and **Hannah**
(**L o v e l**); Beebe d 2/1870 in Joliet, LaSalle Co., IL. He m
5/15/1837 in Washington, CT, **Susan Bishop**, d1872, Joliet, IL.
(*Hist. of LaSalle Co., IL*, p. 383-4)
Rev. **Charles G.** - b 4/8/1796 in Preston, CT, s/o **Shubel** and **Esther**
(**Tracy**); Rev. Charles G. d 10/2/1871 age 75 in Ann Arbor, Wash-
tenaw Co., MI. He m 8/30/1830 in Ann Arbor, MI, **Elizabeth Platt**.
(*Pioneer Collection of MI*, v. 9, p. 157-9)
Deacon **Daniel** - b 10/13/1752 in Middletown, CT, s/o **John, Jr.** and
S a r a h; Deacon Daniel d 4/14/1854, age 101-6-4 years, in
Plymouth, VT. He m 1/1780 **Lydia Davison** of Brooklyn, CT, d
9/27/1844 in 84th year. (*A Memorial to Deacon Daniel Clark* by
Norman Mason)
Elizur - b 10/5/1807 in Saybrook, CT, d 12/27/1895 in Syracuse,
Onondaga Co., NY. Elizur m (1) 1825 **Jerusha N. Spencer**, and m
(2) 1869 **Augusta M. Peck**. (*Onondaga Hist. Soc. of 1914*, p. 167 -
paperback)
Griffin - bc1792 in CT, d 10/18/1868 age 77, buried Spring Road
Cem., Tunbridge, VT. Griffin m **Julia Abbott**, bc1796, d 3/11/1869
age 73 in Tunbridge, VT. (*1850 Orange Co. Census, Tunbridge, VT*)
Dr. **Herman** - b 8/29/1789 in Waterbury, CT, s/o **John, Jr.** and **Milla**
(**Munson**); Dr. Herman d 3/15/1865 in Ashland, OH. He m 2/8/1816
in Southbury, CT, **Laura Downs**, b 3/18/1798 in S. Britain, CT, d

50

5/20/1863 in S. Amherst, OH, d/o **Philo** and **Hannah (Mallory)**. (*Residents of CT Who Migrated to Huron Co., OH - Deacon George Clark*, p. 136, 189)

Jeremiah - b1782 in CT, d 11/18/1872 in Strafford, VT, (Kibling Cem. stone). Jeremiah m (1) **Polly**, d 3/15/1825 age 44 (gravestone), and m (2) **Minerva Blanchard**, d 10/18/1868 age 68. (Strafford Cemetery called Kibling - gravestones)

Jeremiah - b 7/18/1734 in Plainfield, CT, s/o **James** and **Thankful**; Jeremiah d 10/17/1817 in 84th year in Shaftsbury, Bennington Co., VT. He m (1) 4/17/1755 in Preston, CT, **Susanna Clark** of Plainfield, CT, bc1733, d 4/29/1787 in Shaftsbury, VT, d/o **Benjamin**, and m (2) **Mary** bc1749 d 5/6/1840 in 91st year in Shaftsbury, VT. (*Gravestone Rec. of Shaftsbury*, p. 12 - *DAR Patriot Index*, p. 134 - *Bennington Co. Gazetteer*, p. 198-9 - *Hist. of Bennington Co.*)

John, Jr. - b 10/1/1732 in Milford, CT, s/o **John** and **Billing (Baldwin)**; John Jr. d 7/12/1816 age 86 in Vienna, Trumbull Co., OH. He m **Elizabeth Rogers**, b 2/4/1740 (or 1741), d 3/22/1833 age 94 in Vienna, OH, d/o **Joseph** and **Elizabeth (Clark)**. (*Ezra Thompson Clarks Anc. and Des.*, p. 76-88)

Moses - b 9/24/1761 in Lebanon, CT, s/o **Moses** and **Mehitable (Bridges)**; Moses (the younger) d 1/2/1844, and is buried in Walker Cem., Alpine, Kent Co., MI. He m **Patty Bill**, b1765, d1846. (*Connecticut Revolutionary Soldiers Buried in Michigan* - *DAR Patriot Index*, p. 135)

Roswell - b 6/5/1761 in Cheshire, CT, d 9/19/1837 age 75 in Wells, VT. Roswell m (1) **Thankful Hotchkiss**, d 2/10/1809 age 50 in Wells, VT, and m (2) **Susanna Cook**, wid/o ---- Cook. (*Hist. of Wells, VT*, p. 73-4 - *DAR Patriot Index* p. 135)

Hon. Samuel - b 2/28/1777 in Lebanon, CT, s/o **Samuel** and **Sarah (Cushman)**; Hon. Samuel d 4/19/1861 age 84 in Brattleboro, Windham Co., VT. He m **Susan Johnson**, b 9/1778 in Ellington, CT, d/o **David**. (*1850 Census of Windham Co., VT* - *Gazetteer of Windham Co.*, p. 114 - *VT Hist. Magazine*, v. 5, p. 127)

Stephen, Jr. - b1750 in Cheshire, CT, d 2/8/1827 age 77 in Wells, VT. Stephen, Jr. m (1) 9/12/1770 in Wallingford, CT, **Patience Grannis**, d 3/8/1809 age 59 in Wells, VT, and m (2) **Roxanna Beck**, wid/o ---- Beck. (*Hist. of Town of Wells, Vermont*, p. 46, by Grace Wood)

Stephen - b 3/3/1745 in Plainfield, CT, d 8/29/1834 in Otsego Co., NY. Stephen m (1) **Mary** ----, and m (2) **Anne** ----. (*DAR Patriot Index*, p. 135 - *New Eng. Gen. Register*, 10/1976)

Timothy - b 4/9/1767 in CT, s/o **Timothy**; d 9/19/1848 in Rockingham, Windham Co., VT. Timothy m 12/28/1794 **Sarah Burk**, b 7/8/1778, d 5/2/1851 in Rockingham, VT, d/o Major **Silas** of Westminster, VT. (*Hist. of Rockingham*, p. 629-30)

William, Jr. - b1753 in Hampton, CT, s/o **William**; William Jr. d 10/4/1840 age 87 in Preston, NY. He m 4/15/1783 in Hampton, CT, **Eunice Ford Preston**, d 10/31/1856 age 98 years. (*History of Chenango Co.*)

CLEVELAND

Deacon **Benjamin** – b 8/30/1733 in Windham, CT, d prob. in King's
Co., Nova Scotia. Deacon Benjamin m (1) 2/20/1754 in Windham,
CT, **Mary Alderkin**, b 12/16/1735 in Windham, CT, and m (2) in
Scotland, CT, **Sarah Hibbard** or **Hubbard**. (*King's Co. – Family
Sketches*, p. 606–7)

Camden – b 4/1778 in Canterbury, CT, d 3/13/1826 in Youngstown,
OH. Camden m 5/25/1800 **Betsey Adams**. (*Trumbull and Mahoning
Counties, OH*)

Chester – b 3/22/1771 (or 3/28/1771?) in CT, s/o **Samuel** and **Ruth**
(Darbe); Chester d after 1820 in Tunbridge, VT. He m (1) 5/7/1795
in Royalton, VT, **Mary Hibbard**, b 5/7/1777 in Royalton, VT, d
5/20/1817 in Royalton, VT, and m (2) 3/1820 **Elizabeth Sophia
Dodge** in Tunbridge, VT. (*1850 Orange Co. Census for Tunbridge –
Cleveland Gen.*, p. 270–1, 706–8)

Gardner, Sr. – b 9/25/1763 in Pomfret, CT, d 4/22/1851 prob.
Chautauqua Co., NY. Gardner, Sr. m (1) **Mary Holmes**, d1830, and
m (2) **Huldah Demming**. (*DAR Patriot Index*, p. 138 – *Chautauqua
Co., NY*)

George – b 1/9/1769 in Norwich, CT, s/o **Aaron** and **Abiah (Hyde)**;
George d 2/2/1851 in Middlebury, Addison Co., VT. He m **Catey
Caldwell**, b 8/29/1766 in Guilford, CT, d 5/11/1853 in Middlebury,
VT. (*Cleveland Gen.*, p. 503, 1079 – Middlebury Cem. gravestone)

Henry – b 5/11/1746 in Mansfield, CT, d 1/5/1841 age 95 in Dalton,
MA. Henry m **Elizabeth Royce**. (*American Monthly*, v. 41 – *DAR
Patriot Index*, p. 138)

John – b 10/4/1779 in CT, d 4/16/1861 in Huron, OH. John m1808 in
Bristol, NY, **Silva Phillips**, b 6/8/1783, d 2/14/1868. (*Residents of
Connecticut in Huron, OH – 1812 War Index*)

Squire – b 7/29/1754 in Canterbury, CT, s/o **Eleazer** and **Anna
(Bradford)**; Squire d 6/14/1834 age 79–11 years in Royalton, VT.
He m 11/16/1788 **Pamelia Green** of Royalston, MA, b 3/3/1764, d
4/25/1851. (*Cleveland Gen.*, v. 1, p. 129, 261, 604–5 – *DAR Patriot
Index*, p. 138)

Samuel – b 6/7/1730 in Canterbury, CT, s/o **Joseph** and **Sarah
(Ensworth)**; Samuel d 9/1809 age 79 years in Royalton, Windsor
Co., VT. He m (1) 3/7/1751 in Canterbury, CT, **Ruth Darby** (or
Derby?), b 9/21/1732, d 8/13/1782 in Bethel, VT, and m (2)
3/11/1784 **Ann Welch**. (*Cleveland Gen.*, v. 1, p. 139–140 – *DAR
Patriot Index*, p. 138 – *History of Royalton, VT*, p. 724–8)

Thomas – b 3/24/1769 in CT, d 12/22/1861 age 93 years in Hartland,
VT. Thomas m (1) 1/2/1794 in Pomfret, CT, **Anna Crafts**, b
7/5/1772 in Pomfret, CT, d 9/30/1835 in Hartland, VT, and m (2)
6/2/1836 Mrs. **Abigail (Roberts) True**, b 12/12/1792 in Plainfield,
NH, d 10/8/1880 in Bolton, Quebec. (*1850 Windsor Co. Census for
Hartland, VT – Cleveland Gen.*, p. 328–9)

Tracy – b 5/8/1752 in Canterbury, CT, s/o **David** and **Rebecca
(Tracy)**; Tracy d 2/27/1836 age 87 in Kirtland, Lake Co., OH. He
m 4/25/1773 in Canterbury, CT, **Phebe Hyde**, bc 4/2/1748, d
11/5/1829 age 77, d/o **Jonathan** and **Lucy (Tracy)**. (*Rev. Soldiers
Buried In Lake Co., OH – DAR Patriot Index*, p. 138 – *Cleveland
Gen.*, p. 617–620)

COBB

Bennett – b 11/1785 in Plymouth, CT, d 4/8/1870 age 84 in Camden, Oneida Co., NY. Bennett m (1) **Mercy Doten**, d 4/18/1838 age 49, and m (2) widow of **Nathaniel Brown**. (*Pioneer Hist. of Camden, NY*, p. 234-238)

G i d e o n – b 7/7/1716 in Stonington, CT, d 7/24/1797 age 81 year in Orwell, Rutland Co., VT. Gideon m (1) 11/5/1739 in Canterbury, CT, **Abigail Dyer**, d 6/10/1808 age 91-7-23 in Orwell, VT, d/o **John** and **Abigail (Fitch)**. (*Hist. of Rutland Co.*, p. 702)

Jeduthan, Jr. – b 6/25/1791 in Tolland, CT, s/o Lt. **Jeduthan** and **Sarah (Chapman)**; Jeduthan, Jr. d1827 in Berlin, Erie Co., OH. He m 11/5/1811 **Harriet Griggs**, d/o **Stephen** of Tolland, CT. (*Hist. of Cuyahoga Co., OH*, p. 338-9)

Jerome T. – b 12/29/1821 in Goshen, CT, d 11/15/1893 age 71-10-16 in Schoolcraft, MI. Jerome T. m (1) 8/1846 **Juliana Benton** of Amenia, NY, dc1850, and m (2) **Harriet Felt**. (*Pioneer Collections of MI*, v. 13, p. 110)

Dr. Samuel – b 8/2/1746 in Tolland, CT, s/o **Samuel**; Dr. Samuel d1806 in Norwich, Windham Co., VT. He m (1) 12/14/1769 **Esther Grant**, d/o **Ephraim**, and m (2) 12/16/1773 **Ann Steel**. (*Cobb History*, p. 141 – *DAR Patriot Index*, p. 140 – *VT Antiquarian*, p. 41)

COE

Ithamar – b 9/10/1755 in Durham, CT, d 8/26/1826 in LeRoy, Onondaga Co., NY. Ithamar m **S a r a h   B a l l** of Granville, MA, b 11/25/1763. (*Onondaga Hist. Soc. of 1914*, p. 194 – *DAR Patriot Index*, p. 141)

Oliver – b 9/3/1738 in Torrington, CT, s/o **Jonathan**; d 12/31/1775 during the Revolution – lived Burke VT. He m 10/7/1761 **Mary A g a r d**. (*DAR Patriot Index*, p. 141 – *Gazetteer of Caledonia Co., VT*, p. 155 – *Robert Coe, Puritan*, p. 168)

COGSWELL

L e v i – b 9/6/1759 in Farmington, CT, s/o **S a m u e l** and **M a r y (Langdon)**; Levi d 11/29/1853 in Charlotte, Chittenden Co., VT. He m 12/1/1786 **Rachel F. Whiteley**, b 5/22/1762, d 6/22/1846 in Charlotte, VT, d/o **William**. (*Cogswell in America*, p. 253-4 – *1850 Census Chittenden Co., VT*)

COLE

B e n j a m i n – b 2/18/1761 in Plainfield, CT, s/o **E b e n e z e r** and **Elizabeth (Wheler)**; d 4/10/1842 age 81 (gravestone) in S. Royalton, VT. He m (1) **Eunice Pierce**, and m (2) **Jemima (Poor) L a t h a m**. (*History of Royalton, Vermont*, p. 729 – *DAR Patriot Index*, p. 143)

Samuel – b 7/23/1775 in Voluntown, CT, d 11/8/1832 age 57-3-15 in Oxford, Chenango Co., NY. Samuel m 12/20/1798 **Alice Pullman** of West Greenwich, RI, b 6/22/1783, d 1/21/1858 age 74-6-29 in Sterling, IL. (*Annals of Oxford, NY*, p. 468-71 – *Tree Talks*, June 1974, p. 80)

Thomas – b 8/25/1733 in Voluntown, CT, d 10/25/1825 age 92-2 in Norwich, Chenango Co., NY. Thomas m **Mariam Kinnee**, d 12/15/1827 age 89-8. (*DAR Patriot Index*, p. 144 – *Tree Talks*, June 1974)

COLEMAN
Ozias – b 1/2/1739 in Colchester, CT, d 9/17/1817 in Fort Ann, PA. Ozias m 6/24/1760 in Lebanon, CT, **Hulda Brewster**, b 4/23/1744 in Lebanon, CT, d/o **Ichabod** and **Lydia (Barstow)**. (*First Hundred Years in Townville, PA*)

COLLIN
David – b 5/1/1772 in Milford, CT, s/o **John** and **Hannah (Merwin)**; David d 12/17/1818 prob. in Hillsdale, Columbia Co., NY. He m (1) 2/19/1764 **Lucy Smith** of Dutchess Co., NY, d 3/15/1767, and m (2) 1/19/1772 **Esther Gellett**, d 5/8/1824. (*Hist. of Hillsdale, NY*, p. 6)

John – b 7/15/1732 in Milford, CT, s/o **John** and **Hannah (Merwin)**; John (the younger) d 8/21/1809 in Hillsdale, Columbia Co., NY. He m (1) **Sarah Arnold** of Dutchess Co., NY, d 12/29/1791, and m (2) 5/13/1792 **Diedama Morse Davidson**. (*Hist. of Hillsdale, Columbia Co., NY*, p. 5)

COLLINS
Archibald – b 12/1764 in Guilford, CT, d 12/1842 in Ferrisburgh, Addison Co., VT. Archibald m 12/1787 **Rhoda Bates**. (*Gazetteer of Addison Co., VT*)

Gen. Oliver – b 8/21/1762 in CT, d 8/14/1838 age 76 in New Hartford, Oneida Co., NY. Gen. Oliver m (1) **Lois Cowls**, and m (2) **Betsey Wyman**, and m (3) **Melinda Peirce**, and m (4) **Keturah Kellogg**. (*Annals of Oneida Co.*, p. 282 – *DAR Patriot Index*, p. 145)

Oliver – b 8/25/1762 in Wallingford, CT, s/o **Jonathan** and **Agnes (Linn)**; Oliver d 8/14/1838 in New Hartford, NY. He m 1/25/1784 in Wallingford, CT, **Lois Cowles**. (*History of Cuyahoga County, OH*, p. 341)

COMSTOCK
Abijah – b 9/2/1781 in New Canaan, CT, d 2/1/1857 in Norwalk, OH. Abijah m1810 in Huron Co., OH, **Esther Iseft**, bc1790. (*Residents from CT in Huron Co., OH*)

Anselm A. – b 8/25/1762 in Lyme, CT, d 7/28/1845 age 84 in Sweden Twp., Monroe Co., NY. Anselm A. m **Betsey Jewett**. (*DAR Patriot Index*, p. 147 – Tombstone Rec.)

David – b 1/30/1761 in Norwalk, CT, d 4/23/1844 age 83 in Clinton, Oneida Co., NY. David m **Hannah Marvin**, d 5/19/1844 age 79. (*Clinton-Memorial – Kirtland Ave. Cemetery*, p. 96 – *CT Hist. Soc. Collection*, v. 8, p. 217)

Serajah – b 10/17/1758 in Norfolk, CT, d 2/23/1826 age 66 in Camden, Oneida Co., NY. Serajah m (1) **Ann Benedict**, and m (2) **Clemina Austin**. (*Pioneer Hist. of Camden, NY*, p. 313-14 – *DAR Patriot Index*, p. 147)

CONE

Daniel – b 7/7/1759 in East Haddam, CT, d 6/28/1842 age 83 in Peru, MA. Daniel m1785 **Olive Ackley**, d 9/12/1840 age 76. (*DAR Patriot Index*, p. 148 – *American Monthly*, v. 41)

Linus – b 10/12/1802 in Haddam, CT, d 10/17/1875 in Avon, Oakland Co., MI. Linus m 8/12/1827 **Mary Crooks**, d/o **David** and **Eunice Cone**. (*Pioneer Collections of MI*, v. 9, p. 188)

CONVERSE

Gov. **Julius** – b 12/27/1798 in Stafford, CT, s/o **Joseph** and **Mary M.**; Gov. Julius d 8/16/1885 in Dixville, Notch, NH. He m (1) **Melissa Arnold**, d 12/14/1872, and m (2) **Jane Martin**, b1842. (*Gazetteer of Orange Co., VT – Randolph*, p. 133)

COOK

Charles C. – b 6/22/1799 in Wallingford, CT, d 9/26/1863 in Youngstown, OH. Charles C. m **Mary E. L. Salter**, b 2/15/1800 in New Haven, CT, d 1/3/1862. (*Trumbull and Mahoning Counties, Ohio*, p. 406)

Chauncey – b1794 in Wallingford, CT, s/o **Joseph** and **Rachel (Langdon)**; Chauncey d 1/26/1871 in N. Monroeville, OH. He m1816 **Dorcas** ----, b1801, d 11/23/1867 in N. Monroeville, OH. (Residents from CT in Huron Co. OH)

Elijah – b 9/10/1759 in CT, d 6/30/1839 near Homer, MI, buried in Cook's Prairie Cem., Homer, MI. Elijah m **Charity Lockwood**. (*CT Rev. Soldiers Buried in MI – DAR Patriot Index*, p. 150)

Lemuel – b 9/10/1763 in CT, d 5/20/1866 age 102-8-10 in Clarendon, Onondaga Co., NY. Lemuel m **Hannah Curtis**. (*DAR Patriot Index*, p. 151 – *Onondaga Hist. Soc. of 1914*, p. 19 – *Pioneer Hist. Orleans Co., VT*, p. 208-9)

Martin – b 3/3/1772 in Litchfield, CT, s/o **Oliver**; Martin d 3/20/1855 in Camden, NY. He m **Clarissa Rossiter**, d 8/28/1848. (*Pioneer Hist. of Camden, NY*, p. 106-9 Oneida Co.)

Oliver – b 10/3/1750 in Windsor, CT, s/o **Samuel**; Oliver d 12/30/1838 age 88 in Camden, Oneida Co., NY. He m at Harwinton, CT, 2/17/1768 **Submit Cogsdell**, d 7/20/1846. (*Pioneer Hist. of Camden, NY*, p. 104-6 – *DAR Patriot Index*, p. 151)

Richard – b1751 in CT, d 8/13/1833 in Plainfield, Otsego Co., NY, buried in Family Cemetery. Richard m (1) **Mary Rowley**, and m (2) **Susanna** ----. (*DAR Mag., 1977*, p. 915)

Samuel – b 5/18/1765 in Preston, CT, s/o **Thaddeus** and **Zervia (Hinckley)**; Samuel d 9/25/1852 prob. in Mt. Holly, Rutland Co., VT. He m 1/1/1791 **Sally Chamberlain**, b 12/19/1766 in CT, d 5/24/1861 age 95, d/o **Oliver**. (*Hist. of Rutland Co.*, p. 676-7 – *1850 Rutland Co. Census*)

Solon – b 9/30/1795 in Harwinton, CT, s/o **Martin** and **Clarissa**; Solon d 7/2/1876 prob. in Camden, Oneida Co., NY. He m (1) 4/1815 **Elvira Byington**, b 3/28/1797, d 5/4/1822, and m (2) 10/25/1824 **Elizabeth Peck**, b 11/8/1794, d 9/12/1845, d/o **Henry Peck**. (*Pioneer History of Camden, New York*, p. 137-143 – War of 1812)

COPELAND

Willard - b 10/27/1769 in Brooklyn, CT, d 2/20/1852 in Braintree, VT. Willard m (1) **Alice Lyon**, d1804, and m (2) 12/12/1805 **Rebecca White**. (*Hist. of Braintree, VT*, p. 127)

William - b 8/5/1755 in Pomfret, CT, s/o **William** and **Sarah** **(Smith)**; William (the younger) d 11/19/1815 in Salisbury, Addison Co., VT. He m 12/7/1780 **Anna Weeks**, b 12/24/1760, d 3/5/1826 in Salisbury, Addison Co., VT. (*Copeland Fam.*, p. 75-6 - *Hist. of Salisbury, VT*, p. 338)

CORBIN

Clement - b 2/15/1764 in Thompson, CT, d 6/2/1853 age 89 in Charlestown, NH. Clement m1789 **Sabra (or Sara) Chamberlain**. (*DAR Patriot Index*, p. 154 - *American Monthly*, v. 41)

Elijah - b 6/28/1767 in Killingly, CT, s/o **Elijah** and **Elizabeth** **(Prince)**; Elijah (the younger) d 11/15/1812 age 46 (gravestone) in Royalton, Windsor Co., VT. Elijah m 6/23/1790 in Thompson, CT, **Orinda Childs**, b1768, d 9/30/1855 age 87 (gravestone). (*History of Royalton, Vermont*, p. 730 - *Corbin Gen.*, p. 40-41, 62 - *1850 Windsor Co. Census*)

Joseph - b 5/31/1751 in Killingly, CT, d 10/3/1838 age 87 in Champlain, Clinton Co., NY. Joseph m1772 **Mary Tallmadge**, d 8/6/1838. (*DAR Patriot Index*, p. 154 - *DAR Magazine*, v. 41 p. 174)

Micaiah - bc1776 in CT (a Quaker), d1836 in Roxbury, NY. Micaiah m **Maria Borden**. (*Hist. of the Town of Roxbury, NY*, p. 33 - *Corbin Gen.*, p. 323-4)

CORNWELL

Levinus - b 11/1791 in CT, s/o **Benjamin** and **Esther (Carrington)**; Levinus d 11/3/1878 in Concord, NY. He m **Lois Wheat**, b 11/28/1794 in Whitehall, Washington Co., NY, d 5/5/1871 in Sardinia, NY. (*Hist. of the Original Town of Concord, NY*, p. 858)

COTTON

Charles - b 4/4/1778 in Pomfret, CT, d prob. in Roxbury (or Brookfield), VT. Charles m (1) **Alice Spaulding**, b1779, d 2/26/1831 in W. Brookfield, VT, and m (2) 1/12/1832 **Lydia Richardson**. (*Short Biog. of Rev. John Cotton*, p. 51)

Ebenezer - b 5/5/1768 in Pomfret, CT, s/o **Thomas** and **Sarah** **(Holbrook)**; Ebenezer d 9/26/1819 in Hartland (?), VT. He m **Tirza Grow**, b 7/18/1782, d 11/19/1853, d/o **Joseph** and **Tirza (Sanger)**. (*Short Biog. of Rev. John Cotton*, p. 48)

COUCH

Daniel - b1764 prob. in Redding, CT, d 9/16/1846, and is buried in Johnson Cem., Hillsdale Co., MI. Daniel m **Sally ----**, b1774, d1847. (CT Rev. Soldiers Buried in MI)

COVELL

Edward - b 1/10/1790 in Glastonbury, CT, d in Ogden Twp., Monroe Co., NY. Edward m (1) 9/14/1815 **Mary Gilman**, d 6/11/1822, and

m (2) 1/12/1824 **Rhoda Town**, d1864, and m (3) **Harriet Terry.**
(*Hist. of Monroe Co., NY*, p. 182)
Leonard Eleazer - b1810 in CT, d 1/25/1851 in Upper Sandusky,
Wyandot Co., OH.   Leonard Eleazer m in OH **Lydia A. Har-
denbrook**, b1821, d 3/21/1892 age 70 in Sand Creek, OH (?).
(*Detroit Soc. Gen. Research*, p. 22 Fall 1972 issue)

COVILLE
Ebenezer H. - b1784 in Burlington, CT, d1838 in Oxford, Chenango
Co., NY.   Ebenezer H. m **Thankful Cook**, b1786 in Burlington, CT,
d1884. (*Annals of Oxford*, p. 210)

COWDREY
William, Jr. - b 9/5/1765 in E. Haddam, CT, s/o **Wm.** and **Hannah
(Emmons)**; William Jr. d 2/26/1847 in Kirtland, OH. He m (1)
Rebecca Fuller, b 1/2/1768, d 9/3/1809, and m (2) Mrs. **Keziah
(Pearce) Austin** of Poultney, VT, b 7/1/1773, d 7/10/1860 in
Ellery, NY, and m (3) ----. (*Hist. of Wells, VT*, p. 50 - *Cowdrey
Gen*, p. 95-6, 170-188)

COWLES
Samuel - b 6/8/1776 in Norfolk, CT, s/o **Joseph** and Sarah **(Mills)**;
Samuel d 11/1837 in Cleveland, OH. He m1832 in Lenox, MA, **Cor-
nelia Whiting**, d/o **Bradford**. (*Hist. of Cuyuoga Co., OH*, p. 345 -
Cowles Gen., v. 1, p. 382)
Dr. Edwin Weed - b 5/3/1794 in Bristol, CT, s/o Rev. Dr. **Giles
Hooker Cowles**; Dr. Edwin Weed d 6/6/1861 in Cleveland, OH. He
m 11/5/1815 **Almira Mills Foot**, b 1/5/1788 in Norfolk, CT, d
4/9/1846 in Cleveland, OH, d/o **Asa**. (*Hist. of Cuyahoga Co., OH -
Cowles Gen.*, v. 1, p. 275)

CRAFTS
Ebenezer - b 9/22/1740 in Pomfret, CT, s/o **Joseph**; Ebenezer d
5/24/1810 in 70th year in Craftsbury, VT.   He m 12/9/1762
Mehitable Chandler, b 2/28/1740, d 9/29/1712. (*DAR Patriot In-
dex*, p. 160)
Hon. **Samuel** - b 10/6/1768 in Woodstock, CT, s/o **Ebenezer** and
Mehitable Chandler; Hon. Samuel d 11/19/1853 age 85 in
Craftsbury, VT. He m 1/9/1798 in Farmington, CT, **Eunice Todd**, b
7/31/1773, d 8/25/1829, wid/o ---- **Beardsley**. (*Genealogy of
Woodstock Families*, v. IV, p. 159-161 - *Gazetteer of Orleans Co.,
Vermont*, p. 243)

CRANE
Abiah - b 2/8/1751 in Tolland, CT, s/o **Abiah** and **Mary (Tyler)**;
Abiah d 2/6/1805 in Surry, NH. He m 12/9/1779 **Experience Smith**,
d 3/27/1814, d/o **Jonathan** of Surry, NH. (*Hist. of the Town of
Surry, NH*, p. 546-7 - *Crane Genealogy*, p. 69-70)
Frederick M. - b 5/12/1815 in Salisbury, CT, s/o **Aaron** and **Polly
(Conklin)**; Frederick M. d 1/8/1877 in Honesdale, Wayne Co., PA.
He m **Olivia Sims** of Philadelphia. (*History of Wayne County, Pen-
nsylvania*, p. 375)

Joel – b 1/19/1772 in E. Windsor, CT, s/o **Hezekiah**; Joel d
1/14/1835 prob. in Pharsalia, Chenango Co., NY. He m1796 **Sally
Graves**, b 2/17/1777 in Worcester, MA, d 8/22/1852. (*History of
Chenango Co., NY*, p. 425)

Roger – b 5/4/1762 in Mansfield, CT, s/o **Ebenezer** and **Sarah
(Curtis)**; Roger d 6/3/1841 in Painesville, OH. He m 5/20/1784 in
Ashford, CT, **Sarah Whiton**. (*DAR Patriot Index*, p. 161 – Rev.
Soldiers Buried in Lake Co., OH)

Dr. **Rufus** – b 3/19/1774 in CT, s/o **Isaac** and **Thankful (Putnam)**; Dr.
Rufus d 9/18/1846 in Warren, NY. He m1796 in Warren, Herkimer
Co., NY, **Philotheta Marshall**, b Colchester, CT. (*Biog. Rec. of
Otsego Co., NY*, p. 626 – *Crane Gen.*, p. 69, 112–113)

CRARY

Christopher – b 6/24/1759 in New London, CT, s/o **Oliver**; Chris-
topher d 6/2/1846 in Union Co., OH. He m 11/4/1784 Preston, CT,
Polly Witter. (*Rev. Soldiers Buried in Lake Co., OH*, p. 20-1 –
DAR Patriot Index, p. 162 – *Crary Family Records*, p. 26)

CRIPPEN

Samuel – b1743 in Simsbury, CT, dc1783.   Samuel m (1) **Esther
Wheeler**, d 3/1824, and m (2) ---- **Selden**. (*Hist. of Pittsford, VT*,
p. 34-5 – *DAR Patriot Index*, p. 163)

CRUTTENDEN

Jeremiah – b 8/19/1767 in New Haven, CT, d 12/2/1859 in Morris,
Otsego Co., NY.   Jeremiah m **Mary Brooks**, bc1770, d 9/22/1836
age 68 in Morris, NY, d/o **Benjamin** and **Thankful (Hickok)**. (*Biog.
Rec. of Otsego Co., NY*, p. 231 – *Families of Ancient New Haven*, p.
512)

CROCKER

James – b 11/11/1757 in Colchester, CT, s/o **James**; James (the
younger) d 3/19/1825 age 68 in Thetford, Orange Co., VT.   He m
Mary Buckingham, b1761 (or 1762), d 11/10/1850 in Randolph, VT,
d/o **Jedediah** and **Mary (Haynes)**. (*Gazetteer of Orange Co., VT*, p.
441 – *Crocker Gen.*, p. 86, 136-7)

James Dyer – b 11/30/1788 in Litchfield, CT, s/o **James** and **Mary
(Buckingham)**; James Dyer d 7/22/1861 age 72 in Thetford, VT. He
m (1) **Achsah Ladd**, d 3/15/1859 age 68 in Brookfield, CT, and m
(2) 10/26/1859 **Betsey (Worthley) Lougee**, b NH. (*Crocker Genealogy*, p. 86, 136-7)

CROSS

Ichabod – b 6/16/1736 in Mansfield, CT, s/o **Daniel, Jr.** and
Elizabeth (Abbe); Ichabod d 1/6/1827 in 91st year in Shatfsbury,
Bennington Co., VT. He m (1) **Jemima Cobb**, d 11/2/1785 in 52nd
year, and m (2) **Olive ----**, d 8/20/1817 age 88 years in Shaftsbury,
VT. (*Gravestone Rec. of Shaftsbury, VT*, p. 16 – *Hist. of Pittsford,
VT*, p. 209 – *Bennington Co. Gazetteer* – *DAR Patriot Index*)

CRUM

Nathan - b 11/4/1808 in Stonington, CT, d 4/20/1882 in Adrian, Lawrence Co., MI. Nathan m 8/21/1835 in Exeter, Otsego Co., NY, Elizabeth Caswell, b 9/12/1812 in Exeter, NY, d 10/3/1879 in Adrian, MI, d/o Jonathan and Margery (Markham). (*Detroit Soc. Gen. Research*, 1973, p. 15)

CUMMINGS

Ezra - bc1771 in CT, d 10/13/1814 age 43 in E. Thetford, VT. Ezra m Esther ----, d 1/30/1836 age 67 in E. Thetford, VT. (Information from gravestones in E. Thetford Cemetery.)

CURTIS

Abel - b 6/13/1755 in Lebanon, CT, s/o Simeon and Sarah (Hutchinson); Abel d 10/7/1783 in Norwich, Windsor Co., VT. He m Kezia Brown. (*A Hist. of Norwich, VT*, p. 193-8)

Amos, Jr. - b 8/27/1768 in Suffield, CT, d 5/8/1854 age 86 in Pawlet, Rutland Co., VT. Amos Jr. m (1) 2/4/1790 in Weathersfield, VT, Eunice Upham, b 8/17/1769 in Sturbridge, MA, d 2/7/1836, d/o Asa and Lydia (Pierce), and m (2) 10/12/1839 in Suffield, CT, Sarah Mather, d 3/30/1854 age 75, wid/o William of Suffield. (*1850 Rutland Co. Census - TAG*, v. 15, p. 88)

Gen. Elias - b 10/16/1747 in Lebanon, CT, d 10/18/1827 age 79 in Tunbridge, Orange Co., VT. Gen. Elias m Sarah Hutchinson. (*On the Beginnings of Tunbridge, VT*)

Gideon - b 11/19/1767 in Woodbury, CT, d 7/7/1843 in either Jericho or Essex, VT. Gideon m (1) Rebecca Hardy, d 2/6/1816, and m (2) 8/5/1816 Hannah Stimson, d 11/26/1872 age 84 in Essex, VT. (*Chittenden Co. Gazetteer*, p. 235)

Jesse - bc1767 in Plymouth, CT, d 1/19/1850 age 83 in Clinton, NY, and buried in Kirkland Cem. Jesse m Lola ----. (*Clinton, New York, Memorial*, p. 50)

CURTISS

Benjamin, Jr. - b 2/13/1735 (or 1736) in Plymouth, CT, d 9/27/1825 in Camden, Oneida Co., NY. Benjamin, Jr. m (1) Content Pond, and m (2) Aurelia Sterne. (*Pioneer Hist. of Camden, NY*, p. 61-2 - DAR Patriot Index, p. 170)

Major Jesse - b 9/22/1733 in Waterbury, CT, s/o Daniel and Lottie; Major Jesse d 5/28/1821 age 88 in Camden, NY. He m Sarah Curtiss, d 1/19/1818 age 81. (*Pioneer Hist. of Camden, NY*, p. 53-4 - DAR Patriot Index, p. 170)

CUSHMAN

Eleazer - b 9/30/1752 in Willington, CT, d 5/17/1822 in Clinton, NY, and buried in Kirkland Cem. Eleazer m Mehitable Hinckley, b 4/21/1752, d 3/11/1811 (or 3/16/1811) age 59. (*Clinton Memorial*, p. 43 - *Cushman Gen.*)

Capt. Solomon - b 8/2/1745 in Lebanon, CT, d 11/12/1798 age 54 in E. Tunbridge, VT. Capt. Solomon m 5/26/1768 in Lebanon, CT, Sarah Curtiss, d 6/14/1842 age 92. (*On the Beginnings of Tunbridge - Cushman Gen.*, p. 163-4 - *DAR Patriot Index*, p. 172)

CUTLER

Benoni – b 8/17/1737 in Killingly, CT, d1807 in Guildhall, Essex Co., VT. Benoni m 12/22/1763 in Killingly, CT, **Laurana Leavens**, d/o **James**. (*History of Guildhall, Vermont – Cutler Genealogy*, p. 64, 111-114 – *DAR Patriot Index*, p. 172)

Charles – b 5/7/1765 in Killingly, CT, s/o **Benoni**; Charles d 11/1854 in WI (had lived in Guildhall, VT). He m **Chloe Blake**, b 12/20/1767 in Sturbridge, MA, d 10/20/1827. (*Cutler Memorial*, p. 111)

Ephraim – b 4/13/1767 in CT, d 7/8/1853 age 86 prob. in Washington Co., OH. Ephraim m (1) **Leah Attwood**, and m (2) 4/13/1808 **Sally Parker**. (*Washington Co., Ohio*, vol. 2, p. 507)

DAILEY

William – b1788 in CT, d1861 in Bridgewater, VT (?). William m **Lucy Lamb**, d1861 in Bridgewater, VT (?). (*Car Del Scribe* Query 7/1977, p. 25)

DAINS

Ephraim – b 7/4/1752 in CT, d 7/7/1836 in MI. Ephraim m **Irene Stedman** (?). (*DAR Patriot Index*, p. 173 – *Connecticut Rev. Soldiers Buried in MI*)

DAKIN

Timothy – b 3/13/1763 in Quaker Hill, CT, s/o **Timothy**; Timothy (the younger) d 2/1/1838 in Ferrisburg, VT. He m **Lydia Akin**, b 7/24/1770, d 4/14/1852. (*Gazetteer of Addison Co., VT*, p. 107 – *Des. of Thomas Dakin of Concord, MA*, p. 34)

DANA

Isaac – b 11/28/1765 in Pomfret, CT, s/o **John W.** and **Hannah Pope (Putnam)**; Isaac d 5/2/1831 in Pomfret, VT. He m (1) 12/31/1789 in Pomfret, VT, **Sarah Dean**, b 5/4/1770, d 4/3/1812 in Pomfret, VT, and m (2) 2/23/1813 in Hartford, VT, **Laura Miner**, b 5/6/1785, d 12/18/1855 in Windsor, VT. (*Dana Genealogy*, p. 280-1 – *Pomfret, VT*, v. 2, p. 473)

Capt. James – b 10/10/1732 in CT, d 10/16/1817 in Lawyerville, Otsego Co., NY. Capt. James m **Elizabeth Whittemore**. (*DAR Mag.*, v. 107, p. 417 – *DAR Patriot Index*, p. 174)

John Winchester – b 1/29/1739 (or 1740) in Pomfret, CT, s/o **Isaac**; John Winchester d 2/9/1813 in Pomfret, VT. He m 10/25/1764 **Hannah Putnam**, b 8/25/1744, d 4/2/1820 in Pomfret, VT, d/o Gen. **Israel**. (*Dana Genealogy*, p. 253-5 – *Pomfret, VT*, v. 2, p. 472)

DANIELS

Gad – b 1/27/1764 in Killingly, CT, d 4/15/1812 in W. Rutland, Rutland Co., VT. Gad m **Zipporah Herrick**, b 1/5/1764 in Canterbury, CT, d 2/5/1861 in W. Rutland, VT, d/o **Phineas** and **Sarah (Leonard)**. (*Daniels Family*, v. 2, p. 390)

DARBE

Jonathan – b 7/4/1726 in Hebron, CT, s/o **John** and **Hannah**; Jonathan d 1/19/1794 in Orford, NH. He m 7/31/1748 in Lebanon, CT, **Abigail Dewey**, b 9/3/1730, d 10/12/1815 in Orford, NH, d/o **Noah** and **Abigail (Plumley)**. (*DAR Patriot Index*, p. 176 – *NEGR* 4/1950, p. 114)

DARROW

G u r d o n – bc1791 in Groton, CT, d1885 in 94th year in New Milford, Susquehanna Co., PA. Gurdon m1815 **Sally Moxley**, d1864 age 75. (*Hist. of Susquehanna County, PA*, p. 619)

DART

Josiah – b 5/3/1759 in Bolton, CT, s/o **Joshua** and **Deborah**; Josiah d 8/26/1829 in Weathersfield, VT. He m **Betsey Delano**. (*History of Surry, NH*, p. 572-3 – *DAR Patriot Index*, p. 176)

Thomas – b 4/25/1724 in CT, d 4/9/1792 in Gilsum, NH. Thomas m 5/31/1745 **Sarah Belden (Belding)**, b CT. (*DAR Patriot Index*, p. 176 – *History of Town of Gilsum, NH*, p. 296)

Timothy – b 11/15/1756 in Bolton, CT, s/o **Jonathan** and **Lucy**; Timothy d 6/27/1814 in Gilsum, NH. He m 11/13/1776 **Margaret Taylor**, b 11/22/1756 in Bolton, CT. (*DAR Patriot Index*, p. 176 – *Hist. of Surry, NH*, p. 580)

DARTE

Eliphalet – b 2/7/1741 in Bolton, CT, s/o **Daniel** and **Jemimah**; Eliphalet d 11/9/1821 in Surry, NH. He m 5/15/1764 **Anna Field**, d/o Ensign **Moses**. (*History of Town of Surry, NH*, p. 571-2 – *DAR Patriot Index*, p. 176)

Joshua – b 8/14/1727 in Bolton, CT, s/o **Daniel, Jr.** and **Jemima**; Joshua d1790 in Weathersfield, VT. He m 4/3/1751 in Bolton, CT, **Deborah Spencer**. (*DAR Patriot Index*, p. 176 – *History of Town of Surry, NH*, p. 571)

DARTT

Justus – b 5/28/1757, s/o **Joshua** and **Deborah**; Justus d1838 in Wellsboro, PA. He m 2/25/1777 in Keene, NH, **Hannah Gleason** of Surry, NH. (*Hist. of Surry, NH*, p. 572 – *DAR Patriot Index*, p. 176)

DAVIS

George – bc1800 in CT, d 3/16/1879 age 79-6 in Sherburne, Chenango Co., NY. George m **Sarah ----**, b NY, d 9/11/1864 age 56-6-13. (*1850 Census Chenango Co., NY*)

Joseph – b 6/13/1801 in Bristol, CT, s/o **Clark** and **Hannah**; Joseph d 3/29/1874 in Rush, Monroe Co., NY. He m 12/8/1830 **Parthenia Green**, d/o **James** and **Mary**. (*History of Monroe County, NY*, p. 196, 197, 259, 284)

DAVISON

Nathan – b 12/20/1796 in Brooklyn, CT, s/o **Joseph** and **Lydia (Clark)**; Nathan d 5/29/1848 in Alaiedon Twp., Ingraham Co., MI. He m 4/4/1822 in CT, **Loretta Hicks**, b 2/2/1797 in Pomfret, CT, d 4/11/1849, d/o **Israel** and **Phebe**. Had resided in Homer, NY, until 1836. (*DSGR*, v. 39 #2 1975, p. 83)

DAY

Benjamin – b 9/13/1731 in Colchester, CT, s/o **Benjamin** and **Margaret (Foote)**; Benjamin (the younger) d 1/26/1811 age 78 in Royalton, VT. He m (1) **Abigail**, and m (2) 5/9/1764 **Eunice Rood**, b1735, d 8/13/1806 age 71 in Royalton, VT, d/o **Jabez** and **Mehitable (Standish)**. (*History of Surry, NH*, p. 585 – *History of Royalton, VT*, p. 745-6 – *DAR Patriot Index*, p. 181 – *Descendants of Robert Day*, p. 63, 67)

Noah, Sr. – b 2/14/1757 in CT, d 1/10/1840 in Granville, NY. Noah, Sr. m **Alice Whitney**. (*History of Washington Co., NY* – *DAR Patriot Index*, p. 182)

Stephen – b 2/20/1746 in Colchester, CT, s/o **John**; Stephen d 4/11/1820 in Catskill, Greene Co., NY. He m **Demmis Ransom**. (*DAR Patriot Index*, p. 182 – *Hist. of Greene Co., NY*, p. 451)

Wareham – b 3/19/1790 in Avon, CT, d prob. in Canaan, PA. Wareham m (1) **Lucretia Hoadley**, d/o **Abraham**, and m (2) 11/19/1819 **Olive Samson**. (*Descendants of Robt. Day*, p. 21, 32 – *History of Wayne Co., PA*, p. 178)

DEAN

Ashbel – b 5/18/1763 in Cornwall, CT, s/o **Moses**; Ashbel d 5/5/1823 in Addison Co., VT. He m **Rachel Barnum**, d 2/7/1842. (*Some Vermont Ancestors*, p. 17 – *DAR Patriot Index*, p. 182)

Daniel – b1744 in CT, d1811 age 67 in Camden, NY. Daniel m **Anna Surtliff**. (*Pioneer Hist. of Camden, Oneida Co., NY*)

James – b 8/20/1743 in Groton, CT, d 9/10/1823 prob. in Oneida Co., NY. James m (1) 10/11/1786 **Lydia Camp**, and m (2) Mrs. **Cynthia Phelps**. (*Oneida, Our County and Its People*, p. 605 – *DAR Patriot Index*, p. 182 – *Hist. of Mohawk Valley*, v. II, 1176)

John – b 7/5/1780 in Waterbury, CT, d 11/18/1862 age 82 in Camden, Oneida Co., NY. John m1805 **Betsey Woods**, d 8/12/1850 age 67, d/o **Samuel**. (*Pioneer Hist. of Camden, NY*, p. 150)

DEARBORN

Capt. Asa – bc1755 in CT, d 10/17/1830 age 75 in Chelsea, Orange Co., VT. Capt. Asa m **Ann Emerson**, d 9/10/1852 age 93, d/o **Samuel** and **Dorothy (Sanborn)**. (Chelsea – Old Cemetery stone – *DAR Patriot Index*, p. 183)

DELANO

Jonathan – b 11/23/1735 in CT, s/o **Jabez** and **Prudence (Hebert)**; Jonathan d 9/28/1811 age 79 in Hartford, Windsor Co., VT. He m **Anna Ladd**, b 10/31/1734 in Coventry, CT, d 2/11/1816 age 82. (*DAR Patriot Index*, p. 185 – *Hist. of Hartford, VT*, p. 412-13)

DEMING

Noadiah – b 7/14/1749 in Wethersfield, CT, s/o **Solomon** and **Sarah (Kirkham)**; Noadiah d in Pittsford, Rutland Co., VT. He m

4/11/1794 in Pittsfield, MA, Mrs. **Eunice W. Moore**. (*Hist. of Pittsford, VT*, p. 285)

DENISON
Daniel – b 7/20/1740 in Stonington, CT, s/o **William** and **Hannah (Tyler)**; Daniel d 3/17/1818 age 77 in Norwich, Chenango Co., NY. He m 5/28/1771 **Martha Geer**. (*History of Chenango County*, p. 423 – *Denison Genealogy*, p. 35-6)
Gilbert – b 9/18/1762 in Stonington, CT, s/o **George** and **Jane (Smith)**; Gilbert d 9/16/1834 in Brattleboro, Windham Co., VT. He m (1) **Huldah Palmer**, and m (2) **Abigail Stone**. (*1850 Census Windham Co., VT* – *DAR Patriot Index*, p. 188)
Joseph – b 2/14/1735 in Stonington, CT, s/o **William** and **Hannah (Burrows)**; Joseph d 11/15/1785 age 50 in Pharsalia, Chanango Co., NY. He m **Mary Babcock**, d 12/15/1798 age 52. (*History of Chenango Co., NY*, p. 423 – *History of Stonington, CT*, p. 344, 350)
Dr. **Joseph Adam** – b 12/22/1774 in Stonington, CT, s/o **James** and **Eunice (Stanton)**; Dr. Joseph Adam d 9/4/1855 in Royalton, VT (gravestone). He m 6/9/1802 in Cornish, NH, **Rachel Chase** of NH, b 6/10/1774, d 8/23/1858 (gravestone). (*History of Royalton, VT*, p. 749-58 – *Denison Genealogy*, p. 101-2 – *1850 Windsor County, Vermont, Census*)
W i l l i a m – b1705 in No. Stonington, CT, d 1/29/1760 in Oxford, Chenango Co., NY. William m **Martha Geer** of Groton, CT. (*Annals of Oxford, NY*, p. 290-2 – *History of Chenango County, NY*, p. 259-60)

DENTON
Jabez – b1767 in Greenwich, CT, d1859 age 90 in Fitchville, OH. Jabez m **Rachel** ----, b in Greenwich, CT, d age 89 in Fitchville, OH. (*The Fire Lands Pioneer*, p. 84)

DERBY
Apollos – b 4/28/1768 in Hebron, CT, d 9/8/1842 age 74-4-11 in Bridport, Addison Co., VT. Apollos m 2/5/1780 **Lois Frizzell**, b 4/9/1770 in Northfield, MA, d 4/6/1858, d/o **John** and **Martha**. (*Gen. Rec. of John Derby*, p. 25, 37, 44, 47)
Benjamin – b 6/6/1756 in Hebron, CT, d 11/14/1829 age 73 in Huntington, Chittenden Co., VT. Benjamin m 6/8/1780 in Lebanon, CT, **Esther Finley**, b 2/6/1762 in Lebanon, CT, d1842 age 79 in Huntington, VT. (*Gen. Rec. of Des. of John Derby*, p. 22, 33-5)
Benjamin, Jr. – b 1/7/1783 in Hebron, CT, s/o **Benjamin** and **Esther (F i n l e y)**; Benjamin Jr. d 12/9/1838 in Wilna, NY., in the War of 1812. He m 11/3/1804 in Huntington, VT, **Polly Brewster**, b 8/5/1781 in Tinmouth, VT, d 8/15/1848 in Wilna, NY, d/o **Charles, Jr.** and **Anna (Turner)**. (*Gen. Rec. of John Derby*, p. 22, 33, 59)
Moses – b 10/1/1759 in Colcheater, CT, d1834 in Dallas, PA. Moses m 12/27/1781 in CT, **Dorothy Tiffany**, b 6/19/1762 in Hartland, CT, d/o **Consider** and **Sarah (Wilder)**. (*Gen. Rec. of Des. of John Derby of Greenwich*, p. 20)

DERTHICK
James - b 8/10/1773 in Colchester, CT, s/o **Ananias** and **Mary A.**
(Welch); James d 4/9/1855 in Bronson, MI. He m **Huldah ----,** b
10/1787, d 4/20/1847 in Portage Co., OH. (*Nutmegger* Query 6/81,
p. 84)

DEWEY
Asa - bc1775 in CT, d 3/7/1850 age 75 in Bethel, VT, buried Royalton, VT. Asa m **Jerusha ----,** d 1/6/1825 age 47-7. (*1850 Census
of Windsor Co., VT*)

Ebenezer - b 3/7/1740 in Hebron, CT, s/o **Ebenezer** and **Martha**
(Wilcox); Ebenezer (the younger) d 2/28/1820 in Royalton, Windsor
Co., VT. He m 7/24/1760 **Temperance Holdridge,** b1736, d
6/15/1822 in Royalton, VT. (*Hist. of Royalton, VT,* p. 759-64 -
DAR Patriot Index, p. 190 - Town of Gilsum, NH - *Dewey Geneal-
ogy,* p. 418)

Ebenezer - b 8/11/1762 in Hebron, CT, s/o **Ebenezer**; Ebenezer (the
younger) d 2/12/1843 in Royalton, Windsor Co., VT. He m
9/21/1788 **Jerusha Kimball,** b 4/3/1767 in CT, d 8/1/1833 in
Royalton, VT, d/o **John** and **Jerusha (Meacham)**. (*Hist. of Royalton, VT,* p. 760-1)

Ebenezer - b 1/24/1712 in Lebanon, CT, s/o **Ebenezer** and **Elizabeth**
(Wright); Ebenezer (the younger) d 10/19/1794 in Royalton,
Windsor Co., VT. He m (1) 3/12/1735 in Hebron, CT, **Martha**
Wilcox, b 1/3/1711, d 5/29/1761, d/o **Ebenezer,** and m (2) **Chris-
tiana Phelps,** and m (3) **---- Young.** (*Hist. of Royalton, VT,* p.
759-64 - *Dewey Gen,* p. 401, 417-420 - *DAR Patriot Index,* p. 190)

Nathan - b 5/7/1742 in Hebron, CT, s/o **Samuel** and **Elizabeth (Allen)**;
Nathan d 2/2/1779 in Orford, NH. He m 12/3/1760 in Hebron, CT,
Mindwell Horsford, d/o **Joseph** and **Eunice (Beach)**. (*NEGR* April
1950, p. 114)

Rodolphus - b 10/17/1766 in Hebron, CT, s/o **Ebenezer**; Rodolphus d
5/25/1839 in Royalton, Windsor Co., VT. He m (1) 5/23/1793
Jemima Kinney, b 5/2/1766 in Preston, CT, d 6/27/1804 at Royal-
ton, VT, d/o Capt. **Joseph** and **Jemima (Newcomb)**, and m (2) **Diana**
Wright, b 10/22/1773, d 8/1851 in Canton, IL, d/o Deacon
Nathaniel of Hanover, NH. (*Hist. of Royalton, VT,* p. 761)

Capt. Simeon - b 8/20/1770 in Lebanon (or Colchester), CT, s/o **Wil-
liam** and **Rebecca (Corwin)**; Capt. Simeon d 1/11/1863 in
Montpelier, Washington Co, VT. He m 2/27/1794 **Prudence**
Yemans of Norwich, VT, d 4/1/1844 in Berlin, VT. (*Washington
Co., VT, Gazetteer,* p. 386)

Timothy - b 3/27/1755 in Hebron, CT, s/o **Ebenezer** and **Martha**
(Wilcox); Timothy d 12/28/1852 age 97 in Tunbridge, Orange Co.,
VT. He m 7/29/1780 in Keene, NH, **Jemima Griswold,** b 7/1755 in
Keene, NH, d 4/1/1822 in Tunbridge, VT, d/o **Stephen** and **Hannah.**
(*1850 Orange Co., VT, Census - DAR Patriot Index,* p. 90 - *Dewey
Gen.,* p. 401, 419-20, 453-4)

DEWOLF
Matthew - b 1/6/1744 in Bolton, CT, s/o **Matthew** and **Eunice**
(Baker); Matthew (the younger) d 5/3/1834 in Surry, NH (or Gilsum,

NH). He m **Esther Higley**. (*History of Surry, NH*, p. 589 - *DAR Patriot Index*, p. 191)

DEXTER

Austin - b 6/20/1803 in Mansfield, CT, s/o **Jonathan** and **Olive (Parker)**; Austin d 4/10/1878 in Cortland, NY. He m 4/24/1825 in Marcellus, NY, **Anna Tripp**, b 10/16/1806 in Otsego Co., NY, d 3/3/1860 in Colon Twp., St. Joseph Co., MI. (*DSGR Quarterly*, Spring 1973)

John - b 10/28/1753 in Mansfield, CT, s/o **Isaac** and **Esther (Davis)**; John d 12/10/1840 in Pomfret, Windsor Co., VT. He m (1) 4/15/1779 in Mansfield, CT, **Sarah Parker**, b 11/17/1759, d 2/12/1817, d/o Lt. **Zachariah** and **Peace (Ames)**, and m (2) 4/15/1817 Widow **Sarah Howard**. (*Pomfret, Vermont*, v. 2, p. 479 - *DAR Patriot Index*, p. 191)

DICKINSON

Joseph - b1774 in CT, d 4/19/1862 in Oxford, Chenango Co., NY. Joseph m 11/2/1797 **Mary Rowland** of CT, bc1776, d 1/15/1863. (*Annals of Oxford, NY*, p. 93-4 - *1850 Census Chenango Co., NY*)

DIMMICK

Eber - b 3/18/1794 in Stafford, CT, s/o **Ephraim** and **Polly (Saxton)**; Eber d 8/10/1876 age 82-4-23 in Smyrna, Chenango Co., NY. He m1818 **Rosetta Foote**, b in CT, d 10/13/1876 age 79-8, d/o Capt. **Jesse**. (*Smyrna* by Munson, p. 87-8 - *1850 Census Chenango Co., NY* - *Tree Talks* Dec. 1974 p. 151)

Joseph - b 2/27/1746 in Mansfield, CT, s/o **Peter**; d 2/26/1820 prob. in Bridgewater, VT. Joseph m **Prudence** ----, d1824. (Query in *NEGR* Oct. 1967 - *DAR Patriot Index*, p. 194)

DIMON

Moses - b1776 in Weston, CT, s/o **Moses** and **Grace (Dimon) Dimon**; Moses d 10/16/1869 age 93-7-8 prob. Fairfield, Franklin Co., VT. He m (1) **Sarah** ----, d 2/23/1814 age 21, and m (2) **Lucy Gilbert**, d 11/17/1827 age 47-3-21. (*Franklin Co., VT, Census* - *Franklin Co. Gazetteer*)

DIX

Charles - b 11/8/1764 in Wethersfield, CT, d 7/13/1850 in Vernon, Oneida Co., NY. Charles m 3/5/1786 **Prudence Wells**, d/o **John**. (*Oneida, Our Country and Its People*, p. 574-5)

DODGE

Amos - b1758 in Colchester, CT, d 1/11/1852 age 92 in Clinton, Oneida Co., NY. Amos m **Elizabeth** ----, d 5/6/1828 age 74 in Clinton, NY. (*Clinton Memorial - Kirtland Ave. Cemetery*, p. 16)

DOOLITTLE

Benjamin - b in CT, d prob. in New Milford, PA (or in OH). Benjamin m **Fanny Ward**, d/o **Ichabod**. (*History of Susquehanna County, PA*, p. 616)

Philo – b 10/1/1793 in Wallingford, CT, s/o **Theophilus** and **Abiah**; Philo d 1/1862 in Burlington, Chittenden Co., VT. He m (1) 7/11/1820 **Harriet E. Hayes**, d 8/1/1837, d/o **Newton**, and m (2) 7/10/1839 **Eliza C. Hayes** (sister-in-law), d 11/11/1843, and m (3) 9/1846 **Catherine Esther Brush**, d/o **Reuben**. (*VT Historical Mag.*, v. 1, p. 641 by Hemingway)

DORR

Matthew, Jr. – b 5/29/1756 in Lyme, CT, d 5/23/1843 age 87 in Sparta, Livingston Co., NY. He m **Dinah Mudge**. (*DAR Magazine*, v. 41, p. 175 – *DAR Patriot Index*, p. 199)

DORT

Eliphalet – b 2/7/1741 in Bolton, CT, s/o **Daniel** and **Jemimah**; Eliphalet d 11/9/1821 in Surry, NH. He m 5/15/1764 **Anna Field**, b 11/12/1744 in Northfield, MA, d 7/4/1818 in Surry, NH, d/o **Moses** and **Ann (Dickinson)**. (*Hist. of the Town of Gilsum, NH*, p. 295)

Timothy – b 11/15/1756 in CT, s/o **Jonathan** and **Lucy (Whitney)**; Timothy d 6/27/1814 prob. in Gilsum, NH. He m **M a r g a r e t Taylor**, b 11/22/1756 in Bolton, CT. (*Town of Gilsum, NH*, p. 297)

T i t u s – b 1/6/1779 in Bolton, CT, d 3/3/1844 in Plainfield, OH. Titus m 11/13/1800 **Charlotte Clark**, d/o **Samuel**. (*History of Surry, NH*, p. 580-1)

DOUBLEDAY

Asahel – b 4/11/1751 in Hartford, CT, d 2/24/1843 in Woodstock, Windsor Co., VT. Asahel m in Woodstock, VT, **Betsey Gray**, d 10/1/1821. (*Hist. of Woodstock, VT*, p. 103)

DOUGLAS

Benajah – b 8/5/1780 in Cornwall, CT, d 7/23/1828 in Cornwall, VT. Benajah m (1) 7/1803 **Saloma Scott**, b 3/27/1783, d 8/16/1810 in Cornwall, VT, and m (2) 2/19/1811 **Elizabeth Preston**, b 3/3/1787, d 9/24/1871 in Cornwall, VT. (*Douglas Genealogy*, p. 215-16 – *Gazetteer of Addison Co., VT*)

B u r n h a m – b 11/3/1782 in Cornwall, CT, d 6/28/1814 in Granville, Washington Co., NY. He m **Weltha Williams**, b 5/31/1785, d 12/30/1864. (*Douglas Gen.*, p. 216)

C a l e b – b 4/16/1760 in New London, CT, d prob. in Chelsea, Orange Co., VT. Caleb m 2/20/1786 **Grace Morgan**, d/o **Edward** of New London, CT. (*Douglas Genealogy*, p. 249-50 – *Gazetteer of Orange Co., VT*, p. 225)

Elias – b 2/27/1775 in Cornwall, CT, s/o **James** and **Rhoda**; Elias d 6/10/1828 in Cornwall, Addison Co., VT. He m 7/26/1797 **Rebecca Gibbs**, b 12/9/1780 in Litchfield, CT, d 11/8/1824 prob. in Cornwall, VT. (*Douglas Gen.*, p. 214)

J o h n – b 11/18/1776 in Cornwall, CT, s/o **J a m e s** and **R h o d a (Burnham)**; John d 6/6/1836 in Cornwall, Addison Co., VT. He m 2/8/1810 **Huldah Hunt**, b 3/29/1785 in Canaan, NY, d 1/5/1855. (*Douglas Gen.*, p. 214-15)

DOUGLASS

James Marsh - bc1735 in Cornwall, CT, s/o **James** and **Rachel** **(Marsh)**; James Marsh d 8/28/1790 age 55 in Cornwall, Addison Co., VT. He m **Rhoda Burnham**, d1822. (*History of Cornwall, VT*, p. 75 - *Douglas Gen.*, p. 132)

DOWD

Jesse - b 6/20/1754 in Middletown, CT, s/o **Jacob** and **Mary** **(Wetmore)**; Jesse d 8/25/1831 in Wells, VT. He m (1) **Bethany** **Green**, and m (2) **Rebecca Grannis Shepherd**. (*Hist. of Town of Wells, VT*, by Wood p. 52)

DOWNER

Cushman - b 3/7/1762 in Lebanon, CT, s/o **Joseph** and **Alcessa** **(Cushman)**; Cushman d 4/24/1843 age 81 in E. Thetford, Orange Co., VT. He m 6/15/1786 in Thetford, VT, **Hannah Garcy** of Lebanon, CT, d1814 age 54 in E. Thetford, VT. (*Downers of America*, p. 56-8)

Joseph - b 2/9/1732 in Norwich, CT, s/o Deacon **Joseph** and **Mary** **(Sawyer)**; Joseph (the younger) d 7/21/1821 age 88 in E. Thetford, Orange Co., VT. He m (1) 4/7/1755 in Norwich, CT, **Alcessa** **Cushman** of Coventry, CT, and m (2) **Asenath** ----, b1755, d 8/12/1831 age 90 in E. Thetford, VT. (*Downers of America*, p. 31, 56 - *Gazetteer of Orange Co., VT*, p. 429-30)

DRIGGS

Elias - b 7/22/1777 in Middletown, CT, s/o **Joseph** and **Chloe** **(Beach)**; Elias d in Fairlee, Orange Co., VT, age almost 91 years. He m1796 **Abigail Coe**, b 4/21/1779 in Middletown, CT, d in 87th year in Fairlee, VT. They lived together 68 years. (*Driggs Fam. Hist.*, p. 55 - *1850 Orange Co. Census of VT*)

DUDLEY

Benajah, Sr. - b 5/27/1763 in Killingworth, CT, d 6/20/1850 in West Brattleboro, Windham Co., VT. He m 8/23/1786 in Killingworth, CT, **Elizabeth Redfield**, d1846. (*Gazetteer of Windham County, Vermont*, p. 143)

James - b 11/19/1772 in Guilford, CT, s/o **John** and **Tryphena** **(Stone)**; James d 1/26/1835 prob. in Dutchess Co., NY. He m **Lydia Leete**, d 8/22/1842. (*Com. Biog. Record of Dutchess County, NY*, p. 97-8)

DUNBAR

Capt. **Joel** - b1752 in Plymouth, CT, d 12/31/1827 age 75 in Camden, Onondaga Co., NY. He m **Rebecca Curtiss**, d 1/24/1831 age 69, d/o **Abel**. (*Pioneer Hist. of Camden, NY*, p. 169 - *DAR Patriot Index*, p. 205)

DUNHAM

Deacon **Daniel** - b 2/2/1744 in Colchester, CT, d 5/21/1822 age 69. Deacon Daniel m 2/23/1768 **Anna Moseley**, d/o **Increase**.

(Pompey Reunion–Onondaga Co., NY – *DAR Patriot Index*, p. 206 – *Dunham Gen.*, p. 81)

Lt. **Daniel** – b 2/2/1744 in Lebanon, CT, s/o **Samuel** and **Esther**; Lt. Daniel d 5/21/1822 in Onondaga Co., NY, buried in Orange Cem. He m 12/27/1767 in Windham, CT, **Anna Moseley**, d 3/6/1815 in 69th year. (*Clinton Memorial*, p. 37 – *DAR Lineage*, v. 50, p. 311 – *DAR Patriot Index*, p. 206 – *CT Hist. Soc. Collection*, v. 8 p. 4, 163)

Josiah – b 2/2/1746 in Coventry, CT, d1834 age 88–4 in Woodstock, Windsor Co., VT. Josiah m 11/22/1770 **Experience Williams**, d1854 age 95–5, d/o **Phineas** of Mansfield, CT. (*Hist. of Woodstock, VT*, p. 35–7)

Capt. **Samuel** – b1780 in Windham, CT, s/o Deacon **Daniel**; Capt. Samuel d in Pompey, Onondaga Co., NY, at age 69. He mc1805 **Mary Parmerlee** of Cazenovia, NY. (*Pompey Reunion*, p. 301–2)

DUNLAP

Ephraim – b 4/17/1746 in Windham, CT, d 4/6/1814 in Pittsford, Rutland Co., VT. Ephraim mc1790 **Betsey Tedder**, b 9/2/1765 in New Ipswich, NH, d 4/15/1809. (*Hist. of Pittsford, VT*, p. 311, 700)

DURAND

Jeremiah – b 8/8/1749 in Derby, CT, dc1798 in Fair Haven, VT. Jeremiah m (1) 11/12/1772 in Derby, CT, **Hannah Trowbridge**, d1777, and m (2) **Sarah Andrus**. (*History of Fair Haven, Rutland County, VT*)

DURKEE

Bartholomew – b 1/14/1739 in Woodstock, CT, s/o **Andrew** and **Mary (Bartholomew)**; Bartholomew d1807 in Sheldon, VT. His will was dated 4/3/1807. Bartholomew m 10/6/1761 **Ruth Keyes**, d/o **Elnathan** of Woodstock, VT. (*Woodstock Fam.* by Bowen, v. 4, p. 602–3 – *Pomfret, VT*, v. 2, p. 485)

Col. **Heman** – b 6/17/1759 in Woodbury, CT, s/o Lt. **Timothy**; Col. Heman d 10/5/1797 age 38 in Royalton, Vt (gravestone). He m 9/19/1781 **Susannah Rix**, b 6/30/1765 in Preston, CT, d 9/9/1852 in Royalton, VT (gravestone), d/o **Daniel** and **Rebecca (Johnson)**. She m (2) **Hezekiah Hutchinson** of Tunbridge, VT. (*History of Royalton, VT*, p. 772)

Lt. **Timothy** – b 5/1737 in Woodbury, CT, s/o **Nathaniel** and **Mary (Baker)**; Lt. Timothy d 3/22/1797 age 59–10 (gravestone). He m **Lucy Ann Smalley**. (*Hist. of Royalton, VT*, p. 771–5)

DUTTON

Samuel – b 3/1/1707 in E. Haddam, CT, s/o **Joseph**; Samuel d1802 in Royalton, VT. He m 5/6/1729 **Abigail Merriam**, bc1708, d 4/6/1799. They had lived in Hartford, VT, and Norwich, VT. (*Hist. of Norwich, VT*, p. 202–3 – *Hist. of Hartford, VT*, p. 414–15)

Samuel – b 1/24/1737 in Wallingford, CT, s/o **Thomas**; Samuel d 2/22/1813 in Hartford, Windsor Co., VT. He m (1) 12/6/1754 **Joanna Root**, b 1/1/1737, d1772 in Woodstock, VT, and m (2) 10/7/1772 **Rachel Benedict**, b 4/14/1751, d 7/21/1828 in Hartford,

VT. (*History of Norwich, Vermont*, p. 203 - *History of Hartford, Vermont*, p. 414-415)

EASTMAN

Amos - b 2/17/1763 in Norwich, CT, s/o **Jonathan** and **Elizabeth (Wood)**; Amos d1861 in Bristol, Addison Co., VT.   He m **Sally Hewitt**, b 2/12/1773. (*History and Genealogy of Eastman Family of America*, p. 137)

Calvin - b 5/25/1760 in Norwich, CT, s/o **Jonathan** and **Elizabeth (Wood)**; Calvin d 10/5/1856 age 95 in Bristol, Addison Co., VT. He m **Lois Standish**, b 8/23/1757, d 4/25/1845 age 86 in Bristol, VT. (*Hist. and Gen. of Eastman Family*, p. 136)

Cyprian - b 1/29/1749 in Norwich, CT, s/o **Jonathan** and **Elizabeth (W o o d)**; Cyprian d 5/23/1798 age 49 in Bristol, Addison Co., VT. He m **Rosamond Nelson** of Rupert, VT. (*History and Genealogy of Eastman Family*, p. 66, 133)

Jonathan - b1753 in Norwich, CT, s/o **Jonathan** and **Elizabeth (Wood)**; Jonathan (the younger) d 12/16/1816 in Bristol, Addison Co., VT. He m (1) **Ruth Davis**, d in Bristol, VT, and m (2) **Ruth Dean**, d in OH. (*Hist. and Gen. of Eastman Family*, p. 134)

Oliver - b1762 in Norwich, CT, s/o **Jonathan** and **Elizabeth (Wood)**; Oliver d in OH. He m **Sophy** ----. (*History and Genealogy of Eastman Fam.*, p.* 136)

EASTON

Michael Perry - b 1/8/1790 in Woodbury, CT, s/o **Norman** and **Merab (Perry)**; Michael Perry d 5/9/1858 in Monroesville, Huron Co., OH. He m1815 **Sallie Raymond**, b1795 in Great Barrington, MA, d 12/29/1872 in Monroesville, OH. (*Des. of Joseph Easton*, p. 59, 96-7 - Residents from CT in Huron Co., OH)

EATON

General **William** - b 2/23/1764 in Woodstock, CT, s/o **Nathaniel**; General William d 6/1/1811 in Brimfield, MA. He m 8/21/1792 in Union, CT, **Eliza (Sikes)**, b 9/17/1767 in Brimfield, MA, d1830 in Auburn, NY, d/o **Benjamin** and **Mary (Danielson)**. (*Gen. of Woodstock Fam.*, p. 633)

ECCLESTON

David - bc1757 in Stonington, CT, d1845 age 88 in Preston, Chenango Co., NY. David m **Catherine Fanning** of Stonington, CT. (*Hist. of Chenango Co.*, p. 359)

EDDY

Joel - b 12/21/1777 in Woodstock, CT, s/o **Jonathan** and **Mercy (C a d y)**; Joel d 1/30/1871 in Randolph, Orange Co., VT. He m (1) 9/8/1805 in Bethel, VT, **Sarah McKinstry**, bc1783, d 9/28/1834 in Randolph, VT, d/o **Paul**, and m (2) **Abiah Hopson**, bc1789, d 5/12/1869 age 80. (*Eddy Fam. in America*, p. 265-6)

EDGERTON

Asa - b 3/28/1736 in Norwich, CT, s/o **William** and **Lydia (Barstow)**; Asa d 5/1/1798 age 62 in Randolph, Orange Co., VT (gravestone). He m **Eunice** ----, d 12/18/1802 age 59 in Randolph, VT. (*Norwich, CT, Vital Records*, p. 152, 358)

Ezra - b 1/17/1752 in Norwich, CT, s/o **William** and **Lydia (Barstow)**; Ezra d 2/6/1802 in Randolph, Orange Co., VT (gravestone). He m **Anne** ----, d 3/4/1819 age 68 (gravestone) in Randolph, VT. She m (2) Deacon **Isaac S. Palmer**. (*Norwich, CT, Vital Records*, v. 1, p. 300)

Capt. Lebbeus - b 5/4/1773 in Norwich, CT, s/o **Asa** and **Eunice (Storrs)**; Capt. Lebbeus d 8/18/1846 age 73 in Randolph, Orange Co., VT. He m (1) **Catherine** ----, d 8/22/1826 age 52-7-12 in Randolph, VT, and m (2) **Elizabeth Potter**, b 3/25/1781, d 9/5/1848 in Randolph, VT. He was in the War of 1812. (*Norwich Vital Records*, v. 1, p. 358)

Levi - bc1785 in Coventry, CT, d 6/13/1869 age 84 in Hyde Park, Lamoille Co., VT. Levi m **Sarah G. Fitch** (or possibly his son married her.) (*Gazetteer of LaMoille Co., VT*, p. 101)

Oliver - b 11/16/1765 in Norwich, CT, s/o **Asa** and **Hannah (Griswold)**; Oliver d 8/22/1814 age 49 in Randolph, Orange Co., VT (gravestone). He m 12/7/1788 **Lucy Brainerd**, b in Haddam, CT, d 3/5/1844 age 83-1 in Randolph, VT (gravestone), d/o **Elijah**. (*Norwich Vital Records*, p. 357)

Roger - b 12/12/1761 in CT, d 5/24/1844 age 83 in Coventry, Chenango Co., NY. Roger m **Betsey Cole**. (*DAR Mag.*, v. 41, p. 217 - *DAR Patriot Index*)

Capt. Simeon - b 3/9/1732 in Stamford, CT, d 8/27/1809 age 70 in Rutland or Pawlet, Rutland Co., VT. Capt. Simeon m **Abiah Hough**, d 10/17/1821. (*Hist. of Rutland Co.*, p. 327, 703 - *Rutland Co. Gazetteer*, p. 217)

William - b 8/28/1763 in Norwich, CT, s/o **Asa** and **Hannah (Griswold)**; William d prob. in Randolph, Orange Co., VT. He m **Hannah** ----, b 3/3/1769, d 2/2/1849 age 79-11 in Randolph, VT. (*Norwich Vital Records*, p. 357)

EDSON

Eliab - b 10/27/1760 in Stafford, CT, s/o **Timothy** and **Lydia (Joy)**; Eliab d 11/27/1833 in Randolph, Orange Co., VT. He m 8/22/1787 in Stafford, CT, **Prudence Whittaker**, bc1767, d 6/20/1829 in Randolph, VT. (*Edsons in England and America*, p. 60-1)

Erwin - b 9/19/1854 in Stafford, CT, s/o **Collins** and **Mary E. (Johnson)**; Erwin d 2/13/1916 in Kansas City, MO. He m 9/20/1877 **Nellie Hudson** at Byron, WI, d/o **Augustus** and **Sarah**. (*Edson Fam. Hist. and Gen.*, v. II, p. 1043-4 - *1880 Census of Portage Co., WI*)

Josiah - b1758 in Stafford, CT, s/o **Timothy** and **Lydia (Joy)**; Josiah d 10/27/1819 age 61. He m 7/1/1779 in Stafford, CT, **Sarah Pinney**, d 12/16/1805 in Randolph, VT, d/o **Isaac** and **Susanna (Phelps)**. (*Edsons in England and America*, p. 58-9)

Luther - b 3/4/1785 in Stafford, CT, s/o **Timothy** and **Susanna (Orcutt)**; Luther d 7/26/1856 in Randolph, VT. He remained unmarried. (*1850 Orange County, VT, Census - Edsons in England and America*, p. 58)

Timothy - b 3/26/1754 in Stafford, CT, s/o **Timothy** and **Lydia (Joy)**; d 6/19/1831 in Randolph, VT. Timothy (the younger) m 6/28/1764 in Stafford, CT, **Susanna Orcutt**, b1758 in Stafford, CT, d 2/17/1847 in Randolph, VT, d/o **Solomon** and **Mary (Rockwell)**. (*Edsons in England and America*, p. 57-8)

Timothy - b1750 in Stafford, CT, s/o **Jonathan** and **Mehitabel (Lilly)**; Timothy d 9/30/1834 age 68 in Brookfield, VT (gravestone). He m 12/23/1790 in Whately, MA, **Hannah Bardwell**, d 9/13/1798 in Whately, MA, d/o **Ebenezer** and **Sarah (Tute)**, and m (2) **Mercy G r a v e s**, b 8/27/1771, d 3/25/1841 in Brookfield, VT. (*Edsons in England and America*, p. 62)

EDWARDS

I s a a c - b 1/29/1764 in CT, s/o Nathaniel; Isaac d 2/18/1848 in Greenfield, Saratoga Co., NY, buried in family cemetery. He m **Esther Foote**. (*DAR Magazine* 1977, p. 915 - *Hist. of Saratoga Co., NY*, p. 393 - *DAR Patriot Index*)

EELLS

Nathan - b 6/28/1769 in Lebanon, CT, d 9/22/1850 in Cornwall, Addison Co., VT. Nathan m (1) c1795 **Chloe Morgan**, d 10/6/1811 age 35, d/o **Enos** and **Lois**, and m (2) **Huldah Scott Stowell**. (*Hist. of Cornwall, VT*, p. 104)

Dr. O l i v e r - b 10/26/1795 in Coventry, CT, d 4/4/1860 in Cornwall, Addison Co., VT. Dr. Oliver m (1) 10/25/1818 in East Hartford, CT, **Harriet Warner**, and m (2) **Charlotte ----**, b in VT. (*Hist. of Cornwall, VT*, p. 209)

EGGLESTON

Andrus - b 11/5/1785 in Stonington, CT, s/o **Benedict** and **Content (Brown)**; Andrus d1860 age 75 prob. in Danby, Rutland Co., VT. He m1811 **Nancy Curtis** of Dorset, VT, b in VT. (*1850 Rutland Co., VT. Census - Hist. of Danby, VT*, p. 141-2)

ELDEN

John - b in Plymouth, CT, s/o **John** and **Elizabeth (Curtis)**; John (the younger) d1848 age 64 in Camden, Oneida Co., NY. He m **Lucy Cook**, b in Plymouth, CT, d1840 age 55. (*Pioneer Hist. of Camden, NY*, p. 288)

ELLIS

Gen. J o h n - b1763 in Hebron, CT, d 6/20/1820 age 56 in Onondaga Co., NY. Gen. John m1795 **Submit Olds**. (*Onondaga Hist. Society of 1914*, p. 170 - *DAR Patriot Index*, p. 219)

ELLSWORTH

Samuel - b 10/1/1718 in Windsor, CT, s/o **Samuel**; Samuel (the younger) dc1803 age 85 at Arlington, VT. He m 12/2/1746 in Simsbury, CT, Widow **Anna (Halladay) Matson**, d at age 75. (*Hist. of Pittsford, VT*, p. 40)

ELY

Seth - bc1764 in Lyme, CT, s/o Deacon **Seth** and **Lydia (Reynolds)**; Seth (the younger) d 12/11/1847 in Ripley, NY. He m 4/14/1799 **Phebe Marvin**, b 11/28/1772 in Lyme, CT, d/o **Elisha** and **Elizabeth (Selden)**. (*Chautauqua County, New York*, p. 522 - *Ely Anc.*, p. 191)

ENO

Stephen - b 10/4/1764 in Simsbury, CT, s/o **William** and **Lillie (Hix)**; Stephen d 8/1/1854 age 90 in Pine Plains, Dutchess Co., NY. He m (1) 12/17/1795 prob. in Amenia, NY, **Mary Denton**, b 2/11/1769, d 9/17/1807 in Amenia, NY, d/o **Benjamin** and **Joanna (Peck)**, and m (2) 1/14/1811 Mrs. **Olive (Shores) Watkins**. (*The Eno and Enos Fam. in America*, p. 182-193 - *Little Nine Partners*, p. 331 - *Comm. Biog. Rec. Dutchess Co., NY*, p. 94)

ENSIGN

Otis - b 2/8/1762 in Hartford, CT, s/o **Eliphalet**; Otis d 10/4/1855 in Sheridan, Chautauqua Co., NY. He m (1) **Mary Patrick**, d 1/8/1842 age 73, and m (2) **Mary Briggs**, and m (3) **Hannah Dickinson**. (*DAR Patriot Index*, p. 222 - *Soldiers of Am. Revolution - Chautauqua Co.*, p. 44)

EVEREST

Lt. **Benjamin** - b 1/12/1751 (or 1752) in Salisbury, CT, s/o **Benjamin**; Lt. Benjamin d 3/3/1843 age 81. He m1784 **Patty Fuller (Martha)**, b 11/25/1763 in Norwich, CT, d 3/6/1842 age 79, d/o **J a c o b** and **Abigail (Webb)** of Shelburne, VT. (*Everest Gen.*, p. 158, 186-196)

Capt. **Zadock** - b 3/5/1743 (or 1744) in Saybrook, CT, s/o **Benjamin**; Capt. Zadock d 4/30/1825 age 81 in Addison, Addison Co., VT. He m (1) 1769 **Sarah Moss**, b 7/5/1751 in New Milford, CT, d before 1778, d/o **John** and **Lydia (Roberts)**, and m (2) 3/9/1778 in Bennington, VT, **Sarah (Cook) Meacham**, wid/o Capt. **William M e a c h a m**, b 4/22/1752, d 7/13/1828 age 75 in Moriah, NY. (*Everest Gen.*, p. 98 - *VT Hist. Magazine*, v. 1, p. 10-13)

EVERTS

Luther - b 3/6/1771 in Salisbury, CT, s/o **Luther** and **Sarah**; Luther (the younger) d1846 prob. in New Haven, Addison Co., VT. He m 8/13/1767 in Salisbury, CT, **Deborah Newcomb**. (1812 War Index - *Gazetteer of Addison Co., VT*, p. 171)

FAIRCHILD

B e n j a m i n - b1760 in Trumbull, CT, d 1/21/1837 age 71 in Pitcher, Chenango Co., NY. Benjamin m **Dolly Blackman**, b1767 in CT, d 1/27/1831 age 64 in Pitcher, NY. (*Hist. of Chenango Co.*, p. 431)

FAIRMAN

John - b 6/12/1752 in Somers, CT, s/o **Benjamin** and **Hannah (Gregory)**; John d 1/14/1827 poss. in Vernon, Windham Co., VT.

He m **Elizabeth Pelton,** b 11/14/1762, d 3/12/1826. (*Fairman Gen. of Enfield*, p. 14-21 - *DAR Patriot Index*, p. 227)

FANCHER

Lt. **Thomas** - bc1745 in CT, d 8/22/1815 in Clinton, Oneida Co., NY. Lt. Thomas m **Olive Dunbar.** (*Clinton Memorial-Kirtland Ave. Cemetery*, p. 16-17 - *DAR Patriot Index*, p. 228 - *Waterbury, CT, History*, p. 34, 341 - *History of Oneida Co., NY*, p. 81 - *Records of CT*, v. 1, p. 278)

FARGO

William, Jr. - b 3/20/1791 in New London, CT, s/o **William**; William, Jr. d poss. in Pompey, NY, or Buffalo, NY. He m 8/10/1817 **Tacy Strong,** b 9/14/1799 in Hebron, CT, d 11/9/1870 in Buffalo, NY. (*Pompey Reunion-Onondaga Co.*, p. 373-7)

FARNHAM

Capt. **Samuel** - b 12/16/1775 in New London, CT, d 4/20/1822 age 47 in Oxford, Chenango Co., NY. Capt. Samuel m **Sally Balcom,** d 12/16/1859 in 79th year, d/o **Henry.** (*Annals of Oxford, NY*, p. 144)

FARNSWORTH

Hon. **Joseph D.** - b 12/22/1771 in Middletown, CT, d 9/9/1857 in Franklin Co., VT. Hon. Joseph D. m at least twice (poss. also to **Catherine** ----, d 5/24/1799). Married (1) **Sarah** ----, d 4/1/1813 age 33, and m (2) **P o l l y** ----, d 7/1/1823 age 39. (*Franklin Co. Gazetteer*, p. 94 - *Farnsworth Memorial*, p. 18-19)

FARRAND

Daniel - bc1760 in Canaan, CT, s/o Rev. **Daniel** and **Jerusha (Bordman)**; Daniel d 10/13/1825 in Burlington, VT. He m 5/1/1794 in Haverhill, MA, **Mary Porter,** b/8/23/1773, d 3/24/1812, d/o Col. **Asa** in Burlington, VT. (*Hist. of Newbury, VT*, p. 542-3)

FARWELL

A s a - b 1/4/1757 in Mansfield, CT, s/o **J o h n**; Asa d 6/16/1815 (or 1/16/1815) in Dorset, Bennington Co., VT. He m 3/23/1780 in Mansfield, CT, **Keziah Freeman,** b 4/24/1761, d 12/2/1843 in Dorset, VT, d/o **Skiff** and **Anna (Sargent).** (*Farwell Gen.*, p. 156)

Elisha - b 7/1/1754 in Mansfield, CT, s/o **William**; Elisha dc1826 in Genesee Co., NY. He mc1775 **Sarah Parker.** They lived in Charlestown, NH, Springfield, VT, Georgia, VT, and Genesee Co., NY. (*Farwell Gen.*, p. 158 - *DAR Patriot Index*, p. 230)

J o h n - b 9/5/1742 in Mansfield, CT, s/o **J o h n**; John (the younger) d 8/24/1823 in Dorset, Bennington Co., VT. He m 8/25/1763 in Mansfield, CT, **Esther Dimmick,** b 1/4/1743 in Mansfield, CT, d 8/11/1831 in Dorset, VT, d/o **Shubael** and **Esther (Pierce).** (*Farwell Gen.*, p. 154-5 - *DAR Patriot Index*, p. 230 - *Bennington Co. Gazeteer*, p. 92, 126)

Joseph - b 3/29/1756 in Mansfield, CT, s/o **William**; Joseph d 11/15/1833 in Dalton, NH. He m **Polly Carpenter,** b1763, d

7/30/1813, d/o **Amos** and **Polly (Gould)** of Westminster, VT. First settled in Charlestown, NH. (*Farwell Gen.*, p. 159)

FELLOWS

Abiel - b 10/17/1764 in Canaan, CT, d1833 at Fellows Farm near Schoolcraft, Kalamazoo, MI. Abiel m (1) **Anna Andrus**, b1767, d1789, and m (2) **Catherine Mann**, b1773, d1803, and m (3) **Dorcas Hopkins**, b1786. (CT Rev. Soldiers Buried in MI – *DAR Patriot Index*, p. 232 – 1812 Index)

FELT

Jehiel - b 12/5/1769 in Somers, CT, s/o **Samuel, Jr.** and **Mehitabel**; Jehiel d 3/19/1842 in Rochester, NY. He m 2/25/1794 in Somers, CT, **Mehitabel Davis**, b 5/29/1776, d in OH, d/o **James** and **Elizabeth (Belknap)**. (1812 Index – *Felt Gen.*, p. 126)

FENN

Titus - b 4/27/1761 in Watertown, CT (?), d 9/26/1844 age 44 in Cornwall, Addison Co., VT. Titus m 3/16/1779 in Watertown, CT, **Rhoda Andrus**, b1761. (*Hist. of Cornwall, VT*, p. 101, 285 – *Des. of Edward Fenn*, p. 10)

FENTON

Jacob - b 11/5/1765 in Mansfield, CT, d 1/25/1822 age 57 in Fluvanna, Chautauqua Co., NY. Jacob m in Milford, CT, 9/13/1790 **Lois Hurd** of New Milford. (*Fenton Fam.* by Weaver, p. 615 – *DAR Patriot Index*, p. 233 – *Chautauqua Co., NY*, p. 338)

Nathaniel - b 3/26/1763 in Mansfield, CT, d 1/25/1846 age 83 in Poland, NY, buried in Allen Cem. Nathaniel m **Rachel Fletcher**, b1766, d 9/1/1842. (Soldiers of the American Rev. – *Chautauqua Co., NY*, p. 10 – *DAR Patriot Index*, p. 233)

Capt. Solomon - b 6/23/1749 in Mansfield, CT, d 12/25/1831 age 82 in Oxford, Chenango Co., NY. Capt. Solomon m **Sybil Snow**, b 9/19/1749, d 9/29/1824. (*Annals of Oxford, NY*, p. 72 – *DAR Patriot Index*, p. 233)

FIELD

David - b 5/7/1790 in E. Guilford, CT, s/o **David** and **Lois (French)**; David (the younger) d 9/7/1877 age 72 in NY City. He m (1) **Widow Conklin** of Jericho, VT, and m (2) **Phebe Ward** of NY. Had lived in Jericho, VT, and Pompey, NY. (*Field Gen.*, p. 602)

James - bc1765 in CT, d 6/30/1823 in Niagara Falls, Oakwood Cemetery, NY. James m **Anna Spencer**. (*DAR Magazine* 1977, p. 916 – *DAR Patriot Index*, p. 235)

Jedediah - b 5/28/1765 in E. Guilford, CT, s/o **David** and **Anna (Stone)**; Jedediah d 9/30/1842 in Jericho, Chittenden Co., VT. He m 5/7/1787 **Mabel Stevens**, b 4/9/1768 in E. Guilford, CT, d 8/21/1849 in Jericho, VT, d/o **Nathaniel** and **Sarah (Griswold)**. (*Field Gen.*, v. 1, p. 409-10, 606-7 – *Chittenden Gazeteer*, p. 230)

FITCH

Asabel – b 3/21/1769 in Norwich, CT, d 8/21/1849 in Rochester, Monroe Co., NY. Asabel m **Polly** ----, b 4/29/1778 in CT, d 9/2/1857. (Tombstone Records)

Ebenezer – b 9/9/1755 in CT, d 5/14/1817 in Old Saratoga, NY, buried in family cemetery. Ebenezer m **Sarah Hobby** of North Castle, NY. (*Hist. of Saratoga Co., NY*, p. 199, 438 – *DAR Patriot Index*, p. 238 – *DAR Magazine* 1977, p. 916)

Ephraim – b 3/29/1736 in Norwalk, CT, d 2/2/1832 in Oxford, Chenango Co., NY. Ephraim m 4/28/1757 **Lydia Root**. (*Annals of Oxford*, p. 445 – *DAR Patriot Index*, p. 238)

Col. **John** – b 7/2/1749 in Lisbon, CT, d 8/8/1840 in Kirkland, Oneida Co., NY. Col. John m 3/5/1772 **Irene Warner**, d 11/1/1817, d/o **Timothy** of Windham, CT. (*Onondaga Hist. Soc. of 1914*, p. 198 – *DAR Patriot Index*, p. 238)

John – b 9/14/1783 in Windham, CT, d 1/25/1856 age 73 in Bristol, Addison Co., VT. John m **Hannah** ----, bc1786 in VT, d 8/30/1864 age 78 in Bristol, VT. (*Gazetteer of Addison Co. VT*, p. 145)

Hon. **Peletiah** – b in Norwich, CT, d 12/11/1832 in 82nd year in Salem, Washington Co., NY. Hon. Peletiah m **Sarah** ----, d 8/18/1835 age 77 in Salem, NY. (*The Salem Book, NY* – Rev. War Cemetery, Salem, NY)

Roswell – b 12/7/1765 in CT, d1842 in Pomfret, Chautauqua Co., NY, buried in Fredonia Cem. Roswell m **Sarah Sheffield**. (*Soldiers of Am. Rev. – Chautauqua Co.*, p. 15-16 – *DAR Patriot Index*, p. 238)

FLINT

Amasa – b 8/25/1774 in Hampton, CT, s/o **Nathaniel, Jr.** and **Lucy (Martin)**; Amasa d 12/11/1851 age 62 in Braintree, VT. He m (1) 9/10/1795 in Hampton, CT, **Hannah Martin**, d 3/15/1837 age 62, and m (2) Mrs. **Lucy B. Bartlett**, d 7/30/1838 age 56-6, and m (3) 7/25/1839 Mrs. **Phebe Rumrill**. (*Thos. and Wm. Flint of Salem, MA*, p. 88)

Ashel – b 5/28/1765 in Windham, CT, s/o **Silas** and **Abigail (Robinson)**; Ashel d 3/16/1855 in Braintree, Orange Co., VT. He m (1) 1/7/1790 in Braintree, VT, **Betsey King**, and m (2) **Sally Parish**, b 9/7/1784 in NY, d 1/31/1868. (*Thomas and William Flint of Salem*, p. 39 – *1850 Orange Co. Census*)

Augustus – b 9/23/1791 in Hampton, CT, d 1/2/1872 age 82-9 prob. in Braintree, VT. Augustus m (1) 10/29/1813 **Nancy Vinton**, and m (2) 9/2/1847 **Maria (Lyon) Smith**, wid/o **Jabez**; Marie was b in CT, d 1/18/1883 age 82-9 in Braintree, VT. (*Thomas and William Flint of Salem*, p. 89 – *1850 Orange Co. Census*)

Charles – b 8/20/1780 in Windham, CT, s/o **John** and Sarah (Tilden); Charles d 7/3/1866 age 89 in Williamstown, Orange Co., VT. He m 5/31/1807 **Sarah Rood**, b1785, d 4/22/1834 age 49. (*Thomas and William Flint of Salem, MA*, p. 77, 113-114)

Daniel – b 12/7/1761 in Windham, CT, s/o **Nathaniel, Jr.** and **Mary (Henry)**; Daniel d 3/12/1841 in Braintree, Orange Co., VT. He m (1) **Elizabeth Martin**, b 12/24/1761 in Hampton, CT, d 10/24/1804, d/o **Joseph** and **Elizabeth (Ford)**, and m (2) possibly Mrs. **Sarah**

Sumner. (*Thomas and William Flint of Salem, MA*, p. 48 – *History of Braintree, VT*, p. 138-9)

Diah – b 3/26/1771 in Windham, CT, s/o **Samuel, Jr.** and **Lucy (Martin);** Diah d 4/17/1855 age 84 in Williamstown, VT. He m (1) 12/1/1796 **Polly Brainerd,** d 2/6/1805 age 27, and m (2) 5/9/1805 **Eleanor Stebbins,** d 3/29/1858 age 78. (*Thomas and William Flint of Salem, MA*, p. 71-2)

Elijah – b 3/7/1798 in Hampton, CT, d 3/8/1882 in Braintree, Orange Co., VT. Elijah m 9/5/1824 in Braintree, VT, **Patience Neff,** b 2/4/1805 in Braintree, VT, d 5/7/1881, d/o **Joseph** and **Abigail (C a b l e).** (*Thomas and William Flint of Salem, MA*, p. 91 – *1850 Orange Co. Census*)

Elisha – b 4/7/1787 in Ashford, CT, s/o **Jonathan** and **Molly;** Elisha d prob. in Braintree, Orange Co., VT. He m (1) **Huldah Carpenter,** b 4/7/1789 in VT, d 2/22/1854 age 65, in Braintree, VT, and m (2) **Hannah Fitts,** d 10/27/1864 age 69, in Braintree, VT. (*Thomas and William Flint of Salem, MA*, p. 88 – *1850 Orange Co. Census*)

Elisha – b 11/30/1780 in Windham, CT, s/o **James;** Elisha d 9/1862 in Williamstown, Orange Co., VT. He m (1) 6/19/1806 **Nancy Carpenter,** b 12/1786, and m (2) **Lovisa Barnes.** (*Thomas and William Flint of Salem, MA*, p. 82-3)

Elisha – b 8/30/1781 in Windham, CT, s/o Capt. **Benjamin** and **Bethia (Cheney);** Elisha d in S. Royalton, VT. He m (1) **Betsey Ormsbee,** and m (2) **Betsey Orvis,** and m (3) **Polly Keyes.** (*Thomas and William Flint of Salem, MA*, p. 46, 86-7)

Gideon – b 10/26/1781 in Windham, CT, s/o **John** and **Philena;** Gideon d in Roxbury, Washington Co., VT. He m (1) **Olive Emerson,** and m (2) Mrs. **Luana Loomis,** b in MA. (*Thomas and William Flint of Salem, MA*, p. 126 – *1850 Census Washington Co., VT*)

Jabez – b 5/2/1756 in Windham, CT, s/o **Asher;** Jabez d 3/28/1844 in Amenia, NY. He m (1) 5/16/1782 **Eliza (Merritt ?) Willson,** and m (2) 5/10/1790 **Elizabeth Paine.** (*History of Surry, NH*, p. 616 – *Thomas and William Flint of Salem, MA*, p. ? – *DAR Patriot Index*, p. 241)

James – b 8/10/1751 in Windham, CT, s/o **Samuel** and **Mary (Hall);** James d in Randolph, VT, or Williamstown, VT. He m 4/22/1773 in Scotland, CT, **Herusha Lillie,** b 5/20/1757, d/o Capt. **Elisha** amd **Huldah (Tilden).** (*Thomas and William Flint of Salem, MA*, p. 41-2 – *DAR Patriot Index*, p. 241)

James, Jr. – b 3/10/1779 in Windham, CT, s/o **James;** James, Jr. d 6/17/1870 in Williamstown, Orange Co., VT. He m (1) 3/31/1803 **Hannah Ford,** b 5/22/1777, d 7/13/1821, and m (2) 6/9/1822 **Sally Kelsey.** (*Thomas and William Flint of Salem, MA*, p. 82, 122-4)

Jeremiah – b 11/16/1784 in Hampton, CT, s/o **Phineas** and **Hannah (Clark);** Jeremiah d 10/26/1842 in Braintree, Orange Co., VT. He m 4/7/1830 **Jerusha Pratt,** b 2/24/1803 in Braintree, VT. (*Thomas and William Flint of Salem, MA*, p. 90)

John – b 2/13/1760 in Windham, CT, s/o **Gideon** and **Sarah (Walcutt);** John d 1/24/1832 in Granville, VT. He m (1) 11/30/1780 **P h i l e n a Flint,** b 4/4/1762, d1805 in Royalton VT, d/o **Bartholomew** and **Mary (Welch),** and m (2) Mrs. **Desiah (King) Gilligan,** d/o **Samuel**

King of Tolland, CT. (*Thomas and William Flint of Salem, Massachusetts*, p. 43-4, 84-5)

Jonathan - b 11/22/1755 in Windham, CT, s/o **Nathaniel** and **Mary (Hovey)**; Jonathan d 12/3/1846 age 93 in Braintree, Orange Co., VT. He m **Mary Amidon**, bc1762, d 8/26/1840 age 78 in Braintree, VT. (*DAR Patriot Index*, p. 241 - *Thomas and William Flint of Salem, MA*, p. 47, 88-9)

Joseph - b 3/15/1789 in Ashford, CT, s/o **Jonathan** and **Molly (Hovey)**; Joseph d 12/23/1879 in Braintree, Orange Co., VT. He m 11/21/1811 **Anna Bass**, b 6/6/1790 in VT. (*1850 Orange Co., VT, Census* - *Thomas and William Flint*, p. 88-9)

Leonard - b 4/29/1782 in Windham, CT, s/o **John** and Sarah **(Tilden)**; Leonard d 7/23/1870 in Williamstown, Orange Co., VT. He m (1) 4/14/1808 in Williamstown, VT, **Anna Luce**, b 2/5/1786 in Williamstown, VT, d 2/19/1846 in Williamstown, VT, d/o **Ephraim**, and m (2) 10/20/1848 **Betsey Palmer**, b 5/14/1804 (or 5/14/1809) in Tunbridge, VT, d 1/13/1879, d/o **Roderick** and **Hannah (Palmer)**. (*Thomas and William Flint of Salem, MA*, p. 78-9 - *Orange Co. Gazetteer*, p. 524 - *1850 Orange Co. Census*)

Nathan - b 4/17/1762 in Windham, CT, s/o **Gideon** and Sarah; Nathan d 9/25/1851 age 89-5 in Chelsea, VT, buried in Flint Cem., Chelsea, VT. He m (1) 1783 **Olive Redington**, b1755, d 12/1/1838 age 83, and m (2) **Polly** ----, d 8/20/1851 age 62-6. (*Thomas and William Flint of Salem, MA*, p. 44 - *Gazetteer of Orange Co., VT*, p. 226-7 - West Hill Cemetery and Flint Cem.)

Nathaniel - b 7/11/1745 in Windham, CT, s/o **Nathaniel** and **Sarah (Bidlake)**; Nathaniel (the younger) d1803 in Braintree, Orange Co., VT. He m 5/23/1767 **Lucy Martin**, b 5/8/1747 in Windham, CT, d/o **Ebenezer** and **Jerusha (Durkee)**. (*Thomas and William Flint of Salem, MA*, p. 46)

Nathaniel - b 3/2/1795 in Hampton, CT, d 7/17/1873 age 77-4 in Braintree, Orange Co., VT. He m **Polly N.** -----, bc1793, d 1/29/1887 age 93-8 in Braintree, VT. (*1850 Orange Co. Census*)

Nathaniel - b 7/2/1772 in Windham, CT, s/o **Nathaniel, Jr.** and **Lucy**; Nathaniel (the younger) d 7/9/1841. He m 6/20/1793 in Hampton, CT, **Eunice Moulton**, d1840 age 65, d/o **Samuel** and Sarah **(Rinde)**. (*Thomas and William Flint of Salem, MA*, p. 87-8)

Phineas - b 7/23/1757 in Windham, CT, s/o **Nathaniel** and **Mary (Henry)**; Phineas d 6/25/18-- in Braintree, Orange Co., VT. He m 2/24/1780 in Hampton, CT, **Hannah Clark**, b 12/29/1757 in Windham, CT, d 4/14/1827, d/o **Jeremiah** and Hannah (Clark). (*Thomas and William Flint of Salem, MA*, p. 47 - *History of Braintree, VT*, p. ?)

Phineas - b 8/17/1782 in Hampton, CT, s/o **Phineas** and **Hannah (Clark)**; Phineas (the younger) d 6/9/1826 in Braintree, Orange Co., VT. He m 3/18/1813 **Abigail Weld**. (*Thomas and William Flint of Salem, MA*, p. 89)

Rufus - b 4/3/1768 in Windham, CT, s/o **Silas** and **Abigail**; Rufus d 5/12/1837 in Madison, OH. He m **Hannah Hawes**, b 7/10/1773, d 7/12/1842 prob. in Madison, OH. He went to Braintree, VT, then c1830 to Madison, OH. (*Thos. and Wm. Flint of Salem, MA*, p. 70)

Samuel, Jr. – b 10/25/1746 in Windham, CT, s/o **Samuel** and **Mary**; Samuel, Jr. d 7/9/1827 in Randolph, VT. He m 12/17/1767 in Windham, CT, **Lucy Martin**, b 5/6/1749 in Windham, CT, d 3/3/1827 in Randolph, VT. (*Thomas and William Flint of Salem, MA*, p. 39-40, 71-77)

Samuel, Sr. – b 4/9/1712 in Windham, CT, s/o **John** and **Christian (Read)**; Samuel, Sr. d1802 in Randolph, VT. He m (1) 4/13/1736 **Mary Lamphere**, d 1/1/1744 in Windham, CT, and m (2) 4/11/1745 **Mary Hall**, b 9/27/1717, dc1778 (or 1779), d/o **James**, and m (3) 1772 **Sarah Blackman**, b 4/15/1744. (*Thomas and William Flint of Salem, MA*, p. 19, 40)

Silas – b 3/19/1737 in Windham, CT, s/o **Samuel** and **Mary (Lamphere)**; Silas d in Canada. He m (1) 12/4/1757 **Sarah Norton**, and m (2) 4/19/1762 in Windham, CT, **Abigail Robinson**, b 2/22/1737, d/o **Israel** and **Sarah (Sabin)**. (*Thomas and William Flint of Salem, MA*, p. 39 – *History of Braintree, VT*, p. 77)

Thomas – b 1/18/1779 in Windham, CT, s/o **John** and **Sarah (Tilden)**; Thomas d 9/8/1864 in Williamstown, Orange Co., VT. He m 5/29/1803 **Azubah Wiley**, b1782 in Wilbraham, MA, d 2/16/1859, d/o **Judah** and **Deborah (Harvey)**. (*Thomas and William Flint of Salem, MA*, p. 77-8 – *Gazetteer of Orange Co., VT*, p. 526)

William – b 3/17/1795 in CT, d 8/16/1879 in Braintree, Orange Co., VT. William m **Anna Thomas**, b 12/6/1798 in VT, d 9/21/1879. (*Thomas and William Flint of Salem, MA*, p. 48 – *1850 Orange Co. Census of Braintree, VT*)

William – b 4/29/1769 in Hampton, CT, s/o **Nathaniel** and **Mary (Hovey)**; William dc1850 in Braintree, Orange Co., VT. He m **Patty Randall**. (*Hist. of Braintree, VT*, p. ? – *Thomas and William Flint of Salem, MA*, p. 48)

FLOWER

Timothy – bc1774 in CT, d 1/17/1861 in 90th year in Rupert, Bennington Co., VT. Timothy m **Clarissa ----**, b 2/16/1785 in VT, d 4/11/1868 in Rupert, VT. (*1850 Bennington Co. Census – Gravestone Record of Rupert*, p. 24)

FOOT

Bronson – b 9/5/1757 in Waterbury, CT, s/o Capt. **Moses**; Bronson d 8/30/1836 age 79 in Clinton, Oneida Co., NY. He m 5/7/1782 **Thankful Pond**, b 2/16/1757 in Woodbury, CT, d 6/9/1843 age 86. (*Clinton Memorial-Kirtland Ave. Cemetery*, p. 17 – *Hist. of Waterbury, CT*, p. 349 – *Foote Gen.*, p. 63, 153)

Daniel – b 4/3/1760 in Watertown, CT, d 8/24/1848 age 89 in Cornwall, Addison Co., VT. Daniel m (1) 1783 **Sarah Johnson** of Rutland, VT, d 12/6/1790 age 25 in Cornwall, VT, and m (2) 1792 **Ellen Scott** of Watertown, CT, d 4/4/1847 age 78 in Cornwall, VT. (*DAR Patriot Index*, p. 243 – *Hist. of Cornwall, VT*, p. 285 – *VT Hist. Magazine*, v. 1, p. 26 – *Foot History and Gen.*, p. 182, 314)

David, Sr. – b 1/24/1753 in Watertown, CT, d 9/27/1821 in W. Cornwall, VT. David, Sr. m1777 **Mary Scovel** of Watertown, CT, d 7/11/1838 in W. Cornwall, VT. (*Foot Hist. and Gen.*, p. 179-181 – *Hist. of Cornwall*, p. 91, 285)

Elijah - b 5/10/1788 in Watertown, CT, s/o **David** and **Mary (Scovel)**;
   Elijah d 1/1/1868 in Cornwall, Addison Co., VT. He m (1)
   11/17/1812 **Orpha Ward** of Cornwall, VT, d 12/29/1815, and m (2)
   11/4/1817 **Mehitable Gale**, b1796, d 5/20/1877. (*Foot Hist. and
   Gen.*, p. 311-12, 443)
Jared - b 8/28/1728 in CT, d 1/28/1806 in Cornwall, Addison Co.,
   VT. Jared m (1) 1753 **Hannah Buell**, b 11/9/1735 in Marlboro, CT,
   d 4/5/1774, d/o Capt. **Timothy** and **Hannah (Bradford)**, and m (2)
   Hepzibah Phelps, d/o **Charles** (they were divorced), and m (3)
   Widow **Joanna Jennings**, d 5/17/1823 age 75. (*Foot Hist. and Gen.*,
   p. 49-51, 102-3 - *DAR Patriot Index*, p. 243)
Capt. **Justus** - b 6/24/1782 in Simsbury, CT, d 6/10/1829 in Middel-
   bury, VT. Capt. Justus m 4/15/1810 **Harriet Swan Graham**, b
   3/9/1789 in W. Suffield, CT, d 4/30/1865 age 76, d/o Rev. **John** of
   Suffield, CT. (War of 1812 Index - Middlebury Cem. stone - *Foote
   Hist. and Gen.*, p. 121, 240-1, 371)
Dr. **Nathan** - b 2/10/1738 in Watertown, CT, d 7/25/1808 at son Uri's
   in Charlotte, VT, buried in Cornwall, Addison Co., VT. Dr. Nathan
   m 6/12/1759 **Marian Silkriggs**, b1840 in Waterbury, CT, d
   12/26/1811 age 75 in Cornwall, VT. (*Foot Hist. and Gen.*, p. 71-2
   - *Hist. of Cornwall*, p. 45, 54, 204 - *DAR Patriot Index*, p. 244)
Russell - b 5/17/1786 in Watertown, CT, d 5/19/1842 in Cornwall,
   Addison Co., VT. Russell m (1) 1/1809 **Belinda Mead** of Cornwall,
   VT, d 1/1832, and m (2) 1832 **Huldah Gibbs** of Middlebury, VT.
   (*Foote Hist. and Gen.*, p. 310-11, 441-3)
Dr. **Solomon** - b1768 in Colchester, CT, s/o **Jonathan** and **Sarah
   (Fenner)**; Dr. Solomon d 10/26/1811 in W. Rutland, VT. He m1798
   Betsey Crossett, b1771, d 8/13/1845 age 74 in Rutland, VT, d/o
   Archibald of Pelham, MA. (*Hist. of Cornwall, VT*, p. 208, 285 -
   Foote Hist. and Gen., p. 112-115, 232)

FOOTE

Calvin - b 2/28/1785 in Northford, CT, s/o **Luther** and **Temperance**;
   Calvin d 6/12/1879 in PA, prob. in Mill Creek. He m 11/6/1812
   Polly Burton, d 7/23/1867 in Mill Creek, PA, d/o **David**. (War of
   1812 Index - *Foote Hist. and Gen.*, p. 257)
David - b 2/1780 in Watertown, CT, d prob. in Cornwall, Addison Co.,
   VT. David m1802 **Mehitabel Post** of Cornwall, VT, d 9/16/1872
   age 90 in Crown Point, NY. (*Foot Hist. and Gen.*, v. 1, p. 309-10,
   440-1)
Fenner - b 10/5/1754 in Colchester, CT, d 4/27/1847 age 92 in Lee,
   MA. Fenner m1779 **Sarah Wilcox**, d 1/14/1840 age 76. (*Am.
   Monthly*, v. 41 - *DAR Patriot Index*, p. 243)
Hon. **Isaac** - b 1/4/1746 in Colchester, CT, s/o **Daniel**; Hon. Isaac d
   2/27/1842 in Smyrna, Chenango Co., NY. He m **Mary Kellogg**, b
   5/31/1768 in Colchester, CT, d 11/19/1826 age 82 in Smyrna, NY.
   (*DAR Patriot Index*, p. 243 - *Smyrna*, p. 16-17)

FORD

Abijah - b 12/23/1765 in Hebron, CT, d 2/19/1813 in Salisbury,
   Herkimer Co., NY. Abijah m **Rebecca Salisbury**, b 2/5/1762 in

Swansea, MA, d 11/14/1815. (*NEGR* 4/1976, p. 157 - *DAR Patriot Index*, p. 244)

Abraham - b 8/29/1744 in Windham, CT, s/o **Nathaniel** and **Dinah** (**Holt**); Abraham d 3/19/1832 in Brookfield, VT. He m 11/8/1763 in Windham, CT, **Abigail Woodward**, b 4/21/1740, d 5/23/1826, d/o **Jacob** and **Abigail (Flint)**. (*Descendants of Andrew Ford of Weymouth*, p. 43-4 - *NEGR* 1/1966, p. 49-50 - *Hist. of Braintree, VT*, p. 141-3)

FOWLER

Asahel - b 9/9/1771 in Coventry, CT, s/o **Ichabod** and **Ruth (Glover)**; Asahel d 12/25/1851 age 82 in Thetford, Orange Co., VT. He m **Mary** - - - -, bc1782 in NH, d 2/2/1862 age 80. (*1850 Orange Co. Census* - Thetford, VT)

Dr. Benjamin - b1821 in Northford, CT, d 9/8/1858 in Poughkeepsie, NY. Dr. Benjamin m 9/11/1850 **Mary Payne**. (*Comm. Biog. Record - Dutchess Co., NY*, p. 256)

Frederick William - b 1/6/1789 in Guilford, CT, d 8/20/1868 (poss. in Milan, Huron Co., OH). Frederick William m (1) 1814 **Elizabeth Barrett**, bc1793, d1826 in Milan, OH, and m (2) 1826 in Norwalk, OH, **Mary Inman**, d/o **Malvery**. (Residents from Connecticut in Huron Co., Ohio)

FOX

Amasa - b 2/14/1767 in East Haddam, CT, d 10/20/1866 age 91-3 in Sherburne, Chenango Co., NY. Amasa m **Abigail**, b in CT, d 10/20/1866 age 97-9 in Sherburne Chenango Co., NY. (*1850 Census of Chenango Co., NY*)

Stephen - b1760 in CT, d 2/25/1842 in IN. Stephen m **Mary Bates**. (1812 Index - *DAR Patriot Index*, p. 249)

Veniah - b1763 in New Hartford, CT, d 2/2/1851 in Pomfret, NY, buried in Fredonia Cem. Veniah m **Sarah Cadwell**, b1764, d 6/21/1840. (*Soldiers of Am. Rev. - Chautauqua Co.*, p. 16 - *DAR Patriot Index*, p. 249)

FRANCIS

Joel - bc1771 in Wallingford, CT, s/o **James**; Joel d 1/23/1844 age 73 in Wells, VT. He m (1) **Sybil Butts**, d1809, and m (2) **Clarissa Colvin** of Manchester, VT. (*The Francis Family*, p. 121 - *Hist. of Wells, VT*, by Paul, p. 88)

John - b 2/28/1752 in Wallingford, CT, d1813 in Middletown, VT. John m1783 **Sarah Blakeley**. After John's death she m (2) **Robert Hotchkiss**. (*Hist. of Wells, VT*, by Paul - *Hist. of Wells, VT*, by Wood, p. 53)

Nathan - b1756 in Wallingford, CT, s/o **James** and **Mary**; Nathan d 9/5/1798 age 72 in Wells, Rutland Co., VT. He m (1) 9/21/1780 **Abigail Thompson** of Wallingford, CT, and m (2) **Lucinda Coy**. (*The Francis Family*, p. 149-50 - *Hist. of Wells, VT*, by Wood, p. 52 - *Hist. of Wells, VT*, by Paul, p. 86)

FRANKLIN
Amos A. - b 6/27/1785 in Stonington, CT, d 4/14/1858 in Oxford, Chenango Co., NY. Amos A. m (1) 1809 **Anne Howe,** d 7/12/1811 age 21, and m (2) 1814 **Minerva Cary,** d 5/23/1859. *(Annals of Oxford, NY,* p. 329-30)
John - bc1715 in Canaan, CT, s/o **John;** John (the younger) killed by Indians 7/3/1778 in Hanover Twp., PA. He m **Elizabeth** ----. *(Hist. of Hanover Twp., PA,* p. 412)

FREEMAN
Samuel - b 2/1/1753 in CT, d 10/11/1837 in Brookfield, Orange Co., VT. Samuel m **Jemima Bigelow,** b 5/27/1763 in Colchester, CT, d/o **Amasa** and **Jemima (Strong).** *(DAR Patriot Index,* p. 251)

FRENCH
Andrew - b 3/24/1755 in Stratford, CT, s/o **Samuel** and **Elizabeth (Loring);** Andrew d 8/11/1840 in Dorset, Bennington Co., VT. He m (1) 3/24/1788 in Dorset, VT, **Catherine Barto,** b 4/4/1765, d 5/9/1808, d/o **Samuel** and **Anna,** and m (2) **Eunice** ----, b1772, d 3/16/1842. *(Anc. and Des. of Samuel French the Joiner,* p. 144)
Bronson - b 7/26/1767 in Southbury, CT, s/o **William** and **Anne (Bennett);** Bronson d 11/2/1852 in Poughkeepsie, Dutchess Co., NY. He m 5/5/1805 in Woodbury, CT, **Mary Ann Burritt,** b 3/4/1783 in Southbury, CT, d 1/21/1872 in Poughkeepsie, NY, d/o Dr. **Anthony** and **Anna.** *(Ancestors and Descendants of Samuel French the Joiner,* p. 150)
Ebenezer - b 1/29/1756 in CT, d 9/25/1826 in S. Milton, Ulster Co., NY. Ebenezer m **Rachel Hinman.** *(DAR Mag.,* 1977, p. 916 - *DAR Patriot Index,* p. 251)
Elijah - b 9/12/1751 in Stratford, CT, s/o **Samuel** and **Elizabeth (L o r i n g);** Elijah d 9/18/1830 in Dorset, VT. He m 5/13/1777 in Manchester, VT, **Abigail Beardslee,** b1757 in Stratford, CT, d 12/14/1831, d/o of **B e n n i t .** *(Anc. and Des. of Samuel French the Joiner,* p. 141)
Jeremiah - b 8/3/1786 in Huntington, CT, s/o **Jonas** and **Susanna (Winton);** Jeremiah d 4/1/1855 in Granville, OH. He m 5/4/1823 **Elizabeth Dudley,** b 4/4/1801 in Derby, CT, d 8/31/1887 in Williamsport, IN, d/o **Josiah** and **Sabra.** *(Anc. and Des. of Samuel French the Joiner,* p. 258)
Jeremiah - b 7/8/1743 in Stratford, CT, s/o **Jeremiah** and **Hannah (Edwards);** Jeremiah (the younger) d 12/5/1820 in Maple Grove, Canada. He m1762 **Elizabeth Wheeler,** b 12/14/1745, d 7/14/1838 in Maple Grove, Canada. *(Anc. and Des. of Samuel French the Joiner,* p. 154)
Jeremiah - b 8/19/1764 in Huntington, CT, s/o **Thomas** and **Abigail (Mallory);** Jeremiah d 2/11/1835 in Williston, Chittenden Co., VT. He m (1) **Hannah Ormsby,** b 4/4/1768 in Manchester, VT, d 6/16/1801 in Williston, VT, d/o Major **G i d e o n ,** and m (2) 10/10/1802 **Polly Lyon,** b1776 in CT, d 4/10/1859 in Williston, VT, d/o **Gershom.** *(Anc. and Des. of Samuel French the Joiner,* p. 289-90, 292)

Jeremiah – bc1712 in Stratford, CT, s/o **Samuel** and **Mary (Price)**; Jeremiah dc1793 in S. Dover, Dutchess Co., NY. He m (1) 7/28/1737 in Stratford, CT, **Hannah Edwards**, b1715 in Stratford, CT, d 10/29/1776, d/o **William**, and m (2) **Martha Beardslee**, d/o **Abraham** and **Esther**. (*Ancestors and Descendants of Samuel French the Joiner*, p. 147)

John – b 12/23/1746 in Stratford, CT, s/o **John** and **Elizabeth (Nichols)**; John (the younger) d 10/2/1831 in Dorset, VT. He m (1) **Catherine Beardslee**, b 2/1753 in Stratford, CT, d 9/30/1819 in Manchester, VT, d/o **Israel** and **Elizabeth (French)**, and m (2) **Submit Sargent** (or **Sargence**). (*Anc. and Des. of Samuel French the Joiner*, p. 190–3)

Joseph – b 7/26/1748 in Stratford, CT, s/o **Samuel** and **Elizabeth (Loring)**; Joseph d 6/14/1813 in Manchester, Bennington Co., VT. He m 5/13/1777 **Mary Beardslee**, b1755 in Stratford, CT, d 3/17/1839 in Manchester, VT, d/o **Israel** and **Elizabeth (French)**. (*Anc. and Des. of Samuel French the Joiner*, p. 130–1, 136, 138, 141)

Joshua – b 2/20/1767 in Ripton Parish, Fairfield Co., CT, s/o **Samuel** and **Hannah (Nichols)**; Joshua d 8/28/1857 in Newark, OH. He m **Grace Bassett**, b1765 in Newtown, CT, d 11/30/1852 in Clinton, OH, d/o **Joel** and **Grace (Livingston)**. (*Anc. and Des. of Samuel French the Joiner*, p. 57)

Peter Price – b 10/15/1762 in Huntington, CT, d 12/26/1841 in Wells, Bradford Co., PA. Peter Price m (1) 10/20/1782 in Manchester, VT, **Lucy Benedict**, b 5/24/1760 in New Milford, CT, d 11/23/1793 in Hampton, Washington Co., NY, d/o **Jonathan** and **Lucy**, and m (2) **Jerusha Dart**, b 4/17/1772 in Hartford, CT, d 11/13/1798 in Hampton, NY, d/o **Jabish**, and m (3) **Sarah Sterne**, b 7/22/1777 in Claremont NH. (*Anc. and Des. of Samuel French the Joiner*, p. 268)

Nathaniel Loring – b 5/1/1737 in Stratford, CT, s/o **Samuel** and **Elizabeth (Loring)**; Nathaniel Loring d after 1787 prob. in Ferrisburgh, Addison Co., VT. He m **Sarah Lane**, bp. 4/1735, d after 1787 (her will dated 5/2/1777), d/o **Charles** and **Achsah (Mallory)**. (*Anc. and Desc. of Samuel French the Joiner*, p. 50)

Samuel – b 3/9/1739 in Stratford, CT, s/o **Samuel** and **Elizabeth (Loring)**; Samuel (the younger) d 3/28/1809 in Manchester, Bennington Co., VT. He m 5/29/1766 in Stratford, CT, **Hannah Nichols**, d 2/8/1813 age 70 at Manchester, VT, d/o **Samuel** and **Comfort (Mansfield)**. (*Ancestors and Descendants of Samuel French the Joiner*, p. 51–61)

Thomas – b 7/4/1726 in Stratford, CT, d 7/1776 in Manchester, Bennington Co., VT. Thomas m **Abigail Mallory**, b 11/10/1732 in Stratford, CT, d 3/10/1813 in Williston, VT. (*Anc. and Des. of Samuel French the Joiner*, p. 266–7)

FRISBEE

Benjamin – b 8/17/1768 in Sharon, CT, d 2/18/1841 in Roxbury, Delaware Co., NY. Benjamin m 2/8/1790 **Ruth Dolph**. (*Frisbee-Frisbie Fam.*, p. 66 – *Hist. of Roxbury, NY*, p. 61)

FRISBIE

William - b 2/14/1737 in Bethlehem, CT, d 3/1/1813 age 76 in Middletown, Rutland Co., VT.   William m **Sarah Campbell**.   (*DAR Patriot Index*, p. 253 - *Hist. of Rutland Co., VT*, p. 649)

FRIZZLE

Ebenezer - b 1/10/1766 in Wethersfield, CT, d1849 in Northfield (?), Washington Co., VT.   Ebenezer m **Azubah Hayward**, b 3/12/1771, d1847.   (*Early Settlers of Northfield, VT*, p. 130)

FULLER

Abraham - b 10/1737 in CT, d 9/20/1807 in E. Bainbridge, Chenango Co., NY.   Abraham m **Lydia Gillette** 1/4/1762 (or 11/4/1762). (French's *Hist. Gazetteer*, p. 225 - *DAR Patriot Index*, p. 254)

David - b 3/16/1778 in Mansfield, CT, s/o Dr. **Jonathan** and **Sybel (Meacham)**; David d 4/13/1854 age 76-6 in Chelsea, Orange Co., VT.   He m **Sally ----**, b in MA, d 9/29/1866 age 86-8 in Chelsea, VT.   (*1850 Orange Co. Census - Chelsea*).

Joshua - b 10/2/1728 in Bolton, CT, d 3/19/1816 in Surry, NH. Joshua m 12/3/1750 in Bolton, CT, **Joanna Taylor** d 7/25/1823 age 89.   (*DAR Patriot Index*, p. 255 - *Town of Gilsum, NH*, p. 175, 310)

Luther - b 5/10/1766 in Union, CT, s/o **William** and **Mehetable (Tyler)**; Luther d 10/1841 in NH.   He m (1) ----, and m (2) **Lydia Hutchins**, d1837.   (1812 Index - *Fuller Gen.*, p. 102, 104)

FYLER

Roman - b1768 in Winsted, CT, d1828 prob. in Burke, Caledonia Co., VT.   Roman m **Sally Lyman**.   (*VT Hist. Mag.*, v. 1, p. 307)

GAINES

David - b 6/25/1732 in Glastonbury, CT, s/o Nathaniel; David d 7/31/1813 in Guilford, VT.   He m in Glastonbury, CT, **Prudence Risley**, b 9/25/1735, d 4/15/1815 in Guilford, VT.   (*NEGR* 1/1931, p. 52-3)

GALLUP

John Adam - b 4/6/1795 in Sterling, CT, s/o **Benadam** and 1st wife **Elizabeth (Dorrance)**; John Adam d1875 in IL.   He m **Polly Barber** 11/26/1818.   (1812 Index - *Gallup Family*, p. 79, 137-9)

Levi - b 3/25/1760 in Stonington, CT, s/o **Nathaniel** and **Hannah Gore (Burrows)**; Levi d 2/18/1850 age 90 in Old Jefferson, NY.   He m **Abigail Packer** of Groton, CT, b1758, d 7/11/1826 in Old Jefferson, NY.   (*DAR Patriot Index*, p. 258 - *Biog. Rev. of Otsego Co.*, p. 80 - *Gallup Gen.*, p. 33, 57)

GALPIN

Judson Benjamin - b 5/15/1816 in Washington, CT, s/o **Benjamin** and **Polly (Judson)**; Judson Benjamin d 2/20/1893 in Oxford, Chenango Co., NY.   He m 5/16/1841 **Catherine Jane Brownson**, b 12/2/1818 in Warren, CT.   (Annals of Oxford)

GALUSHA

Jonas – b 2/11/1753 in Norwich, CT, d 10/8/1834 in 82nd year in Shaftsbury, VT. Jonas m (1) **Mary Chittenden**, d 4/20/1794 in 36th year, and m (2) **Patty ----**, d 11/10/1797 in 33rd year, and m (3) **Abigail Ward**, d 5/6/1809 in 39th year, and m (4) ----. (May have m **Nabby ----**, d 7/30/1831 in 68th year.) (*Gravestone Rec. of Shaftsbury, VT*, p. 24-5 – *DAR Patriot Index*, p. 258 – *Hist. of VT*, v. 5, p. 79-80)

GARDNER

Michael – bc1814 in New Fairfield, CT, d 5/16/1884 age 70 in Dutchess Co., NY. Michael m 10/15/1837 **Anna Davis**, d/o **Daniel** and **Mermelia (Hodge)**. (*Comm. Biog. Rec. – Dutchess Co.*, p. 446)

GATES

Caleb – b 8/22/1735 in Preston, CT, d 4/22/1816 in Charlton, Saratoga Co., NY, and is buried there in the Old Cemetery. Caleb m **Elizabeth Branch**. (*DAR Mag.* 1977, p. 916 – *DAR Patriot Index*, p. 262)

Ezra – b1749 in CT, d 10/6/1841 in NY. Ezra m **Mercy Gates**. (1812 War Index – *DAR Patriot Index*, p. 262)

Joshua – b 11/3/1730 in Preston, CT, s/o **Caleb** and **Mary (Forbes)**; Joshua d 12/27/1798 age 69 in NY state. He m 5/22/1755 in Preston, CT, **Anna Branch**, b 2/17/1733 (or 2/17/1734) in Preton, CT, d/o **Samuel** and **Anna (Lamb)**. (*DAR Patriot Index*, p. 262 – *For King or Country*, Orange Co., CA, Bicentennial Project, p. 129)

Luther – b 6/1/1761 in Preston, CT, d 9/1/1826 in Pomfret, Chautauqua Co., NY, and buried in Fredonia Cemetery. Luther m 1/1/1789 in Stephentown, NY, **Anna Brown**, d 1/2/1846. (*Soldiers of Am. Rev. – Chautauqua Co.*, p. 16 – *DAR Patriot Index*, p. 262)

Nathaniel – b 3/4/1756 in CT, d 11/7/1793 age 37 years. Nathaniel m **Lucy Gallup**. (*Hist. of Luzerne-Lackawanna-Wyoming Co., PA*, p. 313 – *DAR Patriot Index*, p. 262)

GAYLORD

Rev. Elijah – b1800 in Bristol, CT, d age 92 in Camden, Oneida Co., NY. Rev. Elijah m1821 **Eliza Stearns** of Florence, NY. (*Pioneer Hist. of Camden, NY*, p. 216-17)

GEAR (or GEER)

Hezekiah – b 12/17/1791 in Middletown, CT, d1877 (or 1878) in Okohama, IA. Hezekiah m (1) 1817 in Manlius, NY, **Charlotte Clark**, and m (2) Mrs. **Deborah Rose**, d1850, and m (3) 1853 **Fr999 cenia Trego**. (War of 1812 Index – *George Geer and Des.*, p. 133-4)

Rezin – b 8/3/1737 in Norwich, CT, s/o **Oliver** and **Elizabeth**; Rezin d 7/3/1778 in Brooklyn, Susquehanna Co., PA. He m **Mary Vanderburgh**. (*DAR Patriot Index*, p. 264)

GIBBS

David – b 6/4/1788 in Windsor, CT, d 3/16/1840 in Norwalk, Huron Co., OH. David m 5/20/1810 in Norwalk, OH, **Elizabeth Lockwood**, b 3/23/1791, d 10/4/1873 in Norwalk, OH. (War of 1812 Index)

GIDDINGS

James - b1780 in Groton, CT, s/o **Solomon** and **Sarah (Waterman)**; James d1863 (poss. in Herrick Twp.) in Susquehanna Co., PA. He m1802 **Lucy Demming** of Norwich, CT, b 6/17/1783, d 6/18/1861. (*Giddings Family*, p. 193-7 - *History of Susquehanna County, Pennsylvania*, p. 349-50)

Lyman - b 6/17/1785 in Hartland, CT, s/o **David** and **Lois (Borden)**; Lyman d 7/31/1846 in Farmington, Oakland Co., MI. He m (1) ----, and m (2) 4/4/1824 in NY state, **Sarah Mead Bush**, b 4/17/1792 in Rutland, VT, d 1/23/1878 in Farmington, MI, d/o **Timothy** and **Phoebe (Crippen)**. (*DSGR* Summer 1972, p. 193)

Marsh - b 11/19/1816 in Sherman, CT, s/o **William** and **Jane (Ely)**; Marsh d 6/3/1875 in Santa Fe, NM. He m1836 **Louisa Mills**, d/o **Augustus** of Richland, MI. According to a Kalamazoo County lawyer, he went to Richland, MI in 1830. (*Pioneer Collections of MI*, v. 11, p. 300-303)

GIFFORD

John - b 10/23/1766 in Norwich, CT, s/o **Ziba** and **Edith**; John d at age 90, prob. in Randolph, Orange Co., VT. He m **Cynthia Kimball**, b 3/29/1769 in Pomfret, CT, d1864 age 95, d/o **John** and **Jerusha (Macham)**. (*Hist. Souvenir of Randolph*, p. 111-112 - *Gazetteer of Orange Co., VT*, p. 353)

GILBERT

Butler - b 10/22/1747 in Middletown, CT, s/o **Nathaniel** and **Mary (Butler)**; Butler d 5/3/1827 in Morris, Otsego Co., NY. He m 5/7/1777 **Abigail Woodhouse**, b 3/31/1753 in Wethersfield, CT, d 1/20/1823, d/o **William** and **Mary (Walker)**. (*Gilbert Family* by Brainerd, p. 208-9 - *DAR Pat. Index*, p. 267 - War of 1812 Index)

Isaiah - b 3/29/1733 in CT, d 2/15/1825 age 93 in Cornwall, Addison Co., VT. Isaiah m (1) **Esther Bull** 2/14/1758 in Woodbury, CT, and m (2) **Experience** ----. (*DAR Patriot Index*, p. 267)

John - b 3/9/1779 in CT; d 11/10/1867 age 88-8 in Ludlow, Windsor Co., VT. John m **Eunice** ----. (*1850 Census of Windsor Co., VT*)

Nathan - bc1767 in CT, s/o **John** and **Lydia (Merwin)**; Nathan d 9/10/1804 age 37 in Fairfield, Franklin Co., VT. He m **Lucy Sherwood**, d 9/21/1817 age 41 years, d/o **Nathan** and **Joanna (Noble)**. She m (2) Col. **Horace Barber**. (*Some Early Records of Fairfield, VT*, p. 6 - *Franklin Co. Gazetteer*, p. 106)

Samuel - b1772 in Litchfield, CT, d1845 in LeRoy, Genesee Co., NY. Samuel m **Deborah Sanford**. (*Yankee Magazine* August 1977)

Samuel - b 3/1/1712 (or 5/1/1712) in Lebanon, CT, d 10/16/1774 in Lyme, Grafton Co., NH. Samuel m (1) 2/7/1732 (or 2/7/1733) **Elizabeth Curtis**, b 1/31/1707 (or 1/31/1708), d 6/25/1739, d/o **Samuel** and **Mary**, and m (2) 5/22/1740 in Hebron, CT, **Abigail Rowley**, b 2/13/1716 in E. Haddam, CT, d 10/23/1764 in Hebron, CT, d/o Deacon **Samuel** and **Elizabeth (Fuller)**, and m (3) 1/27/1765 **Susannah (Gross) Phelps**, bc1722, d1795, d/o **Jonah** and **Susanna Gross** of Hartford. (*Gilbert Family*, p. 102-3, 137-9 - *Hist. of Surry, NH*, p. 631)

Col. **Thomas** - b 9/15/1743 in CT, s/o **Samuel** of Hebron, CT; Col. Thomas d1790, prob. in Lyme, NH. He m **Lydia Lathrop**. (*Gazetteer of Grafton Co., NH*, p. 526 - *DAR Patriot Index*, p. 267)

GILKEY

Jonathan - b 2/1/1782 in Lisbon, CT, s/o **Charles**; Jonathan d 9/1/1869 in Strafford, VT. He m **Polly Spaulding**, b 11/8/1784 in NH, d 3/9/1858. (*1850 Orange Co., VT, Census - Hist. of Early Gilkeys and Their Des.*, p. 40, 48)

GILLET

Gideon - b 4/14/1781 in Hartford, CT, s/o **Thomas B.** and **Rhoda**; Gideon d1866 in Mendotta, IL. He m1806 **Ruth Goddard**, b1787 in Hartford, CT. (*Hist. of LaSalle Co., IL*, p. 412)

John - b 4/7/1745 in Lebanon, CT, s/o **Ebenezer**; John d 1/19/1829 age 85 in Hartford, VT, buried in Christian Cemetery. He m1773 **Jemima Smalley**, d 1/21/1835 age 86. (*Hist. of Hartford, VT*, p. 424 - *DAR Patriot Index*, p. 269)

GILLETT

Asa - b 6/11/1764 in Litchfield, CT, d1839 in Washtenaw Co., MI. Asa m **Naomi Hosford**. (CT Rev. Soldiers Buried in MI - *DAR Patriot Index*, p. 268)

Ebenezer - b 6/5/1705 in CT, s/o **John, Jr.**; Ebenezer d 10/19/1776, a proprietor of Hartford, VT, but may never have come there. He m 9/23/1730 **Mary Ordway**, d 9/4/1791, d/o **Jacob** and **Rebecca (Wright)**. (*History of Hartford, Vermont*, p. 421-2 - Hazen Family in America)

Lt. **Israel** - b 9/17/1738 in Lebanon, CT, s/o **Ebenezer**; d 7/8/1829 age 91, prob. in Hartford, VT. He m (1) 1/8/1761 **Martha Throope**, d/o **William** and **Elizabeth**, b 5/17/1739, d 7/4/1763, and m (2) 11/15/1764 **Susannah Durkee** of Woodbury, CT, d 7/26/1821 age 77. (*Hist. of Hartford, VT*, p. 421-2 - *VT Antiquarian*, p. 24 - *DAR Patriot Index*, p. 268)

Samuel - bc1717 in Lebanon, CT, d 7/29/1780 age 63 years. Samuel m **Elizabeth** ----, d 12/9/1783 in E. Thetford, VT, age 58 years. (*Gazetteer of Orange Co., VT*, p. 431)

William - b 2/1/1758 in Colchester, CT, d 3/2/1838 in Townville, Crawford Co., PA. William m **Abigail Bishop**, b1765 in CT. (*First Hundred Years in Townville, Pennsylvania*, p. 76-80 - *DAR Patriot Index*, p. 269)

GILLETTE

Zaccheus Phelps - b1776 in Goshen, CT, d1865 in WI. Zaccheus Phelps m in Goshen, CT, **Clarissa Humphrey**, d/o **Charles** and **Naomi (Worcester)**. (War of 1812 Index - *Humphrey Gen.*, p. 287)

GLASS

Rufus - b 4/7/1755 in Canterbury, CT, s/o **Anthony**; Rufus d 3/21/1813 in Wells, VT, in an epidemic. He m 11/16/1779 in E. Haddam, CT, **Huldah Fuller**, d 4/4/1813 age 58 in the same epidemic as Rufus. (*Hist. of Wells, VT*, p. 92 - *Glass Gen.*, p. 69)

Samuel – b 4/1/1758 in Canterbury, CT, s/o **Anthony** and **Eunice (Bennett)**; Samuel d 4/4/1813 age 85 in Wells, VT, in an epidemic. He m **Abigail Munger**, d 7/27/1831 in Wells, VT, age 76. (*Hist. of Wells, VT*, p. 92-3)

GLEASON

Hiram North – b 9/17/1800 in Farmington, CT, d prob. in Chautauqua Co., NY. Hiram North m1825 **Sarah Root** of Farmington, CT. (*Gleason Gen.*, p. 352 – *Chautauqua Co., NY*, p. 549-50)

Ira Fay – b 1/27/1806 in Sharon, CT, s/o **Ira** and **Esther (Fay)**; Ira Fay d 9/6/1874 prob. in Chautauqua Co., NY. He m 4/12/1827 in Eaton, NY, **Caroline Force**, b 2/1/1810. (*Chautauqua Co., NY*, p. 300 – *Gleason Gen.*, p. 362)

Job – b 1/28/1754 in Enfield, CT, s/o **Isaac**; Job d prob. in Surry, NH. He m 2/28/1754 **Hannah Pease**. (*Hist. of Surry, NH*, p. 637 – *Gleason Gen.*, p. 67)

Jacob – b 7/23/1768 in Thompson, CT, d 10/12/1842 in Stockton, Chautauqua Co., NY. Jacob m (1) 3/3/1792 **Rachel Barnes**, and m (2) 1/16/1796 **Mehitable Hudson**. (*Soldiers of Am. Rev. - Chautauqua Co.*, p. 16)

James – b1759 in Farmington, CT, d d 10/4/1834 in Roxbury, Delaware Co., NY. James m **Lovina Drake**. (*Hist of the Town of Roxbury, NY*, p. 12 – *DAR Patriot Index*, p. 271)

GLOVER

James A. – b 4/24/1793 in Plainfield, CT, d 5/23/1875 in Oxford, Chenango Co., NY. James A. m **Ann Bradley**, b 7/8/1792, d 12/21/1871. (*Annals of Oxford, NY*, p. 239-40 – *1850 Census of Chenango Co., NY*)

GOFF

Hezekiah – b 6/26/1753 (or 6/26/1754) in Middletown, CT, s/o **Hezekiah** and **Bethiah**; Hezekiah (the younger) d 2/27/1848 in VT. He m (1) **Anna Ward**, and m (2) **Rebecca Smith Woodward**. (1812 War Index – *DAR Patriot Index*, p. 273)

GOLD

Joseph Wakeman – b in Cornwall, CT, d at about age 40 years in Pompey, Onondaga Co., NY. Joseph Wakeman m Mrs. **Rhoda Gold**, b1777 in Harwinton, CT, d prob. in Milwaukee, WI, 50 years after her husband. (*Pompey, NY*, p. 309-310

GOODELL

Abial – b 8/13/1747 in Pomfret, CT, d1830 at age 83 years in Westminster, VT. Abial m **Margaret Brown**. (*Caledonia Gazetteer*, p. 256)

Ebenezer – bc1796 in CT, d 4/12/1880 age 84 years in Fairlee, Orange Co., VT, buried in Ely Cem. Ebenezer m **Mercy ----**, bc1794 in NH. (*1850 Orange Co. Census for Fairlee*)

Elijah – bc1760 in Pomfret, CT, s/o **Abijah** and **Lucy (Tyler)**; Elijah d in Ecorse, Wayne Co., MI. He mc1785 **Achsah Pickert**, d/o **Bartholomew**. (*DSGR* Winter 1978, p. 64)

GOODRICH

David – b in Glastonbury, CT, d prob. in Wells, VT. David m **Rachel Bidwell**, d/o **Jonathan** and **Hannah (Matson)**, b 4/18/1772 in Glastonbury, CT. (*Hist. of the Town of Wells, VT*, by Wood, p.57)

George – b 8/24/1751 in Glastonbury, CT, d 8/16/1843 age 93 years in Gill, MA. George m **Lucinda Wells**. (*Am. Monthly*, v. 3. – *DAR Patriot Index*, p. 275)

Simon – b 9/11/1759 in CT, d 2/7/1852 age 92 years in Benson, VT. Simon m **Sally Howard**, d1839 age 73 years. (*1850 Census of Rutland County – History of Rutland Co.*, p. 937, 457 – *DAR Patriot Index*, p. 275)

Timothy – b1755 (or b1756) in Woodbury, CT, d 2/17/1829 in 73rd year in Fair Haven, VT. Timothy m (1) **Kezia Hines**, d 10/10/1803 in 43rd year, and m (2) Widow **Rebecca (Stoddard) Steele**, d 2/23/1829 age 70. (*Hist. of Fair Haven, VT*, p. 374)

GOODSELL

Thomas – b 11/30/1746 in E. Haven, CT, s/o **Isaac** and **Elizabeth (Penfield)**; Thomas d1840 at nearly 100 years of age in Clinton, Oneida Co., NY. He m ----. (*Clinton Memorial-Kirtland Ave. Cem.*, p. 19 – *New Haven Gen. Mag.*, v. 3:666 – *Connecticut in the Rev.*, p. 521)

GOODYEAR

Edward – b1788 in Cheshire, CT, d1862 age 74 years prob. in Camden, Oneida Co., NY. Edward m1814 in Wolcott, CT, **Leva Alcott**, gr/d/o Capt. **John Alcott**, d1863. (*Pioneer History of Camden, New York*, p. 341-2)

Jared – b1792 in CT, d 10/24/1874 in Otsego Co., NY. Jared m **Ann Eliza Collier**, d 3/30/1878. (*Biog. Review of Otsego County, New York*, p. 81)

GORE

Obadiah – b 4/7/1744 in Norwich, CT, s/o **Obadiah** and **Hannah (Parke)**; Obadiah (the younger) d 3/22/1821 in PA. He m 3/22/1764 in Norwich, CT, **Anna Avery**. (War of 1812 Index – *DAR Patriot Index*, p. 276)

GORHAM

Demming – b 6/6/1789 in Fairfield, CT, s/o **Seth** and **Millicent (Dunks)**; Demming d 11/14/1861 prob. in Pittsford, Rutland Co., VT. He m 2/11/1808 **Sabra Gates**, b 8/22/1790 in Rutland, VT, d 6/23/1869. (*Hist. of Pittsford, VT*, p. 402-3)

George – b 7/20/1759 in Groton, CT, d 11/13/1848 age 89-3-28 in Montgomery, MA. George m **Mary Welles**. (*Am. Monthly*, v. 37 – *DAR Patriot Index*, p. 276

Seth – b 1/18/1763 in Kent, CT, d 8/28/1852 in Poultney, Rutland Co., VT. Seth m (1) **Amelia Dunks**, and m (2) **Louisa Everson**. (*Hist. of Rutland Co.*, p. 772 – *DAR Patriot Index*, p. 276 – *1850 Census of Rutland Co., VT*)

GORTON

Joseph – b 3/25/1773 in New London, CT, d1851 in NY state. Joseph m 1/8/1796 **Charlotte Schriver** of Dutchess Co., NY, b 1/8/1774. (1812 War Index – *Gorton Fam.*, p. 287, 439-40)

GOTT

Daniel – b 7/10/1793 in Hebron, CT, s/o **Hazael** and **Abigail (Phelps)**; Daniel d 7/6/1864 in Syracuse, NY. He m 9/12/1819 **Ann (Baldwin) Sedgwick**, wid/o **Stephen**. (*Pompey, NY*, p. 410)

GOULD

Ebenezer – b 8/1/1755 in Killingly, CT, s/o **Samuel** and **Martha**; d1809 prob. in Granville, Washington Co., NY. Ebenezer m **R h o da Robbins**. (War of 1812 Index – *Hist. of Washington Co., NY*)

GOVE

Nathaniel – b 4/21/1739 in Coventry, CT, d 9/9/1813 in Rutland, Rutland Co., VT. Nathaniel m **Esther Tyler**. (*Hist. of Rutland Co.*, p. 324 – *DAR Patriot Index*, p. 278)

GRANGER

A m o s   P . – b 6/3/1789 in suffield, CT, d 8/20/1866 age 77 in Syracuse, Onondaga Co., NY. Amos P. m **Charlotte Hickox**, b1790, d 7/4/1882. (*Onondaga Hist. Soc. of 1914*, p. 171, paperback)

Elihu – b 4/30/1771 in Simsbury, CT, s/o **Elisha** and **Sarah (Pierce)**; Elihu d 7/16/1842 in Phelps, NY. He m **Apena Granger**, d/o **Aaron** and **Mary (Ward)**, b 8/1/1772, d 7/21/1853. (War of 1812 Index – *Granger Gen.*, p. 152-5)

Lancelot – b 10/5/1779 in Suffield, CT, s/o **Enoch** and **Catherine (Kent)**; Lancelot d prob. in Fairlee, Orange Co., VT. He m **Betsey ----**, bc1778 in NH. (*1850 Orange Co., VT, Census*)

GRANNIS

Eli – b 4/3/1822 in Southington, CT, s/o **Harvey** and **Mindwell (Dutton)**; Eli d prob. in Pine Grove, Portage Co., WI. He m in Sherman, NY, **Pamela Skinner**, b in CT. (*1880 Census, Portage Co., Wisconsin*)

GRANT

Noah – b1772 in Stonington, CT, s/o **Noah** and **Mary (Palmer)**; Noah (the younger) d prob. in Pharsalia, Chenango Co., NY. He m 11/25/1789 **Polly Browning**. (*Hist. of Chenango Co.*, p. 424 – *Hist. of Stonington, CT*, p. 403-4)

Zebulon – b 12/9/1776 in Tolland, CT, s/o Capt. **Ephraim** and **Mary**; Zebulon d 10/1/1835 in NY City, NY. He m **Anna Moore**, d/o **Richard** and **Catherine (Berrien)**, b 11/6/1791 in Newtown, LI, NY, d 10/4/1832 in New York City. (War of 1812 Index – *Grant Family*, p. 34, 468)

GRAVES

Chauncey – b1762 in CT, s/o **Joshua**; Chauncey d 8/7/1832 in Salisbury, Addison Co., VT. Chauncey m **Olive Graves**. (Salisbury from Birth to Bicentennial – *DAR Patriot Index*, p. 280)

Edmund – bc1766 in Guilford, CT, d 6/15/1827 age 61-7-15 in Sunderland, VT (gravestone). Edmund m **Bulah Hill**, bc1776, d 7/24/1844 in 68th year in Sunderland, VT, d/o **Abner**. (*Bennington Co. Gazetteer* – gravestones in Sunderland, VT)

Ezra H. – bc1807 in Sherman, CT, d 5/6/1886 age 79 in Sweden Twp., Monroe Co., NY. Ezra H. m **Julia** ----, bc1813 in Wilton, CT, d 7/7/1907 age 94 (possibly 2nd w). (*Hist. of Monroe Co., NY*, p. 156, 162 – Tombstone Rec. of Brockport Cemetery)

GRAY

Abisha – b 9/21/1809 in New London, CT, s/o **Jonas** and **Lucy (Spicer)**; Abisha d 4/27/1882 in Rush, Susquehanna Co., PA. He m 8/31/1831 **Mary Green**, b 8/19/1812 in RI, d/o **Abel** and **Polly (Whitford)**. (*Hist. of Susquehanna Co., PA*, p. 447)

Hiram B. – b 3/22/1801 in Fairfield, CT, d 1/27/1872 in NY City, NY. Hiram B. m 12/20/1847 **Nancy Hager**. (*Comm. Biog. Rec. – Dutchess Co., NY*, p. 204)

James – b 8/3/1759 in Sharon, CT, s/o **John** and **Catherine (Gardner)**; James d 3/1/1846 in PA. He m **Parthenia White**. (War of 1812 Index – *DAR Patriot Index*, p. 281)

John – bc1727 (or bc1728) in Kent, CT, d 11/28/1806 in 80th year in Arlington, VT. John m (1) ----, and m (2) 3/12/1761 **Mary Morgan**. (*VT Hist. Magazine*, v. 1:136)

Jonas – b1762 in CT, s/o **Philip**; Jonas d 8/16/1832 in Rush, Susquehanna Co., PA. He m (1) **Lucy Spicer**, d1813, and m (2) 1/1/1819 Mrs. **Mary Vorse Gardner**. (*Hist. of Susquehanna Co., PA*, p. 446-7 – *DAR Patriot Index*, p. 281)

Joseph – b 6/12/1732 in Windham, CT, s/o **John** and **Ann**; Joseph d 3/29/1796 in Greene, Chenango Co., NY. He m ----. (*NEGR* Query 1/1961, p. 78 – *DAR Patriot Index*, p. 282)

GREEN

Benjamin – bc1797 in CT, d prob. in Halifax, Windham Co., VT. Benjamin m **Mary A.** ----, b in CT. (*1850 Census of Windham County, Vermont*)

David – b1769 in New Milford, CT, d 7/22/1848 in 87th year in Pompey, NY. David m1796 **Hannah Pease**, d 4/22/1838 in 82nd year. (*Pompey, NY*, p. 310 – *Onondaga Hist. Soc. of 1914*, p. 310)

GREENFIELD

Enos – b1749 in CT, d 11/23/1824 in Onondaga Co., NY. Enos m **Mary Curtis**. (*Onondaga Hist. Soc.*, p. 199 – *DAR Patriot Index*, p. 284)

GREENSLIT

John – b 6/5/1767 in Windham, CT, d 4/1/1856 in Warren, Washington Co., VT. John m **Saloma Pitts**, bc1766 in CT. (*1850 Washington Co. Census – DAR Patriot Index*, p. 284)

GREGORY

George – b 11/12/1786 in Wilton, CT, s/o **Abraham** and **Dorothy (L a m b e r t)**; George d 6/16/1865 in New London, OH. He m 12/31/1810 in Southeast, NY, **Polly Warring**, d/o **John** and **Mary (Elwell)**, b 11/25/1792 in Southeast, NY, d 12/29/1833 in New London, OH. (Residents from CT in Huron Co., OH – *Gregory Genealogy*, p. 185)

Ralph – bp 5/27/1743 in Wilton, CT, s/o **Samuel**; Ralph d 8/21/1797 age 55. He m 5/30/1764 in Newtown, CT, **Pamela Terrill**, b1740, d 4/16/1809. (*Some Early Records of Fairfield, VT*, p. 15 – *Gregory Gen.*, p. 116–117)

Seeley – b 8/19/1776 in Danbury, CT, s/o **Seeley**; Seeley (the younger) d 9/30/1857 age 81 prob. in Otsego Co., NY. He m **Mary Gregory**, d/o **Hezekiah**, b 5/29/1783, d 3/4/1850. (*Biog. Rec. of Otsego Co., NY*, p. 652 – *Gregory Gen.*, p. 161)

U r i a h – b 3/21/1754 in CT, d 10/2/1844 in Ballston, Saratoga Co., NY, buried in Briggs Cemetery. Uriah m **Tamor Rowland**. (*DAR Mag. 1977*, p. 917 – *DAR Patriot Index*, p. 285)

GRIDLEY

Abraham – b 5/16/1742 in Kensington, CT, d 3/12/1827 age 84 years in Clinton, Oneida Co., NY. Abraham m 7/7/1768 **T h e o d o c i a Hoisington** of Kensington, CT, b1742, d 9/11/1830 age 88. (*Clinton Memorial-Kirtland Ave. Cem.*, p. 19 – *CT in the Rev.*, p. 396 – *Farmington Family Notes* by Julius Gay)

Clement – b 6/23/1800 in Berlin, CT, d 1/11/1870 in Rochester, Monroe Co., NY. Clement m ----. (Tombstone Record in Mt. Hope Cemetery)

Hezekiah, Jr. – b 6/13/1732 in Stonington, CT, s/o **Hezekiah, Sr.** and **Sarah (Newell)**; Hezekiah, Jr. d 2/18/1816 in Clinton, Oneida Co., NY. He m1754 **Abigail Peck**, b 5/20/1736 in Bristol, CT, d 4/21/1826, d/o **Zebulon** and **Mary (Edwards)**. (*Clinton Memorial-Kirtland Ave. Cem.*, p. 20 – *DAR Patriot Index*, p. 286)

Theodore – b1758 in Farmington, CT, d 2/26/1826 age 67 in Clinton, NY. Theodore m (1) **Ruth Lewis**, b1754, d 7/26/1808 age 54, and m (2) **Penelope** ----, b1764, d 9/13/1817 age 54, and m (3) **Amy Ely**, b1777, d after her husband, d/o **Wells** and **Rebecca (Selden)**. (*Clinton Memorial-Kirtland Ave. Cem.*, p. 20-1 – *Farmington, CT, Family Notes* by Julius Gay – *DAR Patriot Index*, p. 286)

GRIFFIN

Nathaniel – bc1761 in Hampton, CT, d 12/26/1836 in Clinton, Oneida Co., NY. Nathaniel m **Miss Clark**. (*Clinton Memorial-Kirtland Ave. Cem.*, p. 44)

GRIFFITH

Jeremiah – b 7/28/1758 in Norwich, CT, d 6/11/1842 in Chautauqua Co., NY. Jeremiah m **Mary Cropsy**, b 2/8/1764. (*Chautauqua Co., NY*, p. 315, 323-4 – *DAR Patriot Index*, p. 286)

GRIGGS
Charles – b 4/27/1874 in Chaplin, CT, s/o **Waterman**; Charles d prob. in Surry, NH. He m 9/5/1897 **Katherine Roach**, b 7/31/1877 in E. Windsor, CT, d prob. in Surry, NH, d/o **David** and **Ellen (Meade)**. (*Hist. of Surry, NH*, p. 641)

GRINNELL
Jonathan – b 3/6/1742 (or 3/6/1743) in Saybrook, CT, s/o **Pabody** and **Sarah (Barnes)**; Jonathan d 12/4/1821 in Dorset, Bennington Co., VT. He m 1/7/1771 in Westbrook, CT, **Judith Waterhouse**, b1750, d 6/8/1817, d/o **Abraham** and **Abigail (Wolcott)**. (Dorset, VT, Vital Records)

GRISWOLD
Chester – b 9/8/1782 in Litchfield, CT, s/o **Elizur** and **Tryphena**; Chester d1868 in MD. He m **Rhoda Griswold**, d/o **Elias** and **Rhoda (Flower)**. (War of 1812 Index – *Griswold Family*, v. 3:239)

Dr. Elihu – b 8/17/1756 in Windsor, CT, s/o **Matthew**; Dr. Elihu d 1/12/1812 age 55 in Herkimer, Herkimer Co., NY. He m 12/25/1776 **Mary Wolcott**, b 8/7/1756, d/o Dr. **Alexander** and **Mary (Richards)**. (*Hist. of Herkimer Co.* by Benton, p. 317 – *DAR Patriot Index*, p. 288 – *Griswold Family*, p. 50-1)

Gaylord – b 12/18/1767 in Windsor, CT, s/o **Silvanus** and **Mary (Collins)**; Gaylord d 3/1/1809 age 41-2/11 in Herkimer, Herkimer Co., NY. He m **Mary Hooker**, b 11/26/1769, d 8/2/1811, d/o **Horace** and **Elizabeth (Filer)**. (*Hist. of Herkimer Co.*, p. 314 – *Griswold Fam.*, p. 26, 113)

Hezekiah – b1773 in Windsor, CT, s/o **Noah** and **Azubah (Strong)**; Hezekiah d1836 in NY state. He m **Mary Denslow Thrall**. (War of 1812 Index)

Isaac, Jr. – bc1779 in Norwich, CT, s/o **Isaac** and **Abigail**; Isaac, Jr. d1844 age 65 years, in MI while visiting his son. He m (1) **Naomi Barber**, d 5/4/1814 age 32, and m (2) **Huldah Dickinson**, d1858 age 80. (*Rutland Co., VT, Gazetteer*, p. 80)

Isaac, Sr. – b 4/3/1735 in Norwich, CT, d 2/22/1817 age 82 prob. in Benson, Rutland Co., VT. Isaac Sr. m **Abigail Latham**, d1817 age 79. (*Rutland Co. Gazetteer*, p. 79 – *DAR Patriot Index*, p. 288)

Jabez, Jr. – b 5/12/1764 in Sharon, CT, s/o **Jabez** and **Deborah (Prout)**; Jabez, Jr. d 11/4/1827 in Spencertown, NY. He m **Anna Spencer**, b1766. (War of 1812 Index – *DAR Patriot Index*, p. 288 – *Griswold Fam.*, v. 3:241)

Joab – b 6/29/1760 (or 6/29/1769) in Goshen, CT, s/o **Giles** and **Mary (Stanley)**; Joab d 8/20/1811 (?) in Herkimer, Herkimer Co., NY. He m in Herkimer, NY, **Nancy Myers**, d/o Gen. **Michael** and **Catherine (Harter)**. (*Hist. of Herkimer Co.*, p. 316-17 – *Griswold Fam.*, p. 27, 117)

John E. – b 3/19/1795 in CT, d 6/6/1868 in Chautauqua Co., NY. John E. m 5/24/1821 **Lucia Ann Meacham**. (*Chautauqua County, New York*, p. 540)

Samuel – b 3/29/1759 in Norwich, CT, s/o **Ebenezer** and **Lydia**; Samuel d 10/16/1851 age 93 prob. in Orwell, Addison Co., VT. He m1783 **Lucretia Abell**, b1765, d 5/7/1850, d/o **Isaiah** and **Rhoda**.

(*Gazetteer of Addison Co., VT*, p. 21-2 – *Griswold Fam.*, p. 34, 129 – *DAR Patriot Index*, p. 288)

GROW

Asa – bc1784 in CT, d 6/29/1871 in Bethel, VT. Asa m (1) ___ and m (2) **Abigail (Hale) Bill**, bc1799, d 1863 in Bethel, VT. (*1850 Windsor Co., VT, Census*)

Elijah – b 8/24/1810 in Pomfret, CT, s/o **Elisha** and **Louisa**; Elijah d 4/24/1887 prob. in Oakland Co., MI. He m 1/19/1833 in Homer, NY, **Charity Baker**, d 5/6/1885. (*Pioneer Collections of Michigan*, v. 11, p. 125-6)

Rev. **Stillman T.** – b 4/15/1807 in Pomfret, CT, s/o **Elisha**; Rev. Stillman T. d 4/25/1889 age 82 in Goodrich, Genesee Co., NY. He m1828 **Derinda Graham**. (*Pioneer Collection of MI*, v. 13:263-4)

GUERNSEY

John – b 4/6/1709 in Milford, CT, s/o **Joseph** and **Elizabeth (Disbrow)**; John d 4/3/1783 in Amenia, NY. He m 12/28/1733 in Waterbury, CT, **Ann Peck**, b 3/10/1713, d 10/12/1794, d/o Rev. **Jeremiah** and **Rachel (Richards)** of Taunton, MA. (*Comm. Biog. Rec. – Dutchess Co., NY*, p. 197 – *DAR Patriot Index*, p. 290 – *Garnsey-Guernsey Gen.*, p. 412-413)

Sylvanus – b 10/7/1767 in Bethlehem, CT, s/o **Solomon**; Sylvanus d prob. in Castleton, Rutland Co., VT. He m 11/30/1797 **Esther Higley**, d/o Deacon **Brewster Higley**. (*History of Rutland County, VT*, p. 531)

GUILE

Samuel – b 11/11/1781 in Preston, CT, s/o **Samuel** and **Lydia (Geer)**; Samuel (the younger) d1847 in PA. He m **Hannah Coleman**. (War of 1812 Index)

GURLEY

Jason – b 11/4/1779 in Mansfield, CT, d1873 age 64 in Troy Grove, IL. Jason m **Susan Bryant**, d1875 age 64. (*Hist. of LaSalle Co., IL*, p. 407-8 – *Gurley Fam.*, p. 104-8)

GUTHRIE

Eben – b 2/9/1770 in Litchfield, CT, d 10/20/1855 in Bronson Twp., Huron, OH. Eben mc1790 **Nabby Herrick**, b1770, d1826 in Peru, OH. (*Res. of CT who Migrated to Huron, OH*, p. 3)

William, Jr. – b 12/3/1768 in CT, s/o **William** and **Susan**; William, Jr. d 3/14/1813 in Bainbridge, Chenango Co., NY. He m1799 **Sarah Whitney** of Binghamton, NY, b 5/8/1775. (*History of Chenango Co., NY*, p. 160-1)

HACKETT

Josiah – b 6/15/1758 in Lyme, CT, d 7/4/1845 in Oxford, Chenango Co., NY. Josiah m **Mary Booth**. (*Annals of Oxford, NY*, p. 100 – *DAR Patriot Index*, p. 292)

HACKLEY

Aaron - b1745 in Wallingford, CT, d 10/18/1823 in Sangerfield, NY. Aaron m 11/18/1773 in Wallingford, CT, **Elizabeth Moss**. (*Hist. of Herkimer Co., NY*, p. 337-8)

HALE

Deacon **Asa** - b 11/6/1759 in Galstonbury, CT, s/o **Moses** and **Mary (Edwards)**; Deacon Asa d 12/2/1843 age 84 in Rutland, VT. He m **Dorcas Mead**, bc1762, d 10/16/1824 age 62 in Rutland, VT, d/o Col. **James**. (*Hale, House, and Related Families*, p. 127-8 - *DAR Patriot Index*, p. 294)

Ashbel - b 8/31/1773 in Glastonbury, CT, s/o **Josiah** and **Anne (Welles)**; Ashbel d1861 in Greensboro, VT. He m 5/8/1803 in Glastonbury, CT, **Patience Munn**, d1868 in Greensboro, VT. (*Hale, House, and Related Families*, p. 104 - Glastonbury Deeds 15:266, 17:493 - *VT Hist. Mag.*, v. 3:213, 216)

Isaac - b 3/21/1763 in Waterbury, CT, s/o **Samuel** and **Judith (Hodge)**; Isaac d 11/1/1839 in Oakland, Susquehanna Co., PA. He had gone to VT with his grandfather, then westward. Isaac m **Elizabeth Lewis**, b 11/19/1767 in Litchfield, CT. (*DAR Patriot Index*, p. 294 - *Hale, House, and Related Families*, p. 267)

John - b 10/12/1746 (or 10/12/1747) in Ashford, CT, s/o **James** and **Elizabeth (Bicknell)**; John d1810 in Burlington, Otsego Co., NY. He m 4/14/1772 in Ashford, CT, **Mehitable Knowlton**, b1750, d 7/22/1825 age 75 in New Lisbon Co., NY. (*DAR Magazine*, v. 107:418 - *DAR Patriot Index*, p. 294 - *Hale, House and Related Families*, p. 295-7)

Josiah - b1757 in Glastonbury, CT, s/o **Moses** and **Mary (Edwards)**; Josiah d 7/1/1811 in Georgia, Crittenden Co., VT. He m 8/5/1778 in Rutland, VT, **Abigail Williams**, bc1760, d 1/5/1808 in Georgia, Crittenden Co., VT. (*Hale, House and Related Families*, p. 126-7 - *DAR Patriot Index*, p. 294)

Lt. **Moses** - b 7/29/1728 in Glastonbury, CT, s/o **Thomas** and **Susanna (Smith)**; Lt. Moses d 11/21/1819 in Rutland, VT. He m 7/29/1752 in Middletown, CT, **Mary Edwards**, bc1733, d 12/15/1797 age 66 in Rutland, VT. (*Hale, House, and Related Fam.*, p. 71-2 - *DAR Patriot Index*, p. 291)

Thomas - bc1755 in Glastonbury, CT, s/o **Moses** and **Mary (Edwards)**; Thomas d 10/29/1812 age 57 in Rutland, VT. He m (1) 1/13/1777 in Rutland, VT, **Ruth Maynard**, bc1757, d 1/27/1801 age 44 in Rutland, VT, and m (2) 4/4/1802 **Hannah Spooner**, bc1775, d 10/15/1825 age 50. She m (2) 4/2/1817 **Moses Turner**. (*Hale, House, and Related Families*, p. 125-6)

HALL

Abner - b 4/9/1774 in CT, d 7/26/1867 in Tunbridge, Orange Co., VT. Abner m **Elizabeth Rano**, b 10/5/1771 in NH. (*1850 Orange Co. Census* - Tunbridge, VT - East Hill Cem.)

Alpheus - b 1/10/1757 in Plainfield, CT, s/o **John** and **Jemima (Read)**; Alpheus d 4/19/1841 prob. in S. Hero, VT. He m **Mercy Blinn**. (War of 1812 Index - *DAR Patriot Index*, p. 294)

Amos - b 11/21/1761 in CT, d 12/28/1827 in W. Bloomfield, Ontario Co., NY. Amos m **Phoebe Coe**. (*DAR Mag.* 1977, p. 917 - *DAR Patriot Index*, p. 294)

Asa, Sr. - b 6/20/1767 in CT, d 3/14/1832 age 65 in Chautauqua Co., NY. Asa, Sr. m ----. Removed to Stratford, NH, and in 1811 to Chautauqua Co. (*Chautauqua Co., NY,* p. 600-1)

Asahel - b 4/6/1792 in Wallingford, CT, s/o **Aaron** and **Elizabeth (Cook)**; Asahel d1877 in NY state. He m **Catherine R. Vandenburgh**. (War of 1812 Index)

Asbury - bc1792 in Fairfield Co., CT, d 2/13/1879 age 87 in Aurelius, NY. Asbury m1812 **Nancy Foster**, d/o **Dan** of Windham Co., CT. (*Hist. of Cayuga Co., NY*, p. 238-9)

David - b 11/8/1764 in Colchester, CT, d 11/7/1841 in Pittsford, Rutland Co., VT. David m 4/5/1784 **Abigail Hitchcock**, b 4/12/1762 in Bolton, CT, d 8/28/1833 in Sudbury, VT. (*Hist. of Pittsford, VT*, p. 319, 368, 704)

Elias - b in Southington, CT, d 10/29/1820 in Williston, VT. Elias m1779 **Sarah Hitchcock**, d/o **Jotham** and **Mary (Hull)**, b 2/11/1749, d1815. (*Hist. of Pittsford, VT*, p. 205)

Henry G. - b 5/4/1789 in Colchester, CT, s/o **Joshua** and **Hannah (Caverly)**; Henry G. d1872 in MI. He m **Ruth Stark**. (War of 1812 Index)

Hiland - b 5/3/1754 in Guilford, CT, s/o **Abraham** and **Jerusha (Bowen)**; Hiland d 7/10/1789 in Norfolk, CT, at the home of his father where he had traveled for his health. In 1783 he resided in Cornwall, VT. He m **Hannah Parker**, b in CT, d 8/25/1847. She had remarried after his death. (*Halls of New England*, p. 14 - *Hist. of Cornwall, VT*, p. 113 - *DAR Patriot Index*, p. 295)

Hiland - bc1791 in Norfolk, CT, s/o **Samuel** and **Lucy (Parmelee)**; Hiland d 5/5/1860 in Bristol, VT. He m (1) **Sophia Smith**, bc1809, d/o **Levi**, and m (2) **Samantha** ---- (could be his sister rather than wife). (*Halls of New England*, p. 16)

John - bc1757 in CT, d 11/26/1832 in Portland, NY. John m 6/7/1781 in Pownal, VT, **Sarah Reynolds**, d/o **Caleb**. (Soldiers of Am. Rev., Chautauqua Co., NY)

John - b 7/3/1747 in Canaan, CT, dc1842 in Luzerne, Warren Co., NY. He m **Mary Stevens** of Canaan, CT. (*Hist. of Pittsford, VT*, p. 50, 704 - *DAR Patriot Index*, p. 295)

Moses - bc1754 in CT, d 5/11/1827 in Providence, Saratoga Co., NY. Moses m **Lucy Hart**. (*DAR Magazine* 1977, p. 917 - *DAR Patriot Index*, p. 296)

Deacon **Moseley** - b 3/15/1772 in Wallingford, CT, s/o **Isaac**; Deacon Moseley d1861 in Rutland Co., NY. He m **Mary** ----. (*Hist. of Rutland Co., NY*, p. 836 - *1850 Rutland Co., NY, Census*)

Rufus - b 10/31/1782 in Mansfield, CT, s/o **Isaac** and **Anna (Palmer)**; Rufus d prob. in Newbury, Orange Co., VT. He m **Phebe** ----, bc1787 in MA. (*1850 Orange Co. Census - Newbury*)

Samuel - b 10/5/1759 in Guilford, CT, s/o **Abraham** and **Jerusha (Bowen)**; Samuel dc1838 in Bristol, VT. He m 8/17/1786 **Lucy Parmelee**, d1858. (*Halls of New England*, p. 15-16 - *DAR Patriot Index*, p. 296)

HAMLIN

Dr. Asa - b 3/30/1780 in Sharon, CT, s/o Capt. **Nathaniel** and **Deborah (St. John)**; Dr. Asa d in PA. He m 12/26/1802 in Sharon, CT, **Asenath Delano**, b 4/6/1780, d/o **Stephen** and **Huldah (Doty)**. (*Hamlin Fam.*, p. 245-6 - *Hist. of Wayne Co., PA*, p. 274-5)

Salmon - b 8/5/1763 in Sharon, CT, d1821 in Beekman Twp, NY. Salmon m **Margaret Vanderburg**. (*Hamlin Fam.*, p. 253 - War of 1812 Index)

HAMMOND

Calvin - b 12/2/1775 in Bolton, CT, s/o **Nathaniel** and **Dorothy (Tucker)**; Calvin d 10/4/1826 in Bath, OH. He m1798 **Roxanna Field** of Coventry. (*NEGR* 4/1850, p. 116)

Theodore - b 5/11/1789 in Bolton, CT, s/o **Jason** and **Rachel (Hale)**; Theodore d 9/3/1856 in Galesburg, IL. He m (1) **Rebecca Farnham**, b 2/1/1791, d 11/4/1824, d/o **John** and **Mary (Everett)**, and m (2) 3/20/1825 **Mary Fisk**, b 9/18/1802, d 5/9/1885 in Victoria, IL, d/o **Jonathan** and **Mary (Arnold)**. (*Hammond Gen.*, v. 2:382-3 - War of 1812 Index)

William - b 9/19/1735 in Windham, CT, d 10/18/1793 in Norwich, Windsor Co., VT. He m **Sarah Crane**, b 11/30/1735 in Wethersfield, CT, d 12/9/1820 in Norwich, VT, d/o **John, Jr.** and **Rebecca (Huntington)**. (*DAR Patriot Index*, p. 299 lists his wife as **Sarah Hutchins**)

HANFORD

Levi - b 9/1759 in CT, d 10/19/1854 in Walton, Delaware Co., NY. Levi m 8/1782 in Norwalk, CT, **Polly Mead**. (*Hist. of Delaware Co.*, p. 342 - *DAR Patriot Index*, p. 301)

HANKS

Arunah - b 3/24/1770 in Mansfield, CT, d 9/14/1830 in Rupert, VT. Arunah m 4/10/1791 **Lucy Perkins**, d 5/16/1860 age 88, d/o **Jacob** and **Lucy (Fitch)**. (*NEGR* Jan. 1932, p. 16)

Asa - b 8/20/1764 in Mansfield, CT, s/o **Richard** and **Hannah (Barrows)**; Asa d prob. in Thetford, VT. He m 12/1/1785 in Mansfield, CT, **Mary Harris**, b in Mansfield. (*NEGR* January 1932, p. 19)

Consider - b 4/29/1764 in Mansfield, CT, s/o Ensign **Silas**; Consider d 2/8/1818 in Dorset, VT. He mc1792 **Sarah Baldwin**, d 4/12/1820 in Dorset, Vermont. (*NEGR* January 1932, p. 23 - *DAR Patriot Index*, p. 301)

Isaac - b 1/15/1752 in Mansfield, CT, s/o Deacon **John** and **Tabitha (Hall)**; Isaac d 1/24/1826 in Greenwich, NY. He m (1) ----, and m (2) **Lois Case**, d 9/22/1838, d/o **Jonathan**. (*NEGR* Jan. 1932, p. 17)

Levi - b 5/28/1761 in Mansfield, CT, d 12/19/1835 in Addison, VT. Levi m (1) 1786 **Mercy Waterman**, and m (2) 6/11/1804 in Addison, VT, **Chloe Squires**, d 9/29/1863. (*NEGR* Jan. 1932, p. 16)

Theophilus - b 3/1/1769 in Mansfield, CT, s/o **John** and **Tabitha (Hall)**; Theophilus d 1/23/1830 in E. Bethel, VT (gravestone). He m 6/11/1797 **Patty (Martha) Stevens**, b 8/8/1772 in Rindge, NH, d 9/13/1849 age 77 in E. Bethel, VT (gravestone), d/o **Oliver** and

Sarah (Hosmer). (*Hist. Souvenir of Randolph*, p. 142 – *NEGR* Jan. 1932, p. 18)

HARDING

Abraham - b 4/14/1744 in CT, d 10/22/1815 in PA. Abraham m **Huldah Tryon**. (War of 1812 Index – *DAR Patriot Index*, p. 302)

Samuel - b 1/7/1727 in Woodstock, CT, s/o **Samuel**; Samuel (the younger) d 6/1805 in Deerfield, MA. He m (1) 10/24/1748 **Abigail Fisher**, b 11/14/1725 in Wrentham, MA, d 12/17/1756 age 30 in Woodstock, CT, d/o **Cornelius** and **Hannah (Partridge)**, and m (2) 1757 **Dinah Johnson**, b 11/16/1722 in Woodstock, CT, d 6/22/1808 age 85 in Deerfield, MA, d/o **Isaac** and **Abigail (Peck)**. (*Woodstock Fam.*, v. 6, p. 650 – *Pomfret, VT*, v. 2:498)

Timothy - b 11/22/1749 in Woodstock, CT, s/o **Samuel** and **Abigail (Fisher)**; Timothy d 3/14/1823 in Pomfret, Windsor Co., VT. He m (1) 6/1/1775 **Levina Perrin**, b 3/2/1748 in Woodstock, CT, d 2/6/1796 in Pomfret, VT, and m (2) 1/11/1798 **Hannah Curtis** of Barnard, VT, d 1/10/1833 in Pomfret, VT. (*Gen. of Woodstock Family*, v. 6:651)

HARLEY

Thomas - b 2/1746 in Fairfield Co., CT, d 10/1814 poss. in Roxbury, Delaware Co., NY. Thomas m 11/24/1771 **Mary Payne**, d/o **Elisha** of Shelter Island, NY. (*Hist. of Town of Roxbury, NY*, p. 10-11 – *DAR Patriot Index*, p. 304)

HARMON

John - b 12/11/1789 in Suffield, CT, s/o **Elias** and **Unice (Hanchet)**; John d1871 in OH. He m **Philinda Chapman**. (War of 1812 Index)

Seth - b 1/28/1752 in CT, d 6/8/1838 age 87 in Rupert, VT. Seth m (1) **Elizabeth Sheldon**, and m (2) **Anna Foster**. (*Gravestone Rec. of Rupert, VT*, p. 19, 30, 32 – *Rupert, VT, Historical and Descriptive* – *DAR Patriot Index*, p. 304)

HARPER

Col. **Alexander** - b 2/22/1744 in Middletown, CT, d 9/10/1798 in Harpersfield, OH. Col. Alexander m **Elizabeth Bartholomew**. (*DAR Patriot Index*, p. 305)

HARRINGTON

Stephen - b 7/17/1777 in Simsbury, CT, s/o **Elisha**; Stephen d1812 in OH. He m **Sarah Holcomb**. (War of 1812 Index)

HARRIS

Jedediah H. - b1784 in CT, d1855 in Strafford, Orange Co., VT. Jedediah H. m **Judith ----**, b1787 in RI, d1850. (*1850 Orange Co., VT, Census*)

John - b 4/1744 in Wallingford (or Derby), CT, s/o **John** and **Rachel (Moss)**; John (the younger) d 11/27/1814. He mc1770 **Mary Gamble**, b 2/25/1752, d 12/20/1834 in Pine Plains, NY. (*DAR Patriot Index*, p. 306 – *Little Nine Partners*, p. 351-2)

HARRISON

Samuel – b 4/26/1756 in CT, d 4/6/1813 (or 4/26/1813) age 57 in N. Chittenden, VT, buried in Wetmore Cemetery. Samuel m **Rebecca Keeler**, d 5/1/1832 age 76. (*DAR Patriot Index* – Gravestone Inscriptions)

HART

Hon. **Alvin N.** – b 2/11/1804 in W. Cornwall, CT, d 8/22/1874 in Lansing, MI. Hon. Alvin N. m 7/8/1828 in Utica, NY, **Charlotte F. Ball**, d/o Dr. **Benjamin.** (*Pioneer Collections of Michigan*, v. 1:184, 270-2)

Amasa – b 6/19/1754 in Bristol, CT, s/o **Thomas** and **Hannah (Coe)**; Amasa d1794 in Clinton, NY. He m **Phebe Roberts**, b 4/27/1755. (*Clinton Memorial-Kirtland Ave. Cem.*, p. 21 – *DAR Patriot Index*, p. 308 – *CT in the Rev.*, p. 501)

Dennis – b 9/3/1798 in Northington (now Avon), CT, s/o **Linas** and **Mary Ann (Wilcox)**; Dennis d 9/8/1868 age 70 in Sherman, NY. He m 2/1/1825 in Farmington, CT, **Elvira Dutton** of Farmington, b 12/22/1802, d/o **Joseph.** (*Hart Family*, p. 279-80 – Chautauqua County, NY)

Jonathan – b 3/22/1746 in Farmington, CT, s/o **Thomas** and **Hannah (Coe)**; Jonathan d 3/2/1806 in Paris, NY. He m (1) **Mary Coe**, dc1787, and m (2) **Lucy** (or **Lucia**) **Clark** of Southington, CT, b 11/4/1760, d 2/26/1803 age 42. (*Clinton Memorial*, p. 37 – *Tuttle Gen.*, p. 6 – *Hart Gen.*, p. 388)

Joseph – b 11/1775 in Berlin, CT, d 7/1855 in Barre, NY. Joseph m **Lucy Kirtland**, b Saybrook, CT, d 1/1868 in Adrian, MI age 89. (*Pioneer Hist. of Orleans Co., NY*, p. 169-70)

Capt. **Joseph** – bc1765 in Wallingford, CT, d 9/1813 in Tallmadge, OH. Capt. Joseph m **Anna Hotchkiss.** (*OH Gen. Soc.* Oct. 1972)

Rufus – b (poss. 3/15/1773 in Cornwall, CT), d1840 in OH. Rufus m **Esther Cotter.** (War of 1812 Index)

Seth – b 6/21/1763 in Kensington, CT, d 3/16/1832 in Hempstead, LI, NY. Seth m **Ruth Hall**, d 11/3/1841, d/o Hon. **Benjamin** of Cheshire, CT. (*Comm. Biog. Rec. – Dutchess Co., NY*, p. 816)

Thomas, Jr. – b 9/10/1749 in Bristol, CT, s/o **Thomas** and **Hannah (Coe)**; Thomas, Jr. d 2/9/1811 in 61st year in Clinton, NY. He m1772 **Mary Hungerford**, d 8/21/1823 age 71, d/o **Benjamim.** (*Clinton Memorial-Kirtland Ave. Cem.*, p. 21-2 – *Gen. of the Hart Family*, p. 389)

Timothy Thompson – bp 5/6/1781 in Farmington, CT, s/o **William, Jr.** and **Abigail**; Timothy Thompson d 9/28/1857 in Porter Twp., Cass Co., MI. He m **Sarah Wright**, b1788 in Guilford, CT, d1847 in Bergen, NY, d/o **Benjamin** and **Susanna (Murray).** His home was Bergen, NY, but he d at his granddaughter's, **Mary Smith Tubbs.** (*DSGR* Spring 1979, p. 114)

William – b1786 in CT, d1834 in NY state. William m **Delia Willis.** (War of 1812 Index)

HARTSHORN

Ryal – b1789 in CT, d1857 in NY state. Ryal m **Jane Kingsley.** (War of 1812 Index)

HARVEY

Capt. Thomas – b 4/20/1740 in Lyme, CT, s/o **John** and **Elizabeth (R a t h b o n e)**; Capt. Thomas d 3/28/1836 in Surry, NH. He m 7/18/1763 in E. Haddam, CT, **Grace Willey** of E. Haddam, b 10/6/1742, d 3/8/1812 age 69. (*Hist. of Surry, NH*, p. 660 – *DAR Patriot Index*, p. 310)

HASKINS

Frederick – b 7/6/1786 in Sharon, CT, s/o **Noah** and **Betsey**; Frederick d 7/11/1853 age 67. He m **Percy** ----, d 5/11/1856 age 66–15da. (*1850 Census Chenango Co., NY – Smyrma*)

Henry – b 8/24/1798 in CT, d 5/1/1877 in Bristol, VT. Henry m **Ursula Chapman**, b 11/11/1803, d 4/13/1876 in Bristol, VT. (Addison County, Vermont)

HATCH

Asher – b 8/27/1752 in Preston, CT, s/o **John** and **Sarah (Richards)**; Asher d1826 age 73 in Brookfield, Orange Co., VT. He m **Lucy Storey** of Norwich, CT. (*VT Hist. Mag.*, v. 2:867)

Darius – b 7/19/1779 in CT, s/o **Ichabod**; Darius d 1/1860 in Roxbury, Washington Co., VT. He m 4/10/1804 **Anna Gould** of Roxbury, VT, b MA, d1859. (*Hatch Gen.*, v. 2:339, 575 – *1850 Census of Washington Co., VT*)

Gilbert – b 8/14/1764 in Preston, CT, d 2/22/1835 in Northfield, Washington Co., VT. Gilbert m (1) **Sally Nichols**, b 1/22/1767, and m (2) **Martha Royce**. (*Early Settlers of Northfield, VT*, p. 83 – *DAR Patriot Index*, p. 312)

Isaac – b 5/24/1763 in Tolland, CT, s/o **Joseph**; d 2/6/1853 in Windsor Co., VT. Isaac m 5/27/1790 in Sharon, Windsor Co., VT, **Mary (Polly) Shepherd**, d/o **Isaac**. (Hatch Gen. 148)

J o e l – b 8/29/1764 in CT, d 3/26/1855 in Sherburne, Chenango Co., NY. Joel m **R u t h G r a y**. (*1850 Census Chenango Co., NY – DAR Patriot Index*, p. 312)

Dr. Johnson – b 9/20/1792 in Kent, CT, s/o **Clark** and **Polly (Camp)**; drowned 8/24/1854 in IL. Dr. Johnson m 9/6/1819 **Hannah Swift Dexter** of Kent, CT. (*Hist. of LaSalle Co., IL*, p. 389 – *Hatch Genealogy*, p. 195–6)

John – b 6/9/1727 in Preston, CT, s/o **John** and **Jerusha (Herrick)**; John (the younger) d 4/24/1806 age 79 in Norwich, VT (stone obliterated). He m 4/7/1748 in Preston, CT, **Sarah Richards** of Preston, d 4/14/1806 age 78 (gravestone) in Norwich, VT. (*A History of Norwich, VT*, p. 210–11 – *DAR Patriot Index*, p. 312)

Capt. Joseph – b 5/13/1738 in Preston, CT, s/o **John** and **Jerusha (Herrick)**; Capt. Joseph d 11/12/1811 age 73 in Norwich, Windsor Co., VT. He m (1) 3/19/1761 in Preston, CT, **Elizabeth Brown**, d1773, and m (2) **Harriet Freeman**, d1810 age 69. (*A Hist. of Norwich, VT*, p. 211–12 – *DAR Patriot Index*, p. 312)

Nathan – b 9/17/1757 in Tolland, CT, s/o **Joseph**; Nathan d 6/1/1841 in Ft. Miller, Washington Co., NY. He m in S. Reading, VT, **Hannah Marcy**, b1756 in Reading, VT, d 10/15/1841 in Ft. Miller, NY. (*Hatch Gen.*, p. 160 – *DAR Patriot Index*, p. 312)

Hon. **Reuben** - b 7/7/1763 in Preston, CT, s/o **Joseph** and **Elizabeth (Brown)**; Hon. Reuben d 1/5/1818 age 55 in Norwich, Windsor Co., VT. He m **Eunice Dennison**, d1842 age 78. (*A Hist. of Norwich, VT*, p. 212-14 - *DAR Patriot Index*, p. 312 - *On the Beginnings of Tunbridge, VT*)

HATHEWAY
Heman - b 1/4/1794 in Suffield, CT, s/o **John King**; Heman d 4/14/1871 in Laurens, Otsego Co., NY. He m **Olive Hopkins** of Otsego Co., b1796, d 5/8/1849 age 53, d/o **Duty** and **Wealthy**. (*Hatheways of America*, p. 346 - *Biog. Record of Otsego County, New York*, p. 605)

HAWKINS
William - b 3/15/1737 in CT, d 9/23/1819 in Milton, Saratoga Co., NY, buried in W. Bloodville Cemetery. William m **Sarah Belknap**. (*DAR Mag.* 1977, p. 917 - *DAR Patriot Index*, p. 314)

HAWLEY
Deacon **Abel, Jr.** - b 10/5/1750 (or 1755) in Farmington, CT, d 4/4/1836 age 85 in Clinton, NY. Deacon Abel, Jr. m **Elizabeth Peck**, d/o Capt. **Zebulon**. (*Clinton Memorial-Kirtland Ave. Cem.* - *DAR Patriot Index*, p. 314 - *Am. Genealogy* v. 9 #2, p. 87, 89)

Col. **Alpheus** - bc1786 in Farmington, CT, d 5/5/1844 age 58 in Jamestown, NY. Col. Alpheus m in Sandy Hill, NY, vicinity **Kezia Berry**, d/o Col. **John**. Kezia m (2) Gen. **Thomas W. Harvey**. (*Chautauqua Co., NY*, p. 363)

Gideon - b 4/2/1725 in Newtown, CT, s/o **Joseph** and **Sarah (Smith) Bristol**; Gideon d 3/3/1795 in Sandgate, VT. He m 6/20/1752 in Southbury, CT, **Miriam Wooster**, d/o **Moses** and **Mary (Hawkins)**. (Jillson Papers for Hawley-Hurd - *New Haven Fam.*, v. 2:313)

Gideon - b 7/20/1763 in Stratford (or Bridgeport), CT, s/o **Aaron** and **Elizabeth**; Gideon d1813 in VT. He m 10/9/1784 in Fairfield, CT, **Lavina Darrah (Darrow)**, bc1765, d1845. (1812 War Index - *Hawley and Nason Anc.*, p. 15-16)

James - b 5/8/1760 in Huntington, CT, s/o **Matthew** (or **Wolcott**); James d 4/14/1836 in Sheldon, VT. He m (1) 10/26/1780 **Bridget Stanton**, d 8/1791 age 26-3 in Fairfield, VT, and m (2) 2/12/1793 Mrs. **Martha (Stevens) Waterhouse**. (*Some Early Rec. of Fairfield, VT*, p. 15 - *DAR Patriot Index*, p. 315)

Capt. **Jehiel** - b 2/24/1712 in New Milford, CT, s/o **Ephraim** and **Sarah (Curtis)**; Capt. Jehiel d 11/2/1777 in 65th year in Shelburne, VT. He m 3/30/1731 in New Milford, CT, **Sarah ----**, b 8/14/1713. (*Bennington Co. Gazetteer*, p. 72 - *Hawley Family Society*, p. 5-8)

John - bp. 3/25/1750 (or 3/25/1751) in Durham, CT, d1811 in PA. John m **Mary Newton**. (War of 1812 Index)

Joseph - b1763 (or 1765) in CT, d 9/15/1818 in Greenfield, Saratoga Co., NY, buried in St. John Family Cemetery. Joseph m **Phebe Smith**. (*DAR Mag.* 1977, p. 917 - *DAR Patriot Index*, p. 315)

Josiah - b1731 in CT, d 10/22/1791 in Arlington, VT. Josiah m (1) 2/8/1753 in Roxbury, CT, **Hannah Warner**, b 8/4/1737, d/o Dr.

Benjamin and **Silence (Hurd)**, and m (2) 4/20/1759 in Stratford, CT, **Ruth Burton**, d1780, and m (3) 10/5/1783 in Stratford, CT, **Phebe (McEwen) Finch**, d/o **Timothy** and **Abigail (Hurd) McEwen**. (*Jillson Papers* for Hawley, p. 3 - *DAR Patriot Index*, p. 315)

HAYDEN

Chauncey - b 10/8/1771 in CT, s/o Lt. **Thomas** and **Abigail (Parsons)**; Chauncey d1858 age 87 prob. in Randolph, Orange Co., VT. He m (1) 2/28/1795 in Torrington, CT, **Anna Dibble**, bc1770 in CT, d1822 age 52, and m (2) 10/8/1834 **Aurelia Dibble**, b 3/5/1772 in Torrington, d1856 age 84, d/o **D a n i e l** and **A n n a**. (*1850 Orange Co., VT, Census - Hayden Gen.*, p. 141)

Capt. **Jacob** - b1760 in Killingworth, CT, d1849 in Rochester, Monroe Co., NY. Capt. Jacob m **Mary ----**. (*DAR Patriot Index*, p. 315 - Tombstone Rec. Mt. Hope Cem. - *Hist. of Monroe Co., NY*, p. 174)

Peletiah - b 1/10/1768 in Newington, CT, s/o **David** and **Jemima (Ellsworth)**; Peletiah d prob. in Pompey, Onondaga Co., NY. He m wid **Hepzibah Case**. (*Pompey, Onondaga Co., NY*, p. 317 - *Hayden Gen.*, p. 136, 169)

HAYES

Ezekiel - b 11/11/1724 in CT, s/o **Daniel** and **Martha (Holcombe)**; Ezekiel d 10/17/1807 age 83 prob. in Brattleboro, VT. He m (1) 12/26/1749 **Rebecca Russell**, b 2/6/1723, d 5/27/1773 in New Haven, CT, d/o Judge **John** and **Sarah**, and m (2) 5/5/1749 **Abigail (Hitchcock) Brown**, d/o **Jacob** and **Abigail (Butler)**. (*Gazetteer of Windham Co., VT*, p. 121-3 - *DAR Patriot Index*, p. 315 - *George Hayes of Windsor*, p. 18-22)

Gaylord - b 12/29/1790 in Granby, CT, s/o **Ezekiel** and **Mary (Cossitt)**; Gaylord d 4/29/1838 in Farm Ridge, LaSalle Co., IL. He m 1/1/1820 in Torrington, CT, **Mary Goodrich Humphrey**, d 12/1845, d/o **Daniel** and **Mary (Goodrich)**. (*Hist. of LaSalle Co., IL*, p. 345-6 - *Hayes Fam.*, p. 152-3)

John - b 5/25/1742 in Lyme, CT, s/o **Richard** and **Patience (Mack)**; John d 4/1/1813 prob. in Woodstock, VT. He m 9/20/1764 **Azubah Rowland**, b in Lyme, CT, d 4/7/1813, d/o **Uriah** and **Lydia (Lee)**. (*Lyme, CT, Vital Rec.*, p. 85, 233 - *Hist. of Woodstock, VT*, p. 111)

Lester - b1790 in CT, d1828 in OH. Lester m **Matilda Bushnell**. (War of 1812 Index)

Robert "Daniel Robard" - b 7/11/1762 in Danbury, CT, d 3/29/1846 in Strafford, Orange Co., VT. Robert mc1785 **Abigail Merrill**, d 11/6/1819 age 48. (*Gazetteer of Orange Co., VT*, p. 406 - *NEGR* 4/1966, p. 159 - For King and Country, Orange Co., CA, Bicent. Project - Kibling Cem. stone)

Rutherford - b 7/29/1756 in Branford, CT, s/o **Ezekiel** and **Rebecca (R u s s e l l)**; Rutherford d 9/25/1836 in W. Brattleboro, VT. He m1789 in Brattleboro, VT, **Chloe Smith**, b 11/10/1762 in S. Hadley, MA, d 2/17/1847 in Brattleboro, VT, d/o Col. **Israel** and **Abigail (Chandler)**. (*DAR Patriot Index*, p. 316 - *Geo. Hayes of Windsor*, p. 22, 38-45 - *VT Hist. Soc.*, v. 5, p. 56 - *Windham Co. Gazetteer*, p. 121-3.

HAYS

Isaac - bc1783 (or 1784) in CT, d 3/6/1873 age 89-10-10 in Rupert, Bennington Co., VT. Isaac m **Clarissa** ----, bc1788, d 7/25/1849 in Rupert, VT, age 61. (*1850 Bennington Co. Census - Gravestone Rec. of Rupert*, p. 5)

HAYWARD

Charles - b 4/28/1808 in Killingly, CT, s/o **John** and **Eunice**; Charles d 7/20/1849 in Ottawa, IL. He m -----. She m (2) **Henry J. Reid**. (*Hist. of LaSalle Co., IL*, p. 233)

HAZEN

Capt. Asa - b 11/16/1749 in Woodbury, CT, s/o **Thomas**; Capt. Asa d 3/12/1819 age 69 in Hartford, VT, buried in Christian Cemetery. He m 12/7/1780 **Susannah Tracy**, d/o **Thomas** and **Elizabeth (Warner)**. (*Vermont Antiquarian*, p. 23 - *History of Hartford, Vermont*, p. 432 - *Hazen Fam. in America*, p. 125-6 - *DAR Patriot Index*, p. 318)

Daniel - b 7/17/1761 in Woodbury, CT, s/o **Thomas**; Daniel d 11/22/1814 in Hartford, VT. He m 2/5/1789 in Litchfield, CT, **Olive Bartholomew**, b 11/1/1759 in Litchfield, CT, d 4/9/1845, d/o **Noble** and **Mabel (Parmelee)**. (*Hazen Fam. in America*, p. 130 - *The Old and the New*, p. 34-5 - *DAR Patriot Index*, p. 318)

Capt. Joshua - b 10/8/1745 in Woodbury, CT, s/o **Thomas** and **Ann (Tenney)**; Capt. Joshua d 4/19/1796 in Hartford, VT, buried in Christian Cem. He m 11/17/1767 in Woodbury, CT, **Mercy Hazen**, b 1/30/1748 in Norwich, CT, d 8/12/1824 in Hartford, VT, buried in Christian Cem., d/o **Joseph** and **Elizabeth (Durkee)**. (*Hist. of Hartford, VT*, p. 187 - *Hazen Fam. in America*, p. 123-4, 262-7 - *DAR Patriot Index*, p. 318)

Reuben - b 4/7/1768 in Woodbury, CT, s/o **Thomas** and **Ann (Tenney)**; Reuben d 6/18/1852 in W. Hartford, Windsor Co., VT. He m (1) 4/15/1790 **Lucretia Noble**, b 1/8/1772 in Westfield, MA, d 12/1/1823 in W. Hartford, VT. (*Hazen Fam. in America*, p. 131, 298 - *Hist. of Hartford, VT*, p. 425-446)

Capt. Solomon - b 11/2/1759 in Woodbury, CT, d 7/26/1849 age 89 in Hartford, VT, buried in Christian Cem. Capt. Solomon m (1) 12/17/1780 **Theodora Pease**, b 3/28/1762, d 5/21/1824 in Hartford, VT, d/o **Christopher** and **Anna**, and m (2) **Sarah Kilburn**, bc1763, d1853 age 90. (*1850 Orange Co., VT Census* for Chelsea - *Hazen Fam. in America*, p. 288 - *DAR Patriot Index*, p. 318)

Thomas - b 9/30/1719 in Norwich, CT, s/o **Thomas** and **Sarah (Ayer)**; Thomas d 8/19/1782 age 63 in Hartford, VT, buried Christian Cem. He m 3/7/1742 **Ann Tenney**, b 2/5/1726 (or 1727), d 7/29/1802 age 75 in Hartford, VT, buried in Christian Cem., d/o **Joseph** and **Abigail (Wood)**. (*Hist. of Hartford, VT*, p. 425-446 - *VT Antiquarian*, p. 22-3 - *Hazen Fam. in America*, p. 64-6 - *DAR Patriot Index*, p. 318)

HEATH

Daniel – b 3/26/1760 in CT, d 10/1/1841 in Coventry, Indiana. Daniel m (1) **Hannah Gates**, and m (2) **Azuba Reynolds**. (War of 1812 Index - *DAR Patriot Index*, p. 319)

Samuel Corbin – b 3/18/1759 in East Haddam, CT, d 5/19/1836 in Malone, NY, buried in Maplewood Cem. Samuel Corbin m **Leah Tracy**. (*DAR Mag*. 1977, p. 917 – *DAR Patriot Index*, p. 319)

HEBARD

Abel – b 11/26/1784 in Windham, CT, s/o **Diah** and **Zerviah** (**Hebard**); Abel d prob. in Randolph, Orange Co., VT. He m **Rosanna Lee**, d1858. (*Hubbard Family*, p. 99 – *1850 Orange Co., VT, Census*)

Marvin – b 8/25/1797 in Mansfield, CT, s/o **Andrew** and **Ruth** (**Loomis**); Marvin d prob. in Randolph, Orange Co., VT. He m 8/30/1826 in Ashford, CT, **Zilpah Robbins**, b 9/2/1802. (*Hibbard Fam.*, p. 179, 302-3 – *1850 Orange Co., VT, Census*)

Milan – b 1/30/1762 in Windham, CT, s/o **Samuel** and **Mary** (**Burnap**); Milan d1830 in Randolph, VT. He m 2/12/1793 **Betsy Burnham** of Hampton, CT. (*Hibbard Fam.*, p. 32, 51 – *Gazetteer of Orange Co., VT*, p. 353 – *Hist. Souvenir of Randolph, VT*, p. 103)

William – b 11/26/1800 in Windham, CT, s/o **Diah** and **Zerviah** (**Hibbard**); William d 10/20/1875 in Chelsea, Orange Co., VT. He m 9/12/1830 **Elizabeth Starkwether Brown**, bc1807 in VT, d 4/16/1870. (*Hibbard Fam.*, p. 100 – *Gazetteer of Orange Co., VT*, p. 89-92)

Zebulon, Jr. – b 2/17/1747 (or 2/17/1748) in Windham, CT, s/o **Zebulon** and **Hannah** (**Bass**); Zebulon, Jr. d 3/1/1814 prob. in Randolph, Orange Co., VT. He m 4/18/1776 **Lucy Hebbard**, b 1/27/1753 in Windham, VT, d 11/18/1828, d/o **Samuel** and **Mary**. (*Hibbard Fam.*, p. 37, 66-8 – *VT Hist. Mag.*, v. 2, p. 1049 – *Hist. Souvenir of Randolph, VT*, p. 102-3)

HEMPSTEAD

Stephen – b 10/1/1812 in New London, CT, d 2/16/1883 in Dubuque, IA. Stephen m ----. He became the 2nd Governor of IA. (*History of IA*, p. 125)

HENDEE

Caleb – b 8/30/1745 in Coventry, CT, s/o **Jonathan** and **Martha**; Caleb d 10/2/1823 in Pittsford, VT. He m (1) 4/27/1767 **Caroline Ellsworth**, b 3/1748, d 5/12/1791, and m (2) **Mary Squires**. (*Hist. of Pittsford, VT*, p. 43-4, 705 – *DAR Patriot Index*, p. 321)

Gen. Caleb – b 10/21/1768 in CT, s/o **Caleb** and **Caroline** (**Ellsworth**); Gen. Caleb d prob. in Pittsford, VT. He m 1/14/1789 **Lydia Rich**, d/o Elder **Elisha**. (*1850 Rutland Co. Census, Pittsford, VT* – *Hist. of Pittsford, VT*, p. 230-3)

Richard – b 6/14/1744 in Coventry, CT, s/o **Jonathan** and **Martha** (**Millinton**); Richard d1797 in Pittsford, VT (killed in barn raising). He m **Hannah Parsons** of Windsor, CT. She m (2) **David June** of Brandon, VT. (*Hist. of Pittsford, VT*, p. 206, 706)

HENDERSON
Gideon - b1789 in New Hartford, CT, d1869 in Rose, Wayne Co., NY.
Gideon m1813 **Deborah (Benham) Goodwin** (widow), d1876. (*Rose
Neighborhood Sketches*, p. 70)

HENRY
James, Jr. - b1765 in CT, d1840 in OH. James, Jr. m 11/1/1792
Hannahritta Waterman of Coventry, RI. (War of 1812 Index)

HENSHAW
D a n i e l - b 3/26/1762 in Middletown, CT, d 5/4/1825 in Middelbury,
Addison Co., VT. Daniel m 4/18/1788 **Sarah E. Prentiss**, b
11/10/1770 in New London, CT, d 11/26/1849. (Middlebury, VT,
Cemetery stones)

HERRICK
Lemuel - b 4/7/1758 in Preston, CT, d 10/18/1822 in Milton, Ulster
Co., NY. Lemuel m ----. (Rock City, Cemetery - *DAR Magazine*
1977, p. 917)

HEWITT
James - b 2/23/1771 in Stonington, CT, s/o **Henry** and **Rachel
(Kenney)**; James d 4/8/1858 in Pittsford, Rutland Co., VT. He m
6/1794 **Phebe Mead**, b 2/13/1774, d 8/8/1855. (*1850 Rutland Co.
Census - Hist. of Pittsford, VT*, p. 707)
Richard - b1737 in CT, d 9/3/1825 in Milton, Ulster Co., NY, buried
in Hoyt Cemetery. Richard m **Experience Leeds**. (*DAR Mag.*
1977, p. 917 - *DAR Patriot Index*, p. 326)

HIBBARD
Augustine - b. 4/7/1748 in Windham Co., CT, d 12/4/1831. Augustine m (1) **Eunice Ashley**, b 12/28/1751 in Claremont, NH, d
8/1/1800, and m (2) **S o p h i a S t o n e**, d 5/4/1842. (*Forests and
Clearings-Stanstead, Quebec*, p. 120 - *DAR Patriot Index*, p. 326)
Daniel - b1763 in Greenwich, CT, s/o **Jonathan**; Daniel d1840 age 75
in Northeast, PA. He m **Bethiah Gray** of Sherburne, NY, d1854 age
75 in Jamestown, NY. (*Chautauqua County, New York*, p. 540 -
Hibbard Fam., p. 64)
David - b 12/2/1755 in Windham, CT, d 2/18/1844 (or 2/18/1845) age
90 in Concord, Essex Co., VT. David m **E u n i c e T a l c o t t**.
(*Gazetteer of Essex Co.*, p. 425-6 - *DAR Patriot Index*, p. 326)
John - b 12/9/1727 in Canterbury, CT, s/o **John**; John d1786 in Royal-
ton, Windsor Co., VT. He m 2/14/1749 **Elizabeth Pearl** of
Hampton, CT. (*History of Royalton, Vermont*, p. 820 - *DAR Patriot
Index*, p. 326)
J o h n - b1756 in Hampton, CT, s/o **J o h n**; John (the younger) d
7/18/1800 in Royalton, Windsor Co., VT. He m 3/17/1777 **Abigail
Cleveland**, b 8/6/1758 in Canterbury, CT, d/o **Samuel** and **Ruth
(Darbe)**. (*Royalton, VT*, p. 820-1)
Lovell - b 3/28/1774 in Canterbury, CT, s/o **James** and **Susannah
(Shepard)**; Lovell d 3/20/1848 in Royalton, Windsor Co., VT. He
m (1) 12/8/1793 **Lois Whitney** of Tunbridge, VT, d 10/7/1818, and

m (2) 11/29/1819 **Elizabeth Paul**, widow, d 7/2/1836, and m (3) 3/20/1839 **Eunice Parkhurst**, d 4/30/1860. (War of 1812 Index – *Hibbard Fam.*, p. 169)

HIGBY

John – b 6/5/1757 in Middletown, CT, s/o **John**; John (the younger) d 2/18/1817 in Fly Creek, NY. He m 12/21/1780 **Sarah Clinton**, bp 8/29/1760 in Green Farms, CT, d 4/18/1812 in Fly Creek, NY, d/o **John** and **Elizabeth (Beecher)**. (*Edward Higby and His Des.*, p. 169-171 – *DAR Patriot Index*, p. 327)

HIGGINS

Jehiel – b 6/19/1774 in CT, s/o **Heman** and **Eunice (Sexton)**; Jehiel d 9/1850 age 76 in Camden, Oneida Co., NY. He m (1) **R a c h e l Rebecca Hungerford**, d 2/11/1831 age 76, and m (2) **Chloe (Scoville) Kinne**, widow. (*Pioneer Hist. of Camden, NY*, p. 95-6 – *Richard Higgins and Des.*, p. 281)

Ornan – b 4/21/1788 in Chatham, CT, s/o **Moses** and **Dorcas (Brainerd)**; Ornan d 5/8/1857 age 69 in Smyrna, Chenango Co., NY. He m **Eleanor P. ----**, b in CT, d 9/3/1880 age 89 in Smyrna, NY. (*1850 Census Chenango Co. – Smyrna, NY*)

Samuel – b1743 in Killingworth, CT, d 6/30/1811 in Benson, Rutland Co., VT. Samuel m **Temperance Kelsey**, d 2/6/1831 age 73. (*Rutland Co. Gazetteer*, p. 79 – *DAR Patriot Index*, p. 327)

HIGLEY

Brewster – b 12/12/1709 in Simsbury, CT, d 3/21/1794 in Castleton, Rutland Co., VT. Brewster m (1) **Esther Holcombe**, and m (2) Mrs. **Mindwell Bull**. (*History of Rutland County, Vermont – DAR Patriot Index*, p. 328)

HILL

Caleb – b1770 in CT, d1814 in VT. Caleb m **Cynthia Strong**. (War of 1812 Index)

Charles – b 4/13/1796 in Woodbury, CT, d prob. in Rochester, Monroe Co., NY. Charles m 6/15/1823 **Salome Morgan**, b in MA. (*Hist. of Monroe Co., NY*, p. 145-6)

Uriah – b1796 in CT, s/o **Uri** and **Chloe (Hale)**; Uriah d 6/1843 age 46 in Camden, Oneida Co., NY. He m 3/1824 **Rhoda Baldwin Tibbals** of Durham, NY, d 4/5/1833 age 29. (*Pioneer History of Camden, New York*, p. 152-3)

Zimri – b1762 in Winchester, CT, d 11/1844 in Portland, Chautauqua Co., NY. Zimri m (1) **---- Hurlburt**, and m (2) **Malinda Palmer** of Ferrisburg, VT. (*Soldiers of Am. Rev., Chautauqua Co., NY*, p. 16-17 – *DAR Patriot Index*, p. 330)

HILLS

E l l i o t t – b 12/8/1774 in Lebanon, CT, d 12/17/1860 in Bennington, VT. Elliott m 3/12/1798 in VT, **Nabby Cushman**. (*Car Del Scribe* Query 7/1977, p. 32)

HILLIARD

John – b1729 in Saybrook, CT, d1793 in Danby, Rutland Co., VT. He m **Elizabeth Smith**, d1791 age 57. (*Hist. of Danby, VT*, p. 164-5 – *DAR Patriot Index*, p. 330)

Capt. **Miner** – b 4/29/1764 in Norwich, CT, s/o **John** and **Elizabeth**; Capt. Miner d1847 age 84 in Danby, Rutland Co., VT. He m (1) **Abigail Hill**, and m (2) Mrs. **Silence Story**. (*Hist. of Danby, VT*, p. 164 – *DAR Patriot Index*, p. 330)

Rev. **Samuel** – b 11/16/1747 in Stonington, CT, d 11/16/1831 in Clarendon, VT, buried in Cornish, NH. Rev. Samuel m (1) **Phebe Yerrington**, b1747, d 7/18/1798 age 52 in Cornish, NH, and m (2) **Caroline Lathrop**, b 6/1/1770, d 2/21/1845. (*Hist. of Cornish, NH*, p. 199 – *DAR Patriot Index*, p. 330)

HINCKLEY

Amasa – b 7/26/1772 in CT, s/o **Benjamin** and **Peninah (Nye)**; Amasa d 9/6/1858 in Rome, NY. He m (1) 8/23/1800 **Irene Woodward**, d1802, and m (2) **Betsey Woodward**, d 7/24/1805, and m (3) 3/27/1806 **Lucretia McDonald**. (*Hinckley Heritage and Hist.*, p. 57-8 – War of 1812 Index)

Elijah – b 3/25/1765 in Pomfret, CT, s/o **Samuel** and **Mary (Vinant)**; Elijah d 3/29/1822 in Russia, Herkimer Co., NY. He m (1) **Sally Vincent**, b1770 in Westerly, RI, d 12/1808 in Russia, NY, d/o Dr. **William**, and m (2) **Zeruiah Sarviah Vincent**, d 6/8/1847 in Russia, NY. (*Hist. of Herkimer Co.* by Hardin, p. 521-3)

Gilbert – b1778 in CT, d1843 in OH. Gilbert m **Betsey Turner**. (War of 1812 Index)

Jared – b 11/8/1759 in Lebanon, CT, d 4/12/1828 age 69 in Oxford, NY. Jared m **Hopestill Brewster**, d1849 age 89. (*Annals of Oxford, NY*, p. 544 – *DAR Patriot Index*, p. 331)

Orramel – b 2/29/1766 (or 2/29/1768) in Lebanon, CT, d 10/23/1811 in E. Thetford, VT. Orramel m **Lydia Strong**, b 11/12/1768, d 12/3/1811 age 44 in E. Thetford, VT. (Gravestones, East Thetford, Vermont)

HINE

Homer – b 7/25/1776 in New Milford, CT, s/o **Nobel**; Homer d 7/1856 age 80 in Youngstown, OH. Homer m 10/5/1807 **Mary Skinner**, d/o **Abraham** of Painesville, OH. (*Trumbull and Mahoning Counties, Ohio*, p. 211)

HINMAN

Major **Benjamin** – b1757 in Southbury, CT, d 4/7/1821 in 66th year. Major Benjamin m **Anna Keyser**, d 8/20/1863 in 95th year in Rushville, IL, d/o **John**. (*Hist. of Oneida Co., NY – Oneida, Our Country and Its People*, p. 282 – *DAR Patriot Index*, p. 331)

Edward – b1773 in CT, d1843 in OH. Edward m **Lucy Mather**. (War of 1812 Index)

Timothy – b 7/21/1762 in Southbury, CT, d 4/29/1850 in Derby, Orange Co., VT. Timothy m 12/18/1786 in Woodbury, CT, **Phebe Stoddard**, b 11/5/1769. (*DAR Mag.*, v. 71:89 – *Gazetteer Orange Co., VT – DAR Patriot Index*, p. 332)

HINSDELL
David - b 6/30/1754 in Salisbury, CT, d 11/8/1822 in Pompey, Onondaga Co., NY. David m in Lenox, MA, **Farozina Remus** (or **Bemus**). (*Pompey, NY*, p. 318 - *DAR Patriot Index*, p. 332)

HITCHCOCK
James - bc1790 in CT, d 11/27/1871 age 81-6-13 in Ludlow, VT. James m **Tamesin** ----, bc1794 in VT, d 9/27/1872 age 78-2-14. (*1850 Census of Windsor Co., VT*)

John - b 4/5/1741 in Colchester, CT, s/o **Eliakim**; John d 6/14/1813 in Pittsford, Rutland Co., VT. He mc1758 **Abigail Chapman**, b 9/3/1736 in Saybrook, CT, d 5/2/1808 in Pittsford, VT, d/o **Benjamin** and **Lydia (Streeter)**. (*Hist. of Pittsford, VT*, p. 206-7, 707 - *Hitchcock Gen.*, p. 15-16)

Willard - b 7/22/1799 in Bristol, CT, s/o **Oliver**; Willard d1842 prob. in W. Haven, VT. He m1822 **Adaline Welton**, d age 77. (*Rutland Co. Gazetteer*, p. 256)

HOWARD
Hezekiah - bc1780 in Pomfret, CT, d1859 age 79 prob. in Fair Haven, Rutland Co., VT. Hezekiah m (1) **Ruth Stanley**, d 4/24/1857 in 73rd yr., and m (2) ----, wid/o **Joseph Sheldon**. (*History of Fair Haven, Vermont*, p. 401-2)

HOADLEY
Abraham - b 11/11/1768 in Branford, CT, s/o **Isaac**; Abraham d1822 in Canaan, Wayne Co., PA. He m 10/10/1791 **Olive Price**, d/o **John**. (*Hoadley Genealogy*, p. 64-5, 114-15 - *History of Wayne Co., PA*, p. 178-9)

Calvin - b 7/2/1769 in Waterbury, CT, s/o **Lemuel** and **Urane (Mallery)**; Calvin d 7/21/1846 in Columbia, OH. He m1791 in Naugatuck, CT, **Miriam Terrell**, b 9/8/1770 in Waterbury, CT, d 5/12/1841 in Columbia, OH. (*Hoadley Genealogy*, p. 34-5 - War of 1812 Index)

Silas - bp 5/15/1757 in Branford, CT, s/o **Nathaniel** and **Anna (Scarrit)**; Silas d 10/28/1835 in Canaan, Wayne Co., PA. He m 1/6/1785 in Branford, CT, **Rachel Hoadley**, b 1/23/1764, d 5/20/1839 (in 5/30/1839) in Canaan, PA, d/o **Samuel** and **Sibyl (Jones)**. (*Hist. of Wayne Co., PA*, p. 178 - *Hoadley Gen.*, p. 30-31 - *DAR Patriot Index*, p. 333)

HOISINGTON
Joab - b 9/19/1736 in Farmington, CT, s/o **John** and **Sarah (Templar)**; Joab d 2/1/1777 prob. in Woodstock, Windsor Co., VT. He m **Mary Boardman**. (*Hist. of Woodstock, VT*, p. 17 - *DAR Patriot Index*, p. 336)

HOLBROOK
Samuel - b 12/16/1776 in Lebanon, CT, s/o **Timothy**; Samuel d 6/17/1849 in Freeport, Cumberland Co., ME. He m (1) 10/13/1811

Hannah **Webster**, d 11/7/1820, and m (2) Mrs. **Elizabeth How** of Portland, ME. (*Hist. of Cumberland Co., ME*, p. 285)

HOLCOMB

Amos – b 6/1/1732 in Simsbury, CT, s/o **Nathaniel**; Amos d in VT. He m 9/1756 **Mary Dibble**. (War of 1812 Index)

Diadorus – b1780 in CT, d1859 in NY. Diadorus m **Sybil Spaulding Wright**. (War of 1812 Index)

Joel H. – b 2/5/1761 in Granby, CT, d 6/1/1847 in LeRoy, Lake Co., OH. Joel H. m **Sarah Warner**. (*A Rec. of Rev. Soldiers Buried in Lake Co., OH*, p. 32 – *Holcombe Gen.*, p. 84)

Philo – bc1786 (or bc1787) in CT, s/o **Abraham**; Philo d 3/12/1857 in Smyrna, Chenango Co., NY. He m **Charlotte Holmes**, b1786, d 10/5/1866. (*1850 Census of Chenango Co., NY*, p. 77–78)

HOLLISTER

A m a s a – b 5/30/1768 in Glastonbury, CT, s/o **N a t h a n i e l** and **Mehitable (Mattison)**; Amasa d 3/30/1847 prob. in Salem, Wayne Co., PA. He m1790 **Mehitable Everts**, b 4/1768, d 6/26/1843. (*History of Wayne County, Pennsylvania*, p. 273 – *Hollister Fam.*, p. 87, 134/5 261–4)

Benjamin – b 2/5/1694 in Glastonbury, CT, s/o **John** and **Abiah (Hollister)**; Benjamin d near Leedsville, Dutchess Co., NY. He m **Ruth Hale**, d before 1735, d/o **Thomas** and **Naomi (Kilburn)**. (*Hist. of Dutchess Co., NY – Hollister Fam.*, p. 38, 57 – *Hale House and Related Families*, p. 24)

Hon. **H o r a c e** – b 7/4/1791 in E. Hartford, CT, d at age 76 prob. in Marshfield, Washington Co., VT. Hon. Horace m **Ruth P. Rich**, d/o Capt. **Stephen**. (*Washington Co. Gazetteer*, p. 297)

J o n a t h a n – b1745 in CT, d1837 prob. in Hinesburg, VT. Jonathan m **Mehitable** ----. (*Am. Genealogist*, v. 11, p. 124–5)

William – b 2/11/1792 in Glastonbury, CT, s/o **John** and **Mary (W e l l e s)**; William d 6/27/1873 in Hollisterville, PA. He m 3/25/1814 in Salem, PA, **Polly Jones**, b 9/26/1794 in Colchester, CT, d 9/19/1876 in Hollisterville, PA, d/o **Asa** and **Polly**. (*Hist. of Wayne Co., PA*, p. 283 – *Hollister Fam.*, p. 128, 249–50)

HOLLY

Myron – b 4/29/1779 in Salisbury, CT, s/o **Luther** and **Sally**; Myron d 3/4/1841 in Rochester, Monroe Co., NY. He m ----. The Liberty Party of the USA erected his monument as a friend of the slave and the most effective as well as one of the earliest of the founders of the party. (Tombstone Records – Mt. Hope Cem. – *Hist. of Monroe Co.*, p. 30, 41, 42, 83, 158)

HOLT

Erastus – b 9/8/1778 in Mansfield, CT, s/o **Paul** and **Sarah (Welch)**; Erastus d 3/28/1875 in Rutland Co., VT. He m **Sally Parmenter**, bc1782 in MA. (1812 War Index – *1850 Rutland Co., VT, Census* – *Rutland Co. Gazetteer*, p. 177)

John - bc1792 in CT, d 10/31/1853 age 61 in Sherbourne, Chenango Co., NY. John m **Abigail** ----, b1791 in NH, d 5/13/1858 age 66-11 in Sherburne, NY. (*1850 Census Chenango Co., NY*)

HOOKER

David - b 7/9/1771 in CT, d 8/6/1847 in Ridgeway, Orleans Co., NY. David m (1) 1795 **Betsey Saunders**, d 3/1813, and m (2) 2/1814 **Polly Pixley**. (*Pioneer Hist. of Orleans Co., NY*, p. 340)

Horace C. - b 8/3/1797 in Stafford, CT, s/o **Oliver**; Horace C. d 6/20/1877 age 83 prob. in Otsego Co., NY. He m **Sophia Anderson**, b 12/25/1802 in Mansfield, CT, d/o **Lemuel**. (*Biog. Rec. of Otsego Co., NY*, p. 273)

HOPKINS

Ebenezer - b 6/24/1699 in Hartford, CT, s/o **Ebenezer** and **Mary (Butler)**; Ebenezer dc1784 in Shaftsbury, VT. He m 6/7/1727 in Hartford, CT, **Susannah Messenger**, b 11/30/1704 in Wallingford, CT, d/o Capt. **Daniel** and **Lydia (Royce)**. (*Hist. of Pittsford, VT*, p. 32-3, 708 - *DAR Patriot Index*, p. 342)

Capt. Frederick - bc1768 in Derby, CT, d 6/23/1855 age 87 prob. in Oxford, Chenango Co., NY. Capt. Frederick m (1) ---- Pickett, and m (2) **Susan Smith**, bc1780, d 6/16/1858 age 78. (*Annals of Oxford, NY*, p. 476-7 - *1850 Census of Chenango Co., NY*)

Col. Hezekiah - b 2/20/1758 in Harwinton, CT, poss. s/o **Hezekiah** and **Sarah (Davis)**; Col. Hezekiah d 5/18/1834 in Pompey Hill, NY. He m 6/1783 **Eunice Hubbell**, b 12/21/1762, d 9/2/1839 in Pompey Hill, NY, d/o **Richard** of Newtown, CT. (*Pompey, NY*, p. 321 - *DAR Patriot Index*, p. 342)

Nehemiah - b 4/14/1730 in Harwinton, CT, s/o **Ebenezer** and **Susanna (Messenger)**; Nehemiah dc1814 in Crown Point, NY. He m **Tryphena Smith**, d1803 in Pittsford, VT. (*Hist. of Pittsford, VT*, p. 62, 221 - *DAR Patriot Index*, p. 342)

Samuel Miles - b 5/9/1772 in Waterbury, CT, d 10/8/1837 in Geneva, NY. Samuel Miles m 10/5/1800 **Sarah Elizabeth Rogers** of NY city, b 2/1/1778, d 12/17/1866. (*Annals of Oxford, Chenango County, NY*, p. 82-7)

HOPSON

John Collins - b 5/3/1769 in Wallingford, CT, s/o **Samuel, Jr.** and **Mamre (Hall)**; John Collins dc1856 age 87 in Wells, Rutland Co., VT. He m (1) **Persis Swift**, d 11/27/1811 age 40 in Wells, VT, and m (2) **Bethiah Lewis**, widow, d 6/4/1840 age 61 in Wells, VT. (*Hist. of Wells* by Parks, p. 103-5 - *Hist. of Wells* by Wood, p. 59-60 - *1850 Rutland, VT, Census*)

HORR

John - b 7/21/1765 in Ashford, CT, s/o **Elijah**; John d 2/3/1827 in Pomfret, VT. He m 9/7/1786 in Pomfret, VT, **Theodosia Durkee**, d 5/2/1827, d/o Capt. **Bartholomew**. (*Pomfret, VT*, v. 2, p. 515)

HORTON

Major **Gideon, Sr.** - bc1769 in Colebrook, CT, d 10/2/1842 age 73 in Hubbardton, Rutland Co., VT. He m **Thyrsa Farrington** of Brandon, VT. (*Hist. of Rutland Co.*, p. 625)

Horace - b 12/29/1793 in Glastonbury, CT, s/o **Sampson** and **Lucy (Phelps)**; Horace d1883 in IL. He m **Clarissa Stevens.** (War of 1812 Index)

Joel - b 1/6/1784 in Wolcott, CT, s/o **Elisha** and **Ruth (Bishop)**; Joel d 4/17/1872 in Trumansburg, NY. He m 3/10/1815 in Covert, NY, **Abigail Pratt**, b 9/5/1793 in Sandisfield, MA, d 7/1/1882 in Trumansburg, NY, d/o **Justin** and **Sarah (Herbert)**. (*Portrait and Biog. Record of Seneca and Schuyler Co., NY*, p. 389 - *Des. of Thomas Horton*, p. 57)

Solomon - b 10/20/1787 in Ashford, CT, d1864 in WI. Solomon m (1) in VT, **Philena Peters**, and m (2) in Erie Co., PA, **Elizabeth ----**. (*Nutmegger* Query June 1981, p. 59)

HOSFORD

Aaron - b 12/25/1747 in Hebron, CT, s/o **Joseph**; Aaron d 7/9/1818 age 70 in N. Thetford, Orange Co., VT. He m 2/2/1769 in Chatham, CT, **Lucy Strong**, d 4/5/1818 age 69. (*Gazetteer of Orange Co., VT*, p. 430 - *DAR Patriot Index*, p. 344)

Lt. **Elihu** - b 6/25/1749 in Hebron, CT, s/o **Joseph**; Lt. Elihu d 2/28/1810 age 61 in E. Thetford, VT (gravestone). He m (1) 4/3/1770 in Hebron, CT, **Abigail Chamberlain**, d 2/15/1785 in 33rd year, and m (2) **Mary ----**, d 11/22/1820 age 60. (*Gazetteer of Orange Co., VT*, p. 430)

Joseph - b 6/21/1743 in Hebron, CT, s/o **Joseph**; Joseph (the younger) d 11/3/1819 age 76 in E. Thetford, Orange Co., VT. He m 9/27/1764 in Hebron, CT, **Mary Peters**, b 1/19/1743 (or 1/19/1744) in Hebron CT, d 8/30/1826 age 82, d/o **John**. (*Gazetteer of Orange Co., VT*, p. 430)

Obadiah - b 3/27/1756 in Hebron, CT, s/o **Joseph** and **Eunice**; Obadiah d 11/15/1822 age 67 in N. Thetford, Orange Co. VT. He m 6/20/1779 **Abigail Carrier**, b 12/13/1760 in Hebron, CT, d 11/27/1840 age 80 in E. Thetford, VT. (*Gazetteer of Orange County, VT*, p. 430)

HOSMER

John B. - b 11/20/1787 in Mansfield, Windham Co., CT, d 7/2/1854 in Sardinia, NY. John B. m 6/9/1809 **Lura Abbe**, b 1/30/1791 in Chatham, CT, d in Racine, WI. (*History of Original Town of Concord, NY*, p. 863-4)

Sherman - b 9/20/1786 in Canaan, CT, s/o **Thomas** and **Hannah**; Sherman d1877 in NY. He m **Fanny Slack.** (War of 1812 Index)

HOTCHKISS

Eber - b1788 in Guilford, CT, s/o **Eber** and **Leah (Page)**; Eber (the younger) d 6/1837 in Oakland Twp, Oakland Co., MI. He m1813 **Rhoda Morrill**, b 6/9/1792 in Danville, VT, d/o **Abraham** and **Sarah (Hoyt)**. (*DSGR* Spring 1972, p. 124 - War of 1812 Index)

Freeman – b 10/17/1799 in Litchfield, CT, d 4/23/1888 in Marshall, Calhoun Co., MI. Freeman m 1/19/1825 **Lydia Tompkins,** d 4/13/1869. (*Pioneer Collections of MI*, v. 13, p. 157-8)

Hon. **Roswell** – b 7/24/1762 in Cheshire, CT, s/o **Joseph**; Hon. Roswell d 12/28/1845 in Harpersfield, Delaware Co., NY. He m1785 **Margaret Harper,** d/o Col. **John.** (*Hist. of Delaware Co.*, p. 229 – *DAR Patriot Index*, p. 345)

Dr. **Socrates** – b 5/4/1774 in Cheshire, CT, d 2/27/1810 age 36 in Wells, Rutland Co., VT. He m (1) 12/1/1796 in Wells, VT, **Bethiah Lathrop,** bc1779, d 6/24/1803 age 24, d/o **Samuel,** and m (2) **Mary Ann Doolittle.** (*Hist. of Wells, VT* by Paul, p. 105-6 – *Hist. of Wells* by Wood, p. 60)

HOUGH

David – b 3/13/1753 in Norwich, CT, s/o **David** and **Desire (Clark);** David (the younger) d1828 in NH. He m **Abigail Huntington.** (War of 1812 Index – *DAR Patriot Index*, p. 345)

Matthew – b 3/1/1763 in Meriden, CT, d1813 in Turin, Lewis Co., NY. He m (1) **Martha Cowles,** and m (2) **Mrs. Barnes Woodruff.** (*NEGR* Query Oct. 1960, p. 321)

HOUSE

H a r r y – b 11/6/1787 in Hartford, CT, d prob. in Concord, Erie Co., NY. Harry m **Annie Martinsdale.** (*Hist. of Original Town of Concord, NY*, p. 866-7)

Israel – bc1758 in CT, s/o **William;** Israel d 1/21/1831 age 73 in Berlin, Washington Co., VT. He m (1) 4/23/1780 in Glastonbury, CT, **Abigail Hubbard,** bc1758, d 4/18/1811 age 53 in Berlin, VT, d/o **Eleazer** and **Abigail (Hollister),** and m (2) 2/1812 **Hannah Work,** d/o Lt. **Joseph** and **Betty (Hayward),** b 7/23/1774 in Ashford, CT. (*Hale, House and Related Families*, p. 353-4)

HOVEY

Alvan – b 3/3/1779 in Lyme, CT, s/o Elder **Samuel** and **Abigail (Cleveland);** Alvan d 1/29/1864 in E. Brookfield, Orange Co., VT. He m (1) 4/3/1803 in Brookfield, VT, **Nancy Seabury,** b 8/8/1780 in CT, d 11/27/1856 in E. Brookfield, VT, d/o **Benjamin** and **Lucretia (Kingsbury),** and m (2) 10/12/1857 in Brookfield, VT, Mrs. Nancy **B e a n** (his cousin), b 3/8/1791 in Brookfield, VT. (*Hovey Book*, p. 158 – *1850 Orange Co., VT, Census*)

D a n i e l – b 7/24/1764 in Windham, CT, d 3/2/1850 age 85 in Lyme, NH. Daniel m 2/18/1789 **Beulah Pingree,** b 2/1/1769 in Coventry, CT, d 11/26/1857 age 88 in Lyme, NH, d/o **Sylvanus** and **Mary (Sawyer).** (*The Hovey Book*, p. 218 – *DAR Patriot Index*, p. 346)

Rufus – b 8/29/1770 in Canterbury, CT, s/o Elder **Samuel;** Rufus d 7/5/1817 in Brookfield, VT. He m 7/17/1794 in Lyme, NH, **Grace Billings,** b 11/22/1777 in New London, CT, d 7/29/1819 age 41 in Brookfield, VT. (*The Hovey Book*, p. 224-5, 280-5)

Elder **Samuel** – bc1780 in Windham, CT, d 5/12/1833 age 90-2 in E. Brookfield, Orange Co., VT. Elder Samuel m 12/29/1764 in Windham, CT, **Abigail Cleveland,** b 8/13/1746 in Canterbury, CT, d

6/2/1832 in 84th year in E. Brookfield, VT, d/o **Benjamin** and **Rachel (Hall)**. (*Hovey Book*, p. 154-161)

HOWARD

Abijah - b1750 in CT, d 5/6/1818 in Thetford, VT (fell through mill floor). Abijah m 3/6/1783 **Priscilla Cushman**, d 8/31/1823 age 74. (*Gazetteer of Orange County, Vermont*, p. 432-3 - *DAR Patriot Index*, p. 347)

Capt. Elijah - b 6/4/1765 in Hebron, CT, s/o **Isaiah** and **Hannah**; Capt. Elijah d 9/23/1815 in E. Thetford, Orange Co., VT. He m **Mary ----**, d 2/3/1845 in E. Thetford, VT. (*Gazetteer of Orange Co., VT*, p. 431)

William - b 8/2/1753 in Pomfret, CT, s/o **John**; William d 3/1/1834 in Royalton, Windsor Co., VT. He m 12/29/1774 **M a r y D a n a**, b 5/11/1751 in Pomfret, CT, d 3/1/1834 in Royalton, VT, d/o **Samuel, Jr.** and **Sarah (Holdrich)**. (*History of Royalton, Vermont*, p. 823-4)

Zebedee - bc1734 in Hebron, CT, d 1/22/1800 age 66 in E. Thetford, Orange Co., VT. Zebedee m **Mercy Mann**, b 9/7/1736, d/o **Joseph** and **Mercy**. (*Mann Memorial*, p. 87 - *Gazetteer of Orange County, Vermont*, p. 431)

Zephaniah - b1788 in CT, d1847 in NY. Zephaniah m **Olive Smith**. (War of 1812 Index)

HOWE

Joseph - b1777 in CT, d1862 in NY. Joseph m **Amy Reed**. (War of 1812 Index)

Joshua - b 9/14/1731 in Wallingford, CT, s/o **Joshua** and **Elizabeth (Judd)**; Joshua d 1/25/1800 age 70 in Wells, VT. He m 10/14/1756 **Miriam Blakeslee**. She m (2) **Matthias Button**. (*Hist. of Wells, VT* by Paul, p. 106-7 - *DAR Patriot Index*, p. 348)

Squire - b 11/2/1752 in Plainfield, CT, s/o **Jonas**; Squire d 2/6/1834 in Barnston, Canada. He m **P h e b e P i e r c e**, b1760, d1848 in Barnston, Canada, d/o **Nathaniel** and **Priscilla (Shepard)**. (*Royalton, VT*, p. 224)

HOYT

Aaron - b1778 in CT, d1847 in NY. Aaron m **Sophia Brooks**. (War of 1812 Index)

David - bc1756 in Ridgefield, CT, s/o **David**; David (the younger) d 5/21/1804 age 48 in Fairfield, Franklin Co., VT. He m **Ellen ----**, d 3/20/1812 age 50. She m (2) **John Andrews**. (*Some Early Rec. of Fairfield, VT*, p. 15)

Noah - b 11/3/1753 in CT, d 12/23/1827 in NY. Noah m (1) **Jerusha Abbott**, and m (2) **Mary Seeley**. (War of 1812 Index)

HUBBARD

Capt. George - b 2/12/1765 in Tolland, CT, d 7/2/1839 age 76 in Lebanon, NH. Capt. George m **Mehetable Tyler**. (*DAR Mag.*, v. 43, p. 403 - *DAR Patriot Index*, p. 351)

Col. Josiah - b 9/13/1758 in Middletown, CT, s/o **Hezekiah** and **Ruth (Center)**; Col. Josiah d 7/13/1833 age 75 in Thetford, Orange Co.,

VT. He m **Mary Hovey**, b 9/24/1755, d 3/15/1846, age 91, d/o **Edmond**. (*Gazetteer of Orange County, Vermont*, p. 435 - *DAR Patriot Index*, p. 351)

Noadiah - b 10/11/1765 in Middletown, CT, s/o **Noadiah** and **Phebe (Crowel)**; Noadiah d1859 in NY. He m **Eunice Ward**. (War of 1812 Index)

Perez - b1802 in Glastonbury, CT, d prob. in Bristol, VT. Perez m (1) **Cornelia Felt**, and m (2) **Mehitable** ----. (*One Thousand Years of Hubbard History*, p. 221)

Solomon - b 5/9/1788 in Haddam, CT, s/o **Giles**; Solomon d1864 in New London, OH. He m 1810 in Livingston Co., NY, ----. (*Residents of CT Who Migrated to Huron Co., NY*, p. 3)

Capt. **Timothy** - b 8/17/1776 in Windsor, CT, d 8/28/1850 in Montpelier, Washington Co., VT. Capt. Timothy m (1) 1801 **Lucy Davis**, d1839, d/o Col. **Jacob**. (*Hist. of Montpelier, VT*, p. 228-231 - *Washington Co., VT, Gazetteer*)

William - b 7/24/1787 in Hamden, CT, s/o **John**; William d1863 in OH. He m **Katherine Hurlburt**. (War of 1812 Index)

HUBBEL

Vernon - b1788 in CT, d1870 in MI. Vernon m **Lucy Deake** (or **Dake**). (War of 1812 Index)

HUBBELL

Elijah - bc1771 in Danbury, CT, s/o **Parnach** (or **Andrew**); Elijah d 2/1847 age 76 in Otsego Co., NY. He m **Hannah Fields** of MA, bc1764, d 3/20/1837 age 73. (*Biog. Rec. of Otsego Co., NY - Hist. of Hubbell Fam.*, p. 248, 329)

HUBBLE

Addison - b 1/18/1795 in Danbury, CT, s/o **Elijah** and **Hannah**; Addison d in Westville, Otsego Co., NY. He m (1) **Nancy Green**, and m (2) Mrs. **Elizabeth Stowell**. (*Hist. of Hubbell Fam.*, p. 248, 329 - *Biog. Rec. of Otsego Co., NY*, p. 578)

HUDSON

Eli - b 11/17/1774 in Southington, CT, d 4/18/1821 in Pittsford, Rutland Co., VT. Eli m 12/6/1798 **Eunice Chase**, b 3/16/1776, d1844, d/o **Isaac**. (*Hist. of Pittsford, VT*, p. 293, 709)

James Ogden - b 11/4/1794 in Haddam, CT, s/o **Lot**; James Ogden d 4/12/1869 in Braintree, Orange Co., VT. He m (1) **Asenath Hildreth** of Roxbury, b 3/23/1797 in NH, d 9/26/1865, and m (2) **Abiah (Trask) Pratt**. (*Hist. of Braintree, VT*, p. 152-3 - *1850 Orange Co., VT, Census*)

HULBERT

John - b 1/29/1735 in CT, d 6/7/1815 in MA. John m **Mercy Hamlin**. (*DAR Patriot Index*, p. 358 - War of 1812 Index)

HULETT

Daniel - b 5/11/1748 in Killingly, CT, d 8/27/1838 in Paulet, Rutland Co., VT. Daniel m **Abigail Paul**. (*Hist. of Rutland Co., VT*, p. 705 - *DAR Patriot Index*, p. 353)

HULL

Daniel, Jr. - b1766 in CT, d1842 in NY. Daniel, Jr. m **Phebe Green**. (*DAR Patriot Index*, p. 353 - War of 1812 Index)

Ebenezer - b1776 in CT, s/o **John** and **Martha (Pardee)**; Ebenezer d 7/24/1849 age 73 in Oxford, Chenango Co., NY. He m 1/2/1803 in No. Haven, CT, **Bedee Jacobs**, d 2/24/1844 age 64. (*Annals of Oxford, NY*, p. 134-5)

John - b 4/21/1771 in CT, s/o **John** and **Martha (Pardee)**; John (the younger) d 9/4/1864 in Oxford, Chenango Co., NY. He m 7/2/1797 **Hannah Wood**, b 5/14/1778, d 1/16/1845. (*Annals of Oxford, New York*, p. 133)

William - b 6/24/1753 in Derby, CT, s/o **Joseph, Jr.** and Mrs. **Elizabeth (Clark)**; William d 11/29/1825 in MA. He m **Sarah Fuller**. (*DAR Patriot Index*, p. 354 - War of 1812 Index)

Zephaniah - b1763 in Cheshire, CT, d 3/22/1841 prob. in Wallingford, Rutland Co., VT. Zephaniah m **Rachel Gilbert**. (*Rutland Co. Gazetteer*, p. 256-7 - *DAR Patriot Index*, p. 354)

HUMPHREY

Allen - b1773 (or b1777) in CT, d1825 in OH. Allen m **Polly Bodwell**. (War of 1812 Index)

Decius - b1789 in CT, d1873 in IA. Decius m **Laura Adams**. (War of 1812 Index)

George - bc1804 in Canton, CT, s/o **George**; George (the younger) d 8/13/1883 in 79th year in Smyrna, Chenango Co., NY. He m (1) ---- **Mills**, d1839, and m (2) 10/1839 **Louise M. Webb**. (*Smyrna by Munson*, p. 103-4)

Thomas - b 2/22/1791 in CT, s/o **Ephraim**; Thomas d age 81 years in St. Johnsbury, Caledonia Co., VT. He m **Susannah Olmstead**, b 5/14/1791, d 7/21/1883 age 92. (*Caledonia, VT, Gazetteer*, p. 326)

HUNGERFORD

Abner G. - b 2/21/1805 in New Milford, CT, d 10/4/1892 in Dutchess Co., NY. Abner G. m 5/7/1828 **Maria Sabin**, b 6/10/1803, d 12/9/1888, d/o **Jeptha** and **Anna (Starr)**. (*Comm. Biog. Rec. - Dutchess Co., NY*, p. 444)

Elijah Hurlburt - b1790 in CT, d 10/17/1857 in Highgate, VT. Elijah Hurlburt m (1) **Anna Skeels**, d 7/19/1821 age 39, and m (2) **Sarah Ann Skeels**, b1797, d1873 in Evanston, IL, buried in Highgate, VT. (*Thomas Hungerford of Hartford, CT, and LI, NY*, p. 20-1)

Simeon - b1766 in New Fairfield, CT, s/o **Samuel**; Simeon d 10/7/1819 in 53rd year in Swanton, VT. He m **Elizabeth Birchard**, d 7/28/1827 age 57. (*Thomas Hungerford of Hartford, CT, and LI, NY*, p. 17)

HUNT

Daniel – b CT 8/17/1708 s/o **Ebenezer** and **Hannah (Clark)**; Daniel d 10/1/1808 age 99 at Tunbridge, Orange Co., VT. He m **Hannah** ----, d 4/18/1829 age 87. (*Hunt Families of Tunbridge, VT*)

James – bc1781 in CT, prob. s/o **Daniel, Jr.**; James d 2/20/1862 in Tunbridge, Orange Co., VT, buried in Hunt Cemetery. He m **Betsey Brigham**, bc1790 in NH, d 9/11/1870 age 80. (*1850 Orange County, VT, Census*)

Deacon **Simeon** – b 12/20/1762 in CT, s/o **Daniel** and **Hannah**; Deacon Simeon d 10/14/1852 age 89-10 in Tunbridge, Orange Co., VT, buried in Hunt Cemetery. He m (1) 1/30/1793 in Sandersfield, MA, **Ruth Cowdry**, b 1/22/1773, d 11/25/1815 in Tunbridge, VT, and m (2) 3/17/1816 in Tunbridge, VT, **Elizabeth Folsom**, bc1781, d 11/17/1864 (or 11/19/1864) in Tunbridge, VT, d/o **Abraham** and **Elizabeth**. (*Hunt Fam. of Tunbridge*, p. 6-8 – *1850 Orange County, VT, Census*)

HUNTER

John – b1784 in CT, d1850 in NY. John m **Susanna** ----. (War of 1812 Index)

HUNTINGTON

Chandler – b1778 in CT, d1845 in Indiana. Chandler m **Anna Wallace**. (War of 1812 Index)

Rev. **Elijah** – b 8/21/1763 in Mansfield, CT, s/o **Christopher** and **Mary (Dimmock)**; Rev. Elijah d 6/24/1828 in Braintree, Orange Co., VT. He m (1) 12/1792 **Sally Field** of Tunbridge, VT, d 11/1794, and m (2) 6/9/1801 (or 6/9/1807) **Lydia Parmly**, b 8/6/1779 in Newtown, CT, d 5/27/1851 age 71. (*Hist. of Braintree, VT*, p. 51, 153 – *Huntington Family Memoir*, p. 156-7)

James – b 4/25/1728 in Lebanon, CT, s/o **Caleb** and **Lydia (Griswold)**; James d 12/10/1812 in Orange, Orange Co., VT. He m **Hannah Marsh**, d1795 in Norwich, VT, d/o **Jonathan**. (*Huntington Gen.*, p. 801)

Joseph Clark – b 10/3/1798 in Mansfield, CT, d 12/6/1852 in Chicago, IL. Joseph Clark m **Julia A. Warner**, b 12/24/1804, d/o **Levi**. (*Huntington Gen.*, p. 801)

Miller – b 8/15/1770 in Norwich, CT, s/o **William** and **Anne (Pride)**; Miller d 1859 in Randolph, VT. He m **Betsey Miller**, bc1774 in CT. (*1850 Orange Co., VT, Census*)

Samuel – bc1765 in Norwich, CT, d 2/1817 in Painesville, OH. Samuel m1793 ----, d/o **Andrew Huntington** of Norwich, CT. (*Trumbull and Mahoning Cos., OH*, p. 210)

Solon – b 1/15/1812 in Harwinton, CT, s/o **William**; Solon d 8/11/1890 in Oneonta, NY. He m 6/2/1840 **Harriet Saunders** of NY. (*Biog. Rev. of Otsego Co., NY*, p. 588)

Whitman – b 7/12/1763 in Windham, CT, d 11/3/1847 in New Haven, Addison Co., VT. Whitman m 2/16/1787 in Mansfield, CT, **Susan Clark**, b 8/24/1768 in Mansfield, CT, d 3/4/1837 in New Haven, VT. (*Huntington Gen.*, p. 799-800)

William - b 5/26/1775 in Lebanon, CT, d 11/3/1826 in Washington, Orange Co., VT. William m **Elizabeth Derby**, b 10/22/1778. (*Gazetteer of Orange Co., VT*, p. 503 - *Huntington Gen.*, p. 809)

HUNTLEY

Seth - b 5/1/1779 in Lyme, CT, s/o **Elihu** and **Naomi**; Seth d1856 in IA. He m ----. (War of 1812 Index)

HURD

James - bc1768 in Woodbury, CT, d prob. in Sandgate, Bennington Co., VT. James m **Betsey** ----, bc1776 in NY. (According to the 1850 Bennington Co. Census, he was 82 and she was 74.)

Justus - b 4/2/1722 in Killingworth, CT, s/o **Robert** and **Elizabeth**; Justus d 3/31/1804 poss. in Gilsum, NH. He m 5/20/1746 in Killingworth, CT, **Rachel Fuller**. (*Town of Gilsum, NH*, p. 338-341)

Capt. Lewis - b 5/26/1759 in Roxbury, CT, d 12/18/1848 age 90 prob. in Sandgate, VT. Capt. Lewis m **Catherine Sanford**. (*VT Hist. Magazine*, v. 1, p. 230 - *DAR Patriot Index*, p. 357 - *Bennington County Gazetteer*)

Zera - b1789 in CT, d1866 in IL. Zera m **Abigail Gilbert**. (War of 1812 Index)

HURLBURT

Jehiel - b 1762 (?) in Middletown, CT; d1813 in OH. Jehiel m **Sibyl Martindale**. (War of 1812 Index)

Robert W. - b 3/22/1783 in Roxbury, CT, d1876 in Clarksfield, OH. Robert W. m (1) ----, b1785, d1818, and m (2) ---- **Croxford** (widow). (*Residents of CT Who Migrated to Huron Co., OH*)

HURLBUT

Elisha - b 6/3/1760 in Canaan, CT, d (drowned) 5/29/1824 age 64 in Middlebury, VT. Elisha m (1) **Hannah Landon**, b 4/29/1761, d 2/16/1804 in Cornwall, VT, and m (2) **Hannah** ----, d 6/27/1867 age 89 in Cornwall, VT. (*Hist. of Cornwall, VT*, p. 59-60, 286 - *DAR Patriot Index*, p. 358)

Salmon - b 5/19/1710 in Woodbury, CT, d 6/13/1789 in Charlotte, VT. Salmon m **Abigail Hickok**, b 12/11/1714 in Woodbury, CT, d 3/4/1800 in Charlotte, VT, d/o **Samuel** and **Ellen**. (*Nutmegger* Query June 1981, p. 62)

HUSTEAD

Samuel - b1779 in Danbury, CT, s/o **Andrew**; Samuel d1863 in Clarksfield, OH. He m (1) 11/25/1799 **Esther Wildman**, b1779 in Danbury, CT, d1842, d/o **Samuel**, and m (2) **Fanny Barnum Husted**, wid/o **Platt**, d1863. (*Residents of CT Who Migrated to Huron County, OH*, p. 3)

HUTCHINS

Francis - b 9/16/1826 in Litchfield, CT, d prob. in Warren, OH. Francis m 12/11/1851 **Elizabeth M. Sanderson**. (*Trumbull and Mahoning Cos., OH*, p. 198)

116

HUTCHINSON

Rev. **Aaron** - b 3/1722 in Hebron, CT, s/o **Jonathan** (or **Aaron**); Rev. Aaron d 9/27/1800 in Pomfret, VT. He mc1750 **Margery Carter** of Hebron, CT, d 8/8/1818 age 90. (*Vermont Antiquarian*, p. 24 - *A Biographical Sketch of Rev. Aaron Hutchinson of Pomfret-Hebron*)

Abijah - b 7/4/1756 in Lebanon, CT, d 2/11/1843 in Tunbridge, VT. Abijah m **Miriam Farnum**, d 5/4/1815 age 54 in Tunbridge, VT. (*On the Beginnings of Tunbridge - DAR Patriot Index*, p. 359)

Rev. **Elisha** - b 12/22/1749 in Sharon, CT, s/o **Samuel**; Rev. Elisha d 4/19/1833 in Newport, NH. He m (1) 7/16/1778 in Westford, CT, **Jerusha Cadwell**, and m (2) **Martha Eddy**, d/o **Samuel** of Washington, NY. (*Pomfret, VT*, v. 2, p. 520)

Hezekiah - b 10/6/1752 in Lebanon, CT, s/o **Timothy** and **Mercy** (**Samson**); Hezekiah d prob. in Tunbridge, VT. He m (1) perhaps **Phebe Farnham**, d 11/26/1819 age 68, and m (2) **Susan** ----, bc1766 in CT. At the time of the 1850 census, he was 97, Susan was 84; his children: Amos was 67, and Jerusha was 69. (*1850 Orange Co., VT, Census-Tunbridge*)

Jerome - b 3/2/1763 in Ashford, CT, s/o **John** and Mary (**Wilson**); Jerome d1849 in Norwich, Windsor Co., VT. He m **Content Smith**. (*Hist. of Norwich, VT*, p. 215-16)

John - b1741 in Ashford, CT, s/o **Samuel**; John d 6/22/1778 in Philadelphia, PA. He m **Mary Wilson**, b 8/1744 in Ashford, CT. She m (2) **Solomon Story**. (*A History of Norwich, Vermont*, p. 25-6, 214-217)

Samuel - b 9/6/1751 in CT, s/o **Samuel**; Samuel (the younger) d 10/1/1839 prob. in Norwich, Windsor Co., VT. He m 8/16/1779 **Hannah Burr**, b 3/5/1761. (*Hist. of Norwich, VT*, p. 215 - *DAR Patriot Index*, p. 359)

Zenas - b 11/21/1770 in Lebanon, CT, s/o **Paul** and **Susanna** (**Sprague**); Zenas d1854 in NY. He m **Fannie Tyler Smith**. (War of 1812 Index)

HYDE

Judge **Austin** - b 1/21/1789 in Franklin, CT, d 2/25/1850 poss. in Oxford, NY. He m 10/1818 **Elizabeth Mygatt**, b 6/2/1799, d/o **Noadiah** and **Clarissa** (**Lynes**) of New Milford, CT. (*Hist. of Chenango Co., NY*, p. 262)

Daniel - b 9/11/1782 in Lebanon, CT, d poss. in Bainbridge, NY. Daniel m 10/28/1828 **Clarissa Graham**, b 12/27/1786 in Sharon, CT, d/o **James** and **Eunice** (**Guthrie**). (*History of Chenango County, New York*, p. 166)

Jacob - b 8/1/1730 in Norwich, CT, d 2/1815 in N. Hero, VT. Jacob m **Hannah Hazen**. (*Franklin Co., VT, Gazetteer*, p. 129 - *DAR Patriot Index*, p. 360)

Capt. **Jedediah** - b 8/24/1738 in Norwich, CT, s/o Rev. **Jedediah** and **Jerusha** (**Perkins**); Capt. Jedediah d 5/29/1822 age 84 in Hyde Park, Lamoille Co., VT. He m (1) 1/28/1761 **Mary Waterman**, d 9/2/1780, and m (2) 1781 **Elizabeth** (**Brown**) **Parker**, b1751 in Stonington, CT, d 11/28/1825, d/o **Humphrey Brown**, wid/o **David Parker**. (*Vermont Hist. Magazine*, v. 2, p. 635 - *DAR Patriot Index*, p. 360)

Pitt W. - b 12/29/1776 in Norwich, CT, s/o Capt. **Jedediah;** Pitt W. d 5/29/1823 prob. in Sudbury, Rutland Co., VT. He m 10/19/1796 **Mary Kilbourne** of Litchfield, CT. (*History of Rutland County, Vermont*, p. 817)

Septy - bc1785 in CT, d prob. in Tunbridge, VT. Septy m **Mary** ----, bc1795 in CT, d prob. in Tunbridge, VT. In the 1850 Census, Septy was 65 and Mary was 55. (*1850 Orange Co. Census-Tunbridge, VT*)

Thomas - bc1773 in CT, d prob. in Sudbury, Rutland Co., VT. Thomas m **Clarissa** ----, bc1779 in CT, d prob. in Sudbury, Rutland Co., VT. In the 1850 census Thomas was 77 and Clarissa was 71. (*1850 Rutland Co., VT, Census*)

William - bc1776 in CT, d prob. in Randolph, Orange Co., VT. William m **Sarah** ----, bc1780 in MA, d prob. in Randolph, Orange Co., VT. In the 1850 census William was 74 and Sarah was 70. (*1850 Census Orange Co., VT*)

INGALLS

Edmund - b 9/7/1770 in CT, s/o **Ephraim** and **Mary (Sharp);** Edmund d 11/25/1850 age 80 in Cavendish, VT. He m **Dorantha** ----, bc1775 in MA. (Mt. Union Cem. - *1850 Windsor Co., VT, Census*)

Simeon - b 5/28/1754 in Pomfret, CT, s/o **Ephraim** and **Mary (Sharpe);** Simeon d 5/23/1827 in Hartwick, NY. He m (1) 8/27/1781 **Olive Grosvenor**, b 5/12/1760, d 4/17/1782, d/o **Joshua**, and m (2) 1/10/1786 **Eunice Wheeler**, b 11/1/1756, d 10/5/1807, d/o **Benjamin**, and m (3) 3/8/1808 **Rachel Harris**. (*Ingalls Gen.*, p. 120-1 - *DAR Patriot Index*, p. 361 - *Biog. Review of Otsego Co., New York*, p. 151)

Waldo - bc1799 in Pomfret, CT, s/o **Harvey** and **Ella (Ford);** Waldo d prob. in Brookfield, Orange Co., VT. He m **Minerva** ----, bc1802 in VT. In 1850 census Waldo was 51, Minerva was 48, and Ella, her mother, b in CT, age 75. (*1850 Orange Co., VT, Census*)

INGHAM

Alexander, 3rd - b 4/26/1788 in CT, s/o **Alexander, Jr.** and **Polly (Chester);** Alexander 3rd d 4/6/1870 in Brooklyn, OH. He m 8/20/1808 **Lydia Fish** of Groton, CT, b 12/5/1784, d 1/15/1869 in Brooklyn, OH. (*Joseph Ingham and His Des. 1639-1948*, p. 8)

Alexander, Jr. - b 12/16/1764 in Hebron, CT, s/o **Alexander** and **Catherine (Trumbull);** Alexander, Jr. d 12/10/1858 age 94 in Brooklyn, OH. He m 11/23/1789 **Polly Chester** of Groton, CT, b 1/5/1761, d 7/19/1830. (*Joseph Ingham and His Des.*, p. 8)

David - b 4/15/1756 in Saybrook, CT, s/o **Ebenezer, II;** David d 7/8/1839 in Farmington, Franklin Co., ME. He m (1) 4/27/1782 **Mary Larabee**, d 1/5/1792, and (2) 4/18/1797 **Rebecca Butterfield**, d 11/17/1848. (*Joseph Ingham and His Des.*, p. 15)

INGRAHAM

Samuel - b 4/2/1754 in Hebron, CT, d 8/18/1834 age 80 in Cornwall, Addison Co., VT. Samuel m **Sarah Lewis**, d 4/6/1816 age 56 in Cornwall, VT. (*Hist. of Cornwall, VT*, p. 52, 287)

Simeon - bc1775 in CT, d prob. in Thetford, Orange Co., VT. Simeon m **Mehitabel** ----, bc1777 in RI. In the 1850 census, Simeon was

75, Mehitabel was 73, and son, David was 32. (*1850 Orange Co. Census-Thetford, VT*)

ISBELL

Eli – bc1759 in CT, d 1/26/1797, buried in Potter Cem., south of E. Galway, NY. Eli m ----. (*DAR Mag.* 1977, p. 918)

Seymour – bc1780 in CT, s/o **Peruda** and **Mercy (Hurlburt)**; Seymour d 10/12/1860 in Smyrna, NY. He m **Lois Nearing**, b 10/30/1782 in Newbury, CT, d 1/30/1863 in Smyrna, NY, d/o **Henry** and **Lois (Blackman)**. In the 1850 census Seymour was 70 and Lois was 67. (*Des. of Robert Isbell*, p. 26, 48 – *Smyrna*, p. 69-70 – *1850 Census of Chenango Co., NY*)

ISHAM

Daniel – b 1/17/1779 in Colchester, CT, s/o **Daniel** and **Rhoda (Lord)**; Daniel d 3/27/1831 in St. George, Chittenden Co., VT. He m (1) **Hannah Hull**, d 10/11/1848, and m (2) **Alma** ----, bc1791, d 2/5/1861 age 70. (*Ishams in England and America*, p. 308, 438-9)

David – b 12/11/1776 in Colchester, CT, d 10/22/1853 in St. George, VT. David m 12/28/1806 **Mary Greene**, b 7/10/1778 in Hinesburg, VT, d 6/25/1867 in St. George, VT, d/o **Jonathan**. (*Ishams in England and America*, p. 307-8, 434-437)

Ebenezer – b 12/2/1762 in Bolton, CT, s/o **Timothy** and **Rebekah Fuller**; Ebenezer d 10/27/1819 prob. in Gilsum, NH. He m 12/21/1793 **Chloe Carpenter**, b 3/24/1763 in Rehoboth, MA, d 5/15/1831. (*Town of Gilsum, NH*, p. 343-4)

Jehiel – b 6/17/1761 in Colchester, CT, s/o **Isaac**; Jehiel d 9/17/1851 (or 9/17/1852) in St. George, VT. He m 9/1783 in E. Haddam, CT, **Sarah Mobbs**, b 5/7/1762 (or 9/1762), d 6/5/1847 (or 12/1847), d/o **Pierce** and **Eunice (Sawyer)**. (*Chittenden Co. Gazetteer*, p. 256 – *Ishams in England and America*, p. 176 – *DAR Patriot Index*, p. 363)

Jirah – b 4/22/1760 in CT, d 12/9/1837 in VT. Jirah m **Lois Kellogg**. (War of 1812 Index – *DAR Patriot Index*, p. 363)

IVES

Ambrose – b 5/22/1736 in CT, d1810 in MA. Ambrose m **Deborah** ----. (War of 1812 Index – *DAR Patriot Index*, p. 363)

Jesse – b 6/21/1776 in Litchfield, CT, d 11/27/1857 age 81 in Homer, NY. Jesse m ----. (*Pioneer Hist. of Cortland Co., NY*, p. 164)

JACKSON

Abraham, Sr. – b 1/16/1726 in CT, d 9/18/1791 perhaps in Mt. Holly, VT. Abraham, Sr. m **Eleanor Bump**. (*Rutland Co. Gazetteer*, p. 161 – *DAR Patriot Index*, p. 363)

Abraham, Jr. – b 7/10/1751 in Cornwall, CT, s/o **Abraham** and **Eleanor Bump**; Abraham, Jr. d 8/9/1833 prob. in Mt. Holly, VT. He m (1) **Jerusha Steele**, and m (2) **Mary Button Kinne**. (*Rutland Co. Gazetteer*, p. 161 – *DAR Patriot Index*, p. 363)

Levi – b 3/7/1779 in New Milford, CT, s/o **David** and **Priscilla (Benedict)**; Levi d1847 in PA. He m **Hannah Mechum**. (War of 1812 Index)

William - bc1794 in CT, d prob. in Meredith, Delaware Co., NY. William m **Martha** ----, bc1797 in Delaware Co., NY, d prob. in Meredith, Delaware Co., NY. In the 1855 census William was 61 and Martha was 58. (*1855 Census Delaware Co.*)

Rev. **William** - b1768 in Cornwall, CT, d 10/1842 prob. in Dorset, Bennington Co., VT. Rev. William m1797 **Susanna Cram**, b1771 in Brentford, NH. (*VT Hist. Mag.*, v. 1, p. 193-4)

JAKEWAY

William - bc1754 in CT, d 7/1848 age 94-2 in Palmyra, NY. William m **Mary** ----, bc1754, d 2/15/1826 age 72. (*Am. Monthly*, p. 43)

JENKINS

Edward - bc1805 in Winsted, CT, s/o **Benjamin** and **Elizabeth**; Edward d1854 age 49 in Prompton, Wayne Co., PA. He m ----. (Honesdale, PA, Courthouse, loose sheets on deaths)

Col. **John** - b 11/27/1751 in Colchester, CT, s/o **John** and **Lydia** (**Gardner**); Col. John d 3/19/1827 prob. in Kingston, PA. He m 6/23/1788 **Bethia Harris** of Colchester, CT. (War of 1812 Index – *DAR Patriot Index*, p. 367 – *Hist. of Luzerne-Lackawanna and Wyoming Co., PA*, p. 306B)

JENNINGS

Levi, Jr. - bc1792 in CT, d1852 age 60 in LaSalle Co., IL. Levi Jr. m **Emily Allis**. (*Hist. of LaSalle Co., IL*, p. 447)

JEWEL

Ebenezer - b 2/8/1789 in Salisbury, CT, s/o **Joseph** and **Mary** (**Crane**); Ebenezer d in MI. He m **Anna Jones**. (War of 1812 Index)

JEWELL

Marcus - b 9/6/1792 in Salisbury, CT, s/o **Oliver, Jr.** and **Clarinda** (**Chittenden**); Marcus d 5/5/1876 in Rochester, Monroe Co., NY. He m ----. (Tombstone Records, Mt. Hope Cemetery)

JEWETT

Nathan - bc1783 in E. Haddam, CT, d1861 age 78 in Brooklyn Susquehanna Co., PA. Nathan m1808 **Electa Fox**, d/o **Moses** and **Caroline** (**Mack**), d 2/23/1865 age 77. (*Hist. of Susquehanna Co.*, p. 659 – *Jewett Gen.*, p. 1029)

Thomas - b 7/19/1736 in Norwich, CT, s/o **Eleazer** and **Elizabeth** (**Grigs**); Thomas d 5/29/1812 in VT. He m **Eunice Slafter**. (War of 1812 Index – *DAR Patriot Index*, p. 369)

JOHNSON

Abel - b 3/26/1758 in Woodstock, CT, s/o **Edward** and **Mary** (**Phillps**); Abel d 3/2/1811 in Weston, VT. He m (1) 5/16/1781 **Lydia Mumford**, bc1758, d 6/16/1803 in Weston, VT, and m (2) 6/15/1804 **Eunice Olcott**, b 9/8/1768, d 9/24/1815 age 47 in Weston, VT. (*William Johnson* - typescript p. 297-8)

Abel - b 3/11/1784 in Woodstock, CT, d prob. in Weston, Windsor Co., VT. Abel m **Anna** ----, bc1785 in MA, d prob. in Weston,

Windsor Co., VT. In 1850 census Abel was 66 and Anna was 64. (*1850 Census of Windsor Co., VT*)

Abram - b 2/25/1793 in Litchfield, CT, s/o **Eliphalet** and **Mary**; Abram d 8/1866 age 73 in Richfield, MI. He m **Amanda Preston**, d 10/3/1865, d/o **Caleb**. (*Pioneer Hist. of Camden, NY*)

Anson - b1790 in CT, d1865 in OH. Anson m **Maria Oviatt**. (War of 1812 Index)

Asahel - b 10/3/1745 in Woodstock, CT, s/o **Edward** and **Mary (Phillips)**; Asahel d1790 in Chester, VT. He m **Phebe** ----. (*William Johnson*, typescript p. 180)

Calvin - b 12/20/1755 in Willington, CT, s/o Capt. **William**; Calvin d 10/7/1843 in Norwich, Windham Co., VT. He m **Sarah Armstrong**. (*VT Antiquarian*, p. 42 - *DAR Patriot Index*, p. 370)

Christopher - b 1/3/1755 in Middletown, CT, d 1/2/1823 in NY City. Christopher m (1) 5/15/1777 in New Hartford, CT, **Mary Austin**, d 6/18/1801 in Salisbury, VT, and m (2) **Phoebe Watrous (Waterhouse)**, d 4/15/1850 age 89-9 in Salisbury, VT. (*Branches and Twigs*, v. 1 #3, p. 25 - *DAR Patriot Index*, p. 370)

Daniel - b 9/5/1775 in Chatham, CT, s/o **James, Jr.** and **Sarah (Clark)**; Daniel d1869 in NY. He m **Lucretia Prout**. (1812 Index)

Eliakim - bc1779 in CT, d prob. in Woodstock, Windsor Co., VT. Eliakim m **Mary** ----, bc1787 in CT, d prob. in Woodstock, Windsor Co., VT. (*1850 Census of Windsor Co., VT*)

Enos - b 3/1777 in Canterbury, CT, s/o **Joseph**; Enos d 7/8/1864 age 87 (blind) in Camden, Oneida Co., NY. He m **Patricia Curtiss**, d 4/30/1865 age 88. (*Pioneer Hist. of Camden, NY*, p. 181-2)

Hezekiah - b 3/12/1733 in Mansfield, CT (?), d 2/21/1810 prob. in Norwich, Windham County, Vermont. Hezekiah m **Ruth Merriman**. (*Vermont Antiquarian*, p. 41 - *DAR Patriot Index*, p. 370)

Isaiah - b 2/5/1741 (or 2/5/1741) in Woodstock, CT, s/o **Edward**; Isaiah d 1799 (or 1800) in Chester, VT. He m **Dorcas Day**, b 7/27/1746 in Sutton, MA, d/o **John** and **Abiel (Chapman)**. She m (2) 2/25/1800 **John Russell** of Sutton. (*Wm. Johnson*, typescript p. 178, at CT Hist. Soc.)

John - b 1/26/1732 (or 1/26/1733) in Woodstock, CT, s/o **Edward**; John d 12/20/1810 in 78th year at Chester, VT. He m (1) 5/13/1756 **Rachel Haywood**, and m (2) **Ruth** ----, bc1733, d 12/28/1810 in Chester, VT. (*Wm. Johnson*, typescript p. 176, at Connecticut Hist. Soc.)

Levi - b 4/26/1760 in Middletown, CT, s/o **Henry**; Levi d prob. in Rupert, VT. He m **Elizabeth** ----. (*Wm. Johnson*, typescript p. 125b - Gravestone Rec. of Rupert, VT)

Moses - b 2/23/1741 in Stafford, CT, d 9/5/1835 in Putney, VT. Moses m (1) **Margaret Nathan Moore**, wid/o **Benjamin**, d1779, and m (2) **Lydia Wheeler**, d/o **Peter**. (*Putney, Vermont*, p. 6 - *DAR Patriot Index*, p. 371)

Ozias - b 4/21/1758 in Middletown, CT, s/o **Henry**; Ozias d 2/27/1841 age 83 in Benson, Rutland Co., VT. He m (1) **Hannah** ----, and m (2) **Rhoda** ----, bc1761, d 4/25/1840 age 79 in Benson, VT. (*Wm. Johnson*, typescript p. 125a)

Russell - b 6/7/1782 in Harwinton, CT, d 8/4/1858 age 76 prob. in Camden, Oneida Co., NY. Russell m in Harwinton, CT, **Tirzah**

Smith, b1786 in Harwinton, CT, d 6/19/1877 age 91. (*Pioneer Hist. of Camden, NY*, p. 257-8)

Solomon - b 12/17/1755 in Woodbury, CT, d 3/6/1825 age 69 in Clinton, NY, buried in Kirtland Avenue Cemetery. Solomon m (1) 5/22/1782 **Olive Curtiss**, and m (2) 4/18/1798 **Mabel Strong** of Southbury, CT, (divorced), d1846 age 80, and m (3) **Julia** ----. (*Clinton Mem.*, p. 45 - *Southbury, CT, V. Rec.*, v. 1, p. 123, 125)

Stephen - b 11/29/1786 in Willington, CT, d1860 in NY. Stephen m **Mercy Pierce.** (1812 Index)

Stephen Curtiss - b 8/31/1786 in Stratford, CT, s/o **Solomon** and **Olive (Curtiss)**; Stephen Curtiss d prob. in Camden, Oneida Co., NY. He mc1810 **Lois Heacock.** (*Pioneer History of Camden, New York*, p. 117-118)

Willard - b 2/11/1761 in Woodstock, CT, s/o **Edward**; d 10/27/1823 age 57 in Chester, VT. He m 2/17/1788 **Sarah Holbrook** of Woodstock, CT, d 11/22/1803 age 41. (*William Johnson*, typescript p. 302)

William, Jr. - b 8/2/1725 in Willington, CT, d 9/12/1804 prob. in Norwich, Windham Co., VT. William, Jr. m 1/25/1750 **Dorcas Chamberlain.** (*VT Antiquarian*, p. 41 - *DAR Patriot Index*, p. 372)

Wyllys (or Willis) - b 7/24/1768 in CT, s/o **Fenn** and **Rebecca (Bishop)**; Wyllys d 3/11/1853 age 84-2-16 in Chelsea, Orange Co., VT. He m 4/24/1793 **Mary Davis**, d/o **Philip** and **Abigail**, b 1/9/1775 in CT, d 9/1/1856 in Chelsea, VT. (*1850 Orange Co. Census* for Chelsea - *DSGR* Winter 1972 p. 67-8 - Old Cemetery in Chelsea, VT, gravestone)

JONES

Asa - b 6/9/1739 in Colchester, CT, d 6/15/1810 in Claremont, NH. Asa m 4/19/1760 in Colchester, CT, **Sarah Treadway**, d1822. (*DAR Patriot Index*, p. 373)

Asa - b 7/18/1762 in Colchester, CT, d 6/4/1828 in Claremont, NH. Asa m 1/30/1783 in Claremont, NH, **Mary Pardee**, b 7/7/1759 in Hamden, CT, d 5/17/1833 in Claremont, NH. (Colchester, Connecticut, V. Records)

Benajah - b 8/12/1755 in Hebron, CT, s/o **Benajah** and **Experience (Northam)**; Benajah d 8/19/1839 age 84 in Jonesville, MI. He m 2/7/1781 **Jemima Skinner.** (*Rev. Soldiers Buried in Lake Co., OH*, p. 33-4 - *DAR Patriot Index*, p. 373)

Lewis - b1771 in CT, d1848 in PA. Lewis m **Sarah Benedict.** (1812 Index)

JUDD

Allyn Southmayd - b 10/1756 in Waterbury, CT, s/o **Timothy** and **Millicent (Southmayd)**, wid/o **John** (nee **Gaylord**); Allyn Southmayd d prob. in Windsor, Broome Co., NY. He m1776 **Joanna Seymour**, b 9/1759, d 10/5/1833. (*Thomas Judd and His Des.*, p. 46)

Chauncey - b 1/5/1796 in Coventry, CT, s/o **Elias** and **Beulah (Laribee)**; Chauncey d age 72 in Schuylers Lake, Otsego Co., NY. He mc1818 **Amelia Tunercliff.** (*Biog. Rec. of Otsego Co. NY*, p. 398 - *Thomas Judd and His Des.*, p. 137, 152)

Demas - b 5/26/1753 in Watertown, CT, s/o **William** and **Mary (Castle)**; Demas d 1/4/1841 possibly in Schoharie, NY. He m **Maranah Garnsey**, d 9/22/1840. (*Thomas Judd and His Des.*, p. 41, 56-7 - *DAR Patriot Index*, p. 376)

Eben Warner - b 4/12/1761 in Hartland, CT, s/o **Stephen** and 3rd w **Lydia (Warner)**; Eben Warner d 9/18/1837 age 76 in Middlebury, VT. He m 2/27/1791 in Hartland, CT, **Lydia Giddings**, d 8/8/1848 age 81. (*Thomas Judd and His Descendants*, p. 50 - *DAR Patriot Index*, p. 376)

Elnathan - b 8/7/1724 in CT, s/o Capt. **William**; Elnathan d 1/3/1777 in NY. He m 12/28/1752 **Miriam Richards**, b 4/12/1735, d 1/12/1806 in Paris, NY, d/o **Samuel**. (*Thomas Judd and His Descendants*, p. 40-1)

Dr. Elnathan - b 12/7/1773 in CT, s/o **Elnathan**; Dr. Elnathan d 9/4/1845 in Troy, MI. He m1802 **Betsey Hastings**. (*Thomas Judd and His Des.*, p. 55-6)

Erastus - b 6/29/1771 in Waterbury, CT, s/o **Stephen** and **Else (Matthews)**; Erastus d 5/22/1837 in Jefferson, NY. He m **Ruth Hickox**, d 11/7/1836. (*Thomas Judd and His Des.*, p. 51-2)

Ethan - bc1797 in CT, d prob. in Rutland, Rutland Co., VT. Ethan m **Mary ----**, bc1805 in CT, d prob. in Rutland, Rutland Co., VT. (*1850 Rutland Co. Census*)

Freeman - b 8/10/1755 in CT, s/o **Stephen** and Lydia **(Warner)**; Freeman d 3/5/1840 age 85 in Lockport, Niagara Co., NY. He m 9/7/1786 **Deborah Boughton**, b 8/7/1770 in Norwalk, CT, d 5/13/1845 age 75 in Lockport, NY. (*Thomas Judd and His Des.*, p. 47-8 - *DAR Patriot Index*, p. 376)

Rev. Gaylord - b 10/7/1784 in Watertown, CT, s/o **Allyn S.** and **Joanna (Seymour)**; Rev. Gaylord d prob. in Candor, Tioga Co., NY. He m (1) 6/24/1805 **Sally Higley**, b 5/18/1787, d 12/22/1820, and m (2) 1/16/1825 **Jane M. Mather**, b 11/28/1790. (*Thomas Judd and His Des.*, p. 46)

Ira - b 5/19/1771 in Hebron, CT, s/o **Philip** and **Mary (Peters)**; Ira d 1/28/1853 age 82 in Strafford, Orange Co., VT. He m (1) 1796 **Hannah Ladd**, b 10/22/1777, d 12/12/1815 age 39, and m (2) 9/1816 **Polly Abbott**, bc1780, d 8/18/1855 age 73. (*Philip Judd and His Des.*, p. 24-5, 62-5 - *1850 Orange Co., VT, Census* - Strafford Old City Cem.)

Jesse - b1785 (or b1786), poss. 10/11/1786 in Waterbury, CT, s/o **Stephen, Jr.** and **Sarah**; Jesse d1859 in NY. He m **Anna (Alvira) Dayton**. (1812 Index - *Waterbury, CT, V. Rec.*, 2:129)

Marvin - b 5/16/1775 in CT, s/o **William** and **Mary (Castle)**; Marvin d prob. in Jefferson, Schoharie Co., NY. He m (1) 8/29/1800 **Eloisae Gibbs**, d 12/8/1845, d/o Dr. **Caleb** of Pownall, VT, and m (2) **Sarah Maria Hinman**, d 5/27/1847 age 33. (*Thomas Judd and His Descendants*, p. 58-9)

Oliver - b 6/9/1782 in New Britain, CT, s/o **John** and **Lydia (Mather)**; Oliver dc1859 (or dc1860) in 78th year in Cherry Valley, NY. He m 3/11/1804 **Elizabeth Belden**, b 4/3/1784, d/o **Jonathan** and **Mary (Allen)**. (*Biog. Rec. of Otsego Co.*, p. 402)

Philip - b 12/31/1715 (?) in Glastonbury, CT, d 9/15/1776 in Hebron, CT. Philip m 1/17/1764 in Hebron, CT, **Mary Peters**, b1743, d

1/20/1838 in Bethany Center, NY. Mary went by ox cart in 1764 with six children to Strafford, VT. She married four times. (*Philip Judd and His Des.*, p. ? – *DAR Patriot Index*, p. 377)

Philip – b 12/14/1765 in Hebron, CT, s/o **Philip** and **Mary (Peters)**; Philip (the younger) d 12/28/1831 age 67 (gravestone) in Strafford, VT. He mc1785 **Lovey West**, b 3/12/1769, d 2/25/1830. (Strafford Cem., [Kibling gravestones] – *Philip Judd and His Des.*, p. ?)

Sheldon – b 10/17/1768 in CT, s/o **William** and **Mary (Castle)**; Sheldon d 5/12/1806 in Scipio, Cayuga Co., NY. He m **Beulah Burr**. (*Thomas Judd and His Des.*, p. 58)

Thomas – b 2/9/1744 in Watertown, CT, s/o **Stephen** and **Margery (Clark)**; Thomas d 8/1820 age 76 in Mayfield, Cuyahoga Co., OH. He m **Mercy Scott**, d1840 age 90 in Willoughby Lake, OH. (*Thomas Judd and His Des.*, p. 47)

Timothy – b 9/13/1780 in Watertown, CT, s/o **Allyn S.** and **Joanna (Seymour)**; Timothy d prob. in Windsor, Broome Co., NY. He m 2/20/1823 **Lucy Lounesbury**, b 12/19/1803. (*Thomas Judd and His Des.*, p. 46, 61-2)

William – b 1/12/1730 in CT, s/o Capt. **William**; William (the younger) d 11/22/1815 in Jefferson, NY. He m (1) 1752 **Mary Castle**, d/o **Isaac**, d 3/12/1777, and m (2) 10/1778 **Sarah Greene** of Stamford, CT. (*Thomas Judd and His Des.*, p. 41)

JUDSON

Alfred – b 10/2/1800 in Woodbury, CT, d 1/14/1887 age 86 in Pontiac, Oakland Co., MI. Alfred m (1) 1829 **Louisa Bartlett**, d1870, and m (2) 1877 **Mrs. Bell**. (*Pioneer Collections of Michigan*, v. 11, p. 108)

David – b 2/28/1786 in Stamford, CT, d 2/15/1862 in Oxford, Chenango Co., NY. David m (1) 1812 in Stamford, CT, **Jerusha Stillson**, b 6/14/1791, d 4/9/1832 in Oxford, NY, and m (2) 4/4/1833 in Preston, NY, **Melinda Billings** of Preston, NY, d 10/4/1892 in Oxford, NY. (*Annals of Oxford, NY*, p. 289-90 – *1850 Chenango Co., NY, Census*)

Philo – bc1789 in Stamford, CT, d 1/9/1872 in Omaha, Nebraska. Philo m **Charity ----**, bc1795, d 7/26/1851. (*Annals of Oxford, Chenango Co., NY*, p. 289)

William – bc1804 in CT, d prob. in NY. William m **Betsey ----**, bc1800 in Delaware Co., NY. (*1855 Census of Delaware Co., NY* – Sidney, NY)

JUNE

David – b 9/9/1746 in Stamford, CT, d 6/24/1819 in 74th year in Brandon, Rutland Co., VT. David m **Prudence Ambler**, d 4/17/1797 age 45, d/o **John**. (*Hist. of Rutland Co.*, p. 475-6 – *Rutland Co. Gazetteer*, p. 88)

Joshua – bc1756 in CT, dc1812 Pittsford, Rutland Co., VT. Joshua m1779 **Sarah Cox**, dc1840, d/o **William**. (*DAR Patriot Index*, p. 377 – *Hist. of Pittsford, VT*, p. 62, 710)

KAPLE

John - b 11/12/1750 in CT, d1834 prob. in Otsego Co., NY. John m
Sarah Richardson. (*DAR Magazine* v. 107, p. 418 - *DAR Patriot
Index*, p. 377)

KASSON

Marvin - b1784 in Pomfret, CT, d 6/18/1881 age 98-6 in Newbury,
Orange Co., VT. Marvin m1830 Elizabeth Dick. (*Orange County,
Vermont*, p. 321)
Thomas - bc1781 in CT, d prob. in Topsham, Orange Co., VT.
Thomas m Clarissa Hutchins, bc1795 in VT, d prob. in Topsham,
Orange Co., VT. (*1850 Orange Co. Census - Topsham, VT*)

KEELER

Daniel - b 7/13/1750 in Ridgefield, CT, s/o Samuel and Mary; Daniel
d in NY. He m Abigail Isaacs. (1812 Index)
Lot - b 6/7/1752 (or 6/7/1762) in Ridgefield, CT, s/o Joseph and
Elizabeth (Whitney); Lot d prob. in Pittsford, Rutland Co., VT. He
m Catherine Goodnough of Brandon, VT. (*Hist. of Pittsford, VT*, p.
212-13, 710)

KEEN

Timothy - bc1779 in CT, dc1847 in MD. Timothy m Harriet Bayliss.
(1812 Index)

KEENEY

Thomas - bc1751 in CT, d1840 in PA. Thomas m Mercy Lamb.
(1812 Index)

KEETH (or KEITH)

William H. - b1790 in CT, d after 1875 in Hamilton, NY., buried in
Blossom Cemetery. William H. m Esther A. ----, b1791 in CT, d
9/28/1865 in Hamilton, NY. (*DSGR* v. 39 #2, p. 107, 1975)

KELLER

Edward - b1761 in CT, d1826 in NJ. Edward m Elizabeth Gray.
(1812 Index)

KELLEY

Hon. Alfred - b 11/7/1789 in Middlefield, CT, s/o Daniel and Jemima
(Stone); Hon. Alfred d 12/2/1859 in OH. He m 8/25/1817 Mary
Seymour Wells, b 11/10/1799 in NY, d 5/19/1882, d/o Melancthon
and Abigail (Buel). (*Hist. of Cuyahoga Co., OH*, p. 364 - *Gen.
Hist. of the Kelley Fam.*, p. 62-75)
Thomas Moore - b 3/17/1797 in Middlefield, CT, s/o Daniel;
Thomas Moore d 6/12/1878 in Cleveland, OH. He m 5/6/1833
Lucy Harris Latham, d/o William Harris Latham. She d
6/16/1874 in Cleveland, OH. (*Gen. Hist. of the Kelley Fam.*, p.
84-91 - *Hist. of Cuyahoga Co., OH*, p. 365)

KELLOGG

Amos - b 7/7/1760 in Lebanon, CT, s/o **Joseph** and **Mary**; Amos d 3/6/1826 in Pittsford, VT. He m 12/7/1782 in Bennington, VT, **Lucretia Harwood** b 3/9/1764 in Bennington, VT, d 9/1850. (*Hist. of Pittsford, VT*, p. 194, 711 - *Kelloggs in the New World*, v. 1:204 - *DAR Patriot Index*, p. 380)

Bradford - b 3/24/1759in CT, d1832 prob. in Hudson, OH. Bradford m **Mary Thompson**. (*Reminiscences of Hudson Co., OH*, booklet - *DAR Patriot Index*, p. 380)

Eleazer - b 4/10/1749 in New Hartford, CT, s/o **Isaac, Jr.** and **Martha (Merrill)**; Eleazer d 5/13/1813 in NY. He m **Esther Fuller**. (1812 Index - *DAR Patriot Index*, p. 380)

Isaac - b 1/14/1745 in CT, d 4/5/1829 in Malta, NY, buried in Armstrong Cem. Isaac m (1) **Hannah Fitch**, and m (2) **Sarah (Burgess) Gardner**. (*DAR Magazine* 1977, p. 918 - *DAR Patriot Index*, p. 380)

Jonathan - b 5/4/1767 in Colchester, CT, s/o **Martin** and **Sarah (Treadway)**; Jonathan d1869 in PA. He m **Elizabeth Smith**. (1812 Index)

Joseph - b 8/13/1738 in Hartford, CT, s/o **Edward**; Joseph d 9/20/1828 age 90 in Henderson, Jefferson Co., NY. He m 5/31/1759 in Bozrah, CT, **Mary Cushman**, b 9/9/1740, d 3/12/1828 age 88, d/o **Thomas** and **Mary (Harvey)** of Lebanon, CT. (*Kelloggs in the New World*, v. 1:105 - *Hist. of Pittsford, VT*, p. 194)

KELLUM

Luther - b1760 in Stonington, CT, d 6/5/1846 in 86th year in Susquehanna Co., PA. Luther m **Elvira Baldwin**, d/o **David**. (*Hist. of Susquehanna Co., PA*)

KELSEY

Asa - bc1748 in Litchfield, CT, d 4/20/1818 age 70 in Camden, Oneida Co., NY. Asa m **Sarah** ----, d 2/2/1841 age 84. (*Pioneer Hist. of Camden, NY*, p. 320-1)

Daniel - b 3/17/1786 in Killingworth, CT, s/o **Ezra** and **Phebe (Carter)**; Daniel d 9/2/1843 in Whiting, VT. He m 9/14/1809 in Whiting, VT, **Marcia Needham**, b 7/20/1788 in Whiting VT, d 8/3/1863 in Kalamazoo, MI. (*Kelsey Gen.*, p. 322-3)

Eber - bc1763 in Killingworth, CT, s/o **Joseph** and **Sarah (Lewis)**; Eber d 8/18/1839 in Jefferson Co., NY. He mc1787 in Killingworth, CT, **Lucy Ann Leete**, d/o **Gideon** and **Anne Parmelee** (or Gideon's 2nd w **Lucretia Buckingham Leete**). (*Hist. of Jefferson Co., NY*, p. ? - *Kelsey Genealogy*, v. 2:40)

Ezra - b 3/20/1761 in Killingworth, CT, s/o **Ezra** and **Mary (Clark)**; Ezra (the younger) d 3/20/1847 in Whiting, Addison Co., VT. He m 3/16/1785 in Killingworth, CT, **Phebe Carter** b 10/12/1761 in Killingworth, CT, d 9/13/1818 in Whiting, VT, d/o **Benj.** and **Phebe**. (*Gazetteer of Addison Co., VT*, p. 248 - *DAR Patriot Index*, p. 381)

James - bc1763 in CT, d 7/9/1849 age 86, buried in Kelsey Mt. Cem. between Tunbridge and E. Randolph, VT. James m **Parmela** ----, bc1762, d 1/12/1841 age 79. (Kelsey Mt. Cemetery gravestones - *Branches and Twigs* v. 6 #2)

KENDRICK

Rev. **Ariel** - b 3/31/1771 in Coventry, CT, s/o **Ebenezer** and **Anne (Davenport)**; Rev. Ariel d 3/23/1856 age 75 in Cavendish, VT, buried in Mt. Union Cem. He m (1) 10/25/1792, **Penelope Cotton**, b 12/25/1769, d 4/14/1844 age 74, and m (2) c1850 Mrs. **Emma Parker**, b 5/20/1787, d 6/23/1876 age 89. (*Hist. of Cornish, NH*, p. 239 - *1850 Windsor Co., VT, Census*)

KENTNER

Amos - b 2/16/1790 in Middletown, CT, s/o **John P.** and **Mary**; Amos d1858 in NY. He m **Lucinda Clark**. (1812 Index)

KETCHUM

Joseph, 2nd - bc1720 in CT, d 5/6/1793 in Dutchess Co., NY. Joseph, 2nd m **Elizabeth Hurlburt**. (*Hist. of Little Nine Partners*, p. 365 - *DAR Patriot Index*, p. 385)

KIBBY

Walter - bc1795 in CT, d1868 in NY. Walter m **Lydia Barber**. (1812 Index)

KIDDER

Ephraim - bc1715 in CT, d 1/8/1796 in his 81st year in Austerlitz, NY. Ephraim m **Freedom** ----, d 8/5/1788 age 73. (French's *Historical Gazetteer*, p. 243)

KILBORN

Col. **Charles** - b 3/3/1758 in Litchfield, CT, d 6/19/1834 prob. in Stanstead, Quebec, Canada. Col. Charles m1784 **Margaret Young**, d 8/21/1841. (*Forests and Clearing - Stanstead, Quebec*, p. 153)

KILBOURN

William - b 1/11/1758 in New Britain, CT, s/o **Josiah** and **Isabella (Whaples)**; William d 6/22/1816 age 58 in Chelsea, Orange Co., VT. He m 8/21/1786 **Sarah Sage**, b 1/29/1769 in Middletown, CT, d 4/1/1860, d/o **Jedediah** of Berlin, CT. (*Kilbourn Genealogy*, p. 138-9, 233-7 - Chelsea, Vermont, Cemetery stones - *DAR Patriot Index*, p. 386)

KILBOURNE

Ralph - b 8/29/1796 in Berlin, CT, d 3/19/1854 in Montpelier, Washington Co., VT. Ralph m **Sarah Dearborn**. (*1850 Census of Washington Co., VT - Hist. of Kilbourn Family*, p. 235)

KILBURN

Josiah - b 5/28/1706 in Glastonbury, CT, s/o **Ebenezer** and **Sarah**; Josiah d1793 perhaps in Gilsum, NH. He m (1) 7/14/1741 **Mary Mack**, dc1770 age 60, and m (2) **Mrs. Abial Day**. (*Town of Gilsum, NH*, p. 169, 347-8 - *DAR Patriot Index*, p. 386)

KIMBALL
Richard – b 8/21/1762 in Pomfret, CT, s/o Capt. **John** and **Jerusha (Macham)**; Richard d 11/23/1828 in Randolph, Orange Co., VT. He m 2/7/1778 **Susanna Holden**, b 5/23/1765 in Mendon, MA, d 4/29/1826 in Randolph, VT. (*Hist. of Kimball Fam.*, p. 254 – *Hist. Souvenir of Randolph*, p. 61 – *DAR Patriot Index*, p. 387)

KIMBERLY
Hazard – b 12/8/1776 in Guilford, CT, s/o **Abraham** and **Thankful (Chittenden)**; Hazard d1827 in New York. He m **Eliza Robbins**. (1812 Index)

KIMBLE
Abel – b 11/17/1754 in CT, s/o **Jacob** and **Esther (Phillips)**; Abel d1832 age 77, and is buried in Paupack Cem., Wayne Co., PA. Abel m **Sibyl Chapman**, d/o **Uriah** and **Sibyl (Cook ?)**. (*History of Kimball Family*, p. 135 – *DAR Patriot Index*, p. 386 – Gravestones in Paupack Cem.)

Ephraim – b 5/11/1761 in Preston, CT, s/o **Jacob** and **Esther (Phillips)**; Ephraim d in Wayne Co., PA. He m **Eunice Ainsley**. (*Wayne, Pike, and Monroe Co., PA*, p. 960 by Matthews)

Jacob – b 12/1/1735 in Preston, CT, s/o **Jacob** and **Mary (Parke)**; Jacob (the younger) d 5/18/1826 age 91, and is buried in Paupack Cem., Wayne Co., PA. He m **Esther Phillips** of Plainfield, CT, d/o **John**. (*Wayne, Pike, and Monroe Co., PA*, p. 813 – *DAR Patriot Index*, p. 386)

Walter – b 4/26/1756 in Norwich, CT, s/o **Jacob**; Walter d prob. 1810 in Kilbuck, Holmes Co., OH. He m **Betsey Jennings**. (*DAR Patriot Index*, p. 387 – *Wayne, Pike, and Monroe Co., PA*, p. 813)

KING
Dan – b1791 in CT, d1864 in RI. Dan m **Cynthia Pride**. (1812 Index)

James W. – b 7/12/1807 in Hartford, CT, d 4/23/1884 age 77 in Clinton, Lenawee Co., MI. James W. m **Hannah Rose**. (*Pioneer Collection of MI*, v. 7, p. 446)

Leicester – b 5/1/1789 in Suffield, CT, d1856 in Bloomfield, Trumbull Co., OH. Leicester m 10/12/1814 **Julia Ann Huntington**. (1856 Trumbull and Mahoning Counties, OH)

Moses – b 11/4/1794 in Suffield, CT, s/o **Gideon** and **Ruth**; Moses d 7/5/1881 age 86 in Rochester, Monroe Co., NY. (Tombstone Records – Mt. Hope Cem., Rochester, NY)

Walter – b 12/26/1792 in Suffield, CT, d 4/5/1855 in Warren, OH. Walter m 3/19/1820 **Cynthia Halladay**, d/o **Jesse** and **Sarah (Hover)**. (*Trumbull and Mahoning Cos., OH*, p. 357)

KINGMAN
John – b1770 in CT, d1859 in NY. John m **Mariam Isbel**. (1812 Index)

KINGSBURY
Rev. Ebenzer – b 8/30/1762 in Coventry, CT, d in Honesdale, Wayne Co., PA. Rev. Ebenzer m ----. (*Hist. of First Presbyterian Church of Honesdale*)

Nathaniel - b 5/8/1785 in Franklin, CT, s/o Capt. **Daniel** and **Martha** (**Adams**); Nathaniel d 2/1/1864 age 78-9 in Brookfield, Orange Co., VT. He m **Aptha Woodbury**, bc1806 in MA, d 10/24/1883 age 77 in Brookfield, VT. (*Kingsbury Family*, p. 250 - *1850 Orange Co., VT, Census-Brookfield*)

Solomon - b 5/2/1812 in CT, d prob. in MI. Solomon m1836 **Melinda Bond**, b in Rutland, VT, prob. d in MI. (*Pioneer Collections of MI*, v. 11, p. 86-7)

KINGSLEY

Elijah - b1740 in Lebanon, CT, d 10/30/1839 in Bernardston, MA. Elijah m **Dorothy ----**, d 11/23/1824 age 87. (*American Monthly*, p. 43 - *DAR Patriot Index*, p. 389)

Rufus - b 4/11/1763 in Windham, CT, d 5/26/1846 age 84 prob. in Harford, PA. Rufus m **Lucinda Cutler**, d 5/29/1846 age 76. (*DAR Mag.*, v. 43, p. 514 - *DAR Patriot Index*, p. 389)

Zephaniah - b 10/7/1761 in Lebanon, CT, d 2/6/1836 in Townville, Crawford Co., PA. Zephaniah m (1) 3/18/1783 in Fort Ann, NY, **Hulda Coleman**, b in Colchester, CT, d/o **Ozias** and **Huldah** (**Brewster**), and m (2) 2/21/1796 **Eunice Hunter**, b1766, d 9/1/1835. (*First Hundred Years of Townville, PA*, p. 48-53)

KINNE

Lt. **Asa** - b 9/26/1723 in Preston, CT, s/o **Joseph** and **Keziah** (**Peabody**); Lt. Asa d 1/12/1810 in Clarendon, Rutland Co., VT. He m 11/12/1743 **Bethiah Kimball**, b 2/18/1724, d 10/15/1802. (*Gen. of Henry and Ann Kinne*, p. 50-1 - *DAR Patriot Index*, p. 390)

Asa - b 8/26/1752 in Preston, CT, s/o **Asa** and **Bethiah** (**Kimball**); Asa (the younger) d 4/9/1842 in 90th year in Rupert, Bennington Co., VT. He m (1) 12/31/1772 in Preston, CT, **Thankful Bellows**, b 9/22/1756, d1785, d/o **Daniel** and **Deborah** (**Rix**), and m (2) 1790 **Mary Colton**, b1758, d 12/25/1846 in 88th year. (*Gravestone Rec. of Rupert, VT*, p. 36-7 - *Gen. of Henry and Ann Kinne*, p. 58-9 - *DAR Patriot Index*, p. 390)

KINNEY

David - b 1/9/1762 in Preston, CT, s/o Col. **Joseph** and **Jemima** (**Newcomb**); David d 3/26/1838 (or 5/26/1838) age 76 in Thetford, VT, and buried in Kinney Cem. He m **Jemima Fowler**, d 1/26/1849 age 84 in Thetford, VT. (*Gen. of Henry and Ann Kinne*, p. 38-9)

Rev. **Jonathan** - b 6/9/1763 in Preston, CT, s/o **Joseph** and **Jemima** (**Newcomb**); Rev. Jonathan d 5/7/1838 in Berlin, Washington Co., VT. He m (1) 1/20/1785 in Hanover, NH, **Lydia Kendrick**, b 3/6/1763 in Coventry, CT, d 7/4/1838 in Plainfield, VT, and m (2) 4/20/1834 in Croyton, NH, Mrs. **Rebecca Cummings**, b 7/26/1788, d 10/10/1865. (*Gen. of Henry and Ann Kinne*, p. 41-4)

KIRBY

Reuben - b in Litchfield, CT, his will was dated 4/1/1828 in E. Bainbridge, NY. Reuben m (1) **Ann Guthrie**, d1793, and m (2) 1794 **Naomi Patterson** of Washington, CT, d about age 90. (*French's Historical Gazetteer*, p. 225)

KIRKLAND

John – b1807 in Saybrook, CT, d in Grand Rapids, Kent Co., MI. John m (1) c1836 in W. Winfield, NY, **Emily Jane Green**, and m (2) c1854 (or c1855) **Sarah Rauch**. (*Pioneer Collections of Michigan*, v. 11, p. 91-2)

KNAPP

Abraham – bc1804 in Danbury, CT, s/o **Elijah** and **Currance (Barnes)**; Abraham d 3/4/1878 in Novesta Twp., Tuscola Co., MI. He mc1830 in Steuben Co., NY, **Sarah Hunter**, b 11/1/1811 in PA, d 3/4/1878 in Novesta Twp., MI, d/o **William** and **Anna**. (*DSGR* v. 37 #4 1974, p. 188)

Auren – bc1795 in CT, d1876 in OR. Auren m **Sarah Maria Burrell**. He may have m a second time. (1812 Index)

Dr. **David A.** – b 6/13/1820 in New Fairfield, CT, s/o **Isaac** and **Amy (Brush)**; Dr. David A. dc1907 prob. in Dutchess Co., NY. He m1846 **Rebecca Vincent**, b1827 in N. Clove, NY, d1902, d/o **Jonathan** and **Loretta (Williams)**. (*Comm. Biog. Record, Dutchess Co., NY*, p. 122 – *Knapp Gen.*, p. 240)

KNOWLES

Hezekiah – b 6/23/1785 in Haddam, CT, s/o **Walker** and **Elizabeth (Wells)**; Hezekiah d 3/22/1846 age 60 in Rome, MI. He m 10/22/1807 **Anna Smith**, b1790 in Haddam, CT, d1870 age 80 in Rome, MI, d/o **Henry** and **Susan**. (*Des. of Richard Knowles*, p. 204 – *Yesteryears* Winter 1973, p. 88)

Leonard D. – b 7/17/1792 in Haddam, CT, s/o **Walker** and **Elizabeth (Wells)**; Leonard D. d 3/11/1888 in Chenango Co., NY. He m 6/15/1815 **Beulah Merriam**, b 2/1/1797, d 12/29/1867. (*Des. of Richard Knowles*, p. 206 – *Yesteryears* Winter 1973, p. 89)

Simon – b 7/12/1786 (or 7/22/1786) in Haddam, CT, s/o **Walker** and **Elizabeth (Wells)**; Simon d 11/16/1884 age 98 in Meredith, Delaware Co., NY. He m 3/26/1812 **Susanna Brainerd**, b 8/10/1786 in Haddam, CT, d 9/30/1863 age 78 in Andes, NY, d/o **William** and **Susanna (Tyler)**. (*Des. of Richard Knowles*, p. 205 – *Yesteryears* Winter 1973, p. 89 – *1855 Census Delaware Co., NY*)

LADD

Nathaniel – b 10/4/1751 in Coventry, CT, s/o **Samuel**; Nathaniel d 10/31/1837 prob. in Woodstock, VT. He m **Abigail Scripture**, d/o **Simeon** and **Ann (Slafter)**. (*Ladd Gen.*, p. 37, 66 – *Hist. of Woodstock*, p. 64 – *DAR Patriot Index*, p. 397)

LAKE

Edward – b1776 in CT, d1831 in NY. Edward m **Lois Dennison**. (1812 Index)

LAMB

Elisha – b1801 in Groton, CT, d 5/10/1852 age 51 in Penfield Twp., Monroe Co., NY. Elisha m **Sarah O---**, b in Groton, CT, d

2/28/1885 age 78. (*History of Monroe County, New York*, p. 218 – Tombstone Record)

Joseph – bc1735 in Norwich, CT, d 1/21/1808 (or 1/21/1809) age 74 in Wells, VT. Joseph m **Betsey** ---- , d 11/1825 age 92 in Wells, VT. (*History of Wells, Vermont* by Parks, p. 109 – *Rutland Gazetteer*, p. 256)

Rev. Shubael – bc1770 in Norwich (or New London), CT, s/o **Joseph**; Rev. Shubael d1850 age 80 in Wells, Rutland Co., VT. He m (1) **Rhoda Patterson**, and m (2) **Clarissa Bushnell** of New London, CT, d1866 age 86. (*Hist. of Wells, VT* by Paul and Parks, p. 112-113 – *1850 Rutland Co., VT, Census*)

LANDON

Alson – b 4/18/1789 in Litchfield, CT, s/o **Thaddeus** and **Anne (Marsh)**; Alson d 5/ 23/1863 in MI. He m 6/26/1817 **Belinda Reynolds**. (*Landon Gen.*, p. 162-3)

Birdsey – b 6/21/1786 in Litchfield, CT, d 10/11/1836 in Montpelier, Washington Co., VT. Birdsey m 2/27/1815 **Susan Lane**, b 12/6/1787, d 7/3/1875. (*Landon Gen.*, p. 152, 159)

Thaddeus – b 12/1/1766 in CT, s/o **David, Jr.** and **Mary (Osborn)**; Thaddeus d 6/17/1846 in S. Hero, VT. He m **Anne Marsh Baldwin**, b 3/24/1771, d 5/26/1849 in S. Hero, VT. (*Landon Gen.*, p. 143-4)

LANGDON

George – b 1/14/1814 in New London, CT, d prob. in Gilsum, NH. George m 10/6/1840 **Emma Olivia Barstow**, d/o **Spaulding** and **Emma (Holmes)**, b 8/19/1820 in Canterbury, CT, d prob. in Gilsum, NH. (*Town of Gilsum, NH*, p. 351)

James Hooker – b 3/3/1783 in Farmington, CT, d 1/7/1831 in Montpelier, Washington Co., VT. James Hooker m **Nabby Robins** of Lexington, MA. (*Hist. of Montpelier, VT*, p. 204-7)

LANE

Job – b 4/22/1787 in Plainfield, CT, s/o **Hezekiah** and **Deborah**; Job d1859 in Addison Co., VT. He m **Sarah Terrill**. (1812 Index)

LARKIN

Joseph – b1758 in New Haven, CT, dc1811 age 53 in Fairfield, Franklin Co., VT. Joseph m1785 **Hannah Winslow** of Brandon, VT. (*Franklin Co. Gazetteer*, p. 107)

LARNED

Joseph – b 7/14/1779 in CT, dc1867 age 89 in Fairfax, Franklin Co., VT. Joseph m1808 **Lydia Powell** of Milton, VT. (*Franklin Co. Gazetteer*, p. 97)

William – b 4/1/1752 in Thompson, CT, d 2/22/1828 age 75 in Providence, RI. William m (1) **Mrs. Angell**, and m (2) **Sarah Smith**. (*American Monthly*, p. 43 – *DAR Patriot Index*, p. 406)

LATHAM

Joseph – b1789 in CT, d1867 in NY. Joseph m **Polly Crosby**. (1812 Index)

LATHROP

Adgate - b 8/29/1764 in Lebanon, CT, s/o **Cyprian** and **Mary (Stark)**; Adgate d 4/10/1840 in Stafford, VT. He m (1) **Anne House**, and m (2) 1/23/1799 **Martha Morse**, b 3/9/1771, d1850 in Geneva, NY, d/o **Joseph**. (*History of Pittsford, VT*, p. 267, 712 - *Lathrop Family*, p. 118, 178)

Asa - b 2/2/1756 in Norwich, CT, s/o **Ezekiel** and **Mary (Fellows)**; Asa d1827 age 72 in Susquehannah Co., PA. He m 9/17/1782 **Allis Fox** of Bozrah, CT. (*Hist. of Susquehanna Co., PA*, p. 370 - *Norwich V. Rec. of CT*, p. 327 - *Lathrop Family*, p. 117, 177 - *DAR Patriot Index*, p. 424)

Asher - b 7/11/1770 in Norwich, CT, d 4/24/1849 age 79 in Henrietta Twp. (?), NY. Asher m 9/25/1791 **Temperance Tillotson**, d/o **Simeon**. (*Lathrop Family Memoir*, p. 120 - Tombstone Record)

Daniel - b 3/23/1789 in Franklin, CT, s/o **Walter** and **Esther (Fox)**; Daniel d1842 in PA. He m ---- **Perkins**. (1812 Index)

Elias, Jr. - b 2/18/1763 in Norwich, CT, s/o **Elias** and **Hannah (Gurdon)**; Elias, Jr. d 3/5/1851 age 88 in Vershire, Orange Co., VT. He m 1/12/1797 in Chelsea, VT, **Dorcas Bohonon**, b 2/23/1799 in NH, d 10/30/1862 age 84 in Vershire, VT, d/o **Andrew** and **Susannah (Webster)**. (*Lathrop Fam. Rec.*, p. 170, 246 - *Gazetteer of Orange Co., VT*, p. 495 - *1850 Census Orange Co., VT* - *History of Salisbury, NH*)

Elias - b 10/28/1732 in Norwich, CT, s/o Capt. **Elisha**; Elias d 8/8/1802 age 69 in Chelsea, VT. He m 1/28/1762 **Hannah Gurdon**, b 12/3/1742, d 12/9/1788 in Canaan, NH, d/o **Joseph**. After death of wife, Elias left New Hampshire and went to Vershire, VT, with one of his sons, and is perhaps buried there. (*Lathrop Family Memoir*, p. ? - Vershire Cemetery)

Ezekiel - b 9/5/1724 in Norwich, CT, s/o **Israel, Jr.** and **Mary (Fellows)**; Ezekiel prob. d1771 (date of probate) in Susquehanna Co., PA. He m 10/18/1753 in Norwich, CT, **Abigail Lyon**, d 2/14/1806 age 86. (*Hist. of Susquehanna Co., PA*, p. 371 - *Norwich, CT V. Rec.*, p. 73, 327)

Horace - b in Windham, CT, s/o **Eliphalet**; Horace d1862 in Cooperstown, NY. He m **Eunice Ripley**, d1835 in Cherry Valley, NY, d/o **Ralph**. (*Biog. Rec. of Otsego Co., NY*, p. 153)

Jedediah - b 1/29/1745 (or 1/29/1746) in Norwich, CT, s/o **Ezra Lo** and **Charity (Perkins)**; Jedediah d 12/1879 perhaps in Brooklyn, Susquehanna Co., PA. He m 10/29/1767 in Norwich, CT, **Sarah Tracy** of Newent, CT, b 1/25/1747 age 82, d/o Deacon **Andrew** and **Ruth**. (*Hist. of Susquehanna Co., PA*, p. 131 - *Lathrop Family Memoir*, p. 105-6, 147 - *Norwich, CT, V. Rec.*, p. 222, 389)

Rufus - b 2/12/1765 in Norwich, CT, d 9/16/1842 in Orange Co., VT (prob. Tunbridge). Rufus m 3/8/1790 **Margaret Huntington**, d/o **Theophilus** and **Lois (Gifford)**, d 11/29/1849 age 82. (*Lathrop Fam. Memoir*, p. 170 - *Gazetteer of Orange Co., VT*)

Urban - b 3/24/1770 in New London, CT, s/o **Elijah** and **Elizabeth (Elderkin)**; Urban d 12/31/1858 age 89 in Chelsea, Orange Co., VT. He m **Lydia** ----, d 10/18/1845 age 73 in Chelsea, VT. (*Lathrop Fam.*, p. 252-3 - *1850 Orange Co., VT. Census-Chelsea*)

Walter - b 11/19/1749 in Norwich, CT, s/o **Benjamin**; Walter d1817 age 68 prob. in Susquehanna Co., PA. He m (1) ----, and m (2) 5/13/1779 **Esther Fox**, d1838 age 83. (*Lathrop Fam. Memoir*, p. 177 - *Hist. of Susquehanna Co., PA*, p. 295)

Gen. William Edward - b 8/31/1794 in Guilford, CT, s/o **Jedediah** and **Mary (Caldwell)**; Gen. William Edward d 4/28/1877 age 83 in Rochester, Monroe Co., NY. He m 4/11/1839 **Jemima Wight** of Mendon, MA, d/o **Dr. Wight**. (*Lathrop Fam. Memoir*, p. 221-2, 147, 286 - Tombstone Rec. of Mt. Hope Cem., Rochester, NY)

LAW

John Archibald - b1789 in CT, d1879 in RI. John Archibald m **Asha Carnal Aldrich**. (1812 Index)

LAWRENCE

Amos - b 3/12/1758 in CT, d 1/2/1842 age 83 in Chittenden, Rutland Co., VT. Amos m **Sabra Eggleston**, d 2/17/1840, age 86, in Chittenden, VT, buried in Baird Cem. (Gravestone Inscriptions - *DAR Patriot Index*, p. 403)

Elisha - bc1764 in Canaan, CT, d 9/11/1835 age 71 in Weybridge, Addison Co., VT. Elisha m (1) **Esther Kingsbury**, b 9/2/1770, d 11/5/1799, and m (2) **Patience Clark**, b 6/19/1777, d/o **Stephen** of Cheshire, CT. (*Gen. of the Fam. of John Lawrence*, p. 179)

James - b1858 in CT, d 3/19/1834 age 76 in Cornwall, VT. James m **Lois Teller**, d 2/3/1797 age 38 in Cornwall, VT. (*DAR Patriot Index*, p. 404)

LAY

Ezra D. - b 12/6/1807 in Saybrook, CT, d 4/28/1890 age 82-4-22 in Ypsilante Plains, MI. Ezra D. m 12/4/1834 **Melinda Kinne**, d/o **Rev. J. Kinne** of Monroe, NY. (*Michigan Colonial and Pioneer Collections*, v. 17, p. 198-201)

LEACH

Daniel - b 10/14/1777 in Harwinton, CT, d1831 in NY. Daniel m **Eve Corbett**. (1812 Index)

Hezekiah - bc1774 in Litchfield Co., CT, d 1/1840 age 66 in New Milford, PA. Hezekiah m ----, d/o **Robert Corbett**. (*Hist. of Susquehanna Co., PA*, p. 615-16)

John - b 8/10/1735 in New Fairfield, CT, s/o **Amos** and **Mercy (Martin)**; John d 6/27/1811 age 77 prob. in Fairfield, Franklin Co., VT. He m (1) **Martha Wanzer**, d 6/18/1844 age 80, and m (2) **Hannah Page**, d 12/1/1823 age 72. Possible error unless divorced from first wife. (*Some Early Records of Fairfield, VT*, p. 7 - *DAR Patriot Index*, p. 405)

LEAVENWORTH

Gideon - b 1/30/1809 in Huntington, CT, s/o **Capt. Gideon** and w (2) **Mary (Hull)**; Gideon d 8/16/1897 in Rochester, Monroe Co., NY. He m **Eleanor Dannells**, b 7/8/1816, d/o **George**. (*Gen. of the Leavenworth Fam.*, p. 177-8 - Tombstone Rec. of Mt. Hope Cem.)

Nathan, Jr. - b1764 in Washington, CT, s/o **Nathan** and **Rachel**; Nathan, Jr. d 6/1849 age 85 in Hinesburgh, Chittenden Co., VT. He m (1) **Anna Buckingham**, d 2/1805 age 35, and m (2) ---- **Hurlburt**. (*1861 Hist. and Tales of Hinesburgh, VT*, p. 8-9)

Nathan - bc1730 in Washington, CT, dc1802 age 72 in Hinesburgh, Chittenden Co., VT. Nathan m **Rachel Castle**, d1806 age 72 in Hinesburgh, VT. (*Look Around Hinesburgh*, p. 1 - *Hist. and Tales of Hinesburgh, VT*, p. 8)

LEAVIN

Rufus - b 4/22/1769 in Killingly, CT, d prob. in W. Windsor, Windsor Co., VT. Rufus m **Hannah** ----, bc1773 in NH, d prob. in W. Windsor, Windsor Co., VT. (*1850 Census of Windsor Co., VT*)

LEE

Abner - b 2/20/1759 in Middletown, CT, d 6/30/1843 age 84-4-10 in Brutus, Cayuga Co., NY. Abner m **Mary (or Maria)** ----. (*NEGR* 1/1966, p. 20 - *DAR Patriot Index*, v. 2:129)

Daniel - b 1/20/1753 in Ellington, CT, s/o **Elias** and **Sarah (Royce)**; Daniel d 7/1/1806 prob. in Stanstead, Quebec, Canada. He m **Sarah Whittaker**. (*Forests and Clearing-Stanstead, Quebec*, p. 156 - *DAR Patriot Index*, p. 407)

David - b1784 in CT, d1862 in NY. David m **Mary Whitcomb**. (1812 Index)

Ebenezer, Jr. - b 1/7/1757 in Farmington, CT, d 10/29/1837 in Granby, NY. Ebenezer, Jr. m (1) **Martha Parsons**, and m (2) **Anna Hyde**. (Tombstone Rec. Mt. Hope Cem., Rochester, Monroe Co., NY - *DAR Patriot Index*, p. 407)

Elisha - b 3/18/1763 (or 3/18/1764) in Lyme, CT, s/o Capt. **Elisha, Jr.** and **Abigail (Murdock)**; Elisha d 12/17/1847 age 84 (living with son, **Enoch**). He m **Sarah Smith**. (*Clinton Memorial-Kirtland Ave. Cem., Clinton, NY*, p. ?)

George - b 8/23/1767 in Lyme, CT, s/o **Benjamin, Jr.** and **Mary (Dorr)**; George d in NY. He m **Elizabeth Bennett**. (1812 Index)

Jedediah - b 4/7/1755 in Ellington, CT, s/o **Elias** and **Sarah (Royce)**; Jedediah d 10/24/1824 prob. in Quebec. He m (1) 1776 **Elizabeth Wood**, and m (2) **Mary Perry**, and m (3) 3/1/1797 **Mary Denison**, widow, d1793. (*Forests and Clearing-Stanstead, Quebec, Canada*, p. 155-6, 167-8 - *DAR Patriot Index*, p. 407)

Col. **Noah** - b 10/15/1745 in Norwalk, CT, d 5/5/1840 in Castleton, Rutland Co., VT. Col. Noah m **Dorcas Bird**. (*Rutland Co., VT, Gazetteer*, p. 103 - *DAR Patriot Index*, p. 408 - *History of Rutland Co., VT*, p. 517-19)

Oliver - b 12/23/1791 in Lebanon, CT, d 7/28/1846 in Buffalo, NY. Oliver m 10/30/1813 in CT, **Elizabeth Downer**, b 7/22/1794. (*Chautauqua Co., NY*, p. 421)

Vene - b 11/27/1770 in Guilford, CT, s/o **Elon** and **Elizabeth**; Vene d prob. in Canaan, Wayne Co., PA. He m 5/16/1793 **Hannah Rebeckah Palmer** of Branford, CT, d prob. in Canaan, Wayne Co., PA. (*Hist. of Wayne Co., PA*, p. 178)

LEET

Anson – b1777 in CT, d 6/25/1843 in Stockton, NY. Anson m1799 in CT, **Abigail Dudley**, b1780, d when over 95. (*Chautauqua County, New York*, p. 273)

Samuel M. – b1794 in Chester, CT, d Feb. 1882 in IL. Samuel M. m **Anna Atwood.** (1812 Index)

LEONARD

William – b1752 in CT, d1828 in RI. William m **Mrs. Angell.** (1812 Index)

LEWIS

Arba – b1799 in Derby, CT, s/o **Ezra**; Arba d 1/17/1879 in 80th year in Marshall, Calhoun Co., MI. He m 6/1/1828 **Mary Redfield.** (*Pioneer Collections of MI*, p. v. 2:231-2, v. 3:374-5)

Barnabas – b 8/17/1733 in Cheshire, CT, d 7/3/1811 age 80 in Wells, VT. Barnabas m (1) 5/1/1753 **Jerusha Doolittle**, d/o **Ebenezer**, and m (2) 2/22/1759 **Deborah Brooks**, and m (3) **Rachel P. Curtis**, d/o **Enoch** and **Rachel (Plumb)**, d 10/6/1817 age 76. (*Hist. of Wells, VT* by Paul, p. 112-114 – *Hist. of Wells, VT* by Wood, p. 65 – *DAR Patriot Index*, p. 413)

Birdseye – b 2/20/1750 in Huntington, CT, d 11/27/1822 in Dutchess Co., NY. Birdseye m 11/11/1773 **Jerusha Thompson**, d 6/8/1821. (*Comm. Biog. Rec. of Dutchess Co., NY*, p. 870)

Charles – bc1799 in CT, d 9/11/1884 age 85 in Sherburne, Chenango Co., NY. Charles m **Deborah ----**, b1797 in CT, d 9/1/1872 age 75 in Sherburne, Chenango Co., NY. (*1850 Census of Chenango County, New York*)

Cyrus – b 11/15/1778 in Trumbull, CT, s/o **Birdseye** and **Jerusha (Thompson)**; Cyrus d 8/25/1861 in Dutchess Co., NY. He m 11/28/1809 **Alice Hawley**, b 10/29/1793, d 5/26/1861. (*Comm. Biog. Rec. of Dutchess Co., NY*, p. 870)

David – b 4/29/1757 in Cheshire, CT, s/o **Barnabus**; David d 3/3/1845 age 88 in Wells, VT. He m (1) **Elizabeth Burnham**, and m (2) in Wells, VT, **Rebecca Hotchkiss**, d1857 age 76 in Poultney, VT. (*Hist. of Town of Wells, VT* by Woods, p. 65 – *DAR Patriot Index*, p. 413)

Horatio Gates – b1780 in CT, d1847 in MA. Horatio Gates m **Betty Bailey.** (1812 Index)

Dr. Joseph – b 11/1746 in Old Lyme, CT, d 6/18/1833 in Norwich, Windsor Co., VT. Dr. Joseph m1771 **Experience Burr**, d 1/18/1819. (*A History of Norwich, Vermont*, p. 219-221 – *DAR Patriot Index*, p. 413)

Levi – bc1724 in Cheshire, CT, dc1811 age 87 in Wells, VT. Levi m **Bethiah Lumbard.** (*Hist. of Town of Wells, VT* by Wood, p. 65)

Miles B. – b in Trumbull, CT, d 4/1892 in Dutchess Co., NY. Miles B. m in Milford, CT, **Maria Kelsey**, d/o **Horace**. (*Comm. Biog. Rec. of Dutchess Co., NY*, p. 870)

Martin – b 4/1761 in CT, d 8/23/1854 in MI. Martin m **Abigail Thayer.** (1812 Index – *DAR Patriot Index*, p. 414)

Deacon **Robinson** - bc1789 in CT, d1858 age 69 in New Milford, PA. Deacon Robinson m **Abigail** ----, d1879 in 84th yr. (*Hist. of Susquehanna Co., PA*, p. 619)

Samuel - b 5/20/1744 in Voluntown, CT, d 2/9/1818 in Oxford, Chenango Co., NY. Samuel m **Sarah Edwards**, b 8/18/1750, d 5/1/1831. (*Annals of Oxford, New York*, p. 496-500 - *DAR Patriot Index*, p. 414)

William - b 6/11/1727 in Lyme, CT, s/o **William** and **Elizabeth**; William d 12/15/1806 prob. in Norwich, VT. He m **Naomia Brockway**, d 4/28/1803. (*A Hist. of Norwich, VT*, p. 218-19 - *DAR Patriot Index*, p. 414 - 1812 Index)

LILLEY

Jared - bc1759 in CT, d1827 in Butternuts, NY (near Gilbertville). Jared m **Susanna Tuckerman**. (*DAR Magazine* 1977, p. 918 - *DAR Patriot Index*, p. 415)

LILLIE

Elisha - b 5/21/1764, s/o **Elisha** and **Huldah (Tildon)**; Elisha (the younger) d age 86 prob. in Randolph, Orange Co., VT. He m **Lavina Story**, d prob. in Randolph, Orange Co., VT. Living with son, **Horatio**, and his wife, **Betsey**, in 1850. (*1850 Census - Gazetteer of Orange Co., VT*, p. 351)

LINCOLN

Levi - b 4/25/1774 in Windham, CT, s/o **Samuel, Jr.** and **Phyliss (Austen)**; Levi d 8/1849 age 76 in Chelsea, Orange Co., VT. He m ----. (*1850 Orange Co., VT, Census-Chelsea*)

Luther - b1787 in CT, d1862 in NY. Luther m **Samantha Sanford**. (1812 Index)

Samuel - b 6/2/1753 in Windham, CT, s/o **Samuel** and **Phebe (Fenton)**; Samuel d 10/10/1844 age 91-2-20 in Chelsea, Orange Co., VT. He m 11/29/1781 **Prudence Lincoln**, d/o **Thomas** and **Mercy (Lamb)**, b 2/20/1754, d 7/6/1820 age 72-4-16. (Allen Cemetery of Chelsea, VT)

Deacon **Samuel** - b 12/27/1724 in Windham, CT, s/o **Samuel** and **Ruth (Huntington)**; Deacon Samuel d 12/1/1800 age 76 in Chelsea, Orange Co., VT. He m (1) 10/1/1747 **Phebe Fenton**, and m (2) 3/9/1758 **Phyliss Austen**, d 2/25/17766 in Windham, CT. (*Gazetteer of Orange Co., VT*, p. 226 - Chelsea Old Cem.)

LINDSEY

Stephen - b 3/22/1759 in Stratford, CT, d 8/14/1846 in Sandy Creek, NY. Stephen m **Sally McNitt**, b1766, d1833. (*For King and Country*, p. 180, Orange Co., CA, Bicentennial Project - *DAR Patriot Index*, p. 417)

LINSLEY

Abiel, Sr. - bc1730 in Woodbury, CT, s/o **Abiel**; Abiel, Sr. d 5/7/1800 age 70 in Cornwall, Addison Co., VT. He m 10/5/1752 in N. Branford, CT, **Thankful Pond**, b 4/27/1733 in Branford, CT. (*Des. of*

Francis Linsley of CT and NJ, v. 1, p. 103, 202-3 – *DAR Patriot Index*, p. 416 – *Hist. of Cornwall, VT*, p. 66)
Hon. **Joel** – b 2/7/1756 in N. Branford, CT, s/o **Abiel**; Hon. Joel d 2/13/1819 age 63 in Cornwall, Addison Co., VT. He m **Lavina Gilbert**, d 4/30/1843 age 84 in Cornwall, VT, d/o **Isaiah**. (*Hist. of Cornwall*, p. 46-7 – *Des. of Francis Linsley of CT and NJ*, v. 1:318 – *VT Hist. Mag.*, p. 27)

LOBDELL
Ebenezer, Jr. – b 7/13/1735 in Ridgefield, CT, s/o **Ebenezer** and **Rebecca (Benedict)**; Ebenezer, Jr. d1783 in Fairfield, Franklin Co., VT. He m **Eunice Bradley**, d/o **James** and **Abigail (Sanford)**. (*Lobdell Gen.*, p. 214, 219 – *Some Early Rec. of Fairfield, VT*, p. 15 – *DAR Patriot Index*, p. 420)

LOCKWOOD
Ebenezer – b 3/31/1737 in CT, d 7/29/1821 in NY. Ebenezer m (1) **Hannah Smith**, and m (2) **Sarah ----**. (1812 Index – *DAR Patriot Index*, p. 421)
Ebenezer – b 7/4/1776 in Greenwich, CT, s/o **Timothy** and **Abigail**; Ebenezer dc1860 age 84 prob. in Concord, NY. He m **Betsey Seymour**. (*Hist. of Orig. Town of Concord, NY*, p. 921)
Homer – b 11/17/1793 in Brookfield, CT, d 2/12/1875 age 82 in Cayuga Co., NY. Homer m 10/2/1816 **Sally Benedict**, b 10/27/1795 in Ridgefield, CT, d 8/24/1897 age 82. (*History of Cayuga County, New York*, p. 273)
William A. – b 5/6/1806 in Stamford, CT, s/o **Daniel** and **Sally (Jessup)**; William A. d 10/30/1864 in Perinton, Monroe Co., NY. He m 4/27/1831 in Stamford, CT, **Polly Hubbard**, d/o **Nathaniel** and **Polly (McCay)**, b 10/28/1806 in Stamford, CT, d 10/19/1878 in Fairport, NY. (*Hist. of Monroe Co., NY*, p. 231, 222 – *Des. of Robert Lockwood*, p. 461, 576)

LONG
Reuben – b 3/29/1764 in Coventry, CT, s/o **Lemuel** and **Martha (Brewster)**; Reuben d 4/27/1846 in Sardinia, NY. He m **Esther Bingham**, b 4/12/1776, d 1/26/1851. (*Hist. of Original Town of Concord, NY*)
Levi – b 7/23/1758 in Coventry, CT, d 9/11/1849 in Rutland, VT. Levi m (1) **Abigail Baker**, and m (2) **Martha Kimball**. (*Rutland Co. Gazeteer*, p. 219 – *DAR Patriot Index*, p. 422)

LONGBOTTOM
Jesse – b 7/11/1762 in Norwich, CT, s/o **David**; Jesse d 7/22/1847 prob. in Orwell, Addison Co., VT. He m 2/19/1784 Mrs. **Betsey Bennett** of Norwich, CT, b 3/6/1765, d 3/24/1856. (*Gazetteer of Addison Co., VT*, p. 189 – *Orwell, Vermont*, p. 25 – *Bottum (Longbottom)*, p. 176-7)

LOOMIS
Hon. **Beriah, Jr.** – b 3/1/1753 in Bolton, CT, s/o **Beriah** and **Lydia (Northam)**; Hon. Beriah, Jr. d 9/21/1819 age 66 in E. Thetford,

Orange Co., VT. He m **Mary ----**, d 11/29/1820 age 69 in E. Thetford, VT. (East Thetford gravestones)

Daniel - b 6/5/1761 in Colchester, CT, s/o **Daniel, Jr.** and **Alice (Chamberlain)**; Daniel (the younger) d 8/19/1833 in NY. He m **Mary Huston**. (*DAR Patriot Index*, p. 423 - 1812 Index)

Israel, Jr. - b 9/27/1768 in Colchester, CT, s/o **Israel** and **Irene (Chamberlain)**; Israel, Jr. d1835 in MI. He m **Mary Lee**. (1812 Index)

Hon. Jeduthan - b 1/5/1779 in Tolland, CT, d 11/12/1843 prob. in Montpelier, Washington Co., VT. He m (1) 3/11/1807 **H a n n ah Hinckley**, d 12/24/1813, and m (2) 10/10/1814 **Charity Scott**, d/o Col. **Oramel** of Thetford, VT, d 6/13/1821, and m (3) 10/8/1822 **Sophia Brigham** of Salem, MA, d1855. (*History of Montpelier, Vermont*, p. 208-10)

Oliver - b 9/24/1763 in CT, d 1/4/1837 in Pawlet, Rutland Co., VT. Oliver m (1) **Judith Adams**, and m (2) Mrs. **Deborah Hamlin**. (*Hist. of Rutland Co., VT*, p. 706 - *DAR Patriot Index*, p. 423)

Reuben - b 10/9/1785 in Torrington, CT, d prob. in PA. Reuben m1807 **Sarah Westland**, b 11/25/1787 in Windsor, CT, d prob. in PA. (*Hist. of Wayne, Pike, and Monroe Cos., PA*, p. 588)

Samuel - b 3/26/1776 in Colchester, CT, d 4/17/1855 age 79 in Elba, NY. Samuel m **Jerusha ----**, d 2/14/1841 age 66. (*Tombstone Inscriptions from Abandoned Cemeteries and Farm Burials of Genesee Co., New York*, p. 69)

LORD

David Edwin - b 9/28/1795 in Lyme, CT, s/o **Richard** and **Deborah (Jewett)**; David Edwin d 7/22/1830 in Ann Arbor, Washtenaw Co., MI. He m 2/1/1817 in Herkimer Co., NY, **Mary Jeannette Fargo**, b 5/25/1799 in German Flats, Herkermer Co., NY, d 1/13/1871 in Manchester, MI, d/o **Daniel** and **Mary**. (*Michigan Pioneer Collections*, v. 1:337)

Jonathan - b 2/17/1752 in Colchester, CT, s/o **Jonathan** and **Ruth**; Jonathan (the younger) d 2/27/1821 in Norwich, VT. He m 10/14/1772 (or 10/14/1782) **Mary Smith**, b 2/18/1753, d 6/6/1851. (*Gen. of Descendants of Thomas Lord*, p. 94-102 - *History of Norwich, VT*, p. 222-3)

LOUNSBERRY

Nathan - b 9/8/1755 in Woodbridge, CT, s/o **John** and **Ruth**; Nathan d 4/26/1857 in Clarendon, VT, when over 100 years old. He m **L u c y Pelton**. (*Biog. Project of Some VT Ancestors*, p. 8 - *History of Wells, Vermont*, p. 67)

LOVELAND

Aaron - b 5/26/1775 in Hebron, CT, s/o **Israel**; Aaron d1866 in Townshend, VT. He m 2/21/1799 **Hannah Reed** of Swanzey, NY, b 10/4/1780, d 10/1/1852 in Glen Falls, VT, d/o **J o s i a h**. (*Hist. of Surry, NH*, p. 754 - *Loveland Gen.*, v. 3:103)

Eliphaz - b 12/31/1745 in Marlborough, CT, d 8/28/1823 in Franklin, Delaware Co., NY. Eliphaz m (1) **Jemima Porter**, and m (2) Mrs.

Rachel Kneeland. (*Hist. of Delaware Co., NY*, p. 173 - *DAR Patriot Index*, p. 426)

H a r r y - bc1800 in CT, d prob. in Marshfield, Washington Co., VT. Harry m **J e r u s h a** ----, bc1806 in VT, d prob. in Marshfield, Washington Co., VT. In the 1850 Census he was 50 and she was 44 years old. (*1850 Census of Washington Co., VT*)

Israel - b1731 (or b1732) in Glastonbury, CT, s/o **Thomas**; Israel dc1827 in Grafton, VT. He m 10/19/1755 **Dinah Loveland** (his cousin), b 1/20/1738 in Glastonbury, CT, d1826 in Grafton, VT. (*Town of Gilsum, NH*, p. 355-7 - *Loveland Gen.*, v. 3:82)

J o s e p h - b 4/14/1747 in Glastonbury, CT, s/o **J o h n**; Joseph d 9/8/1813 in Norwich, Windsor Co., VT. He m 11/12/1772 in Colchester, CT, **Mercy Bigelow**, d/o **David** and **Mercy (Lewis)**, b 11/23/1753 in Marlboro, CT, d 8/3/1832 in Norwich, VT. (*A Hist. of Norwich, VT*, p. 223-5 - *Loveland Genealogy*, v. 1:81 - *DAR Patriot Index*, p. 426)

Robert - b 3/19/1765 in Hartford, CT, s/o **Robert** and **Elizabeth (Gaines)**; Robert d 5/13/1856 in Pittsford, Rutland Co., VT. He mc1794 **Ruth Milber**, d 3/18/1846. (*1850 Rutland Co., VT, Census* - *Loveland Gen.*, v. 2:105-6 - *Hist. of Pittsford, VT*, see index)

Solomon - b1787 in CT, d1866 in NY. Solomon m **Clorinda Chidester**. (1812 Index)

S y l v e s t e r - bc1794 (or bc1781) prob. in Glastonbury, CT, d prob. in Marshfield, Washington Co., VT. Sylvester m **Ruth** ----, bc1799 in CT, d prob. in Marshfield, Washington Co., VT. During 1850 Census he was 56 and she was 51 years old. A Sylvester m **Ruth Riley** - perhaps this Sylvester. (*1850 Census of Washington Co., VT*)

LUCE

R o w l a n d - bc1776 in CT, d1862 in ME. Rowland m (1) ----, and m (2) **Eunice Mason**. (1812 Index)

LYMAN

Francis - b 2/23/1756 in Woodbury, CT, s/o **David** and **Mary**; Francis d 3/23/1840 in OH. He m **Abigail Coles**. (*DAR Patriot Index*, p. 430 - 1812 Index)

Jeremiah - bc1765 in Coventry, CT, d 8/19/1845 in 80th year prob. in Windham, OH. Jeremiah m ----, d 6/16/1811 in Utica, NY. (*Semi-Centennial Windham, OH*, p. 56-7)

John - b1760 in Salisbury, CT, s/o **Simeon**; John d1840 prob. in Jericho, Chittenden Co., VT. He m **Huldah Brinsmade**, d 1/1/1833 age 69. (*DAR Patriot Index*, p. 430 - *Gazetteer of Chittenden Co.*, p. 229 - *Lyman Gen.*, p. 370-4)

Noah - b 3/10/1753 in Salisbury, CT, s/o **Simeon**; Noah d 6/3/1831 age 73 in Jericho, Chittenden Co., VT. He m (1) 5/12/1784 **H o p a B u n n**, b 3/13/1765, d 5/12/1813 age 48, and m (2) 3/30/1816 **Urania Knowles**. (*Lyman Gen.*, p. 368-9)

Stephen - b 1/30/1785 in CT (possibly in Salisbury), s/o **Noah**; Stephen d prob. in Jericho, Chittenden Co., VT. He m 12/24/1817 **Ermina Knowles**, d prob. in Jericho, Chittenden Co., VT. In 1850 Census he was 65 and she was 60 years old. (*1850 Census of Chittenden Co., VT*)

LYNDES

Luther - bc1790 in CT, d prob. in Corinth, Orange Co., VT. Luther m **Nancy ----**, bc1801 in VT, d prob. in Corinth, Orange Co., VT. During 1850 Census he was 60 and she was 49 years old. (*1850 Orange Co., VT, Census* for Corinth)

LYON

Alvin - b 11/26/1777 in CT, s/o **Robert**; Alvin d 2/16/1848 age 70 in Braintree Hill, Orange Co., VT. He m (1) 1/20/1807 **Philena French** of Stockbridge, MA, d 3/8/1820 age 43 in Braintree Hill, VT, and m (2) 2/11/1821 **Sarah E. French** (w #1's sister), b 7/10/1785, d 10/19/1873. (*Hist. of Braintree, VT*, p. 162)

Burr - b1794 in CT, d1867 in NY. Burr m **Melinda Churchill**. (1812 Index)

Charles - b in Greenwich, CT, d1844 in Fitchville, OH. Charles m **Deborah ----**, d1847. (*The Fire Lands Pioneer*, p. 84)

Chester - b 5/25/1772 in CT, s/o **Robert**; Chester d 3/17/1812 age 41 in Braintree Hill, VT. He m **Thirza Poola** of Brooklyn, CT, d 10/18/1843 age 71 in Braintree Hill, VT. (*History of Braintree, Vermont*, p. 161-2)

Daniel - b 2/16/1796 in Woodstock, CT, s/o **Daniel, Jr.** and Mrs. Esther **(Perrin)**; Daniel d1842 in NY. He m **Polly Strickland**. (1812 Index)

Jabez - b 1/26/1756 in Woodstock, CT, s/o **John**; Jabez d 3/16/1843 age 87 in Brandon, Rutland Co., VT. The marriage intentions published 8/31/1778 to **Mehitable Woodward**, d/o **Thomas** and **Mehitable**, b 3/11/1757 in Brookline, MA, d 3/25/1837 age 80 in Brandon, VT. (*DAR Patriot Index*, p. 431 - *Lyon Memorial*, p. 99 - *Rutland Co. Gazetteer*, p. ?)

Josiah - b 12/3/1772 in Woodstock, CT, d1866 age 94 prob. in Derby, Orleans Co., VT. Josiah m 1/4/1798 **Polly Cole**, d1865 age 88. (*Gazetteer of Orleans Co., VT*, p. 259)

Noah - b 3/16/1759 in CT, d 9/23/1820 age 64 prob. in Cayuga Co., NY. Noah m **Mary Mead**. (*Hist. of Cayuga Co., NY*, p. 491 - *DAR Patriot Index*, p. 431)

Robert - bc1809 in CT, d 10/13/1859 age 50 in Braintree Hill, Orange Co., VT. Robert m (1) **Mary B---**, d 5/10/1840 age 30 in Braintree Hill, VT, and m (2) **Lucinda ----**, d 7/13/1843 in Braintree Hill, VT, age 23. (*Hist. of Braintree, VT*, p. 161-2)

Thomas - b1700 in Greenwich, CT, s/o **Thomas** and **Abigail (Ogden)**; Thomas d1770 in Rye, NY. He m **Phebe Vowles**. (*Connecticut Nutmegger* Query June 1981, p. 77)

Zebulon - b 3/1750 in Woodstock, CT, s/o **Jacob** and **Mehitable (Bugbee)**; Zebulon d 10/16/1822, Royalton, VT. He m (1) 2/7/1782 Mrs. **Eleanor (Porter) Skinner**, b 5/1/1753 in Thompson, VT, d 9/15/1813 age 61 in Royalton, VT, d/o **Samuel Porter**, wid/o **Calvin Skinner**, and m (2) 4/7/1814 **Hannah Dana**, d/o **John** and **Hannah (Pope)**, b 6/28/1775 in Pomfret, CT, d 4/14/1850 in Pomfret, VT. (*Lyon Memorial*, p. 43-4, 136 - *Woodstock Families*, v. 7:257 - *DAR Patriot Index*, p. 431)

MCCALL

Dyar - bc1799 in CT, d prob. in Oxford, Chenango Co., NY. Dyar m **Sophia A---**, bc1812 in NY, d prob. in Oxford, Chenango Co., NY. In the 1850 Census he was 51 and she was 38 years. (*1850 Census of Chenango Co. NY*)

Elijah - b 6/22/1794 in Lebanon, CT, d 8/6/1868 in Oxford, NY. Elijah m 11/19/1829 **Mehitable Smith**, b 4/9/1807 in Hadley, MA, d 7/14/1895 in Buffalo, NY. During the 1850 census he was 56 and she was 43 years old. (*Annals of Oxford, NY*, p. 308-9 - *1850 Census of Chenango Co., NY*)

MCLEAN

Charles - bc1769 in CT, d1813 in NY. Charles m **Anna Babcock**. (1812 Index)

MACK

Bezaleel - b 9/18/1760 in CT, d 7/22/1829 prob. in Gilsum, NH. Bezaleel m (1) 7/28/1785 **Rachel Hurd**, d 10/15/1820, and m (2) 3/25/1822 Mrs. **Olive (Gibbs) Temple**, d/o Isaac and Lois, b1757 in Marlboro, d 2/22/1827, and m (3) **Lucy (Hill) Smith**. (*Town of Gilsum, NH*, p. 358 - *DAR Patriot Index*, p. 432)

Joseph - b 7/22/1729 in Lyme, CT, s/o **Jonathan** and Sarah; Joseph dc1792 in Alstead, NH. He m (1) **Lois ----**, and m (2) **Lydia ----**. (*Town of Gilsum, NH*, p. ? - *Hist. of Surry, NH*, p. ?)

Solomon - b 9/26/1735 in Lyme, CT, s/o **Ebenezer** and Hannah (**Huntley**); Solomon d 8/23/1820 prob. in NH. He m 1/4/1759 in Lyme, CT, **Lydia Gates**, b 9/3/1735 in E. Haddam, CT, d/o **Daniel**. (*Town of Gilsum, NH*, p. 357-8 - *Hist. of Surry, NH*, p. 757 - *DAR Patriot Index*, p. 432)

Stephen - b 1764 in Lyme, CT, d 11/11/1826 in 72nd year in Pontiac, MI. Stephen m ----. (*The City of Detroit*, v. II:1388)

MALLORY

Aurora - bc1809 in CT, d1870 in E. Montpelier, VT. Aurora m1831 **Martha Templeton**, d/o **Levi**. (*Washington County, Vermont, Gazetteer*, p. 275)

James - b 7/28/1773 in Redding, CT, d1825 in NY. James m **Amelia Hunt**. (1812 Index)

MALTBY

Jonathan - b 7/10/1746 in Bolton, CT, d1801 prob. in Vershire, Orange Co., VT. Jonathan m ----. (*Gazetteer of Orange Co., VT*, p. 496)

Jonathan - bc1772 in CT, s/o **Jonathan**; Jonathan (the younger) d prob. in Vershire, Orange Co., VT. He m **Susannah Hosford**, bc1775 in VT, d prob. in Vershire, Orange Co., VT. During the 1850 census he was 78 and she was 75. (*1850 Census of Orange Co., VT*)

MANN

James - b 2/24/1768 in Hebron, CT, s/o **Joseph**; James d 3/21/1856 age 88 in Ballston, Saratoga Co., NY. He m1790 **Tryphena Tarbox** of Hebron, CT, b 12/27/1765, d 11/1/1850 age 84. (*History of Saratoga Co., NY*, p. 257-8, 484)

John - b 12/25/1743 in Hebron, CT, s/o **John** and **Margaret (Peters)**; John d 5/9/1828 prob. in Orford, NH. He m (1) 1765 in Hebron, CT, **Lydia Porter**, d/o **John** and **Lydia (Tarbox)**, and m (2) **Mrs. Barber**. (*Hist. of Norwich, CT*, p. 24-5 - *DAR Patriot Index*, p. 435)

S a m u e l - bc1772 in New Haven, CT, d1842 age 70 prob. in NH (possibly in Benton, NH). Samuel m **M a r y H o w e**. (*Gazetteer of Grafton Co., NH*)

MANNING

Dr. **H e n r y** - b 1/15/1787 in Lebanon, CT, d 1/11/1869 nearly 82 in OH (blind). Dr. **Henry** m (1) 9/1814 **Lucretia Kirtland** of Poland, OH, d 7/13/1819 age 22, and m (2) 6/1821 **Mary Bingham**, d 7/21/1845 age 47, and m (3) Mrs. **Catherine Ruggles** of Canfield, OH. (*Trumbull and Mahoning Cos., OH*, p. 404-5)

J a m e s - b 4/3/1792 in Coventry, CT, s/o **C a l v i n** and **L y d i a (Robertson)**; James d 12/26/1867 in Wappingers Falls, NY, buried in Glen Dyberry Cem. in Honesdale, PA. He m 3/17/1821 **Charity Brink Wilder**, b 3/1/1804 in Cochecton, NY, d 1/22/1887 in Bethany, PA, buried in Glen Dyberry Cem. in Honesdale, PA, d/o **David**. (*Hist. of Wayne Co., PA*, p. 314 - *Manning Family*, p. 246-7, 339-40, 470)

MANROSS

Theodore - b 1/6/1760 in Southington, CT, d 7/22/1825 age 66 in Clinton, Oneida Co., NY. Theodore m **Martha White**, d 3/21/1847 age 83. (*Clinton Memorial-Kirtland Ave. Cem.*, p. 25 - *DAR Patriot Index*, p. 436 - *Connecticut Records of Rev. War*, p. 203 - *DAR Lineage*, v. 136:57)

MANSER

George Barney - b 8/8/1803 in New Haven, CT, s/o **John** and **Sarah (B a r n e y)**; George Barney d 11/17/1862 in Bennington, VT. He m 6/12/1831 **Mary Clark**, d/o **Augustin** of Danville, VT. (*Washington Co., VT, Gazetteer*, p. 93)

MANSFIELD

Henry E. - b 8/16/1803 in Wallingford, CT, s/o Major **Ira**; Henry E. d prob. in Portage Co., OH. He m (1) **Jane Stanley**, b in OH, d 4/2/1837, and m (2) **Ann S. Stanley** (sister of w #1), d/o **Nathaniel** and **Mary (Moore)**, b 8/16/1815, d prob. in Portage Co., OH. (*Hist. of Portage Co., OH*, p. 583)

Isaac - b 11/1815 in Hamden, CT, s/o **Ebenezer, Jr.** and **Laura (S t i l e s)**; Isaac d in Butternuts, NY. He m 5/15/1842 **M a r i a Hitchcock**. (*Biog. Rec. of Otsego Co., NY*, p. 806)

MANSON

S a m u e l - b 7/9/1762 in Farmington, CT, b 2/27/1841, buried in Portland Cem., Portland, NY. Samuel m 2/3/1784 in Hartford, CT, **Martha Barnes**, d 12/6/1845 in Portland, NY. (*Soldiers of the Am. Rev. - Chautauqua Co., NY*, p. 18 - *DAR Patriot Index*, p. 487)

MANVILL

Ira – b 6/29/1763 in Woodbury, CT, s/o **Nicholas** and **Lurana (Rose)**; Ira d1803 in PA. He m **Mary Reynolds**. (1812 Index)

MAPLES

D a r i u s – bc1785 in New London, CT, d1857 age 72 in Delaware Co., NY (possibly in Cannonsville, NY). Darius m1812 **Lucy Little** of Windham, CT. (*Hist. of Delaware Co., NY*, p. 314)

J o s i a h – b 5/15/1762 in New London, CT, d 7/2/1847 in E. Aurora, NY, buried in Oaksville Cem. Josiah m (1) **Deidamia Comstock**, and m (2) **Esther Hedges**. (*DAR Mag.*, v. 107:418 – *DAR Patriot Index*, p. 436)

MARCY

C h e s t e r – b1760 in Woodstock, CT, d in Hartland, VT. Chester m **Matilda Waldo**, wid/o Dr. **S. A. Waldo**. (*Rec. of the Marcy Fam.*, p. 312 – *NEGR*, July 1875)

Samuel – b 10/8/1739 in Woodstock, CT, s/o **Samuel**; Samuel (the younger) d 2/1820 age 80 possibly in Woodstock, VT. He m **Esther** (or **Lois**) **Peak**. (*Rec. of the Marcy Fam.*, p. 306 – *NEGR* July 1895 – *DAR Patriot Index*, p. 437)

MARKHAM

Capt. Ebenezer – b1749 in Enfield, CT, d 2/1813 age 64 prob. in Middlebury, Addison Co., VT. Capt. Ebenezer m (1) 1775 **C a t h e r i n e Lydius**, d/o **John**, and m (2) 1784 **Sarah Gold Kellogg**, d/o **Benjamin**, d 1/1850 age 84. (*Gazetteer of Addison Co., VT*, p. 148-9)

William – b 8/19/1762 in E. Haddam, s/o **William** and **Abigail**; William (the younger) d 1/3/1826 in NY. He m **Phebe Dexter**. (1812 Index – *DAR Patriot Index*, p. 437)

MARKS

Ira – b1787 in Wallingford, CT, s/o **Levi** and **Hope (Treadwell)**; Ira d 5/3/1869 in Starrville, Cottrellville, MI. He m 2/26/1811 in Pownal, VT, **Hannah Thurber**, b 9/30/1792 in Williamstown, MA, d 11/8/1883. (*DSGR* Winter 1977, p. 79)

MARSH

Abel – b1735 in Lebanon, CT, s/o **Joseph** and **Mercy (Bill)**; Abel d1822 prob. in Hartford, Windsor Co., VT. He m 12/26/1754 in Lebanon, CT, **Dorothy Udall** of Stonington, CT. (*VT Antiquarian*, p. 23 – *John Marsh of Hartford*, p. 161-2 – *DAR Patriot Index*, p. 438)

Amos – bc1795 in New Hartford, CT, d1866 age 69 prob. in Wayne Co., NY. Amos m **Polly Deady**, d1873 age nearly 75. (*Rose Neighborhood Sketches*, p. 49-50)

A r c h i – b 5/23/1794 in Litchfield, CT, s/o **J a m e s** and **S a r a h (McNeal)**; Archi d1852 in Liberty, Susquehanna Co., PA. He m1820 **Lois Merriman** of Cheshire, CT. (*History of Susquehanna County, Pennsylvania*, p. 510)

Charles – b 7/19/1765 in Lebanon, CT, s/o Gov. **Joseph** and **Dorothy (Mason)**; Charles d 1/11/1849 in Woodstock, VT. He m (1) **Nancy Collins**, b 5/17/1768 in Litchfield, CT, d 6/18/1793 in Woodstock,

VT, d/o **John** and **Lydia (Buell)**, and m (2) 6/3/1798 **Susan Arnold**, b 10/9/1776, d 1/31/1853 age 76 in Woodstock, VT, wid/o **Josiah**, d/o **Elisha Perkins** of Plainfield, CT. (*Hist. of Woodstock, VT*, p. 468-70 - *John Marsh of Hartford, CT*, p. 153-7)

Elisha - b1738 in Lebanon, CT, s/o Ensign **Joseph** and **Mercy (Bill)**; Elisha d prob. in Hartford, Windsor Co., VT. He m - - - - **T e r r y**. (*John Marsh of Hartford*, p. 116, 167 - *VT Antiquarian*, p. 23)

Eliphalet - b1742 in CT (possibly in Lebanon), s/o **Joseph** and **Mercy (Bill)**; Eliphalet d1828 prob. in Hartford, Windsor Co., VT. He m **Sarah** ----. (*John Marsh of Hartford, CT*, p. 116 - *VT Antiquarian*, p. 23 - *DAR Patriot Index*, p. 438)

Frederick - b1794 in Hartford, CT, s/o **John** and **Susan (Bunce)**; Frederick d1868 age 74 prob. in Montpelier, Washington Co., VT. He m (1) **Harriet Hills** of E. Hartford, CT, d 1/22/1839, d/o **Amos**, and m (2) **Clara Cloe W. Robbins**, b 1/1808. During 1850 census he was 55 and Clara was 48. (*John Marsh of Hartford, CT*, p. 85 - *Washington County Gazetteer*, p. 198 - *1850 Census of Washington County, VT*)

Joseph - b 12/5/1699 in Hartford, CT, s/o **Joseph** and **Hannah (M a r s h)**; Joseph (the younger) d1753 in Lebanon, CT. He m 9/25/1723 **Mercy Bill**, b 1/12/1701, d 5/20/1786 age 85, buried in Quechee Village Cem., VT. (*John Marsh of Hartford, CT*, p. 116 - *VT Antiquarian*, p. 23)

Silas - b 5/26/1764 in CT (possibly in Lebanon, CT), d 2/23/1848 (or 2/23/1851) in Pomfret, Chautauqua Co., NY. Silas m 1/18/1787 **Mary Hare**. (*Soldiers of Am. Rev. - Chautauqua Co.*, p. 18 - *DAR Patriot Index*, p. 439)

MARSHALL

John - b 8/19/1787 in Hartford, CT, d 12/29/1860 in Royalton, Windsor Co., VT. John m **Polly Bachelder**, b in VT, d 4/25/1875 age 88-3 in Royalton, VT. In the 1850 census he was 63 and she was 64 years old. (*1850 Census Windsor Co., VT*)

Dr. **John Ellis** - b 3/18/1785 in Norwich, CT, s/o **Thomas** and **Sarah (Edgerton)**; d 12/27/1838 in Chautauqua Co., NY. Dr. John Ellis m 9/20/1810 **R u t h   H o l m e s**, d/o **O r s a m u s** of Sheridan, NY. (*Chautauqua Co., NY*, p. 274-5)

MARTIN

A a r o n - b 7/29/1742 in Windham, CT, s/o **G e o r g e**; Aaron d 3/12/1819 in Williamstown, Orange Co., VT. He m 11/13/1766 in Windham, CT, **Eunice Flint**, b 3/10/1748 in Windham, CT, d 11/12/1810 in Williamstown, VT, d/o **Samuel** and **Mary (Hall)**. (*George Martin of Salisbury, Massachusetts*, p. 32-4 - *DAR Patriot Index*, p. 440)

Aaron, Jr. - b 2/25/1772 in Windham, CT, s/o **Aaron** and **Eunice (Flint)**; Aaron, Jr. d 4/13/1865 age 89 in Williamstown, Orange Co., VT. He m (1) **Nancy Martyn**, b 8/5/1772 in CT, d 1/20/1804, d/o **Richard** and **Susannah (Low)**, and m (2) 5/6/1804 **Hannah Wise**, b1781, d 2/19/1809, and m (3) 10/5/1809 **Polly E. Burnham**, b 11/3/1788 in Bradford, VT, d 8/26/1864, d/o **Elijah** and **Abina (Bowen)**. (*George Martin of Salisbury, MA*, p. 42-3)

Daniel - b 7/12/1770 in Windham, CT, s/o **Aaron**; Daniel d 11/18/1836 in Williamstown, Orange Co., VT. He m 1/10/1793 in Northfield, VT, **Betsey Mosley**, d 2/28/1842 in Williamstown, VT. (*Geo. Martin of Salisbury, MA*, p. 42)

David - b 7/26/1790 in Lebanon, CT, s/o **Aaron** and **Eunice (Flint)**; David d 9/11/1873 in Williamstown, Orange Co., VT. He m (1) 12/2/1813 in Williamstown, VT, **Ruhamah Russell**, b1794, d 1/4/1848 in Williamstown, VT, and m (2) 5/12/1859 **Betsey (Goodrich) Wolcott Gale**. (*George Martin of Salisbury, MA*, p. 48 - *1850 Census Orange Co., VT* for Williamstown)

Erastus - b1786 in Windham, CT, s/o **Gideon**; Erastus d 4/15/1864 in Randolph, Orange Co., VT. He m **Sally Standish**, b1788, d 9/4/1861. (*Geo. Martin of Salisbury, MA*, p. 40-41)

George - b 3/14/1742 (or 3/14/1743) in Windham, CT, s/o **Ebenezer** and **Jerusha (Durge)**; George d 3/27/1827 prob. in Rochester, Windsor Co., VT. He m 6/7/1764 in Windham, CT, **Dorothy Brown**, b1752 in Wells, ME, d 8/2/1836. (*Geo. Martin of Salisbury, MA*, p. 27, 36, - *DAR Patriot Index*, p. 440)

Gideon - b 9/24/1740 in Windham, CT, s/o **George, Jr.** and **Sarah (Durkee)**; Gideon d 1/19/1808 in VT (possibly in Randolph, VT). He m 1/24/1765 in Windham, CT, **Rachel Heath**. (*Gazetteer of Orange Co., VT*, p. 209 - *Geo. Martin of Salisbury, MA*, p. 32, 38 - *Hist. Souvenir of Randolph, VT*, p. 71-2)

Gurdon - b 10/4/1786 in Windham, CT, s/o **Aaron**; Gurdon d 9/18/1834 in Williamstown, Orange Co., VT. He m 6/9/1808 in Williamstown, VT, **Sarah Wise**, b 10/1/1790, d 5/31/1880 in Williamstown, VT. (*Geo. Martin of Salisbury, MA*, p. 47-8)

James - b 12/14/1768 in Windham, CT, s/o **Aaron**; James d 9/13/1838 in Williamstown, Orange Co., VT. He m 6/25/1788 in Hampton, CT, **Martha Coburn**, b1771 in Windham, CT, d 10/27/1844 in Williamstown, VT. (*George Martin of Salisbury, Massachusetts*, p. 41-2)

John - b 12/31/1775 in Windham, CT, s/o **Aaron** and **Eunice (Flint)**; John d 3/3/1853 in Williamstown, Orange Co., VT. He m (1) **Nancy Smith**, b1778, d 11/13/1812, and m (2) 5/10/1813 **Philomena Lyman**, b 8/28/1786 in Lebanon, CT, d 6/9/1833, and m (3) **Olive Mower**, d/o **Ezra** and **Phebe (Thomas)**, b1798 in Barre, VT, d 6/13/1864. (*Geo. Martin of Salisbury, MA*, p. 44, 69-71 - *1850 Orange Co., VT, Census*)

Jonathan - b 8/8/1767 in Windham, CT, s/o **Aaron**; Jonathan d 2/24/1840 in Williamstown, Orange Co., VT. He m 3/3/1791 **Susannah Martyn**, d/o **Richard and Susannah (Low)**, b 8/19/1769 in Windham, CT, d 12/28/1845 in Williamstown, VT. (*George Martin of Salisbury, MA*, p. 41)

Rufus - b 5/25/1773 in Windham, CT, s/o **Gideon**; Rufus d 6/14/1864 in Randolph, Orange Co., VT. He m (1) **Abigail Brown**, b 9/16/1769, d 8/27/1827 in Rochester, VT, d/o **Henry and Sarah**, and m (2) **Lydia (Turner) Pinkham** (or **Tinkham**), b 10/9/1788, d 2/9/1875, widow. In the 1850 census he was 77 and Lydia was 63 years old. (*George Martin of Salisbury, MA*, p. 38-9 - *1850 Census for Windsor Co., VT*)

Samuel - b 2/7/1783 in Windham, CT, s/o **Aaron**; Samuel d 10/2/1848 in Lawrenceville, NY, buried in Williamstown, VT. He m 12/5/1803 **Hannah Russell**, b 4/8/1787, d 9/29/1848, buried Lawrenceville, NY. (*Geo. Martin of Salisbury, MA*, p. 46)

Stedman - b 12/10/1791 in Hampton, CT, s/o **Jonathan**; Stedman d 7/12/1844 in Williamstown, Orange Co., VT. He m **Huldah Bixbee**, d/o **Ebenezer** and **Hannah (Flint)**. (*George Martin of Salisbury, MA*, p. 57)

MARVIN

Dudley - b 5/9/1786 in Lyme, CT, s/o **Elisha** and **Elizabeth (Selden)**; Dudley d prob. in (possibly in Canandaigua) Chautauqua Co., NY. He m1818 Canandaigua, NY, **Mary Whalley**, d prob. in Chautauqua Co., NY. (*Chautauqua Co., NY*, p. 641)

John - b 1/30/1727 in Lyme, CT, s/o **John** and **Mehitable (Champin)**; John d 12/24/1792 prob. in Gilsum (or Surry), NH. He m 2/10/1746 (or 2/10/1747) in Lyme, CT, **Sarah Brooker** of Saybrook, CT. (*Town of Gilsum, NH*, p. 175 - *Hist. of Surry, NH*, p. 764 - *DAR Patriot Index*, p. 441)

Ozias, Jr. - b 2/10/1763 in Norwalk, CT, s/o **Ozias** and **Sarah (Lockwood)**; Ozias, Jr. d 4/9/1848 in 86th year in Clinton, Oneida Co., NY. He m (1) **Mary Bennett**, d 9/17/1815 age 49, and m (2) **Eunice Parmelee**, d 4/19/1838 age 62, and m (3) **Althea Herrick**, d 12/20/1866 age 83. (*Clinton Memorial-Kirtland Ave. Cem.*, p. ? - Connecticut Soc. Collection, v. 8:217)

MASON

Edwin - b 8/17/1803 in Litchfield, CT, s/o **Elisha** and **Lucretia (Webster)**; Edwin d 2/21/1901 in Richland, Kalamazoo Co., MI. He m 12/13/1826 in Litchfield, CT, **Clarissa Johnson**, d/o **Amos** and **Sarah Hubbard**, b 8/29/1805 in Litchfield, CT, d 10/13/1890 in Richland, MI. (*DSGR* Winter 1975, p. 84)

Elijah - b 9/26/1756 in Lebanon, CT, s/o **Peleg** and **Mary (Stanton)**; Elijah d 6/27/1833 in OH. He m (1) 1778 **Mary Marsh**, d/o Lt. **Joseph** of Hartford, VT, b1758, d1794, and m (2) 1795 **Lucretia Green**. (*VT Antiquarian*, p. 372-3 - *Hist. of Hartford, VT*, p. 372-3 - *DAR Patriot Index*, p. 442)

Henry - b 6/9/1819 in Woodstock, CT, s/o **Leonard** and **Sally (Breese)**; Henry d 1/15/1860 in Royalton, Windsor Co., VT. He m 3/22/1853 in Royalton, VT, **Jerusha Mosher**, d/o **Nicholas** and **Polly (Wilson)**, b1827 in Sharon, VT. (*Genealogies of Woodstock, CT, Families*, v. 7:405)

Gov. **Joseph** - b 1/12/1726 in Lebanon, CT, s/o **Joseph** and **Mercy (Bill)**; Gov. Joseph d 2/9/1811 in Hartford, Windsor Co., VT. He m 1/10/1750 **Dorothy Mason**, b 4/9/1732 in Norwich, CT, d 4/14/1810, d/o **Jeremiah** and **Mary (Clark)**. (*John Marsh of Hartford*, p. 131-6 - *Vermont Antiquarian*, p. 370-2 - *DAR Patriot Index*, p. 438)

Marshall - b 10/18/1765 in Woodstock, CT, s/o **Elias** and **Lydia (Brown)**; Marshall d 7/11/1836 in S. Woodstock, VT. He m 6/30/1788 in Pomfret, VT, **Polly Sessions**, b 1/30/1770 in Woodstock, VT, d 12/29/1814 in Woodstock, VT, d/o **Simeon** and

Sarah (Dana) Sessions, and m (2) 6/17/1817 in Pomfret, VT,
Christiana Bartholomew, b 9/23/1770 in Woodstock, CT, d after
1848, d/o **John** and **Candace (Ainsworth).** (*Pomfret, VT*, v. 2:536 -
Descendants of Hugh Mason, p. 455, 477-8 - *Woodstock, CT,*
Families, v. 7:400)
Peter - b 10/16/1786 in Salisbury, CT, s/o **Peter** and **Elisheba**
(Farnum); Peter d1856 in OH. He m **Sebra Day.** (1812 Index)
William - b1790 in CT, d1882 in MN. William m **Lovina Lyon.**
(1812 Index)

MATHER
Dan - b 10/1/1774 in Lyme, CT, s/o **Jehoiada** and **Unice (Miller);**
Dan d 9/1/1856 in Burlington, NY. He m (1) 10/27/1799 **S a l l y**
Frost, d1810 in NY, and m (2) 1811 **Susan Onderdonk,** d 3/9/1853
age 77. (*Biog. Rec. of Otsego Co., NY*, p. 267)
Demas - b1767 in Torrington, CT, d1833 in VT. Demas m **Louise**
Marine. (1812 Index)
J o s e p h - b 1/28/1756 in Lyme, CT, d 3/21/1848 in Chautauqua Co.,
NY. Joseph m1780 **Ruth Adams.** (*Soldiers of the Am. Rev. -*
Chautauqua Co., NY, p. 47 - *DAR Patriot Index*, p. 443)
S t e p h e n - b 2/9/1758 in Lyme, CT, d 6/7/1837 age 79 in Ellington,
NY, buried Clear Creek Cem. Stephen m1781 **Elizabeth Peck,** b
1/5/1760 in Lyme, CT, d 4/12/1839 age 79. (*Soldiers of the Am.*
Rev. - Chautauqua Co., NY, p. 10 - *DAR Patriot Index*, p. 443)
Timothy - b 3/2/1757 in Suffield, CT, s/o **Timothy** and **Hannah**
(Fuller); Timothy d 3/8/1818 prob. in Marlboro, Windham Co., VT.
He m1779 **Hannah Church,** b1756, d 10/1827. (*The Mather Family*,
p. 131-2, 175 - *Gazetteer of Windham Co., VT*, p. 252 - *DAR*
Patriot Index, p. 443)
William H. - b 5/17/1822 in Darien, CT, d 12/20/1893 in Tecumseh,
MI. William H. m 3/1846 **Clarissa F. Brewster.** (*Michigan Coll.*,
v. 26, p. 155)

MATHEWS
Timothy - b 8/26/1723 in Suffield, CT, d 10/28/1802 age 79 prob. in
Marlboro, Windham Co., VT. Timothy m (1) **Sarah Fuller,** d1757
in Suffield, CT, and m (2) ---- **Kent,** d1777 in Marlboro, VT,
widow, and m (3) **Lydia Curtis Allen,** d in Dover, VT, widow. (*VT*
Hist. Mag., v. 5:445-6)

MATTHEWS
Hon. **D a r i u s** - b 12/11/1766 in Cheshire, CT, d 10/8/1819 in
Cornwall, VT. Hon. Darius m ----. (*Gazetteer of Addison Co., VT*,
p. 98-9 - *Salisbury from Birth to Bicentennial*, p. 87)

MATTOON
Rev. **Gershom** - b 9/18/1781 in Wallingford, CT, s/o Capt. **Gershom**
and **R u t h (P a r k e r);** Rev. Gershom d 10/22/1847 in Owosso,
Shiawassee Co., MI. He mc1805 in NY, **Anna Nancy Sayre,** b
7/23/1783 in Elizabeth, NJ, d 1/16/1868 in Owosso, MI, d/o **Abner**
and **Joanna (Meeker).** (*DSGR* vol. 39 #3, p. 139)

MAY

Capt. Asa - b 9/4/1764 in Woodstock, CT, s/o **Stephen** and **Mary (Child)**; Capt. Asa d 2/9/1791 in W. Fairlee, VT. He m 2/9/1791 **Anne Fillebrown**, d 5/1814 in W. Fairlee, VT. (*Gazetteer of Orange Co., VT*, p. 508 - *Woodstock Fam.*, v. 7:424-5)

Thomas - bc1759 in Woodstock, CT, s/o **Thomas**; Thomas (the younger) d 12/12/1849 age 89 in Fairlee, Orange Co., VT. He m 3/8/1789 in Woodstock, Connecticut, **Polly Mills**. (*NEGR* April 1950, p. 120)

MEAD

Peter - b1781 in Greenwich, CT, s/o **Peter**; Peter (the younger) d1854 age 73 in Fitchville, OH. He m1790 in Greenwich, CT, **Rachel ----**, b1770, d 7/3/1884 in Fitchville, OH. (*The Firelands Pioneer*, p. 82 - *Res. of CT Who Migrated to Huron Co., OH*, p. 4)

Rufus - bc1793 in Greenwich, CT, d1857 age 64 in Cornwall, Addison Co., VT. Rufus m **Betsey Rockwell**. (*History of Cornwall, Vermont*, p. 90, 93)

Solomon - b1769 in CT, d1861 in NY. Solomon m **Hannah Knapp**. (1812 Index)

MEEKER

Forrest - b1768 in CT, d1840 in Delaware. Forrest m **Patience Hulburd**. (1812 Index)

MEIGS

Daniel Bishop - b 1/13/1762 (or 1/13/1763) in CT, d 12/19/1849 in VT. Daniel Bishop m (1) **Hulda Brownson**, and m (2) **Esther ----**. (1812 Index - *DAR Patriot Index*, p. 462)

Henry - b1782 in CT, d1861 in NY. Henry m **Julia Austin**. (1812 Index)

MERRILL

Correll - b 12/14/1766 in Hartford, CT, s/o **Ebenezer**; Correll d 8/29/1849 in 83rd year in Addison, Addison Co., VT. He m (1) **Huldah Valance**, b1771, d 12/23/1797, and m (2) 2/18/1806 **Nancy Jones**, b 12/27/1784 in Nobletown, NY, d 2/8/1828. (*Gazetteer of Addison Co., VT*, p. 71 - *Merrill Memorial*, p. 461)

Elijah - b 3/6/1793 in CT, d 10/4/1857 in Sherburne, Chenango Co., NY. Elijah m **Isabelle ----**, b in NY. In the 1850 census he was 56 and she was 51. (*1850 Census Chenango Co., NY*)

Enos - bc1769 in CT, d prob. in Castleton, Rutland Co., VT. Enos m **Susan (Noble) Willard**, bc1782 in VT, d prob. in Castleton, Rutland Co., VT. In the 1850 census he was 81 and she was 68. (*History of Rutland Co.*, p. 523 - *1850 Rutland Co., VT, Census*)

Timothy - b 3/26/1781 in Farmington, CT, d 7/27/1836 in Montpelier, Washington Co., VT. Timothy m1812 **Clara Fassett**, d prob. in Montpelier, Washington Co., VT, d/o **Dr. Fassett** of Bennington, VT. (*Washington Co. Gazetteer - Hist. of Montpelier, VT*, p. 211)

MERRIMAN

Capt. **Abel** - bc1736 in Wallingford, CT, d1790 in Wells, VT. Capt. Abel m 3/9/1756 in Wells, VT, **Elizabeth Merriman**, d before 1797. (*Hist. of the Town of Wells, VT* by Wood, p. 68 - *DAR Patriot Index*, p. 465 - *Merriman Reunion and Gen.*, p. 162)

Joel - bc1799 in Connecticut, d1886 in Michigan. Joel m **Chloe Gaylord.** (1812 Index)

Samuel Sedgwick - b 4/2/1762 in Wallingford, CT, s/o **Abel** and **Elizabeth**; Samuel Sedgwick d 9/19/1847 age 85 in Wells, VT. He m **Polly Cross**, d/o **Joseph**, d 1/19/1845 age 74. (*Hist. of Town of Wells* by Wood, p. 68 - *Merriam Reunion and Gen.*, p. 163 - *DAR Patriot Index*, p. 465)

MERRITT

Michael - b 7/27/1738 in Killingworth, CT, d 8/18/1815 age 77 in Fair Haven, VT. Michael m (1) **Lucy Chittenden**, d 9/15/1810 in 77th yr. in Fair Haven, VT, and m (2) 12/13/1810 **Sarah (Olney) Hawkins.** (*Hist. of Fairhaven, VT*, p. 432-3 - *Hist. of Rutland Co.*, p. 593 - *DAR Patriot Index*, p. 465)

Peter - b 4/23/1778 in CT, d1861 in Angelica, NY. Peter m (1) **Polly Ann Mallory**, d 6/15/1810 age 25, and m (2) 11/25/1810 **Ruth Hurd**, d1844 in Royal Oaks, MI. (*Hist. of Fairhaven, VT*, p. 433-4)

MERWIN

James - b1777 in CT, d1865 in NY. James m **Esther Smith**. (1812 Index)

William J. - b 11/3/1833 in Bridgewater, CT, d1892 in Pauling, NY. William J. m **Elizabeth Van Burgh**, d/o **Hexton**. (*Comm. Biog. Rec. of Dutchess Co., NY*, p. 345)

MESSINGER

Forest - b 11/12/1799 in CT, d 9/30/1884 in Monroeville, OH. Forest m (1) 1828 in Huron Co., **Cecilia Hubbell**, d1849, and m (2) 1850 **Hannah Patterson**. (*Residents of CT Who Migrated to Huron Co., OH*, p. 4)

METCALF

Jonathan - b 6/26/1787 in Lebanon, CT, d 7/30/1869 in 83rd year in Hudson, OH. Jonathan m 12/26/1814 **Abigail L. Root** of Aurora, OH. (*Reminiscences of Hudson, OH*, p. 30-32)

Simeon - bc1778 in CT, d 8/1859 age 81 in Washington, VT. Simeon m **Hannah ----**, bc1782 in CT. In the 1850 census he was 72 and she was 68 years old. (*1850 Orange Co., VT, Census*)

MIDDLEBROOK

Hezekiah - b 5/18/1740 in CT, d 12/1/1832 prob. in Ballston, Saratoga Co., NY. Hezekiah m (1) **Phebe Nash**, and m (2) **Sarah White**, and m (3) **Mercy Fitch**. N.Y. (*Hist. of Saratoga Co.*, p. 248 - *DAR Patriot Index*, p. 467)

MILES

Daniel - bc1786 in CT, d prob. in Shaftsbury, Bennington Co., VT. Daniel m **Minerva** ----, bc1789 in CT, d prob. in Shaftsbury, Bennington Co., VT. In the 1850 census he was 64 and she was 61. (*1850 Bennington Co., VT, Census*)

Reuben - b 4/5/1782 in Pomfret, CT, d1844 in NY. Reuben m **Sarah Hallock**. (1812 Index)

Samuel - bc1800 in CT, d prob. in Oxford, Chenango Co., NY. Samuel m **Sarah** ----, bc1807 in CT, d prob. in Oxford, Chenango Co., NY. In the 1850 census he was 50 and she was 43. (*1850 Census Oxford, NY*)

Simon - bc1798 in CT, d prob. in Meredith, Delaware Co., NY. Simon m **Sally** ----, bc1807 in Delaware Co., NY, d prob. in Meredith, Delaware Co., NY. In the 1850 census he was 57 and she was 48 years old. (*1850 Census Delaware Co., NY*)

MILLER

Andrew - b 2/15/1743 in CT, d 4/11/1812 in S. Oxford, Chenango Co., NY. Andrew m **Sarah Lyon**, b 1/28/1748, d 3/22/1813 in S. Oxford, NY, d/o **Gilbert** and **Jane (Kniffen)**. (*Annals of Oxford, NY*, p. 230)

Eliphas - b 1/31/1756 in Middletown, CT, d 1/29/1813 in Pomfret, Windsor Co., VT. Eliphas m 4/9/1776 in Granville, MA, **Esther Doud**, b 10/24/1758, d 7/3/1845 in Pomfret, VT. (*Pomfret, New York*, p. 541)

Epaphras - b 6/2/1778 in Glastonbury, CT, d 7/5/1860 in Oxford, Chenango Co., NY. Epaphras m 7/14/1810 **Elizabeth Baldwin**, b 3/26/1787 in MA, d 7/14/1853. During the 1850 census he was 72 and she was 63 years old. (*Annals of Oxford, NY*, p. 255-60 - *1850 Census of Chenango Co., NY*)

George - bc1788 in CT, d prob. in Hartland, Windsor Co., VT. George m **Lucy** ----, bc1787 in VT, d prob. in Hartland, Windsor Co., VT. In the 1850 census he was 62 and she was 63. (*1850 Census of Windham Co., VT*)

MILLS

Asa - b1765 in Norfolk, CT, d1827 age 62 in Ann Arbor, Washtenaw Co., MI. Asa m1790 **Arthusa Phelps**. (*Pioneer Collections of Michigan*, v. 5:393-7)

Edward - b1781 in CT, d1869 in IL. Edward m **Locina Stewart**. (1812 Index)

Hon. Merrill J. - b 11/14/1818 in Canton, CT, d 9/14/1882 in Detroit, Wayne Co., MI. Hon. Merrill J. m1850 **C. Barbour**. (*Pioneer Collections of MI*, v. 6:517)

Oliver - b 11/23/1777 in Simsbury, CT, d 11/1861 in Hudson, OH. Oliver m **Amelia Mills**. (*Reminiscences of Huron Co., OH*, p. 49)

Stone - bc1774 in CT, d prob. in Bethel, Windsor Co., VT. Stone m **Sarah** ----, bc1783 in VT, d prob. in Bethel, Windsor Co., VT. In the 1850 census he was 76 and she was 67 years of age. (*1850 Census of Windsor Co., VT*)

MINARD

Lynde - b 6/30/1793 in CT, d 5/10/1878 possibly in Erie Co., OH. Lynde m1813 in CT, **Experience** ----, b1792, d 10/8/1862. (*Residents of CT Who Migrated to Huron Co, OH*, p. 4)

MINER

Gideon - b 3/2/1728 in Woodbury, CT, s/o **Samuel** and **Rachel** (**Galpin**); Gideon d 12/9/1806 in Middletown, VT. He m1764 **Elizabeth Lewis**, d 11/16/1815, wid/o **John Strong**. (*Miner Gen.*, p. 17 - *Hist. of Rutland Co.*, p. 649-50)

Thomas - b 11/25/1746 (or 11/25/1743) in Norwich, CT, d 7/12/1827 in Canaan, NH. Thomas m1765 **Eleanor Lamb** of Norwich, CT, d 7/17/1815. (*Miner Gen.*, p. 169, 173 - *Gazetteer of Grafton Co., NH*, p. 221 - *DAR Patriot Index*, p. 472)

William - b 2/14/1774 in Stonington, CT, d 5/12/1840 age 66 in Cayuga Co., NY. William m **Polly** ----, d 4/4/1817 age 33. (*Hist. of Cayuga Co., NY*, p. 493)

MITCHELL

John - b1760 in CT, d 9/6/1842 age 82 in Fairfield, Franklin Co., VT. John m 10/30/1783 in Stratford, CT, **Jemima Sunderland**, b1760, d1862 age 102, d/o **John**. (*Some Early Rec. of Fairfield, VT*, p. 18 - *Franklin Co. Gazetteer* - *DAR Patriot Index*, p. 473)

Minot - b 9/24/1784 in Norwalk, CT, s/o **Justus** and **Patty (Sherman)**; Minot d1862 in NY. He m **Elizabeth Leeds Silliman**. (1812 Index)

Timothy - b 10/4/1790 in Woodbury, CT, s/o **Abijah** and **Ruth E.** (**Root**); Timothy d 8/29/1879 in Tecumseh, Lenawee Co., MI. He m (1) **Lovina Dawley**, b 3/2/1806 in Oneida Co., NY, d 2/4/1841 in Lenawee Co., MI, d/o **Ebenezer** and **Mary (Babcock)**, and m (2) **Martha Brooks Ives**, and m (3) **Jerusha Brooks Calkins**. (*DSGR* Winter 1972, p. 77)

Rev. William - bc1797 in CT, d prob. in Wallingford, Rutland Co., VT. Rev. William m **Sarah** ----, bc1799 in NY, d prob. in Wallingford, Rutland Co., VT. In 1850 census he was 53 and she was 51. (*1850 Rutland Co., VT, Census*)

MIX

Amos Davenport - bc1767 in Wolcott, CT, d 9/6/1846 age 79 prob. in Camden, Oneida Co., NY. Amos Davenport m **Urzula Cook**, bc1781, d 9/17/1862 age 81. (*Pioneer History of Camden, New York*, p. 47-8)

MONROE

Jesse - bc1771 in Canterbury, CT, d prob. in Poultney, Rutland Co., VT. Jesse m **Hannah** ----, bc1777 in MA, d prob. in Poultney, Rutland Co., VT. In the 1850 census he was 79 and she was 73 years old. (*1850 Rutland Co., VT, Census*)

William - b 5/16/1761 in Willington, CT, d 4/29/1838 in Plymouth, Chenango Co., NY. William m (1) **Sally Barney**, and m (2) **Rebecca W. B. Prentis**. (*DAR Mag.*, v. 43:594 - *DAR Patriot Index*, p. 475)

MOORE

Asa - bc1777 in CT, d prob. in Pomfret, Windsor Co., VT. Asa m **Celia ----**, bc1780 in CT. In the 1850 census he was 73 and she was 70 years old. (*1850 Windsor, VT, Census*)

Elam - bc1787 in CT, d prob. in Castleton, Rutland Co., VT. Elam m **Lydia ----**, bc1785 in CT. In the 1850 he was 63 and she was 65 years old. (*1850 Rutland Co., VT, Census*)

Hon. **Grove** - b 2/3/1761 in Simsbury, CT, s/o **James** and **Mary (Norton)**; Hon. Grove d 11/9/1837 age 76-8 in N. Rupert, Bennington Co., VT. He m **Mary Buell**, d 2/16/1814 in 50th year. (*Gravestone Records of Rupert*, p. 48)

Jabez - bc1787 in CT, d prob. in Calais, Washington Co., VT. Jabez m **Ruth ----**, bc1792 in VT, d prob. in Calais, Washington Co., VT. In the 1850 census he was 63 and she was 58 years old. (*1850 Census of Washington Co., VT*)

James - bc1780 in Simsbury, CT, killed 5/1/1800 age 65 by falling tree in Rupert, VT. James m **Mary Norton**. (*Gravestone Rec. of Rupert, VT*, p. ? - *Rupert, VT, Hist.*, p. 154-5)

Jehiel - bc 9/17/1774 in CT, s/o Capt. **Roger**; d 12/1817 age 43 in Hamilton Co., OH. Jehiel m ----. (*Chautauqua Co., NY*, p. 413)

MOREHOUSE

David - b 11/25/1764 in Norwalk, CT, d 11/16/1839 age 75 in Sharon, VT. David m **Tryphena Bidwell**. (*American Monthly*, v. 43 - *DAR Patriot Index*, p. 479)

Gershom - b 10/23/1763 in CT, d 5/14/1857 in Greenfield, Saratoga Co., NY, buried in St. John Cemetery. Gershom m **Hannah Smith**. (*DAR Mag.* 1977, p. 917 - *Hist. of Saratoga Co., NY*, p. 435)

Gould - b 2/23/1781 in Fairfield, CT, s/o **Abijah** and **Mary**; Gould d1866 in NY. He m **Betsey Meeker**. (1812 Index)

MOREY

Gen. **Israel** - b 5/27/1735 in Lebanon, CT, s/o **Lunsford** and **Sarah (Dewey)**; Gen. Israel d 8/10/1809 prob. in Fairlee, Orange Co., VT. He m **Martha Palmer**. (*Gen. Rec. of Des. of John Derby*, p. 14)

Jonathan - b 3/31/1730 in CT (possibly in Canaan), d 3/31/1790 in Stillwater, Saratoga Co., NY. Jonathan m **Lydia Campbell**, d/o Rev. **Robert**. (*History of Saratoga Co., NY*, p.290 - *DAR Patriot Index*, p. 479)

Moulton - b 7/4/1765 in Hebron, CT, d1854 in Fairlee, Orange Co., VT. Moulton m 11/10/1793 **Patty Frizzell**. In the 1850 census he was 85 living with **Samuel** and **Belinda Morey**. (*Gazetteer of Orange Co., VT*, p. 44 - *1850 Orange Co., VT, Census*)

MORGAN

Christopher - b 10/15/1777 in Groton, CT, s/o **Christopher** and **Deborah (Ledyard)**; Christopher d 10/4/1834 in Cayuga Co., NY. He m 7/15/1805 **Nancy Barber**, b 8/29/1785, d 8/4/1864, d/o **John** of Groton, CT. (*Hist. of Cayuga Co., NY*, p. 399-400)

Daniel - bc 3/1776 in Groton, CT, d prob. in Hartland, Windsor Co., VT. Daniel m **Rhoda Marsh**, bc1782 in VT, d prob. in Hartland,

Windsor Co., VT. In the 1850 census he was 74 and she was 68 years old. (*1850 Windsor Co., VT, Census*)

Capt. **David** - bc1785 in Litchfield, CT, d prob. in Brooklyn, Susquehanna Co., PA. Capt. David m **Esther Brink**, b1794, d1872, prob. in Brooklyn, Susquehanna Co., PA, d/o **Thomas** and **Mary (Marsh)** of Bradford Co., PA. (*History of Susquehanna County, Pennsylvania*, p. 657)

Jesse - b 1/27/1758 (poss. in Salem, CT), s/o **Timothy**; Jesse d 8/30/1846 age 89 in Canaan, Wayne Co., PA. He m 3/6/1783 **Matilda Fish**, d 5/15/1837 age 80, d/o **Jonathan** and **Abigail**. (*Hist. of Wayne Co., PA*, p. 184 - *Morgan Fam.*, p. 65, 123 - *DAR Patriot Index*, p. 479)

Jonathan - b 2/15/1779 in Simsbury, CT, s/o **Jonathan**; Jonathan (the younger) d 3/22/1859 age 74 in Poultney, Rutland Co., VT. He m **Submission Canfield**, bc1785 in VT. In the 1850 census he was 71 and she was 65 years old. (*1850 Rutland Co., VT, Census - Rutland Co. Gazetteer*, p. 191)

Samuel - b1789 in CT, d1861 in PA. Samuel m **Mary Holmes**. (1812 Index)

MORLEY

Thomas - b 3/26/1758 in Glastonbury, CT, s/o **Timothy** and **Mary**; Thomas d 8/6/1852 in Chester, Geauga Co., OH. He m **Editha Marsh**. (Rev. Soldiers Buried in Lake Co., OH)

MORRIS

Asa - b 12/2/1755 in Woodstock, CT, s/o **Asa** and **Anna (Childs)**; Asa (the younger) d 5/1826 in Richford, Franklin Co., VT. He m (1) 12/7/1775 **Bethiah Goff**, b 2/2/1752 in Middletown, CT, d 6/10/1803 age 53 in Richford, VT, and m (2) 2/5/1816 **Penelope Thomas**, d prob. 1826. (*Gen. and Hist. Rec. of Deacon Edward Morris*, p. 64 - *Pomfret, VT*, p. 543 - *Woodstock Families*, p. 472)

Edward - b 9/15/1801 in Stafford, CT, s/o **Ephraim**; Edward d 4/17/1881 in W. Lebanon, NH. He m (1) 11/18/1821 **Lucetta Kinstry** of Bethel, CT, d 5/19/1829 in Barnard, VT, and m (2) 12/8/1830 **Harriet Bowman** of Barnard, VT, b 1/15/1812 in Barnard, VT, d 1/1/1885 in W. Lebanon, NH. (*1850 Windsor Co. Census of VT* - Gen. and Hist. Reg. of Edward Morris)

Elijah - bc1771 in CT, d after 1857 in Surry, NH. Elijah mc1799 **Anna Kendrick**, b1773 in Hanover, NH, d 5/28/1827 in Surry, NH. (*Hist. of Surry, NH*, p. 785)

Sylvester - bc1798 in Stafford, CT, d prob. in Norwich, Windsor Co., VT. Sylvester m **Susan J. Weston**, bc1802 in VT. In the 1850 census he was 52 and she was 48 years old. (*1850 Census of Windsor County, Vermont*)

William Munroe - b 8/28/1783 in Woodstock, CT, d 2/9/1873 in Vershire, VT. William m 5/11/1815 in W. Fairlee, VT, **Esther P. Southworth**, b 4/30/1792 in W. Fairlee, VT, d 4/25/1868, d/o **Lemuel**. In the 1850 census he was 66 and she was 56 years old. (*Southworth Gen.*, p. 267-8 - *Woodstock Families*, v. 7:478 - *1850 Orange Co., VT, Census*)

MORRISON

Roderick – b 12/29/1763 in Hebron, CT, d 8/21/1843 prob. in Westmoreland, Oneida Co., NY. Roderick m **Charlotte Besse**. (*Oneida, Our Country and Its People*, p. 608 – *DAR Patriot Index*, p. 482)

MORSE

Abial – b 5/28/1760 in Woodstock, CT, s/o **John, Jr.** and **Elizabeth**; Abial d 2/22/1857 prob. in Pomfret, Windsor Co., VT. Abial m (1) **Mary Johnson**, and m (2) **Lucy Swift Miller**. In the 1850 census he was 90 years old. (*Pomfret, VT*, v. 2, p. 544 – *1850 Census Windsor Co., VT* – *DAR Patriot Index*, p. 482)

Amos – b 2/24/1764 in Woodstock, CT, s/o **John** and **Elizabeth** (**Bugbee**); Amos d 3/12/1855 age 91 (gravestone) in W. Fairlee, VT. He m 2/10/1791 in Killingly, CT, **Tamar Bush** of Killingly, CT, d 7/26/1834 age 69 (gravestone). (*Morse Gen.*, p. 217–18)

Amos – b 10/26/1763 in Canterbury, CT, s/o **Peter** and **Sarah** (**Raynsom**); Amos d prob. in W. Fairlee, Orange Co., VT. He m **Sarah** ––––, bc1771 in CT, d prob. in W. Fairlee, VT. In the 1850 census he was 87 and she was 79 years old. (*1850 Orange Co., VT, Census-West Fairlee*)

Ben – bc1770 in CT, d prob. in Sharon, Windsor Co., VT. Ben m **Phebe** ––––, bc1771 in CT, d prob. in Sharon, Windsor Co., VT. In the 1850 census he was 80 and she was 79 years old. (*1850 Census of Windsor Co., VT*)

Calvin – b 6/30/1752 in Woodstock, CT, s/o **Jedediah** and **Sarah** (**Child**); Calvin d 4/7/1830 in W. Fairlee, VT. He m (1) 1/6/1774 in Woodstock, CT, **Sophia Nason** (or **Mason**), b 6/5/1755, d 9/14/1805 in 31st year in W. Fairlee, VT, d/o **Elias** and **Lydia**, and m (2) 10/4/1806 **Lucy Simpson** of Bradford, VT. (*Morse Gen.*, p. 215–16 – *Woodstock Fam.*, v. 7: 491, 495)

John – bc1780 in CT, d prob. in Middletown, Delaware Co., NY. John m **Martha** ––––, bc1793 in CT, d prob. in Middletown, Delaware Co., NY. In the 1850 census he was 75 and she was 62 years old. (*1850 Census of Delaware Co., NY*)

Miner – b 12/22/1780 in Guilford, CT, s/o **John** and **Deborah** (**Lines**); Miner d1851 in MI. He m **Minerva Everetts**. (1812 Index)

Timothy – b 3/3/1754 in Preston, CT, s/o **Daniel, Jr.** and **Anne** (**Willcocks**); Timothy d1821 in NY. He m **Miriam Lee**. (1812 Index)

Walter – b 10/24/1794 in Woodstock, CT, s/o **Jonathan** and **Azubah** (**Lyon**); Walter d1844 prob. in Wardsboro, Windham Co., VT. He m1827 **Laura Taylor** of Wardsboro, VT, b 9/30/1801, d 6/1848. (*Windham Co., VT, Gazetteer*, p. 304)

MORTON

Rockwell – b1783, s/o **Diodate** and **Jemima** (**Rockwell**); Rockwell d 8/15/1862 in Williston, Chittenden Co., VT. He m (1) Mrs. **Mary** (**Dolly Kimball**) **Miner**, b1794, d 3/29/1833 in Williston, VT, wid/o **John**, and m (2) **Eliza Atwater**, b1802, d 3/30/1863, d/o **Linus** and **Esther** (**Hotchkiss**). In 1850 census he was 66 and Eliza was 48 years old. (*1850 Census of Chittenden Co., VT - William Morton of Windsor, CT*, p. 34)

MOSES
Schuyler - b 12/31/1798 in Simsbury, CT, d 3/13/1889 in Rochester, Monroe Co., NY. Schuyler m ----. (Rochester, NY - Tombstone Rec. - Mt. Hope Cem.)

MOSELEY
Increase, Sr. - b 5/18/1712 in Norwich, CT, d 5/2/1795 in Clarendon, VT. Increase, Sr. m **Deborah Tracy**. (*Hist. of VT*, v. 5:52-3 - *DAR Patriot Index*, p. 484)

MOULTHROP
Josiah - b1794 in CT, d1853 in WI. Josiah m **Sophia Lanckton**. (1812 Index)

MOULTON
Benjamin - b1755 in Windham, CT, d1850 (or d1851) age 95 prob. in W. Windsor, Windsor Co., VT. Benjamin m **Phebe** ----, b1754, d1815. In the 1850 census he was 95 living with son, **Nathaniel**, age 62. (*Branches and Twigs* Fall 1973, p. 27 - *1850 Windsor Co., VT, Census*)

MOXLEY
Jonathan - b1763 in Groton, CT, s/o **Joseph**; Jonathan d1849 age 84 in New Milford, PA. He m **Sally Woodmansee**, d1826 age 67. (*Hist. of Susquehanna Co., PA*, p. 620 - *DAR Patriot Index*, p. 486)
Nathan - b 7/1/1771 in Stonington, CT, s/o **Thomas** and **Hannah (Smith)**; Nathan d 7/5/1858 age 87 in Tunbridge, VT, buried in Spring Road Cem. He m **Clarinda** ----, bc1771 in CT, d 12/23/1854 age 85. In the 1850 census he was 78 and she was 79 years old. (*1850 Orange Co. Census-Tunbridge, VT*)

MOZENA
Dennis - b1786 in CT, d1873 in OH. Dennis m **Rachel McLarin**. (1812 Index)

MULFORD
Nathan - b 7/25/1759 in Branford, CT, d 5/19/1825 in Rochester, Monroe Co., NY. Nathan m **Sabrina Barker**, b 4/12/1763, d 10/4/1828 in Rochester, NY, d/o Capt. **Samuel**. (Tombstone Rec. - Mt. Hope Cem. - *DAR Patriot Index*, p. 486)

MUNGER
Daniel - b 8/26/1725 in Guilford, CT, d 2/10/1805 in 80th year in Fairhaven, VT. Daniel m 8/16/1753 in Bethlehem, CT, **Eunice Barnes**. (*Munger Gen.*, p. 15-16, 33-5 - Hist. of Fair Haven, VT - *DAR Patriot Index*, p. 487)
Simeon - b 12/18/1787 in Guilford, CT, d1849 in NY. Simeon m **Damaris Evarts**. (1812 Index)

MUNROE

Daniel - bc1774 in CT, d1854 in NY. Daniel m **Deborah Sexton.** (1812 Index)

MUNSELL

Gurdon - b 10/27/1760 (or 10/28/1760) in Windsor, CT, s/o **Gurdon** and **Lucy (Stiles);** Gurdon (the younger) d 11/15/1807 age 47 in Bristol, VT. He m 4/20/1785 **Olive Carver,** d 6/1/1811, d/o **Samuel** of Bolton, CT. (*Vermont History Magazine*, v. 1, p. 22-3 - *Gazetteer of Addison Co.*, p. 87 - Stiles, *The History of Ancient Windsor*, p. 511-12)

MUNSON

Bimon - bc1798 in CT, d prob. in Wells, VT. Bimon m **Huldah ----,** bc1805 in VT, d prob. in Wells, VT. In the 1850 census he was 52 and she was 45 years old. (*1850 Rutland Co., VT, Census*)

Caleb - b 5/22/1746 in Wallingford, CT, s/o **Moses** and **Phebe (Merriman);** Caleb d 12/1/1802 in Canada. He m 3/19/1767 **Mary Lee,** b 1/13/1747 in Goshen, CT, d 3/29/1835 in Williston, VT. (*The Munson Record*, p. 1069, 1077-83 - *Gazetteer of Orange Co., VT*, p. 259 - *DAR Patriot Index*, p. 487)

Caleb - bc1776 in CT, d 10/3/1857 in Williston, Chittenden Co., VT. Caleb m **Elizabeth Corse,** bc1783 in MA, d prob. in Williston, Chittenden Co., VT. In the 1850 census he was 74 and she was 67 years old. (*1850 Census of Chittenden Co., VT*)

Edmund - b 5/2/1805 in Barkhamsted, CT, s/o **Samuel;** Edmund d prob. in Utica, NY. He m (1) **Elizabeth Stuart,** b 7/24/1812, d 7/20/1837, and m (2) 10/13/1838 **Sarah Gardner.** (*Oneida, Our County and Its People*, p. 3-5 of Biography Section)

Elizur - bc1798 in CT, d prob. in Wallingford, Rutland Co., VT. Elizur m **Sarah (Smith) Dale,** bc1807 in NH, d prob. in Wallingford, Rutland Co., VT. In the 1850 census he was 52 and she was 43 years old. (*1850 Rutland Co., VT, Census*)

Isaac - b 4/5/1771 in New Haven, CT, d1835 in W. Haven, Rutland Co., VT. Isaac m **Sarah Bradley.** (*Hist. of Rutland, VT*, p. 904)

Israel - b 3/18/1808 in New Haven, CT, s/o **Isaac** and **Sarah (Bradley);** Israel d1836 prob. in W. Haven, Rutland Co., VT. He m 9/9/1845 **Matilda Clark,** d/o **Chauncey.** (*Hist. of Rutland*, p. 904)

John - b 11/23/1769 in Goshen, CT, s/o **Caleb;** John d1864 in VT. He m **Betsey Taylor.** (1812 Index)

Levi - b 8/29/1738 in Wallingford, CT, s/o **Abel** and **Sarah (Peck);** Levi d1815 age 77 prob. in Camden, Oneida Co., NY. He m 11/27/1760 **Mary Cooley,** b1743, d1826 age 84. (*Munson Record*, v. II, p. 845 - *Pioneer History of Camden, NY*, p. 38-40 - *DAR Patriot Index*, p. 487)

Peter - b 9/9/1783 in Watertown, CT, s/o **Heman;** Peter d 11/4/1868 in Meredith, Delaware Co., NY. He m **Maranah Hecock,** b in CT, d 1/29/1859. In the 1850 census he was 73 and she was 72 years old. (*1855 Census of Delaware Co., NY - Munson Rec.*, p. 270, 298)

Reuben - b 7/31/1781 in CT, s/o **Caleb;** Reuben d 4/4/1871 in Duxbury, Washington Co., VT. He m 4/26/1807 **Mary Miller,** b9/19/1787 in Marlow, NH, d 4/4/1871 in Duxbury, VT, d/o

Bethuel. They died within 10 minutes of one another. In the 1850 census he was 69 and she was 63 years old. (*1850 Census of Washington Co., VT - Munson Record*, p. 1082-3, 1107-11)

MURDOCK

Joshua - b 10/9/1763 in Windham, CT, d 12/13/1845 age 82 in Venice, NY. Joshua m1787 **Eunice Moore** of Athol, MA, d 8/21/1839 age 78 in Venice, NY. (*Hist. of Cayuga Co., NY*, p. 434)

Hon. **Thomas** - bc1720 in CT, d 12/5/1803 in Norwich, Windsor Co., VT. Hon. Thomas m 11/8/1753 in Preston, CT, **Elizabeth Hatch**, d1814. (*A Hist. of Norwich, VT*, p. 226-8 - *Murdock Gen.*, p. 238-9 - *DAR Patriot Index*, p. 488)

MURRAY

Eber - b 11/12/1745 in Killingworth, CT, s/o **Jonathan** and **Dorcas**; Eber d 11/23/1826 in Orwell, Addison Co., VT. He m (1) **Azubah** ----, d1774 (or 1775) in Cheshire, MA, and m (2) c1781 **Abigail Dunning**, b 11/17/1752, d 6/1/1836 in Orwell, VT. (*Gazetteer of Addison Co., VT*, p. 186-7 - *Des. of Jonathan Murray of E. Guilford, CT*, p. 32-3 - *DAR Patriot Index*, p. 488)

Seymour - b Norwich, CT, 7/26/1792 s/o **Seymour** and **Philena (Willet)**; Seymour d 1852. He m **Ann Elizabeth Ellsworth Sickles**. (New York State 1812 Index)

MYERS

James - b 2/21/1787 in CT, d in Perry, Wyoming Co., NY. James m (1) **Mary DeWitt**, and m (2) **Huldah Wallis**. (*Car Del Scribe* Query July 1977)

MYGATT

Henry - b 11/7/1783 in New Milford, CT, s/o **Noadiah** and **Clarissa (Lynde)**; Henry d 5/5/1835 in Oxford, Chenango Co., NY. He m (1) 1809 **Sarah S. Washburn** of Oxford, NY, b 3/27/1791, d 9/26/1818 in Meredith, NY, and m (2) Mrs. **Susan Hosmer** of CT. (*History of Chenango, NY*, p. 261 - *Annals of Oxford, NY*, p. 429-432)

William - b 10/25/1785 in New Milford, CT, d 2/5/1868 in Oxford, Chenango Co., NY. William m 1/29/1817 in New Milford, CT, **Caroline Northrup**, b 7/27/1797 in New Milford, CT, d 5/15/1866, d/o **Cyrus**. (*Annals of Oxford, NY*, p. 450)

NARRAMORE

Asa - b 4/19/1761 in CT, d 4/11/1851 age 90 prob. in Charlotte, Chittenden Co., VT. Asa m (1) **Mary Lake**, and m (2) **Caty Conger**, and m (3) **Sally Joslin**. (*Chittenden Gazetteer*, p. 171 - *DAR Patriot Index*, p. 490)

NASH

Daniel - b1763 in Ridgefield, CT, d1850 in Butternuts, NY, buried in Prentiss Cem. Daniel m ----. (Otsego Co., NY - *DAR Magazine* 1977, p. 917)

Silas - b 6/14/1762 in Norwalk, CT, d 1/6/1852 age 92 in Hanover, Chautauqua Co., NY. Silas m (1) **Adri Adams**, and m (2) **Hannah**

Peacock. (*Soldiers of the American Rev., Chautauqua Co. - DAR Patriot Index*, p. 490)

NAUGHTON

Solomon - b 5/1750 (or 5/1751) in Farmington, CT, d1844 in Villenova, Chautauqua Co., NY. Solomon m ----. (*Soldiers of the Am. Rev., Chautauqua*)

NEAL

Levi - bc1717 in CT, d prob. in Pitcher, Chenango Co., NY. Levi m **Hulda** ----, bc1787 in CT, d prob. in Pitcher, Chenango Co., NY. In the 1850 census he was 73 and she was 63 years old. (*1850 Census Chenango Co., NY*)

William - b 9/15/1764 in New Hartford, CT, d 12/1842 age 78 (possibly in Tallmadge, OH). William m (1) **Abigail Denison**, and m (2) **Abigail Lewis**. (*OH Gen. Soc. Quarterly* Oct. 1972, p. 33 - *DAR Patriot Index*, p. 491)

NEARING

Henry - b 1/29/1758 in New Milford, CT, d 9/15/1845 age 88 in New Lisbon, NY, buried in Cem. at Welcome, NY. Henry m (1) **Lois Blackman**, and m (2) **Jane (Treat) Blackman**. (*DAR Magazine*, v. 107:418 - *DAR Patriot Index*, p. 491 - *Biog. Rev., Otsego County, NY*, p. 441)

NEFF

Joseph - b 12/2/1769 in Windham, CT, d 5/8/1862 in Burlington Green, NY. Joseph m (1) 1791 **Miriam Walcott**, b 5/4/1774 in Windham, CT, d 2/11/1837 in Burlington Green, NY, and m (2) **Sally** ----. (*Biog. Rev. Otsego Co., NY*, p. 437 - Descendants of William Neff #72)

Joseph - b 7/27/1746 in Windham, CT, s/o **William and Grace (Webster)**; Joseph d 9/30/1807 in Randolph, VT. He m **Abigail Cables** of Hartford, CT, b 1/2/1780, d 11/20/1878 in Braintree, VT. (*Hist. of Braintree, VT*, p. 166 - Des. of Wm. Neff #19)

Thomas - b 7/31/1744 in Windham, CT, s/o **William and Grace (Webster)**; Thomas d 12/23/1817 in Randolph, VT. He mc1770 **Eunice Walcott**, b 3/5/1743 in Windham, CT, d in Randolph, VT, d/o **Stephen** and **Marcy (Broughton)**. (*Des. of Wm. Neff*, p. 34-6 #55 - *Hartford Times* Query)

NEWCOMB

Benjamin - bc1786 in Durham, CT, d1816 in Norwalk, OH. Benjamin mc1806 in Durham, CT, **Stata Crosby**, b1798, d1816 in Norwalk, OH. (*Res. of CT Who Migrated to Huron Co., OH*, p. 4)

Bethuel - b 12/17/1751 in Lebanon, CT, s/o **Jacob** and **Elizabeth (Hamilton)**; Bethuel d 2/2/1826 age 74 in Thetford, VT. He m 4/16/1778 **Mabel Thomas**, b 3/12/1752, d 3/20/1841 age 82 in Thetford, VT, d/o **Ezekiel**. (*Caledonia Gazetteer*, p. 249 - *Newcomb Gen.*, p. 62-3, 113-15, 225-7 - *DAR Patriot Index*, p. 493)

Bradford - b 2/17/1777 in Mansfield, CT, d 10/1/1867 prob. in Williamstown, VT. Bradford m 11/8/1804 **Hannah Clark**, b 5/10/1781 in Greenwich, MA, d 11/22/1854, d/o Deacon **Rowland** and **Mary (Wild)**. In the 1850 census he was 73 and she was 69 years old. (*Newcomb Gen.*, p. 253, 460-1 - *1850 Orange Co., VT, Census*)

Henry B. - b 7/3/1803 in Enfield, CT, s/o **Silas**; Henry B. d 5/22/1878 in Charlotte, NY. He m 3/15/1829 in Charlotte, NY, **Philocha Clark**, b 1/7/1810 in Clifton Springs, NY, d 3/11/1872, d/o **Samuel**. (*History of Monroe Co., NY*, p. 315 - *Newcomb Genealogy*, p. 458, 663)

Jacob - bc1780 in Lebanon, CT, d prob. in Norwich, Windsor Co., VT. Jacob m (2) **Relief Burnham**, widow, bc1785 in MA, d prob. in Norwich, Windsor Co., VT. In the 1850 census he was 70 and she was 65 years old. (*1850 Census of Windsor Co., VT*)

Justus - b 8/5/1766 in CT, d 12/11/1852 in Thetford, VT. Justus m **Mary Gilbert**, b 12/30/1769 in Warren, CT, d 4/1855 in Thetford, VT. In the 1850 census he was 84 and she was 80 years old. (*Newcomb Gen.*, p. 154, 303-4 - *1850 Orange Co., VT, Census*)

NEWELL

Capt. Daniel - b 9/14/1755 in Windsor, CT, s/o **Nathaniel** and **Abigail**; Capt. Daniel d 12/23/1824 prob. in Burke, Caledonia Co., VT. He m **Nancy Curtis**. (*VT History Magazine*, v. 1:307 - *DAR Patriot Index*, p. 494)

Jesse - bc1790 in CT, d1880 in NY. Jesse m **Amaryllis Cowles**. (1812 Index)

NEWTON

Anson - b1798 in Colchester, CT, d prob. in Sherburne, Chenango Co., NY. Anson m **Mariah** ----, bc1803 in NY, d prob. in Sherburne, Chenango Co., NY. In the 1850 census he was 52 and she was 47 years old. (*1850 Census of Chenango Co., NY*)

Asahel - b 10/7/1763 in Colchester, CT, d 1/5/1852 age 88 in Strafford, Orange Co., VT. Asahel m **Sarah** ----, d 9/5/1829 age 74 in Strafford, VT. In the 1850 census he was 86 years old. (*1850 Orange Co., VT, Census*)

David - b 3/25/1753 in Milford, CT, s/o **Ezekiel** and **Mary (Collins)**; David d 12/29/1839 in Hartford, VT, buried in the Christian St. Cem. He m 9/16/1773 **Mary Hazen**, b 9/11/1754 in Norwich, CT, d 2/4/1823 in Hartford, VT, d/o **Joseph** of Norwich, CT. (*Vermont Antiquarian*, p. 24 - *Hazen Fam. in America*, p. 118-120 - *DAR Patriot Index*, p. 495)

Eben - b 10/16/1795 in Goshen, CT, s/o **Isaac** and **Rebecca**; Eben d prob. in Canfield, OH. Eben m 5/20/1826 in Canfield, OH, **Mary S. Church**, d prob. in Canfield, OH. (*Trumbull and Mahoning Counties, Ohio*, p. 215-16)

Isaac - b 3/12/1801 in Huntington, CT, s/o **Louis** and **Betsey**; Isaac d 12/10/1864 in Concord, Erie Co., NY. He m 12/24/1820 **Zilpah Ford**. (*Hist. of Original Town of Concord, NY*, p. 418-19)

Isaac - bc1768 in Colchester, CT, d 4/8/1833 in Pomfret, Windsor Co., VT. Isaac m **Betsey Quitterfield**, bc1769 in CT, d 2/2/1861. (*Pomfret, VT*, v. 2:544)

John - b 8/2/1775 in CT, s/o **Isaac**; John d in Darien, NY. He lived in Randolph, VT, for a time. John m 2/10/1799 in Randolph, VT, **Anna Cole**, b 10/15/1781, d 9/12/1875. (*Newton Gen.*, p. 190-1)

Capt. Joel - bc1758 in Cheshire, CT, s/o **Joseph** and **Sarah (Hull)**; Capt. Joel d1842 age 84 prob. in Salisbury, Addison Co., VT. He m Mrs. **Ruth (Nichols) Manning** of Manchester, CT, b1756, d1833 in Salisbury, VT. (*Newton Gen.*, p. 711 - *Hist. of Salisbury, VT*, p. 329 - *DAR Patriot Index*, p. 495)

Phineas - bc1803 in CT, d prob. in Sidney, Delaware Co., NY. Phineas m **Martha ----**, bc1808 in Greene Co., NY, d prob. in Sidney, Delaware Co., NY. In the 1850 census he was 52 and she 47 years old. (*1855 Census Delaware Co., NY*)

Stephen - bc1761 in CT, d1831 in MA. Stephen m **Esther Witter**. (1812 Index)

NOBLE

Rev. Calvin - b 1/9/1778 in New Milford, CT, s/o **Morgan**; Rev. Calvin d 4/20/1834 age 56 in Chelsea, Orange Co., VT. He m 12/30/1807 **Sophia Lucy Thompson**, b 8/24/1791, d 7/10/1856 age 66 in Chelsea, VT, d/o Rev. **Lathrop** of NY. (*Des. of Thomas Noble*, p. 102-3 - Gravestones, Chelsea Old Cem.)

Deodatus - b 7/29/1766 in New Fairfield, CT, s/o Hon. **David** and **Abigail (Bennett)**; Deodatus d 1/27/1853 age 86 in Monroe Co., NY. He m 2/27/1794 in Colchester, CT, **Betsey Buckley**, b 2/22/1772 in Colchester, CT, d 10/9/1846 age 75, d/o **Charles** and **Betsey (Taintor)**. (*DSGR* Fall of 1973, p. 16)

Goodman - b 7/3/1756 in New Milford, CT, d 8/7/1834 in Cairo, NY. He m **Sarah Tyler**, b1757, d 12/29/1837 in Cairo, NY. (Query *NEGR* Oct. 1967, p. 320 - *DAR Patriot Index*, p. 498)

James - b 10/3/1721 in New London, CT, s/o **John** and **Mercy (Williams)**; James d 2/2/1805 age 83 in Royalton, Windsor Co., VT. He m Mrs. **Hannah (Leffingwell) Vibber**, d/o **Samuel** and **Hannah (Gifford)**. (*Noble Gen.* by Boltwood, p. 730 - *Some Des. of Wm. Billing*, p. 11)

Thomas - b 2/5/1785 in New Milford, CT, s/o **Jesse**; Thomas d prob. in Sidney, NY. He m **Eliza Ann Beach**, b 2/26/1797 in Greene Co., NY, d prob. in Sidney, NY, d/o **Abijah** of Unadilla, NY. In the 1850 census he was 70 and she was 59 years old. (*1850 Census Delaware Co., NY*)

NORTH

Abijah - b 10/19/1743 in Farmington, CT, s/o **John** and **Esther (Stanley)**; Abijah d 5/3/1785 in Bridport, VT. He m 9/6/1764 in Goshen, CT, **Triphena Grant**, b 1/16/1737 in Windsor, CT, d 3/17/1783 in Shoreham, VT. (*John North of Farminton*, p. 49-50 - *DAR Patriot Index*, p. 499)

Alvin - b 3/2/1790 in Berlin, CT, s/o Col. **Simeon** and **Lucy (Savage)**; Alvin d 8/31/1845 age 55 in Hartford, CT. No certainty that he ever went to VT but often listed as doing so. Alvin m1812 **Mary Goodrich**, b1791 in New Britain, CT, d1868. (*Hist. of Pittsford, VT*, p. 478 - *John North Gen.*, p. 142)

Edward D. - bc1800 in Farmington, CT, d 1871 in W. Windsor, Windsor Co., VT. Edward m **Lucina Lincoln,** bc1805 in VT, d prob. in W. Windsor, Windsor Co., VT. In the 1850 census he was 50 and she was 45 years old. (*1850 Census of Windsor, VT*)

NORTHRUP

Amos - b1765 in Sherman, CT, s/o **Thomas** and **Joanna (Leach)**; Amos d1849 age 83 prob. in Fairfield, Franklin Co., VT. He m **Zurah Hungerford,** b1763, d 2/18/1832 in 69th year. (*Franklin Co. Gazetteer,* p. 105 - *Northrup Gen.,* p. 78, 175-7 - *Thos. Hungerford of Hartford and New London,* p. 16)

Burr - b 11/12/1799 in Trumbull, CT, s/o **Abel G.** and **Sally (Beach)**; Burr d 5/4/1877 in Rochester, Monroe Co., NY. He m 12/10/1821 **Sarah Fisk,** b 3/10/1802, d age 83 in Rochester, NY. (*Hist. of Monroe Co., NY,* p. 301, 220 - *Northrup Gen.,* p. 88, 201)

Eliakim - bc1791 in CT, d prob. in Oxford, Chenango Co., NY. Eliakim m **Julia ----,** bc1804 in CT. In the 1850 census he was 51 and she was 46 years old. (*1850 Census of Chenango Co., NY*)

Gideon - b 11/11/1753 in Plymouth, CT, s/o **Joseph**; Gideon d 6/18/1842 age 89 in Pine Grove, PA. He m **Esther Munson,** d 9/20/1824 in Camden, NY. (*Pioneer Hist. of Camden, NY,* p. 168 - *Northrup Gen.,* p. 381 - *DAR Patriot Index,* p. 499)

Nathaniel - b 3/26/1752 prob. in Salisbury, CT, d 8/6/1830 age 78 prob. in Castleton, Rutland Co., VT. Nathaniel m (1) 2/24/1773 **Sarah Norton,** b 9/23/1750, d 1/18/1817, and m (2) **Abigail Kilburn,** d 8/16/1831 age 67. (*Rutland Co. Gazetteer - Northrup Genealogy,* p. 40-1)

Nehemiah - b 9/18/1801 in Trumbull, CT, s/o **Abel G.** and **Sally (Beach)**; Nehemiah d 10/1/1878 prob. in Rochester, Monroe Co., NY. He m (1) 1/10/1831 **Laura Hartwell** of Pittsford, NY, d 3/2/1839, and m (2) 9/1/1840 in Buffalo, NY, **Elizabeth Chauncey Langdon** of Portsmouth, NH. (Tombstone Rec. - *Mt. Hope Cem., Monroe Co., NY,* p. 201-2)

Thomas - b 11/7/1762 in New Fairfield, CT, s/o **Thomas**; Thomas (the younger) d 9/2/1847 prob. in Fairfield, VT. He m 10/29/1783 in New Milford, CT, **Clarissa Cone,** d 2/6/1853 age 85, d/o **Thomas.** (*Some Early Rec. of Fairfield, VT,* p. 15 - *Northrup Gen.,* p. 77-8, 174-5)

NORTON

Aaron - b 5/12/1776 in Goshen, CT, s/o **Aaron**; Aaron (the younger) d prob. in Tallmadge, OH. Aaron m **Abigail Filer,** b1780 in VT, d prob. in Tallmadge, OH. (*OH Gen. Soc.* Oct. 1972, p. 33)

Elihu - b 1/11/1732 in Durham, CT, s/o **Joseph** and **Prudence (Osborn)**; Elihu d 4/1802 age 72 (gravestone) in Strafford, VT. He mc1755 (or mc1756) near Durham, CT, **Dinah Snow,** d 4/22/1806 age 73 in Strafford, VT (gravestone). (*Norton Gen.,* p. 15-20 - Gravestones in Strafford, VT)

Isaac - bc1790 in CT, d prob. in Benson, Rutland Co., VT. Isaac m **Louisa ----,** bc1798 in MA. In the 1850 census he was 60 and she was 52 years old. (*1850 Rutland Co., VT, Census*)

Josiah - b 10/12/1747 in Berlin, CT, s/o **Jedediah** and **Eunice** (Curtiss); Josiah d 3/26/1803 age 55 in Fairhaven, VT. He m (1) **Rebecca Cogswell**, d 1/14/1797 age 42, and m (2) **Margaret Cole**, widow. (*Hist. of Fairhaven, VT*, p. 115, 444-5)

Levi - b 5/30/1759 in Goshen, CT, d 1/21/1823 prob. in Clinton, Wayne Co., NY (or PA). Levi m1784 **Olive Wheeler**. (*Hist. of Wayne Co.*, p. 323-4 - *DAR Patriot Index*, p. 500)

Noah - bc1776 in CT, d 10/30/1853 age 78 in Strafford, VT (gravestone). Noah m (1) Mrs. **Peggy** ----, d1809, and m (2) **Sally** ----, bc1779 in NH, d 5/8/1853 age 75 in Strafford, VT (gravestone). In the 1850 census he was 74 and Sally was 71 years old. (*1850 Orange Co., VT, Census*)

Peter - b 5/11/1770 in Norfolk, CT, d 8/1822 age 52 poss. in Tallmadge, OH. Peter m **Elethina Thompson**, b1771 in Hartford, CT. (*OH Gen. Soc.* Oct. 1972, p. 33)

Salmon - b1782 in Berlin, CT, s/o **Josiah** and **Rebecca (Cogswell)**; Salmon d 1/7/1813 in 32nd year in Fairhaven, Rutland Co., VT. He mc1802 **Rebecca Merritt**, d/o **Michael**. (*History of Fairhaven, Vermont*, p. ?)

Zerah - b 7/17/1763 in Goshen, CT, s/o **Elihu** and **Dinah (Snow)**; Zerah d 10/13/1840 in Freedom, NY. He m (1) **Ruth Chamberlain**, d 6/6/1796 age 30 in Strafford, VT (gravestone), and m (2) 9/11/1796 in Strafford, VT, **Elizabeth Newman**. (*Norton-Lathrop-Tolles Gen.*, p. 15-20 - Strafford Cem. gravestones - *DAR Patriot Index*, p. 500)

NOYES

Gershom - b 7/8/1764 in Stonington, CT, d1843 in WI. Gershom m **Mary Stanton**. (*History of Chenango Co., NY*, p. 361 - *DAR Patriot Index*, p. 501)

John - b 9/8/1745 in Groton, CT, s/o **John** and **Mercy (Breed)**; John (the younger) d 10/16/1827 over 80 years old, poss. in Guilford, VT. He m 3/5/1767 **Elizabeth Rogers**. (*Gazetteer of Windham Co., VT*, p. 205 - *Des. of Rev. James Noyes of Stonington, CT*, p. 101)

Judge John - bc1769 in Stonington, CT, d 9/4/1830 age 61 in Norwich, NY. Judge John m **Priscilla Packer**, b in VT, d 10/15/1849 age 78 in Norwich, NY. (*Hist. of Chenango Co., NY*, p. 360-1)

Russell - b 10/29/1823 in Sharon, CT, d 4/16/1866 in Rochester, Monroe Co., NY. Russell m ----. (Tombstone Rec. - Mt. Hope Cemetery, NY)

Samuel - b 8/28/1807 in Stonington, CT, s/o **John B.**; Samuel d prob. in Cayuga Co., NY. He m 2/15/1827 **Catherine R. Jackson**, d prob. in Cayuga Co., NY, d/o **Asa** of Fleming, NY. (*History of Cayuga Co., NY*, p. 479)

NYE

David - b 9/29/1760 in Glastonbury, CT, s/o **Meletiah**; David d 9/9/1832 age 72 prob. in Berlin, Washington Co., VT. He m **Honor Tryon**, d 6/13/1811 in Berlin, VT. (*Nye Family*, p. 219-220, 350 - *Washington Co. Gazetteer*, p. 191 - *DAR Patriot Index*, p. 502)

Elijah - bc1766 (or bc1768) in Glastonbury, CT, d prob. in Montpelier, Washington Co., VT. Elijah m **Susannah** ----, bc1782 in NH, d prob. in Montpelier, Washington Co., VT. In the 1850 census he was 84 and she was 68 years old. (*1850 Census of Washington County, VT - Nye Family*, p. 130-1, 221, 351-3 - *Washington County Gazetteer*, p. 191)

Solomon - b 10/22/1763 in Glastonbury, CT, (br/o **Elijah** and **David**), s/o **Meletiah**; Solomon d 3/1/1857 age 93 in Berlin, Washington Co., VT. He m (1) 4/4/1784 **Lois Fuller** (his cousin), d 2/16/1826 age 64, d/o **Daniel** and **Lois (Nye)**, and m (2) **Mary Woods**, d 12/30/1866 age 91. (*Washington Co. Gazetteer*, p. 191 - *Nye Family*, p. 220, 251 - *DAR Patriot Index*, p. 502)

OATMAN

Eli - bc1777 in CT, d 1851 in Middletown, Rutland Co., VT. Eli m **Mary Simonds**, bc1781 in VT, d prob. in Rutland Co., VT. In the 1850 census he was 73 and she was 69 years old. (*1850 Rutland Co., VT, Census*)

OCAIN

John Henry - b 7/9/1902 in Goshen, CT, s/o **Ernest** and **Edith (Wright)**; John Henry d prob. in Surry, NH. He m 1/2/1921 **Genevieve K. Hall**, b 10/20/1900 in Wassaic, NY, d prob. in Surry, NH, d/o **John Henry** and **Katherine (Barley)**. (*History of Surry, New Hampshire*, p. 787)

OLCOTT

Abel - b 10/26/1768 in New Hartford, CT, s/o **Thomas** and **Lydia**; Abel d1813 in NY. He m **Mary Rounds**. (1812 Index)

Benjamin - b1732 in CT (poss. in E. Haddam), d 9/26/1813 prob. in Gilsum, NH. Benjamin m **Naomi Comstock**. (*Town of Gilsum, NH*, p. 176 - *DAR Patriot Index*, p. 504)

Elias - b 2/28/1744 in Bolton, CT, s/o **Timothy** and **Eunice (White)**; Elias d 10/29/1794 age 51 (gravestone) in Rockingham, VT. He m **Sybil Dutton** of Rockingham, VT, d 8/27/1802 age 75. (*VT Hist. Mag.*, v. 5:503 - *Gazetteer of Windham Co., VT*, p. 300 - *Hist. of Rockingham, VT*, p. 721-2)

Hon. Peter - b 4/25/1733 in Bolton, CT, s/o **Titus** and **Wid. Damaris (Marshall)**; Hon. Peter d 9/12/1808 age 75 at home of son, **Mills**, in Hanover, NH. He m 10/11/1759 **Sarah Mills**, d/o **Peletiah** of Windsor, CT. (*History of Norwich, VT*, p. 229-231 - *History of Vermont*, v. 5:56)

Timothy, Jr. - b 10/11/1739 in Bolton, CT, d 6/24/1832 in Chester, VT. Timothy m **Elizabeth Chandler**. (1812 Index)

OLMSTEAD

A. Borden - b 3/25/1824 in Wilton, CT, d 8/13/1849 in Sweden Twp., Monroe Co., NY. A. Borden m ----. (Tombstone Rec-Brockport Cem.)

Ashbel - b 12/18/1750 in E. Haddam, CT, s/o **Ichabod** and **Dorothy (Bates)**; Ashbel d1832 in NY. He m **Ruth Cone**. (1812 Index)

Asher - bc1772 in Danbury, CT, d prob. in Benson, Rutland Co., VT. Asher m (2) **Sally Barber**, bc1775 in MA, d prob. in Benson, Rutland Co., VT. In the 1850 census he was 78 and she was 75 years old. (*1850 Rutland Co., VT, Census*)

David - bc1745 in Norwalk, CT, d 11/29/1829 in Jessup, (PA). David m **Sarah Waller**. (*DAR Patriot Index*, p. 505 - *Susquehanna Co., Pennsylvania*, p. 361)

George B. - b 11/25/1805 in Wilton, CT, d 2/23/1858 in Sweden Twp., Monroe Co., NY. George B. m **Sarah A. Belden**, b 10/12/1804 in Wilton, CT, d 8/19/1882. (Tombstone Rec-Brockport Cemetery - *Hist. of Monroe Co., NY*, p. 279)

James - b 4/5/1755 in Norwalk, CT, d 1/4/1841 in Arkwright, Chautauqua Co., NY. James m ----. (*Soldiers of Am. Rev. - Chautauqua Co., NY*, p. ?)

ORCUTT

John - bc1788 in CT, d 5/3/1876 in Hartland, Windsor Co., VT. John m **Sally** ----, bc1789 in CT, d prob. in Hartland, Windsor Co., VT. In the 1850 census John was 62 and Sally was 63 years old. (*1850 Windsor Co., VT, Census*)

ORMS

Jonathan - bc1764 in CT, d1812 in VT. Jonathan m **Eunice Hines**. (1812 Index)

ORTON

Oliver - b 8/15/1809 in CT, s/o **William**; Oliver d prob. in Dutchess Co., NY. He m **Ruth Burton**, d prob. in Dutchess Co., NY. (*Comm. Biog. Rec. of Dutchess Co., NY*, p. 695)

ORVIS

Loren - b 9/22/1768 in Norfolk, CT, s/o **Roger** and **Ruth (Howe)**; Loren d 10/5/1853 in Ferrisburg, VT. He m (1) **Elizabeth Brooks**, b 2/27/1773, d 1/1/1802 age 29, and m (2) **Lillis Brown**, b 6/13/1781, d 6/6/1867. (*Gazetteer of Addison Co., VT*, p. ? - *Orvis Fam. of America*, p. 36)

Philander - b 10/11/1772 in Norfolk, CT, s/o **Roger** and **Ruth (Howe)**; Philander d perhaps in Starksboro, Addison Co., VT. He m **Phebe Chase**. (*Gazetteer of Addison Co., VT*, p. 222 - *Orvis Fam. in America*, p. 36)

OSBORN

Amos - b 11/30/1764 in Trumbull, CT, d perhaps in Waterville, Oneida Co., NY. Amos m **Rosanna Swetland**, d perhaps in Waterville, Oneida Co., NY, d/o **Benjamin**. (*Hist. of Oneida Co.*, p. 521 - *Oneida, Our County and Its People*, p. 537 of Biog. Section)

David - b1782 in Litchfield, CT, d1859 in Camden, Oneida Co., NY. David m 12/22/1802 **Esther Potter**, b1779 in Plymouth, CT. (*Pioneer Hist. of Camden, NY*, p. 291)

PADDOCK

Ephraim - b 5/7/1768 in Tolland, CT, d 7/27/1859 in St. Johnsbury, VT. Ephraim m ----. (*Hist. of CT* by Crockett, v. 5:98)

Zenas - b1751 in Mansfield, CT, d 4/11/1827 in Pomfret, VT. Zenas m **Eunice** ----, d 5/28/1814 age 59. (*Pomfret, Vermont* by Vail, v. 2:546)

PAGE
Gilbert - bc1798 in CT, d prob. in Columbus, Chenango Co., NY. Gilbert m **Lydia** ----, bc1812 in NY, d prob. in Columbus, Chenango Co., NY. In the 1850 census he was 52 and she was 38 years old. (*1850 Census of Chenango Co., NY*)

PACKARD
Simeon - bc1777 in CT, d prob. in Halifax, Windham Co., VT. Simeon m **Deborah** ----, bc1777 in CT, d prob. in Halifax, Windham Co., VT. In the 1850 census he and she were both 73 years of age. (*1850 Census of Windham Co., VT*)

PACKER
Hon. **Asa** - b 12/29/1805 in Groton, CT, s/o **Elisha**; Hon. Asa d 5/17/1879 in Susquehanna Co., PA. He m **Sarah Minerva Blakeslee**, d/o **Zophar** and **Clarinda (Whitmore)**. (*Hist. of Susquehanna Co., PA*, p. 391)

PADDLEFORD
Jonathan - b in Ashford, CT, d 7/13/1783 prob. in Enfield, NH. Jonathan m ----. (*Gazetteer of Grafton Co., NH*, p. 251)

PAINE
Asa - b 9/17/1744 in Woodstock, CT, s/o **Ebenezer** and **Mary (Grosvenor)**; Asa d 6/7/1832 in Woodstock, VT. He m **Keziah Child**, b 12/20/1748, d 4/20/1841 in Woodstock, VT, d/o **Charles** and **Keziah (Hutchins)**. (*Gen. of Woodstock, CT, Families*, p. ? - *Pomfret, VT*, v. 2:548)

Capt. **Edward** - b 1/17/1746 in Bolton, CT, d 8/28/1841 in Painesville, OH. Capt. Edward m (1) 9/7/1769 **Elizabeth King**, and m (2) **Rebecca (White) Loomis**, and m (3) **Lorena Horey** (?). (*Rev. Soldiers Buried in Lake Co., OH*, p. ? - *DAR Patriot Index*, p. 511)

Eleazer - b1764 in E. Windsor, CT, s/o **Stephen**; Eleazer d 2/10/1804 in Painesville, OH. He m **Aurel Ellsworth**. (*Rev. Soldiers Buried in Lake Co., OH*, p. 43 - *DAR Patriot Index*, p. 511)

Elijah - b 1/21/1757 in Pomfret, CT, s/o **Seth** and **Mabel (Tyler)**; Elijah d 4/28/1842 in Williamstown, Orange Co., VT. He m 6/7/1790 **Sarah Porter**, d 5/31/1851 in Williamstown, VT, d/o **John** of Plymouth, NH. (*Gazetteer of Orange Co., VT*, p. 160-1 - *Gen. of Woodstock, CT, Families*, v. 8:13 - *Paine Gen.*, p. 111-112, 128 - *Washington Co., VT, Gazetteer*, p. 415)

Ezra - b 7/3/1770 in Pomfret, CT, d 10/17/1857 age 87 prob. in Barre, VT. Ezra m 5/3/1793 in Thetford, VT, **Mehitable Chamberlain**, b 8/31/1775 in Thetford, VT, d 3/18/1841 in Barre, VT. In the 1850 census he was 80 years old. (*Paine Gen.*. p. 269, 280 - *1850 Census of Washington Co., VT*)

Moses - bc1780 in CT, s/o **Asa** and **Keziah (Child)**; Moses d prob. in W. Windsor, Windsor Co., VT. He m **Mary** ----, bc1784 in NH, d

165

prob. in W. Windsor, Windsor Co., VT. In the 1850 census he was 70 and she was 66 years old. (*1850 Windsor Co., VT, Census*)

PAYNE

John Calvin - b 9/9/1778 in Ashford, CT, s/o **Noah** and **Surviah**; John Calvin d1846 in NY. He m **Philena Pierce**. (1812 Index)

Joseph A. - b 3/12/1786 in Lebanon, CT, d 2/8/1831 in Newburgh, OH. Joseph A. m **Betsey Cochran** of Blanford, MA. (*Branches and Twigs*, VT Gen. Soc., vol. 1:29 issue #3)

PAINTER

Gamaliel - b 5/22/1743 in New Haven, CT, s/o **Shubael** and **Elizabeth**; Gamaliel d 5/21/1819 age 76 in Salisbury, VT. He m (1) 8/20/1767 **Abigail Chipman**, d 4/21/1790 age 40 in Salisbury, VT, and m (2) **Victoria Ball**, d 6/9/1806 age 46, and m (3) **Ursula Gillett Bull**, widow, d 2/28/1824 age 77. (*New Haven Families*, p. 1337 - *Hist. of Salisbury, VT*, p. 272 - *Gazetteer of Addison Co., VT*, p. 142-3 - *Salisbury from Birth to Bicentennial*, p. 4-5)

PALMER

Abijah - b1773 in Greenwich, CT, d 10/18/1840 age 67 in Fitchville, OH. Abijah m **Clarinda ----**, b1783 in Dutchess Co., NY, d 9/13/1863 age 79 in Fitchville, OH. (*Firelands Pioneer*, p. 82-3)

Alvah - b 5/1/1794 in Greenwich, CT, d 5/27/1827 age 33 in Fitchville, OH. Alvah m ----. (*Firelands Pioneer*, p. 83 - *Residents of CT Who Migrated to Huron Co., OH*, p. 4)

Beriah - b 12/25/1741 in CT, d 5/20/1812 prob. in Ballston, Saratoga Co., NY. Beriah m **Deborah White**. (*Hist. of Saratoga Co., NY*, p. 248 - *DAR Patriot Index*, p. 512)

Daniel - b 4/22/1763 in Voluntown, CT, d 10/9/1851 in PA. Daniel m **Joanna Youngs**. (*DAR Patriot Index*, p. 512 - 1812 Index)

George - b 9/22/1719 in Stonington, CT, s/o **George** and **Hannah (Palmer)**; George (the younger) d 12/15/1809 age 90 in Stillwater, NY. He m 4/13/1738 **Hannah Marsh**, d/o **James**. (*Hist. of Saratoga Co., NY*, p. ? - *DAR Patriot Index*, p. 513)

George - bc1761 in Stonington, CT, d 3/15/1856 age 95 in Hinesburg, VT. George m ----. (*Hist. and Tales of Hinesburg*, p. 5 - *Chittenden Co. Gazetteer*, p. 205 - *American Monthly*, v. 39 p. 15)

Humphrey - b 12/25/1758 in Stonington, CT, d 7/25/1848 in Otsego Co., NY. Humphrey m (1) **Wealthy Wheeler**, and m (2) Mrs. **Eunice Tiffany**. (*Biog. Rec. of Otsego Co., NY*, p. 645 - *DAR Patriot Index*, p. 513)

Humphrey - b 3/11/1790 in Stonington, CT, s/o **Humphrey**; Humphrey (the younger) d 8/16/1878 in Otsego Co., NY. He m **Marie C. Wilber**. (*Biog. Rec. of Otsego Co., NY*, p. 645)

Jared - bc1772 in CT, d prob. in Castleton, Rutland Co., VT. He m **Philinda ----**, bc1789 in MA, d prob. in Castleton, Rutland Co., VT. In the 1850 census he was 78 and she was 61 years old. (*1850 Rutland Co., VT, Census*)

Deacon Joel - b 6/22/1788 in North Branford, CT, d 3/24/1877 in Clarkson Twp., Monroe Co., NY. Deacon Joel m **Phebe ----**, b

2/18/1790 in Granville, MA. (Tombstone Rec.-Clarkson Twp. - *Hist. of Monroe Co., NY*, p. 167-9)

John - b 6/22/1751 in Tolland, CT, d 7/7/1838 prob. in Charlotte, Chittenden Co., VT. John m **Ruth Chapman**. (*Chittenden Gazetteer*, p. 171 - *DAR Patriot Index*, p. 513)

John - b 12/19/1796 in Stafford, CT, d age 75 in Detroit, MI. John m ----. (*Pioneer Collections of MI*, v. 4:428)

Jonathan - b 12/6/1724 in CT, d1813 in NY. Jonathan m **Hannah Rundle (or Randle)**. (1812 Index - *DAR Patriot Index*, p. 513)

Joseph - bc1773 in CT, d 10/24/1849 age 76 in Vershire, Orange Co., VT. Joseph m (1) **Rachel** ----, bc1774, d 3/20/1851 age 77 (gravestone), and m (2) ----, d 6/7/1874 (gravestone). (Vershire Cemetery, Orange Co., VT)

L i n u s - b1802 in Greenwich, CT, d 4/15/1860 age 58 in Fitchville, OH. Linus m ----. (*The Firelands Pioneer*, p. 83)

M a s o n - bc1788 in CT, d 1/1870 age 81 in Detroit, Wayne Co., MI. Mason m (1) ----, and m (2) ----. (*Pioneer Collections of Michigan*, v. 4:427-8)

Noah - b 8/30/1765 in Branford, CT, s/o **Micah, Jr.** and **Hannah (H o w d)**; Noah d1835 in Pompey, Onondaga Co., NY. He m ----. (*Onondaga Co., NY*, p. 334)

Othniel (or Othnid) - b 2/13/1743 (or 2/13/1743) in Stonington, CT, s/o **Christopher** and **Esther (Prentice)**; Othniel d 5/1790 in Cayuga Co., NY, (prob. in Throopsville). He m **Silence Stevens**. (*Hist. of Cayuga Co., NY*, p. 335 - French's *Gazetteer of NY*, p. 206 - *DAR Patriot Index*, p. 513 - *History of Stonington, CT*, p. ? - *Genealogy by Wheeler*, p. 517)

William - b 4/27/1782 in Plainfield, CT, s/o **Walter** and **Mary**; William d1857 in VT. He m **Cynthia Branch**. (1812 Index)

William A. - b 9/12/1781 in Hebron, CT, s/o **Stephen** and **Susannah**; William d 12/3/1860 in Danville, Caledonia Co., VT. He m1813 **Sarah Blanchard**, d/o Capt. **Peter**. (*Hist. of VT*, v. 5:84 by Crockett - *VT Hist. Mag.*, v. 1:319 - *Gazetteer of Orange Co., VT*, p. 85)

PARDEE

William - bc1794 in CT, d poss. in Oxford, Chenango Co., NY. William m **Zeruah** ----, bc1796 in MA, d poss. in Oxford, Chenango Co., NY. (*1850 Census of Chenango Co., NY*)

PARISH

Daniel - b 10/29/1775 in CT, s/o **Jacob** and **Mehitabel Flint**; Daniel d 9/25/1852 (in Beloit, WI). He m 3/10/1800 in Braintree, VT, **Nabby Kidder**, b 2/6/1778, d 5/5/1856 in Braintree, VT. In the 1850 census he was 74 and she was 72 years old. (*1850 Orange Co., VT, Census - New England Parish Families*, p. 122)

Jacob - b 1/30/1752 in CT (prob. in Preston), s/o **Zebulon** and **Hannah (Kimball)**; Jacob d 6/23/1838 in Randolph, Orange Co., VT. He m 2/2/1773 **Mehitable Flint**, b 6/18/1753 in Windham, CT, d 9/14/1832. (*New England Parish Families*, p. 73-4 122 - *Thomas and William Flint of Salem, MA*, p. 42 - *DAR Patriot Index*, p. 514)

Jeremiah - b 2/17/1765 in Plainfield, CT, s/o **Nehemiah** and **Patience (Smith)**; Jeremiah d 7/16/1851 in Stockbridge, Windsor

Co., VT. He m **Thankful Abbot,** b 2/16/1769, d 9/17/1818. (*New England Parish Fam.*, p. 54, 23-4, 96 - *DAR Patriot Index*, p. 514)

Nathan - b 6/30/1769 in Windham, CT, s/o **Zebulon**; Nathan d 2/2/1849 in Westford, Chittenden Co., VT. He m 6/1792 **Huldah Dryer,** b 3/23/1769 in Rehoboth, MA, d 4/15/1843. (*New England Parish Families*, p. 77-8, 133-4)

Stephen - b 1/28/1755 in CT, dc1830 in MI. Stephen m **Lena Houghtaling.** (1812 Index - *DAR Patriot Index*, p. 514)

PARK

Avery - b 12/23/1781 in Preston, CT, s/o **Roswell** and **Eunice** (Starkweather); Avery d1876 in NY. He m **Betsey Meech.** (1812 Index)

Dr. Silas - b 12/1/1778 in Litchfield, CT, d1824 in Pompey, Onondaga Co., NY. Dr. Silas m **Dolly Clapp,** d1867 age 95, d/o Col. **Amasa.** (Onondaga Co., NY - *Pompey, NY*, p. 334)

PARKE

Daniel - b 4/6/1758 in E. Haddam, CT, s/o **Joseph** and **Amity (Cady)**; Daniel d 10/8/1836 age 86 in Camden, Oneida Co., NY. He m (1) 4/13/1779 **Esther Ranney,** b 1/8/1751 in E. Haddam, CT, d 5/24/1818 age 57 in Camden, NY, and m (2) Mrs. **Catherine Hurlburt,** d1840. (*Pioneer History of Camden, NY*, p. 87-92 - *Parke Fam. of CT*, p. 95 - *DAR Patriot Index*, p. 514)

Dr. Ezra - b 4/4/1793 in Middle Haddam, CT, s/o **John** and **Bethia (Smith)**; Dr. Ezra d 6/20/1844 in Oakland Co., MI. He m1821 **Rhoda Sperry,** d1846. (*Pioneer Hist. of Camden, NY*, p. 151 - *Parke Families of CT*, p. 145)

Capt. Hervey - b 4/1790 in Middle Haddam, CT, d 1-/3/1879 age 89-6 in Pontiac, Oakland Co., MI. Capt. Hervey m ----. (*Pioneer Collections of MI*, v. 3:591)

Ranney - b 3/19/1790 in E. Haddam, CT, s/o **Daniel**; Ranney d 9/6/1877 age 88 in Ruscoe, IL. He m 12/11/1817 **Phoebe Parker** of Vienna, NY, b 5/31/1795, d 8/21/1888 in Ruscoe, IL, in 93rd year. (*Pioneer History of Camden, NY*, p. 476-7 - *Parke Families of CT*, p. 143)

Sage - b 6/7/1783 in E. Haddam, CT, s/o **Daniel** and **Esther** (Ranney); Sage d 9/1848 age 65 in Amboy, Oswego Co., NY. He m 11/1/1803 in Camden, NY, **Almira Preston,** d 12/1846 in Amboy, NY, d/o **Caleb.** (*Pioneer History of Camden, NY*, p. 85 - *Parke Fam.*, p. 142-3)

PARKS

Amaziah - b1758 (or b1759) in Voluntown, CT, s/o **Amaziah**; Amaziah (the younger) d 11/4/1838 in Painesville, Lake Co., OH. He m 2/1798 **Sabra Barrett,** d1845 in Painesville, OH. (*Rev. Soldiers Buried in Lake Co., OH*, p. 43-4 - *DAR Patriot Index*, p. 514 - *Gen. of the Parke Family*, Appendix #367h)

Elijah - b 4/25/1756 in Canterbury, CT, s/o **Simeon** and **Anna**; Elijah d 4/6/1821 age 63 in Granville, NY. He m (1) 3/16/1780 **Anna Smith** of Canterbury, CT, d1793, and m (2) 8/4/1793 in Wells, VT, **Margaret Walker** of Granville, NY. (*History of Wells, VT* by Paul and Parks, p. 128-9 - *History of Wells, VT*, by Wood, p. 71 - *DAR Patriot Index*, p. 514)

Simeon - b 3/21/1768 in Canterbury, CT, s/o **Simeon** and **Ann**; Simeon (the younger) d1817 age 49 in Wells, VT. He m **Betsey Curtis**, who m (2) **Joseph Button**. (*History of Wells, Vermont*, by Paul and Parks, p. 131)

PARKER

Col. **Amasa** - b 10/28/1784 in Washington, CT, d 3/1/1855 in Delhi, Delaware Co., NY. Col. **Amasa** m ----. (*History of Delaware Co.*, p. 166)

A m a s a S. - b1805 in Washington, CT, d 9/4/1878 in Richland, Kalamazoo Co., MI. Amasa S. m ----. (*Pioneer Collections of Michigan*, v. 5, p. 378-9)

Chester - b1800 in Chester, CT, d 12/1856 in Dubuque, IA. Chester m in Poughkeepsie, NY, **Sarah DeGroff**, b1804 in Poughkeepsie, NY, d/o **Cornelius**. (*Comm. Biog. Rec. of Dutchess Co., NY*, p. 617)

Enos - b 3/12/1744 in Wallingford, CT, d 1/1815 in NY. Enos m **Damarius (Parker)**. (1812 Index - *DAR Patriot Index*, p. 515 - *For King and Country*, Orange Co., CA Bicent. Proj. of 1975)

Ezra - b 12/2/1745 in Wallingford, CT, s/o **Andrew** and **Susannah (Blacksley)**; Ezra d 7/7/1842 in MI. He m (1) **Sarah Tuttle**, and m (2) **Elizabeth Perry**. (1812 Index - *DAR Patriot Index*, p. 515)

J o h n - bc1790 in CT, d poss. in Chelsea, Orange Co., VT. John m **Hannah** ----, bc1795 in VT. In the 1850 census he was 60 and she was 45 years old. (*1850 Orange Co., VT, Census*)

Levi - bc1781 in CT, d poss. in New Berlin, Chenango Co., NY. Levi m **Polly** ----, bc1787 in MA, d poss. in New Berlin, Chenango Co., NY. In the 1850 census he was 69 and she was 63 years old. (*1850 Census of Chenango Co., NY*)

PARKILL

David - b in CT, d1832 in Cornwall, VT. David m ----. (*Gazetteer of Addison Co., VT*, p. 95)

PARKHURST

David - b1761 in CT, d1824 in NY. David m **Polly Burroughs**. (1812 Index)

Ebenezer - bc1767 in CT, d poss. in Royalton, Windsor Co., VT. Ebenezer m **Susan** ----, d poss. in Royalton, Windsor Co., VT. In the 1850 census he was 83 and she was 69 years old. (*1850 Census of Windsor Co., VT*)

J a r e d - bc1769 in CT, d poss. in Sharon, Windsor Co., VT. Jared m **Lucy** ----, bc1772 in VT, d poss. in Sharon, Windsor Co., VT. In the 1850 census he was 81 and she was 78 years old. (*1850 Census of Windsor Co., VT*)

PARMELEE

Asaph - b 4/2/1745 (or 4/2/1746) in Chatham, CT, s/o **Jonathan** and **Sarah (Taylor)**; Asaph d 10/4/1834 in 90th year in Bristol, VT. He m (1) 11/21/1769 in Woodbury, CT, **Sarah Everett**, b 11/14/1749 in Woodbury, CT, d 8/25/1806 age 35 in Starksboro, VT, d/o **D a n i e l** and **Elizabeth (Steele)**, and m (2) **Huldah Marshall**, b1763, d 5/4/1855 in Starksboro, VT. (*Parmelee Data*, v. 1:2 – *DAR Patriot Index*, p. 517)

Asaph, Jr. – b 1/6/1778 in CT, s/o **Asaph** and **Sarah (Everett)**; Asaph, Jr. d poss. in Bristol, Addison Co., VT. He m (1) **H a n n a h Hall**, b1780 in Norfolk, CT, d/o **Hiland** and **Dolly (Tuttle)**, and m (2) Mrs. **B e t s e y F o o t e**, d poss. in Bristol, Addison Co., VT. (*Parmelee Data*, v. 1:2 – *Hall Gen.*, p. 22–3)

Major **Danforth** – b 2/27/1783 in Killingworth, CT, s/o **Oliver** and **Lucretia (Smith)**; Major Danforth d 5/18/1867 in Almont, Lapeer Co., PA. He m before 1818 in Claremont, NH, **Patience Strobridge**, b 2/28/1794 in Claremont, NH, d 3/20/1862 in Almont, PA, d/o Capt. **John** and **Patience (Tyler)**. (*DSGR* Fall 1971, p. 25)

Daniel Everett – b 2/4/1776 in Bethlehem, CT, s/o **Asaph** and **Sarah (Everett)**; Daniel Everett d 1/2/1864 age 88 in Bristol, VT. He m (1) 6/4/1803 **Samantha Fuller**, b1784, d 9/27/1806, and m (2) 11/1/1809 in Middlebury, VT, **Charlotte Norton**, b1788 in VT, d 4/30/1867 age 79 in Bristol, VT. (*Parmelee Data*, v. 1-2, p. 71, 394–5)

Dr. **Jeremiah** – b 5/4/1769 in Killingworth, CT, s/o **Jeremiah** and **Temperance (Blackley)**; Dr. Jeremiah d 8/24/1833 age 64 in Wilmington, Windham Co., VT. He m 9/20/1791 **R u t h C o o k**, b 7/27/1769, d 3/9/1841 in Wilmington, VT. (*Parmelee Gen.*, v. II, p. 388-9, 518 – *Windham Co., VT, Gazetteer*, p. 304)

Simeon – b 8/3/1740 in Durham, CT, s/o **Hezekiah** and **Mehitable (Hall)**; Simeon d 5/3/1820 poss. in Pittsford, Rutland Co., VT. He m 10/22/1774 in Berkshire Co., MA, **Jemima Hopkins**, b 7/2/1753 in Tyringham, MA, d 5/14/1831, d/o **Nehemiah** and **Tryphena (Smith)**. (*Hist. of Pittsford, VT*, p. 218, 718 – *DAR Patriot Index*, p. 517 – *Parmelee Fam.*, p. 94A)

Thomas – b 7/31/1742 in Guilford, CT, d1826 (or d1827) age 85 in Clinton, Oneida Co., NY. Thomas m (1) **Elizabeth Roots**, and m (2) **Olive Curtis**, d 2/25/1836 age 84. (*Clinton Memorial-Kirtland Ave. Cem.*, p. 26-7 – *DAR Lineage*, v. 52, p. 448 – *DAR Patriot Index*, p. 517 – *CT Hist. Coll.*, v. 8:173)

PARMLY

Jehiel – b 10/11/1742 in Newtown, CT, s/o **Stephen** and **Elizabeth (S h a r p e)**; Jehiel d 7/14/1804 in Braintree, Orange Co., VT (gravestone). He m 11/1764 **Eunice Hendee**, b 5/31/1744, d 9/20/1823, d/o **Joshua** and **Elizabeth (Wheelock)**. (*Hist. of Braintree, VT*, p. 170-1 – *Parmelee Gen.*, p. 114)

PARSONS

George – b 4/10/1781 in Enfield, CT, d 8/20/1865 in OH. George m 12/10/1807 **Frances M. Austin**, d 6/19/1850. (*Trumbull and Mahoning Cos., OH*, p. 335)

J a b i s h – b in Suffield, CT, d 11/4/1792 by accident in Rupert, VT. Jabish m ––––. (*Hartford Courant*, iss. 12/3/1792)

Lt. **J o h n** – b 1/1/1737 (or 1/1/1738) in Durham, CT, d 3/2/1821 in Sandersfield, MA. Lt. John m (1) 1760 **Hannah Wadsworth**, and m

(2) **Mercy Gibson.** (*New Eng. Gen. Reg.* Query 4/1956, p. 160 - *DAR Patriot Index*, p. 518)

Joseph - b1763 in CT, d1851 in OH. Joseph m **Elizabeth Westcott.** (1812 Index)

Moses - b 2/17/1782 in Enfield, CT, d 3/23/1869 age 87 in Hambden, OH. Moses m 10/25/1807 **Eleaba Pease**, b 4/9/1786 in Longmeadow, MA, d 4/22/1856 in Hambden, OH. (*History of Geauga Co., OH*, p. 355)

S a m u e l - b 12/15/1765 in Redding, CT, d 5/27/1846 age 80 in Hubbardton, Rutland Co., VT. Samuel m **Esther Selleck**, d 2/21/1848. (*Rutland Gazetteer*, p. 142 - *VT Hist. Mag.*, v. 4, p. 1173-4)

Samuel Like - b 10/30/1831 in CT, d in MI. Samuel Like m **Sarah Cook.** (*VT Hist. Mag.*, v. 5, p. 303)

PARTCH

John - b 9/29/1780 in Danbury, CT, dc1872 age 92 in Hinesburgh, Chittenden Co., VT. John m **Ruby ----**, b in VT. In the 1850 census he was 70 and she was 56 years old. (*Chittenden Co. Gazetteer*, p. 211 - *1850 Census of Chittenden Co., VT*)

PARTRIDGE

Elias - b 7/1/1758 in Preston, CT, s/o **Samuel** and **Ruth (Woodward)**; Elias d 9/29/1826 (poss. in Norwich) in VT. He m 12/31/1778 in Norwich, VT, **Sarah Brown.** (*Partridge Gen.*, p. 19, 24 - *DAR Patriot Index*, p. 518)

Elisha - b1743 (or b1744) in Preston, CT, s/o **Samuel** and **Ruth (Woodward)**; Elisha d 4/1/1823 (perhaps in Norwich) in VT. He m 11/14/1765 in Norwich, VT, **Margaret Murdock**, d/o **Thomas.** (*History of Norwich, VT*, p. 31-3 - *Partridge Gen.*, p. 19, 23 - *DAR Patriot Index*, p. 518

I s a a c - b 8/21/1761 in Preston, CT, s/o **S a m u e l** and **R u t h (Woodward)**; Isaac d 5/15/1835 in Norwich, VT. He m 11/3/1785 **Lois Newton.** (*Partridge Gen.*, p. 19, 25)

James - b 3/9/1748 in CT, dc1830 age 82 in Edinburgh, Saratoga Co., NY. James m 2/8/1776 **Amy Herrick**, d age 99-9-29, d/o **Nathan** of CT. (*Hist. of Saratoga Co., NY*, p. 369, 377-8)

Samuel - b 4/23/1722 in Preston, CT, s/o **Samuel** and **Deborah (R o s e)**; Samuel (the younger) d 8/24/1806 age 85 in Norwich, Windsor Co., VT (gravestone). He m **Ruth Woodward**, b 2/23/1719 in Preston, CT, d 4/29/1786 in Norwich, VT (gravestone), d/o **Daniel** and **Thankful (Gates).** (*History of Norwich, VT*, p. 231-2 - *Partridge Gen.*, p. 19)

S a m u e l - b 12/28/1748 in Preston, CT, s/o **S a m u e l** and **R u t h (W o o d w a r d)**; Samuel (the younger) d 7/22/1834 in Norwich, Windsor Co., VT. He m 12/6/1770 in Norwich, VT, **Elizabeth Wright.** (*Partridge Gen.*, p. 19, 24)

PATCHIN

Freegift - b 2/20/1758 in CT, d 8/30/1830 in NY. Freegift m **Molly Morehouse.** (War of 1812 Index - *DAR Patriot Index*, p. 519)

PATRICK

Ralph - b 9/16/1764 in CT, d 8/8/1846 in NY. Ralph m **Mary** ----.
(*DAR Patriot Index*, p. 519 - 1812 Index)

PATERSON

John - b1744 in CT, d 7/10/1808 in NY.   John m **Elizabeth Lee.**
(1812 Index - *DAR Patriot Index*, p. 520)

PATTERSON

Charles - b 9/22/1745 in New Fairfield, CT, s/o **Andrew**; Charles d
5/29/1837. He m **Martha Hall.** (*Hist. of Little Nine Partners*, p. ?
- *DAR Patriot Index*, p. 520)

Josiah Lee - b 10/11/1766 in Farmington, CT, s/o Gen. **John** and
Elizabeth; Josiah Lee d 3/2/1846 in Parma, NY. He m 1/1788 in
Lenox, MA, **C l a r i s s a   H y d e**, b 4/27/1767 in Lebanon, CT, d
4/16/1837 in Parma, NY, d/o Gen. **C a l e b**. (Tombstone Rec., Mt.
Hope Cem. - *Hyde Gen.*, v. 1:270-1)

Oliver - bc1787 in CT, d perhaps in Castleton, Rutland Co., VT.
Oliver m **Charlotte** ----, bc1803 in VT, d perhaps in Castleton,
Rutland Co., VT. In the 1850 census he was 63 and she was 47
years old. (*1850 Rutland Co. Census*)

Sherman - b 12/15/1753 in CT, d 7/6/1842 age 90. Sherman m **Huldah Beach.** (*American Monthly*, v. 43 - *DAR Patriot Index*, 520)

PEABODY

Asa - b1784 in CT, d1826 in NY. Asa m **Mary Ann Ness.** (1812 Index)

PEAK

Asa - bc1800 in CT, d perhaps in Stamford, Bennington Co., VT.   Asa
m **Hannah** ----, bc1802 in MA, d perhaps in Stamford, Bennington
Co., VT. In the 1850 census he was 50 and she was 48 years old.
(*1850 Bennington Co., VT, Census*)

Jonathan - b 1/13/1765 in Woodstock, CT, s/o **Lemuel** and **Joanna**
(Ellington); Jonathan d 11/28/1855 in Bethel, VT. He m (1) **Sarah**
(or **Sally**) **W a l k e r**, d 3/20/1809 in Randolph, VT, and m (2)
3/8/1810 **Rebecca Cumins**, d 11/28/1855 in Bethel, VT. In the
1850 census he was 87 and **F a n n y**, a daughter, was 55 years old.
(*1850 Orange Co., VT, Census - Peake Fam. Hist.*, #1765)

PEAKE

E p h r a i m - b 3/27/1736 in Woodstock, CT, s/o **J o n a t h a n** and
Mehitable (Perrin); Ephraim d 2/6/1813 in Pomfret, Windsor Co.,
VT. He m 4/1/1773 **Peggy Smith**, bc1740, d 8/19/1798 in Pomfret,
VT. (*Peak-Peake Fam. Hist.*, p. ?)

Lemuel - b 9/30/1733 in Woodstock, CT, s/o **Jonathan and Mehitable**
(Perrin); Lemuel d in VT, had lived in Pomfret, Randolph, and
Chelsea, VT. He m 3/13/1760 **Johanna Ellingwood**, b 7/29/1739, d
3/9/1794, d/o **Jonathan** and **Johanna (Hunt)**. (Gen. of Woodstock
Fam. v. 8:93 - Pomfret, VT v. 2 - Peak-Peake Fam. Hist. #1773)

W i l l i a m - b1769 in Woodstock, CT, s/o **S a m u e l** and **J o a n n a**
(Ellingwood); William d 4/26/1853 in Stamford, Bennington Co.,

VT. He m 10/19/1797 in Woodstock, CT, **Sally Bugbee**. (*Peak-Peake Fam. Hist.*, #1733)

PEASE

Aaron – bc1786 in CT, d prob. in Marlboro, Windham Co., VT. Aaron m **Tabithy** ----, bc1788 in CT. In the 1850 census he was 64 and she was 62 years old. (*1850 Census of Windham Co., VT*)

Calvin – b 9/9/1776 in Suffield, CT, s/o **Joseph** and **Mindwell (King)**; Calvin d 9/17/1839 in Warren, OH. He m1804 **Laura Want Risley**. (*Trumbull-Mahoning Co., OH*, p. 174, 216 – 1812 Index)

Dudley – b 3/5/1785 in Norwalk, CT, s/o **Nathaniel** and **Jerusha (Hall)**; Dudley d 3/17/1855 in Poughkeepsie, NY. He m (1) 11/14/1805 **Lewrelly Loomis**, and m (2) **Maria Sears**, and m (3) **Sarah Rilley**. (*Comm. Biog. Rec., Dutchess Co., NY*, p. 239 – *Pease Record*, p. 79, 206)

Elijah – bc1770 in CT, d perhaps in Weston, Windsor Co., VT. Elijah m **Polly** ----, bc1785 in NH, d perhaps in Weston, Windsor Co., VT. In the 1850 census he was 80 and she was 65 years old. (*1850 Census of Windsor Co., VT*)

Gains – b 10/21/1771 in Enfield, CT, d1855 age 83 prob. in Jericho, Chittenden Co., VT. Gains m **Abigail** ----, bc1775 in MA. In the 1850 census he was 78 and she was 75 years old. (*Chittenden Gazetteer*, p. 230 – *1850 Census of Chittenden Co., VT*, for Jericho)

Lemuel – b 9/1771 in CT, d perhaps in Liverpool, Onondaga Co., NY. Lemuel m1793 in CT, **Esther Butler**, b 12/19/1774, d perhaps in Liverpool, Onondaga Co., New York. (*NEGR* Bible Record July 1964, p. 237-9)

Pelatiah – b1737 in Enfield, CT, s/o **Peletiah** and **Jemima (Booth)**; Pelatiah d 2/15/1811 prob. in Gilsum, NH. He m 10/19/1766 **Anna Parsons**, b1741 in Springfield, MA, d 5/29/1787, d/o **John** of Springfield, MA. (*Pease Rec.*, p. 33 – *Town of Gilsum, NH*, p. 374)

Salmon – b 6/14/1783 in Norfolk, CT, s/o **Calvin** and Sally **(Ives)**; Salmon d perhaps in Charlotte, Chittenden Co., VT. He m 6/14/1803 **Matilda Huntington**, d perhaps in Charlotte, Chittenden Co., VT, d/o Dr. **Thomas** of Canaan, CT. In the 1850 census he was 67 and she was 69 years old. (*1850 Chittenden Co., VT, Census – Pease Record*, p. 199)

PECK

Elias – b 1/5/1785 in Greenwich, CT, s/o **Robert** and **Ann (Read)**; Elias d 8/10/1867 in LaSalle, IL. He m 10/11/1812 in Greenwich, CT, **Eunice Williams**, d 4/26/1865 in Stamford, CT. (*NEGR* Query Jan. 1956, p. 69)

Eleazer – b 1/6/1793 in CT, d 5/29/1848 age 55 prob. in Camden, NY. Eleazer m 2/16/1815 **Hannah** ----, b 7/27/1796 in Chatham, CT (?), d 5/6/1869 age 74. (*Pioneer Hist. of Camden, NY*, p. ?)

Enos – b1752 in Greenwich, CT, s/o **Peter** and **Sarah**; Enos d 5/23/1835 in Camillus, NY. He m (1) **Anna Marsh**, and m (2) **Lavina Wilcox**. (*Des. of Wm. Peck* by Darius Peck, p. 24, 45)

Henry – b 3/7/1764 in New Haven, CT, d 2/14/1833 in Camden, Oneida Co., NY. Henry m **Elizabeth Clark**, b 7/19/1766, d 9/21/1842. (*Pioneer Hist. of Camden, NY*, p. ?)

173

Josiah - b1793 in CT, d1849 in OH. Josiah m **Elizabeth C. Bogue**. (1812 Index)

Luther - bc1793 in CT, d perhaps in Pitcher, Chenango Co., NY. Luther m **Mary** ----, bc1796 in RI, d perhaps in Pitcher, Chenango Co., NY. In the 1850 census he was 57 and she was 54 years old. (*1850 Census of Chenango Co., NY*)

Nathaniel - b1782 in CT, d1871 in NY. Nathaniel m **Abigail Starr**. (1812 Index)

Peter - b 1/1746 in Litchfield, CT, d 6/17/1813 prob. in Queensbury, Warren Co., NY. Peter m 12/7/1768 in New Milford, CT, **S a r ah Terrill**, d/o **Paul**. (*Hist. of Warren Co., NY*, p. 389, 610 - *DAR Patriot Index*, p. 524)

Peter - b 6/15/1769 in CT, s/o **Charles**; Peter d 8/8/1835 prob. in Danville, Caledonia Co., VT. He m **Diana Peck**, d/o **Peleg**. (*Peck Gen.*, p. 126-7)

Silas - b1787 in New London, CT, s/o **Daniel**; Silas d1864 age 77 in Otsego Co., NY. He m 10/28/1810 **Abigail Cutting**, b in MA. In the 1850 census he was 62 and she was 59 years old. (*Biog. Rev., Otsego Co., NY*, p. 845 - *1850 Census of Chenango Co., NY*)

Thomas - b 8/15/1762 in Canterbury, CT, s/o **Reuben** and **Charity** (**F r e n c h**); Thomas d 3/18/1826 age 64 in Brookfield, Orange Co., VT. He m **Priscilla Howard**, d 2/2/1849 age 77 in Brookfield Center, VT. She m (2) Dr. **Walter Burnham**. (1812 Index - *Gazetteer of Orange Co., VT*, p. 215 - Brookfield Center Cemetery Gravestones)

PELTON

Amos - bc1799 in CT, d prob. in Woodstock, Windsor Co., VT. Amos m **Betsey** ----, bc1805 in VT, d prob. in Woodstock, Windsor Co., VT. In the 1850 census he was 51 and she was 45 years old. (*1850 Census Windsor Co., VT*)

Enoch - b 8/7/1770 in E. Windsor, CT, s/o **Nathan** and **Ruth**; Enoch d1829 in VA. He m **Matilda Backman**. (1812 Index)

Frederick - b 3/24/1827 in Chester, CT, s/o **Russell**; Frederick d in Brooklyn, OH. He m 8/26/1848 **Susan Dennison** of Brooklyn, OH. (*Hist. of Cuyahoga Co., OH*, p. 371)

Jesse - b1778 in CT, d1862 in PA. Jesse m **Ruhama Wolf**. (1812 Index)

Russell - b 7/20/1803 in Portland, CT, d in Brooklyn, OH. Russell m 8/20/1821 **Pamelia Abby**, d/o **Asaph**. (*Hist. of Cuyahoga Co., OH*)

PEMBER

Andrew - b 11/25/1753 in Norwich, CT, s/o **John**; Andrew d1812 in Quebec, Canada. He m **Jemima** ---- of Amenia, NY. (*Pember Fam.*, p. 74 - *DAR Patriot Index*, p. 525)

Eli - b 8/17/1762 in Norwich, CT, s/o **John**; Eli d 6/22/1851 in Carlisle, Lorain Co., OH. He m (1) 9/24/1789 in Poultney, VT, **Susan Haskell**, and m (2) 12/23/1839 in Carlisle Twp., OH, Mrs. **Clarissa B o w e n**, b 5/10/1787, d 9/1/1858 in Wood Co., OH. (*Pember Family*, p. 78)

Elijah - b1729 in Norwich Farms, CT, s/o **John** and **Mary (Hyde)**; Elijah d 3/15/1812 in Randolph, VT. He m **Hannah Cross** of Ellington, CT. (*Historical Souvenir of Randolph*, p. 104 - *DAR Patriot Index*, p. 525)

Frederick - b 4/24/1781 in Lebanon Crank (or Columbia), CT, s/o **John**; Frederick d 9/21/1859 in Wells, VT. He m 2/1803 **Sarah Polley Stephens**, b 7/27/1785 in Wells, VT, d 2/2/1862 in Wells, VT. In the 1850 census he was 69 and she was 65 years old. (*Hist. of the Town of Wells, VT*, p. 76 - *1850 Census of Rutland Co., VT*)

Jabez - b178- in Norwich Farms, CT, s/o **Jacob**; Jabez d after 1821 in Middlebury, Addison Co., VT. He m 1/17/1809 in Middlebury, VT, **Rebecca Selleck**, d/o **Seymour**. (*Pember Fam.*, p. 100)

Jerah A. - b 4/1/1806 in New London, CT, s/o **Thomas**; Jerah A. d 3/24/1886 in Attica, Wyoming Co., NY. He m **Wealthy** ----, b 1/21/1809, d 7/3/1887 age 78. (*Pember Family*, p. 104)

PEMBER

John - b 10/31/1751 in Franklin, CT, s/o **John**; John (the younger) d 9/27/1827 in Harmony Twp., Chautauqua Co., NY. He m 11/24/1774 **Lucretia Bill**, d1815, d/o **Ebenezer**. (*Pember Fam.*, p. 64 - *DAR Patriot Index*, p. 525 - *Hist. of Town of Wells, VT*, p. 76)

John - bc1777 in Lebanon Crank (or Columbia), CT, s/o **John**; John (the younger) d in Lysander (Hannibal), Onondaga Co., NY. He mc1798 in Poultney, VT, **Diana Willson**. (*Pember Family*, p. 111-112)

Lucius - b 2/7/1817 in Franklin, CT, s/o **Thomas**; Lucius d1859 in KY. He m **Elizabeth Ann Travis**, b 8/25/1825, dc1890. (*Pember Fam.*, p. 154)

Parley - b 4/26/1797 in Ellington, CT, s/o **Elisha**; Parley d 10/13/1856 in Willet, Cortland Co., NY. He m 10/18/1818 in Butternuts, NY, **Abigail Covey**, b 7/18/1793 in Butternuts, NY, d 9/6/1856 age 63. (*Pember Fam.*, p. 147)

Samuel - bp 1/4/1750 in Stafford, CT, s/o **Elijah**; Samuel d 3/14/1826 age 76 in Randolph, Orange Co., VT. He mc1777 **Esther Reade** of Ellington, CT, b 6/27/1758 in CT, d 8/10/1826 in Randolph, VT. (*Pember Fam.*, p. 85-7 - *Gazetteer of Orange Co., VT*, p. 348-9 - *Hist. Souvenir of Randolph, VT*, p. 104 - *DAR Patriot Index*, p. 525 - *Hartford Courant* iss. 4/17/1826)

Stephen - b 10/14/1760 in Stafford, CT, s/o **Elijah**; Stephen d 1/8/1827 in Randolph, Orange Co., VT. He m in E. Windsor, CT, **Sybil Bissell** of Windsor, CT, b1763, d1837 in Randolph, VT. (*Hist. Souvenir of Randolph, VT*, p. 104 - *Pember Fam.*, p. 89-90)

Thomas - b 2/28/1790 in New London, CT, s/o **Thomas**; Thomas (the younger) d 1/4/1843 in Batavia, Genesee Co., NY. He m 1/9/1811 in CT, **Pamelia Williams**, b 2/9/1794, d 1/27/1873 in Batavia, NY. (*Pember Fam.*, p. 102)

Thomas - b 3/2/1753 in New London, CT, s/o **Jonathan**; Thomas d 8/6/1824 prob. in Waterford, Genesee Co., NY. He m 4/8/1789 in New London, CT, **Esther Daniels**. (*Pember Fam.*, p. 53)

Thomas - b 3/2/1757 in Stafford, CT, s/o **Elijah**; Thomas d 10/16/1780 age 23 in Royalton, VT (killed by Indians). He m 10/1780 **Lorenza Havens**. She m (2) **Daniel Lovejoy**. (*Pember Fam.*, p. 88-9)

175

PENDLETON

Nathan - b 4/2/1754 in Stonington, CT, d 1/26/1841 prob. in Oxford, Chenango Co., NY. Nathan m (1) **Amelia Babcock**, and m (2) **Rhoda Babcock Gavitt.** (*Annals of Oxford, NY*, p. 439 - *DAR Patriot Index*, p. 525)

PENFIELD

Daniel - b 4/25/1759 in Guilford, CT, d 8/24/1840 age 81 in Penfield Twp., Monroe Co., NY. Daniel mc1784 **Mary Fellows**, b 9/10/1762 in Sheffield, MA, d 8/18/1828 age 65, d/o Gen. **Jonathan** and **Mary** (**Ashley**). (*Hist. of Monroe Co., NY*, p. 18, 216-8, 236 - *Gen. of Des. of Samuel Penfield*, p. 25, 87 - Tombstone Records - *DAR Patriot Index*, p. 525)

Jesse - b1759 (or b1760) (in Plymouth, CT); d 12/18/1838 in Camden, NY. Jesse m (1) **Sarah Hall**, and m (2) **Polly Upson.** (*Pioneer Hist. of Camden, NY*, p. 309-10 - *DAR Patriot Index*, p. 525)

John - b 11/25/1747 in Fairfield, CT, s/o **Peter** and **Mary (Allen)**; John d 11/11/1829 in Pittsford, VT. He m 11/1/1770 **Eunice Ogden**, b 6/17/1753, d 5/3/1815 in Pittsford, VT, d/o **David** and **Jane** (**Sturgis**). (*History of Pittsford, VT*, p. 286, 340 - *History of Rutland Co., VT*, p. 743 - *Penfield Gen.*, p. 10, 21-23 - *DAR Patriot Index*, p. 525)

Samuel - b 2/20/1763 in Wallingford, CT, d 8/24/1851 age 88 in Westfield, Chautauqua Co., NY. Samuel m **Elizabeth** ----, d 9/27/1845 age 88. (*Soldiers of Am. Rev., Chautauqua Co., NY*, p. ? - *DAR Mag.* 1977, p. 920)

Sturgis - b 9/1/1780 in CT, s/o **John** and **Eunice (Ogden)**; Sturgis d 4/26/1866 prob. in Pittsford, Rutland Co., VT. He m 1/12/1806 **Laura Gidding**, b 1/23/1785 in CT, d 10/13/1854. In the 1850 census he was 69 and she was 65 years old. (*1850 Rutland Co., VT, Census*)

PENNOCK

Ira - bc1767 in CT, d 6/19/1852 age 85 in Strafford, Orange Co., VT. Ira m **Molly** ----, b in New Milford, CT, d 3/4/1861 age 96. In the 1850 census he was 83 and she was 85 years old. (*1850 Orange Co., VT, Census*)

James - bc1712 in CT, d 11/2/1808 age 96. James m **Thankful Root**, d 12/23/1798 age 81. (*Orange Co. Gazetteer*, p. 402 - Old City Cem. of Strafford, VT)

PENNOYER

Hon. Henry - b 2/8/1809 in Norwalk, CT, d 4/30/1886 in Crockney, Kent Co., MI. Hon. Henry m (1) **Harriet Kells**, d1852, and m (2) ----. (*Pioneer Collections of MI*, p. 86-7)

PERKINS

Elijah - b 1/28/1755 in New Haven, CT, d 3/24/1833 in Oneida Co., NY, (poss. in Camden). Elijah m 8/9/1774 **Lydia Sperry**, b 11/16/1754 in New Haven, CT, d1849 age 90, d/o **Jacob** and **Lydia** (**Tuttle**). (*New Haven Families*, p. 1431 - *Hist. of Oneida Co., NY*, p. 433 - *Pioneer Hist. of Camden, NY*, p. 43-4)

Erastus - b 1/18/1778 in Norwich, CT, s/o Capt. **Erastus** and **Anna (Glover)**; Erastus d 5/30/1852 prob. in Oxford, Chenango Co., NY. He m (1) in Oxford, NY, **Abigail Stephens**, d 1/31/1815 age 34, d/o **Alvin**, and m (2) **Ursula Allen** of CT, d 1/2/1821 age 42, wid/o **William**, and m (3) **Agnes Van Wagenen**, b 12/12/1788, d 2/13/1868, d/o **Gerrit**. (*Annals of Oxford, NY*, p. 147 - *Hist. of Chenango Co., NY*, p. 260)

Ethiel - b 1/10/1734 in Derby, CT, s/o **Roger** and **Ann (Russell)**; Ethiel d 2/1826 in Fair Haven, Rutland Co., VT. He m 10/26/1767 **Esther Fox**. (*Hist. of Fair Haven, VT*, p. 450 - *Hist. of Rutland Co., VT*, p. 598 - *Des. of Edward Perkins*, p. 31)

Francis - b 8/27/1758 in New London, CT, d 12/26/1844 age 86 prob. in Middletown, Rutland Co., VT. Francis m (1) 11/29/1781 in Lisbon, CT, **Esther Colburn**, and m (2) **Saloma Dye**. In the 1850 census Saloma was 80 living with **Philo** (46 years old) and **Charlotte Dye** (47 years old). (*Hist. of Rutland Co., VT*, p. ? - *DAR Patriot Index*, p. 527 - *1850 Rutland Co., VT, Census*)

Philo - b1767 in CT, d1836 in VT. Philo m **Chloe Cook**. (1812 Index)

Ralph - bc1797 in CT, d prob. in Fair Haven, VT. Ralph m **Polly A. ----**, bc1801 in VT, d prob. in Fair Haven, VT. In the 1850 census he was 53 and she was 49 years old. (*1850 Rutland County, Vermont, Census*)

Rufus - bc1777 in CT, d prob. in Pawlet, Rutland Co., VT. Rufus m **Selinda ----**, bc1790 in VT, d prob. in Pawlet, Rutland Co., VT. In the 1850 census he was 73 and she was 60 years old. (*1850 Rutland Co., VT, Census*)

Gen. **Simon** - b 9/17/1771 in Norwich, CT, d 11/19/1844 in Warren, Trumbull Co., OH. Gen. Simon m 3/18/1804 **Nancy Ann Bishop** of Lisbon, CT, d 4/1862 in Warren, OH. (*Trumbull and Mahoning Counties, OH*, p. 310-11)

Stephen - bc1790 in CT, d1878 in WI. Stephen m **Eliza Smith**. He was a POW in 1813-1814. (1812 Index)

PERRIN

Asa - b 7/21/1761 in Woodstock, CT, s/o **Asa** and **Olive (Bellows) Daily**; Asa (the younger) d 9/10/1845 in Potsdam, NY. He m 2/26/1784 in Royalton, VT, **Zeruah Bloss**, b 5/22/1763, d 5/28/1855 in Potsdam, NY, d/o **Richard** and **Sarah (Barrett)**. (*Hist. of Royalton, VT*, p. 905-6 - *John Perrin Fam.*, p. 46, 80-2)

Asa - b 5/5/1733 in Woodstock, CT, s/o **Nathaniel** and **Abigail (Jackson)**; Asa d 6/1816 in Royalton, VT. He m 3/1/1759 in Killingly, CT, **Olive (Bellows) Daily**, b1737 in Canterbury, CT, d 9/17/1815 in Royalton, VT. (*Gen. of Woodstock Fam.*, v. 8, p. 124 - *John Perrin Fam.*, p. 25 - *DAR Patriot Index*, p. 528 - *Hist. of Royalton, VT*, p. 904-5)

Calvin - b1793 in CT, d1824 in PA. Calvin m **Polly Newton**. (1812 Index)

Greenfield - b 11/11/1763 in CT, s/o **Asa** and **Olive (Daily)**; Greenfield d 6/2/1854 in Royalton, Windsor Co., VT. He m 6/4/1792 in Northfield, VT, **Sally Ashcraft**, b 12/3/1775, d 6/18/1842 in Northfield, VT, d/o **William** and **Tamasin (Cady)**. In the 1850 census he was 86 and living with **Asa** (34 years old) and **Hannah** (34 years old) **Perrin.** (*John Perrin Family of Rehoboth, MA*, p. 46-7, 82-4 - *History of Royalton, VT*, p. 907 - *1850 Windsor Co., VT, Census*)

Nathaniel - b 1/2/1760 in Woodstock, CT, s/o **Asa** and **Olive (Daily)**; Nathaniel d 10/30/1827 in Royalton, Windsor Co., VT. He m (1) 11/10/1789 **Lydia Metcalf**, bc1761, d 7/15/1812 age 51 (gravestone), d/o **Samuel** and **Mehitable (Hammond)**, and m (2) 3/14/1813 **Joanna Gaines**, b1785, d 3/1/1858 age 73. (*John Perrin Fam.*, p. 45-6, 79 - *Woodstock Fam.*, v. 8, p. 124 - *Hist. of Royalton, VT*, p. 905)

Zachariah - b 3/18/1748 in Hebron, CT, s/o **Thomas**; Zachariah d 5/28/1838 age 88 in Berlin, Washington Co., VT. He m (1) 1/11/1781 in Hebron, CT, **Mary Talcott**, b 6/17/1758 in Gilead, CT, d/o **John** and **Anna (Skinner)**, and m (2) 1/29/1829 **Prudence (Nye) Knapp.** (*John Perrin Fam.*, p. 263, 266-7 - *Washington Co., VT, Gazetteer*, p. 190 - *DAR Patriot Index*, p. 528)

PERRY

Burr - bc1795 in CT, d prob. in Castleton, Rutland Co., VT. Burr m **Eleanor ----**, bc1810 in VT, d prob. in Castleton, Rutland Co., VT. In the 1850 census he was 55 and she was 40 years old. (*1850 Rutland Co., VT, Census*)

Ichabod - b1759 in Greenfield Hills, CT, d prob. in Richmond, Ontario Co., NY. Ichabod m **Rebecca Sturges**, d prob. in Richmond, Ontario Co., NY. (*DSGR*, v. 39 #3, p. 161)

John - b1781 in New London, CT, d 6/3/1857 in Oxford, Chenango Co., NY. John m (1) **Mary Welch** of New London, CT, d 4/21/1830, and m (2) **Lydia ----**, bc1791 in CT. In the 1850 census he was 70 and Lydia was 59 years old. (*Annals of Oxford, NY*, p. 296-8 - *1850 Chenango Co., NY, Census*)

Joseph L. - b 11/30/1794 in Huntington, CT, d 9/17/1845 in Ridgeway, Orleans Co., NY. Joseph L. m 7/15/1819 **Julia Ann Reed**, d/o **Jesse** of Aurelius. (*Pioneer History of Orleans Co., NY*, p. 329-30)

Robert - b 11/1743 in Ashford, CT, s/o **John** and **Abigail (Knowlton)**; Robert d 3/24/1816 in Pomfret, Windsor Co., VT. He m 9/5/1764 in Ashford, CT, **Sarah Hodges**, d 10/10/1833. (*Pomfret, Vermont*, v. 2, p. 556)

PERSONS

Oliver - bc1767 in CT, d prob. in Royalton, Windsor Co., VT. Oliver m **Anna ----**, bc1774 in CT, d prob. in Royalton, Windsor Co., VT. In the 1850 census he was 83 and she was 76 years old. (*1850 Census Windsor Co., VT*)

PETERS

Andrew Barnet - b 1/29/1764 in Hebron, CT, s/o Col. **John** and **Ann (Barnet)**; Andrew Barnet d 8/10/1851 age 87-6-12 in Bradford, Orange Co., VT. He m (1) 1/18/1787 **Anna White** of Newbury, VT, d age 24 in Bradford, VT, and m (2) 12/16/1790 **Lydia Bliss**, b 6/14/1767 in Hebron, CT, d 3/5/1816 age 50, d/o **Ellis** and **Tamar** of Hebron, CT, and m (3) 9/15/1816 **Keziah Howard**, b 11/25/1783 in Bridgewater, MA, d 9/2/1872 age 88. Andrew Barnet was said to be a Loyalist. (*Peters of New England*, p. 189-190 - *Hist. of Bradford, VT*, p. 134-140 - *Gazetteer of Orange Co., VT*, p. 172-3)

John - b 6/30/1740 in Hebron, CT, s/o **John** and **Lydia (Phelps)**; John (the younger), a Loyalist, d 1/11/1788 in 48th year in Paddington, England. He m 11/25/1761 in Hebron, CT, **Ann Barnard**, b 4/30/1740 in Hebron, CT. (*Peters of New England*, p. 186-9 - *A Hist. of Bradford, VT*, p. 126-134)

Joseph Phelps - b 11/7/1761 in Hebron, CT, d 9/21/1843 in Portland, NY. Joseph Phelps m (1) 1784 in VT, **Azubah Case**, and m (2) 4/8/1794 in Pittstown, NY, **Lydia Day**. (*DAR Patriot Index*, p. 529 - *Soldiers of Am. Rev., Chautauqua Co., NY*, p. 18-19)

PETTEBONE

Noah - b 4/16/1714 in Simsbury, CT, d 3/28/1791 prob. in Kingston Twp., PA. Noah m1745 **Huldah Williams**. (*Hist. of Luzerne-Lackawanna-Wyoming Cos., PA*, p. ? - *DAR Patriot Index*, p. 530)

PHELPS

Benajah - bc1770 in CT, d1862 in VT. Benajah m **Catherine Stark**. (1812 Index)

Benjamin - b 12/14/1782 in Simsbury, CT, d 9/29/1840 age 58 in Camden, Oneida Co., NY. Benjamin m **Sally Parke**, b 12/4/1785 in Chatham, CT, d 7/4/1847 age 62, d/o **Daniel** and **Esther**. (*Pioneer Hist. of Camden, NY*, p. 119-127)

Epaphrus Lord - b1779 in CT, d1823 in Indiana. Epaphrus Lord m **Esther Hill**. (1812 Index)

Judge Jabez B. - bc1776 in Hebron, CT, d 12/20/1850 age 74 in Preble, Cortland Co., NY. Judge Jabez B. m ----. (*Pioneer History of Cortland Co., NY*, p. 199)

John - bc1795 in CT, d 6/3/1865 age 70 in Rupert, Bennington Co., VT. John m **Theodotia** ----, bc1797 in CT. In the 1850 census he was 54 and she was 53 years old. (*1850 Bennington Co., VT, Census - Gravestone Rec. of Rupert, VT*, p. 57-8)

Jonathan - b 2/1/1763 in Lyme, CT, c 9/26/1857 in Fredonia, NY. Jonathan m 8/14/1784 in E. Haddam, CT, **Charity Beckwith**. (*Soldiers of Am. Rev., Chautauqua Co., NY*, p. 19 - *DAR Patriot Index*, p. 531)

Dr. Josiah - bc1795 in CT, d prob. in Rochester, Windsor Co., VT. Dr. Josiah m **Ruth** ----, bc1801 in VT, d prob. in Rochester, Windsor Co., VT. In the 1850 census he was 53 and she was 49 years old. (*1850 Census of Windsor Co., VT*)

Samuel Shether - b 5/13/1793 in Litchfield, CT, d 3/25/1855 in Middlebury, Addison Co., VT. Samuel Shether m (1) 11/21/1821 **Frances Shurtleff**, and m (2) 10/23/1825 **Electa Saterlee**, b in Lyons, NY. (*Phelps Gen.*, p. 692 - *History of Vermont*, v. 5, p. 99-102 by Crocket)

Capt. Samuel - b 7/6/1742 in Hebron, CT, d prob. in Lyme, Grafton Co., NH. Capt. Samuel m1764 **Lydia Morey**. (*Gazetteer of Grafton Co., NH*, p. 547)

179

PHILLIPS

Gamaliel – b 9/30/1799 in CT, d 3/4/1853 in Townville, Crawford Co., PA. Gamaliel m1825 **Eliza Emaline Waid**, b 1/11/1806, d 7/24/1887, d/o **Pember**. She m (2) **Hiram Baldwin**. (*First Hundred Years, Townville, PA*, p. ?)

PHINNEY

John – bc1782 in Windham Co., CT, s/o **Samuel**, d1867 age 85 in New Milford, Susquehanna Co., PA. John m **Lucretia** ----, d1853 age 66. (*Hist. of Susquehanna Co., PA*, p. 619)

PIERCE

Nathaniel – b 3/19/1727 in Pomfret, CT, s/o **Nathaniel**; Nathaniel (the younger) d 7/13/1808 in Royalton, VT. He m 9/24/1754 **Priscilla Shepard**, b1734, d 11/10/1827 in Royalton, VT. (*Hist. of Royalton, VT*, p. 908-9)

Willard – b 1/28/1762 in Pomfret, CT, s/o **Nathaniel** and **Priscilla** (**Shepard**); Willard d 11/25/1830 in Royalton, Windsor Co., VT. He m 7/22/1784 **Susannah Waldo**, d/o **Daniel** and **Lois** (**Dana**). (*Hist. of Royalton, VT*, p. 909)

PIERPONT

Robert – b 5/4/1791 in Litchfield, CT, s/o **David** and Sarah (**Phelps**); Robert d 9/23/1864 in Windham Co., VT. He m **Abby Raymond**. (*History of VT* by Crockett v. 5, p. 368)

William – b 6/31/1800 in Litchfield, CT, s/o **David** and Sarah (**Phelps**); William d 3/15/1859 in Watertown, NY. He m **Betsey Terrell**, b 10/20/1803 in Cheshire, CT, d 8/22/1870. (Tombstone Rec., Mt. Hope Cem. – *Pierpont Gen.*, p. 65)

PIERSON

John – bc1783 in CT, d1814 in NY. John m **Cynthia Franklin**. (1812 Index)

PINNEO

Daniel – b1744 in Lebanon, CT, d 6/27/1816 in Hartford, Windsor Co., VT. Daniel m **Jane Hill** of Lebanon, CT. (*Hist. of Hartford, VT*, p. 457 – *VT Antiquarian*, p. 24)

PINNEY

Oliver – b 8/6/1751 in Hebron, CT, s/o **Isaac** and **Susanna** (**Phelps**); Oliver d 11/14/1827 in Randolph, Orange Co., VT. He m 3/31/1774 in Stafford, CT, **Martha Alden** of Stafford, CT. (*Branches and Twigs*, v. 1 #4, p. 50)

PITKIN

Alfred – b 1/6/1792 in CT, s/o **Joshua** and **Ruth** (**Case**); Alfred d 10/26/1855 in Montpelier, Washington Co., VT. He m (1) 11/23/1818 **Jerusha Fairchild**, b 5/20/1794, d 2/8/1823, d/o **Daniel**, and m (2) 1/26/1824 **Orpha Washburn**, b 8/31/1799 in CT, d 6/12/1872, d/o **Asahel**. In the 1850 census he was 58 and Orpha was 50 years old. (*1850 Census Washington Co., VT - Pitkin Genealogy*, p. 86, 166)

Rev. Caleb - b 2/27/1781 in New Hartford, CT, d 2/5/1864 in 83rd year prob. in Hudson, Summit Co., OH. Rev. Caleb m ----, d 12/7/1882 in 99th year. (*Reminiscences of Hudson, OH*, p. ?)

Elisha H. - b 12/11/1812 in CT, s/o **Jonathan** and **Betsey (Cummings)**; Elisha H. d poss. in Hartford, Windsor Co., VT. He m (1) 1/8/1837 **Olive Wilson**, b 7/23/1817 in VT, d 6/3/1863 (or 6/3/1864) age 47, and m (2) 9/12/1863 **Ann Henderson**, b 6/16/1830. (*Pitkin Gen.*, p. 99)

Elizur - b 1/13/1803 in CT, d perhaps in Hartford, Windsor Co., VT. Elizur m 3/28/1831 **Lucy A. Cowen**, b 10/25/1812 in VT, d perhaps in Hartford, Windsor Co., VT. In the 1850 census he was 46 and she was 39 years old. (*Pitkin Genealogy*, p. 98 - *1850 Windsor Co., VT, Census*)

Jonathan - b 7/24/1779 in CT, s/o **Jonathan** and **Lucy (Steele)**; Jonathan (the younger) d 8/1/1870 prob. in Pomfret, Windsor Co., VT. He m 5/28/1802 **Betsey Cummings**, b 3/29/1783 in CT, d 9/1/1869. In the 1850 census he was 73 and she was 68 years old. (*1850 Windsor Co., VT, Census - Pitkin Gen.*, p. 46)

Thomas - b 12/5/1772 in CT, s/o **Thomas** and **Rhoda (Marsh)**; Thomas (the younger) d 5/20/1861 age 88 prob. in Hartford, Windsor Co., VT, buried in Quechee Village Cem. He m (1) 11/2/1800 ---- **Bill**, b 11/8/1777 in NH, d 5/9/1835, d/o **Eliphalet Bill**, and m (2) 11/20/1836 **Betsey Billings**, b 3/22/1786 in NH. (*Pitkin Gen.*, p. 125)

PLATT

Levi - b in Huntington, CT, d1886 in Greenfield Twp., Huron, OH. Levi m1825 in Hopewell, Ontario Co., NY, **Abigail Bodman**, d1881. (*Residents of CT Who Migrated to Huron Co., OH*, p. ?)

PLUMB

Amariah - b 9/5/1733 in CT, d 3/1/1778 prob. in Malta, Saratoga Co., NY. Amariah m **Sarah Aspenwall**. (*Hist. of Saratoga Co.*, p. 290 - *DAR Patriot Index*, p. 538)

POLLEY

Jonathan - b 10/26/1759 in Hebron, CT, s/o **Jonathan**; Jonathan (the younger) d 5/31/1840 in Whitehall, Washington Co., NY. He m **Rachel Hubbard**. (*DAR Patriot Index*, p. 539 - *NEGR* July 1976, p. 235)

POLLOCK

William - b1797 in Lyme, CT, d1858 in Ridgefield Twp., Huron Co., OH. William m (1) 1/22/1830 in Huron Co., OH, **Mary Shelton**, and m (2) 11/1/1832 **Catherine Wisharpt**. (*Residents of CT Who Migrated to Huron Co., OH*, p. ?)

POMEROY

Sylvanus – bc1766 in CT, d1851 prob. in Windsor Co., VT. Sylvanus m **Amy Huggins**, bc1778, d1851 age 72. In the 1850 census he was 85 and she was 67 years old. (*1850 Windsor Co., VT, Census*)

POND

Abel – b 10/27/1753 in CT, s/o **Daniel** and **Mehitable (Munson)**; Abel d 12/29/1828. He m (1) **Eunice Curtis**, d1804 in an accident, and m (2) Widow **Jerusha (Gillett) Barnes**, d 5/13/1842 in Covington, NY. (*DAR Patriot Index*, p. 540 – *First Hundred Years, Townville, Crawford Co., PA*, p. 81-4)

Barnabas – b 10/29/1755 in Waterbury, CT, d 5/9/1841 age 86 in Clinton, Oneida Co., NY. He m (1) 2/17/1784 **Thankful Foote**, b 6/30/1762 in Waterbury, CT, d 10/8/1814 age 52, d/o **Moses**, and m (2) **Sarah ----**, d 7/7/1826 age 65-9, and m (3) **Phebe T. ----**, d 5/30/1859 age 71-1-15. (*Clinton Memorial-Kirtland Ave. Cem.*, p. 27 – *CT Records of the Rev.*, p. 117, 236 – *DAR Patriot Index*, p. 540 – DAR Lineage #80596)

Bartholomew – b 4/13/1736 in CT, s/o **Philip** and **Thankful (Frisbie)**; Bartholomew d 3/21/1810 in Camden, Oneida Co., NY. He m **Lucy Curtiss**. (*Pioneer History of Camden, NY*, p. 351-2 – *DAR Patriot Index*, p. 540)

Beriah – b1758 in CT, s/o **Bartholomew**; Beriah d 3/14/1836 age 78 in Camden, Oneida Co., NY. He m in Plymouth, CT, **Sylvia Sandford**. (*Pioneer History of Camden, NY*, p. 344-5 – *DAR Patriot Index*, p. 540)

Dan – b 3/4/1726 in Branford, CT, s/o **Philip** and **Thankful (Frisbie)**; Dan d 5/27/1783 in Poultney, Rutland Co., VT. He m **Mehitable Munson**, d 1/8/1793 in 62nd yr. (*A Gen. Rec. of Daniel Pond and Des.*, p. 195 – *DAR Patriot Index*, p. 540 – *First Hundred Years of Townville, PA*, p. ? – *Hist. of Rutland Co., VT*, p. 771)

Col. Josiah – b 12/20/1756 in CT, s/o **Dan** and **Mabel (Munson)**; Col. Josiah d 8/3/1842 in Shoreham, VT. He m (1) **Lydia Belden** of Lenox, MA, b 1/1/1757, d 1/25/1789 in Shoreham, VT, and m (2) **Olive Merrills**, b 4/2/1771, d 5/2/1831 in Shoreham, VT. (*Gen. Rec. of Samuel Pond*, p. 15, 27 – *DAR Patriot Index*, p. 540 – *A Gen. Rec. of Daniel Pond and Des.*, p. 195)

Luther – b1790 in CT, d1843 in MI. Luther m **Sarah White**. (War of 1812 Index)

Philip – b 8/20/1777 in Bristol, CT, d 3/13/1853 in Rochester, Monroe Co., NY. Philip m ----. (Tombstone Rec., Mt. Hope Cem., Rochester, NY)

Timothy – b 10/7/1730 in Branford, CT, d 5/22/1801 age 70 in Clinton, Oneida Co., NY. Timothy m (1) 6/19/1751 (or 6/20/1751) **Mary Munson**, b 5/2/1731 in Wallingford, CT, d 1/16/1763, d/o **Abel** and **Sarah (Peck)**, and m (2) 8/30/1764 **Sarah Bartholomew**, b 12/28/1740 in Branford, CT, d 7/7/1826 age 83, d/o **Isaac** and **Martha (Barnes)**. (*Clinton Memorial-Kirtland Ave. Cem.*, p. 27 – *DAR Patriot Index*, p. 540 – *CT Hist. Coll.*, v. 8, p. 22 – *CT Rec. of Rev.*, p. 41, 236, 412)

PORTER

Augustus - b 1/18/1769 in Salisbury, CT, s/o **Joshua** and **Abigail (Buel)**; Augustus d1864 in Niagara Falls, NY. He m ----. (Barbour Collection, Salisbury, CT)

Dr. **Benjamin** - b1788 in Voluntown, CT, d perhaps in Northfield, Washington Co., VT. Dr. Benjamin m **Sophia Fullerton**, d perhaps in Northfield, Washington Co., VT. (*Early Settlers of Northfield, VT*, p. 144)

Hezekiah - bc1784 in CT, d 4/13/1851 age 67, buried Thetford, VT, Cem. Hezekiah m **Mary Howard**, bc1785 in VT, d 10/16/1861 age 76, buried Thetford, VT, Cem. In the 1850 census he was 66 and she was 65 years old. (*1850 Orange Co., VT, Census* for Thetford)

Dr. **Joshua** - b1759 in Salisbury, CT, s/o Col. **Joshua** of Salisbury; Dr. Joshua d 10/26/1831 in Saratoga Springs, NY. He was said to have been a prisoner on *The Jersey*. He m ----. (*Hist. of Saratoga Co.*, p. 203 - *Biog. and Hist. of Saratoga, NY*, p. 383)

Lewis - bc1786 in CT, d1862 in NY. Lewis m **Samantha King**. (War of 1812 Index)

Milo - b1808 in Waterbury, CT, d 8/27/1899 in Oxford, Chenango Co., NY. Milo m ----, d 8/5/1889. (*Annals of Oxford, NY*, p. 367)

Moses - b 9/30/1738 in CT, d 2/17/1803 in Pawlet, Rutland Co., VT. Moses m **Sarah Kilham Part**. (*Hist. of Rutland Co., VT*, p. 707-8 - *DAR Patriot Index*, p. 542)

Thomas - b 2/14/1734 in Farmington, CT, d 5/30/1833 in Granville, NY. Thomas m **Abigail Howe**. (*Hist. of VT*, v. 5 by Crockett, p. 56 - *DAR Patriot Index*, p. 542)

POST

Roswell, Jr. - b 5/10/1753 in Saybrook, CT, d 5/5/1827 age 74 in Cornwall, VT. Roswell, Jr. m (1) ----, and m (2) **Martha Mead**, d 9/11/1807 age 51 in Cornwall, VT. (*Hist. of Cornwall, VT*, p. 86 - *DAR Patriot Index*, p. 543)

POTTER

Horace - bc1781 in CT, d1841 in OH. Horace m **Abrilla Quinby**. (War of 1812 Index)

Rev. **Lyman** - b 3/14/1747 (or 3/14/1748) in Salisbury, CT, d 7/20/1827 age 80 in Steubenville, OH. Rev. Lyman m 9/1/1776 **Abigail Paine**, d/o Col. **Elisha** of Lebanon, NH. (*A Hist. of Norwich, VT*, p. 236-8 - *DAR Patriot Index*, p. 543)

Milton - b 3/6/1763 in New Fairfield, CT, d 7/2/1840 in Pittsford, Rutland Co., VT. Milton m **Esther Cone** of E. Haddam, CT. (*Hist. of Pittsford, VT*, p. 268-9 - *DAR Patriot Index*, p. 543)

Capt. **William** - b 8/5/1749 in New London, CT, d 8/10/1825 age 77 in Wells, Rutland Co., VT. Capt. William m in New London, CT, **Phebe Woodard**, d 8/8/1838 age 85. (*History of Wells, VT*, by Paul, p. 140-1 - *DAR Patriot Index*, p. 544 - *History of Wells* by Wood, p. 75)

183

POWERS

John – b 8/14/1762 in CT, d 2/26/1837 in NY.   John m (1) **Susannah Palmer,** and m (2) **Anna Napier.** (*DAR Patriot Index*, p. 545 – War of 1812 Index)

POYNEER

Alfred N. – b1831 in CT, d 8/28/1897 in Montour, IA. Alfred N. m ----. (*Hist. of IA*, p. 215)

PRATT

George W. – b 7/28/1805 in Hartford, CT, d 7/19/1879 in Rochester, Monroe Co., NY.   George W. m **Mary Byington,** b 4/28/1807 in Redding, CT, d 2/21/1894. (Tombstone Rec., Mt. Hope Cemetery, Rochester, NY)

Harry – b 6/9/1778 in Hartford, CT, d 12/31/1853 in Rochester, Monroe Co., NY. Harry m **Susan Cleveland,** b 9/26/1784 in Norwich, CT, d 8/19/1883. (Tombstone Rec., Mt. Hope Cemetery, Rochester, NY)

Joshua – bc1781 in CT, d 7/1/860 age 79-7 in Sherburne, NY. Joshua m **Jemima Talcott,** bc1784 in CT, d 3/11/1877 age 92-8 in Sherburne, Chenango Co., NY.   In the 1850 census he was 69 and she was 66 years old. (*1850 Census Chenango Co., NY*)

Manoah, Sr. – b1754 in Glastonbury, CT, d prob. in Pompey, Onondaga Co., NY. Manoah, Sr. m **Elizabeth Loveland,** d prob. in Pompey, Onondaga Co., NY, d/o **Solomon.** (*Pompey, NY*, p. 341)

PRAY

John, Jr. – b in CT, d 9/26/1794 in Wells, VT.   John, Jr. m 11/22/1793 in Wells, VT, **Elizabeth Bellamy.** (*History of Wells, VT* by Wood, p. 76)

PRENTICE

James – b 10/30/1755 in Preston, CT, s/o **Nathaniel** and **Huldah** (**Stallion**); James d before 4/1827 in Shaftsbury, VT. He m **Chloe** (?) **Fuller,** b 1/16/1759, d after 3/7/182?, d/o **Elijah** and **Mary** (**Millington**). (Shaftsbury, VT, Rec.)

PRENTISS

Manasseh – bc1778 in CT, d1814 in NY. Manasseh m **Susan Lothrop.** (War of 1812 Index)

Samuel – b 3/31/1782 in Stonington, CT, s/o Dr. **Samuel** and **Lucretia** (**Holmes**); Samuel d 1/15/1857. He m 10/3/1804 in Northfield, MA, **Lucretia Houghton,** b 3/6/1786 in Northfield, MA, d 6/15/1855.   In the 1850 census he was 68 and she was 64 years old. (*Prentice Fam.* by Binney, p. 207-8, 385-401, 219-24 – *1850 Census of Washington Co., VT*)

PRESCOTT

Joshua – b 12/10/1786 in CT, s/o **Dominicus** and **Hannah (Moulton)**; Joshua d age over 80 in Washington, VT. He m 6/11/1807 **Nancy Martin** (or **Mardin**). (*Gazetteer of Orange County, Vermont*, p. 256, 255, 298-9)

Sherburn - b in CT, d 3/24/1867 age 84-6 in Vershire, Orange Co., VT. Sherburn m (1) **Rebecca** ----, d 7/17/1823 age 42, and m (2) **Pauline P.** ----, d 11/14/1889 age 91-8-24. (Vershire, VT, Cem.)

PRESTON

Abner - b1781 in CT, s/o of **Caleb**; Abner d 11/24/1833 age 52 in Camden, Oneida Co., NY. He m **Hannah** ----. (*Pioneer History of Camden, Oneida Co., NY*, p. ?)

Caleb - b 9/10/1772 in Wallingford, CT, s/o **Caleb** and **Ame (Lewis)**; Caleb (the younger) d 5/28/1867 age 96 in Camden, Oneida Co., NY. He m **Sybil Leonard**, d 4/18/1851 age 76. (*Pioneer Hist. of Camden, NY*, p. 171-2)

Caleb - bc1746 in CT, d 2/27/1813 age 67 in Camden, Oneida Co., NY. He m **Ame Lewis**, bc1744, d 6/1/1817 age 73. (*Pioneer Hist. of Camden, NY*, p. 170)

David, Sr. - b 2/25/1758 in Ashford, CT, s/o **David** and **Susannah (Mason)**; David, Sr., d 7/11/1827 age 79 poss. in Tallmadge, OH. He m **Cynthia Sprague**, b 1/1/1756 in Sharon, CT. (*OH Gen. Soc. Quarterly*, Oct. 1972, p. 34 - *DAR Patriot Index*, p. 547)

John Sprague - b 9/9/1784 in Canaan, CT, s/o **David** and **Cynthia (Sprague)**; John Sprague d prob. in Tallmadge, OH. He m **Elizabeth Chamberlain**, b 3/9/1787 in Sharon, CT. (*OH Gen. Soc. Quarterly*, Oct. 1972, p. 34)

Noah - b 2/23/1763 in Harwinton, CT, s/o **John** and **Marion (Bristol)**; Noah d 4/4/1835 age 72 in Camden, Oneida Co., NY. He m 12/29/1785 in Hebron, CT, **Honor Rosseter**, b 5/28/1766, d 11/22/1847 age 82. (*Pioneer Hist. of the Town of Camden, NY*, p. 31-2 - *Preston Gen.*, p. 121, 185 - *DAR Patriot Index*, p. 547)

Major General **Otis** - bc1770 in Woodstock, CT, s/o **Amariah**, d1836 age 66 poss. in Roxbury, NY. Major General Otis m **Dolly Knapp**. (*Hist. of Town of Roxbury, NY*, p. 48)

William - bc1715, d 4/15/1815 age 99-11-10 in Poultney, VT. William m ----. (*Rutland Hist. of Rutland Co., VT*, p. 770 - *Rutland Co. Gazetteer*, p. 191)

William Riley - b 2/4/1790 in Litchfield, CT, s/o **Noah** and **Honor (Rosseter)**; William Riley d 8/19/1834 age 44 in Camden, NY. He m 5/19/1812 **Sarah Ann Smith**, d/o Capt. **John Smith**. (*Pioneer Hist. of Camden, NY*, p. 68-9)

PRIDE

Darius - bc1787 in CT, d prob. in Williamstown, Orange Co., VT. Darius m **Sally** ----, bc1797 in VT, d prob. in Williamstown, Orange Co., VT. In the 1850 census he was 63 (and a merchant) and she was 53 years old. (*1850 Orange Co., VT, Census*)

PRIEST

Philip - b 6/27/1737 in Killingworth, CT, d1816 in Chateauguy, NY. Philip m in CT, **Truba Merritt**. (*Hist. of Fairhaven, VT*, p. 449-50 - *DAR Patriot Index*, p. 548)

PRIME

Grant - bc1766 in CT, d 4/11/1861 age 95 in VT, (poss. Bristol, VT). Grant m **Electa Doud**, d 12/15/1849 age 80-8. (War of 1812 Index)

PRINDLE

John - bc1756 in CT, d1838 in MA. John m **Penelope Johnson**. (War of 1812 Index)

Cyrus - b 5/27/1760 in Newtown, CT, s/o **Joseph, Jr.** and **Huldah (Glover)**; Cyrus d 8/17/1811 in Bedford, NY. He m 4/3/1782 in Newtown, CT, **Mary Beers**, d/o **Daniel** of Woodbury, CT, b 2/2/1762 in VT, d 1/16/1841 age 80. (*Prindle Gen.*, p. 139-141)

Samuel - b 5/15/1771 in New Milford, CT, s/o **Samuel**; Samuel (the younger) d1813 in E. Charlotte, Chittenden Co., VT. He m **Elinor Whalen**. In the 1850 census she was 74 years old. (*1850 Census Chittenden Co., VT - Prindle Gen.*, p. 92-3)

PULSIFER

David - bp. 3/4/1716 in Pomfret, CT, d 8/1/1775 poss. in Rockingham, NH. David m **Elizabeth Stowell**. (*Hist. of Rockingham, NH*, p. 731 - *DAR Patriot Index*, p. 551)

PUMPELLY

Charles - bc1779 in CT, d1855 in NY. Charles m **Frances Avery**. (War of 1812 Index)

RALPH

Daniel - bc1747 in Woodstock, CT, d 3/2/1826 age 79 in Woodstock, Windsor Co., VT. Daniel m **Priscilla ----**, bc1753, d 7/30/1825 age 72. (*Hist. of Woodstock, VT*, p. 126)

RAMSDALL

Horace - bc1797 in Danbury, CT, d1872 in Huron Co, OH. Horace m (1) 1817 in OH, **Sarah Willet**, and m (2) 1825 **Sarah Bullard**, b1807, d1888. (*Residents of CT Who Migrated to Huron Co., OH*, p. 5)

RANDALL

Gurdon - b1795 in Scotland, CT, s/o **Greenfield**; Gurdon d1861, prob. in Northfield, Washington Co., VT. He m **Laura S. Warner** of Putney, VT, b1803, d 2/16/1880 age 76-9. (*Orange Co., VT*, p. 175 - *Washington Co., VT, Gazetteer*, p. ? - *Early Settlers of Northfield, VT*, p. 217-18)

Col. John - b 3/24/1754 in Stonington, CT, s/o **John** and **Lucy (Brown)**; Col. John d prob. in Chenango Co., NY (poss. in Pharsalia). He m (1) 11/7/1775 **Mary Swan**, d 3/29/1813 in Norwich, NY, and m (2) 5/3/1816 **Hannah Mary (Avery) Randall**, d/o **Nathan** and **Hannah (Stoddard) Avery**, and wid/o **Roswell Randall**. (*Hist. of Chenango Co., NY*, p. ? - *Hist. of Stonington*, p. 206, 548)

Levi - bc1800 in CT, d perhaps in Sandgate, Bennington Co., VT. Levi m **Anna ----**, bc1801 in VT, d perhaps in Sandgate, Bennington Co., VT. In the 1850 census he was 50 and she was 49 years old. (*1850 Bennington Co., VT, Census*)

Thomas W. - bc1781 in CT. He m **Ruth** ----, bc1787 in VT. They resided at one time in Masonville, Delaware Co., NY. In the 1855 census he was 74 and she was 68 years old. (*1855 Census Delaware Co., NY*)

Walter - bc1793 in CT. He m **Eunice** ----, bc1797 in CT. They resided at one time in Sandgate, Bennington Co., VT. In the 1850 census he was 57 and she was 53 years old. (*1850 Bennington Co., VT, Census*)

RANNEY

Elijah - b 3/14/1750 in Middletown, CT, s/o **Ephraim, Sr.**; Elijah d 4/29/1833 prob. in Westminster, Windham Co., VT. He m **Elizabeth Root**. (*Windham Co. Gazetteer*, p. 304)

Ephraim, Jr. - b 10/27/1748 in Middletown, CT, s/o **Ephraim** and Si-l e n c e (**W i l c o x**); Ephraim, Jr. d 5/30/1835 in Westminster, Windham Co., VT. He m (1) **Lydia Johnson**, and m (2) **Rhoda Har-l o w**. (*Windham County, Vermont, Gazetteer*, p. 304 - *DAR Patriot Index*, p. 556)

Ephraim, Sr. - b 4/10/1725/6 in Middletown, CT, d 6/9/1811 in Westminster, Windham Co., VT. Ephraim, Sr. m **Silence Wilcox**. (*Windham Co., VT, Gazetteer*, p. 304 - *DAR Patriot Index*, p. 556)

Willett - b 3/28/1731 in Middletown, CT, s/o **Willett** and **Anna**. Willett (the younger) m 11/19/1752 in Middletown, CT, **Mary But-ler**. They resided at one time in the Mohawk Valley, NY. (*Hist. of the Mohawk Valley*, v. II, p. 1181-2 - War of 1812 Index - *DAR Patriot Index*, p. 556)

RANSOM

John - b in Canaan, CT, d 8/1811 in Poultney, Rutland Co., VT. John m **Sarah Roberts Whitney**. (*Hist. of Rutland Co., VT*, p. 770)

George Palmer - b 1/3/1762 in CT, d 9/5/1850 in PA. George Pal-mer m (1) **Olive Utley**, and m (2) **Elizabeth Lamoreux**. (*DAR Patriot Index*, p. 556 - War of 1812 Index)

Dr. Joshua - bc1772 in Colchester, CT, d 3/13/1834, age 52 in Cam-den, NY. Dr. Joshua m **Clarissa Warner**, d 8/8/1855, age 69. (*Pioneer Hist. of Camden, Oneida Co., NY*)

Ensign Joshua, Jr. - b 10/21/1744 in CT, d 10/26/1829 in Otsego Co., NY. Ensign Joshua, Jr. m **Lois Rathbun**. (*DAR Mag.*, v. 107, p. 418 - *DAR Patriot Index*, p. 556)

Russell - b1788 in Tolland, CT, s/o **Joseph** and **Azuba**; Russell d1864 in Berlin Heights, Erie Co., OH. He m1809 in Tolland, CT, **Lucretia Wickham**, b1791, d1855. (*Residents of CT Who Migrated to Huron Co., OH*, p. 5)

RATHBONE

Gen. Ransom - b 4/10/1780 in Colchester, CT, d 7/17/1861 age 81 in Rathbonville, NY. Gen. Ransom m **Catherine Fisher**, d 7/27/1857 in Rathbonville, NY, d/o Capt. **John**. (*Annals of Oxford, New York*, p. 463-6)

RAY

Nathan - bc1791 in CT, d 5/12/1866 age 75-5 in Smyrna, NY. Nathan m **Lucretia** ----, bc1792 in CT, d 12/29/1872 age 80-7 in Smyrna, NY. In the 1850 census he was 59 and she was 58 years old. (*Cemetery Records - Sherburne, Chenango Co., NY*, p. 56 - *1850 Census Chenango Co., NY*)

RAYS

Nathaniel - bc1773 in CT, d prob. in Oxford, Chenango Co., NY. Nathaniel m **Elizabeth** ----, bc1774 in CT, d probably in Oxford, Chenango Co., NY. In the 1850 census he was 77 and she was 76, listed with Loyal (b in CT), 41, and Mary A. (b in CT), 35 years old. (*1850 Census for Oxford-Chenango Co., NY*)

RAYMOND

William - bc1747 in CT, d1832 in NY. William m **Ruth Hoyt**. (War of 1812 Index - *DAR Patriot Index*, p. 558)

REDFIELD

Lewis H. - b 11/26/1793 in CT, d 7/14/1882 in Onondaga Co., NY. Lewis H. m **Ann Marie Treadwell**, d1889 age 89. (*Onondaga Hist. Soc. of 1914*, p. 175, in paperback.)

REDMON

John - bc1800 in CT, d perhaps in Middletown, Delaware Co., NY. John m **Molly** ----, bc1798, d perhaps in Middletown, Delaware Co. NY. In the 1855 census he was 55 and she was 53 years old. (*1855 Census Delaware Co., NY*)

REED

Amasa - bc1793 in CT, d perhaps in Pittsfield, Chenango Co., NY. Amasa m **Syntha** ----, bc1797 in CT, d perhaps in Pittsfield, Chenango Co., NY. In the 1850 census he was 57 and she was 53 years old. (*1850 Census of Chenango Co., NY*)

Rufus - bc1777 in CT, d in Fairlee, Orange Co., VT. Rufus m **Lydia** ----, bc1785 in VT, d perhaps in Fairlee, Orange Co., VT. In the 1850 census he was 73 and she was 65 years old, and they were living in the home of **Sylvester** and **Eliza Slafter**, ages 37 and 34 years. (*1850 Orange Co. Census of Fairlee, VT*)

Samuel - b1794 in CT, d1865 in OH. Samuel m **Hannah Brown**. (War of 1812 Index)

REEVE

Lt. Benjamin - b1739 in CT, s/o of **Abner**; Lt. Benjamin d 10/29/1819 age ca 80. He m 1/31/1764 **Huldah Hill**, d 8/5/1819 age 77 in Cornwall, VT. (*Hist. of Cornwall, VT*, p. 79 - *Reeve-Reeves*, p. 423 - *DAR Patriot Index*, p. 562)

RESSEGNE

James - bc1744 in CT, d 9/7/1830 perhaps in Hubbardton, Rutland Co., VT. James m (1) **Sarah Rumsey**, and m (2) **Eunice** ----. (*Hist. Mag.*, v. 4, p. 1175 - *DAR Patriot Index*, p. 564)

REXFORD

Allen - bc1792 in Barkhamsted, CT, d 12/5/1875 in Sherburne, Chenango Co., NY. Allen m **Almira Hart**, b1792, d1871 in Sherburne, NY. In the 1850 census he was 58 and she was 58 years old. (*1850 Census Chenango Co., NY - Smyrna, NY*, by Munson, p. 20)

Benajah - b in CT, d1862 in Ripley, Chautauqua Co., NY. Benajah m (1) **Zeruiah Squier**, and m (2) **Roxana Ayer**. Removed c1823 from VT to Ripley. (*Chautauqua Co., NY*, p. 587)

Simeon - b 5/7/1776 in Barkhamsted, CT, s/o Joel; d 12/31/1857 in Smyrna, NY. Simeon m (1) **Wealtha Carver** of Smyrna, d 8/31/1806, and m (2) **Bersheba Taylor** of VT, d 2/5/1810, and m (3) **Milly Carver**, b in Bolton, CT, d 5/7/1836, and m (4) 1/1837 Mrs. **Betsey (Merrell) Jones**. In the 1850 census he was 74 and Betsey was 64 years old. (*1850 Census of Smyrna, NY - Rexford Gen.*, p. 51-2)

Zina - bc1777 in CT, d 9/6/1855 age 78 in Sherburne, Chenango Co., NY. Zina m **Lucy ----**, b1792 in NY. In the 1850 census he was 73 and she was 58 years old. (*1850 Census Chenango Co.*)

REYNOLDS

Caleb - b1739 in Greenwich, CT, d1790 in Dutchess Co., NY. Caleb m **Sarah Brown**. (*Hist. of Little Nine Partners*, p. 376-7 - *DAR Patriot Index*, p. 564)

Gamiel - b 5/20/1754 in Norwich, CT, d 6/7/1836 in Rochester, Monroe Co., NY. Gamiel m **Mary Smith**, b 5/12/1757 in Groton, CT, d 8/29/1847, d/o **Nathan** and **Elizabeth (Denison)**. (Tombstone Rec., Mt. Hope Cem. - *DAR Patriot Index*, p. 564)

John - b 3/16/1760 (or 3/16/1761) in Norwich, CT, d 3/3/1840 in Mentor, OH. John m **Mary Morgan**. (*Rev. Soldiers Buried in Lake Co., OH*, p. 44-5 - *DAR Patriot Index*, p. 564)

RHODES

Capt. Henry - b 4/25/1762 in Stonington, CT, s/o Col. **James** and **Anna (Crandall)**; Capt. Henry d 1/7/1848 in Southampton, LI, NY. He m ----. (*Hist. of Southampton, LI, NY*, p. 360)

RICE

Col. Aaron Seth - bc1755 in CT, d1838 age 83 in Camden, Oneida Co., NY. Col. Aaron Seth m Mrs. **Sarah A. Dayton**, d 12/4/1875 age 91. (*Pioneer Hist. of Camden, NY*, p. 69-71)

Amos - bc1784 in CT, b perhaps in Readsboro, Bennington Co., VT. Amos m **Lovisa ----**, bc1796 in CT, d perhaps in Readsboro, Bennington Co., VT. In the 1850 census he was 66 and she was 56 years old. (*1850 Bennington Co., VT, Census*)

Jonathan - bc1780 in CT, d1863 age 83 in Sheldon, Franklin Co., VT. Jonathan m ----. (*Franklin Co. Gazetteer*, p. 156)

Orvis - bc1783 in CT, d perhaps in Readsboro, Bennington Co., VT. Orvis m **Margaret ----**, bc1792 in NY, d perhaps in Readsboro, Bennington Co., VT. In the 1850 census he was 67 she was 58 and **Jacob** (? a son) was 19 years old, b in VT. (*1850 Bennington Co., VT, Census*)

RICHARDS

David - bc1760 in CT, d1837 in PA. David m **Susannah Dilley**. (War of 1812 Index)

Ezra - b 12/16/1750 in New Canaan, CT, d 4/1819 poss. in Southeast, Putnam Co., NY. Ezra m **Patty Sears**. (*New Eng. Gen. Reg.* April 1977, p. 157)

Jacob - bc1740 in CT, d 10/3/1825 in Milton, Ulster Co., NY, buried in Boyce Cemetery. Jacob m ----. (*DAR Mag.* 1977, p. 920)

Jonas - b 8/6/1743 in Stonington, CT, s/o **William** and **Rebecca (Richards)**; Jonas d 3/24/1800 age 56 (gravestone). He m **Hannah Wheeler** of Plainfield, CT, d 9/4/1826 age 87 (gravestone) in Norwich, Windsor Co., VT. (*A Hist. of Norwich, VT*, p. 238-9)

Street - b 12/12/1750 in CT, d 7/13/1835 in VT. Street m **Eunice Culver**. (War of 1812 Index - *DAR Patriot Index*, p. 567)

RICHARDSON

Amos - b 11/26/1754 in Coventry, CT, s/o **Nathan** and **Phebe (Crocker)**; Amos d perhaps in Manchester, Bennington Co., VT. He m 12/5/1776 **Lurena Cheever**, d perhaps in Manchester, Bennington Co., VT. (*Some Des. of Amos Richardson*, p. 28, 54-5)

Andrew Crocker - b 12/13/1750 in Coventry, CT, s/o **Nathan** and **Phoebe (Crocker)**; Andrew Crocker d 2/25/1828 age 78. He m 10/17/1773 **Mercy Closson** (or **Clausson**), b 9/25/1750 in Lebanon, CT, d 5/10/1813 age 64 in Manchester, VT. (*Some Descendants of Amos Richardson*, p. 27-8, 51-3 - *DAR Patriot Index*, p. 568)

Capt. David - b 11/28/1757 in Stonington, CT, d 9/9/1843 in Monroe, OH. Capt. David m1785 **Sarah Hudson**, b1760, d1848. (*DAR Patriot Index*, p. 568)

Diah - bc1794 in CT, d perhaps in Montpelier, Washington Co., VT. Diah m **Louisa Hutchins**, bc1800 in VT, d perhaps in Montpelier, Washington Co., VT. In the 1850 census he was 56 and she was 50 years old. (*1850 Census of Washington Co., VT*)

Eleazer - b 3/21/1774 in Coventry, CT, s/o **Andrew Crocker** and **Nancy (Closson) Richardson**; Eleazer d1835 (or d1834) in Castile, NY. He m **Ophelia Washburn**, d1843, d/o **Azel** and **Beede**. They lived in Manchester, VT, and in Bristol, VT and then moved to Richland, NY. (*Some Des. of Amos Richardson*, p. 51-2, 77)

Elias - b 10/3/1777 in Coventry (or Lebanon), CT, s/o **Amos** and **Lurena (Cheever)**; Elias d 12/6/1837 age 60 in Manchester, Bennington Co., VT. He m 12/8/1814 in Manchester, VT, **Rachel (Boarn) Richardson**, d1861 age 80, wid/o cousin **Andrew**. (*Some Des. of Amos Richardson*, p. 54, 80)

Dr. Frederick - bc1781 in Tolland, CT. Dr. Frederick m (3) **Betsey Jordan**, b1797 in VT. They res. in Waitsfield, Washington Co., VT. In the 1850 census he was 69 and she was 53 years old. (*1850 Washington Co., VT, Census*)

Ira - b 1/23/1788 in Tolland, CT, s/o **Lemuel** and **Rachel (Lathrop)**; Ira d 12/16/1844 in Fayston, VT. He m 2/13/1815 **Rachel Durkee**, b1795, d 12/15/1884 in Wisconsin, d/o **Andrew** and **Phoebe**. (*Some Des. of Amos Richardson*, p. 31, 57, 86-7)

James - b1742 in Haddam, CT, d 3/26/1819 age 75 prob. in Westminster, VT. James m **Molly Dodge**. (*Gazetteer of Windham Co., VT*, p. 304 - *DAR Patriot Index*, p. ?)

John Closson - b 9/1/1776 in Coventry, CT, s/o **Andrew Crocker** and **Mercy (Closson)**; John Closson d 6/27/1860 in Manchester, VT. He m (1) 9/6/1804 in Manchester, VT, **Lucretia Root**, b1784, d 5/29/1823 in Manchester, VT, and m (2) 11/16/1830 **Mabel Howard**. (*Some Des. of Amos Richardson*, p. 52)

John - b 11/16/1756 (or 11/16/1757) in Coventry, CT, s/o **Nathan** and **Phebe (Crocker)**; John d prob. in VT, poss. in Manchester or Dorset. He m **Sarah ----**, d1802 age 40 in Dorset, VT. (*Some Des. of Amos Richardson*, p. 29)

Lemuel - b1761 in Haddam, CT. He m **Jerusha Hedges**, d/o **David** and **Hannah (Shaw)**. Lemuel and Jerusha resided at one time in Westminster, VT. (*Some Des. of Amos Richardson*, p. 44, 75)

Lemuel - b 12/24/1752 in Coventry, CT, s/o **Lemuel** and **Anna (Rust)**; Lemuel (the younger) d 9/26/1826 in Waitsfield, Washington Co., VT. He m 6/2/1774 in Coventry, CT, **Rachel Lothrop**, d 8/27/1811 in CT. (*Richardson Memorial* by Vinton, p. 806 - *Some Des. of Amos Richardson*, p. 31)

Lothrop - b 8/27/1790 in Tolland, CT, s/o **Lemuel** and **Rachel (Lothrop)**; Lothrop d 7/15/1850 in Coventry, CT. He m 4/20/1813 in Waitsfield, VT, **Charity Skinner**, b 7/19/1792, d/o **Eli** and **Lucinda (Nims)**. (*Some Des. of Amos Richardson*, p. 57-8)

Nathan - b 3/20/1725 in Preston, CT, s/o **Amos**; Nathan d1806 in Jericho, VT (living w/dau, **Esther**). He m 11/8/1748 **Phebe Crocker**, d 5/23/1821 age 93-9-18, d/o **John** and **Elizabeth (Champion)**. (*Some Des. of Amos Richardson*, p. 13-14 - *DAR Patriot Index*, p. 568)

Nathan - b 10/27/1760 in Coventry, CT, s/o **Nathan** and **Phebe (Crocker)**; Nathan (the younger) d1785 poss. in Manchester, Bennington Co., VT. He m 5/8/1783 **Elizabeth Powell**. (*Some Des. of Amos Richardson*, p. 29)

Hon. Roderick - b 2/15/1779 in Tolland, CT, s/o **Lemuel** and **Rachel (Lothrop)**; Hon. Roderick d 6/8/1844 in Waitsfield, Washington Co., VT. He m 8/25/1802 **Anna Davis**, b1779, d1857 in Waitsfield, VT, d/o **Noah** of Stafford, CT. (*Some Descendants of Amos Richardson*, p. 31)

Roderick - b 8/7/1807 in Stafford, CT, s/o **Roderick** and **Anna (Davis)**; Roderick (the younger) d 12/13/1882 in Newton, MA. He m 2/28/1839 **Harriet Emeline Taylor**, b 7/31/1811, d/o **Elias, Jr.** and **Content (Erskine)**. In 1809 he came to Waitsfield, VT, w/parents, then in 1855 moved to Montpelier, then in 1870 moved to Newton, MA. (*Some Des. of Amos Richardson*, p. 83)

Roswell - b Nov. 1793 in Stafford, CT, d1886 in NH. Roswell m **Mara Huntington**, bc1795 in CT. In the 1850 census he was 57 and she was 55 years old. (*1850 Washington County, VT, Census* - War of 1812 Index)

Samuel - b 6/15/1750 in Stafford, CT, s/o **Uriah** and **Miriam**; Samuel d1822 poss. in Roxbury, Washington, Co., VT. He m 3/31/1774 in Stafford, CT, **Susanna Pinney**, b 7/1749, d1841. (*Washington Co. Gazetteer*, p. 449-50 - *DAR Patriot Index*, p. 569)

Samuel - b1741 in E. Haddam, CT, s/o **Samuel** and **Sarah (Stanton)**; Samuel d 6/24/1831 (or 6/24/1832) age 90 in Northfield, Washington Co., VT. He m (1) **Clarissa Wanbelton**, and m (2) **Jerusha Royce**, poss. d/o **Benedict**, d1843 age 85. (*Early Settlers of Northfield, VT*, p. 139-40 – *Some Descendants of Amos Richardson*, p. 10, 23)

Sanford - b1761 in Coventry, CT, s/o **David** and **Rachel (Richardson)**; Sanford d 6/7/1818 in 57th year in Bethel, VT. He m1780 in Ellington, CT, **Roxalana Burroughs**, b1762, d 3/12/1837 age 75 in Bethel, VT, d/o **Abner** and **Margaret (Harper)**. (*Some Des. of Amos Richardson*, p. 21-2)

Stanton - b 11/16/1755 in E. Haddam, CT, s/o **Samuel** and **Sarah (Stanton)**; Stanton d 8/2/1822 in Northfield, Washington Co., VT. He m 2/24/1780 in Westminster, VT, **Anna Doubleday**, b 5/29/1760, d 3/7/1816 age 56 in Northfield, VT, d/o **Nathaniel**. (*Early Settlers of Northfield, VT*, p. 136-7 – *Some Des. of Amos Richardson*, p. 24, 45)

Welles - b 2/14/1770 in Coventry, CT, s/o **Nathan** and **Phebe (Crocker)**; Welles dc1797 (or dc1798) prob. in Manchester, Bennington Co., VT. He m **Mollie Joy (?)**, b1767 in Plainfield, MA. She m (2) **Willard Colton**. (*Some Des. of Amos Richardson*, p. 30)

RIDER

Joseph - b1780 in CT, d1877 in NY. Joseph m **Mary Hill**. (War of 1812 Index)

RILEY

Capt. **Ashbel** - b 5/3/1760 in Rocky Hill, CT, d 3/5/1797 in Rochester, Monroe Co., NY. He m (1) **Lovina Wells**, and m (2) **Rachel Springsted**. (Tombstone Rec., Mt. Hope Cem., Rochester, NY - *DAR Patriot Index*, p. 571)

John - bc1767 in CT, d 8/12/1852 age 85 in Thetford, Orange Co., VT. John m (1) **Huldah ---**, d 8/11/1809 age 38, and m (2) **Rachel ----**, bc1773 in CT, d 12/7/1859 age 89 in Thetford, VT. In the 1850 census he was 83 and Rachel was 77 years old. (*1850 Orange Co., VT, Census, Thetford*)

RIPLEY

Phineas - b 8/27/1751 in Windham, CT, d 9/1823 in OH. Phineas m **Experience ----**, b 5/14/1755, d 9/14/1814 in NY. (*Hist. of Pittsford, VT*, p. 192, 324 - *DAR Patriot Index*, p. 572)

RISING

Abner - b 1/20/1748 in Suffield, CT, s/o **Aaron**; Abner d 1/3/1839 in Litchfield, Herkimer Co., NY. He m **Abigail Devotion** of Suffield, b 1/16/1751, d 2/10/1846, d/o **Edward** and **Mary (Tute)**. (*New Eng. Gen. Reg.* July 1931 p. 288 - *DAR Patriot Index*, p. 572)

RIX

Garner - bc1768 in Preston, CT, d prob. in Royalton, Windosr Co., VT. Garner m **Betsey Lyman**, bc1774 in CT, d prob. in Royalton,

Windsor Co., VT. In the 1850 census he was 82 and she was 76 years old. (*1850 Census of Windsor Co., VT*)

Elisha – bc1778 in Preston, CT, d 12/9/1851 age 73 in Roylaton, Windsor Co., VT. Elisha m **Elizabeth Flynn**, b1780, d 5/27/1846 age 65 in Royalton, Windsor Co., VT. In the 1850 census he was 72 years old. (*1850 Census of Windsor Co., VT*)

ROBARDS

William – b 2/10/1749 in Canaan, CT, d 8/9/1802 in Queensbury, Warren Co., NY. William m1774 **Phebe Fuller**. (*Hist. of Warren Co., NY*, p. 343 – *DAR Patriot Index*, p. 575)

ROBBINS

John – bc1756 in Killingly, CT, d1831 age 75 prob. in Cornwall, Addison Co., VT. John m **Esther Chapman**. (*History of Cornwall, VT*, p. 63, 289)

ROBINS

Josiah – bc1776 in CT, d 9/30/1850 age 74-3-8 in Chelsea, Orange Co., VT. Josiah m **Fanny G.** ----, b in NH, d 10/8/1857 age 60-5, buried in the Old Cem., Chelsea, VT. In the 1850 census he was 74 and she was 62 years old. (*1850 Orange Co., VT, Census*)

ROBERTS

Amos – b1786 in CT, d1873 in MI. Amos m **Sally Hurd**. (War of 1812 Index)

Eliphalet – b in CT, d 9/27/1843 in Strafford, Orange Co., VT. Eliphalet m **Sarah** ----, d 2/24/1840 age 76. (Strafford Cemetery gravestones, Kibling)

Eliphalet – bc1788 in CT, d prob. in Marshfield, Washington Co., VT. Eliphalet m **Eldalia** ----, bc1802 in NH. In the 1850 census he was 62 and she was 48 years old. (*1850 Census of Washington Co., VT*)

Lt. **Martin** – bc1780 in CT, d 2/28/1829 age 49 in Henrietta Twp., Monroe Co., NY. Lt. Martin m ----. (*Hist. of Monroe Co., NY*, p. 39, 249-51 – Tombstone Rec.)

ROBERTSON

Samuel – b 8/18/1775 in New London, CT, s/o **Patrick** and **Elizabeth**; Samuel d 9/6/1872 age 97 in Roxbury, Washington Co., VT. He m1801 **Persis Richardson** of Tolland, CT. (*Washington Co. Gazetteer*, p. 452)

William – b1822 in Hartford, CT, s/o **George** and **Margaret (Benson)**; William d1912 prob. in Putney, Windham Co., VT. He m1854 **Abbie A. Benson** of Landgrove, VT. (*Putney, VT*, p. 21-2)

ROBINSON

Amos – b1767 in Lebanon, CT, d prob. in Royalton, Windsor Co., VT. Amos m1797 in Canaan, NY, **Levina Bullock** of Orange, NH, d1806 age 33 in Royalton, VT, and m (2) **Betsey** ----, b1762, d 12/9/1838 in Royalton, VT. (*Royalton* by Nash, p. 237 – *History of Royalton, VT*, p. 931-2)

Chauncey - b 1/5/1792 in Durham, CT, d 5/8/1866 in Holley, Orleans Co., NY. Chauncey m ----. (*Pioneer History of Orleans County*, p. 294-5)

Claghorn - b 4/4/1754 in Windham, CT, d1806 prob. in Addison, Addison Co., VT. Claghorn m 1/29/1777 in Canterbury, CT, **Betty Ransom**, b 10/27/1755 in Canterbury, CT. (*Branches and Twigs*, v. 1 #4, p. 60)

Capt. **Ephraim** - b 5/13/1760 in Windham, CT, d1843 prob. in Pawlet, Rutland Co., VT. Capt. Ephraim m **Mary Upham**. (*History of Rutland Co.*, p. 707 - *DAR Patriot Index*, p. 576)

Jabez - bc1783 in CT, d prob. in Oxford, Chenango Co., NY. Jabez m **Anna** ----, bc1796 in NY, d prob. in Oxford, Chenango Co., NY. In the 1850 census he was 67 and she was 54 years old. (*1850 Census, Oxford, Chenango Co., NY*)

Philo - bc1791 in CT, d perhaps in Sherburne, Chenango Co., NY. Philo m **Damaris** ----, bc1792 in CT, d perhaps in Sherburne, Chenango Co., NY. In the 1850 census he was 59 and she was 58 years old. (*1850 Census Chenango Co., NY*)

Richard - b 5/13/1763 in Windham, CT, d 12/15/1838 in Pawlet, Rutland Co., VT. Richard m **Huldah** ----. (*Hist. of Rutland Co.*, p. 707 - *DAR Patriot Index*, p. 576)

R o b e r t - bc1776 in CT, d perhaps in Roxbury, Washington Co., VT. Robert m **P e r s i s** ----, b1783 in CT, d perhaps in Roxbury, Washington Co., VT. In the 1850 census he was 74 and she was 67 years old. (*1850 Census of Washington Co., VT*)

Timothy - bc1784 in CT, d perhaps in Royalton, Windsor Co., VT. Timothy m **Olivia** ----, bc1794 in VT, d perhaps in Royalton, Windsor Co., VT. In the 1850 census he was 66 and she was 56 years old. (*1850 Census of Windsor Co., VT*)

ROCKWELL

Caleb - bc1779 in CT, d1859 in OH. Caleb m **Sarah Watrous**. (War of 1812 Index)

Edward - b in CT, d1874 in OH. Edward m **Matilda Salter**, d1847. (*Trumbull and Mahoning Cos., OH*, p. 230-1)

Eleazer - bc1784 in CT, d perhaps in Pittsfield, Rutland Co., VT. Eleazer m **Parmelia** ----, bc1794 in VT, d perhaps in Pittsfield, Rutland Co., VT. In the 1850 census he was 66 and she was 56 years old. (*1850 Rutland Co., VT, Census*)

Jabez - b 10/3/1761 in Ridgefield, CT, d 1/18/1847 in Honesdale, PA. Jabez m (1) 7/4/1784 in CT, **Sarah Rundel**, and m (2) 1799 **Elizabeth Mulford**. (*Wayne, Pike, & Monroe Co., PA*, p. 819 - *DAR Patriot Index*, p. 577)

John, Jr. - b 5/12/1734 in Ridgefield, CT, d 9/6/1825 age 91 in Cornwall, VT. John, Jr. m (1) 4/16/1754 **H a n n a h   S c o t t**, b 10/3/1731 in Ridgefield, CT, d in Lanesboro, MA, d/o Capt. **James** and **Hannah**, and m (2) (widow) **Sally Rice Hungerford**, and m (3) ----, a French lady of lower Canada. (*Hist. of Cornwall, VT*, p. ? - *DAR Patriot Index*, p. 577 - *Rockwell and Keeler Gen.*, p. 20, 57-9)

John, Jr. - b 5/7/1755 in Ridgefield, CT, s/o **John** and **Elizabeth** (**Keeler**); John, Jr. d 9/2/1825 in Cornwall, VT, four days before his father. John, Jr. m 7/22/1777 in Rutland, VT, **Rebecca Ives**, d

10/1/1837 in Cornwall, VT. (*History of Cornwall, VT*, p. 89 - *DAR Patriot Index*, p. 577 - *Rockwell and Keeler Gen.*, p. 57-8, 120-121)

Simmons - b in Stonington, CT. Simmons m **Rathana** ----. They once resided in Roxbury, Delaware Co., NY. (*Hist. of Delaware Co.*, p. 38 - *Hist. of Roxbury* by Griffin)

Dr. **William Haydon** - b 2/15/1800 in E. Windsor, CT, d 11/30/1873 prob. in Brattleboro, Windham Co., VT. Dr. William Haydon m 6/25/1835 Mrs. **Maria G. Chapin**, b in Salisbury, CT. In the 1850 census they were both 50 years old. (*1850 Census of Windham Co., VT - Gazetteer Windham Co., VT*, p. 129-130 - *Vermont History Magazine*, v. 5, p. 146)

ROGERS

Abial - b1780 in CT. Abial m **Polly Mack** of Whiting, VT. They once resided in Underhill, Chittenden Co., VT. In the 1850 census he was 69 years old and a pauper. (*Gazetteer of Chittenden Co., VT*, p. 256 - *1850 Census of Chittenden Co., VT*)

Rev. **Ammi** - b 5/26/1770 in Branford, CT. Rev. Ammi m1794 in Ballston, NY, **Margaret Bloore**, d1800, d/o **Joshua** and **Margaret (Brintal)**. (*Hist. of Saratoga Co., NY*, p. 236)

Amos - b in CT, s/o Elder **Davis**. Amos m **Mary Chapin**. They once resided in Chenango Co., NY. In the 1850 census he was 69 and she was 67 years old. (*Hist. of Chenango Co., NY*, p. 362 - *1850 Census of Chenango Co., NY*)

David, Jr. - bc1777 in CT, s/o David; d 10/9/1845 age 68. David, Jr. m **Polly Truman**, d 9/8/1845 age 63, d/o **Jonathan**. (*Hist. of Chenango Co., NY*, p. 362)

Elder **Davis** - b in Waterford, CT. Elder Davis m (1) **Hannah** ----, d 1/4/1821 age 70, and m (2) **Avis Burdick**, d 1/11/1835 age 56 in Pharsalia, NY. They were said to be Seventh Day Baptists; came with son-in-law, **Joseph Truman**, in 1804 to Chenango Co. (*Hist. of Chenango Co., NY*, p. 362)

Deacon **Ebenezer** - b 10/3/1769 in Norwalk, CT, d 1/28/1865 age 96-3-25 prob. in Albion, Orleans Co., NY. Deacon Ebenezer m **Betsey Lyman** of Lebanon, CT, d 8/28/1849. (*Pioneer Hist. of Orleans Co., NY*, p. ?)

Ethan - bc1768 in Waterford, CT, d 4/25/1841 age 73 in Preston, NY. Ethan m **Sally Truman**, d 10/21/1860 age 83 in Preston, NY, d/o **Jonathan** and **Annie**. (*Hist. of Chenango Co., NY*, p. 362)

Jabez - b 3/21/1742 in Montville, CT. Jabez m 4/10/1766 **Sarah Gorton**. They once lived in Middlebury, Addison Co., VT. (*Gazetteer of Addison Co., VT*, p. 145)

Jonathan - bc1798 in CT. Jonathan m **Catherine** ----, bc1802 in VT. They resided in Bennington, Bennington Co., VT. In the 1850 census he was 62 (and a shoemaker) and she was 48 years old. (*1850 Bennington Co., VT, Census*)

Matthew - b1770 in CT, d1847 in IL. Matthew m **Eliza Anna Morse**. (War of 1812 Index)

Nathan - bc1787 in CT. Nathan m **Phebe** ----, bc1796 in NY. They once resided in Preston, Chenango Co., NY. In the 1850 census he was 63 and she was 54 years old. (*1850 Census of Chenango County, New York*)

Rufus - bc1786 in CT. Rufus m **Nancy** ----, bc1801. They resided in Clarendon, Rutland Co., VT. In the 1850 census he was 64 and she was 49 years old. (*1850 Rutland Co., VT, Census*)

S i l a s - b1782 in CT, s/o Elder **D a v i s** ; Silas d 2/21/1870 age 88 in Preston, Chenango Co., NY. He m **Sally** ----, d 10/1/1877 age 92. (*Hist. of Chenango Co., NY*, p. 362)

S i m e o n - b 8/1762 in CT, d 3/27/1856 in Barker, Broome Co., NY. Simeon m1792 **Mary Allen Barker**, d/o **John** of CT and NY. (French's *Hist. Gazetteer*, p. 181 - *DAR Patriot Index*, p. 579)

ROLANDSON

William - bc1772 in CT. William m **Rebecca** ----, bc1780 in VT. They once resided in Pomfret, Windsor Co., VT. In the 1850 census he was 78 and she was 70 years old. (*1850 Windsor County, Vermont, Census*)

ROOD

I s a a c - b in CT, d1775 in Pittsford, Rutland Co., VT. Isaac m **Elizabeth Ellsworth**, b in CT, d/o **Samuel, Sr.** (*Hist. of Pittsford, VT*, p. 35)

J o s e p h - b 5/7/1754 (or 5/7/1750) in Lebanon, CT, d 3/31/1843 in Fredonia, Chautauqua Co., NY. Joseph m **Lois** ----. (*Soldiers of Am. Rev., Chautauqua Co., NY*, p. 19 - *DAR Patriot Index*, p. 580)

Welcome - bc1788 in CT. Welcome m **Roby** ----, bc1794 in RI. They once resided in Pittsfield, Chenango Co., NY. In the 1850 census he was 62 and she was 56 years old. (*1850 Census of Chenango County, New York*)

ROOT

Jeremiah - bc1768 in CT. Jeremiah m **Anna** ----, bc1773 in NH. They once resided in Rochester, Windsor Co., VT. In the 1850 census he was 82 and she was 77 years old. (*1850 Census of Windsor Co., VT*)

William Briscoe - b in CT. William Briscoe m **Wealtha** ----. They once resided in Strafford, Orange Co., VT. (Strafford Cemetery, Kibling, Strafford, VT)

ROSE

James - bc1744 in CT, d1830 in RI. James m **Elizabeth Elred**. (War of 1812 Index)

Lt. Col. **William** - b 11/17/1763 in Canaan, CT, d 1/23/1849 in Binghamton, Broome Co., NY. Lt. Col. William m ----. (*DAR Mag.*, v. 39, p. 90)

ROSS

J o s e p h - bc1771 in CT, d 5/10/1855 age 84 in Middletown, Susquehanna Co., PA. Joseph m **Polly** ----, d 4/27/1864 in 85th year. (*Hist. of Susquehanna Co., PA*, p. 455)

ROUNDY

Capt. **J o h n** - b 10/28/1748 in Simsbury, CT, d 4/23/1805 age 57 in Rockingham, Windham Co., VT. Capt. John m **Ruth Chickerly**, d

3/11/1831 age 76. She m (2) ---- **Emery**. (*History of Rockingham, VT*, p. 743-5 - *DAR Patriot Index*, p. 583)

Ralph - b 9/8/1774 in CT, s/o Capt. **John** and **Ruth**. Ralph m 7/10/1794 **Rosalinda Wright**, b 4/29/1777. They once resided in Rockingham, Windham Co., VT. (*The VT Antiquarian*, p. 104)

ROWE

John - b in Hebron, CT, dc1806 age 100-4 in Sullivan, NH. John m (1) 7/5/1745 in Hebron, CT, **Mary Williams**, and m (2) Mrs. **Hepzibah Comstock**, wid/o **William**. (*Town of Gilsum, NH*, p. 387)

ROWLAND

Aaron - b1780 in Danbury, CT, s/o **Hezekiah** and **Grace** (**Wildman**); Aaron d in Clarksfield, OH. He m1799 **Elizabeth Dean** of Carmel, OH, b1780. (*Res. of CT Who Migrated to Huron, OH*, p. p. 5)

Luke - b1758 in Canaan, CT, d1839 in Clarksfield, OH. Luke m1780 in Salisbury, CT, **Elizabeth Knickerbocker**, b1762, d1841 in Clarksfield, OH. (*Res. of CT Who Migrated to Huron, OH*, p. 5)

ROWLEY

Roger - bc1782 in CT, d1844 in NY. Roger m **Rebecca Latimer**. (War of 1812 Index)

Thomas, Sr. - b 3/24/1721 in Hebron, CT, s/o **Samuel**; Thomas, Sr. d1803 in Benson, VT. He m 7/15/1744 **Lois Cass**. (*VT Hist. Mag.*, p. ? - *Hist. of Rutland Co.*, p. 578 - *Hist. of Danby, VT*, p. 239 - *DAR Patriot Index*, p. 584)

ROYCE

Amasa - bc1793 in Mansfield, CT. Amasa m **Alice Spalding**, bc1801 in VT. They once resided in Royalton, Windsor Co., VT. In the 1850 census he was 55 and she was 49 years old. (*1850 Census of Windsor Co., VT*)

Jonathan - bc1745 in CT, d1826 in NH. Jonathan m **Sarah Marvin**. (War of 1812 Index)

Philip - bc1791 in CT. Philip m **Mary** ----, bc1796 in NH. They once resided in Barnard, Windsor Co., VT. In the 1850 census he was 59 and she was 54 years old. (*1850 Windsor Co., VT, Census*)

Samuel - b 4/20/1757 in Waterbury, CT, s/o **Phineas** and **Elizabeth** (**Palmer**) (**Lord**); Samuel d1847 in 90th year in Clinton, Oneida Co., NY. He m 6/10/1780 in Watertown, CT, **Abigail Hawley**, d 4/9/1832 age 74. (*Clinton Memorial-Kirtland Ave. Cem.*, p. 28)

RUDD

Zebulon - b 7/6/1717 in Windham, CT, s/o **Nathaniel** and **Rebecca** (**Adams**); Zebulon d 7/26/1795 in Dutchess Co., NY. He m1742 **Jerusha Brewster**. (*Comm. Biog. Rec., Dutchess Co., NY*, p. 173 - *DAR Patriot Index*, p. 585)

RUGGLES

Alfred - b1773 in Danbury, CT, s/o **Ashbell**; Alfred d1866 in Huron Co., OH. He m ----. (*Residents of Connecticut Who Migrated to Huron, OH*, p. 5)

197

RUMSEY
David – b 1/28/1759 in Redding, CT, d 6/2/1849 in 91st year in Westfield, NY. David m **Hannah Bronson**, d 2/14/1841 age 80. (*Soldiers of Am. Rev., Chautauqua Co., NY*, p. ? – *DAR Patriot Index*, p. 586)

Stephen – b 6/1/1785 in Woodbury, CT, d 7/31/1873 age 88 in Westfield, NY. Stephen m –––––. (*Chautauqua Co., NY*, p. 609–610)

William – b 6/22/1750 in CT, d 2/22/1836 age 85 in Hubbardton, VT. William m **Elizabeth Walker**. (*VT Hist. Mag.*, v. 4, p. 1177 – *DAR Patriot Index*, p. 586 – *Hist. and Gen. of Old Fairfield, CT*)

RUNDALL
David – b 1/4/1757 in Fairfield, CT, d 1/21/1848 in Amenia, NY. David m (1) 1/7/1777 **Catherine Powers**, d 5/14/1799, and m (2) 3/1801 **Elizabeth Cole**, d 7/6/1821, and m (3) **Alice Allerton**. (*Comm. Biog. Rec., Dutchess Co., NY*, p. 637)

RUNDLE
Reuben – b 3/10/1757 in Greenwich, CT, d 10/25/1848 prob. in Greenville, Greene Co., NY. Reuben m **Sarah Holly**. (*Hist. of Greene Co., NY*, p. 298 – *DAR Patriot Index*, p. 586)

RUSCOE
Bennett – b1782 in CT. Bennett m **Roxy Mathewson**, b1784. He once resided in Camden, Oneida Co., NY. (*Pioneer History of Camden, NY*, p. 272)

RUSSELL
Hamlin – bc1781 in CT, d1852 in PA. Hamlin m **Sarah Norcross**. (War of 1812 Index)

James – bc1793 in CT. James m **Mary** –––––, bc1807 in NH. They once resided in Randolph, Orange Co., VT. In the 1850 census he was 57 and she was 43 years old. (*1850 Orange Co., VT, Census*)

Jonathan – b 5/21/1748 in Killingly, CT, d 7/10/1800 in Chesterfield, MA. Jonathan m1775 **Joanna Goodrich** of Hadley, MA, d/o **Aaron** and **Dorcas (Cook)**. (*New Eng. Gen. Reg.*, April 1964, p. 136)

RUST
Aloney – b 2/19/1766 in CT, d 6/29/1857 in OH. Aloney m **Esther Doud**. (*Hist. of Wells, VT*, p. 146 by Paul and Parks – *DAR Patriot Index* 587 – *Hist. of Wells* by Wood, p. 79)

SABIN
Henry – b 10/23/1829 in Pomfret, CT. Henry m –––––. He was a resident of Clinton, IA and an educator. (*Hist. of IA*, p. 228)

SACKETT
Harvey – b 12/25/1791 in Warren, CT, s/o **Salmon** and **Marsey**; Harvey d 8/11/1875 in Ruggles, Huron Co., OH. He m (1) 4/2/1817 in Summit, OH, **Thalia Eldred**, d 4/20/1843, and m (2) 1844 **Mary**

Van Vranken, a widow. (*Residents of Connecticut Who Migrated to Huron Co., OH*, p. 6)

SAFFORD

David - b 2/8/1743 (or 2/8/1744) in Norwich, CT, s/o **Joseph** and **Anne (Longbottom)**; David d1824. He once resided in Bennington, VT. David m **Anna Brewster**. (*OH Valley Saffords* by Culbertson, p. 169 - *DAR Patriot Index*, p. 589)

Erastus - b 2/6/1764 in Norwich, CT, s/o **Josiah** and **Deborah (Sprague)**; Erastus d 12/5/1849. He served from Fairfax, VT, as a Capt in the Revolution. Erastus m **Clarissa Hopkins**. (*OH Valley Saffords*, p. 170-1 - *DAR Patriot Index*, p. 589)

Jacob - b 11/26/1752 in Norwich, CT (moved with parents to Bennington, VT in 1763), s/o **Joseph** and **Anne (Longbottom)**; Jacob d ----. (*OH Valley Saffords* by Culbertson, p. 169-170)

Jacob - b1762 in Preston, CT, s/o **John**; d 4/20/1829 age 67 in Royalton, VT. He m **Mary (Polly) Searle** (?). (*History of Royalton, Vermont*, p. 944-5)

John - b1729 in Preston, CT, s/o **John**; John (the younger) d 4/9/1815 in CT. He had lived in Royalton, VT. He m 3/15/1759 **Mary Johnson**, d 8/1817. (*Hist. of Royalton, VT*, p. 944)

Joseph - bp. 4/29/1770 in Preston, CT, s/o **John**; Joseph d 8/6/1845 in Royalton, VT. He m (1) 12/1/1796 **Lois Pierce**, b 9/14/1772, d 9/14/1798 in Royalton, VT, d/o **Jedediah** and **Susan (Eaton)**, and m (2) **Desire Culver**, b1775, d 4/12/1819, and m (3) 1821 **Polly Bacon**, b 1/27/1782, d 7/28/1863 in Royalton, VT. (*History of Royalton*, p. 945)

Joseph, Jr. - b 12/1/1741 in Norwich, CT, s/o **Joseph** and **Anne (Longbottom)**; Joseph, Jr. d 12/4/1807 in either Bennington, VT, or Malone, NY. He m **Marcy Robinson**. (*OH Valley Saffords* by Culbertson, p. 168-9 - *DAR Patriot Index*, p. 589)

Josiah - b 2/21/1740 (or 2/21/1741) in Norwich, CT, s/o **John, Jr.** and **Lydia (Hebard)**; Josiah d1825. He m (1) 10/28/1762 **Deborah Sprague**, and m (2) **Polly Leffingwell**. He had moved to Bennington, VT, before his death. (*OH Valley Saffords* by Culbertson, p. 170 - *DAR Patriot Index*, p. 589)

Nathan - bp. 5/22/1774 in Preston, CT, s/o **John**; Nathan d 12/2/1828 age 54 in Royalton, Windsor Co., VT. He m **Anna H.** ----, b1766, d 3/1/1840 age 74 in Royalton, VT. (*Hist. of Royalton, VT*, p. 946)

Gen. Samuel - b 4/14/1737 in Norwich, CT, d 3/3/1813 in Bennington, Bennington Co., VT. Gen. Samuel m **Mary Lawrence**. (*Vermont History Mag.*, v. 1, p. 177 - *OH Valley Saffords*, p. 167 - *DAR Patriot Index*, p. 589)

Silas - b 9/11/1757 in Norwich, CT, d 5/12/1832 age 74. Silas m 12/1780 **Clarinda Hawley** of Arlington, VT, d 8/17/1847 age 82. (*OH Valley Saffords* by Culbertson, p. 171 - *Hist. of Fair Haven, VT*, p. 464-5 - *DAR Patriot Index*, p. 589)

Thomas D. - b in Preston, CT. Thomas D. m1807 **Huldah Palmer**, d/o Rev. **Nathaniel** of Brookfield. They once resided in Pompey, Onondaga Co., NY. (*Pompey, NY*, p. 350)

SAGE

Daniel – bc1796 in CT. Daniel m **Eliza Ann** ----, bc1810 in CT. Once resided in New Berlin, Chenango Co., NY. In the 1850 census he was 54 and she was 40 years old. (*1850 Census of Chenango County, New York*)

Giles – b1780 in CT, d1842 in NY. Giles m **Lydia Herendeen**. (War of 1812 Index)

Ransom – b1780 in CT, d1852 in NY. Ransom m **Mary West**. (War of 1812 Index)

ST. JOHN

John – b 4/11/1753 in CT, d 10/22/1825 in Greenfield, NY. John m **Hannah Fitch**. (*DAR Magazine* 1977, p. 921 – *DAR Patriot Index*, p. 590)

Nehemiah – b1742 in CT, s/o **Noah** and **Jane (Smith)**; Nehemiah d 7/23/1803 age 61 in Hubbardton, Rutland Co., VT. He m 2/18/1767 in Southbury, CT, **Ruth Wheeler**, b1746, d 8/15/1804 age 58. (*Hist. of Rutland Co., VT*, p. 620-1 – *St. John Genealogy*, p. 189-90 – *DAR Patriot Index*, p. 590)

Seth – b1770 in Ridgefield, CT, s/o **Nehemiah** and **Ruth (Wheeler)**; Seth d 8/8/1846 in Hubbardton, VT. He m1793 **Rebecca Foster**, d 1/7/1851. (*Vermont History Magazine*, v. 4, p. 1173 – *St. John Gen.*, p. 190, 318)

Stephen – b 6/15/1780 in CT. Stephen m 3/4/1801 **Polly Graves**, b 1/9/1785. In 1830's they were living in Clymer, NY. (*Car Del Scribe* Query July 1977, p. 27)

Timothy – b 5/3/1757 in Norwalk, CT, s/o **Nathan** and **Lois (St. John)**; Timothy d 12/25/1831 prob. in Hubbardton, Rutland Co., VT. He m (1) **Deborah Gorham**, b 4/27/1755 in Greenfarms, CT, d/o **John** and **Abigail (Wakeman)**, and m (2) 1794 **Rachel Curtis**, d 6/6/1837. (*VT Hist. Mag.*, v. 4, p. 1173 – *St. John Gen.*, p. 252)

SALMON

Gershom – b 9/26/1753 in Fairfield, CT, d 5/11/1843 in E. Bloomfield, Ontario Co., NY. Gershom m ----. (*DAR Mag.*, v. 39, p. 90)

SALTER

Orin – bc1797 in CT. Orin m **Polly** ----, bc1800 in NH. They resided in Mt. Holly, Rutland Co., VT. In the 1850 census he was 53 and she was 50 years old. (*1850 Rutland Co., VT, Census*)

SANFORD

Benjamin – b 6/4/1761 in Litchfield, CT, d 7/1/1883 in Cornwall, VT. Benjamin m **Sarah Marsh**, b 1/8/1766, d 2/28/1818 in Cornwall, VT, d/o **John** and **Anna (Marsh)**. (*Hist. of Cornwall, VT*, p. 82, 289 – *Sanford Fam.*, v. 1, p. 258-9, 448-63)

Burritt – b 6/5/1820 in Plymouth Hollow, CT. Burritt m (1) 1/23/1846 **Margaret Sarah Ann Hart**, b 1/13/1828 in Groton, NY, d 10/15/1857 in Menasha, WI, and m (2) 7/3/1859 **Grace Reed Grant**, b 7/23/1825 in Antwerp, NY. They lived in Portage Co., WI. In the 1880 census he was 60 years old and a carpenter. (*1880 Census Portage Co., WI*)

Clark - bc1791 in CT. Clark m **Mary** ----, bc1794 in CT. They lived in Middletown, Delaware Co., NY. In the 1855 census he was 64 and she was 61 years old. (*1855 Census of Delaware Co., NY*)

David - b1769 in New Milford, CT, s/o **Zachariah** and **Rachel**; David dc1812 possibly in Queensbury, Warren Co., NY. He m **Amy Hartwell**. (*Hist. of Warren Co., NY*, p. 402, 404)

Edmond - b 10/25/1781 in CT, d 1/9/1860 prob. in Sherburne, Chenango Co., NY. Edmond m (1) **Sarah** ----, b 5/24/1779, d 4/20/1843, and m (2) **Betsey** ----, b 5/21/1795 in NH, d 2/21/1861. In the 1850 census he was 69 and Betsey was 55 years old. (*1850 Census of Chenango Co., NY*)

Ephraim - bc1789 in CT, d 12/24/1860 age 71 prob. in Camden, Oneida Co., NY. Ephraim m **Temperance Dunbar**, d 10/30/1874 age 83, d/o Capt. **Joel**. (*Pioneer Hist. of Camden, NY*, p. 187-8)

Gay - bc1787 in CT. Gay m **Hannah** ----, bc1797 in CT. They resided in Bennington, Bennington Co., VT. In the 1850 census he was was 63 and she was 53 years old. (*1850 Bennington Co., VT, Census*)

Jonah - b 7/17/1749 in Litchfield, CT, d 11/15/1824 age 75 in Camden, Oneida Co., NY. Jonah m (1) **Mary Dunbar**, his second cousin, d in Clinton, NY, and m (2) **Miss West** of Rome, NY. (*Pioneer Hist. of Camden, NY*, p. 158-160 - *Thomas Sanford Fam.*, p. 166 - *DAR Patriot Index*, p. 592)

Linus - b 1/16/1782 in Plymouth, CT, d 5/29/1842 in Camden, Oneida Co., NY. Linus m (1) 5/6/1810 **Polly Woods**, d 5/18/1816 (or 5/18/1818), d/o **Samuel**, and m (2) 10/11/1819 **Rhoda Alcott**, b 5/5/1789 in Wolcott, CT, d 5/11/1881 in Verona, NY. (*Pioneer Hist. of Camden, NY*, p. 162 - *Thomas Sanford Emigrant to New England*, p. ? - *VT Hist. Mag.*, v. 1, p. 241)

Lot - b 9/5/1773 in CT, d 4/20/1860 in Shoreham, Addison Co., VT. Lot m 2/19/1801 **Lurana Bush**, b 10/2/1783, d 6/22/1865, d/o **Ebenezer** of Shoreham, VT. (*History of Shoreham, VT*, p. ? - *Gazetteer Addison Co., VT*, p. ?)

Reuben - bc1780 in CT, d1855 in OH. Reuben m **Polly Lewis**. (War of 1812 Index)

Rufus Clark - b 12/6/1785 in New Milford, CT, d 8/7/1861 in Charlotte, VT. Rufus Clark m 1/1816 **Clarinda Conger**, b in VT. In the 1850 census he was 64 and she was 59 years old. (*Thos. Sanford Fam.*, v. 1 part 1, p. 300, 555 - *1850 Census Chittenden Co., VT*)

Sala - bc1784 in CT, d1866 in IL. Sala m **Margaret B. Smith**. (War of 1812 Index)

William - bc1783 in CT. William m **Lucy** ----, bc1787 in CT. They resided in Stamford, Bennington Co., VT. In the 1850 census he was 67 and she was 63 years old. (*1850 Bennington County, Vermont, Census*)

SARGENT

John - b 12/16/1739 in Mansfield, CT, s/o **Isaac** and **Ann (Wood)**; John d 12/6/1826 (or 12/6/1827) in Pawlet (or Dorset), VT. He m 4/3/1760 in Mansfield, CT, **Fear Gibbs**, d/o **John**. (*Sargent Gen.*, p. 41, 50 - *A History of Norwich, Vermont*, p. 244-5 - *DAR Patriot Index*, p. 593)

John, Jr. - b 6/30/1761 in Mansfield, CT, s/o **John** and **Fear (Gibbs)**; d 10/30/1843 prob. in Norwich, Windsor Co., VT. John, Jr. m1786 **Delight Bell**, b 6/28/1761, d 8/29/1835, d/o **Samuel**. (*Sargent Gen.*, p. 69 - *A History of Norwich, VT*, p. 244-5 - *DAR Patriot Index*, p. 593)

SAVAGE

T h o m a s - b 12/15/1714 in Middletown, CT, d 10/10/1798 age 84 in Hartford, Windsor Co., VT. Thomas m 2/24/1744 **Martha Whitm o r e**, b 12/11/1719, d1767. (*Hist. of Hartford, VT*, p. 459 - *VT Antiquarian*, p. 24, 458-9)

Francis Whitmore - b 11/25/1762 in Washington, CT, s/o **Thomas** and **Martha (Whitmore)**; Francis Whitmore d 9/23/1817 age 55, buried in Private Cem., W. Hartford, VT. He m 3/11/1790 **Abigail Hazen**, b 9/14/1768, d 8/20/1847 age 70 in W. Hartford, VT, buried in Private Cem., in W. Hartford, VT, d/o Col. **Joshua** and **Mercy (Hazen)**. (*History of Hartford, VT*, p. 459-60 - *Vermont Antiquarian*, p. 459-60)

S e t h - b 10/6/1756 in Lebanon, CT, s/o **T h o m a s** and **M a r t h a (Whitmore)**; d 9/13/1829 in Hartford, Windsor Co., VT. Seth m (1) 4/15/1779 **Rhoda Bacon**, d 4/19/1823 age 65, and m (2) 6/30/1825 **Miriam (Smith) Richards**, d 12/19/1855, d/o **Sylvanus** and **Diana (Fisk) Smith**, wid/o **Joel Richards**. (*DAR Patriot Index*, p. 594 - *Hist. of Hartford, VT*, p. 458-9 - *VT Antiquarian*, p. 458-9)

T h o m a s , J r . - b 2/9/1759 in CT, d 10/29/1841 age 83 in Hartford, Windsor Co., VT. Thomas, Jr. m (1) 10/11/1784 **Lavinia Chapman**, and m (2) 11/26/1789 **Molly Powell**, d 8/5/1803 age 45, and m (3) 3/22/1804 **Clarissa Noble**, b 2/9/1759, d 9/28/1841 age 83, buried in Delano Cem., Hftd., VT. (*VT Antiquarian*, p. 459)

SAWYER

Conant B. - b 4/8/1756 in Hebron, CT, s/o **Isaac** and **Susanna (Gillet)**; Conant B. d 4/18/1838 age 82 in Norwich, Windsor Co., VT. He m (1) **Deborah Robinson**, and m (2) **Roxalana Miller**, d 6/4/1795 age 41, and m (3) **Ruth Boardman**, d 5/2/1813 age 49, and m (4) **Mary McAllister**, d 12/2/1815 age 56, and m (5) **Margaret (McAllister) S m i t h**, d 3/30/1838 age 70. (*A Hist. of Norwich, VT*, p. 245-6 - *DAR Patriot Index*, p. 594)

Cornelius - bc1773 in CT. Cornelius m **Olive ----**, bc1785 in VT. They resided in Norwich, Windsor Co., VT. In the 1850 census he was 77 and she was 65 years old. (*1850 Census of Windsor Co., VT*)

David - bc1766 in CT. David m **Electa ----**, bc1784 in VT. They resided in Tinmouth, Rutland Co., VT. In the 1850 census he was 84 and she was 66 years old. (*1850 Rutland Co., VT, Census*)

Daniel - b1773 in CT, d1819 in NC. Daniel m **Theodosia Penoyer Bouton**. (War of 1812 Index)

Samuel - b1793 in CT, s/o **Nathan**; Samuel d1860 age 67 in Butternuts, Otsego Co., NY. He m **Cynthia Doolittle** of CT, d age 53. (*Biog. Rec. of Otsego Co., NY*, p. 277)

Thomas - bc1714 in CT, d 9/8/1785 age 71 in Lyme, Grafton Co., NH. Thomas m ----. (*Gazetteer of Grafton Co., NH*, p. 546)

SCARRITT

James - bc1797 (or bc1798) in CT, d 12/1/1870 age 72-11 in Smyrna (or Sherburne), NY. James m **Polly** - - - -, bc1810 in NY, d 11/20/1862 in Smyrna, NY, age 52. In the 1850 census he was 52 (and a miller) and she was 40 years old. (*Cemeteries of Sherburne, Chenango Co., NY*, p. 196 - *1850 Census of Chenango Co., NY*)

James - bc1760 in N. Branford, CT, s/o **Jeremiah** and **Mary (Baker)**; James dc1856 (?) in Chenango Co., NY. He m (1) **Silvia Plumb** (?), bc1778, and m (2) Mrs. **Elizabeth Collins**. (*Scarritt Clan in America*, p. 61)

Lester - bc1783 in CT, s/o **Richard** and **Hannah**; Lester d 12/3/1858 age 75-7-17 in Smyrna, Chenango Co., NY. He m **Tryphena** - - - -, bc1788 in CT, d 3/30/1867 age 79-1-13. (*Scarritt Clan in America*, p. ?, booklet)

SCHOFIELD

Enos - b 1/26/1758 in Stamford, CT, d 12/15/1836 in Hanover, Chautauqua Co., NY. Enos m1779 **Hannah Schofield**. (*Soldiers of American Rev., Chautauqua Co., NY*)

SCOTT

Benjamin Rush - bc1791 in CT, d1843 in SC. Benjamin Rush m **Eliza M. Roper**. (War of 1812 Index)

Daniel - bc1780 in CT, d1867 in NY. Daniel m **Sarah Dunlap**. (War of 1812 Index)

Charles H. - bc1854 in CT. Charles H. m **Frances A.** - - - -, b in WI. They resided in Portage Co., WI. In the 1880 census he was 26 and she was 21 years old. (*1880 Census Portage Co., WI*)

Daniel - b 3/24/1759 in CT, d 9/18/1842 in S. Greenfield, Saratoga Co., NY. Daniel m - - - -. (*DAR Mag.* 1977, p. 921)

Eddy - bc1766 in CT, d prob. in Danby, Rutland Co., VT. Eddy m - - - -. In the 1850 census he was 84 years old. (*1850 Rutland Co., VT, Census*)

Ezekiel - bc1830 in CT. Ezekiel m **Mary F. Perry**, bc1836 in CT. He resided in Portage Co., WI. In the 1880 census he was 50 and she was 44 and her mother, **Harriet** - - - -, age 67, was in the household. (*1880 Census Portage Co., WI*)

Harvey - b in CT, s/o **Caleb**. Harvey m in Delaware Co., NY, **Mary Blair**. They resided in Otsego Co., NY. (*Biog. Records of Otsego Co., NY*, p. 346)

Jesse - b 6/10/1787 in Waterbury, CT, s/o **Simeon** and **Lucy (Hickcox)**. Jesse m 8/7/1811 in Waterbury, CT, **Susan Downs**, d/o **David**. They resided in Springville, Susquehanna Co., PA. (*Hist. of Susquehanna Co., PA*, p. 402)

Jonas - bc1773 in CT. Jonas m **Polly** - - - -, bc1777 in CT. They resided in N. Norwich, Chenango Co., NY. In the 1850 census he was 77 and she was 73 years old. (*1850 Census Chenango Co., NY*)

Justus - b in CT, prob, in Hartford. Justus m - - - -, b in Waterbury, CT. They resided in Danby, Rutland Co., VT. (*Hist. of Danby, VT*)

Moses - b 1/31/1761 in CT, d 2/3/1853 in Waterford, Saratoga Co., NY. Moses m **Hannah Wilkinson**. (*DAR Magazine* 1977, p. 921 - *DAR Patriot Index*, p. 599)

Philo - bc1791 in CT. Philo m **Harriet** ----, bc1791 in CT. They resided in Oxford, Chenango Co., NY. In the 1850 census he and she were 59 years old. (*1850 Census Chenango Co., NY*)

Thomas - bc1791 in CT. Thomas m **Amy** ----, bc1805 in NY. They resided in Columbus, Chenango Co., NY. In the 1850 census he was 59 and she was 45 years old. (*1850 Census Chenango Co., NY*)

Titus - b 9/7/1785 in Waterbury, CT, s/o **Simeon** and **Lucy** (**Hickcox**); Titus d age over 95 in Springville, Susquehanna Co., PA. He m 12/1808 **Rhoda Hall**, b 10/8/1787 in Waterbury, CT, d/o **Nathaniel**. (*Hist. of Susquehanna Co., PA*, p. 402)

William - bc1755 in CT, d 1/2/1815 age 60 in Braintree, Orange Co., VT. William m **Olive Harvey** of CT. (*History of Braintree, Vermont*, p. 179)

Zelotis - bc1776 in CT. Zelotis m **Betsey** ----, bc1782 in NH. They resided in Sharon, Windsor Co., VT. In the 1850 census he was 74 and she was 68 years old. (*1850 Census Windsor Co., VT*)

SCOVELL

Daniel - b in Cornwall, CT, d 1/21/1813 age 51 in Cornwall, Addison Co., VT. Daniel m **Lois Rockwell**, d 7/13/1832 age 65 in Cornwall, VT. (*Hist. of Cornwall, VT*, p. 74 - *Survey of the Scovills in England and America by Brainerd*, p. 511)

Ezra - b in Cornwall, CT. Ezra m **Tryphena Terrill**. They resided in Cornwall, VT. (*Hist. of Cornwall, VT*, p. 74 - *Survey of Scovills in England and America* by Brainerd, 511)

SCOVIL

Moses - b 12/6/1762 in CT, d 7/24/1836 in OH. Moses m **Rachel Baker**. (*DAR Patriot Index*, p. 600 - War of 1812 Index)

SCOVILLE

Ezekiel - b 1/17/1773 in Harwinton, CT, s/o **Ezekiel** and **Rebecca** (**Thompson**); Ezekiel (the younger) d 4/2/1834 age 61 prob. in Camden, Onedia Co., NY. He m **Sabra Dunbar**, b1784, d 6/2/1858 age 74. (*Pionesr Hist. of Camden, NY*, p. 73-4)

Joseph Thompson - b 6/6/1777 in Harwinton, CT, s/o **Ezekiel** and **Rebeckah** (**Thompson**); Joseph Thompson d 4/26/1853 age 76 in Camden, Oneida Co., NY. He m **Anna Cook**, d 3/14/1840 age 62. (*Pioneer Hist. of Camden, NY*, p. 128)

Levi - b 6/29/1762 in CT, d1828 in NY. Levi m **Content Dunbar**. (*DAR Patriot Index*, p. 599 - War of 1812 Index)

SCRANTON

Hamlet - b 12/1/1773 in Durham, CT, s/o **Abraham** and **Hannah** (**Camp**); Hamlet d 4/1851 age 78 prob. in Rochester, Monroe Co., NY. He m **Hannah Dimmick**, b 5/22/1774 in Durham, CT, d/o **Daniel** and **Thankful** (**Merriam**). (*Gen. Reg. Des. of John Scranton*, p. 61, 91 - *Hist. of Genesee Co., NY*, v. II, p. 692-3 - *Hist. of Monroe Co., NY*, p. 73, 75, 77, 81, 89)

SCUDDER

Ezekiel - b1763 in CT, d 3/20/1853 in NY. Ezekiel m **Cynthia Gould**. (War of 1812 Index - *DAR Patriot Index*, p. 600)

SEARS

Benjamin - b1771 in CT, d1822 in OH. Benjamin m **Anne Bigelow**. (War of 1812 Index)

David - b1751 in CT, d 8/19/1842 in W. Milton, Ulster Co., NY. David m ----. (*DAR Mag.* 1977, p. 921)

SEDGWICK

Rev. **Evelyn** - b 8/23/1793 in W. Hartford, CT, d 5/23/1868 in Ogden Twp., Monroe Co., NY. Rev. Evelyn m ----. (*Hist. of Monroe Co., NY*, p. 182 - Tombstone Rec.)

Col. **John Andrews** - b 3/8/1764 in Wallingford, CT, s/o **John** and **Abigail (Andrews)**; Col. John Andrews d 7/15/1831 in Cornwall Hollow, CT. He m **Nancy Buell**, b 1/1774 in Cornwall, CT, d 3/20/1848, d/o Major **Jesse**. (Tombstone Rec., Brockport Cem., Sweden Twp., Monroe Co., NY - *A Sedgwick Gen.*, p. 55-7)

SEELEY

Abram - bc1762 in New Haven, CT, d 4/30/1848 age 86 in Great Barrington, MA. Abram m ----. (*Am. Monthly*, v. 39)

Daniel H. - b 4/13/1805 in Bridgeport, CT, d 6/28/1892 age 86 in Genessee Twp., Genessee Co., NY. Daniel H. m 9/2/1827 in Brockport, NY, **Julia A. Taylor**. (*Am. Monthly*, v. 22, p. 86)

Michael - b1750 in CT, d 5/11/1823 in PA. Michael m **Elsche Van Campen**. (*DAR Patriot Index*, p. 602 - War of 1812 Index)

Nathaniel, Jr. - b 10/16/1748 in CT, d 4/30/1806 in Ballston, Saratoga Co., NY, buried in Hubbell Cem., Ballston, NY. Nathaniel, Jr. m **Rhoda Bennett**. (*DAR Mag.*, 1977, p. 921 - *DAR Patriot Index*, p. 602)

Silas - bc1798 in CT. Silas m **Anna** ----, bc1799 in NY. They resided in Oxford, Chenango Co., NY. In the 1850 census he was 52 (a stone mason) and she was 51 years old. (*1850 Census of Chenango Co., NY*)

SELDEN

Henry R. - b 10/14/1805 in CT, d 9/18/1885 in Rochester, NY. Henry R. m ----. (*Hist. of Genesee County*, v. II, p. 705 - *Hist. of Monroe Co., NY*, p. 168, 296)

Samuel - b1748 in CT, d1814 in NH. Samuel m **Prudence Cook**. (War of 1812 Index)

Samuel L. (Judge) - b1800 in CT, d 9/20/1876 in Rochester, NY. Samuel L. m ----. (*Hist. of Genesee County*, v. II, p. 702)

SESSIONS

Anson - b 4/16/1770 in Windham, CT, d 8/1827 in Painesville, OH. Anson m 12/16/1804 **Asenath A. Fobes**, d/o **Lemuel**. (*Rev. Soldiers Buried in Lake Co., OH*, p. 45-8)

John – bc1793 in CT. John m **Elisa M.** ----, bc1804 in VT. They resided in Randolph, Orange Co., VT. In the 1850 census he was 57 and she was 46 years old. (*1850 Orange Co., VT, Census*)

Resolved – b 6/5/1751 in Pomfret, CT, s/o **Simeon** and **Sarah (Dana)**; Resolved d somewhere in the West when he went to live with his son, **Samuel**. He m **Elizabeth Child**, b 1/17/1750 in Woodstock, CT, d 7/8/1784 in Pomfret, VT, d/o **Samuel** and **Keziah (Hutchins)**. (*Gen. of Woodstock Fam.*, p. 269 – *Pomfret, VT*, v. 2, p. 566)

Simeon – b 2/11/1720 in Pomfret, CT, s/o **Nathaniel**; Simeon d 10/1814 in Pomfret, Windsor Co., VT. He m 3/17/1744 in Pomfret, CT, **Sarah Dana**, b 2/8/1724, d 2/4/1807 in Pomfret, VT, d/o **Isaac** and **Sarah (Winchester)**. (*Genealogies of Woodstock Fam.*, p. 269)

SEWARD

Asahel – b 8/19/1781 in Waterbury, CT, s/o **Col. Nathan**; Asahel d 1/30/1835 prob. in Utica, Oneida Co., NY. He m ----. (*Hist. of Oneida Co., NY*, p. 278)

Col. Nathan – b 10/11/1758 in CT, d 11/9/1815 age 57 in New Hartford, Oneida Co., NY. Col. Nathan m **Martha Gridley**, d 3/24/1838 age 80. (*Oneida, Our Country and Its People*, p. 485 – *DAR Patriot Index*, p. 605 – War of 1812 Index)

SEXTON

Frederick – bc1781 in CT. Frederick m **Huldah** ----, bc1796 in NY. They resided in Sherburne, Chenango Co., NY. In the 1850 census he was 69 and she was 54 years old. (*1850 Census of Chenango County, NY*)

Norman – bc1796 in CT. Norman m **Sarah** ----, bc1804 in CT. They resided in Smyrna, Chenango Co., NY. In the 1850 census he was 54, she was 46, Wells was 20, Martin was 19, and Harriet was 18 years old. (*1850 Census Chenango Co., NY*)

SEYMOUR

Belden – b 11/14/1771 in Norwalk, CT, s/o **Lt. William** and **Lydia (St. John)**; Belden d 10/12/1841 in Vergennes, Addison Co., VT. He m 1/28/1798 **Abigail Beers**, b 5/22/1776 in Newtown, CT, d 4/2/1876. (*Seymour Fam.*, p. 114 – *Gazetteer of Addison Co., VT*)

Epaphro – b 7/8/1783 in Litchfield, CT, s/o Major **Moses** and **Molly (Marsh)**; Epaphro d 6/10/1854 in Brattleboro, Windham Co., VT. He m **Mary Root**. (*Seymour Fam.*, p. 252 – *Gazetteer of Windham Co., VT*, p. 120-1)

Henry – b 3/30/1780 in Litchfield, CT, s/o Major **Moses** and **Molly (Marsh)**; d1837 in Utica, NY. Henry m ----, b 2/18/1785 in Monmouth, NJ, d1859, d/o **Col. Jonathan Forman**. (*Pompey, New York*, p. 392)

Horatio – b 5/31/1778 in Litchfield, CT, s/o **Moses**; Horatio d 11/21/1857 in Middlebury, Addison Co., VT. He m 5/1800 **Lucy Case**, b1779 in Addison, VT, d 10/19/1838 in Middlebury, VT, d/o **Jonah**. (*Seymour Fam.*, p. 246-7, 343-4 – Middlebury gravestones)

Leverett – b1775 in CT, d1848 in NY. Leverett m **Sarah Woodworth**. (War of 1812 Index)

Nathaniel - b 1/28/1757 in CT, d 9/12/1846 in S. Greenfield, NY. Nathaniel m (1) **Mercy Carter**, and m (2) **Marion Dickson**. (*DAR Mag.* 1977, p. 921 - *DAR Patriot Index*, p. 605)

Samuel - b1795 in Norwalk, CT, killed at Enterprise, Erie Co., OH. Samuel m ----. (*Residents of Connecticut Who Migrated to Huron Co., OH*, p. 6)

Samuel - b 9/21/1756 at CT, d 1/23/1834 prob. in Walton, Delaware Co., NY. Samuel m 2/7/1774 in Norwalk, CT, **Anna Whitney**. (*Hist. of Delaware Co., NY*, p. 327 - *DAR Patriot Index*, p. 605)

William - b 11/15/1754 in New Hartford, CT, d 12/22/1841 in Fredonia, Chautauqua Co., NY. William m 3/20/1783 in Stillwater, NY, **Sarah Patrick**, b 10/24/1755, d 3/22/1847. (*Soldiers of Am. Rev., Chautauqua Co., NY*, p. 20 - *DAR Patriot Index*, p. 605)

William Henry - b 7/15/1802 in Litchfield, CT, d 10/6/1903 prob. in Sweden Twp., Monroe Co., NY. William Henry m ----. (Tombstone Rec. of Brockport Cem. - *Hist. of Monroe Co., NY*, p. 159, 161, 162, 310)

SHANNON

William C. - b 6/9/1790 in Belfast, Ireland, s/o **James** of Belfast, Ireland; William C. d 6/23/1854 age 64 in Sidney Centre, Delaware Co., NY. He m in Delaware Co., NY, **Pene Shannon** d 11/1853 age 64. (*Biog. Rec. of Otsego Co., NY*, p. 757)

SHAW

Samuel - b 11/21/1777 in CT, d 2/11/1852 in Springville, NY. Samuel m **Phebe Rushmore**, b 4/19/1784 in Orange Co., NY, d 5/30/1847 in Springville, NY. (*Hist. of Original Town of Concord, NY*, p. 466-7)

William, 2nd - bc1796 in CT. William, 2nd m **Delia** ----, bc1804 in MA. They resided in New Berlin, Chenango Co., NY. In the 1850 census he was 54 and she was 46, with Henry 14 years old. (*1850 Census of Chenango Co., NY*)

SHEEDY

Dr. Daniel - b in Norwalk, CT, s/o **Michael** and **Johanna (Hanlon)**. Dr. Daniel m 4/28/1897 **Agnes Kelly**, d/o **Timothy G.** They resided in Dutchess Co., NY, perhaps in Poughkeepsie. (*Comm. Biog. Rec. of Dutchess Co., NY*, p. 131)

SHEFFIELD

George Scofield - b1786 in CT, d in Huron Co., OH. George Scofield m (1) 1813 **Betsey Woodward**, b1776 in New London, CT, d1816, d/o **Abisha**, and m (2) 1819 **Thurza Baker**, b1791, d1834, d/o **John**. (*Res. of CT Who Migrated to Huron Co., OH*, p. 6)

SHELDON

Aaron - bc1786 in CT, d 8/22/1873 age 87 in Rupert, Bennington Co., VT. Aaron m **Lydia** ----, b1800 in VT. In the 1850 census he was 64, Lydia was 50, with Mary Lewis 19, and Dwight 21 years old. (*1850 Bennington Co., VT, Census*)

Caleb - bc1775 in CT. Caleb m ----. In the 1850 census he was 75 years old and living in county poorhouse. (*1850 Census of Preston, Chenango Co., NY*)

Daniel - bc1772 in CT. Daniel m Sarah ----, bc1775 in NH. They resided in Marlboro, Windham Co., VT. In the 1850 census he was 78 and she was 75 years old. (*1850 Census of Windham Co., VT*)

David - bc1781 in Suffield, CT, d 6/11/1864 age 83-6-16 in Rupert, Bennington Co., VT. David m Jerusha ----, b CT, d 11/16/1855 age 76-3. In the 1850 census he was 70 and she was 72, and they were living with David L. Sheldon and wife, Mary 34 years old. (Gravestone Rec. of Rupert, VT - *1850 Bennington Co., VT, Census*)

Hon. David - b1756 in Suffield, CT, d 2/15/1832 age 75 in Rupert, Bennington Co., VT. Hon. David m Sarah Harmon, d 11/11/1829 age 78. (*Gravestone Rec. of Rupert, VT*, p. 10, 13, 6 - *VT Hist. Mag.*, v. 1, p. 222 - *DAR Patriot Index*, p. 609)

Eppaphras - b 8/2/1753 in Litchfield, CT, d 1/31/1850 in E. Smithfield, Chenango Co., NY. Eppaphras m Hannah Lyman. (French's *Historical Gazetteer*, p. 230 - *DAR Patriot Index*, p. 609)

Isaac - b1752 in CT, d 1/4/1810 age 58 (fell into a well) in Rupert, Bennington Co., VT. Isaac m Mindwell Phelps, d 9/17/1835 age 75 in Rupert, VT. (*Gravestone Records of Rupert, Vermont*, p. 3-4, 37 - *DAR Patriot Index*, p. 609 - *Rupert, Vermont, Historical and Descriptive*, p. 157)

Jacob - b1753 in CT, d 8/1/1821 in Brutus, NY. Jacob m 8/26/1779 in Suffield, CT, Mary Smith, bc1753 in CT, d 9/3/1814. (*Hist. of Cayuga Co., NY*, p. 325)

Joel - b in CT, d 4/11/1859 in Westfield, NY. Joel m in VT, Sarah Edgerton. (*Chautauqua Co., NY*, p. 552)

Joel - b1746 in Suffield, CT, s/o Daniel; Joel d 12/25/1829 age 83 in N. Rupert, VT. He m Mary Hanchett, d 2/10/1841 age 90 in N. Rupert, VT. (*Gravestone Rec. of Rupert, VT*, p. 56 - *Rupert, VT, Hist. and Descriptive*, p. 157-8 - *DAR Patriot Index*, p. 609)

Seth P. - b1762 in Suffield, CT, d 12/13/1827 age 65 in Rupert, VT. Seth P. mc1793 in Suffield, CT, Rhoda Pomeroy, d 6/30/1863 age 89-10-19 in Rupert, VT. (*Gravestone Records of Rupert, Vermont*, p. 12-13, 5, 16)

SHEPARD

Elisha - b 7/17/1776 in Plainfield, CT, s/o Reuben and Rebecca (Spaulding); Elisha d prob. in Stannard, Caledonia Co., VT. He m 3/9/1802 in Nottingham, NH, Ann Davis, b1778, d 3/28/1842 age 64 in Stanard, VT. (*Shepard Families of New England*, v. 1, p. 197 - *Caledonia Gazetteer*, p. 307)

Samuel - b 5/29/1768 in Simsbury, CT, d 12/29/1858 age 91 in Panton, Addison Co., VT. Samuel m (1) 8/19/1790 in Panton, VT, Rachel Grandy, bc1772 in Panton, VT, d 3/29/1810, d/o Edmund and Mary (Hinsdale), and m (2) 6/19/1810 in Weybridge, VT, Lucy Wright, b 4/20/1785 in Weybridge, VT, d 1/12/1848 age 62 in Panton, VT, d/o Ebenezer. (*Gazetteer of Addison Co., VT*, p. 196 - *Shepard Fam. of New Eng.*, v. II, p. 85-6 207-8)

Thomas - bc1772 in CT. Thomas m Abigail ----, bc1774 in NH. They resided in Bethel, Windsor Co., VT. In the 1850 census he was 78 and she was 76, with Isaac 36 years old. (*1850 Census Windsor Co., VT*)

William - bc1785 in CT, d1816 in NY. William m **Tamar Halstead**. (War of 1812 Index)

SHEPPARD

Noah - b 12/29/1778 in Plainfield, CT, s/o **Reuben** and **Rebecca (Spaulding)**; Noah d in Hartland, Windsor Co., VT. He m 4/20/1808 **Charlotte Rogers**, b1770, d 7/3/1845 age 75 in Hartland, VT. In the 1850 census he was 68 with Sylvanus 30 and wife Sarah 38 years old. (*Shepard Families of New England*, v. 1, p. 197, 368-9 - *1850 Windsor Co., VT, Census*)

Peletiah - b1779 in CT, d1870 in OH. Peletiah m **Mary Sweet**. (War of 1812 Index)

SHERMAN

Daniel - b in Brookfield, CT, s/o **Justin**; Daniel d 6/13/1800 in Hinesburg, VT. He m **Ollie Peck**, b in Newtown, CT, d in Hinesburg, VT. (*1861 Hist. and Tales of Hinesburgh, VT*, p. 11)

Daniel - b 3/28/1790 in Norwalk, CT, s/o **Taylor**; Daniel d 9/27/1864 in Monroeville, Huron Co., OH. He m (1) 7/10/1813 in Huron Co., **Abbie Guthrie**, d 4/23/1820 in Sherman, NY, and m (2) 6/3/1824 **Laura Hubbell**, b 1/12/1790 in Charlotte, VT, d 12/31/1876 in Monroeville, OH, d/o **David** and **Elizabeth (Williams)**. (*Residents of CT Who Migrated to Huron Co., OH*, p. 6 - *The New England Shermans*, p. 245)

Edmund - b 11/2/1755 in CT, d 3/2/1839 in Corinth, Saratoga Co., NY, buried in Old Cem. there. Edmund m **Hannah Wise**. (*DAR Mag.* 1977, p. 921 - *DAR Patriot Index*, p. 611)

Eli - b 3/23/1764 in Brookfield, CT, s/o **Justin**; Eli d 6/13/1850 age 86 in Fairfield, Franklin Co., VT. He m 11/27/1788 **Polly Phelps**, b 8/25/1770 in S. Kent, CT, d 1/13/1859 in Fairfield, VT, d/o **Ruthven**. (*Franklin Co. Gazetteer*, p. ?)

Ezra - b 6/2/1759 in Fairfield, CT, s/o **John** and **Hannah (Clark)**; Ezra d 9/23/1844 age 85-3 in Fairfield, Franklin Co., VT. He m **Esther Hard**, b in Newtown, CT, d 11/26/1813 age 52, d/o **James** and **Hester (Booth)**. (*Franklin Co. Gazetteer*, p. 103 - *New England Shermans*, p. 205-6)

J. C. - bc1798 in CT. J. C. m **Sally** ----, bc1802 in CT. They resided in Sherburne, Chenango Co., NY. In the 1850 census he was 52, she was 48 and Mary was 25, Sarah A. 23, Elizabeth 20, Matthew F. 17 years old, all of them b in CT. (*1850 Census Chenango Co., NY*)

Leverett - b 9/26/1790 in Woodbury, CT, s/o **John** and **Molly (Castle)**; Leverett d 3/13/1876 age 85 prob. in Charlotte, Chittenden, VT. He m **Sally Gray**, b in VT, d/o **Elijah** and **Betsey (Dunning)**. In the 1850 census he was 59 and she was 54, with Polly A. 25 and Alfred W. 24 years old. (*New England Shermans*, p. 264-5 - *Chittenden Co. Gazetteer*, p. 187 - *1850 Chittenden Co., VT Census*)

William E. - bc1794 in CT, d 6/15/1859 in Charlotte, Chittenden Co., VT. William E. m ----. In the 1850 census he was 56, with John.

H. 30 and Sarah 28 years old, both born in VT. (*1850 Census Charlotte, VT*)

SHERWOOD

Gabriel - bc1769 in New Fairfield, CT, s/o **Nathan** and **Joanna (Noble)**; Gabriel d before 4/28/1808 in Fairfield, Franklin Co., VT. He m 2/1788 in Fairfield, CT, **Johanna Sunderland**, bp. 5/9/1769 in Stratford, CT. (*Some Early Rec. of Fairfield, VT*, p. 18)

H e n r y - b 2/18/1816 in Danbury, CT, d 3/5/1894 age 78 in Berlin, Ionia Co., MI. Henry m (1) 12/7/1842 in Fairfield, CT, **Phoebe A. Knapp**, and m (2) 7/4/1852 **Charlotte Noddins** of Hartford, NY. (Iona Co., MI)

Hezekiah - bc1775 in CT. Hezekiah m ----. He resided in Oxford, Chenango Co., NY. In the 1850 census he was 75 and living with Joseph H., age 41, and Sylvia S. Fox, age 36 years, both born in NY. (*1850 Census of Chenango Co., NY*)

I s a a c - b1768 in CT. Isaac m Catherine Smith of CT, bc1768. They resided in Oxford, Chenango Co., NY. In the 1850 census he was 60 years old and so was she. (*Annals of Oxford, NY*, p. 480-2 - *1850 Census of Chenango Co., NY*)

Joseph - b 1/15/1754 in Greenfield Hills, CT, s/o **Thomas** and **Anne (Burr)**; Joseph d 1/22/1838 in Chester, NY. He m (1) **Sarah Bradley**, and m (2) Mrs. **Hannah Gregory**. (*Comm. Biog. Rec., Dutchess Co., NY*, p. 129 - *DAR Patriot Index*, p. 612)

M a t t h e w - b1755 in CT, d 6/10/1837 in Ballston, Saratoga Co., NY, buried in Hubbell Cemetery. Matthew m ----. (*DAR Magazine* 1977, p. 921)

Nathan - b 1/16/1738 (or 1/16/1739) in Fairfield, CT, s/o **Joseph** and **M a r y**; Nathan d 2/17/1823 age 84 in Fairfield, Franklin Co., VT. He m **Joanna Noblet**. (*American Gen. Magazine* - *DAR Patriot Index*, p. 612)

Nathan J. - b1793 in CT, s/o **William H.** and **Eunice (Lyon)**; Nathan d1870 in PA. He m (1) 1812 **Sally W. Thorp**, d1821, and m (2) 1822 **Hannah Thorp**, cousin/o Sally, d/o **Wakeman Thorp**. (*Hist. of Susquehanna Co., PA*, p. 443-4)

William - b 6/2/1793 in Green Farms, CT, s/o **Asa T.** and **Mary (Phillips)**; William d 5/9/1875 in Norwich, NY. He m **Abigail Smith** of Oxford, NY, b 9/18/1800, d 8/21/1850. (*Annals of Oxford, NY*, p. 331-3)

SHIPMAN

J o b - b 6/2/1772 in Saybrook, CT, d 1/12/1833 in Carlton, Orleans Co., NY. Job m1815 **Ann Tomblin**, d 2/8/1858, widow. (*Pioneer Hist. of Orleans Co., NY*, p. 196-7)

William - b 4/27/1792 in Saybrook, CT, s/o Col. **Edward**; William d 7/21/1872 in Montrose, PA. He m 7/16/1815 **Sarah Vaughn**, b in Wickford, RI, d 8/14/1871 in Montrose, PA, d/o **Jonathan** and **Mary (Austin)**. (*Hist. of Susquehanna Co., PA*, p. 341 - *Edward Shipman and Des.*, p. 70, 92)

SHOLES

Stanton - b 3/14/1772 in CT, d 3/7/1865 in OH. Stanton m **Abigail Avery**. (War of 1812 Index - *DAR Patriot Index*, p. 614)

SHUMWAY

Capt. **John** - b 7/29/1738 in Mansfield, CT, s/o **John**; Capt. John d 4/1831 age 93 in Dorset, VT. He m **Judith Mills** of Waltham, MA, d 6/7/1820. (*VT Hist. Mag.*, v. 1, p. 189 - *Gen. of Shumway Fam.*, p. 335-6 - *DAR Patriot Index*, p. 615)

SHURTLIFF

Amos - b 6/22/1775 in Tolland, CT, d 3/3/1837 in Stanstead, Quebec. Amos m **Nancy Brown**, b 11/25/1770 in Candia, NH, d 3/9/1837. (*Forests and Clearings, Stanstead, Quebec*, p. 195)

SIBLEY

Abijah - b 11/1/1788 in Willington, CT, d 6/3/1856 in Concord, Erie Co., NY. Abijah m1816 **Lucy Mercy**, d 3/19/1859. (*Hist. of Orig. Town of Concord, NY*, p. 473-4, 476-7)

Benjamin - b in CT (prob. Willington), d 5/16/1849 in Sheboygan, WI. Benjamin m **Anna** ----, d 3/10/1876 age 72 in Sheboygan, WI. (*Hist. of Orig. Town of Concord, NY*, p. 473-4, 476-7)

SILL

Andrew - bc1778 in CT. Andrew m **Sally** -⸺-, bc1804 in NY. They resided in Columbus, Chenango Co., OH. In the 1850 census he was 72 and she was 56 years old. (*1850 Census Chenango Co., NY*)

Daniel - bc1771 in New Fairfield, CT, d 2/17/1826 in Ossian, NY. Daniel m (1) 1/25/1798 **Abigail McKnight**, d1806, and m (2) 2/2/1808 **Albasinda Larnes**. (*Annals of Oxford, NY*, p. 270)

SILLIMAN

Gershom - bc1783 in CT, d1856 in IL. Gershom m **Mary Coleman**. (War of 1812 Index)

SIMMONDS

Asa S. - b in Canterbury, CT, d1861 in Roxbury, Washington Co., VT. Asa S. m1815 **Hannah Spaulding**. (*Washington Co., VT, Gazetteer*)

Augustus - bc1792 in CT. Augustus m **Mary** ----, bc1794 in CT. They resided in New Berlin, Chenango Co., NY. In the 1850 census he was 58 and she was 56 years old. (*1850 Census of Chenango County, NY*)

SIMMONS

Asa S. - bc1790 in CT. Asa S. m **Hannah** ----, bc1790 in NH. They resided in Roxbury, Washington Co., VT. In the 1850 census he was 60 and she was 60 years old, living with William, b in VT age 25, and Lucy, b in VT, age 22 years. (*1850 Census of Washington Co., VT*)

P e l e g - b 6/17/1764 in Middletown, CT, d 10/1/1854 age 93 in Willoughby Plains, OH. Peleg m 5/22/1788 **Amia Barrett**. (*Rev. Soldiers Buried in Lake Co., OH*, p. 48 - *DAR Patriot Index*, p. 617)

SIMONDS

Jacob - bc1719 in Hampton, CT, d 9/3/1797 age 78 prob. in Brandon, Rutland Co., VT. Jacob m twice. (*History of Rutland County, Vermont*, p. 481)

SIMONS

Joseph - b 5/23/1757 in Lebanon, CT, d1843 in Smyrna, Chenango Co., NY. Joseph m (1) **Elizabeth ----**, and m (2) **Elizabeth ----**. (*Smyrna* by Munson, p. 36-7 - *DAR Patriot Index*, p. 617)

Loten - b 12/8/1760 in Enfield, CT, d 8/4/1800 prob. in Fleming, Cayuga Co., NY. Loten m **Bridget ----**, d 4/17/1835 age 73-3-23. (*Twp. of Fleming, Cayuga Co., NY*, p. 7-8)

SKEELE

Erastus - bc1796 in CT. Erastus m **Mary ----**, bc1796 in NY. They resided in Sudbury, Rutland Co., VT. In the 1850 census he was 54 and she was also 54 years old. (*1850 Rutland Co., VT, Census*)

SKIDMORE

Isaac - b 9/15/1780 in Danbury, CT, d 1/14/1842 in Dexter, MI. Isaac m 12/19/1808 in Butternuts, NY, **Sarah Lull**, b 1/8/1791 in Butternuts, Otsego Co., NY, d in Dexter, Washtenaw Co., MI, d/o **Joseph** and **Martha (Knapp)**. (*DSGR* Winter 1971, p. 71)

SKINNER

Capt. **Abraham** - b1755 in Glastonbury, CT, s/o **Abram** and **Phoebe (Strong)**; Capt. Abraham d 1/14/1826 age 71 in Painsville, OH. He m 10/13/1788 in Marlborough, CT, **Mary Ayers**, b1766, d 10/7/1812. (*Rev. Soldiers Buried in Lake Co., OH*, p. 51 - *DAR Patriot Index*, p. 620 - *The Skinner Kinsmen*, p. 105)

Alfred - bc1781 in CT. Alfred m **Betsy ----**, bc1787 in NH. They resided in New Berlin, Chenango Co., NY. In the 1850 census he was 69 and she was 63 years old, with Gara age 20, Emory 16, and Sarah Eastman 88 years old, b in MA. (*1850 Census Chenango County, NY*)

David - bc1787 in CT. David m **Polly ----**, bc1779 in CT. They resided in New Berlin, Chenango Co., NY. In the 1850 census he was 63 and she was 71 years old, with David 35 years old. (*1850 Census, Chenango Co., NY*)

Jedediah - bc1765 in CT, d1842 in NH. Jedediah m **Sarah Hurlburt**. (War of 1812 Index)

Luther - b 10/14/1760 in Woodstock, CT, s/o **William**; Luther d 1/12/1838 age 88 in Royalton, Windsor Co., VT. Luther m 5/8/1788 **Temperance Dewey**, d 8/28/1847 age 86. (*History of Royalton, VT*, p. 959-60)

Gov. **Richard** - b 5/30/1778 in Litchfield, CT, s/o **Timothy** and **Susanna**; Gov. Richard d 5/23/1833 in 55th year in Manchester, VT. He m ----. (*Vermont Hist. Magazine*, v. 1, p. 205 - *Hist. of VT* by Crockett, v. 5, p. 81)

Silas - bc1796 in CT. Silas m **Betsey ----**, bc1799 in NH. They resided in Plainfield, Washington Co., VT. In the 1850 census he was 54 and she was 51 years old, with Nathan 22 years old. (*1850 Census of Washington Co., VT*)

SLACK

Joseph S. - bc1796 in CT. Joseph S. m **Mary A.** ----, bc1796 in VT. They resided in Chelsea, Orange Co., VT. In the 1850 census he was 54 and she was 54 years old, too, with Job. M 22, Mary A. 25, and Sarah 10 years old. (*1850 Orange Co., VT, Census*)

William - bc1753 in CT, d 4/10/1832 age 79 (gravestone) in Strafford, VT. William m **Alice** ----, bc1755, d 1/26/1833 age 78 in Strafford, VT. Both William and Alice were buried in Kibling Cemetery, Strafford, Orange Co., VT. (Strafford, Orange Co., VT, Kibbling Cem.)

SLADE

William - b 10/26/1753 prob. in E. Windsor, CT, s/o **William, Jr.** and **Esther (Davis)**; William d 11/24/1826 age 73 in VT (perhaps in Cornwall). He m (1) 4/15/1779 in Washington, CT, **Rebecca Plumb**, b 10/2/1755, d 3/19/1788, and m (2) 10/30/1788 **Mercy Bronson**, b 1/13/1754, d 7/15/1830, divorced from her, and m (3) 1/8/1818 **Sarah Ann Clarke**, d 1/23/1853. (*VT Hist. Mag.*, v. 1, p. 26-7 - *Hist. of Cornwall, VT*, p. 68-9 - *DAR Patriot Index*, p. 621 - *Wm. Slade and Des.*, p. 11-12, 31-3)

SLAFTER

David F. - bc1785 in CT. David F. m **Amelia** ----, bc1787 in VT. They resided in Royalton, Windsor Co., VT. In the 1850 census he was 65 and she was 63 years old, with Elizabeth 23, b in VT, and Clarinda 21, b in VT. (*1850 Census of Windsor Co., VT*)

John - b 5/26/1739 in Mansfield, CT, s/o **Samuel** and **Dorothy (Fenton)**; John d 10/8/1819 in Thetford, Orange Co., VT. He m (1) **Elizabeth Hovey**, b 6/22/1744, d 1/6/1811, and m (2) **Priscilla Hovey** (half sister of 1st wife), b 4/17/1751, d 5/1/1847 age 96. (*Gazetteer of Orange Co.*, p. 439 - *Slafter Memorial*, p. 30-40)

John - b 10/31/1776 in Mansfield, CT, s/o **John**; John (the younger) d 11/21/1856 in Worth, MI. John m **Persis Grow**, b 6/17/1783 of Hartland, VT, d/o Rev. **Timothy** and **Phalle (Richardson)**. (*Slafter Memorial*, p. 40, 49-50)

Samuel - b 8/1696 in either Lynn, MA, (or Mansfield, CT), d 7/31/1770 age 80 prob. in Thetford, Orange Co., VT. Samuel m 1/24/1721 (or m 1/24/1722) **Dorothy Fenton** of Mansfield, CT, b 9/4/1700, d 9/29/1783. (*Slafter Memorial*, p. 8-9 - *Gazetteer of Orange Co., VT*, p. 438-9 - *VT Antiquarian*, p. 41)

SLASON

Francis - b 3/23/1790 in Stamford, CT, d 1/14/1882 age 94 (or poss. 1884) in Rutland, Rutland Co., VT. Francis m (1) 7/1814 in W. Rutland, VT, **Mary Gordon**, b 1/3/1796, d 5/2/1821, d/o **Samuel**, and m (2) 8/6/1822 in Hardwick, MA, **Celia Harmon**, b 12/1/1793 in MA, d 6/11/1887. (*Slason-Slauson-Slosson*, p. 48, 90 - *Hist. of Rutland, VT*, p. 333 - *Rutland Co. Gazetteer*, p. 220)

SLATER

Joseph - bc1778 in CT. Joseph m **Relief** ----, bc1780 in CT. They resided in Preston, Chenango Co., NY. In the 1850 census he was 72 and she was 70 years old. (*1850 Census of Chenango Co., NY*)

SLOCUM

John - bc1768 in CT. John m **Elizabeth** ----, bc1773 in VT. They resided in Manchester, Bennington Co., VT. In the 1850 census he was 82 and she was 77 years old, with Joseph 26 (b in VT) and Mary 6 years old (b in VT). (*1850 Bennington Co., VT, Census*)

SMILEY

William - b in Farmington, CT, s/o **William** from Ireland; William (the younger) d 1/1825 in Chautauqua Co., NY. He m **Hannah Wilcox** of Exeter, RI, d 3/1831. (*Chautauqua Co., NY*, p. 325-6 - *DAR Patriot Index*, p. 623)

SMITH

Aaron - b 7/25/1752 in Hartford, CT, d 7/31/1840 age 87 in Bradford, Orange Co., VT. Aaron m **Abigail Kendrick**, dc1838 age 87. (*Gazetteer of Orange Co., VT*, p. 180)

Abial - b 10/11/1770 in CT, s/o **Ebenezer** and **Dorothy (Child)**. Abial m **Lora Manning**, bc1775 in Canada. They resided in Williamstown, Orange Co., VT. In the 1850 census he was 79 and she was 75 years old. (*1850 Orange Co., VT, Census*)

Abida - b 6/21/1750 in Woodstock, CT, s/o **Ebenezer, Jr.** and **Dorothy**; Abida d 3/30/1815 in Pomfret, Windsor Co., VT. He m (1) 1774 **Frances Sessions**, b 1/17/1753 in Pomfret, VT, d 5/28/1790 in Pomfret, VT, d/o **Simon** and **Sarah (Dana)**, and m (2) 6/10/1792 in Norwich, CT, **Polly Peabody**, b 12/3/1751, d 1/27/1823, d/o **Asa** and **Mary (Prentice)**. (*Pomfret, VT*, v. 2, p. 570 - *Woodstock Fam.*, v. 8, p. 314)

Abijah - b 9/9/1792 in Ashford, CT, s/o **Abijah** and **Judith (Whiton)**. Abijah m **Sally Plumley**, bc1794 in VT. They resided in Orange Co., VT, (either in Brookfield or Randolf). In the 1850 census he was a farmer, 57 years old and she was 56, with Harriet C. 22 and Nelson 19 years old. (*Hist. Souvenir of Randolph*, p. 139-140 - *1850 Orange Co., VT, Census*)

Abijah - bc1758 (or bc1760) in Ashford, CT, d 12/9/1831 in Randolph, VT. Abijah m 8/28/1783 in Ashford, CT, **Judith Whiton**. (*Hist. Souvenir of Randolph*, p. 139-40 - *DAR Patriot Index*, p. 623)

Abisha, Jr. - b 3/26/1785 (or 3/26/1788) in Suffield, CT. Abisha, Jr. m **Susan Remington**, b in Suffield, CT, d age 85, d/o **Simon**. They resided in Otsego Co., NY. (*Biog. Rec. of Otsego Co., NY*, p. 237)

Ahira - bc1807 in CT. Ahira m **Caroline E. Pellet**, bc1812 in CT. They resided in Brookfield, Orange Co., VT. In the 1850 census he was 43 and she was 38 years old, with Lucretia 20 (b in CT), Eunice 13 (b in CT), John 16 (b in VT), Chauncey 8 (b in VT), Lydia 5 (b in VT), and Lewis 4 (b in VT). (*1850 Orange Co., VT, Census*)

Deacon **Albert Gallatin** - b 3/29/1804 in Groton, CT, d 3/29/1855 in Rochester, Monroe Co., NY. Deacon Albert Gallatin m 5/12/1830

Julia A. Burrows, b 8/20/1811 in Groton, CT, d 1/6/1890, d/o Rev. **Roswell** and **Jerusha (Avery).** (Tombstone Rec., Mt. Hope Cem., Rochester, NY - *Robert Burrows and Des.*, v. 2, p. 987, 1057)

Alva O. - b in North Haven, CT, d1870 in LaSalle Co., IL. Alva O. m **Olive Warren.** (*Hist. of LaSalle Co., IL*, p. 438)

Apollos - b 12/5/1756 in Suffield, CT, d 2/25/1810 age 53 in W. Haven (or Fair Haven), VT. Apollos m 12/3/1778 **Anna Gay.** (*Hist. of Fair Haven, VT*)

Arnold - b 2/7/1778 in Lyme, CT, s/o **Richard** and **Lois;** Arnold d1839 in Windsor Co., VT (prob. in Woodstock). He m ----. (*Hist. of Woodstock, VT*, p. 108)

Capt. Asahel - b1756 in Farmington, CT, d1846 in W. Windsor, VT. Capt. Asahel m (1) **Hannah** ----, d1807, and m (2) **Betsey** ----, d1837 age 67. (*Branches and Twigs*, Spring 1974, p. 60)

Asher - bc1766 in CT. Asher m **Elizabeth** ----, bc1776 in CT. They resided in Dorset, Bennington Co., VT. In the 1850 census he was 84 (a mechanic) and she was 74 years old. (*1850 Bennington Co., VT, Census*)

Capt. Benoni - b 10/6/1740 in Glastonbury, CT, d 7/17/1799 age 59 in Pawlet, Rutland Co., VT. Capt. Benoni m (1) **Elizabeth Hall,** and m (2) **Elizabeth Smith.** (*Rutland Co. Gazetteer*, p. 170 - *DAR Patriot Index*, p. 624)

Charles - bc1786 in CT. Charles m **Elizabeth** ----, bc1790 in CT. They resided in Bennington, Bennington Co., VT. In the 1850 census he was 64 and she was 60 years old. (*1850 Bennington Co., VT, Census*)

Charles - bc1781 in Lyme, CT, d 1/17/1846 age 65 in Rochester, Monroe Co., NY. Charles m ----. (Tombstone Rec., Mt. Hope Cem., Rochester, NY)

Judge Chauncey - b 5/4/1785 in Suffield, CT, d 8/8/1853 in Butler, Wayne Co., NY. Judge Chauncey m **Priscilla Pinney,** d 12/20/1877 age 86 in Flint, MI. (*Rose Neighborhood Sketches*, p. 74)

Christopher - bc1776 in CT. Christopher m **Lucretia** ----, bc1782 in NH. They resided in Williamstown, Orange Co., VT. In the 1850 census he was 74 and she was 68 years old. (*1850 Census Orange Co., VT*)

Clark - bc1782 in CT. Clark m **Jemima** ----, bc1774 in CT. They resided in Oxford, Chenango Co., NY. In the 1850 census he was 68 and she was 76 years old. (*1850 Census Chenango Co., NY*)

Dan - b 1/28/1759 in Suffield, CT, d 2/15/1833 in Panton, VT. Dan m ----. (*Hist. of Fair Haven, Rutland Co., VT*)

David - b 5/23/1758 in CT, d 3/23/1841 in Braintree, Orange Co., VT. David m **Mary Seabury,** b 4/4/1759, d 10/23/1843. (*Hist. of Braintree, VT*, p. 180-1 - *DAR Patriot Index*, p. 624)

David - bc1791 in CT. David m **Laura** ----, bc1792 in NY. They resided in Pitcher, Chenango Co., NY. In the 1850 census he was 59 and she was 48 years old, with Cornelia 25 (b in NY), Orcella 22 (b in NY), Eliza 20 (b in NY), Charlotte 18, David 16 (b in NY), Samantha 13 (b in NY), Manrow 11 (b in NY), Eben L. 9 (b in NY), Adella 6 (b in NY), and Joseph 86 (b in CT). (*1850 Census Chenango Co., NY*)

Diodate - bc1772 in CT, d1834 in PA. Diodate m **Rachel Alworth.** (War of 1812 Index)

Ebenezer - b in Woodstock, CT, d1767 in Williamstown, Orange Co., VT. Ebenezer m **Dorothy Childs.** (*Smiths in Williamstown, Vermont*, p. 13)

Ebenezer - bc1787 in CT. Ebenezer m **Betsey ----,** bc1806 in NY. They resided in Castleton, Rutland Co., VT. In the 1850 census he was 63 and she was 44 years old, with Charles 20, Leonora 6 and Dwight R. 1 year old. (*1850 Rutland Co., VT, Census*)

Eldad - b 7/23/1768 in Litchfield, CT, s/o **Jonathan, Jr.** and **Bethiah;** Eldad d1813 during epidemic, prob. in Camden, Oneida Co., NY. He m 12/12/1792 **Martha Moss.** (*Pioneer Hist. of Camden, NY*, p. 40-41 - *Hist. of Oneida Co.*, p. 433)

Elias - bc1791 in CT. Elias m **Sarah ----,** bc1796 in VT. They resided in Woodstock, Windsor Co., VT. In the 1850 census he was 59 and she was 54, with Sarah 29, Lucia 22, Edwin 18, Clara 16, Henry 10 years old, all b in VT. (*1850 Census of Windsor County, VT*)

Elijah - bc1763 in CT. Elijah m **Jerusha ----,** bc1794 in VT. They resided in Rutland, Rutland Co., VT. In the 1850 census he was 87 and she was 56 years old, with Elijah 40, Lavina 28, Edmond 15, Walter 13, Darwin 11, Willard 5, Frank 4, and Mary 2 years old, all b in VT. (*1850 Rutland Co., VT, Census*)

Enoch - b 2/14/1798 in Chatham, CT. Enoch m **Sally Adams.** They resided in Hardwick, Caledonia Co., VT. (*Caledonia Gazetteer*, p. 213)

Ephraim - bc1752 in Wolcott, CT, d 12/11/1831 age 79 in Camden, Oneida Co., NY. Ephraim m **Annie ----,** bc1754, d 9/14/1827 age 73. (*Pioneer Hist. of Camden, Oneida Co., NY*, p. 217-18)

Ephraim - bc1750 in CT. Ephraim m **Anna Baldwin,** d/o **Josiah,** dc age 105. They resided in Otsego Co., NY. (*Biog. Rec. of Otsego Co., NY*, p. 709)

Ephraim - bc1776 in CT, s/o **Ephraim** and **Susannah (Hotchkiss);** Ephraim d 11/4/1856 age 80 in Franklin, Susquehanna Co., PA. He m ----. (*Hist. of Susquehanna Co., PA*, p. 517)

Ephraim - b in CT, s/o **Ephraim** and **Anna (Baldwin);** Ephraim d in Cleveland, OH. He m **Sibyl Stephens,** d in Palmyra, Wayne Co., PA. (*Biog. Rec. of Otsego Co., NY*, p. 709)

Frank Lester - b 11/16/1867 in N. Haven, CT, s/o **Robert W.** Frank Lester m **Alice Marion Seibold,** b 1/6/1891 in Tarrytown, NY, d/o **John** and **Lena (Rauchenbach).** They resided in Surry, NH. (*Hist. of Surry, NH*, p. 881)

Lt. Frederick - b 12/20/1743 in Hebron, CT, d 9/11/1832 age 88 in Strafford, VT, buried in Old City Cem., Strattford, VT. Lt. Frederick m (1) ---- **Williams,** and m (2) **Sarah (Sloan),** wid/o Lt. **Benjamin Grant** of Lyme, NH, d 10/6/1841 age 87 in Strafford, VT. (*Gazetteer of Orange Co., VT*, p. 404 - *DAR Patriot Index*, p. 625)

Fuller - bc1785 in CT. Fuller m **Marion ----,** bc1787 in NH. They resided in Rochester, Windsor Co., VT. In the 1850 census he was 65 and she was 63 years old, with Isaac 26 (b in VT), and Chester M. 30 (b in VT). (*1850 Census of Windsor Co., VT*)

Harmon - bc1795 in CT. Harmon m **Lucinda ----**, bc1798 in NY. They resided in Pittsfield, Chenango Co., NY. In the 1850 census he was 55 and she was 52 years old, with Henry 25, Clarissa 24, Harmon 21, and Russel 16, all b in NY. (*1850 Census of Chenango Co., NY*)

Hewlett - bc1793 in CT, d1879 in PA. Hewlett m **Eunice Wheeler**. (War of 1812 Index)

I r a - bc1800 in Glastonbury, CT, d1880 age 80 in Marshfield, Washington Co., VT. Ira m **Hannah Jacobs**, d/o Deacon **Silas** and **Lydia (Pike)**. (*Washington Co., VT, Gazetteer*, p. 296)

Isaac - b1790 (or b1791) in CT, d1883 in NY. Isaac m **Elizabeth Edwards**. (War of 1812 Index)

I s a a c - bc1738 in Greenwich, CT, d 6/11/1820 in Dutchess Co., NY. Isaac m **Tammy Mead**. (*Hist. of Little Nine Partners*, p. 379)

Isaac - bc1791 in CT. Isaac m **Polly ----**, bc1792 in CT. They resided in Pitcher, Chenango Co., NY. In the 1850 census he was 59 and she was 58 years old, with Augustus 12 (b in NY). (*1850 Census of Chenango Co., NY*)

Hon. **I s r a e l** - b1741 in Colchester, CT, d1809 in Alstead, NH. Hon. Israel m **Jemima Payne**, d 1/15/1789 age 42 in E. Thetford, VT. (*Gazetteer of Orange County, Vermont*, p. 431-2 - *DAR Patriot Index*, p. 626)

James - bc1790 in Suffield, CT. James m **Sally Austin**, b in VT. They lived in Wilmington, Windham Co., VT. In the 1850 census he was 60 and she was 48 years old with Horatio 28, Lorenzo 26, and Alfred D. 25 years old, all b in VT. (*1850 Census Windham County, VT*)

J a m e s - b1787 in Stonington, CT, d1866 in Lyme Twp., Huron Co., OH. James m1815 in Stonington, CT, **Mary L. Doolittle**, d1866. (*Res. of CT Who Migrated to Huron Co., OH*, p. 6)

James - b 8/22/1764 in Woodstock, CT, s/o **Ebenezer** and **Dorothy (Child)**; James d 4/16/1838 in Williamstown, Orange Co., VT. He m **Martha Howard**, b 3/19/1767, d 5/5/1826, d/o **David** and **Priscilla (Knowlton)**. (*Gen. of Woodstock Families*, p. ? - *DAR Patriot Index*, p. 626)

Jedediah - b1762 in Ashford, CT, s/o **Samuel** and **Mehitabel (Watkins)**; Jedediah d 2/25/1847 prob. in Randolph, VT. He m1787 in Monson, MA, **Esther Fuller**. (*Car Del* Scribe Query Jan. 1976, p. 29 - *DAR Patriot Index*, p. 626)

J o e l - b 12/9/1781 in Southington, CT, d 10/27/1878 prob. in Oxford, Chenango Co., NY. Joel m (1) 11/22/1809 **Almira Bradley** of Northampton, MA, and m (2) 5/13/1812 **Sophia Andrews** of Southington, CT, b 3/20/1787, d 10/9/1877 in Newark Valley. (*Annals of Oxford, NY*, p. 283-5)

Joel Beers - b 2/2/1788 in New Milford, CT, s/o **Joel** and **Patience (Beers)**; Joel Beers d 5/14/1850 age 62 in Penfield, OH. He m **Harriet Brownson**, b 1/1/1791 in Warren, CT, d 12/4/1860 age 75 in La Peer, MI. (*Pioneer Hist. of Camden, NY*, p. 244-6)

J o h n - bc1761 in Groton, CT, d 6/5/1838 age 77 in Marlboro, Windham Co., VT. John m **Lucy Rowe** of Suffield, CT, d age 83. (*VT Hist. Mag.*, v. 5, p. 447)

Col. **John** - b1774 in CT, s/o **Ephraim**; Col. John d1860 in Camden, Oneida Co., NY. He m **Lois Alcott**, b1780, d1840. (*Pioneer Hist. of Camden, NY*, p. 271-2)

John - b1730 in Salisbury, CT, d 7/24/1806 age 77 in Rutland, Rutland Co., VT. John m **Phebe** ----, d 8/4/1803 age 68. (*Hist. of Rutland Co.*, p. 317-18 - *DAR Patriot Index*, p. 627)

John - bc1781 in CT. John m **Nancy** ----, bc1792 in MA. They resided in Rutland, Rutland Co., VT. In the 1850 census he was 69 and she was 58 years old, with Judson 18 years old. (*1850 Rutland Co., VT, Census*)

John F. - bc1792 in CT, d 10/23/1865 age 73-7-23 in Cuyhoga Falls, OH. John F. m **Hannah** ----, d 7/27/1867 in Cuyhoga Falls, OH. In the 1850 census Hannah was 56 living with John F., who was 55 years old. (*1850 Census Chenango Co., NY*)

John H. - b 6/1/1821 in Lyme, CT, s/o **Nathan** and **Nancy** (**Waterman**); John H. d in Dutchess Co., NY. He m 6/1/1847 in Amenia, NY, **Maria Reed**, d/o **Myron**. (*Comm. Biog. Rec. of Dutchess Co., NY*, p. 622)

Joseph Lee - bc1779 in CT, d1846 in FL. Joseph Lee m **Frances Marvin Kirby**. (War of 1812 Index)

Joshua - bc1775 in Glastonbury, CT. Joshua m **Catury Loveland**, bc1781 in CT. They resided in Marshfield, Washington Co., VT. In the 1850 census he was 75 and she was 68 (or 69) years old, with Ira 50 and Otis 49 years old. (*Washington Co. Gazetteer*, p. 296 - *1850 Census of Washington Co., VT*)

Josiah - bc1781 in CT. Josiah m **Fanny** ----, bc1801 in NH. They resided in Rochester, Windsor Co., VT. In the 1850 census he was 69 and she was 49 years old, with Julia 10 years old, b in VT. (*1850 Census for Windsor Co., VT*)

Lemuel - bc1770 in CT. Lemuel m **Phoebe** ----, bc1790 in NH. They resided in Randolph, Orange Co., VT. In the 1850 census he was 80 and she was 60 years old, with Emeline 38 years old, b in VT. (*1850 Census of Orange Co., VT*)

Lewis - bc1788 in CT, d1831 in OH. Lewis m Mrs. **Marilla Curtis Stillman**. (War of 1812 Index)

Lorentz - b 6/29/1789 in Litchfield Co., CT, d 7/18/1864 in Amenia, NY. Lorentz m in Amenia, NY, **Sally Fields**, d1848, d/o **Jesse**. (*Comm. Biog. Rec. of Dutchess Co., NY*, p. 864)

Loudon - bc1773 in CT. Loudon m **Mariam** ----, bc1778 in VT. They resided in Woodstock, Windsor Co., VT. In the 1850 census he was 77 and she was 72 years old, with Royal D. 50 and Elira 32 years old, both b in VT. (*1850 Census Windsor Co., VT*)

Martin - bc1718 in Litchfield, CT, d 3/1804 age 86 in Rupert, Bennington Co., VT. He m ----. (*VT Hist. Mag.*, v. 1, p. 223)

Moses, Jr. - b1783 in CT, d1866 in OH. Moses, Jr. m **Sarah Niles Haley**. (War of 1812 Index)

Nathan W. - b 1/12/1818 in N. Lyme, CT, s/o **Nathan** and **Nancy** (**Waterman**). Nathan W. m (1) 1/1847 **Adeline E. Holly**, d 10/1848, and m (2) 2/4/1850 in Washington, NY, **Esther J. Odell**, b1828, d/o **Peter** and **Sarah** of Jefferson Co., NY. They resided in Dutchess Co., NY. (*Comm. Biog. Rec. of Dutchess Co., NY*, p. 492)

Capt. **Nehemiah** - b in Lyme, CT, d 12/1835 in Oxford, Chenango Co., NY. Capt. Nehemiah m **Elizabeth Gee** of Lyme, CT, d1858 in Oxford, NY. (*History of Chenango Co., NY*, p. 260 - *Annals of Oxford, NY*, p. 484-5)

N e w e l l - bc1804 in CT, d 10/11/1857 age 57 in Cavendish, VT, and buried in Baltimore Cemetery. Newell m (1) **Joanna** ----, b1806 in MA, and m (2) **Jerusha Green**, d 2/1/1889 age 77 in Cavendish, VT. In the 1850 census he was 46 and Jerusha was 44 years old. (*1850 Windsor Co., VT, Census*)

Oliver - bc1761 in CT, d1838 in PA. Oliver m **Betsy Lothrop**. (War of 1812 Index)

Peter - b 2/3/1729 in Horse Neck, CT, s/o **Benjamin**; Peter d 11/16/1820 in Dutchess Co., NY. Peter m **Sarah Winans**, d/o **James**, d 10/3/1801. (*Hist. of Little Nine Partners, NY*, p. ? - *DAR Patriot Index*, p. 628)

Phelps - bc1794 in CT, s/o **Eli** and **Deborah**; Phelps d 8/26/1829 age 35-7 in Columbia, NY (tombstone). Phelps m ----. (*Hist. of Monroe Co.*, p. 82, 89)

Hon. **P l i n y** - b 12/19/1761 in Suffield, CT, d 7/5/1840 age 79 in Orwell, Addison Co., VT. Hon. Pliny m **Sarah Porter**. (*History of Orwell, VT*, p. 22-24 - *DAR Patriot Index*, p. 628)

Reuben - bc1770 in CT, d1856 in NY. Reuben m **Elizabeth Moss**. (War of 1812 Index)

Richard - bc1777 in CT. Richard m **Mary** ----, bc1778 in Canada. They resided in Preston, Chenango Co., NY. In the 1850 census he was 73 and she was 72 years old, with Ursula 11 years old. (*1850 Census Chenango Co., NY*)

Ruel - b 4/19/1811 in Ashford, CT. Ruel m **Lucinda Adams**. They resided in Windham Co., VT. (*Windham County, Vermont, Gazetteer*, p. 93, 304)

Rufus - bc1790 in CT. Rufus m **Kezih** ----, bc1800 in MA. They resided in Wilmington, Windham Co., VT. In the 1850 census he was 60 and she was 50 years old, with Cyrus 21 years old. (*1850 Census Windham Co., VT*)

Samuel - bc1774 in CT. Samuel m **Rebecca** ----, bc1779 in MA. They resided in Pitcher, Chenango Co., NY. In the 1850 census he was 76 and she was 71, with Lucy 40 and Adeline 25 years old, both b in NY. (*1850 Census Chenango Co., NY*)

Simeon - b 1/20/1783 in CT, s/o **Apollos, Sr.**; Simeon d 12/6/1830 age 47 in Rutland Co., VT. He m in Lenox, MA, **Susan C. Babcock**, d 5/9/1840 age 51. (*Hist. of Fair Haven, VT*, p. 32-3)

Solomon, Jr. - b1754 in CT, s/o **Solomon**; Solomon, Jr. d 5/27/1838 prob. in Lyme, Grafton Co., NH. He m **Esther Porter**. (*Gazetteer Grafton Co., NH*, p. 530-1 - *DAR Patriot Index*, p. 629)

Sylvanus - bc1783 in CT, d1872 in OH. Sylvanus m **Thankful Kelsey**. (War of 1812 Index)

Sylvester - b 2/16/1758 in Woodstock, CT, s/o **Ebenezer**. Sylvester m 1/18/1787 **Hannah Hayward**, b 2/19/1766, d/o Capt. **Benjamin** and **Hannah (King)**. They resided in Williamstown, Orange Co., VT. (*Woodstock Fam.*, p. 311)

Thaddeus - bc1768 in CT. Thaddeus m **Deborah Sheldon**, bc1781 in VT. They resided in Rupert, Bennington Co., VT. In the 1850 census he was 82 and she was 69 years old, with Diantha 47 years old, b in VT. (*1850 Bennington Co., VT, Census*)

Thomas – b1784 in CT, d1870 in Indiana. Thomas m **Phoebe Lush Johnson**. (War of 1812 Index)

Walter – b 3/21/1800 in Wethersfield, CT, d 9/21/1874 in Chautauqua Co., NY. Walter m **Minerva Abell**, d 2/25/1855, d/o **Mosely**. (*Chautauqua, NY*, p. 309–12)

SNOW

Erastus – bc1783 in Ashford, CT, s/o **James**; Erastus d 2/23/1850 in Windham, OH. He m – – – – **Willoughby**. (*Semi-Centennial Windham, OH*, p. 60)

James – bc1749 in Ashford, CT, d 2/11/1829 in 80th year in Windham, OH. James m – – – –. (*Semi-Centennial Windham, OH*)

SOULE

Joseph – bc1747 in CT, s/o **Timothy**; d 5/12/1820 age 73 in Fairfield, Franklin Co., VT. Joseph m **Eunice Hungerford**, bc1751, d 8/19/1839 age 88, d/o **Samuel**. (*Some Early Rec. of Fairfield, VT*, p. 7 – *Soule Fam.*, v. 1, p. 486)

Samuel – b 12/13/1771 in CT, s/o **Joseph** and **Eunice (Hungerford)**; Samuel d 6/16/1858 in 86th year in Fairfield, Franklin Co., VT. He m **Sarah Bradley**, d/o **Andrew** and **Ruth (Wakeman)**; b 5/23/1779, d 5/23/1846 in 67th year. (*Franklin Co. Gazetteer*, p. 104 – *Soule*, v. 1, p. 488)

Timothy – bc1767 in Dover, NY, s/o **Joseph** and **Eunice (Hungerford)**; Timothy d 12/27/1861 age 93 in Fairfield, Franklin Co., VT. He m **Betsey Elliot** of CT, bc1770, d 4/19/1843 in 73rd year. (*Franklin Co., VT, Gazetteer*, p. ? – *Sole, Solly, Soule, Soulis*, v. 1, p. 487)

SOUTHWORTH

Asa – b 8/28/1756 in Mansfield, CT, s/o **Josiah** and **Esther (Proctor)**. Asa m (1) 6/15/1780 in Mansfield, CT, **Hannah Allen**, d/o **Seth**, and m (2) **Phebe Ketchum** of Hanover, NH. They resided in Fairlee, VT. (*New Eng. Gen. Reg.* Oct. 1950, p. 265 – *DAR Patriot Index*, p. 634)

Gurdon B. – bc1779 in CT. Gurdon B. m **Laura** – – – –, bc1799 in VT. They resided in Dorset, Bennington Co., VT. In the 1850 census he was 71 and she was 51 years old. (*1850 Bennington County, Vermont, Census*)

Isaac Crippen – b 1/25/1759 in Sharon, CT, d 5/4/1846 in Claredon, Addison Co., VT. Isaac Crippen m **Martha Boland**. (*Branches and Twigs*, v. 3 #1, p. 29 – *DAR Patriot Index*, p. 634)

Lemuel – b 6/11/1758 in Mansfield, CT, d 2/4/1841 in Vershire, Orange Co., VT. Lemuel m 11/28/1782 **Elizabeth Stoddard**, b 10/30/1760, d 3/29/1833 in Vershire, VT. (*New England Gen. Reg.* Oct. 1950, p. 265)

Ralph – b 4/7/1768 in Mansfield, CT, s/o **Josiah** and **Irene (Reed)**. Ralph m **Eunice Ludden**, b 4/26/1767 in Chesterfield, MA, d/o **Benjamin** and **Esther (Capen)**. They resided in W. Fairlee, Orange Co., VT. (*New Eng. Gen. Reg.* Oct, 1950, p. 266)

William – b1758 in either Ashford or Mansfield, CT, d 1/6/1849 in E. Springfield, PA. William m **Charlotte Bicknell**, bc1760, d 4/25/1846 in E. Springfield, PA. (*New Eng. Gen. Reg.* July 1960, p. 242 – *DAR Patriot Index*, p. 634)

SPAFFORD
Asa – bc1792 in CT. Asa m **Pethena ----**, bc1796 in NY. They resided in Pittsfield, Chenango Co., NY. In the 1850 census he was 58 and she was 54 years old, with Harvey 19 and Betsey 17 years old, both b in NY. (*1850 Census of Chenango Co., NY*)

SPALDING
Simon – b 1/16/1742 in CT, d 1/24/1814 in PA. Simon m **Ruth Shepard**. (War of 1812 Index – *DAR Patriot Index*, p. 635)
Timothy – bc1749 in CT, d1825 age 76 in Panton, Addison Co., VT. Timothy m ----. (*Gazetteer of Addison Co., VT*, p. 193)

SPAULDING
Darius – b 7/24/1760 in Plainfield, CT, s/o **Philip** and **Deborah (Woodward)**; Darius d 5/13/1835 in Roxbury, Washington Co., VT. He m (1) 1782 **Hannah Ingram**, d 5/19/1814, and m (2) 2/10/1817 **Mary Fenton**. (*The Spaulding Memorial*, p. 188)
Gilbert Richmond – bc1784 in CT, d1870 in NY. Gilbert Richmond m **Orinda McClure**. (War of 1812 Index)
Nathan – b 6/20/1769 in Plainfield, CT, s/o **Philip**; Nathan d 9/30/1844 in Pawlet, VT. He m (1) 12/4/1792 **Elizabeth Hill**, b in Danby, VT, d 11/23/1818, and m (2) 3/18/1821 **Catherine Maharr** of Pawlet, VT. (*Spaulding Memorial*, p. 189, 338 – *History of Danby, VT*, p. 266)
Samuel B. – bc1782 in CT. Samuel B. m **Sally ----**, bc1785 in NH. They resided in Roxbury, Washington Co., VT. In the 1850 census he was 68 and she was 65 years old, with John 10 years old, b in VT. (*1850 Census of Washington Co., VT*)

SPELLMAN
Cyrus – b1850 in CT, s/o **Michael**, d1937 in Ontonagon, MI. Cyrus m **Helen Fleming**, b1852 in NY. (*MI Heritage*, v. 9, p. 173)

SPENCER
Alford B. – bc1818 in Westbrook, CT, d1/17/1851 age 33-9 in Greece Twp., Monroe Co., NY. Alford B. m ----. (Tombstone Rec., Greece Twp., NY)
Asa – b 3/20/1744 (or 3/25/1744) in CT, s/o **Joel** and **Sarah**; Asa d 3/20/1784 poss. in Pittstown, NY. He m **Asenath Graves**, bp 8/12/1750 in E. Haddam, CT. (Jacobus – Spencer file CT Historical Soc.)
Chester – b in CT, d 7/26/1868 in Springville, NY. Chester m **Abigail Badgely**, d at age 54. (*History of Orig. Town of Concord, Erie Co., NY*, p. 534-5)
Daniel – bc1790 in CT. Daniel m **Rebecca Bliss**, bc1790 in MA. They resided in Marshfield, Washington Co., VT. In the 1850 census he was 55 and she was 56, with Stephen 16, Mary 27, Sarah 25,

Gardner 20, Gardner 82 (b in CT), and Mary 76 years old (b in CT). (*1850 Census of Washington Co., VT*)

Dr. **Ebenezer** – bc1775 in CT. Dr. Ebenezer m **Cynthia** ----, bc1773 in NH. They resided in Vershire, Orange Co., VT. In the 1850 census he was 75 and she was 77 years old. (*1850 Orange County, Vermont, Census*)

Ephraim – bc1793 in CT, d 4/25/1853 age 60 prob. in Camden, Oneida Co., NY. Ephraim m **Cornelia Woodin** of W. Stockbridge, MA. (*Pioneer Hist. of Camden, NY*)

Gideon – b 9/14/1741 in Windham, CT, s/o **Ebenezer** and **Sarah Hebbard**; Gideon d 10/15/1819 in VT. He m **Zerviah Buck**. (War of 1812 Index – *DAR Patriot Index*, p. 636)

Jabez – b 3/18/1764 in New Haven, CT, s/o **Nathaniel** and **Abigail (English)**; Jabez d 5/2/1839 age 75 in Salisbury, Addison Co., VT. He m 6/28/1786 **Joanna Ives**, d/o **Joseph** and **Abigail (Grannis)**. (*Gazetteer of Addison Co., VT*, p. 206 – *New Haven Fam.*, p. 1665 – *DAR Patriot Index*, p. 636)

James – b 6/14/1736 in E. Haddam, CT, s/o **Phineas** and **Martha (Stevens)**; James d1805 age 70 in Benton, Yates Co., NY. He m **Anna Spencer**, d1806 age 64 in Benton, NY. (*DAR Patriot Index*, p. 636 – *TAG* Four Spencer Bros., p. 250-1 – *History of Yates Co.* by Aldrich, p. 358 – *Am. Genealogist*, p. 250-1)

John – b 3/30/1689, s/o **Nathaniel**; John dc1773 age 85 in Spencertown, NY. He m 2/18/1713 (or 2/18/1714) **Mary** ----, bc1694 (or bc1696), d at age 85. (Jacobus File on Spencer at CT Hist. Soc.)

Joel – bc1719 in Haddam, CT, s/o **John** and **Mary**; Joel d 2/225/1806 age 87 in Maryland, Otsego Co., NY. He m (1) before 1745 **Mary Bevins**, b 11/1719 in Middletown, CT, d/o **Thomas** and **Martha**, and m (2) **Elizabeth** ----, and m (3) after 1789 **Sarah Haskell**, b 4/8/1747 in Hardwick, MA, d/o **Zachariah** and **Kezia (Goss) Rose**. (*TAG* Four Spencer Brothers, p. 243-4)

John – bc1793 in CT, d1883 in NY. John m **Nancy Carr**. (War of 1812 Index)

John – bc1774 in CT, s/o **Caleb** and **Hannah (Goodrich) (Stokes)**; John d1825 in Oxford, OH. He m (1) 2/29/1798 in Madison, CT, **Elizabeth Wilcox**, bc1774, d 4/29/1803, and m (2) **Alma Harrison**, bc1786 in Branford, CT, d1882. (*TAG* – Four Spencer Brothers, p. 176 – War of 1812 Index)

Joseph – b 7/2/1733 in CT, s/o Sgt. **John** and **Elizabeth**. Joseph m 8/30/1753 in Bolton, CT, **Lucy Dart**, b 12/7/1735 in Bolton, CT, d/o **Daniel** and **Jemima (Shailor)**. They resided in Surry, NH. (*TAG*, v. 29, p. 55-6 – *Town of Gilsum, NH* by Hayward – *History of Surry, NH*, p. 882-3)

Reuben – b 6/8/1752 in E. Haddam, CT, s/o **Gideon** and **Elizabeth (Hurd)**; Reuben d in Villenova, Chautauqua Co., NY. He m (1) 3/7/1774 in E. Haddam, CT, **Elizabeth Cone**, d 5/9/1791 age 35, and m (2) **Mehitable Warner**, bc1762, d 3/4/1850 age 88, d/o **John**. (*Soldiers of American Revolution, Chautauqua Co., NY*, p. ? – *TAG*, p. 52 vol. 30)

Dr. **Silas** – b 12/16/1788 in CT. Dr. Silas m **Harriet Goodrich**, d/o **Gideon** of Ripley, NY. They resided in Chautauqua Co., NY. (*Chautauqua Co., NY*, p. 611)

Truman - b 1/3/1806 in Litchfield, CT, s/o **Ephraim** and **Sarah (Stoddard)**; Truman d 12/7/1854 in Camden, NY. He m 4/1828 **Electa Merriman**, d 10/5/1862 age 59 in Camden, NY. (*Pioneer Hist. of Camden, Oneida Co., NY*, p. 465-6 - *TAG*, v. 30, p. 180-1)

Hon. **William** - b 8/6/1781 in Hartford, CT, s/o **Ashbel** and **Abigail (Birdwell)**; Hon. William d 1/19/1871 age 90 in Corinth, Orange Co., VT. He m 9/6/1807 in Corinth, VT, **Resign M. Nutting**, d 11/28/1847 age 57. (*Gazetteer of Orange Co., VT*, p. 46 - *TAG*, v. 28, p. 113-114)

SPERRY

Allen - bc1791 in CT, d 4/26/1869 age 72 in Camden, Oneida Co., NY. Allen m **Abigail** ----, bc1798, d 4/18/1835 age 37. (*Pioneer Hist. of Camden, NY*, p. ?)

Josiah Clark - bc1788 in CT, d1869 age 81 in Camden, Oneida Co., NY. Josiah Clark m (1) 1812 **Charry Sperry**, bc1774, d1854 age 80, and m (2) 1856 Mrs. **Lydia Perkins Plumb**, bc1799, d1895. (*Pioneer Hist. of Camden, NY*, p. 214)

Levi - b 11/15/1767 in New Haven, CT, s/o **David** and **Sarah (Peck)**; Levi d1828 in Cornwall, VT. He m **Lydia** ----. (*Gazetteer of Addison Co., VT*, p. 98 - *Ancient New Haven Fam.*, p. 1688-9, v. 3)

SPICER

Jabez - b 9/11/1753 in Norwich, CT, s/o **Zephaniah** and **Sarah (Starkweather)**; Jabez d 1/6/1823 in Richmond, VT. Jabez m 1/14/1779 **Faith Ripley**, b 10/13/1757 in Windam, CT, d 5/31/1824 in Richmond, VT, d/o **William** and **Lydia (Brewster)**. (*Spicer Genealogy*, p. 74 - *History of Cornish, NH*, p. 345 - *DAR Patriot Index*, p. 636/7)

Miner - b1776 in CT, d1855 in OH. Miner m **Cynthia Allyn**. (War of 1812 Index)

Simeon A. - b1798 in Hebron, CT. Simeon A. m (1) **Fanny H. Waterman**, d 11/16/1846, and m (2) **Harriet Standish**. They resided and perhaps d in Hyde Park, LaMoille Co., VT. (*Gazetteer of LaMoille Co., VT*, p. 102)

SPRAGUE

Daniel - b in Salisbury, CT, d 6/2/1853 in Poultney, Rutland Co., VT. Daniel m ----. He was a blacksmith. (*History of Rutland County, Vermont*, p. 775)

David - bc1769 in CT. David m ----. He resided in Poultney, VT, with son, George. In the 1850 census he was 81 with George, his son, a physician (b in VT), 36 years old. (*1850 Rutland County, Vermont, Census*)

John - b in CT. John m **Fannie West**. They resided in Smyrna, Chenango Co., NY. In the 1850 census he was 64 years old, with Marcia 31 and Fanny 18 years old, both b in NY. (*1850 Census Chenango Co., NY*)

Jonathan - b 4/2/1766 in Sharon, CT, s/o **Jonathan** and **Lydia (Barrows)**; Jonathan d 2/6/1837 age 69 poss. in Tallmadge, OH. He m 6/25/1795 **Sarah Tousley**, b 6/17/1778, d 8/10/1842. (*OH Gen. Soc. Quarterly* Oct. 1972, p. 34 - *Sprague Gen.*, p. 46)

Paremas – b1780 in CT, d1871 in NY. Paremas m (1) **Rebecca Nobles**, and m (2) **Mary Ann Fellows**. (War of 1812 Index)

Roger – bpc1767 (or bpc1769) in Lebanon, CT, s/o **Silas** and 2nd wife **Abigail (Hill)**; Roger d 7/1843 (or d 7/1848) in Rochester, MI. He m (1) **Althea Baughton**, b 7/5/1778, d 8/29/1827 in Rochester, MI, d/o **Hezekiah** and **Huldah (Wilson)**, and m (2) **Ann Jane**. (*Sprague Gen.*, p. 46 – *Detroit Soc. Gen. Research* Winter 1976)

SPRING

Asahel – bc1795 in CT. Asahel m **Elizabeth** ----, b in MA. They resided in Marlboro, Windham Co., VT. In the 1850 census he was 55 and she was 34 years old, with Benjamin H. 21 (b in MA), Julia T. 18 (b in MA), Ellen 6 (v in VT), Rosette 4 (b in VT), and Asahel 1 year old (b in VT). (*1850 Census of Windham Co., VT*)

SPRINGER

Joshua – bc1766 in CT, d 6/19/1843 age 77 in E. Thetford, VT (gravestone). Joshua m ----. (E. Thetford Cemetery, VT)

SQUIER

Daniel – bc1762 in CT. Daniel m ----. He resided in Hubbardton, Rutland Co., VT. In the 1850 census he was 88 years old, with Asa 53, Clara 45, Daniel 38, Lettice 29, and Laura 5 years old, all b in VT. (*1850 Rutland Co., VT, Census*)

SQUIRE

Jesse – bc1725 in Canaan, CT, d 10/1/1804 in Ontario, NY. Jesse m (1) 1763 **Lydia Clothier**, and m (2) **Mary Whitney**. (*CT Nutmegger* Quarterly June 1981, p. 43 – *DAR Patriot Index*, p. 639)

SQUIRES

Alanson – bc1785 in CT. Alanson m **Bathsheba** ----, bc1800 in VT. They resided in Bennington, Bennington Co., VT. In the 1850 census he was 65 (a shoemaker) and she was 50 years old, with George 19 years old, b in VT. (*1850 Bennington Co., VT, Census*)

Asa – bc1764 in CT, d 4/3/1852 in Strongsville, OH. Asa m 10/23/1783 **Eunice Wakeman**, d/o **Ebenezer**. (*Wakeman Gen.*, p. 186 – *DAR Lineage*, v. 124, p. 21 – *DAR Patriot Index*, p. 639 – *Some Early Rec. of Fairfield, VT*, p. 16)

Henry – bc1769 in CT. Henry m ----. He resided in Sandgate, Bennington Co., VT. In the 1850 census he was 81 years old. (*1850 Bennington Co., VT, Census*)

Stoddard – b 11/8/1758 in Woodbury, CT, s/o **Reuben** and **Joanna** (or **Jemima**) (**Stoddard**). He m1781 **Theodosia French**. They resided in Russia, Herkimer Co., NY. (*History of Herkimer Co., NY*, p. 457-8, 107)

Sturges – b1791 in CT, d1879 in PA. Sturges m **Almira Wood**. (War of 1812 Index)

STAFFORD

Amos – bc1794 in CT. Amos m **Fanna** ----, b1800 in NY. They resided in Sherborne, Chenango Co., NY. In the 1850 census he was

56 and she was 50 years old, with Susan 20, Erva 18, Janes 15, Mary 13, Levi 11, and Amanda 8 years old, all b in NY. (*1850 Census Chenango Co., NY*)

STANARD
Asa - bc1776 in CT, d1837 in NY. Asa m **Sarah Bidwell**. (War of 1812 Index)

STANLEY
Nathaniel - bc1768 in CT, d1848 in OH. Nathaniel m **Mary Moore**. (War of 1812 Index)

William - bc1774 in CT, d1835 in OH. William m **Margaret Bratton**. (War of 1812 Index)

STANNARD
Heman - b 12/27/1780 in Killingworth, CT, s/o **Samuel** and **Jemima (Wilcox)**; Heman d 5/16/1863 in Fair Haven, Rutland Co., VT. He m **Minerva A. Smith**, bc1784 in CT. In the 1850 census, he was 69 and she was 66, with Mary A. 26, Heman Jr. 24, Edward 21, and Charlotte 18 years old, all b in VT. (*1850 Rutland Co., VT, Census*)

Samuel - b1749 in Killingworth, CT, d 4/8/1815 in 67th year in Fair Haven, Rutland Co., VT. Samuel m **Jemima Wilcox**, b1746, d 6/25/1834 age 88. (*History of Fair Haven, VT*, p. ? - *DAR Patriot Index*, p. 641)

STANTON
Amos - b1773 near Stonington, CT, d in Otselic, NY, (once lived in Smyrna, NY). Amos m **Sabra Palmer** of Penobscot, ME. (*Smyrna, NY*, p. 105-6)

Asa - b 3/2/1760 in Preston, CT, s/o **David** and **Sarah (Kimball)**; Asa d 11/12/1817 (drowned) perhaps in Canaan, Wayne Co., PA. He m 3/13/1788 **Keziah Kimble**, b 10/15/1771 in Norwich, CT, d 9/9/1848. (*Hist. of Wayne Co., PA*, p. 174-7 - *DAR Patriot Index*, p. 641 - *Thomas Stanton Fam.*, p. 160-1, 144)

Joshua - b 4/1740 in Preston, CT, d1803. Joshua m **Abigail Sackett**. Once resided in Colchester, VT. (*Hist. of Town of Colchester, VT*, p. ? - *DAR Patriot Index*, p. 641 - *Stanton Fam.*, p. 172)

Samuel - b 4/17/1759 in Preston, CT, d 4/15/1816 prob. in Wayne Co., PA. Samuel m 12/3/1786 in Preston, CT, **Martha Carpenter Morse**, b 10//15/1764 in Preston, CT, d1830 Port Allegany, PA, d/o **Paul** and **Anna (Carpenter)**. (*Thomas Stanton Family*, p. 164-6, 235-6 - *DAR Patriot Index*, p. 642 - *History of Wayne County, Pennsylvania*, p. 175, 188)

STAPLES
Peter - bc1788 in CT. Peter m **Hannah ----**, bc1789 in VT. They resided in Roxbury, Washington Co., VT. In the 1850 census he was 62 (a shoemaker) and she was 61 years old, with Hannah A. 37, and Jane 21 years old, both b in VT. (*1850 Census of Washington Co., VT*)

STARK

Capt. John - bc1743 in CT, d 9/26/1806 prob. in S. Hero, Grand Isle, VT. Capt. John m **Eunice Adams**, d/o Capt. **Samuel**. (*Gen. Hist. of Henry Adams of Braintree*, p. 124 - *DAR Patriot Index*, p. 642)

Nathan - bc1743 in CT, s/o **Daniel**; Nathan d1830 age 87 poss. in Guilford, VT. He m (1) **Olive Morgan**, and m (2) **Esther Gallup**. (*Bicentennial, Some VT Ancestors*, p. ? - *DAR Patriot Index*, p. 642)

STARKS

David - bc1765 in CT, s/o **David** and **Martha (Edgerton)**; David d1805 in Pittsford, Rutland Co., VT. He m1785 **Jemima Mead**, b1767 in Manchester, VT, d1834 in Buffalo, NY. (*History of Pittsford, Vermont*, p. 202, 726)

James - bc1793 in CT. James m **Sybil** ----, bc1796 in VT. They resided in Halifax, Windham Co., VT. In the 1850 census he was 57 and she was 54 years old, with Royal 29, George 21, Sybil 18, Horace 10, and Harriet 20 years old, all b in VT. (*1850 Census of Windham Co., VT*)

William - bc1770 in CT, d perhaps in Halifax, Windham Co., VT. William m ----. In the 1850 census he was 80 years old, with Martha 49 years old, b in NY. (*1850 Census of Windham Co., VT*)

STARKWEATHER

Amos - b 8/1/1759 in Stonington, CT, s/o **John**; Amos d 7/8/1815 in Northfield, Washington Co., VT. He m 1/25/1787 in Preston, CT, **Jemima Gates Brown**. (*Early Settlers of Northfield, VT*, p. 119-120 - *Starkweather Gen.*, p. 93)

Avery - b 10/3/1790 in Preston, CT, d 10/3/1865 in Barre, Orleans Co., NY. Avery m (1) **Abigail Bracket**, m (2) **Electa Ward Moon**. (*Pioneer Hist. of Orleans Co.*, p. 113)

Samuel - b 3/19/1719 in CT, d 3/26/1786 in MA. Samuel m **Sarah Purple**. (War of 1812 Index - *DAR Patriot Index*, p. 642)

STARR

John - 8/16/1774 in S. Farms, CT, s/o **Josiah**; John d 5/7/1833 in Huron, OH. He m1810 in Saratoga, NY, **Sara Chandler**, b1783, d 8/12/1861 in Huron, OH, d/o **Joseph** and **Charity (Andrews)**. (*Res. of CT Who Migrated to Huron, OH*, p. ? - *Starr Fam.*, p. 153)

Leander - bc1803 in Danbury, CT, d 3/21/1885 age 61 in Hudson, OH. Leander m 12/1831 **Ruth Thompson**, b 10/17/1813 in Hudson, OH, d 3/14/1890, d/o Dr. **Moses** and **Elizabeth**. (*Reminiscences of Hudson, Ohio*)

Thomas - b 9/3/1784 in Groton, CT, s/o **William**; Thomas d 8/14/1868 in Rochester, Lorain Co., OH. He m1791 in Berlin Hts., OH, **Clementine Clark** of Pompey, NY, b 4/9/1791, d 8/7/1873 in Berlin Hts., OH. (*Res. of CT Who Migrated to Huron Co., OH*, p. 6 - *Starr Family*, #44, p. 35-6)

STEARNS

Eleazer - b near Bristol, CT, s/o **Eleazer**; d1809 in Easton, NY. Eleazer mc1789 **Aurelia Castle** of Plymouth, CT, b1771, d 1/28/1857 age 86. She m (2) **Benjamin Curtis**, d1825. (*Pioneer*

Hist. of Camden, NY, p. 43 - *Stearns Gen.*, v. 1, p. 623, 629 - *DAR Patriot Index*, p. 643)

STEBBINS
Seth - bc1784 in CT. Seth m **Jemima Hutchinson**, bc1788 in VT. They resided in Norwich, Windsor Co., VT. In the 1850 census he was 66 and she was 64 years old, with Charlotte 24 and Levi 24 years old, too. (*1850 Census of Windsor Co., VT*)

STEDMAN
Levi - b 11/3/1758 in CT, d 10/26/1834 in Pleasantville, Westchester Co., NY. Levi m ----. (*DAR Magazine* 1977, p. 922 - *DAR Patriot Index*, 644 ?)

Lyman - b1785 in CT, d1847 in NY. Lyman m **Elizabeth Wilson**. (War of 1812 Index)

STEDSON
Winslow - bc1767 in CT. Winslow m **Mary** ----, bc1770 in CT. They resided in Warren, Washington Co., VT. In the 1850 census he was 83 and she was 80 years old, with Alexander 29, Oscar 12, and Charlotte 83 years old, all b in VT. (*1850 Census of Washington County, Vermont*)

STEELE
David - bc1767 in Tolland, CT. David m1793 **Phebe Edgerton**. They resided in Lyme, Grafton Co., NH. (*Gazetteer of Grafton County, New Hampshire*, p. 543)

Levi - bc1776 in CT, d1837 in NY. Levi m **Sarah Van Benthuysen**. (War of 1812 Index)

STEPHENS
Eliphalet - bc1731 in CT, d 8/31/1814 in PA. Eliphalet m **Elsa Halloway**. (War of 1812 Index - *DAR Patriot Index*, p. 646)

STERLING
Richard - bc1778 in CT. Richard m **Priscilla** ----, bc1782 in VT. They resided in Warren, Washington Co., VT. In the 1850 census he was 72 and she was 68 years old, with Seth 31 (b in VT) and Eliza 36 years old (b in VT). (*1850 Census of Washington Co., VT*)

Seth - b 3/18/1763 in Lyme, CT, s/o **Joseph** and **Lydia (Ransom)**; Seth d 4/27/1846 in Woodstock, VT. He m (1) **Polly Brewster**, d 7/23/1795, d/o **Ephraim**, and m (2) 1/4/1796 Mrs. **Huldah Tinkham**, b1766, d 4/22/1818, and m (3) 11/18/1818 Mrs. **Lucy (Woods) (Wing) Hammond**, b1767, d 8/23/1846. (*Sterling Genealogy*, p. 385-6 - *DAR Patriot Index*, p. 645)

STERLING (or STARLING)
Joseph - b 3/8/1739 in Lyme, CT, d 9/17/1814 prob. in Woodstock, VT. Joseph m 2/1762 **Lydia Ransom**, b 6/26/1742 in Lyme, CT, d 11/20/1805, d/o **Matthew** and **Sarah (Way)**. (V. Rec. of Lyme, CT - *Hist. of Woodstock, VT*, p. 110)

Joseph - b 11/28/1770 Lyme, CT, s/o **Joseph** and **Lydia (Ransom)**. Joseph (the younger) m **Lucy ----**, bc1775 in VT. They resided in Barre, Washington Co., VT. In the 1850 census he was 79 and she was 75 years old. (*1850 Census of Washington Co., VT*)

STEVENS

Asa - b 4/6/1754 in Plainfield, CT, s/o **David** and **Sarah (Spaulding)**; Asa d 8/31/1817 in Pittsford, Rutland Co., VT. He m **Sally Dunlap** of Plainfield, CT, d1833 age 77. (*Hist. of Pittsford, VT*, p. 222-3)

Gen. **Elias** - b 10/15/1754 in Plainfield, CT, d 11/9/1848 in Royalton, Windsor Co., VT. Gen. Elias m **Sarah Rude**, b 10/9/1753 in Lebanon, CT, d 3/15/1841 in Royalton, VT, d/o **Rufus** and **Sarah (Swetland)**. (*Hist. of Royalton, VT*, p. 979-80)

Elihu - b 4/8/1731 in CT, d 1/8/1814 in NH. Elihu m (1) **Rachel Meigs**, and m (2) Mrs. **Jerusha (Smith) Leonard**. (War of 1812 Index - *DAR Patriot Index*, p. 646)

Hezekiah - b1793 in Killingworth, CT, d 1/1838 age 37 in Pompey, Onondaga Co., NY. Hezekiah m **Lois Field** of Jericho, VT. (*Pompey, NY*, p. 417)

Linus - b 11/29/1800 in Cheshire, CT, d1875 in 75th year in Johnstown, NY. Linus m 12/6/1821 in Naugatuck, CT, (Waterbury) **Fannie Smith**, d 4/1885 in Camden, NY. (*Pioneer History of Camden, NY*, p. 372-3)

Martin - b1767 in Naugatuck, CT, s/o **William**; Martin d 1/24/1839 age 72 prob. in Camden, NY. He m **Thirza Tyrell**, b1778 in Naugatuck, CT, d1850 age 82, d/o **Thomas**. (*Pioneer History of Camden, Oneida Co., NY*, p. 369)

Martin H. - b 12/25/1806 in Naugatuck, CT, s/o **Martin** and **Thirza**; Martin H. was living at age 91 in Camden, Oneida Co., NY. He m (1) 1831 **Helen Preston**, d1835, d/o **Riley**, and m (2) 1836 **Emma A. Fish**, d 12/10/1875 age 65, d/o **Jesse**. (*Pioneer History of Camden, NY*, p. 369-71)

Nelson - bc1827 in CT, d1892 in Seneca Falls, NY. Nelson m **Hannah Opson**, d1893, d/o **Erastus**. (*Pioneer History of Camden, Oneida Co., NY*, p. 500)

Peter - b1741 in Canterbury, CT, s/o **Peter** and **Abigail**; Peter (the younger) d 5/26/1821 age 83 in Wells, VT. He m 11/1/1759 in Canterbury, CT, **Lois Glass**, d 6/6/1820 age 78, d/o **Anthony** and **Eunice (Bennett)**. (*History of Wells* by Paul-Parks, p. 148 - *History of Wells* by Wood, p. 80 - *DAR Patriot Index*, p. 647 - *Pember Fam.*, p. 121-2)

Peter - b 5/6/1759 in Glastonbury, CT, d1838 in Pawlet, Rutland Co., VT. Peter m **Mercy House**. (*Hist. of Rutland Co., VT*, p. 708 - *DAR Patriot Index*, p. 647)

Reuben - b 9/14/1739 in Fairfield, CT, s/o **Daniel**. Reuben m 4/27/1760 **Mary Williams**, b 9/8/1742. They resided in Greenville, Greene Co., NY. (*Hist. of Greene Co., NY*, p. 313-14)

William - bc1734 in Wolcott, CT, d 2/17/1814 age 80 in Camden, NY. William m ----. (*Pioneer Hist. of Camden, NY*, p. 243-4)

STEWARD

Eliphalet - b 8/15/1759 in Stonington, CT, s/o **William, Jr.** and **Elizabeth (Stevens)**; Eliphalet d 11/3/1837 in Busti, NY. He m **Mercy Coates**, b 9/6/1764, d 4/19/1813. (*Chautauqua Co., NY*, p. 441-2 - *DAR Patriot Index*, p. 648)

STEWART

Cephas - b1814 in Ridgefield, VT, d 9/23/1878 in Bennington, MI. Cephas m 11/11/1840 in Romulus, NY, **Mary Barnes**. (*Pioneer Collections of MI*, v. 3, p. 618)

Daniel - b1762 in CT, d1853 in OH. Daniel m **Ruth Fulford**. (War of 1812 Index)

Daniel - b1753 in CT, d 7/29/1845 in W. Galway, Saratoga Co., NY. Daniel m ----. (*DAR Mag.* 1977, p. 922)

Russel - bc1782 in CT. Russel m **Caroline** ----, bc1782 in CT. They resided in Pitcher, Chenango Co., NY. In the 1850 census he was 68 and she was 68 years old, too. (*1850 Census of Chenango Co., NY*)

STILES

David - b1766 in Litchfield, CT, d1873 in Huron Co., OH. David m (1) 1795 in Toronto, Canada, **Martha Ransom**, b1775, d1806, and m (2) 1807 in NY, **Elizabeth Cummins**. (*Res. of CT Who Migrated to Huron Co., OH*, p. 7)

Gould - bc1784 in CT. Gould m **Laura (Haynes) Huntington**, bc1788 in VT. They resided in Wells, Rutland Co., VT. In the 1850 census he was 66 and she was 62 years old, with **Miriba Stevens** 66 years old, b in CT. (*1850 Rutland Co., VT, Census*)

Henry - bc1798 in Danbury, CT, d 8/13/1869 prob. in OH. Henry m1821 **Mary Reeves**, d 12/1859. (*Trumbull and Mahoning Counties, OH*, p. 335)

Samuel - b 1/1/1758 in CT, d1814 in NY. Samuel m **Sarah Rose**. (War of 1812 Index - *DAR Patriot Index*, p. 649)

STILLMAN

Amos - b1785 in CT, d1813 in NY. Amos m **Susannah French**. (War of 1812 Index)

STILSON

Beers - bc1762 in New Milford, CT, s/o **Enoch** and **Freelove (Stilson)**. Beers m **Eunice Dodge**. They resided in Monkton, Addison Co., VT. (*Gazetteer of Addison Co., VT*, p. 158 - *Stilson-Stillson Fam.*, p. 22, 49, 49a - *Gazetteer of Addison Co., VT*, p. 158)

Nathan - bc1783 in CT. Nathan m **Sophia** ----, bc1793 in Albany Co., NY. They resided in Meredith, Delaware Co., NY. In the 1855 census he was 70 and she was 62 years old, with **Milan Seeley** (gr/s) 19 years old. (*1855 Census of Delaware Co., NY*)

William - bc1784 in CT. William m **Affa Ward**, bc1783 in CT. They resided in Meredith, Delaware Co., NY. In the 1855 census he was 71 and she was 72 years old, with Reuben 30, Allen 28 (b in Deleward Co., NY), Helen M. (w/o Allen) 24 (b in CT), and Ida (d/o Allen) 1 month old (b in PA). (*1855 Census of Delaware Co., NY*)

229

STIMSON

Joel – b 8/10/1751 in Tolland, CT, d 4/15/1813 age 62 prob. in Norwich, VT. Joel m 4/15/1779 in Norwich, CT, **Susanna Growe**. (*A Hist. of Norwich, VT*, p. 246-7 – *DAR Patriot Index*, p. 650)

STOCKING

Joseph – bc1784 in CT. Joseph m **Eliza ----**, bc1806 in NH. They resided in Weathersfield, Windsor Co., VT. In the 1850 census he was 66 and she was 44 years old. (*1850 Census of Windsor Co., VT*)

STODDARD

Cheselton – bc1817 in CT, s/o **Stephen**; Cheselton d1901 in Cavendish, VT, buried in Hillcrest Cemetery. He m **Elsa Gassett**, bc1823 in CT, d1893 in Cavendish, VT. In the 1850 census he was 33 and she was 27 years old, with Lucius G. 4, Stella 3, and Eliza S. Archer 14 years old. (*1850 Windsor Co., VT, Census*)

Eliakim – b 8/10/1779 in CT, s/o **John** and **Mary (Atwood)**. Eliakim m (1) 4/26/1801 **Lois Mathews**, b 4/23/1781 in Claremont, NH, d 12/12/1842, d/o Deacon **Abner**, and m (2) 7/13/1843 **Nancy Adset**, b 12/20/1794, d 10/29/1860. They resided in Camden, NY. (*Pioneer Hist. of Camden, Oneida Co., NY*, p. 86-7 – *Stoddard Fam.*, p. 11, 15, 44-5)

Israel – b 2/15/1776 in Watertown, CT, s/o **John** and **Mary (Atwood)**; Israel d 4/4/1859 age 83 in Camden, Oneida Co., NY. He m (1) **Polly Wilson** of Harwinton, CT, b 9/27/1799, d1820 age 45, and m (2) **Mary Wilson** (cousin of 1st wife). (*Pioneer Hist. of Camden, NY*, p. 80-83 – *Stoddard Fam.*, p. 14, 43)

Marcus – bc1791 in CT. Marcus m **Julia ----**, bc1793 in VT. They resided in Middletown, Rutland Co., VT. In the 1850 census he was 59 and she was 57 years old, with Alvira 33 years old, b in VT. (*1850 Rutland Co., VT, Census*)

Martin – b1799 in CT. Martin m **Elizabeth ----**, bc1802 in NY. They resided in Masonville, Deleware Co., NY. In the 1855 census he was 56 and she was 53 years old, with Oliver 19, Franklin 17, George S. 14, Cheston 12 years old, and Mary E. (*1855 Census of Delaware Co., NY*)

Orson – b 1/1/1804 in CT, d 6/15/1870 in Gratiot Co., MI. Orson m **Bethia Hulbert**, b 7/1810 in NY, d 4/21/1870 in Washington Twp., MI. (*Portrait and Biog. Album, Gratiot Co., MI*, p. 228)

Rodman – b 7/5/1797 in Woodbury, CT, s/o **Nathan Ashbell** and **Ruth (Judson)**; Rodman d 5/13/1853 in Detroit, MI, buried in Elmwood Cem. He m 5/26/1829 **Mary Matteson**, b 6/25/1809 in NY, d 12/21/1893 in Reed City, MI, buried in Elmwood Cem. (*Detroit Soc. Gen. Res.*, v. 38 #1 1974, p. 15)

Russell – b1789 in CT, d1873 in NY. Russell m **Clarissa Elliott**. (War of 1812 Index)

Stephen – bc1780 in CT, d 6/2/1858 age 79 in Cavendish, Windsor Co., VT. Stephen m ----. In the 1850 census he was 70 years old, with Cheselton 33 (b in CT), Elsa (w/o Cheselton) 27 (b in CT), Lucius G. 4, Stella M. 3, and Eliza Archer 14 years old. (*1850 Windsor Co., VT, Census*)

Wait - bc1781 in CT, d1866 in NY. Wait m **Rosamund Bates**. (War of 1812 Index)

STONE
Andrew J. - bc1816 in Litchfield, CT, d 1/5/1892 age 76 in Camden, Oneida Co., NY. Andrew J. m (1) **Angelina Blake**, and m (2) **Charlotte (Sanford) Merriam**, d 1/10/1892 age 70, wid/o **James**. (*Pioneer Hist. of Camden, NY*, p. 183-4)

Eber - b 9/7/1773 in Guilford, CT, d 11/2/1845 in Chautauqua Co., NY. Eber m1800 **Betsey Atwater**. (*Chautauqua Co., NY*, p. 612)

David - b 10/9/1769 in CT, d 9/2/1845 age 76 in Westford, VT. David m 9/29/1792 **Thankful Smith**. (*Gazetteer of Chittenden Co., VT*, p. 230 - *Hist. of Chittenden Co., VT*, p. 627)

Garrard - bc1788 in Litchfield Co., CT, s/o **Canfield**; Garrard d 9/21/1855 age 67 in Forest Lake, Susquehanna Co., PA. He m ----, d 11/6/1848. (*Hist. of Susquehanna Co., PA*, p. 483)

Hiel - bc1766 in CT, d1839 in NY. Hiel m **Ruth Norton**. (War of 1812 Index)

Ira - bc1777 in CT, d1852 in IL. Ira m **Rhoda Chapman**. (War of 1812 Index)

Judson - b1792 in Litchfield, Co., CT, s/o **Canfield**; Judson d 6/22/1871 age 78 in Forest Lake, Susquehanna Co., PA. He m (1) 1/1/1815 **Polly Turrell**, b1795, d 7/17/1855, d/o **Abel**, and m (2) ----, wid/o **Garrard** (Judson's brother). (*History of Susquehanna Co., PA*, p. 483, 486)

Lorry - bc1788 (or bc1789) in Litchfield Co., CT, s/o **Benajah**; Lorry d1871 in 83rd year in Susquehanna Co., PA. He m **Permelia Mallory**, bc1792, d1846 age 54, d/o **Truman**. (*Hist. of Susquehanna Co., PA*, p. 360)

William - bc1788 in Orange, CT, d 4/2/1872 age 84 in Ogden Twp., Monroe Co., NY. William m **Sybil** ----, bc1790 in Milford, CT, d 10/5/1871 age 81. (Tombstone Record)

William - b 7/10/1759 in Guilford, CT, d 3/20/1840 age 81 in Sodus, Wayne Co., NY. William m **Tamson Graves**. (*DAR Mag.*, v. 39, p. 263 - *DAR Patriot Index*, p. 653)

STORRS
Benjamin - bc1783 in CT. Benjamin m **Mindwell** ----, bc1778 in CT. They resided in Columbus, Chenango Co., NY. In the 1850 census he was 67 (a merchant) and she was 72 years old. (*1850 Census of Chenango Co., NY*)

Huckens - b 11/6/1732 in Mansfield, CT, s/o **Huckens**; Huckens (the younger) d 3/26/1786 in Royalton, Windsor Co., VT. He m 11/16/1757 **Jerusha (Bicknell) Allen** of Ashford, CT. (*Hist. of Royalton, VT*, p. 983-4 - *DAR Patriot Index*, p. 653)

Col. Seth - b 6/24/1756 in Mansfield, CT, s/o **Thomas** and **Eunice (Paddock)**; Col. Seth d 10/9/1837 in Vergennes, VT. He m 11/26/1789 **Electa Strong**, b 11/6/1770 in Addison, VT, d 3/15/1842 age 81, d/o Gen. **John** of Madison, VT. (*Storrs Fam. in America*, p. 345-353 - Middlebury, VT, Cem.)

STORY

Solomon - b1726 in Norwich, CT, d 5/22/1816 age 90 in Salisbury, Addison Co., VT. Solomon m ----. (Salisbury from Birth to Bicentennial - *DAR Patriot Index*, p. 654)

STOUGHTON

Augustus - bc1786 in CT, d1830 in PA. Augustus m **Hannah Perry**. (War of 1812 Index)

STOWELL

Nathan - b 12/17/1771 in Ashford, CT, s/o **Jonathan** and **Rhoda (Wilson)**; Nathan d 2/14/1810 in Cornwall, Addison Co., VT. He m **Huldah Scott**, b 4/18/1775 in Litchfield, CT, d 4/18/1844 in Cornwall, VT, d/o **Sylvester**. (*History of Cornwall, VT*, p. 65 - *Stowell Gen.*, p. 86, 192, 351-2 - *Gazetteer of Addison Co., Vermont*, p. 100)

STRATTON

Joseph - b 7/1751 in Fairfield, CT, s/o **John**; Joseph d1827 in Roxbury, NY, buried in Old School Baptist Cemetery. He m1778 **Eunice Berry** (?), d1842 age 88. (*Hist. of Roxbury, NY*, p. 36 - *A Book of Strattons*, p. 278 - *DAR Patriot Index*, p. 655)

Samuel - b1755 in Fairfield, CT, s/o **John**; Samuel d 10/3/1838 in Roxbury, NY. He m 3/30/1779 **Grace Darrow**. (*Hist. of Town of Roxbury, NY*, p. ? - *A Book of Strattons*, p. 279-80 - *DAR Patriot Index*, p. 655)

STRICKLAND

Jonathan, Sr. - b in CT (poss. in Waterbury), d1816 in Springville, Susquehanna Co., PA. Jonathan, Sr. m **Susanna** ----, d1815. (*Hist. of Susquehanna Co., PA*, p. 397)

Samuel - bc1778 in CT. Samuel m **Dorotha** ----, bc1775 in MA. They resided in W. Windsor, Windsor Co., VT. In the 1850 census he was 72 and she was 75 years old. (*1850 Windsor County, Vermont, Census*)

STRONG

Benajah - b 1/1734 (or b 1/1735), s/o Lt. **Jedediah** and **Elizabeth (Webster)**; Benajah d 3/1815 in Bethel, VT. He m (1) **Polly Bacon** of Lebanon, CT, d 8/8/1790, and m (2) **Elizabeth Wilson** of Bethel, VT, b 5/1748, d 1/26/1821, a widow. (*Strong Gen.*, v. 2, p. 849-851 - *Vermont Antiquarian*, p. 377, 464 - *Hartford, VT*, p. 462 - *DAR Patriot Index*, p. 657)

Daniel - b 7/10/1776 in CT, s/o **Eliakim** and **Remembrance (Wright)**; Daniel d 6/26/1859 in Batavia, NY. He m **Hannah Richmond**, b 1/26/1780, d/o **Robert** and **Sarah (Dean)**. (War of 1812 Index - *Des. of Thos. Strong*, p. 232-3)

Daniel - b1771 in CT, d1816 in OH. Daniel m **Hannah Scribner**. (War of 1812 Index)

Edmund - b 4/28/1781 in Harwinton, CT, s/o Col. **John** and **Mercy (Newell)**; Edmund d 8/25/1844 age 63 poss. in Tallmadge, OH. He m 12/16/1803 **Anna Gillett**, b 6/21/1784 in Torrington, CT, d

8/18/1868 age 84, d/o Deacon **Nathan** and **Lucy (Harrison)** of Morgan, OH. (1972 Spring Issue of *OH Gen. Soc. Quarterly*, p. 37 - *Strong Gen.*, p. 93)

Elijah - b 8/11/1733 in Lebanon, CT, s/o Lt. **Jedediah** and **Elizabeth (Webster)**; Elijah dc1774 (or dc1775) poss. in Hartford, VT. He m 3/18/1756 **Ruth Loomis**, b 6/14/1729 prob. in Lebanon, CT, d/o **Zachariah** and **Joanna (Abel)**. (*Hartford, VT*, p. 463-4 - *Stong Gen.*, v. 2, p. 848 - *DAR Patriot Index*, p. 657 - *Vermont Antiquarian*, p. 377)

Elisha - b 5/30/1727 in Lebanon, CT, s/o **Noah** and **Deborah**; Elisha d 12/11/1775 age 48 in Brandon, VT. He m1751 **Desire Williams**, b 2/22/1731, d 12/19/1821 age 89 in Brandon, VT. (*Strong Gen.*, v. 2, p. 987 - *Branches and Twigs* Quarterly v. 2 #3, p. 41)

Elisha Beebee - b 11/29/1788 in Hartford, CT, d 10/14/1868 in Rochester, Monroe Co., NY. Elisha Beebee m **Polly Goodwin Hooker**, d 2/15/1850 age 63. (Tombstone Record, Mt. Hope Cem. - *History of Monroe County, New York*, p. 32, 33, 38, 42, 80-1, 85, 138, 210, 243)

Elnathan - b 3/25/1787 in Chatham, CT, s/o Rev. **Cyprian** and **Abigail (White)**; Elnathan d 6/19/1843 prob. in Hardwick, Caledonia Co., VT. He m 10/17/1820 **Jane Chamberlain**, b1792, d1853. (*Vermont Hist. Mag.*, v. 1, p. 331-2 - *Strong Gen.*, v. 1, p. 304)

Frederick Ross - b 10/13/1804 in Salisbury, CT, s/o **Jonathan** and **Lydia (Rood)**. Frederick Ross m 6/8/1826 **Sophronia Chaffee**, b 6/8/1807. They resided in Brandon, Rutland Co., VT. In the 1850 census he was 47 and she was 43 years old, with Saloma 17 (b in VT), Caroline 15 (b in VT), and Lydia 73 years old (b in CT). (*1850 Rutland Co., VT, Census*)

Isaac - b 1/28/1765 in Salisbury, CT, d 2/18/1829 in Sennett (then Brutus), NY. Isaac m **Mariam Bacon**, b 12/31/1768 in Shaftsbury, VT, d 6/16/1847 in Sennett, NY, d/o **Rufus** and **Sarah (Slys)**. (*Strong Genealogy*, v. 2, p. 996-7 - War of 1812 Index - *DAR Patriot Index*, p. 657)

Jedediah - b 10/23/1751 in Lebanon, CT, s/o **Jedediah** and **Hepzibah (Webster)**; Jedediah (the younger) d 2/25/1832 age 80 in Hartford, Windsor Co., VT. He m 9/1/1778 **Ruth Harper**, b 9/1/1759, d 9/18/1839 (or d 9/18/1848), d/o Deacon **J a m e s** and **S a r a h (Burroughs)** of E. Windsor, CT. (*Strong Genealogy*, v. 2, p. 842-3 - *DAR Patriot Index*, p. 657)

Capt. John - b 9/5/1723 in Lebanon, CT, s/o Lt. **Jedediah** and **Elizabeth (Webster)**; Capt. John dc1806 in Hartford, Windsor Co., VT. He m (1) **Elizabeth Crouch**, d 1/15/1784 in Woodstock, VT, and m (2) Mrs. **Mary Hoisington**, a widow. (*Strong Gen.*, v. 2, p. 840-1 - *VT Antiquarian*, p. 21 - *DAR Patriot Index*, p. 657)

Gen. John - b 8/16/1738 in Salisbury, CT, s/o **Noah** and **Deborah**; Gen. John d 6/16/1816 in Salisbury, VT. He m 9/2/1759 **Agnes McCure**, b 4/2/1739 in Salisbury, CT, d 3/3/1829. (*Strong Genealogy*, v. 2, p. 1015-16 - *DAR Patriot Index*, p. 657)

John, Jr. - b 4/13/1788 in Glastonbury, CT, s/o **John** and **Sabra (Stocking)**; John, Jr. d 3/9/1857 age 69 in Sandy Hill, Rutland Co., VT. He m1816 **Nancy McNaughton**, b 5/31/1791 of Pawlet, VT, d/o **Finlay** and **Sarah (Cleveland).** (*Strong Gen.*, v. 2, p. 926-7 - *Hist. of Rutland Co., VT*, p. 708-9)

John Stoughton - b 7/19/1771 in Stafford, CT, s/o **David** and **Sarah (Warner)**; John Stoughton d 2/23/1863 age 91 poss. in Marlboro, VT. He m 6/1795 **Tamar Whitney**, b 7/9/1779, d 8/2/1856 age 77, d/o **Jonas** of Marlboro, VT. (*VT Hist. Mag.*, v. 5, p. 447 - *Strong Gen.*, v. 2, p. 1095)

Hon. **Moses** - b1772 in Salisbury, CT, d 9/29/1842 age 70 in Vergennes, VT, at son's home, having once resided in W. Haven, VT. Hon. Moses m (1) 12/20/1801 **Lucy Maria Smith**, b 9/1/1783 in W. Haven, VT, d 11/12/1823, and m (2) 5/6/1825 **Harriet (Woodbridge) Hopkins**, b 4/25/1786 in Manchester, VT. (*History of Rutland Co., VT*, p. 331-2 - *Strong Genealogy*, v. 2, p. 1031-6 - *Gazetteer of Rutland, VT*, p. 911)

Ozias - b 9/3/1734 in CT, s/o **Phineas** and **Mary (Parker)**; Ozias d 11/21/1807 in Homer, NY. He m 8/9/1757 **Susannah West** of Tolland, CT, d 6/1827, d/o **Peletiah** and **Elizabeth (Lathrop)**. (*Strong Gen.*, v. 2, p. 434 - *Hist. of Susquehanna Co., PA*, p. 55)

Nathan - b 1/30/1768 in Southbury, CT, s/o **Selah** and **Esther (Wood)**; Nathan d 2/9/1862 age 94 in Clinton, NY, buried in Kirtland Ave. Cem. He m (1) 2/10/1790 **Phebe Wakely**, b 8/19/1767, d 6/2/1804, d/o **Abner** and **Sarah**, and m (2) 12/10/1804 **Nancy Beardsley**, b 12/24/1778, d 10/22/1845 in 67th year, d/o **Benjamin** and **Thankful**. (*Clinton Memorial*, p. 48 - *Strong Gen.*, p. 507)

Return - b 12/30/1755 Union, CT, s/o **Samuel, Jr.** and **Martha (Stoughton)**; Return d 3/1/1807 (suicide) in Pawlet, VT. He m **Hannah Harman**, d 6/1813 in Pawlet, Rutland Co., VT, d/o **Phineas** of Suffield, CT. (*Hist. of Rutland Co., VT*, p. 708-9 - *Strong Gen.*, v. 2, p. 1114 - *DAR Patriot Index*, p. 657)

Russell - bc1786 in CT. Russell m **Susanna** ----, bc1788 in CT. They resided in Berlin, Washington Co., VT. In the 1850 census he was 64 and she was 62 years old, with **Russell, Jr.** 27 (b in VT), **Octa** 32 (b in VT), and **Lucy A.** 24 years old (b in VT). (*1850 Census of Washington Co., VT*)

Simeon - b 3/4/1731 in CT, s/o **Noah** and **Deborah**; Simeon d in Salisbury, Addison Co., VT. He m 4/1/1756 **Mary Castle** of Sheffield, MA, b1735. (*History of Salisbury, VT*, p. 334 - *Strong Genealogy*, v. 2, p. 1011)

Solomon - b 10/6/1730 in Lebanon, CT, s/o **Jedediah** and **Elizabeth (Webster)**; Solomon d 9/26/1800 (DAR says 12/12/1799) age 71 in Hartford, VT. He m (1) 1756 **Mary White**, b 10/16/1733, d 6/10/1777 age 44, buried in Quechy Village Cem., and m (2) 7/5/1782 **Mary Hutchinson** (nee **Wilson**), b 8/1744 d 3/21/1823 in Hartford, VT, buried in Center Town Cem. (*VT Antiquarian*, p. 377, 463 - *Strong Gen.*, v. 2, p. 844-5 - *DAR Patriot Index*, p. 657)

Solomon, Jr. - b 1/19/1763 in CT. Solomon, Jr. m 3/12/1795 **Ruth Tracy** of Hartford, VT. They resided in Hartford, Windsor Co., VT. (*Strong Gen.*, v. 2, p. 845)

Theodore - b 4/30/1797 in Bolton, CT, d 4/11/1868 in Berlin, Washington Co., VT. Theodore m (1) 2/5/1822 **Ezoa Poor**, d 9/7/1860, and m (2) 2/26/1861 **Octa Lucina Strong**, b 3/12/1818, d/o **Russell** and **Susannah (Webster)**. In the 1850 census he was 53

and she was 53 years old, too, with Julia 16 years old (b in VT).
(*1850 Census of Washington Co., VT - Strong Gen.*, p. 48-9)

Capt. **Timothy** - b 1/16/1764 in Woodbury, CT, s/o **Timothy**; Capt.
Timothy d1842 in Pawlet, Rutland Co., VT. He m ----. (*Strong
Genealogy*, p. 548-9 - *DAR Patriot Index*, p. 657 - *History of Rut-
land Co.*, p. 708-9)

Whiting - bc1786 in CT. Whiting m **Olive** ----, bc1786 in NH. They
resided in Williamstown, Orange Co., VT. In the 1850 census they
were both 64 years old (he was a shoemaker), with Sibel 19 and
Walter 10 years old, both b in VT. (*1850 Orange Co., VT, Census*)

Hon. **William** - b1763 in Lebanon, CT, s/o **Benajah** and **Polly
(Bacon)**; Hon. William d 1/28/1840 in Hartford, Windsor Co., VT.
He m 6/17/1793 **Abigail Hutchinson**, d 6/1860 age 88 in Hartford,
VT, d/o **John** and **Mary (Wilson)** of Norwich, CT. (*Vermont Anti-
quarian*, p. 377 - *Strong Genealogy*, v. 2, p. 851-2 - *History of
Hartford, VT*, p. 377-8)

William - b 2/29/1797 in Sharon, CT, s/o **Caleb, Jr.** and **Amy (Lee)**;
William d prob. in Meredith, Delaware Co., NY. He m1821 **Char-
lotte Whiting**, b 2/15/1800 in CT, d1867 in Meredith, NY, d/o
David and **Nanny (Raymond)**. In the 1850 census he was 58 and she
was 55 years old, with Milton 15 years old. (*1850 Census of
Delaware Co., NY*)

STUART

Albert R. - bc1781 in CT. Albert R. m **Sibel** ----, bc1785 in VT.
They resided in Mendon, Rutland Co., VT. In the 1850 census he
was 69 and she was 65 years old. (*1850 Census of Rutland Co., VT*)

Orlando G. - bc1818 in Sherman, CT, d 5/21/1886 age 68 in Avon, MI.
Orlando G. m ----. (*Pioneer Collections of MI*, v. 9, p. 60)

STURGES

Ezra - bc1774 in Fairfield, CT, s/o **Seth** and **Mary (Burr)**; Ezra d
10/15/1849 age 75 in St. Rocks, VT. He m ----. (*Some Early
Records of Fairfield, VT*, p. ?)

Ward - bc1764 in CT, s/o **Seth** and **Mary (Burr)**; Ward d 4/1/1812 in
48th year, prob. in Fairfield, VT. He m ----. (*Some Early Rec. of
Fairfield, VT*, p. 7)

STURTEVANT

John - bc1775 in Fairfield, CT, d 9/28/1841 age 66 in Fairfield,
Franklin Co., VT. It was said he was in the War of 1812. John m
----. (*Franklin Co., VT, Gazetteer*, p. 103)

SUMMERS

David - bc1761 in CT, d 4/1816 age 55 in New Milford, PA. David m
----. (*Hist. of Susquehanna Co., PA*, p. 615)

SUMNER

Benjamin - b1737 in Hebron, CT, d1815 in NH. Benjamin m **Prudence
Hubbard**. (War of 1812 Index)

Rev. Clement - b 7/15/1731 in Hebron, CT, s/o **William** and **Hannah
(Hunt)**; Rev. Clement d1795 age 64 in Swanzey, NH. He had

resided in Thetford, VT. He m 4/15/1759 in Hebron, CT, Mrs. **Elizabeth Gilbert.** (Pamphlet on Clement Sumner)

Deacon **E l e a z e r** - bc1761 in Middletown, CT, d1855 age 94 in Middlebury, VT. Deacon Eleazer m1780 ---- **Hall,** of Chatham, CT. (*Hist. of Town of Wells, VT*, by Wood, p. 80)

John - bc1736 in Ashford, CT, d 8/6/1804 in Edinburgh, Saratoga Co., NY. John m **Mehitable Perry.** (*DAR Mag.* 1977, p. 922 - *DAR Patriot Index*, p. 660)

Samuel Coit - b 1/27/1799 poss. in Norwich, CT, d 2/23/1873 age 74-0-27 in Braintree, VT. Samuel Coit m 9/23/1819 **Polly Flint,** bc1800 in CT, d 4/26/1888 age 89-5-24 in Braintree, VT. (*Hist. of Braintree, VT*, p. 185 - *Gazetteer of Orange Co., VT*, p. 203)

SUTLIFF

Nathan - bc1782 in CT. Nathan m **Polly ----,** bc1790 in MA. They resided in Sherburne, Chenango Co., NY. In the 1850 census he was 68 and she was 60 years old, with Hopy E. 21 and Esther 18 years old, both b in NY. (*1850 Census Chenango Co., NY*)

SWAN

Adin - b 5/13/1764 in CT, d 12/26/1842 in NY. Adin m **Hannah Gardner.** (War of 1812 Index - *DAR Patriot Index*, p. 661)

Moses - bc1795 in CT. Moses m **Nancy ----,** bc1797 in VT. They resided in Hartland, Windsor Co., VT. In the 1850 census he was 55 and she was 53 years old, with Austin 20, Lucy M. 16, Susan 14, Julia 13, Sylvia 10, and George 8 years, all b in VT. (*1850 Windsor Co., VT, Census*)

SWEATMAN

A m o s - bc1777 in Ellington, CT, d 4/13/1870 age 93 in Camden, Oneida Co., NY. Amos m **M a r y ----,** bc1777, d 4/12/1857. (*Pioneer Hist. of Camden, NY*, p. 334)

SWEET

Chester - bc1791 in CT, s/o **Joseph.** Chester m **Eliza Peck,** bc1797 in CT. They resided in Sidney, Delaware Co., NY. In the 1855 census he was 59 and she was 53 years old, with Joshua 21, Marvin 17 (b in NY), Eunice 20 (b in CT), Eliza 15 (b in NY), and Marion 12 years old (b in NY). (*1855 Census of Delaware Co., NY*)

Joseph - b 4/11/1822 in Coventry, CT, s/o **Chester** and **Eliza (Peck);** Joseph d prob. in Sidney, Delaware Co., NY. He m **M e l i s s a McMullen,** d/o **Archibald** and **Lucretia (Crawford),** d in Sidney, Delaware Co., NY. (*Biog. Rec. of Otsego Co., NY*, p. 259)

SWEETLAND

Eleazer - b1782 in CT, d1838 in VA. Eleazer m **Sallie Hawkins.** (War of 1812 Index)

SWETLAND

L u k e - b 6/16/1729 in Lebanon, CT, d 1/30/1823 poss. in Kingston Twp., PA. Luke m 4/1/1762 **Hannah Tiffany** of Lebanon, PA, d

1/8/1809. (*Hist. of Luzerne-Lackawanna and Wyoming Co., PA*, p. 306 - *DAR Patriot Index*, p. 663)

SWIFT

Rev. **Job** - b 6/17/1743 in CT, d 10/20/1804 in Enosburg, Franklin Co., VT. Rev. Job m **Mary Ann Sedgwick**. (*Hartford Courant* issue 11/4/1804 - *DAR Patriot Index*, p. 663)

SYMONDS

John - bc1788 in CT. John m **Lucia ----**, bc1788 in CT. They resided in Oxford, Chenango Co., NY. In the 1850 census he was 62 and she was 62 years old, too, with Mary 40 years old. (*1850 Census of Chenango Co., NY*)

TAINTER

Loren - bC1799 in CT, d1864 in MN. Loren m **Ruth C. Graves**. (War of 1812 Index)

TALCOTT

Henry - b7/1/1828 in Glastonbury, CT, s/o **Adna** and **Eliza (Wright)**. Henry m in Unadilla, NY, **Maria L. Morgan**, b 7/1/1829, d/o **Gurdin** and **Sophia (Locke)**. They resided in Otsego Co., NY. (*Biog. Rec. of Otsego Co., NY*, p. 205)

Joshua - b1776 in Bolton, CT, d 1/8/1867 age 90 in Smyrna, Chenango County, NY. Joshua m **Sarissa Taylor** of VT. (*Smyrna* by Munson, p. 19)

TALLMADGE

Col. **Benjamin** - b 2/25/1754 in Litchfield, CT, d 3/7/1835 prob. in Tallmadge, OH. Col. Benjamin m **Mary Floyd**. (*DAR Patriot Index*, p. 665)

TANNER

Zera - b1770 in CT, d1837 in NY. Zera m **Janett McWhorter**. (War of 1812 Index)

TAYLOR

Andrew - bc1796 in CT. Andrew m **Maria ----**, bc1801 in NY. They resided in Poultney, Rutland Co., VT. In the 1850 census he was 56 and she was 49 years old. (*1850 Rutland Co., VT, Census*)

Dyer - bc1790 in CT, d1850 in Forest Lake, Susquehanna Co., PA. Dyer m1813 **Lucinda Kellum**, b1792, d1885, d/o **Luther**. (*Hist. of Susquehanna Co., PA*, p. 486)

Eli - b 6/16/1733 in CT, d 9/14/1797 in Greenfield, NY, and buried in Sadler Cem., Saratoga, NY. Eli m ----. (*DAR Mag.* 1977, p. 922)

Gilbert - b1776 in CT, d1840 in NY. Gilbert m **Clarissa Gibbs**. (War of 1812 Index)

James - b1755 in CT, d 7/19/1817 in S. Bangor, Franklin Co., ME. James m **Penuel Fletcher**. (*DAR Mag.* 1977, p. 922 - *DAR Patriot Index*, p. 667)

Josiah - bc1781 in CT, d 3/28/1823 age 42 in E. Thetford, Orange Co., VT. Josiah m **Lydia Cummings**, bc1786, d 8/26/1866 age 80. (E. Thetford, VT Cemetery gravestones)

R. D. - bc1796 in CT. R. D. m **Sarah ----**, bc1803 in MA. They resided in Smyrna, Chenango Co., NY. In the 1850 census he was 54 and she was 47 years old, with **Addison** 22, **William** 24, **Permilla** 16, and **Clarissa** 13 years old, all ch/o R. D. and Sarah b in NY. (*1850 Census Chenango Co., NY*)

Reuben - b 2/8/1759 in Colchester, CT, d in Portland, Chautauqua Co., NY. Reuben m1784 in Hebron, CT, **Anna Skinner**, b 10/7/1763 in Hebron, CT, d 5/3/1842. (*Soldiers of the Am. Rev., Chautauqua Co., NY*, p. 21 - *DAR Patriot Index*, p. 668)

S e t h - bc1782 in Litchfield Co., CT, d 6/26/1869 in 88th year in Forest Lake, PA. Seth m poss. **Abigail Warren**. (*Hist. of Susquehanna Co., PA*, p. 482)

TEALL

Oliver - b 8/5/1788 in CT, d 8/15/1857 prob. in Syracuse, Onondaga Co., NY. Oliver m1809 **Catherine Walter**. (*Onondaga Hist. Soc. of 1914*, p. 177)

TENNANT

Daniel - b1762 in CT, s/o **Daniel**; Daniel (the younger) d1850 in Chautauqua, Chautauqua Co., NY, buried in Mayville Cem., NY. He m 10/11/1792 in Enfield, CT, **Martha Hale**, bc1770 (or bc1771), d/o **Thomas** and **Elizabeth (Bush)**. (*Hale-House and Related Families*, p. 242 - *DAR Magazine* 1977, p. 922 - *DAR Patriot Index*, p. 670)

TERRELL

Asahel - b 9/10/1739 in New Milford, CT, s/o **Nathan** and **Ruth (Buck)**; Asahel d 10/10/1777 during Rev. He m **Hannah Hoyt**. (*DAR Patriot Index*, p. 671 - *For King and Country, Orange Co., CA*, p. 247)

Elijah - b 3/8/1775 in Fairfield Co., CT, s/o **Asahel** and **Hannah (Hoyt)**; Elijah d 4/11/1848 in New Connecticut, OH. He m (1) 1796 **Clarissa Meeker**, and (2) **Sally Weede**. (*For King and Country, Orange Co., CA*, Bicent. Project, p. 247)

TERRILL

Jeremiah - b1770 in CT, d1831 in OH. Jeremiah m **Millicent Hine**. (War of 1812 Index)

Levi - bc1793 in CT. Levi m **Betsey ----**, bc1801 in VT. They resided in Castleton, Rutland Co., VT. In the 1850 census he was 57 and she was 49 years old, with Olive 22 (b in VT), Nathaniel 19 (b in VT), and Clarissa Sanford 73 years old (b in CT). (*1850 Rutland Co., VT, Census*)

TERRY

David - bc1784 in CT. David m **Sally ----**, bc1799 in VT. They resided in Hubbarton, Rutland Co., VT. In the 1850 census he was 66 and she was 51 years old, with John 29, Louisa 21, Daniel 19,

David Jr. 16, and Sarah 14 years old, all b in VT. (*1850 Rutland Co., VT, Census*)

Lorrain - bc1786 in CT. Lorrain m **Mary** ----, bc1787 in VT. They resided in Stockbridge, Windsor Co., VT. In the 1850 census he was 64 (a sadler) and she was 63 years old, with Hannah 59 (b in CT), Oliver 25 (b in VT), and Lucy 23 years old (b in NY). (*1850 Census of Windsor Co., VT*)

THATCHER

Amasa, Jr. - bc1768 in CT, d1844 in OH. Amasa, Jr. m **Phoebe Green.** (War of 1812 Index)

Charles - bc1799 in CT. Charles m **Rachel** ----, bc1804 in VT. They resided in Bennington, VT. In the 1850 census he was 51 and she was 46 years old, with Newell 13 and Alfred H. 11 years old, both b in VT. (*1850 Bennington Co., VT, Census*)

Eli - bc1794 in CT. Eli m **Sally** ----, bc1794 in CT. They resided in Manchester, VT. In the 1850 census he was 59 and she was 56 years old. (*1850 Bennington Co., VT, Census*)

Eliakim - b 3/30/1763 in Lebanon, CT, d 1/14/1848 in Arkwright, Chautauqua Co., NY. Eliakim m **Deborah Swift.** (*Soldiers of the Am. Rev., Chautauqua Co., NY - DAR Patriot Index*, p. 672)

George - bc1785 in CT. George m **Mary** ----, bc1790 in Delaware Co., NY. They resided in Sidney, Delaware Co., NY. In the 1855 census he was 65 and she was 60 years old, with Legrand 25 years old. (*1855 Census Delaware Co., NY*)

THAYER

Capt. Jeremiah - b 4/22/1762 in Bolton, CT, d 6/15/1857 age 95. Capt. Jeremiah m **Cynthia Case** of Coventry, CT. They resided in Vernon, Windham Co., VT. (*Vermont Hist. Mag.*, v. 5, p. 300 - *DAR Patriot Index*, p. 672)

Samuel - bc1784 in CT. Samuel m **Anna** ----, bc1782 in NH. They resided in Rutland, VT. In the 1850 census he was 66 and she was 68 years old. (*1850 Rutland Co., VT, Census*)

Zephaniah, Jr. - b 5/13/1760, s/o **Zephaniah** and **Prudence (Loomis)**; Zephaniah, Jr. d 4/19/1809 poss. in Athens, Windham Co., VT. He m **Polly Church.** (*Branches and Twigs* Quarterly, v. 3 #1, p. 94 - *DAR Patriot Index*, p. 673)

THOMAS

Daniel - b 11/21/1754 in CT, d 4/23/1825 in Ballston, Saratoga Co., NY. Daniel m **Eunice Foster.** (*DAR Mag.* 1977, p. 922 - *DAR Patriot Index*, p. 673)

David - bc1786 in CT. David m **Betsey** ----, bc1787 in VT. They resided in Middletown, Rutland Co., VT. In the 1850 census he was 63 (a farmer) and she was 64 years old. (*1850 Rutland County, Vermont, Census*)

Erastus - bc1794 in CT. Erastus m **Anna** ----, bc1796 in VT. They resided in Cavendish, Windsor Co., VT. In the 1850 census he was 56 and she was 54 years old, with Sam 25, Delia A. 21, Stillman 19, and Julia 16 years old, all b in VT. (*1850 Windsor Co., VT, Census*)

John - bc1777 in CT. John m **Rhoda** ----, bc1777 in MA. They resided in Weathersfield, Windsor Co., VT. In the 1850 census he was 73 and she was 73 years old, too, with one of them being blind. (*1850 Census of Windsor Co., VT*)

THOMPSON

Benjamin - bc1772 in CT. Benjamin m **Betsey** ----, bca1783 poss. in CT. They resided in Barnard, Windsor Co., VT. In the 1850 census he was 78 (blind) and she was 67 years old. (*1850 Windsor Co., VT, Census*)

Calvin - bc1779 in CT. Calvin m **Dimmis** ----, bc1781 in CT. They resided in New Berlin, Chenango Co., NY. In the 1850 census he was 71 (a carpenter) and she was 69 years old. (*1850 Census Chenango Co., NY*)

Edward - bc1790 in CT. Edward m **Olive** ----, bc1787. They resided in Waterbury, Washington Co., VT. In the 1850 census he was 60 and she was 63 years old with Sally 15 years old. (*1850 Washington Co., VT, Census*)

Enos - b 8/18/1717 in New Haven, CT, s/o **Samuel**. Enos m1741 **Sarah Hitchcock**. They resided in Salem, NY. (*Salem Book, NY*, p. 30 - *Hist. of Little Nine Partners*, p. 385)

Jonathan Palmer - b 7/24/1826 in Bloomfield, CT, d 7/6/1880 in Detroit, Wayne Co., MI. Jonathan Palmer m ----. (*Pioneer Collections of MI*, v. 4, p. 452-4)

Dr. **Moses** - b 1/22/1796 in Goshen, CT, d 11/26/1858 in 83rd year in Hudson, OH. Dr. Moses m 12/22/1797 **Elizabeth Mills**, b 6/15/1780 in Canton, CT, d 11/18/1870 age 70, d/o Lt. **Gideon** and **Ruth (Humphrey)**. (*Reminiscences of Hudson, OH*, p. 28-30)

Deacon **Stephen** - b 4/20/1734 in New Haven, CT, d 2/25/1823 in 90th year in OH. Deacon Stephen m **Mary Walter**. (*Reminiscences of Huron, OH*, p. 32)

William, Jr. - b 8/30/1764 in Hebron, CT, d 1/17/1833 in Alstead, NH. William, Jr. m (1) 11/27/1787 **Patty Hale**, d 2/16/1814 in Alstead, NH, and m (2) 2/1/1816 Mrs. **Prudence (Bill) Redding**, d 8/30/1819, and m (3) Mrs. **Fanny (Aldrich) Graves**, d 8/3/1859 in Keene, NH. (*Town of Gilsum, NH*, p. 401)

THORPE

Oreb - b in Cornwall, CT, s/o **Titus**. Oreb m **Lydia M. Loomis**, b in Egremont, MA, d/o **Moses** and **Hannah (Forbes)**. They resided in Otsego Co., NY. (*Biog. Rec. of Otsego Co., NY*, p. 476)

THRALL

Samuel - b 7/11/1737 in Windsor, CT, d 12/3/1821 in Rutland, VT. Samuel m **Lucy Winchell**, d/o **Martin**. They resided in Rutland, VT. (*DAR Patriot Index*, p. 677)

THRASHER

Charles - b1795 in CT, d1863 in IL. Charles m **Melinda Hicks**. (War of 1812 Index)

THRESHER
Stephen - b1788 in CT, d1857 in Northfield, VT. Stephen m **Sally Smith** of Randolph, VT, b 1/11/1790, d1878. (*Early Settlers of Northfield, VT*, p. 224 - *Washington Co., VT, Gazetteer*, p. 425)

THROOP
Benjamin - b 10/8/1754 in Lebanon, CT, d 1/17/1842 in Manchester, Cayuga Co., NY. Benjamin m **Rachel Brown**. (*Am. Monthly*, v. 39 - *DAR Patriot Index*, p. 678)
Major **Dan** - b 4/27/1768 in CT, d 5/19/1824 in Oxford, NY. Major Dan m **Mary Gager**, b in CT, d 10/13/1843 in Norwich, NY. (*Annals of Oxford, NY*, p. 425-9 - *DAR Patriot Index*, p. 678)
John - b 9/11/1733 in Lebanon, CT, d 1/25/1802 in Pomfret, VT. John m **Frances Dana**. (*History of VT*, v. 5, p. 51 by Crockett - *DAR Patriot Index*, p. 678)

TIBBITTS
Jesse - bc1777 in CT. Jesse m **Abigail ----**, bc1787 in MA. They resided in Cavendish, VT. In the 1850 census he was 73 (a blacksmith) and she was 63 years old. (*1850 Windsor Co., VT, Census*)

TIFFANY
Amos - bc1767 in CT. Amos m **Sally ----**, bc1771 in CT. They resided in Bennington, VT. In the 1850 census he was 83 and she was 79 years old. (*1850 Bennington Co., VT, Census*)
Arnold J. - b 11/1802 in CT, poss. in Ashford, s/o **Amasa** and **Sally**; Arnold J. d prob. in Pittsford, Rutland Co., VT. He m (1) 8/16/1826 **Abigail Drury**, b 3/1805, d 10/14/1844, and m (2) 7/11/1848 **Hannah B. Foot**, b1816, d 11/14/1861, and m (3) 11/16/1862 **Harriet W. Wright**. (*Hist. of Pittsford, VT*, p. 727)

TIFT
Joseph Burrows - b1782 in CT, d in FL. Joseph Burrows m **Rebecca A. Braman**. (War of 1812 Index)

TILDEN
Augustus N. - b1798 in Lebanon, CT, s/o **Ebenezer** and **Elizabeth**; Augustus N. d1875 in Forest Lake, PA. He m 11/29/1827 in Lebanon, CT, **Melina Clark**, b1797 in Lebanon, CT, d1882, d/o **Nathan** and **Anna (Goodwin)**. (*Hist. of Susquehanna Co., PA*, p. 494)
Capt. **Calvin** - b 9/23/1744 in CT, d 3/26/1822 in Cornwall, Addison Co., VT. Capt. Calvin m **Lydia Fuller**, d 8/5/1832 age 77. (*DAR Patriot Index*, p. 679)
Stephen - b1724 in Lebanon, CT, d 3/1813 age 89 in Hartford, VT. Stephen m (1) 4/23/1749 **Abigail Richardson**, d1798, and m (2) **Jerusha Farman**, widow, d 3/1813. They resided in Hartford, Windsor Co., VT. (*VT Antiquarian*, p. 24, 465-6)
Elder **William** - b 5/1/1829 in Lebanon, CT. Elder William m1850 **Amelia Russell**, b 5/13/1829 in PA, d/o **Benjamin** and **Sally (Watrous)**. They resided in Forest Lake, PA. (*History of Susquehanna Co., PA*, p. 494)

TILLOTSON

Charles - bc1786 in Lyme, CT, s/o **Nathaniel** and **Elizabeth**; Charles d 2/20/1865 in Underhill, VT. He m 11/1810 in Corinth, VT, **Hannah Woodward** (or **Bradford**). (*Tillotson Fam. of Am.*, v. 1, p. 193 - *Gazetteer of Orange Co., VT*, p. 332)

Hon. Ira - b 11/19/1783 in Farmington, CT, s/o **John** and **Elizabeth**; Hon. Ira d 3/10/1858 in Marshall, Eaton Co., MI. He m 1/8/1809 **Harriet Southworth**, dc1866. (*Pioneer Collections of Michigan*, v. 7, p. 377)

Isaac - b1762 (or b1765) in Farmington, CT, s/o **Ebenezer**; Isaac d 4/4/1849 age 88 in Belvedere, VT, (or Waterville, VT). He m (1) 12/25/1783 **Rachel Mann**, d1803 in Athens, VT, and m (2) 7/24/1803 in Chesterfield, NH, **Sarah Robbins**, b1782, d 3/9/1869 age 87 in Waterville, VT. (*The Tillotson Fam. in Am.*, v. 1, p. 141 - *DAR Patriot Index*, p. 679)

John - b 6/9/1756 in CT, d 7/12/1826 in NY. John m **Elizabeth Brookway**. (War of 1812 Index - *DAR Patriot Index*, p. 679)

Jonathan - b 1/23/1779 in Lyme, CT, s/o **Nathaniel** and **Elizabeth** (**Tillotson**); Jonathan d 3/28/1848 in W. Topsham, Orange Co., VT. He m 5/4/1806 in Corinth, VT, **Jerusha Howland**, b1785 in Lyme, CT, d 3/28/1848, d/o **Richard** and **Jerusha** (**Chadwick**). (*Tillotson Fam. in America*, v. 1, p. 189)

Joseph - b 5/28/1773 in Lyme, CT, s/o **Nathaniel** and **Elizabeth** (**Tillotson**); Joseph d 2/1/1856 age 82 in Wolcott, VT. He m (1) 1/21/1795 in Lyme, CT, **Lucinda Munsell**, d1815, and m (2) 3/10/1816 in Orange, VT, **Esther Sargeant**, b1790, d 3/1842 age 52 in Orange, VT. (*Tillotson Fam. in Am.*, v. 1, p. 186)

Nathaniel - b 1/22/1781 in Lyme, CT, s/o **Nathaniel** and **Elizabeth** (**Tillotson**); Nathaniel d 3/7/1862 age 81-2-16 in Orange, VT. He m 9/6/1812 in Corinth, VT, **Betsey Avery**, d/o **Andrew** and **Eunice**, b 7/7/1787 in VT, d 2/17/1874 age 85-7-10. (*Gazetteer of Orange Co., VT*, p. 332 - *Tillotson Fam. in Am.*, v. 1, p. 190)

TINKER

James - b 4/24/1772 in Waterford, CT, d 1/27/1856 age 83. James m 2/7/1799 **Rebecca Tyler**, b 1/31/1779 in Branford, CT, d 3/17/1848, d/o **Samuel** and **Rachel** (**Bartholomew**). They resided in Henrietta Twp., Monroe Co., NY. (Tombstone Records - *History of Monroe Co., NY*, p. 247)

TITUS

James B. - b 7/19/1794 in Hebron, CT, s/o **Robert**; d1839 prob. in Concord, Erie Co., NY. James B. m 1/2/1817 **Esther Yeomans**, bc1798, d/o **Sterling** of Otsego, NY. (*Hist. of Original Town of Concord, NY*, p. 917-18)

Noah - bc1794 in CT, d 2/12/1861 (gravestone) age 67 in Vershire, VT. Noah m **Jerusha Carrier**, d 6/7/1874 (gravestone). (Gravestones in Vershire Cemetery, Vershire, VT)

Silas - bc1824 in CT, s/o **Noah** and **Jerusha** (**Carrier**); d 5/5/1902 age 78-6 in Vershire, Orange Co., VT. Silas m (1) **Mary Jane ----**, d 6/9/1866 age 39-4, and m (2) **Hannah Dearborn**, d

12/4/1900 age 76-1. (Vershire Cemetery gravestones, Vershire, Vermont)

TOBY

John - bc1790 in CT. John m **Temperance** ----, bc1795 in MA. They resided in Smyrna, Chenango Co., NY. In the 1850 census he was 60 and she was 55 years old, with Antionette 19, E. P. (male) 27, and D. F. (female) 24 years old, all b in NY. (*1850 Census of Chenango Co., NY*)

TODD

Chancy - bc1784 in CT. Chancy m **Susan** ----, bc1793 in CT. They resided in New Berlin, Chenango Co., NY. In the 1850 census he was 66 and she was 57 years old, with Edward 27, Russel 20, Mary 17, and Chancy 15 years old, all b in NY. (*1850 Census Chenango Co., NY*)

George - b 12/11/1773 in Suffield, CT, s/o **David** and **Rachel (Kent)**; George d 4/11/1841 prob. in Brier Hill, OH. He m 10/1797 in New Haven, CT, **Sally Isaacs**, b 1/12/1778, d 9/29/1847 in Brier Hill, OH, d/o **Ralph** and **Mary**. (*Trumbull and Mahoning Counties, Ohio*, p. 209)

Samuel - bc1794 in CT. Samuel m **Eliza** ----, bc1796 in CT. They resided in Middletown, Delaware Co., NY. In the 1855 census he was 61 and she was 59 years old, with James 33, Dudley 31, and Elsey 19 years old, all b in NY. (*1855 Census of Delaware Co., NY*)

TOLLES

Henry - b 8/8/1736 in New Haven, CT, s/o **Henry** and **Deborah (Clark)**. Henry m 11/25/1757 in New Haven, CT, **Hannah Clark**, b1734 in Milford, CT, d/o **John** and **Rebecca**. They resided in Weathersfield, Windsor Co., VT. In the 1850 census he was 82 years old, with Phila 76 (b in MA), Augustus 54 (b in VT) and Phila 52 years old (b in VT). (*1850 Census of Windsor Co., VT*)

Robert - b 8/2/1827 in CT, s/o **Lyman** and **Almira (Andrews)**; Robert d 7/7/1879 in Eau Claire, WI. He m 11/7/1852 **Mary R. Graham**, b 6/21/1825 in Windham, NY. (*History of Chippewa Valley, Wisconsin*, p. 461)

TOMLINSON

Cyreno - bc1799 in CT. Cyreno m **Betsey** ----, bc1801 in CT. They resided in Castleton, Rutland Co., VT. In the 1850 census he was 51 and she was 49 years old. (*1850 Rutland Co., VT, Census*)

TOWN

Dr. Israel - bc1791 in CT, d 9/20/1859 in 68th year in Hudson, OH. Dr. Israel m **Lucy White** of Whitehall, NY, bc1796, d 5/31/1867. (*Reminiscences of Hudson, OH*, p. ?)

TOWNER

Ephraim - bc1775 in CT, d1850 in MI. Ephraim m **Anna Kellogg**. (War of 1812 Index)

TRACY

Amaziah - bc1794 in CT. Amaziah m **Cloe** ----, bc1800 in MA. They resided in Preston, Chenango Co., NY. In the 1850 census he was 56 and she was 50 years old, with Job S. 28, Peter A. 25, Amaziah, Jr. 24, and Cloe A. 21 years old, all b in NY. (*1850 Census Chenango Co., NY*)

Andrew - b 8/1/1754 in CT, s/o **Thomas** and **Elizabeth**; Andrew d 8/26/1802 in Hartford, VT, buried in the Centre Town Cem., Hartford, VT. He m 12/2/1784 **Sarah Bliss**, b1762, d1814 age 52, d/o **David** and **Polly (Porter)**. (*Hist. of Hartford, VT*, p. 468-71 - *DAR Patriot Index*, p. 685)

Cyrus - b 8/6/1757 in Preston, CT, d 5/31/1845 age 88 (gravestone) in Tunbridge, VT. Cyrus m (1) **Elizabeth Palmer**, and m (2) 3/16/1786 **Hannah Leslie**, d 6/29/1845 age 84. (*Tracy Gen.*, p. 133, 199 - *DAR Patriot Index*, p. 685 - *Branches and Twigs*, v. 6 #2 - Kelsey Mt. Cem., between Tunbridge and E. Randolph, VT)

Daniel, 3rd - b 8/3/1774 in Norwich, CT, s/o **Daniel**; d 3/16/1858 age 74 in Townshend, NY. Daniel, 3rd m in Oxford, NY, **Mary Havens**, d 9/22/1854 in Townshend, NY. (*Annals of Oxford, Chenango Co., NY*, p. 59-60)

Elias - b 4/6/1763 in CT, d 5/24/1848 in Poland, Chautauqua Co., NY, buried in Allen Cem., Poland, NY. Elias m **Lydia Gates**, d 4/25/1845 age 79 in Poland, NY. (*Soldiers of the Am. Rev., Chautauqua Co., NY*, p. 11 - *DAR Patriot Index*, p. 685 - *DAR Magazine* 1977, p. 922)

Elijah - b 4/17/1766 in Norwich, CT, s/o **Ebenezer** and **Mary (Freeman)**; d 1/15/1807 (or 6/15/1807) age 42 in Clinton, NY, buried in Kirtland Cem., Clinton, NY. Elijah m 2/21/1788 **Lois Fitch**, d 2/10/1833 age 70. (*Clinton Memorial*, p. 47 - *Norwich, CT, Vital Records*, v. 2, p. 294, 28, 399 - *Lisbon, CT, Vital Records*, v. 6, p. 111)

Elijah - b 4/26/1756 in Preston, CT, s/o **Samuel** and **Amy (Partridge)**; Elijah d 10/1/1835 in Tunbridge, Orange Co., VT. He m (1) 10/1780 **Jerusha Starkweather**, d 4/1/1801 age 50, and m (2) 7/1803 **Diadema Miller**. (*Anc. and Des. of Lt. Thomas Tracy of Norwich, CT*, p. 132)

Ezekiel - bc1754 in CT, d 2/24/1820 (or 2/24/1822) in NY. Ezekiel m **Patience Kimball**. (War of 1812 Index - *DAR Patriot Index*, p. 685)

Hial - b 7/5/1776 in Norwich, CT, s/o **Daniel** and **Mary (Johnson)**; Hial d 1/17/1842 in Oxford, Chenango Co., NY. Hial m in Norwich, CT, **Susanna Gifford**, d 5/22/1857 in Oxford, NY. (*Annals of Oxford, NY*, p. 59)

Hon. John - b 10/26/1783 prob. in Norwich, CT, d 6/1864 age 80 in Oxford, Chenango Co., NY. Hon. John m 8/5/1813 **Susan Hyde**, d 2/3/1864 age 76, d/o **Joseph** of Franklin, CT. In the 1850 census he was 66 (a lawyer and judge) and she was 63 years old, with Susan Eliza 34 years old, b in CT. (*Annals of Oxford, New York*, p. 298-9 - *History of Chenango Co., NY*, p. 261 - *1850 Census Chenango Co., NY*)

Samuel - b 2/28/1731 in Preston, CT, d 11/14/1815 age 84 in Tunbridge, VT, buried in Hutchinson Cem., Tunbridge, VT. Samuel m **Amy Partridge**, d 9/23/1806 age 76 in Tunbridge, VT. (*Hartford Courant* 10/14/1815 issue - *DAR Patriot Index*, p. 685)

Thomas H. R. - b 5/15/1806 in CT, d 5/15/1856 in Honesdale, Wayne Co., PA. Thomas H. R. m ----. (*History of First Presbyterian Soc., Honesdale, PA*, p. 190)

Uri - b 2/8/1764 in Norwich, CT, s/o **Daniel** and **Mary (Johnson)**; d 7/21/1838 age 75 in Oxford, Chenango Co., NY. Uri m **Ruth Hovey**, b 12/8/1775 in Oxford, NY, d 1/31/1846 age 71, d/o Gen. **Benjamin**. (*History of Chenango County, New York*, p. 257 - *Annals of Oxford, NY*, p. 54-61)

TRAVIS

Elijah - bc1792 in CT. Elijah m **Eunice** ----, bc1795 in CT. They resided in Middletown, Delaware Co., NY. In the 1855 census he was 63 and she was 60 years old, with Ethel (male ?) 30, Rebecca 28, and Caroline 26 years old, all b in Delaware Co., NY. (*1855 Census Delaware Co., NY*)

TREADWAY

Rev. James - b 5/12/1730 in Colchester, CT, s/o **James** and **Sarah (Munn)**; Rev. James d1798 in ME. He m **Olive Smith**, b 4/21/1768 (?) in Colchester, CT, d/o of **John** and **Temperance (Holmes)**. (*History of Surry, NH*, p. 909)

TREADWELL

Burr - b 11/23/1791 in Fairfield, CT, s/o **David** and **Phebe (Lyon)**; Burr d 2/7/1850 in Newton Twp., Calhoun Co., PA (?). He m 10/22/1815 in Ontario Co., NY, **Sarah Armstrong**, b in England, d 12/16/1873. (*Detroit Soc. of Gen. Res.* Fall 1976)

Richard - b 5/15/1783 in Weston, CT, d 6/9/1866 age 83 in Gaines, Orleans Co., NY. Richard m (1) 1/17/1809 **Temperance Smith** of Palmyra, NY, d 5/1810, and m (2) **Frances Bennett**. (*Pioneer Hist. of Orleans Co., NY*, p. 216-18)

TROWBRIDGE

A r t e m a s - b 12/7/1789 in Pomfret, CT, s/o **C a l e b**; Artemas d 11/21/1879 age 90 in Palmyra, Oneida Co., NY. He m 6/7/1827 in Westmoreland, NY, **Elizabeth Leaworthy**, b 2/16/1807 in NY City, d 11/11/1876 in Newark, NY. (*Trowbridge Genealogy*, p. 539, 576 - *Pioneer Hist. of Camden, NY*, p. 463)

George - b 8/11/1789 in Pomfret, CT, s/o **Caleb** and **Zilpha Barrows**; d 9/23/1888 in Camden, Oneida Co., NY. George m 9/29/1829 **Julia Allen** of Pomfret, CT. (*Trowbridge Fam.*, p. 270)

Israel - bp. 9/30/1722 in Stamford, CT, s/o **Isaac**. Israel m **Mary Johnson**, d/o **Peter** and **Mary**. They resided in Fair Haven, Rutland Co., VT. (*Hist. of Fair Haven, VT*, p. 480-4)

Levi - b 5/25/1753 in Derby, CT, d 12/14/1843 age 90 in Swan Creek, Gallia Co., OH. Levi m 12/29/1782 **Hannah Smith**, d 2/1832 age 73 in Ames Vill, d/o Capt. **Benjamin** of New Haven, CT. (*History of Fair Haven, VT*, p. ? - *DAR Patriot Index*, p. 688)

Philemon - b 1/13/1751 in Southbury, CT, s/o **Joseph** and **Trial (Morehouse)**; Philemon d 3/9/1812 in Clinton, Oneida Co., NY. He m 11/29/1773 **Eunice Hicock**, bp. 3/31/1754 in Southbury, CT, d 3/22/1842 (or 12/22/1842). (*Trowbridge Gen.*, p. 48, 123, 126, 129, 134, 154, – *DAR Patriot Index*, p. 688 – *Clinton Memorial-Kirtland Ave. Cem.*, p. 29–30)

Willard – b1796 in CT, d1885 in OH. Willard m (1) **Amy Sprague**, and m (2) **Susannah Sessions**. (War of 1812 Index)

TRUESDELL

Alonzo – b 7/14/1822 in Hartford Co., CT. Alonzo m1849 **Esther King**. They resided in Warren, OH. (*Trumbull and Mahoning Cos., OH*, p. 344)

TRUMBULL

David – b 7/1/1773 in E. Windsor, CT. David m 10/19/1810 **Hannah Richardson**, b 1/1778. They resided in Hartford, Windsor Co., VT. (*Hist. of Hartford, VT*, p. 470-1)

H o r a c e – bc1775 in Hartford Co., CT, d 5/14/1855 age 80 in Rupert, VT, buried in Old Cem., Rupert, VT. Horace m1798 **Dorothy Spear**, bc1779, d 2/19/1861 in Rupert, VT. (*Gravestone Records of Rupert, Bennington Co., VT*, p. 29, 31)

TUBBS

Simon – b 1/16/1755 in CT, d 4/2/1824 in Chittenden Co., VT. Simon m **Rozina Lawrence**. (*DAR Patriot Index*, p. 689 – *Branches and Twigs* Quarterly, v. 3 #1)

TUCK

Reuben – bc1774 in CT. Reuben m **Polly ----**, bc1784 in CT. They resided in Brookfield, Orange Co., VT. In the 1850 census he was 76 and she was 66 years old, living with **Solon** and **Eunice Simmons**, both b in VT. (*1850 Census of Orange Co., VT*)

TULLER

Flavel – bc1795 in CT, d1881 in OH. Flavel m **Lucinda Holcomb**. (War of 1812 Index)

TURNER

A s a – b 6/14/1765 in Watertown, CT, d in Stockton, Chautauqua Co., NY. Asa m **Isabel Ketcham**. (*Soldiers of the Am. Rev., Chautauqua Co., NY*, p. 22 – *DAR Patriot Index*, p. 691)

Hon. B a t e s – b 10/1760 in Canaan, CT, d 4/30/1847 in St. Albans, Franklin Co., VT. Hon. Bates m (1) **Mrs. Persis Humphry** of Providence, RI, d1814, and m (2) 1815 Mrs. **Sarah Webb** of N. Hero, VT, d 8/1839. (*Gazetteer of Franklin Co., VT*, p. 190)

S i m o n – bc1788 in Stonington, CT, d 7/8/1879 (drowned) in Preston, Chenango Co., NY. Simon m **Amanda ----**, bc1803 in CT. In the 1850 census he was 60 and she was 47 years old, with **George H.** 23 (b in NY), **Achsa** 21 (b in NY), **Ursula G.** 19 (b in NY), **Simon, Jr.** 16 (b in NY), and **Daniel** 14 years old (b in CT). (*Hist. of Chenango Co., NY*, p. 360 – *1850 Census of Chenango Co., NY*)

Stephen – b 1/14/1772 in New London, CT. Stephen m **Patty Prentiss**. They resided in Oxford, Chenango Co., NY. In the 1850 census he was 78 and she was 75 years old. (*Annals of Oxford, NY*, p. 280-1 - *1850 Census of Chenango Co., NY*)

TURRELL

Leman - b 7/6/1776 in New Milford, CT, s/o **James** and **Sarah**; d 12/28/1848 in 73rd year in Forest Lake, PA. Leman m 3/5/1797 in New Milford, CT, **Lucy Terrill** of Kent, CT, d 12/1864 in 89th year. (*Hist. of Susquehannah Co., PA*, p. 482)

TUTTLE

Amos - b 10/31/1761 in Southbury, CT, d 2/1833 age 72 in Hardwick, Caledonia Co., VT. Amos m 6/12/1782 **Rachel T. Jones**. (*Vermont Hist. Mag.*, v. 1, p. 330-1)

Andrew - b 11/9/1772 in Waterbury, CT, s/o **Noah** and **Thankful (Royce)**; Andrew d 10/191829 age 57 in Camden, Oneida Co., NY. He m 8/12/1795 **Philoma Allen**, b 5/19/1779, d 11/7/1856 age 77 in Camden, NY. (*Pioneer History of Camden, NY*, p. 297 - *Tuttle Fam.*, p. 492)

Anson - bc1795 in CT. Anson m **Anna ----**, b1803 in NH. They resided in Smyrna, Chenango Co., NY. In the 1850 census he was 55 and she was 47 years old, with Susanna 23, Useba 19, S. A. M. (female) 18, Charles 16, and Jerusha 14 years old, all b in NY. (*1850 Census of Chenango Co., NY*)

Cyrus - b1793 in Middlebury, CT. Cyrus m **Catherine Bennett**, d 11/23/1867 age 74. They resided in Oxford, Chenango Co., NY. (*Annals of Oxford, NY*, p. ?)

Gershom, Jr. - bc1767 in CT, d1823 in Indiana. Gershom, Jr. m **Permelia Strong Clark**. (War of 1812 Index)

Jared - b 6/2/1760 in CT, d 3/17/1837 in NY. Jared m **Roxanna Ward**. (War of 1812 Index - *DAR Patriot Index*, p. 692)

Jerrod - bc1782 in CT. Jerrod m **Alma ----**, bc1785 in CT. They resided in Columbus, Chenango Co., NY. In the 1850 census he was 68 and she was 65 years old, with Sylvester 30 years (a wagon maker, b in NY). (*1850 Census Chenango Co., NY*)

Deacon **Lyman** - b 8/14/1796 prob. in CT, s/o **Andrew**; d 10/25/1865 age 69 in CAmden, Oneida Co., NY. Deacon Lyman m (1) 9/20/1820 **Sarah Hungerford**, d 10/16/1833, and m (2) 5/6/1835 **Sabra Whitney** of Henderson, NY, b 8/13/1806, d 10/18/1872 in Henderson, NY. (*Tuttle Fam.*, p. 492 - *Pioneer Hist. of Camden, NY*, p. 297)

Noah - b 12/18/1744 in CT, s/o **Ephraim** and **Hannah (Pangborn)**; Noah d 6/25/1821 age 77 in Camden, Oneida Co., NY. He m 6/6/1771 **Thankful Royce**, b 2/11/1755, d 2/11/1840 age 94. (*New Haven Families*, p. 1903 - *Tuttle Fam.*, p. 491-2 - *Pioneer Hist. of Camden, NY*, p. 297)

Solomon - bc1794 in CT, d1848 in IN. Solomon m **Nancy Holdridge**. (War of 1812 Index)

Timothy - b 7/1/1746 in Cheshire, CT, dc1820 in Clinton, Oneida Co., NY. Timothy m 7/7/1768 **Mehitable Royce**, b 5/29/1749 in CT, d 12/5/1834 in North East, PA, d/o **Phineas** and **Thankful (Merriman)**. (*Clinton Memorial-Kirtland Ave. Cemetery*, p. 30 -

DAR Patriot Index, p. 693 – *Tuttle Gen.*, p. 497 – *Hist. of Waterbury, CT*, p. 350 – *CT Rev. War Archives*, v. 30)
William – bc1786 in CT. William m **Betsey** ----, bc1793 in CT. They resided in Meredith, Delaware Co., NY. In the 1855 census he was 69 and she was 62 years old. (*1855 Census Delaware Co., NY*)

TYLER
Jonathan – bc 4/12/1744 in CT. Jonathan m (1) 4/12/1764 **Honora Hatch** of Willington, CT, and m (2) Mrs. **Alice (Cole) Spaulding**, d age 85. They resided in Strafford, Orange Co., VT. (*Descendants of Job Tyler*, v. 1, p. 134-5)
Jacob – b 10/20/1760 in Branford, CT, s/o **Phineas** and **Abigail (Harrison)**; Jacob d 2/19/1847 in Mentor, OH. He m 9/11/1789 in Catskill, NY, **Abi Wheeler**. (*Rev. War Soldiers Buried in Lake Co., OH*, p. 58 – *DAR Patriot Index*, p. 693)
Darias – bc1774 in CT, s/o **Jonathan**; Darias d 5/21/1857 age 83 in Strafford, Orange Co., VT. He m (1) **Rhoda Bishop** of Hartland, VT, bc1778, d 10/9/1799 age 21 in Strafford, VT, and m (2) 3/5/1801 **Lois Rowell** of Strafford, VT, bc1780 in NH. (*Descendants of Job Tyler*, v. 1, p. 272)
Perley – b 12/6/1778 in Canterbury, CT, s/o **Oliver**; Perley d1855 in Northfield, VT. He m 10/27/1803 **Betsey Rood** of Brookfield, VT, b 9/15/1787, d1849. (*Early Settlers of Northfield, VT*, p. 104-5 – *Des. of Job Tyler*, v. 1, p. 343 and v. 2, p. 582-3)

UFFORD
Josiah – bc1776 in CT. Josiah m **Abiah** ----, bc1778 in CT. They resided in Pitcher, Chenango Co., NY. In the 1850 census he was 74 and she was 72 years old. (*1850 Census Chenango Co., NY*)

UPHAM
Alson – bc1781 in CT. Alson m (1) **Betsey** ---- , bc1781, d 11/14/1840 age 59, and m (2) **Martha** ----, bc1789 in NY, d 6/30/1857 age 69-6. They resided in Sherburne, Chenango Co., NY. In the 1850 census he was 69 and Martha was 61 years old. (*1850 Census Chenango Co., NY*)
Jonathan, Sr. – b 6/26/1761 in Killingly, CT, s/o **Ivory**; Jonathan, Sr. d 7/15/1827 in Windham, Windham Co., VT. He m 5/19/1787 **Mary Wilson** of Dudley, MA, b 10/19/1766 in Spencer, MA, d 10/14/1843 in Windham, VT. (*Windham Co., VT, Gazetteer*, p. 304 – *Upham Gen.*, p. 161-2)

UPSON
Deacon **Alvin** – b 12/4/1799 in Waterbury, CT, d 9/7/1883 age 84 in Michigan City, Indiana. Deacon Alvin m (1) **Mary Sperry**, d 7/27/1844, and m (2) **Mrs. Burke** of Aurora, OH, d 9/9/1877. (*Pioneer Collection of MI*, v. 7, p. 426)
Ashbel – b 4/25/1762 in Northbury Parish, Waterbury, CT, d 6/30/1851 age 71 in Camden, Oneida Co., NY. Ashbel m 3/18/1784 **Mary Munson**, b 2/14/1766, d 3/3/1857 age 91 in Camden, NY, d/o **Levi Munson** of Wallingford, CT. (*DAR Patriot In-*

dex, p. 695 - *Upson Family*, p. 65-6 - *Pioneer History of Camden, NY*, p. 32-3)

Hon. **Charles** - b 5/19/1821 in Southington, CT, d 9/5/1885 in Coldwater, MI.   Hon. Charles m 8/3/1852 in Leroy, NY, **Sophia Upham.** (*Pioneer Col. of MI*, v. 9, p. 188-192)

Stephen - b 7/28/1775 in Southington, CT, d 8/1850 age 77 poss. in Tallmadge, OH.   Stephen m **Sally Weller**, b 12/1/1778 in Westfield, MA. (*OH Gen. Soc. Quarterly*, Spring 1972, p. 35)

UTLEY

Asa - bc1750 in CT, s/o Capt. **William**; Asa d 8/8/1837 age 87 in Landgrove, Bennington Co., VT. He m ----. (*Bennington Co., VT, Gazetteer*, p. 135 - gravestone in Landgrove Cem., Landgrove, VT)

Elijah - b1765 (or b1766) in CT, d1820 (or d1830) in MA.   Elijah m **Lois Swan.** (War of 1812 Index - *DAR Patriot Index*, p. 696)

William - b 2/5/1724 in Windham, CT, s/o **James** and **Anna**; William d 3/17/1790 prob. in Landgrove, Bennington Co., VT.   He m **Sarah Peabody**, d age 92 (or age 93). (*Bennington Co., VT, Gazetteer*, p. 135 - *DAR Patriot Index*, p. 696 - *Vermont History Magazine*, v. 1, p. 197)

VAIL

Allen - bc1779 in CT.   Allen m **Elizabeth** ----, bc1782 in NY.   They resided in Montpelier, Washington Co., VT.   In the 1850 census he was 71 and she was 68 years old, with Catherine 45 (b in VT), Lucinda 44 (b in VT), and Mary 28 years old (b in VT). (*1850 Census of Washington Co., VT*)

Silas - bc1759 in CT, d 2/10/1821 in Greenfield, Saratoga Co., NY. Silas m ----. (*DAR Mag.* 1977, p. 923)

VAUGHN

Johnson - b1783 in CT, d1845 in OH.   Johnson m **Jemima Allen.** (War of 1812 Index)

William - bc1761 in CT.   William m ----.   He resided in Hartland, Windsor Co., VT.   In the 1850 census he was 89 years old, with Darwin 14, James 32, Mary A. 34, Lucia A. 23, all b in CT, living with **Francis** and **Lucy Lamner.** (*1850 Windsor Co., VT, Census*)

VERGASON

Elijah - bc1800 in CT.   Elijah m **Barbary** ----, bc1801 in Delaware Co., NY.   They resided in Sidney, Delaware Co., NY.   In the 1855 census he was 55 and she was 54 years old, with Roswold 28, Emory 21, Sarah 13, and Emily J. 19 years old, all b in NY. (*1855 Census Delaware Co., NY*)

VINTON

John - b 1/6/1765 in CT, s/o Capt. **John** and **Hepzibah**; John (the younger) d 11/17/1826 age 62 in Braintree, Orange Co., VT.   He m intentions 3/20/1784 **Hannah Ripley** of Weymouth, MA, d 7/23/1828 age 63. (*History of Weymouth, Mass.*, 4:603)

WADE

Duran - b 4/7/1716 in Lyme, CT. Duran m 1/3/1741/2 in Lyme, CT, **Phebe Ransom**. They resided in NH. (*Town of Gilsum, NH*, p. 173 - *Surry, NH*, p. 913)

Edward - b1754 in CT, d1845 in NY. Edward m **Susan Florence**. (War of 1812 Index)

Pember - b 1/21/1774 in Lyme, CT, d 2/15/1852 in Blooming Valley, PA. Pember m 5/19/1799 in Hamburg, CT, **Anne Lord**, b 5/22/1776, d 2/1844, d/o **Samuel** and **Elizabeth**. (*Pember Family*, p. 15)

WADHAMS

Luman - bc1781 in CT, d1832 in NY. Lyman m **Lucy Bostwick Prindle**. (War of 1812 Index)

WADSWORTH

Gen. Elijah - b 11/14/1747 in Hartford, CT, d 6/21/1832 in Canfield, OH. Gen. Elijah m 2/16/1780 **Rhoda Hopkins**, b 11/1/1759 in Litchfield, CT. (*Trumbull and Mahoning Cos., OH*, v. 2, p. 32 - *DAR Patriot Index*, p. 709)

Richard - b in CT, d 4/1/1861 prob. in Concord, Erie Co., NY. Richard m **Ann McLean**, d 10/15/1859. (*Hist. of Original Town of Concord, NY*, p. 529)

Timothy - b in CT, d 11/15/1847 in New Hartford, Oneida Co., NY. Timothy m **Lydia** ----, d 6/11/1848. (*History of Herkimer County, NY*, p. 125)

WAGE

Orvis - bc1797 in CT. Orvis m **Polly** ----, bc1797 in NY. They resided in New Berlin, Chenango Co., NY. In the 1850 census he was 53 (a miller) and she was 53 years old, with Hiram 24 years old (a shoemaker b in NY). (*1850 Census Chenango Co., NY*)

WAINWRIGHT

William - b 10/24/1779 in New Haven, CT, d1858 age 79 prob. in Salisbury, Addison Co., VT. He m ----. (*Gazetteer of Addison Co., VT*, p. 206)

WAIT

Norman - bc1766 in CT. Norman m ----. He resided in Warren, Washington Co., VT. In the 1850 census he was 84 years old, with Elizabeth 41, Nelson 2, and Elizabeth 8 years old, all b in VT. (*1850 Washington Co., VT, Census*)

WAKELEE

Arad - bc1790 in Waterbury, CT, s/o **David**; Arad d 6/6/1879 prob. in Springville, Susquehanna Co., PA. He m ----. (*History of Susquehanna Co., PA*, p. 402-3)

WAKELEY

Abel - bc1785 in CT. Abel m **Lucy** ----, bc1783 in CT. They resided in Sherburne, Chenango Co., NY. In the 1850 census he was 65 and she was 67 years old. (*1850 Census Chenango Co., NY*)

A b e l - b 10/7/1759 (or 10/7/1760) in Woodbury, CT, d 4/13/1850 in Greenville, Greene Co., NY. Abel m 3/15/1785 **Annis Hurd**. (*Hist. of Greene Co., NY*, p. 461 - *DAR Patriot Index*, p. 710)

WAKEMAN

Abijah - b1772 in CT, d1838 in MO. Abijah m **Mary Buckley**. (War of 1812 Index)

James - bc1791 in CT. James m **Sarah** ----, b1793 in Delaware Co., NY. They resided in Sidney, Delaware Co., NY. In the 1855 census he was 64 and she was 62 years old, with **James, Jr.** 27 and **Margaret** 28 years old. (*1855 Census Delaware Co., NY*)

WALBRIDGE

Gen. Ebenezer - b 1/1/1738 in Norwich, CT, d 10/3/1819 in Bennington, Bennington Co., VT. He m **Elizabeth Stebbins**. (*VT Hist. Mag.*, v. 1, p. 174-5)

Isaac - b 1/18/1745 in Preston (or Coventry), CT, s/o **John**; Isaac d 4/14/1822 age 76 in Royalton, Windsor Co., VT. He m (1) 5/22/1768 in Hanover, NH, **Hannah Smith**, b1747, d 7/20/1800 age 52 in Royalton, VT. (*Hist. of Royalton, VT*, p. 1005-6)

Roger - bc1787 in CT. Roger m **Polly** ----, bc1773 in CT. They resided in Sharon, Windsor Co., VT. In the 1850 census he was 63 and she was 77 years old, with **Polly Strong** 66 years old, b in CT. (*1850 Census of Windsor Co., VT*)

WALDO

Anson - b 6/12/1806 in Canterbury, CT, s/o **Zachariah** and **Joanna (Butterfield)**; Anson d 10/2/1882 in New Milford, Susquehanna Co., PA. He m 4/10/1845 in Harford, PA, **Jane Leach**, b 4/1/1826 in New Milford, PA, d/o **Samuel** and **Betsey (McFall)**. (*Hist. of Susquehanna Co., PA*, p. 625 - *Waldo Gen.*, v. 2, p. 571)

Jonathan - bc1738 in CT, d1821 in NY. Jonathan m **Ann Palmer**. (War of 1812 Index)

Zachariah - b 12/26/1764 in Pomfret, CT, s/o **Jonathan**; Zachariah d 8/3/1818 age 53 in Royalton, Windsor Co., VT. He m 2/4/1793 in Thompson, CT, **Abigail Corbin**, b 3/16/1774 in Woodstock, CT, d 12/26/1859 age 86 in Royalton, VT, d/o **Moses** and Sarah (Bacon). (*Hist. of Royalton, VT*, p. 1006-7)

WALES

Roger - bc1768 in CT, d1835 in NJ. Roger m **Harriet Bentley**. (War of 1812 Index)

WALKER

Rev. C h a r l e s - b 2/1/1791 in CT. Rev. Charles m 9/22/1823 **Lucretia Ambrose**, b 1/15/1799 in NH. They resided in Pittsford, Rutland Co., VT. In the 1850 census he was 59 and she was 51 years old, with Ann 23, George L. 20, Stephen 14, Henry 11 years old (all b in VT). (*1850 Rutland Co., VT, Census*). See Index: Hist. of Pittsford, VT.

Charles - bc1798 in CT. Charles m **Elizabeth** ----, bc1808 in NY. They resided in Oxford, Chenango Co., NY. In the 1850 census he was 52 (a shoemaker) and she was 42 years old, with Eliza 20, Abigail 16, Jane 11, and Charles B. 6 years old, all b in NY. (*1850 Census of Chenango Co., NY*)

Dyer - bc1789 in CT. Dyer m **Betsey** ----, d 1/7/1876 age 81-7. They resided in Chelsea, Orange Co., VT. In the 1850 census he was 61 and she was 56 years old, with Betsey 30, Olive 22, and Ezra 19 years old, all b in VT. (*1850 Orange Co., VT, Census*)

Freeman - b 12/12/1768 in Woodstock, CT, s/o **Phinehas** and **Susannah (Hyde)**; Freeman d 5/31/1825 age 55 in Strafford, Orange Co., VT. He m 6/14/1792 **Elizabeth Chandler**, b 8/29/1772, d 10/4/1864 age 92, d/o Capt. **Seth** and **Eunice (Durkee)**. In the 1850 census she ("Betsey") was 77 years old, b in CT. (*1850 Orange Co., VT, Census - Genealogy of Woodstock Fam.*, v. 8, p. 432 - *Chandler Family*, p. 521)

Hiram - bc1799 in CT. Hiram m **Lucy** ----, bc1800 in MA. They resided in Manchester, Bennington Co., VT. In the 1850 census he was 51 and she was 50 years old, with Samuel 17 and Harriet 14 years old, both b in VT. (*1850 Bennington Co., VT, Census*)

Horatio - bc1787 in CT. Horatio m **Rhoda** ----, bc1790 in VT. They resided in Manchester, Bennington Co., VT. In the 1850 census he was 63 and she was 60 years old, with Sarah 35 years old, b in VT. (*1850 Bennington Co., VT, Census*)

Leonard - b 10/5/1766 in Woodstock, CT, s/o **Phinehas**; Leonard d 9/9/1851 age 85 in Strafford, Orange Co., VT. He m 3/31/1790 **Chloe Child**, b 3/28/1767 in Woodstock, CT, d 9/1/1843, d/o **Elisha** and **Alice (Manning)**. (*Genealogy of Woodstock Families*, v. 8, p. 432-3)

Lewis - bc1755 in CT, d1826 in Brockton, NY. Lewis m **Sarah Gunn**, b1761, d1845. (*Soldiers of Am. Rev., Chautauqua Co., NY*, p. ?)

WALKLEY

Jonathan - bc1783 in CT, d1828 in OH. Jonathan m **Nancy Niles**. (War of 1812 Index)

WALLACE

Hiram - bc1796 in CT. Hiram m **Rhoda** ----, b in RI. They resided in Bennington, Bennington Co., VT. In the 1850 census he was 58 and she was 56 years old, with Rhoda 24, Mary L. 21, Helen M. 18, and William 12 years old, all children b in either CT or VT. (*1850 Bennington Co., VT, Census*)

WALBRIDGE

Eleazer - b 5/5/1779 in Stafford, CT, d 8/13/1849 in Randolph, Orange Co., VT. Eleazer m (1) 12/1/1808 in Royalton, VT, **Olive Billings**, b 2/24/1784 in Royalton, VT, d 10/4/1814 in Royalton, VT, d/o **John** and **Olive (Noble)**, and m (2) 10/25/1815 **Huldah Lillie** of Randolph, VT, d 8/12/1847. (*Walbridge Gen.*, p. 122)

Eleazer, Sr. - b1748 in Norwich, CT, s/o **Eleazer**; Eleazer, Sr. d 10/31/1815 in Randolph, Orange Co., VT. He m 8/25/1768 in Stafford, CT, **Abigail Washburne**. (*Wallbridge Gen.*, p. 119, 122, 83-4)

WALLER
Homer, Jr. - b1823 in New Milford, CT, s/o **Homer** and **Martha (Merwin)**. Homer, Jr. m 1/31/1850 **Elizabeth Fry**. They resided in Dutchess Co., NY. (*Comm. Biog. Rec., Dutchess Co., NY*, p. 245)
Nathan - bc1753 in CT, d1831 in PA. Nathan m **Elizabeth Weeks**. (War of 1812 Index)

WALLING
Samuel B. - b1799 in CT. Samuel B. m **Elsy ----**, b1798 in VT. They resided in Randolph, Orange Co., VT. In the 1850 census he was 51 and she was 52 years old, with Ransom 21, Lucinda 15, and Belana 12 years old, all b in VT. (*1850 Orange Co., VT, Census*)

WALSTON
William - bc1796 in CT. William m **Sophronia ----**, bc1803 in NY. They resided in Williston, Chittenden Co., VT. In the 1850 census he was 54 and she was 47 years old, with Russel L. 29 years old. (*1850 Census Chittenden Co., VT*)

WALTER
Augustus - b1790 in Hartford, CT. Augustus m **Abigail Porter**. They resided in Burke, Caledonia Co., VT. (*Gazetteer of Caledonia Co., VT*, p. 154-5)

WALWORTH
Benjamin - b 10/13/1792 in Bozrah, CT. Benjamin m1817 in Hoosick Falls, NY, **Charlotte Eddy**. They resided in Chautauqua Co., NY. (*Chautauqua Co., NY*, p. 638)

WANZER
Elihu - b in Fairfield, CT, d 4/21/1887 age 87 in Perinton Twp., Monroe Co., NY. Elihu m **Tamma Hobbie**, d 5/8/1885 age 75, d/o **C. K.** and **Clarina**. (*Tombstone Rec., Fairport Village Cem., NY*)

WARD
Austin - b1796 in Winchester, CT, d 9/30/1857 in Fitchville, OH. Austin m **Vetty Green**, b1800 in Greenwich, CT, d 5/30/1861 age 61, d/o **Ebenezer**. (*The Firelands Pioneer*, p. 83)
Bela - b 9/19/1770 in CT, s/o **James**; Bela d 4/24/1842 prob. in Middlefield, Herkimer Co., NY. He m 1/16/1798 **Abigail Wilcox**, d/o **John** and **Grace (Griswold)**. (*Hist. of Herkimer Co., NY*, p. 398 - *Ward Fam. Gen.*, p. 139, 218-19)
Rev. David - b 11/30/1761 in CT, s/o **Asael** and **Esther (Franklin)**; Rev. David d 12/17/1821 prob. in Wells, VT. He m (1) **Abigail Pray**, and m (2) 9/24/1817 **Mehitable Rider** (or **Wyman**). She m (2) 1824 **Benjamin Ryder**. (*History of Town of Wells, Vermont* by Wood, p. 82)

Ichabod – b 5 /1/1750 in Litchfield Co., CT, d 2/23/1824 prob. in New
Milford, Susquehanna Co., PA. Ichabod m (1) **Lydia Towner**, and m
(2) Mrs. **Mary Mitchell**. (*Hist. of Susquehanna, PA*, p. 152, 632)

Peter – b 12/28/1756 in Killingworth, CT, s/o **James**; Peter d
7/30/1841 in Fairfield, Herkimer Co., NY. He m **Sarah Hilliard**.
(*Hist. of Herkimer Co., NY*, p. 138, 398)

William – b in Litchfield Co., CT, s/o Deacon **Ichabod**; William d
10/1849 age 64 prob. in New Milford, PA. He m1806 **Sally Briggs**
of Roxbury, CT, d 8/1872 age 85. She m (2) **Joseph Williams**.
(*Hist. of Susquehanna Co., PA*, p. 632)

WARE

Joseph – bc1755 in Middletown, CT, d 2/17/1823 age 68 in Thetford,
Orange Co., VT. Joseph m **Dolly Davis**, bc1758, d 10/14/1840 age
82. (*Gazetteer of Orange Co., VT*, p. 434-5)

WARNER

Alexander – bc1778 in CT, d1862 in NY. Alexander m **Loretta Conklin**. (War of 1812 Index)

Asher – bc1777 in CT, d1813 in NY. Asher m **Susan Courtright**.
(War of 1812 Index)

Eliphaz – b1776, d1816 age 73 in Sandgate, Bennington Co., VT.
Eliphaz m **Mercy Drinkwater**, d1813 age 67. (*The Story of
Sandgate, VT*, by Renner, p. 19)

John – b 5/29/1745 in Roxbury, CT, s/o **Benjamin**; d1819 John in St.
Albans, Franklin Co., VT. He m (1) ---- **Hurlburt**, d1773, and m
(2) **Joanna Ames**, d 2/10/1837. (*Des. of John Warner*, p. 31)

Jonathan, Jr. – b 8/27/1778 in CT, s/o **Jonathan**; Jonathan, Jr. d
5/18/1854 (?) in Pittsford, Rutland Co., VT. He m1801 **Anna
Ripley**, d/o **Phineas** and **Experience (Montague)**, b 12/11/1781 in
VT, d 3/27/1859. In the 1850 census he was 71 and she was 67
years old. (*Histpry of Pittsford, VT*, p. ? – *1850 Rutland Co., VT,
Census*)

Nathaniel – b 7/4/1767 in E. Haddam, CT, d 7/28/1843 in Cambridge,
Chautauqua Co., NY. Nathaniel m 7/4/1790 **Lucinda Avery**, b
11/1771 in Stonington, CT. (*Soldiers of American Rev., Chautauqua
Co., NY*, p. ?)

Col. Seth – b 5/17/1743 in Roxbury, CT, s/o **Benjamin** and **Silence
(Hurd)**; Col. Seth d 12/26/1784 in 42nd year. He m (1) **Alma
Hendee**, d soon after marriage, and m (2) 1765 **Hester Hurd** of
Roxbury, CT. (*Story of Sandgate, VT*, p. 19 – *VT Hist. Mag.*, v. 1,
p. 175-6 – *Warner Gen.*, p. 30b, 60)

WARREN

Calvin – b 2/2/1770 in Ashford, CT, s/o **John** and **Elizabeth**; Calvin
d1827 in Stockton, NY. He m ----. (*Chautauqua Co., NY*, p. 570)

Chauncey – b 4/22/1802 in CT, s/o **Calvin**. Chauncey m 4/9/1823 in
Ashford, CT, **Sally Knowlton** of CT. They resided in Chautauqua
Co., NY. (*Chautauqua Co., NY*, p. 570-1)

Moses – bc1774 in CT. Moses m **Lovina** ----, bc1778 in CT. They
resided in Oxford, Chenango Co., NY. In the 1850 census he was 76

(a farmer) and she was 72 years old, with Moses 50 (b in CT) and
Joseph M. 33 years old (b in NY). (*1850 Census Chenango Co., NY*)

WASHBURN

Amasa - bc1768 in CT. Amasa m **Jerusha** ----, bc1766 in VT. They
resided in Putney, Windham Co., VT. In the 1850 census he was
82 and she was 84 years old, with Minerva 55 years old (b in VT).
(*1850 Census Windham Co., VT*)

Philip - bc1772 in CT, d1828 in NY. Philip m **Elizabeth Davenport**.
(War of 1812 Index)

Roger - bc1792 in CT, d1866 in NY. Roger m **Elizabeth Ross**. (War
of 1812 Index)

Rufus - bc1766 in CT, d1817 in NY. Rufus m **Patience Washburn**.
(War of 1812 Index)

WATERMAN

Hon. **Arunah** - b 11/8/1778 in Norwich, CT, s/o **Arunah** and **Hannah**
(**Leffingwell**); Hon. Arunah d 1/31/1859 prob. in Montpelier,
Washington Co., VT. He m (1) 1804 **Rebecca Noyes**, d1812, d/o
Hon. **David**, and m (2) **Mehitable Dodge**. (*Washington Co., VT,
Gazetteer*, p. 372)

Arunah - b 4/24/1749 in Norwich, CT, d 8/27/1838 in 90th year in
Johnson, Lamoille Co., VT. Arunah m **Hannah Leffingwell**.
(*Lamoille Co., VT, Gazetteer*, p. 111)

Dexter - bc1774 in CT. Dexter m **Betsey** ----, bc1774 in CT. They
resided in Royalton, Windsor Co., VT. In the 1850 census they
were both 76 years old. (*1850 Census of Windsor Co., VT*)

Dyer - b 11/10/1770 in Norwich, CT, s/o **John** and **Mary**; Dyer d
3/23/1857 age 87 in Orange, Orange Co., VT. He m **Lany Bell**, b
6/2/1777 in Herkimer NY, d 12/8/1856 age 79. In the 1850 census
he was 79. (*Waterman Genealogy*, v. 1, p. 525-6 - *1850 Orange
Co., VT, Census*)

Ebenezer - b 6/5/1798 in CT. Ebenezer m 12/28/1843 **Polly A.
Fuller**. They resided in Roxbury, Washington Co., VT.
(*Washington Co., VT, Gazetteer*, p. 459)

Joseph - b 5/1753 in Norwich, CT, d 1/9/1834 in Brookfield, Madison
Co., NY. Joseph m 7/13/1780 in Lebanon, CT, **Rebecca Blackman**.
(*For King and Country, Orange Co., CA*, p. 269)

Zebina - bc1794, s/o **Gideon** and Sally (**Lee**); Zebina d 5/4/1872 age
78 at Royalton, VT. He m 1/1/1818 in Tunbridge, VT, **Asenath
Robinson**, b 9/4/1798 in Epsom, NH, d 6/6/1859 age 62-9-2, d/o
John and **Sarah**. In the 1850 census he was 55 (a carpenter) and she
was 53 years old, with Salina 10 years old, b in VT. (*Waterman
Gen.*, v. 3, p. 178 - *1850 Orange Co., VT, Census*)

WATERS

Amos - b in CT, d 1/1884 in Milford, NY. Amos m **Relief Clark**, d/o
John and **Relief**. (*Biog. Rev., Otsego Co., NY*, p. 138)

WATKINS

Hezekiah - b1790 in Haddam, CT, (or nearby), s/o **Robert**; Hezekiah d
12/1/1872 (or 12/1/1892) in Oneonta, NY. He m 1/25/1816 **Hannah**

Scoville, b1789 in CT, d 3/9/1861. (*Biographical Rev., Otsego Co., NY*, p. 111)

Rev. **Holden A.** - bc1799 in CT. Rev. Holden A. m **Louisa ----**, bc1798 in VT. They resided in Rupert, Bennington Co., VT. In the 1850 census he was 51 (a Congregational Minister) and she was 52 years old, with Chauncey L. 22 (b in VT) and Lucia 14 years old (b in VT). (*1850 Bennington Co., VT, Census*)

WATROUS

Benjamin - b1772 in Chester, CT, d1820 prob. in Brooklyn, Susquehanna Co., PA. Benjamin m1791 **Lucy Spencer**, b1770 in Chester, CT, d1839. (*Hist. of Susquehanna Co., PA*, p. 349)

Joseph - b1794 in Chester, CT, s/o **Benjamin** and **Lucy (Spencer)**; d1875 in Brooklyn, Susquehanna Co., PA. Joseph m (1) 1816 **Dolly Benjamin**, and m (2) 1836 **Lucinda Wilson**, and m (3) **Ann Wilson**. (*Hist of Susquehanna Co., PA*, p. 667)

WATSON

Cyprian - b 6/1/1737 in Canaan, CT, d 9/11/1807 prob. in Stillwater, Saratoga Co., NY. Cyprian m **Dorothy Benton**. (*History of Saratoga Co., NY*, p. 290)

Ebenezer - b1777 in CT, d in NY. Ebenezer m **Hannah Sedgwick**. (War of 1812 Index)

WATTS

David - bc1787 in CT. David m **Beulah ----**, bc1790. They resided in Waterbury, Washington Co., VT. In the 1850 census he was 63 and she was 60 years old, with Alfred 18 (b in VT) and Zenas 22 years old (b in VT). (*1850 Census of Washington Co., VT*)

WAUGH

Alexander - b1729 in Litchfield, CT, d1800 in Hamilton, NY. Alexander m 2/12/1766 in Litchfield, CT, **Elizabeth Throop**. (*Pioneer Hist. of Camden, NY*, p. 502 - *DAR Patriot Index*, p. 722)

Gideon - b1797 in Litchfield, CT, d1869 in Huron Co., OH. Gideon m (1) 1818 in Oswego, NY, ----, d1834 in OH, and m (2) 1835 **Mindwell Shepard** of Brownhelm, OH. (*Res. of CT Who Migrated to Huron Co., OH*, p. 7)

WAY

Daniel - b1744 in Lyme, CT, s/o **Thomas**. Daniel m **Ruth Moor**. They resided in Burke, Caledonia Co., VT. (*Gazetteer of Caledonia Co., VT*, p. 169)

Samuel - b 5/16/1763 in Colchester, CT, d 8/14/1843 in Perrysburg, OH. Samuel m **Sarah ----**, b 1/11/1769 in Colchester, CT, d 3/16/1842 in Finley, OH. (Tombstone Record, Brockport Cemetery - *Hist. of Monroe Co., NY*, p. 155-6)

WEAVER

Davis - bc1791 in CT. Davis m **Betsey ----**, bc1794 in CT. They resided in Pitcher, Chenango Co., NY. In the 1850 census he was

59 (an innkeeper) and she was 56 years old, with Henry 33 (b in NY) and Maria 36 years old (b in NY). (*1850 Census Chenango Co., NY*)

Joshua - b 3/3/1753 in Stonington, CT, d 6/4/1811 age 58 poss. in Pharsalia, Chenango Co., NY. Joshua m **Anna Davis**, d 8/12/1819 age 69. (*Hist. of Chenango Co., NY*, p. 423 - French's *Gazetteer of NY*, p. 329 - *DAR Patriot Index*, p. 723)

Lodowick - b 5/18/1763 in Stonington, CT, d 1/31/1848 age 84 in Groton, NY. Lodowich m 9/4/1787 **Patty Brown**, d 2/29/1852 age 82 in Groton, NY, d/o **Nehemiah** and **Rebecca**. (*Hist. of Chenango Co., NY*, p. 423 - French's *Gazetteer of New York*, p. 229)

Russell - bc1795 in CT. Russell m **Sally ----**, bc1800 in VT. They resided in Pitcher, Chenango Co., NY. In the 1850 census he was 55 and she was 50 years old, with Maryett 19 years old, b in NY. (*1850 Census of Chenango Co., NY*)

WEBB

Major **Adin** - b 3/1/1780 in Scotland, CT, s/o **Christopher**. Major Adin m 10/15/1800 **Deborah Carter**. They resided in Homer, Cortland Co., NY. (*Pioneer Hist. of Cortland Co., NY*, p. 368-9)

Calvin - b 7/31/1757 in Windham, CT, s/o **Joshua** and **Hannah (Abbe)**; Calvin d 11/15/1853 in Rockingham, VT. He m (1) **Mary Porter**, d 11/8/1806, and m (2) 5/4/1815 **Mehitable Cross**. (*Vermont Hist. Mag.*, v. 5, p. 504)

Curtis - b1793 in CT, d1876 in NY. Curtis m **Margaret Hitchcock**. (War of 1812 Index)

David - bc1795 in CT. David m **Lovina ----**, bc1795 in NY. They resided in New Berlin, Chenango Co., NY. In the 1850 census he was 55 and she was 55 years old, with Sarah M. 29, Julia F. 25, David 23, and Lovina 19 years old, all b in NY. (*1850 Census of Chenango Co., NY*)

Ebenezer, Jr. - b 5/29/1757 in CT, d 8/14/1846 in Brainerdsville, Franklin Co., NY. Ebenezer, Jr. m **Abigail Rood**. (*DAR Magazine* 1977, p. 923 - *DAR Patriot Index*, p. 723)

James - b1788 in CT, d1877 in NY. James m **Abigail White**. (War of 1812 Index)

Jonathan - bc1785 in CT, d1867 in NY. Jonathan m **Rebecca Cole**. (War of 1812 Index)

Joshua - b 2/19/1722 in Windham, CT, s/o **Samuel** and **Hannah (Bradford) (Ripley)**; Joshua d 4/17/1808 age 86 in Rockingham, Windham Co., VT. He m 5/28/1744 **Hannah Abbe**, b 9/17/1724, d 2/12/1815 age 90. (*VT Hist. Mag.*, v. 5, p. 504 - *Hist. of Rockingham, VT*, p. 774 - *Windham Co., VT, Gazetteer*, p. 300)

Reuben - b in Norwich, CT, d age 86 in Stockholm, NY. Reuben had four wives, one was **Taphner Peters**. In the 1850 census he was 70 years old (a blacksmith), with Melina 50 years old, b in VT. (*1850 Rutland Co., VT, Census - Hist. of Rutland, VT*, p. 628-9)

Thomas Denny - b 5/10/1784 in Windham, CT, s/o **Peter** and **Tamasin (Dewey)**; d 3/7/1865 in 81st year in OH. Thomas Denny m 1/13/1813 in Warren, OH, **Betsey Stanton**. (*Trumbull and Mahoning Cos., OH*, p. 181-2)

Thomas - bc1784 in CT, d1840 in IL. Thomas m **Rebecca Clark**. (War of 1812 Index)

WEBSTER

Abijah - b1762 in Glastonbury, CT, s/o **Ashbel** and **Rachel (Price)**; Abijah 9/8/1832 in Casenovia, Madison Co., NY. He m (1) ----- **Webster**, and m (2) **Sarah Warren**, and m (3) **Olive Kingsley Ward**. (*DSGR*, v. 38 #4, p. 224 - *DAR Patriot Index*, p. 724)

Benoni - bc1763 in CT, d 1/8/1823 age 60 prob. in Roxbury, Washington Co., VT. Benoni m **Sally Metcalf**, bc1772, d1838 age 66. (*Washington Co., VT, Gazetteer*, p. 451)

Elijah - bc1772 in CT, d 7/8/1839 age 67 in Henrietta Twp., Monroe Co., NY. Elijah m -----. (Tombstone Record - *History of Monroe Co., NY*, p. 298)

Elisha - b in CT, (Vernon or N. Bolton), s/o **Ezekiel** and **Chloe (Elsworth)**; Elisha d in Pomfret, NY, buried in Webster Cem., Pomfret, NY. He m **Catherine Butler**. (*Soldiers of Am. Rev., Chautauqua Co., NY*, p. 22)

Elizur - b 8/24/1767 in CT, d 3/1854. Elizur m **Elizabeth Warren**, d1848 age 74 in Ripley, NY. (*Chautauqua Co., NY*, p. 530)

Laban - b 6/7/1767 in Lebanon, CT, s/o **Jonathan** and **Ruth (Holdridge)**. Laban m **Lucy Wright**, bc1766 (or bc1767) in CT. They resided in Hartland, Windsor Co., VT. In the 1850 census he was 83 and she was 84 years old, with Benjamin F. 40 and Theoda 35 years old (his wife, b in VT). (*Webster Gen.*, p. 275-6, 570-7 - *1850 Windsor Co., VT, Census*)

Miner - bc1776 in CT, d1820 in NY. Miner m **Lydia Savage**. (War of 1812 Index)

Simeon - bc1793 in CT. Simeon m **Sibel** ----, bc1797 in CT. They resided in Pitcher, Chenango Co., NY. In the 1850 census he was 57 and she was 53 years old, with Philura 25 (b in NY) and Daniel 9 years old (b in NY). (*1850 Census Chenango Co., NY*)

WEEKS

John M. - b 5/22/1788 in Litchfield, CT, s/o **Holland**; d 8/1858 in Salisbury, Addison Co., VT. John M. m (1) **Harriet Prindle** of Charlotte, VT, d1853, and m (2) Mrs. **Emily Davenport** of Middlebury, VT. (*Gazetteer of Addison Co., VT*, p. 206 - *Hist. of Salisbury, VT*, p. 352)

Jonathan - b 12/8/1705 in Fairfield, CT, d 11/21/1781 in Hanover Twp., PA. Jonathan m **Abigail** ----. (*Hist. of Hanover Twp. of Wyoming Valley, PA*, p. 484-5)

WELCH

Daniel - bc1791 in CT. Daniel m **Lucy** ----, bc1805 in Chenango Co., NY. They resided in Masonville, Delaware Co., NY. In the 1855 census he was 59 and she was 50 years old, with Mary 20 (b in NY), Abner 16 (b in NY), and Lucy 9 years old (b in Broome Co., NY). (*1855 Census Delaware Co., NY*)

John - bc1745 in CT, d1831 in OH. John m **Deborah Moore**. (War of 1812 Index)

WELD

Thomas - bc1771 in CT, d 11/18/1852 in Ridgeway, Orleans Co., NY. Thomas m **Lorana Lewis**, d1820. (*Pioneer History of Orleans Co., NY*, p. 341)

WELLMAN

Barnabas - b 8/15/1756 in CT, d 3/7/1847 in Chautauqua Co., NY. Barnabas m **Lois Page**. (*Chautauqua Co., NY*, p. 230 - *DAR Patriot Index*, p. 727)

WELLS

Alfred - b 10/3/1779 in Colchester, CT, s/o **Amos** and **Lydia**; Alfred d 4/18/1866 in Whitestown, NY. He m **Abigail Lee**, d 1/10/1861 age 79-5-4. (*Welles-Wells Families of Early Oneida Co., NY* by Coleman, p. ?)

Asa - b 8/6/1774 in Colchester, CT, s/o **Levi** and **Jerusha** (**Clark**); Asa d 2/1859 age 79 in Pompey, Onondaga Co., NY. He m **Chloe Hyde Wells**, d 1/1872 age 92. (*Pompey, NY*, p. 390-1)

David - bc1761 in CT, d 8/13/1840 age 79 in Strafford, Orange Co., VT. David m (1) **Mary** ----, bc1762, d 6/27/1825 in 63rd year, and m (2) **Sarah** ----, bc1775, d 9/29/1859 age 84. (Strafford, VT, Cemetery, Kibling, gravestones)

Elijah - b 2/27/1775 in Wethersfield, CT, d 1830 (in the Fall) in Pompey, Onondaga Co., NY. Elijah m 1/16/1800 **Lucy Sellew** of Glastonbury, CT, d1857. (*Pompey, NY*, p. 363-4)

Elisha - bc1793 in CT, d1872 in NY. Elisha m **Anna Gardner**. (War of 1812 Index)

George W. - bc1802 in CT. George W. m **Anna L.** ----, bc1805 in CT. They resided in Meredith, Delaware Co., NY. In the 1855 census he was 53 and she was 50 years old, with Jane 22, George H. 19, and Martin C. 8 years old, all b in Delaware Co., NY. (*1855 Census Delaware Co., NY*)

Joel - bc1791 in CT, d1831 in OH. Joel m **Mila Ingham**. (War of 1812 Index)

Josiah D. - bc1777 in CT. Josiah D. m ----. They resided in Meredith, Delaware Co., NY. In the 1855 census he was 78 years old (a widower), with **Josiah, Jr.** 34, **Miranda** 29 (w/o Josiah, Jr.), **Helen M.** 5, **Albert D.** 2 (all b in Delaware Co., NY), **Abigail Dutton** 50 (m/o Miranda, b in MA) and **Helen Dutton** (sis/o Miranda, b in Delaware Co., NY). (*1855 Census Delaware Co., NY*)

WELTON

Philo - bc1782 in CT, d1852 in OH. Philo m **Sina Blakeslee**. (War of 1812 Index)

WEST

Charles W. - bc1792 in CT. Charles W. m **Betsey** ----, bc1793 in CT. They resided in Columbus, Chenango Co., NY. In the 1850 census he was 58 and she was 57 years old. (*1850 Census of Chenango Co., NY*)

Jonathan - b 5/31/1761 in Lebanon, CT, s/o **Joshua** and **Elizabeth** (**Williams**). Jonathan m 5/26/1785 **Parthena Clark** in Lebanon,

259

CT. They resided in Forest Lake, Susquehanna Co., PA. (*History of Susquehanna Co., PA*, p. 481)

WESTON

William Williston - bc1791 in CT, s/o **Amaziah** and **Mary (Cady)**; William Williston d1853 poss. in Brooklyn, Susquehanna Co., PA. He m (1) 1819 **Eliza Cone**, b1802, d1836, d/o **Daniel** of Middletown, CT, and m (2) **Lovina Smith**, d/o **Latham**. (*Hist. of Susquehanna Co., PA*, p. 650)

WETMORE

Nathaniel - bc1779 in CT, d 3/6/1831 age 52 in Camden, Oneida Co., NY. Nathaniel m **A b i a h** ----, bc1782, d 2/11/1844 age 62. (*Pioneer Hist. of Camden, NY*, p. 174)

Seth - bc1761 in CT, d1836 in NY. Seth m **Lois Bronson**. (War of 1812 Index)

WHALEY

Dr. Christopher - b 6/16/1798 in Montville, CT, d 10/26/1867 in Medina, NY. Dr. Christopher m (1) 3/20/1824 **Mary Ann Coffin**, and m (2) **Sophronia Martin**, and m (3) **Carrie E. Perry**. (*Pioneer Hist. of Orleans Co., NY*, p. 348)

Theophilus - bc1759 in CT, d 9/6/1827 age 68 prob. in Camden, Oneida Co., NY. Theophilus m **Mary Burdick** of Litchfield, CT, d1842 age 74. (*Pioneer Hist. of Camden, NY*, p. 211-12 - *DAR Patriot Index*, p. 732)

WHEAT

Solomon - bc1804 in CT. Solomon m **Ruth M.** ----, bc1810 in Otsego Co., NY. They resided in Sidney, Delaware Co., NY. In the 1855 census he was 51 and she was 45 years old, with Edwin R. 23, Oscar 22, Leonoly 20, Adelia 17, Almeron 14, Eliza 11, and George A. 9 years old, all b in Delaware Co., NY. (*1855 Census Delaware Co., New York*)

WHEATON

Isaac - b 8/17/1770 in Branford, CT, d 11/25/1851 age 81 in Pittsford, VT, buried in Old Cong. Cemetery there. Isaac m 12/6/1797 **Irena Dike**, b 6/25/1779 in Coventry, CT, d 7/5/1855 age 76, buried in Old Cong. Cem, Pittsford, VT. In the 1850 census he was 80 (a farmer) and she was 71 years old. (Gravestones in Pittsford Cem., VT - *Hist. of Pittsford, VT*, p. ? - *1850 Rutland Co., VT, Census*)

Nathan Phillips - b 11/17/1810 in Washington, CT, s/o **Caleb** and **Julia (Phillips)**. Nathan Phillips m1838 **Mary Watson**, b 9/8/1814, d/o **James** and **Sarah (Lounsbury)**. They resided in Franklin, Susquehanna Co., PA. (*Hist. of Susquehanna Co., PA*, p. 522)

Rufus - bc1759 in CT, s/o **James**; d 4/5/1840 (gravestone: 12/6/1842, age 83). Rufus m (1) **Anna Norton**, d 2/9/1832 and m (2) ---- **Gatt**, widow, from Rutland, VT. (Gravestones in Old Cemetery, Pittsford, Vermont - *Hist. of Pittsford, VT*, p. 385-6)

WHEELER

Alvin - bc1790 in CT, d1886 in Indiana. Alvin m **Sara Willa**. (War of 1812 Index)

Cornelius - b in CT, d1814 in Canada. Cornelius m **Abigail Oliver**. (War of 1812 Index)

Ebenezer - bc1770 in CT, d1814 in NY. Ebenezer m **Harriet B. Foster**. (War of 1812 Index)

Capt. Edward - b 3/11/1753 in Preston, CT, d 8/22/1839 age 86-5-11 poss. in Fleming, Cayuga Co., NY. Capt. Edward m **Mary Buck** of Lanesboro, MA, b1755, d 10/20/1830 age 75-6-18. (*The Township of Fleming, Cayuga Co., NY*, p. 6, 95-6)

Eli - bc1770 in CT, d1847 in NY. Eli m **Crisel Wheeler**. (War of 1812 Index)

Elias - bc1771 in CT (poss. 1/1/1772 in Stonington, CT). Elias m **Lucinda** ----, bc1775 in CT. They resided in Windsor, Windsor Co., VT. In the 1850 census he was 79 and she was 75 years old, with Cyrus 52 (b in NH) and Lydia 32 years old (b in VT). (*1850 Census of Windsor Co., VT*)

Jedediah - b in CT, d 10/16/1863 prob. in Halifax, Windham Co., VT, (or Milton, Chittenden Co., VT). Jedediah m **Amanda Hickok**. (*Chittenden Co., VT, Gazetteer*)

Jesse - b 9/2/1792 poss. in Stonington, CT, s/o **Nathaniel** and **Prudence (Breed)**; Jesse d 4/1869 age 77 prob. in Halifax, Windham Co., VT. He m1815 **Prudence Greene**. (*Gazetteer of Windham Co., VT*, p. 222)

Joseph - b 5/27/1738 in Fairfield, CT, s/o **Joseph** and **Abigail (Perry)**; Joseph d in western NY, where he went after his wife died. He m **Frances Hill**, d 7/30/1805 age 68 poss. in Fairfield, VT, d/o **William** and **Abigail (Barlow)**. (*Some Early Records of Fairfield, VT*, p. 5-6)

Josiah - b1750 in Plainfield, CT, s/o **Isaac** and **Hannah (Stearns)**; Josiah d 4/11/1827 in Barnston, Canada. He m (1) **Elizabeth** ----, and m (2) **Hannah Howe**, b1756, d 9/6/1846 in Barnston, Canada, d/o **Jonas** and **Sarah (Wheeler)**. (*Hist. of Royalton, VT*, p. 1023-4 - *Royalton, VT*, p. 248)

Nicholas - bc1783 in CT, d1848 in Otsego Co., NY. Nicholas m1813 **Patty Bunn**, b1793 in Hardwick, NY, d1859 age 65. (*Biog. Rev. of Otsego Co., NY*, p. 557)

Shepard, III - b 3/11/1781 in CT, s/o **Shepard** and **Lucy (Wheeler)**; Shepard, III d1846 in MI. He m **Phoebe Jordan**. (*History of Stonington, CT*, p. 644 - War of 1812 Index)

Thomas J. - b 11/16/1803 in Plainfield, CT, s/o **Hezekiah** and **Abigail (Wheeler)**. Thomas J. m (1) 5/10/1827 **Isabella Glashan**, b1810 in York, NY, d 3/23/1832 and m (2) 10/15/1834 **Christiana D. Gardner**, b 3/9/1807 in Woodstock, VT, d 1/17/1848, and m (3) 12/28/1853 **Hannah Johnson**, b 3/14/1819 in Livonia, NY. They resided in Chautauqua Co., NY. (*Chautauqua Co., NY*, p. 647-8)

Warren - bc1786 in CT. Warren m **Susanna** ----, bc1784 in VT. They resided in Jamaica, Windham Co., VT. In the 1850 census he was 64 and she was 66 years old. (*1850 Census Windham Co., VT*)

WHITE

Hugh – b 2/15/1733 in Middletown, CT, s/o **Hugh** and **Mary**; Hugh d 4/17/1812 age 79 poss. in Whitesboro, Oneida Co., NY. He m (1) 8/23/1753 in Middletown, CT, **Mary Clark**, and m (2) **Lois Davenport**. (*Oneida-Our Country and Its People*, p. 616-17 – *DAR Patriot Index*, p. 736 – *Hist. of the Mohawk Valley*, v. II, p. 1176)

James – bc1754 in CT, d 12/18/1830 in 77th year in Thetford, VT. James m **Eunice ----**, bc1759, d 12/24/1819 age 60 in Thetford, VT. (Cem. gravestones, E. Thetford, VT Cem.)

Joel – b in CT, d1872 in OH. Joel m **Phoebe Blakesly**. (*Hist. of Orig. Town of Concord, NY*, p. 516)

Oliver – b 7/25/1764 in Canaan, CT, d1853 age 89 in Starksboro, Addison Co., VT. Oliver m **----**. (*Gazetteer of Addison County, Vermont*, p. 222)

WHITELEY

Gurdon – b1790 in Lebanon, CT, d 12/24/1864 in Preston, NY. Gurdon m **----** (perhaps unmarried). In the 1850 census he was 59 years old living with **Clark** 59 and **Sophia Hough** 53 years old (both b in CT). (*1850 Census Chenango Co., NY*)

WHITING

Elisha – bc1785 in CT, d1848 in IA. Elisha m **Sally Hulet**. (War of 1812 Index)

John – bc1773 in CT. John m **Lydia ----**, bc1777 in CT. They resided in Bennington, Bennington Co., VT. In the 1850 census he was 77 and she was 73 years old. (*1850 Bennington County, Vermont, Census*)

Samuel – bc1783 in CT, d1851 in NY. Samuel m **Zilpha Mather**. (War of 1812 Index)

William – bc1730 in CT, d1792 in MA. William m **Anna Mason**. (War of 1812 Index)

WHITLOCK

Hezekiah – b 5/30/1770 in CT, d 12/31/1855 age 85 in Fair Haven, VT. Hezekiah m 1/8/1797 **Naomi Taylor**, b 2/3/1774. (*Hist. of Fair Haven, VT*, p. ?)

John Burr – bc1786 in CT, d1863 in NY. John Burr m **Rachel Olmstead**. (War of 1812 Index)

Peter – bc1785 in CT. Peter m **Sarah ----**, bc1793 in CT. They resided in Meredith, Delaware Co., NY. In the 1855 census he was 70 and she was 62 years old (b in Dutchess Co., NY), with Ann M. 35 years old (b Delaware Co., NY). (*1855 Census Delaware Co., NY*)

Samuel – bc1779 in CT. Samuel m **Charity ----**, bc1790 in VT. They resided in Castleton, Rutland Co., VT. In the 1850 census he was 71 and she was 60 years old, with Laura 24 years old (b in VT). (*1850 Rutland Co., VT, Census*)

Salmon – bc1781 in CT. Salmon m **Nabby ----**, bc1784 in CT. They resided in Hubbardton, Rutland Co., VT. In the 1850 census he was 69 and she was 66 years old, with Oren 34, Ansel 29, Russel 12, and Allen 4 years old, all b in VT. (*1850 Rutland Co., VT, Census*)

Zachariah - bc1770 in CT. Zachariah m **Naomi** ----, bc1774 in CT. They resided in Fairhaven, Rutland Co., VT. In the 1850 census he was 80 and she was 76 years old, with Edward 8 years old. (*1850 Rutland Co., VT, Census*)

WHITMORE

Capt. Francis - bc1720 in Middletown, CT, d 5/31/1790 age about 70. Capt. Francis m **Elizabeth** ----, bc1727, d 5/24/1814 age 87. She m (2) **Isaac Pratt**. They resided in Marlborough, Windham Co., VT. (*DAR Patriot Index*, p. 739)

Luther - bc1792 in CT. Luther m **Elsa** ----, bc1802 in NY. They resided in Columbus, Chenango Co., NY. In the 1850 census he was 58 (a merchant) and she was 48 years old, with Samuel 26, Ann F. 22, Augustus C. 21, John L. 19, George 16, Henry 14, Lee 10, and Allie (female) 7 years old, all b in NY. (*1850 Census Chenango Co., New York*)

Samuel - bc1769 in CT. Samuel m **Anna** ----, bc1768 in CT. They resided in Columbus, Chenango Co., NY. In the 1850 census he was 81 and she was 82 years old, with **Drake** 81 and **Abigail Miller** 79 years old, both b in NY. (*1850 Census Chenango Co., NY*)

WHITNEY

Noah Ashley - bc1770 in CT, d1834 in OH. Noah Ashley m **Olive Dorwin**. (War of 1812 Index)

Peter - b 4/10/1738 in Willington, CT, s/o **Josiah**; Peter d 6/19/1826 in Tunbridge, VT. He m 4/21/1763 in Tolland, CT, **Mercy Case**, b 8/15/1745. (*Whitney Gen.*, p. 205-7)

Samuel Platte - bc1775 in CT, d1871 in OH. Samuel Platte m Lois Buttles. (War of 1812 Index)

WHITON

Joseph - bc1760 in CT, d1828 in MA. Joseph m **Amanda Garfield**. (War of 1812 Index)

WHITTLESEY

Elisha - b 10/19/1783 in Washington, CT, s/o **Molly** and **John**; Elisha d 1/7/1863 poss. in Canfield, OH. He m 1/5/1806 in Danbury, CT, **Polly Mygatt**, d/o **Comfort**. (*Trumbull and Mahoning Cos., OH*, p. ?)

WICKHAM

P. D. - bc1797 in CT. P. D. m **Elizabeth** ----, bc1810 in CT. They resided in Manchester, Bennington Co., VT. In the 1850 census he was 53 (a teacher) and she was 40 years old, with Emma 17 years old, b in NY. (*1850 Bennington Co., VT, Census*)

Robert - bc1798 in CT. Robert m **Louisa** ----, bc1804 in CT. They resided in Pawlet, Rutland Co., VT. In the 1850 census he was 52 and she was 46 years old. (*1850 Rutland Co., VT, Census*)

WIGHT

Simeon - b 2/24/1774 in Woodstock, CT, s/o Dr. **Simeon** and **Margaret (Smith)**; Simeon d 5/26/1840 in Williamstown, Orange Co.,

VT. He m 4/29/1798 **Esther Smith**, b 8/10/1775 in Woodstock, CT, d 1/8/1829 in Williamstown, VT, d/o **Ebenezer** and **Margaret (Bowen)**. (*Woodstock Familes* by Bowen, p. 313)

WILBUR

John – bc1794 in CT. John m **Abigail** ----, bc1801 in RI. They resided in Oxford, Chenango Co., NY. In the 1850 census he was 56 (a laborer) and she was 49 years old, with Sarah 18 years old, b in NY. (*1850 Census Chenango Co., NY*)

Rev. **William N.** – b 11/28/1825 in Griswold, CT, d in Rockingham, VT. Rev. William N. m (1) 11/26/1856 **Huldah J. Richards**, b in Preston, CT, d 9/1867, and m (2) 10/13/1868 **Harriet Richards**, b in Preston, CT. (*Hist. of Rockingham, VT*, p. ?)

WILCOX

Darius William – bc1832 in Ashford, CT, s/o **Darius** and **Sophronia**. Darius (the younger) m 10/25/1853 in Honesdale, PA, **Julia Ann Ron** (?), bc1833, d/o **John** and **Rebecca**. They resided in Honesdale, Wayne Co., PA. (Misc. Collection of Marriage Records in Honesdale, PA)

D a v i d – b 5/1783 in Suffield, CT, d 1/1855 in Thetford, Orange Co., VT, buried in Post Mills Cem., Thetford, VT. David m **L u c i n d a Hosford**, b1786, d1853 in Post Mills, Thetford, VT. (*Gazetteer of Orange Co., VT*, p. 437 – Cem. at Thetford, VT)

D a v i d – b 10/30/1773 in Chatham, CT, d 7/12/1841 in Otsego Co., NY. David m 11/4/1793 **Polly Chappell**, b 4/4/1775, d 2/21/1853. (*Biog. Rec. of Otsego Co., NY*, p. 213)

Ezra Erin – bc1789 in CT, d1872 in NY. Ezra Erin m **Sarah Davis**. (War of 1812 Index)

Horace – bc1794 in CT. Horace m **Sophia Lombard**, bc1796 in VT. They resided in Pawlet, Rutland Co., VT. In the 1850 census he was 56 and she was 54 years old, with Francis 24, Julia 20, Helen 17, and Edward 14 years old, all b in VT. (*1850 Rutland Co., VT, Census*)

Dr. **Jeremiah C.** – b 12/6/1790 in Hartland, CT, d1873 prob. in Hudson, OH. Dr. Jeremiah C. m1839 Mrs. **Julia Wilder Pittee**. (*Reminiscences of Hudson, OH*, p. 50)

John Flavel – b1775 in CT, d1860 in OH. John Flavel m **Johannah** ----. (War of 1812 Index)

L e m u e l – b1758 in CT, d 4/1839 in Ballston, Saratoga Co., NY. Lemuel m ----. (*DAR Mag.* 1977, p. 923)

Nathan – bc1777 in CT. Nathan m **Nancy** ----, b1795 in CT. They resided in Pownal, Bennington Co., VT. In the 1850 census he was 73 and she was 55 years old. (*1850 Bennington Co., VT, Census*)

Obadiah – b 4/15/1719 in Guilford, CT, s/o **John** and **Deborah**; d 8/26/1780 in Gilsum, NH. Obadiah m 10/12/1743 **Lydia Wilcox** (his cousin), b1716 in Guilford, CT, d 1/16/1796. (*DAR Patriot Index*, p. 743 – *Town of Gilsum, NH*, p. 176, 417–18)

Obadiah – b 7/24/1724 in CT, d 2/20/1810 in Surry, NH. Obadiah m **Sarah Talcott**, b 3/1734 in CT, d 9/21/1809 in Surry, NH. (*Town of Gilsum, NH*, p. 417 – *DAR Patriot Index*, p. 743)

Philo - b 1/22/1783 in Goshen, CT, d 8/26/1865 in Benson, Rutland Co., VT. Philo m **Sarah ----**, b MA. In the 1850 census he was 67 and she was 67 years old, too. (*1850 Rutland Co., VT, Census*)

Reuben - b 11/1/1762 in Middletown, CT, d 12/10/1853 prob. in Whitestown, Oneida Co., NY. Reuben m **Hannah Johnson**. (*Oneida: Our County and Its People*, p. 620 - *DAR Patriot Index*, p. 743)

William - b 5/1/1790 in Simsbury, CT, s/o **Aaron**; William d 10/14/1867 in Fredonia, NY. He m1817 **Esther S. Cole**, b in VT, d 7/7/1851. (*Chautauqua Co., NY*, p. 227, 625)

WILFORD

Jeremiah - bc1782 in CT, d1860 in PA. Jeremiah m **Clarissa Waldo**. (War of 1812 Index)

WILKINSON

Ichabod - b 12/4/1753 in New Milford, CT, s/o **John** and **Jerusha**; Ichabod d 3/1825 prob. in Fleming, Cayuga Co., NY. He m 4/13/1775 in New Milford, CT, **Anna Taylor**. (*Township of Fleming, Cayuga Co., NY*, p. 6-7 - *DAR Patriot Index*, p. 745)

Reuben - bc1783 in CT. Reuben m **Lucy ----**, bc1789 in VT. They resided in Benson, Hartford Co., VT. In the 1850 census he was 67 and she was 61 years old. (*1850 Rutland Co., VT, Census*)

WILLARD

Charles - b1785 in CT, d1862 in NY. Charles m **Mehitabel Bullard**. (War of 1812 Index)

Joseph - b1750 in Colchester, CT, s/o Capt. **Jonathan**; Joseph d 8/28/1829 age 80 prob. in Pawlet, Rutland Co., VT. He m 4/3/1782 **Sarah Hare**, d1846 age 80. (*Willard Gen.*, p. 150, 279-80 - *VT Gazetteer*, v. 3)

WILLIAMS

Andrew - b1748 in Lebanon, CT, d 2/3/1816 age 69 in Clinton, Oneida Co., NY. Andrew m **Anna Giddings**, d 2/7/1817 age 73. (*Clinton Memorial-Kirtland Ave. Cem.*, p. 30-31 - *CT Soc. Coll.*, v. 8, p. 5)

Caleb - b 4/12/1767 in E. Haddam, CT, s/o **Charles** and **Elizabeth** (**Hubbard**); Caleb d 12/20/1854 in Sunderland, Bennington Co., VT. He m (1) 11/6/1788 **Abigail Andrus**, and m (2) **Eunice** (**Benson**) **Hathaway**. (*DAR Patriot Index*, p. 746 - Query *NEGR* April 1963, p. 160)

Charles - b 3/3/1761 in E. Haddam, CT. Charles m 10/31/1786 Mrs. **Sarah Goodrich**, d 12/20/1843 age 83 in Arlington, VT. They resided in Arlington, Addison Co., VT. (*Hartford Times* Genealogical Page)

Cornelius - bc1750 in CT, d1821 in MA. Cornelius m **Sarah Kellogg**. (War of 1812 Index)

Daniel - bc1771 in CT, d1860 in MI. Daniel m **Vina Hovey**. (War of 1812 Index)

Dudley - bc1771 in CT. Dudley m **Tabitha ----**, bc1782 in VT. They resided in Hartland, Windsor Co., VT. In the 1850 census he was 79 and she was 48 years old, with Harriet 49, Sarah 37, Hannah 25,

Samuel A. 39, and Lewis D. 24 years old. (*1850 Windsor Co., VT, Census*)

Elias H. - b 7/23/1819 in Ledyard, CT, d 8/20/1891 prob. in Garnaville, Clayton Co., IA. Elias H. m ----. (*Hist. of IA*, p. 286-7)

Flavel M. - b1800 in Brooklyn, CT, d1880 in Lathrop, Susquehanna Co., PA. Flavel M. m1826 **Lodema Downing**, b1799, d1875 in Lathrop, PA. (*Hist. of Susquehanna Co., PA*, p. 686)

Henry - bc1788 in CT. Henry m **Clarissa** ----, bc1787 in CT. They resided in Oxford, Chenango Co., NY. In the 1850 census he was 62 and she was 63 years old. (*1850 Census Chenango Co., NY*)

Henry W. - bc 8/20/1791 in CT, d 7/17/1861 in Knox, NY. Henry W. m **Sallie Tarbell**, b 7/28/1795 in Renssaeler Co., NY, d 7/24/1883 in Knox, Albany Co., NY. (*Nutmegger* Query June 1981 p. 66)

Hezekiah - bc1783 in CT, d 6/24/1861 age 79 in Brookfield, Orange Co., VT. Hezekiah m **Lodema** ----, bc1789 in VT, d 11/12/1859 age 71. (*Gazetteer of Orange Co., VT*, p. 216-17)

Isaac - bc1776 in CT, d 9/23/1858 age 82 in Clinton, Oneida Co., NY. Isaac m (1) **Clara** ----, b1776 in Farmington, CT, d 5/25/1810 age 34, and m (2) **Rebecca** ----, bc1783 (or bc1784), d 2/13/1866 in 82nd year. (*Clinton Memorial-Kirtland Ave. Cem., NY*, p. 49)

Isaac - b 1/6/1763 in E. Haddam, CT, s/o **Charles** and **Elizabeth (Hubbard)**; Isaac d 12/1/1815 in Arlington, Addison Co., VT. He m 11/27/1788 in Glastonbury, CT, **Ruth Goodale**, b 4/8/1770, d 9/5/1829 age 58 in Arlington, VT, d/o **Joseph** and **Ruth (Fox)**. (*Hist. of Addison Co., VT*, p. ?)

John - bc1789 in CT, d1865 in OH. John m **Sarah Walker**. (War of 1812 Index)

John - b 2/7/1747 in Poquetannock, CT, s/o **Joseph**; John d 4/9/1813 in Weathersfield, VT. He m1776 in Brattleboro, VT, **Abigail Phelps**, b 8/13/1751 in Brattleboro, VT, d 9/13/1833 in Weathersfield, Windsor Co., VT, d/o **Charles** and **Dorothy (Root)**. (*Des. of John Williams*, p. 60-1)

Nathan Gallup - b 10/31/1844 in Pomfret, CT, s/o **Giles**. Nathan Gallup m (1) 10/4/1871 **Sarah Phillips Carr** of Warren, RI, b 8/20/1851, d 10/4/1884, and m (2) 1/28/1886 **Emily Frances (Cole) Smith**, d 10/29/1901, and m (3) 12/1/1906 **Abbie Lucinda Haines**, b in Waterbury, VT. They resided in Rockingham, Windham Co., VT. (*Hist. of Rockingham, VT*, p. 794)

Peter - bc1758 in CT, d 11/5/1833 in Ballston, Saratoga Co., NY, buried in Hubbell Cemetery there. Peter m ----. (*DAR Magazine* 1977, p. 923)

Peter - b 9/2/1735 in Preston, CT, s/o **Daniel**; Peter d1803 (or d1810) in Rockland Twp., Sullivan Co., NY. He m 11/18/1756 in Norwich, CT, **Sarah Smith**, b 8/10/1739 in Preston, CT, d 3/17/1802 in Rockland, NY, d/o **Samuel**. (*Hartford Times* Genealogy Page)

Phineas - b 11/5/1734 in Mansfield, CT, d 12/28/1820 prob. in Windsor, VT. Phineas m **Mary Fields**, d/o **Bennett**. (*Hist. of Woodstock, CT*, p. ?)

Pollydore - b 7/16/1778 in Pomfret, CT, s/o **Silas**; Pollydore d 3/30/1873 in Royalton, Windsor Co., VT. He m (1) 3/5/1804 in Hanover, NH, **Percia Davis**, d 4/14/1846, and m (2) **Zurviah Cleveland**, b 6/1802, d 4/23/1880, d/o **Squire** and **Permelia**

(Green). In the 1850 census he was 72 and Zurviah was 48 years old. (*1850 Census Windsor County, Vermont - History of Royalton, Vermont*, p. 1034-5)

Silas - b 2/4/1750 in Pomfret, CT, s/o **David**; Silas d 10/20/1843 age 93-8 in Royalton, VT. He m **Mary H. Flynn**, b 1/29/1749 in Pomfret, CT, d 3/13/1835 age 86 in Royalton, VT, d/o **Richard**. (*History of Royalton, Vermont*, p. 1033-4 - *Woodstock Families*, v. 8, p. 503)

WILLIS

Wearam - bc1781 in CT. Wearam m **Hannah ----**, bc1791 in CT. They resided in Masonville, Delaware Co., NY. In the 1855 census he was 74 and she was 64 years old, with Warren 28 years old, b in NY. (*1855 Census of Delaware Co., NY*)

WILLOUGHBY

Bliss - b 2/22/1767 in New London Co., CT, s/o **Joseph** and **Bridget (Wickwier)**; Bliss d 5/21/1849 age 82 in Oxford, Chenango Co., NY. He m 4/20/1791 **Fanny Patton**, b 1/10/1768, d 2/7/1815. (*Annals of Oxford, NY*, p. ? - *DAR Magazine*, v. 45, p. 136 - *DAR Patriot Index*, p. 749)

WILLS

Jesse - b1766 in Windham, CT. Jesse m1796 **Emma Perkins**, d/o **Jacob**. They resided in Chelsea, Orange Co., VT. (*Gazetteer of Orange Co., VT*, p. 224)

John - bc1786 in CT. John m **Betsey ----**, bc1780 in NH. They resided in Randolph, Orange Co., VT. In the 1850 census he was 64 and she was 70 years old. (*1850 Orange Co., VT, Census*)

WILMOT

Timothy - b1756 in Tolland, CT, d 1/23/1825 age 68 in Thetford, Orange Co., VT. Timothy m **Mary Copp**. (*Gazetteer of Orange Co., VT*, p. 436-7)

WILSON

John, Jr. - b 1/17/1784 in Harwinton, CT, s/o **John** and **Elizabeth (Davis)**; John, Jr. d 3/4/1844 in Camden, Oneida Co., NY. He m **Jerusha Dunbar** of Camden, NY, b 1/8/1786 in Plymouth, NY, d 2/4/1856. (*Pioneer Hist. of Camden, NY*, p. 196)

Capt. John - b 3/26/1760 in Harwinton, CT, d 12/1/1839 age 79 in Camden, Oneida Co., NY. Capt. John m 2/7/1781 **Elizabeth Wilson (Davis)**, b 9/4/1760, d 1/22/1844 age 83 in Camden, NY. (*Pioneer Hist. of Camden, NY*, p. 197)

John D. - bc1745 in Middletown, CT, s/o **Archibald**; John d 7/6/1843 age 98 in Whitetown, Oneida Co., NY. He m ----. (*DAR Magazine*, v. 40, p. 33)

Samuel - bc1772 in CT. Samuel m **Sarah ----**, bc1773 in CT. They resided in New Berlin, Chenango Co., NY. In the 1850 census he was 78 and she was 77 years old, with Olive 50, Isaac T. 37, and Sarah 30 years old, all b in NY. (*1850 Census of Chenango Co., NY*)

Sylvanus - b1787 in Harwinton, CT. Sylvanus m1824 **Beulah Doolittle.**
They resided in Camden, Oneida Co., NY. (*Pioneer Hist. of Camden, NY,* p. 95)

Sylvanus - b 11/11/1769 in Harwinton, CT, s/o **Eli** and **Mindwell;**
Sylvanus d 3/17/1833 age 64 in Camden, Oneida Co., NY. He m
Chloe Hall, b1771 in Harwinton, CT, d 3/9/1827 age 56. (*Pioneer Hist. of Camden, NY,* p. 93-4)

WINCHESTER

A m a r i a h - b2/13/1753 in New London, CT, d 3/26/1842 in Amenia,
Dutchess Co., NY. Amariah m in Kent, CT, **Mary Follett,** b
12/4/1759, d 6/9/1832. (*Comm. Biographical Rev., Dutchess Co., New York,* p. 669)

WINTERS

Juvenile - b 3/18/1762 in Pomfret, CT, d 9/11/1841 in Mina, NY.
Juvenile m1780 in Cherry Valley, NY, **Amelia Heath.** (*Soldiers of the American Revolution, Chautauqua Co., NY,* p. ? - *DAR Patriot Index,* p. 754)

WITTERS

H a w l e y - b in CT, d 8/26/1878 prob. in Milton, Chittenden Co., VT.
Hawley m **Clarissa Basford,** d1878. (*Chittenden Co., VT, Gazetteer,* p. 243)

WOLCOTT

Benajah - b1762 in New Haven, CT, d1832 in Huron, OH. Benajah m
(1) 1793 **Elizabeth Bradley** of New Haven, CT, and m (2) 1822 in
Norwalk, OH, **Rachel Miller.** (*Res. of CT Who Migrated to Huron Co., OH,* p. 7 - *DAR Patriot Index,* p. 756)

Joseph - b1775 in CT, d1866 in OH. Joseph m **Lucy Hills.** (War of 1812 Index)

WOOD

Caleb - bc1780 in CT. Caleb m **Abigail** ----, bc1778. They resided
in Sidney, Delaware Co., NY. In the 1855 census he was 70 and she
was 72 years old, with Seeley 33 years and Susan 31 (w/o Seeley),
both b in Delaware Co., NY. (*1855 Census Delaware Co., NY*)

Elisha - bc 1/29/1760 in CT, s/o **Noah,** d age 80 in Otsego Co., NY.
Elisha m **Jennie Hall.** (*Biog. Rev. of Otsego Co., NY,* p. 846-7)

Sanford - b 8/20/1801 in CT, s/o **Jacob** and **Ruth (Dauchy);** Sanford d
8/6/1891 in Washington, Macomb Co., MI. He m 1/8/1823 in
Monroe Co., NY, **Maria Dickinson,** b 8/1/1803 in Haddam, CT,
d1851, d/o **Dan** and **Rachel (Strong).** (*DSGR* Quarterly Summer 1974, p. 188)

S o l o m o n - b in E. Windsor, CT, d 5/8/1847 in Kirkland, NY (or on
McConnell Farm in Clinton, Oneida Co., NY). Solomon m
9/21/1832 **Christiana McConnell,** d in Kirkland, NY. (Clinton Memorial)

WOODS

Samuel – b 8/6/1758 in Windham, CT, s/o **Joseph, Jr.** and **Deborah (Tubbs).** Samuel m **Margaret Morgan,** b 9/20/1762. They resided in Wells, VT. (*Hist. of Wells, VT,* by Wood, p. 82)

Samuel – b 3/15/1755 in CT (poss. in Waterbury), d 7/29/1837 in Camden, Oneida Co., NY. Samuel m **Elizabeth Sperry,** d 7/27/1837. (*Pioneer History of Camden, NY,* p. ? – *DAR Patriot Index,* p. 758)

WOODBRIDGE

William – b 8/20/1780 in Norwich, CT, s/o **Dudley;** William d 10/20/1861 in Detroit, Gratiot Co., MI. He m 6/1806 **Julianna Trumbull.** (*Portrait and Biog. Album of Gratiot Co., MI*)

WOODFORD

Isaac, Jr. – b1774 in CT, d1838 in OH. Isaac, Jr. m **Statira Cowles.** (War of 1812 Index)

WOODRIDGE

William – bc1780 in CT, d1860 in MI. William m **Julia Trumbull.** (War of 1812 Index)

WOODRUFF

Chauncey – bc1791 in Harwinton, CT, d 5/14/1880 age 89 in Camden, Oneida Co., NY. Chauncey m1817 **Rebecca Scoville,** b 5/5/1795 in Harwinton, CT, buried 11/5/1883 in Waterbury, CT, d/o **Daniel.** (*Pioneer Hist. of Camden, NY,* p. 310)

Dr. Hurlburt – b 4/1/1825 in Watertown, CT, d 11/2/1881 prob. in Camden, Oneida Co., NY. Dr. Hurlburt m1847 **Calista Abbott** of New Haven, CT, b in Middlebury, CT, d 11/27/1895. (*Pioneer History of Camden, NY,* p. 495)

Joel – bc1780 in CT. Joel m **Sarah ----,** bc1786 in CT. They resided in Sidney, Delaware Co., NY. In the 1855 census he was 75 (a cooper) and she was 69 years old. (*1855 Census Delaware Co., NY*)

Morris M. – bc1792 in CT, d1875 in NY. Morris M. m **Roxanna T. Bush.** (War of 1812 Index)

Samuel H. – b 12/31/1814 in Farmington, CT, d 8/22/1888 in St. Clair, MI. Samuel H. m 10/1/1840 in NY, **Elizabeth Walker.** (*DSGR Quarterly,* v. 37 #4, p. 192)

WOODWARD

Daniel – b1776 in CT, s/o **Ebenezer, Sr.;** Daniel d 7/27/1836 in Royalton, Windsor Co., VT. He m 2/18/1802 **Polly Hibbard,** b 2/6/1780 in Royalton, VT, d 6/25/1858, d/o **John, Jr.** and **Abigail (Cleveland).** (*History of Royalton, VT,* p. 1040-1 – *Royalton* by Nash, p. 251)

Ebenezer – b 4/5/1771 in Tolland, CT, s/o **Ebenezer;** Ebenezer (the younger) d 12/14/1807 in Royalton, Windsor Co., VT. He m1798 **Lucy Lee,** b 2/7/1772 in Mt. Washington, MA, d 6/7/1864 in Royalton, VT. (*Hist. of Royalton,* p. 1039-40)

Ebenezer – b1751 in Windam, CT, d 2/8/1836 in Royalton, Windsor Co., VT. Ebenezer m (1) **Patience Orms,** b1744, d 9/1808 in

269

Royalton, VT, and m (2) 3/19/1811 **Molly Hayes.** (*History of Royalton, VT*, p. 1039 - *DAR Patriot Index*, p. 761)

John - b 8/7/1757 in Plainfield, CT, d 6/12/1845 age 88 in Poland, NY. John m 3/5/1786 in Conway, MA, **Sally Galloway**, d 2/21/1832 in Ellington, NY, buried in Riverside Cem., Poland, NY. (*Soldiers of the Am. Rev., Chautauqua Co., NY*, p. 11)

Joshua - b 4/11/1755 in CT, d 7/10/1844 in Poland, NY, buried in Allen Cemetery there. Joshua m **Experience Jerald**, d 3/18/1822 age 57. (*DAR Mag.* 1977, p. 923 - *DAR Patriot Index*, p. 761 - *Soldiers of the Am. Rev., Chautauqua Co., NY*, p. 11)

WOODWORTH

Dudley - bc1766 in CT, d1822 in MA. Dudley m ----. (War of 1812 Index)

James - bc1785 in CT. James m **Phebe** ----, bc1786 in VT. They resided in Bethel, Windsor Co., VT. In the 1850 census he was 65 and she was 64 years old, with Laura 34, Alonzo 30, Ellen 30 (w/o Alonzo), Charles 36, and Sarah 34 years old (w/o Charles), all b in VT. (*1850 Census of Windsor Co., VT*)

James - b 7/8/1766 in Coventry, CT, d 11/2/1859 age 93 in Painesville, OH. James m ----. (*Revolutionary Soldiers Buried in Lake Co., OH*, p. 61)

John - bc1793 in CT. John m **Cyrena** ----, bc1798 in VT. They resided in Middletown, Rutland Co., VT. In the 1850 census he was 57 and she was 52, with Paulina 16, Ellen 12, and Martin 8 years old, all b in VT. (*1850 Rutland Co., VT, Census*)

Ziba - b 4/1769) in Bozrah, CT, d 11/27/1826 prob. in Montpelier, Washington Co., VT. Ziba m (1) ----, divorced, and m (2) **Lucy Palmer** of Canaan, NH. (*Washington Co. Gazetteer*, p. 356-7 - *Hist. of Montpelier, VT*, p. 181-4)

WOOSTER

Rev. Benjamin - b 10/29/1762 in Waterbury, CT, s/o **Wait** and **Phebe** (**Warner**); d 12/18/1840 age 78 in Fairfield, Franklin Co., VT. Rev. Benjamin m (1) 1796 **Sarah Harris**, d 10/19/1824 age 51. d/o Capt. **Israel** of Rutland, VT, and m (2) 1825 **Sally Cooper** of Sheldon, VT. (*VT Hist. Mag.*, v. 2, p. 193 - *Hist. of Cornwall, VT*, p. 155 - *DAR Patriot Index*, p. 762)

Sherman - b 2/17/1779 in Danbury, CT, d 5/21/1833 age 54-3-4 in Newport, Herkimer Co., NY. Sherman m ----. (*History of Herkimer Co., NY*, p. 380-5)

WORDEN

Walter - b 3/19/1757 in CT, d 9/20/1814 in NY. Walter m **Lucretia Hicks.** (War of 1812 Index - *DAR Patriot Index*, p. 763)

WORTHINGTON

George - bc1781 in CT. George m **Clarissa Davis**, bc1790 in VT. They resided in Montpelier, Washington Co., VT. In the 1850 census he was 69 (a merchant) and she was 60 years old. (*1850 Census Washington Co., VT*)

WRIGHT

Aaron – b1700 in CT (perhaps in Hebron, CT), s/o **Samuel** and **Elizabeth**; d 1/1/1783 age 83 in Norwich, Windsor Co., VT. Aaron m **Elizabeth Bliss**, d 3/26/1787 age 75 in Norwich, VT, d/o Rev. Samuel and Elizabeth. (*A Hist. of Norwich, VT*, p. 250-1)

Abel – b 8/18/1742 in Lebanon, CT, s/o **Benjamin** and **Ann (Reddington)**; Abel d1828 prob. in Hartford, Windsor Co., VT. He m (1) 11/6/1766 **Mary Lyman**, d 8/1776, and m (2) **Alice** ----, d 4/6/1809. (*VT Antiquarian*, p. 22)

Ambrose – b 10/2/1773 in Saybrook, CT, d 1/12/1851 age 77-4-16 in Concord, Erie Co., NY. Ambrose m **Betsey Pattison**, b 6/12/1779 in CT, d 4/4/1835 age 55-9. (*Hist. of Original Town of Concord, NY*, p. 517-18)

Benjamin – b 3/3/1713 (or b 3/3/1714) in Lebanon, CT, s/o **Abel** and **Rebecca**; dc1798 prob. in Hartford, Windsor Co., VT. Benjamin m **Rachel** ---- (perhaps **Owen**). (*VT Antiquarian*, p. 22 – *DAR Patriot Index*, p. 764)

Benjamin, Jr. – b 7/5/1737 in Lebanon, CT, s/o **Benjamin** and **Rachel**; Benjamin, Jr. d1803 prob. in Hartford, Windsor Co., VT. He m 4/29/1762 **Ann Reddington**. (*Vermont Antiquarian*, p. 22 – *DAR Patriot Index*, p. 764)

Bildad – b1768 in CT, d1853. Bildad m **Chloe Shipman**. (War of 1812 Index)

Daniel – b 9/9/1794 in Hebron, CT, d sometime after age 78 prob. in Pompey, Onondaga Co., NY. Daniel m 4/21/1826 **Eva Helmer** of Manlius, NY, d 7/17/1866. (*Pompey, Onondaga Co., NY*, p. 366-7)

Daniel – b1757 in Lebanon, CT, d 10/10/1822 in Westport, NY. Daniel m 1/20/1777 **Patience Bill**, d 4/15/1829 in Westport, NY. (*Town of Gilsum, NH*, p. 424-5 – *DAR Patriot Index*, p. 764)

David – b 3/14/1749 in Lebanon, CT, s/o **Benjamin** and **Rachel**; David d 2/21/1822 prob. in Hartford, Windsor Co., VT. He m1771 **Hannah Bailey**. (*VT Antiquarian*, p. 22 – *DAR Patriot Index*, p. 764)

Ebenezer – bc1795 in CT, s/o **Nathan** and **Lementa**; Ebenezer d 12/14/1854 age 59 prob. in Salem, Wayne Co., PA. He m ----. (Loose sheet at Honesdale, PA, Courthouse)

Joab – bc1759 in CT, d1844 in OH. Joab m **Mary Olive**. (War of 1812 Index)

Capt. John – b 1/22/1743 in Goshen, CT, s/o **John**; Capt. John d 7/29/1825 age 83 poss. in Tallmadge, OH. He m (1) **Lydia Mason**, and m (2) **Sarah Case**, b 9/9/1758 in Norfolk, CT. (1972 Spring Issue *OH Gen. Soc.*, p. 36 – *DAR Patriot Index*, p. 765)

John, Jr. – b 1/11/1780 in Winsted, CT. John, Jr. m **Saloma Gillett**, b 5/23/1786 in Torrington, CT. They resided in OH, poss. in Tallmadge. (1972 Spring Issue *OH Gen. Soc.*, p. 36)

Phineas – bc1752 in Hartford, CT, d 5/6/1812 in Keene, NH. Phineas m **Zilpah Cooper** of Westmoreland, PA, bc1756 (or bc1760), d 9/30/1841 in Keene, NH. (*History of Surry, NH*, p. 965 – *DAR Patriot Index*, p. 765)

Reuben – b 7/9/1749 in New Britain, CT, d 4/17/1841 in 93rd year in Westfield, NY. Reuben m **Martha Gridley**, d 6/29/1841 in 86th year. (*Soldiers of Am. Rev., Chautauqua Co., NY*)

WYLEY

John - bc1785 in CT. John m **Mary** ----, bc1800 in VT. They resided in Wallingford, Rutland Co., VT. In the 1850 census he was 65 and she was 50 years old, with Julius 16 and Mary 5 years old, both b in VT. (*1850 Rutland Co., VT, Census*)

YALE

Benjamin - b 7/30/1779 in Sharon, CT, d 10/4/1855 in Windham, OH. Benjamin m ----. (*Semi-Cent., Windham, OH*, p. 63-4)

YOEMAN

Andrew - bc1799 in CT. Andrew m **Helena** ----, bc1799 in NY. They resided in Preston, Chenango Co., NY. In the 1850 census he was 51 (a carpenter) and she was 51 years old, with H. Diantha 12 and **Sarah Keeler** 80 years old, both b in NY. (*1850 Census Chenango Co., NY*)

Andrew - bc1778 in CT. Andrew m **Polly** ----, bc1771 in CT. They resided in Preston, Chenango Co., NY. In the 1850 census he was 72 and she was 79 years old. (*1850 Census Chenango Co., NY*)

YEOMANS

Judge Erastus - b 8/11/1791 in New Lebanon, CT, s/o **David** and **Esther**; Judge Erastus d 6/8/1883 in Ionia, MI (1812 Index says 1863). He m 3/19/1815 **Phebe Arnold**, d/o **Job** and **Hannah** of Fairfield, NY. (*Pioneer Coll. of MI*, v. 6, p. 302-4 - War of 1812 Index)

YORK

Dr. Edward - b 8/26/1797 in N. Stonington, CT. Dr. Edward m **Lydia Stratton**, d 2/10/1888 age 80 in Westfield, NY. They once resided in Oxford, Chenango Co., NY. (*Annals of Oxford, NY*, p. ?)

Jeremiah - b 9/25/1794 in N. Stonington, CT, d 4/24/1873 prob. in Oxford, Chenango Co., NY. Jeremiah m (1) 1815 in Norwich, NY, **Catherine Pendleton**, b 7/22/1789 in CT, d 1/14/1826 in Oxford, NY, and m (2) **Mrs. Aruba Sheldon**, b 2/4/1804, d 4/21/1886. (*Annals of Oxford, NY*, p. 448)

YOUNG

Asa - bc1790 in CT. Asa m **Eunice** ----, bc1789 in CT. They resided in Sidney, Delaware Co., NY. In the 1855 census he was 65 and she was 66 years old, with **Daniel Pearsall** 36, **Cynthia** 29 (w/o Pearsall), **Erma** 6, and **Dwight** 3 years old, all b in NY. (*1855 Census Delaware Co., NY*)

John - bc1796 in CT. John m **Sophia** ----, bc1800 in VT. They resided in Jamaica, Windham Co., VT. In the 1850 census he was 56 and she was 50 years old, both b in VT. (*1850 Census Windham Co., VT*)

REFERENCE LIST FOR
SOME CONNECTICUT NUTMEGGERS WHO MIGRATED

Abbe-Nichols - <u>Abbe-Abbey</u> Genealogy, Tuttle Morehouse & Taylor 1916

Abell, Horace and Lewis - The <u>Abell</u> Family in America, Tuttle Pub. Co. 1940

Adams, Andrew N. - A Genealogical History of Henry <u>Adams</u> of Braintree, MA, etc., Tuttle Pub. Co., 1898.

Adams, Andrew N. - A Genealogical History of Robert <u>Adams</u> of Newbury, MA, and His Descendants 1635-1900, Tuttle Pub. Co., 1900.

Allen, Orrin Peer - The <u>Allen</u> Memorial, Published for the author by C.B. Fiske and Co. 1907.

Alvord, Samuel - A Genealogy of the Descendants of Alexander <u>Alvord</u>, A.D. Andrews, Printers Webster, NY 1908

Ames, Faber - The <u>Ames</u> Family of Bruton, Somerset, England 1520-1969, 1969 Los Angeles, CA. By author.

Andrews, A. H. - Genealogical History of John and Mary <u>Andrews</u>, published by A.H. Andrews and Co., Chicago 1872.

Wyman, Mary E. T. - The Genealogy of the Descendants of Lawrence and Mary <u>Antisell</u>, Champlain Printing Co., Columbus, OH. 1908

Atwater, Francis - <u>Atwater</u> History and Genealogy, Journal Publishing Co. 1901 4 v.

Augur, Edwin P. - Family History and Genealogy of the Descendants of Robert <u>Augur</u> of the New Haven Colony, Middletown, CT 1904.

Moore-Day - Descendants of Richard <u>Austin</u> of Charlestown, MA, 1638, no publisher given.

Avery, Catherine - The Groton <u>Avery</u> Clan, 2 vol., Cleveland 1912.

Babcock, Stephen - <u>Babcock</u> Genealogy, Eaton and Mains 1903.

Backus, Mary E. N. - The New England Ancestry of Dana Converse <u>Backus</u>, Private Printing 1949, Newcomb & Ganes Co., Salem, MA.

Baldwin, John D. - A Record of the Descendants of John <u>Baldwin</u> of Stonington, CT, 1880.

Bartholomew, George Jr. - Record of the <u>Bartholomew</u> Family, published by the compiler 1885.

Beadle, Walter J. - Samuel <u>Beadle</u> Family, privately printed 1970.

Holt, Nellie Beardsley - Family of William <u>Beardsley</u>, typed copy W. Hartford 1951.

Benedict, Henry Marvin - The Genealogy of the <u>Benedicts</u> in America, Joel Munsell, Albany, NY, 1870.

Benton, Josiah Henry Jr. - Samuel Slade <u>Benton</u> and His Descendants, privately printed, Merrymount Press, Boston 1901.

273

Bicknell, Zachary - History and Genealogy of the Bicknell Family, published by Thomas W. Bicknell, Providence, 1913.

Howe, Gilman Bigelow - Genealogy of the Bigelow Family of America, printed by Charles Hamilton, Worcester, MA, 1890.

Bingham, Theodore - Bingham Family in the United States, Bingham Assoc., Easton, PA. 1930 3 vol.

Jones, Edward Payson - Descendants of John Bissell of Windsor, CT. Privately printed. 1938.

Bixby, Willard G. - A Genealogy of the Descendants of Joseph Bixby 1621-1701, NY City, 1914.

Bliss, John Homer - Genealogy of the Bliss Family in America, printed by the author, Rockwell and Church Press, 1881.

Thompson, Bradley & Franklin - Descendants of Thomas Blodgett of Cambridge, 6 volumes and index, typed, Concord, NH. 1956.

Goldwaite, Charlotte - Boardman Genealogy 1525-1895, Case Lockwood Brainerd, 1895 by William F. J. Boardman.

Bogue, Virgil T. - Bogue and Allied Families, Herald Printers, MI, 1944.

Bostwick, Henry A. - Genealogy of the Bostwick Family in America, Bryan Printing Co., Hudson, NY, 1901.

Oliver, Rebeckah D. - Bottom-Longbottom Family Album, W. Kelly Oliver Pub., Denver, CO 1970.

Brace, John Sherman - Brace Lineage, George Elwell & Sons, PA. 1927.

Brainerd, Lucy A. - The Genealogy of the Brainerd-Brainard Family in America, Case Lockwood & Brainerd Co. 1908. 3 vols.

Jones, Emma C. Brewster - The Brewster Genealogy 1566-1907, 2 vols., Grafton Press, NY, 1908.

Bridgman, Burt N. - Genealogy of the Bridgman Family, Clark W. Bryan Co., Springfield, 1894.

Brigham, W. I. Tyler - History of the Brigham Family, Grafton Press, NY, 1907.

Welles, Albert - History of the Buell Family in England and America, Society Library, NY, 1881.

Jacobus, Donald Lines - Rev. Peter Bulkeley, Tuttle Morehouse and Taylor, 1933.

Todd, Charles B. - A Genealogical History of the Burr Family in America, E. Wells Sackett, NY, 1878.

Burritt, Lewis L. - The Burritt Family in America, 1635-1940, no date given.

Allen, Orrin Peer - Descendants of Nicholas Cady 1645-1910, published by author, C. B. Fiske & Co., 1910.

no information - Calkin Family Lines in the United States and Canada, typed manuscript.

Carpenter, Amos B. - A Genealogical History of the Rehoboth Branch of the Carpenter Family, Carpenter and Morehouse, 1898.

May, George S. - Some Descendants of Thomas Carrier of Andover and Billerica, MA, booklet, 1978.

Chaffee, William H. - The Chaffee Genealogy 1835-1909, Grafton Press, 1909.

Glazier, Prentiss - Chamberlain Families of Early New England and New York, typed. 1973.

Trowbridge, Francis B. – History of Descendants of Henry Champion, by author at New Haven. 1891.

Chandler, George – The Descendants of William and Annis Chandler, Press of Charles Hamilton, Worcester, MA, 1883.

Child, Elias – Genealogy of Child, Childs & Childe Families, Curtiss and Childs, 1881.

Chipman, John H. – A Chipman Genealogy, Chipman Histories, Norwell, MA, 1970.

Church, John A. – Descendants of Richard Church of Plymouth, MA, 1913.

Pope, Charles Henry – The Cheney Genealogy, pub. by Charles Pope, Boston, MA, 1897.

Gould, Robert F. – Ezra Thompson Clark's Ancestors and Descendants, Bethesda, MD, 1975.

Bryant, George Clarke – Deacon George Clark of Milford, CT, and Some of His Descendants, Anthoensen Press, 1949.

Cleveland, Edmund Janes – The Genealogy of the Cleveland and Cleaveland Families, Case, Lockwood, and Brainerd, 1899.

Cobb, Philip L. – A History of the Cobb Family, 1923.

Bartlett, J. Gardner – Robert Coe, Puritan, His Ancestors and Descendants 1340-1910, pub. by author, Boston, MA, 1911.

Jameson, E. O. – The Cogswells in America, pub. by author, 1884.

Copeland, Warren Turner – The Copeland Family, Tuttle Pub. Co., Rutland, 1937.

Lawson, Rev. Harvey – History and Genealogy of the Descendants of Clement Corbin, Case Lockwood Co., 1905.

Cooley, Laverne – A Short Biography of the Rev. John Cotton of Boston, MA, 1945.

Merling, Mary – Cowdrey-Cowdery-Cowdray Genealogy, Frank Allaben Gen. Co., 1911.

Cowles, Compiler Calvin D. – Genealogy of the Cowles Families in America, 2 vols., Tuttle, Morehouse and Taylor, 1929.

Crane, Ellery – Genealogy of the Crane Family, 3 vols., Charles Hamilton Press, Worcester, MA, 1900.

Crocker, James R. – Crocker Genealogy, 1952. Published bythe author.

Cushman, Henry Wyles – Genealogy of the Cushmans, Little Brown Co., 1855.

Cutler, Nahum – Cutler Memorial and Genealogical History, Hall & Co. 1889.

Dakin, Albert H. – Descendants of Thomas Dakin, Tuttle Pub., 1948.

Dana, Elizabeth Ellery – The Dana Family of America, Wright and Potter, Boston, MA, 1956.

Daniels, James Harrison Jr. – A Genealogical History of the Descendants of William Daniels, 2 vols., N. A. Gossman Pub. Co., 1959.

Denison, E. Glenn – Denison Genealogy, Pequot Press, Stonington, CT, 1963.

Derby, Charles L. and Walter – Genealogical Record of the Descendants of John Derby, typed 1935-1944.

Dewey, Louis M. – Life of George Dewey, Dewey Pub. Co., Westfield, MA, 1898.

Douglas, Charles Henry James - A Collection of Family Records of Douglas, E. L. Freeman & Co., Providence, RI, 1879.

Driggs, Howard R. - Driggs Family History, Book One, Publishers' Press, Salt Lake, 1959.

Dunham, Isaac Watson - Dunham Genealogy, England and American Branches, Bulletin Print, Norwich, CT, 1907.

Rix, Guy S. - History and Genealogy of the Eastman Family of America, 2 vols., Press of Ira C. Evans. 1901.

Easton, William Starr - Descendants of Joseph Easton, 1636-1899, St. Paul, MN, 1899.

Eddy Family Assoc. - The Eddy Family in America, 2 vols., pub. by Caroll A. Edson by Edward Brothers.

Ely, Rev. William and Beach, Moses S. - The Ely Ancestry, Calumet Press, 1902.

Richardson, Douglas - The Eno and Enos Family in America, typed, 1973.

Holman, Winifred L. - Descendants of Andrew Everest, privately printed, 1955.

Allen, Orrin P. - Descendants of John Fairman of Enfield, CT, 1683-1898, C. B. Fiske & Co., Palmer, MA, 1898.

Farnsworth, Moses F. - Farnsworth Memorial Being a Record of Matthias Farnsworth and His Descendants in America, L. A. Lauber, Manti, UT, 1897.

Farwell, John D., Abbott, Jane, and Wilson, Lillian M. - The Farwell Family, v. 1, Published by Frederick and Fanny Farwell, printed by Tuttle Co., 1929.

Morris, John E. - The Felt Genealogy, Case Lockwood Brainerd Co., 1893.

Weaver, William L. - A Genealogy of the Fenton Family, Willimantic, CT, 1867.

Pierce, Frederick - Field Genealogy, 2 vols., Hammond Press, Chicago, 1901.

Smith, Rev. Alven - Thomas Flint and William Flint of Salem, MA, and Their Descendants, typescript, Alvin M. Smith of CA, 1931.

Foote, Abram W. - Foote Family, 2 vols., Tuttle Co., Rutland, VT, 1907, 1932.

Francis, Charles E. - Francis, Des. of Robert Francis of Wethersfield, CT, Tuttle Morehouse, Taylor Co., 1906.

French, Mansfield Joseph - Ancestors and Descendants of Samuel French, the Joiner of Stratford, CT, Edwards Bros., MI, 1940.

Frisbee, Olin E. - Frisbee-Frisbie-Frisby Family Genealogy - no publisher, 1904.

Fuller, William H. - Genealogy of Some Descendants of Thomas Fuller, 1919.

Gallup, John D. - Genealogical History of the Gallup Family in the United States, Hartford Printing Co., Hartford, CT. 1893.

Gallup, Darwin and Peck, Josephine - Gallup Genealogy, The Anthoensen Press, Portland, ME, 1966.

Geer, Walter - The Geer Genealogy, Plimpton Press, Norwood, MA, 1923.

Giddings, Minot - The Giddings Family or Des. of George Giddings, 1635, Case Lockwood, Brainerd, Hartford, CT, 1882.

Brainerd, Homer and Torrey, Clarence - The Gilbert Family, Descendants of Thomas Gilbert, printed by Anthoensen Press, Portland, ME, 1953.

Hazen, Celeste - Glass Genealogical Data, typescript, CT State Lib., Hartford, CT, 1955.

White, John - Genealogy of the Descendants of Thomas Gleason of Watertown, MA, Nicholas Press, Haverhill, MA, 1909.

Gorton, Adelos - Life and Times of Samuel Gorton, Geo. Ferguson Co., Philadelphia, PA. 1907.

Granger, James N. - Lancelot Granger of Newbury, MA, and Suffield, CT. Case Lockwood Brainerd, Hartford, CT, 1893.

Grant, Arthur Hastings - The Grant Family and Gen. History of Des. of Matthew Grant of Windsor, CT, Press of A. V. Haight, Poughkeepsie, NY, 1898.

Gregory, Grant - Ancestors and Descendants of Henry Gregory, published by the compiler, Provincetown, MA, 1938. Tuttle Pub. Co.

Griswold, Glenn E. - Griswold Family, England and America, Pub. by Griswold Family Assoc. of America, v. 3, Tuttle Pub., 1943.

Card, Eva and Guernsey, Howard - Garnsey-Guernsey Genealogy, Interstate Printing & Pub. Co. for Eva and Leslie Card 1963.

Jacobus, Donald and Waterman, Edgar - Hale, House and Related Families, CT Historical Soc., Hartford, CT, Printed by Anthoensen Press, ME, 1952.

Hall, Rev. David B. - Halls of New England, Printed by Joel Munsell's Sons, Albany, NY, 1883.

Andrews, H. Franklin - The Hamlin Family, A Genealogy of James Hamlin of Barnstable, MA, Pub. by the author, Exira, IA, 1902.

Hammond, Frederick S. - History and Genealogies of the Hammond Families in America, v. II, Printers, Ryan and Burkhart, Oneida, NY, 1904.

Andrews, Alfred - Genealogical History of Deacon Stephen Hart and His Descendants 1632-1875, Case Lockwood Brainerd, 1875.

Hatch, Ruth A. and Hatch Gen. Soc. - Genealogy and History of the Hatch Family, A. L. Scoville Pub., Ogden, UT, no pub. date.

Versailles, Elizabeth - Hathaways of America, Gazette Printing Co., Northampton, MA, 1970.

Everett, Elizabeth - Hawley and Nason Ancestry, Pub. Ralph Fletcher Seymour, 1929.

Hayden, Jabez Haskell - Records of the Connecticut Line of the Hayden Family, Case Lockwood and Brainerd Co., 1888.

Hayes, Rev. Charles W. - George Hayes of Windsor and His Descendants, Baker Jones & Co., Buffalo, NY, 1884.

Hazen, Tracy E. - The Hazen Family in America, Tuttle Morehouse and Taylor, 1947.

Hibbard, Augustine George - Genealogy of the Hibbard Family, Case Lockwood and Brainerd Co., 1901.

Higby, Clinton David - Edward Higby and his Descendants, T. R. Marvin & Sons, Boston, MA, 1927.

Higgins, Mrs. Catherine C. - Richard Higgins and His Descendants, Printed for the author, Worcester, MA, 1918.

Hinckley, E. Charles - Hinckley Heritage and History, pub. E. Charles Hinckley, Fort Worth, TX, 1976.

Hitchcock, Mrs. Edward - Genealogy of the Hitchcock Family, Press of Carpenter and Morehouse, Amherst, MA, 1894.

Trowbridge, Francis B. - The Hoadley Genealogy, History of the Descendants of William Hoadley, Tuttle Morehouse and Taylor Co., 1894.

Seaver, Jesse - The Holcombe Genealogy, pub. by the American Historical and Genealogical Society, Philadelphia, PA. 1925.

Case, Lafayette W. - The Hollister Family of America, Fergus Printing Co., Chicago 1886.

Fischer, Carl (Compiler) - Descendants of Thomas Horton of Springfield, MA. I. T. Publishing Corp., Interlaken, NY, 1976.

Hovey, Daniel (Assn.) - The Hovey Book, Press of Lewis R. Hovey, Haverhill, MA, 1913.

Hubbard, Harlan Page - One Thousand Years of Hubbard History, printed by G. W. Rodgers and Co. for the author, 1895.

Hubbell, Walter - History of the Hubbell Family, J. H. Hubbell & Co., 1881, printed by Sherman & Co., Philadelphia, PA.

Leach, F. Phelps - Thomas Hungerford of Hartford and New London, CT, printed privately for use of family, 1924.

Huntington, Rev. E. P. - Genealogical Memoir of the Huntington Family in This Country, pub. for the author by John Stedman Co., 1863.

Huntington Family Assn. - The Huntington Family in America, Hartford Printing Co. for the association, 1915.

Walworth, Reuben - Hyde Genealogy, Descendants of William Hyde of Norwich, J. Munsell Co., Albany, 1864.

Burleigh, Charles - Genealogy and History of the Ingalls Family, pub. by George E. Dunbar, Malden, MA, 1903.

Ingham, Charles S. - Joseph Ingham and His Descendants 1639-1948, paperback, 1933.

Mason, Edna Warren - The Descendants of Robert Isbell in America, Tuttle, Morehouse and Taylor, 1944.

Brainerd, Homer - A Survey of the Ishams in England and America, Tuttle Pub. Co., 1938.

Jewett, Frederic - History and Genealogy of the Jewetts in America, 2 vols., Grafton Press, 1908.

Judd, Sylvester - Thomas Judd and His Descendants, typed and bound. J. & L. Metcalf, 1856.

McDowell, Caroline - Philip Judd and His Descendants, Grinnell Herald Press, 1923.

Ladd, Warren - The Ladd Family, A Genealogical and Biographical Memoir, Edmund Anthony and Sons, 1890.

Landon, James Orville - Landon Genealogy, Part II, Boardman Genealogy, Clark Boardman Co., S. Hero, VT, 1928.

Huntington, E. B. - A Genealogical Memoir of the Lothrop-Lathrop Family, Case Lockwood Brainerd Co., Hartford, CT, 1884.

Lawrence, John - The Genealogy of the Family of John Lawrence, Nichols and Noyes, Boston, MA, 1869.

Leavenworth, Elias Warner - A Genealogy of the Leavenworth Family in the U.S., S. G. Hitchcock & Co., Syracuse, NY, 1873.

Hopkins, Timothy - The Kelloggs in the Old World and the New, Sunset Press and Photo Engraving Co., San Francisco, 1903.

Claypool, Edward and Others – A Genealogy of the Descendants of William Kelsey, 3 vols., private printing 1929 and 1947.

Kilbourne, Payne – The History and Antiquities of the Name and Family of Kilbourn, Durrie and Peck, 1856.

Morrison, Leonard and Sharples, Stephen P. – History of the Kimball Family, 2 vols., Damrell and Upham, 1897.

Kingsbury, Frederick J. – The Genealogy and Descendants of Henry Kingsbury, Case Lockwood, 1905.

Robertson, Florence K. – The Genealogy of Henry and Ann Kinne, Wetzel Pub. Co., Los Angeles, CA, 1947.

Knapp, Alfred Averill – Nicholas Knapp Genealogy, Edwards Bros., Florida, 1953.

Hufbauer, Virginia Knowles – Descendants of Richard Knowles, Ventures International, San Diego, CA, 1974.

Lindly, John M. – The History of the Lindley, Lindsley, Linsley Families in America, vol 1, no published listed, 1930.

Lobdell, Julia Harrison – Simon Lobdell 1646 of Milford and His Descendants, published by the author, no date.

Holden, Frederick and Lockwood, E. Dunbar – Colonial and Revolutionary History of the Lockwood Family in America, privately printed, 1889.

Lord, Kenneth – Genealogy of the Descendants of Thomas Lord, Tuttle Morehouse and Taylor, New Haven, CT 1946.

Loveland, J. B. and George – Genealogy of the Loveland Family v. III, I. M. Keller & Son, Fremont, OH, 1895. Also vol. I.

Coleman, Lyman – Genealogy of the Lyman Family, J. Munsell, Albany, NY, 1872.

Lyons, A. B. & G. (editors) – Lyon Memorial, pub. by Albert Brown Lyons, William Graham Printing Co., Detroit, MI, 1905.

Manning, William H. – Genealogy and Biographical History of the Manning Family of New England and Descendants, Salem Press, Salem, MA, 1902.

Marsh, Dwight W. – Marsh Genealogy: John Marsh of Hartford, CT, pub. by D. W. Marsh by Press of Carpenter and Morebouse, Amherst, MA, 1895.

Watson, Elliot Burnham & Smith, Rev. Alven – George Martin of Salisbury, MA, and His Descendants, pub. by Alven M. Smith, S. Pasadena, CA, 1929.

Mather, Horace E. – Lineage of Rev. Richard Mather, Case Lockwood & Co., 1890.

Mason, Edna Warren – Descendants of Capt. Hugh Mason in America, Tuttle Morehouse and Taylor, New Haven, CT, 1937.

Merrill, Samuel – A Merrill Memorial, privately printed by the author, 1928.

Merriman, Mansfield and Jacobus, Donald – Descendants of Nathaniel Merriman, Donald Jacobus, New Haven, CT, 1914.

Miner, John Augustus – Thomas Miner Descendants 1608-1981, pub. by the author, ME, 1981.

Morgan, Nathaniel H. – Morgan Genealogy: A History of James Morgan, Case Lockwood and Brainerd, 1869.

Morris, Jonathan Flynt – A Genealogical and Historical Register of the Descendants of Edward Morris, Case Lockwood & Brainerd, 1887.

Morse, J. Howard and Leavitt, Emily W. – Morse Genealogy, Auspices of the Morse Society, Inc., 1903.

Munger, J. E. & Francis E. – The Munger Book, Something of the Mungers 1639-1914, Tuttle Morehouse and Taylor, 1915.

Munson, Myron A. – The Munson Record: A Genealogical and Biographical Account of Capt. Thomas Munson and His Descendants, 2 vols., Tuttle Morehouse and Taylor, New Haven, 1896.

Murdock, Joseph B. – Murdock Genealogy: Robert Murdock of Roxbury, MA, C. E. Goodspeed & Co., Boston, MA, 1925.

Murray, William B. – The Descendants of Jonathan Murray of East Guilford, CT. IL Valley Publishing Co., Peoria, IL, 1956.

Curry, Dorothy Neff – The Descendants of William Neff Who Married Mary Corliss Jan. 23, 1665, Haverhill, MA, no pub., 1958.

Newcomb, Bethuel M. – Andrew Newcomb 1618-1686 and His Descendants, Tuttle Morehouse & Taylor, printed for the author, 1923.

Leonard, Ermima Newton – Newton Genealogical, Biographical, Historical, Being a Record of Richard Newton, Tuttle Morehouse & Taylor, 1915.

Boltwood, Lucius M. – History and Genealogy of Thomas Noble of Westfield, MA, Case Lockwood and Brainerd, 1878.

North, Dexter – John North of Farmington, CT, and His Descendants, Rumford Press, Concord, NH, 1921.

Northrup, A. Judd – The Northrup-Northrop Genealogy, Grafton Press, NY, 1908.

Norton, James E. – The Norton-Tolles-Doty American Ancestry, privately printed, 1916.

Noyes, Col. Henry and Noyes, Harriette E. – Genealogical Record of Some of the Noyes Descendants of James, Nicholas and Peter Noyes, privately printed, Boston, MA, 1904.

Nye, George Hyatt and Best, Frank E. – A Genealogy of the Nye Family, pub. by the Nye Family of America, Assoc., 1907.

Penfield, Florence B. – The Genealogy of the Descendants of Samuel Penfield, Harris Press, Reading, PA, no date.

Perkins, Caroline and Derby, Perley – Descendants of Edward D. Perkins of New Haven, CT, pamphlet printed in Rochester, NY, 1914.

Perin, Stanley and Carl Leslie – The John Perrin Family of Rehoboth, MA, Gateway Press, Inc., Baltimore, MD, 1974.

Peters, Edmond F. and Eleanor – Peters of New England, Knickerbocker Press, NY, 1903.

Pitkin, A. P. – Pitkin Family in America: A Genealogy of the Descendants of William Pitkin, Case Lockwood, Hartford, CT. 1887.

Harris, Edward Doubleday – A Genealogical Record of Daniel Pond and His Descendants, pub. by William Parsons Lunt, Boston, MA, 1873.

Binney, C. J. F. – The History and Genealogy of the Prentice or Prentiss Family in New England, printed by Alfred Mudge & Son, 1883.

Preston, Charles Henry – Descendants of Roger Preston of Ipswich and Salem Village, Essex Institute, Salem, MA, 1931.

Prindle, Franklin C. – The Prindle Genealogy, printed by the Grafton Press, NY, 1906.

Paine, H. D. – Paine Family Records, v. 1, no publisher given, 1880.

Parish, Roswell - New England Parish Families, Tuttle Pub. Co., 1938.

Parks, Sylvester - Genealogy of the Parke Families of Connecticut, privately printed, 1906.

Smallwood, Dorothy - Parmalee Data, a Bi-Monthly Magazine, 10 vol. and index published by the editor, Mrs. Smallwood, 1940 on.

Partridge, George Henry - Partridge Genealogy, privately printed, 1915.

Peake, Cyrus H. - The Peak-Peake Family History, privately printed, 1975.

Pease, Rev. David - A Genealogical and Historical Period of the Descendants of John Pease Sr., Samuel Cowles and Co., Springfield, MA, 1869.

Peck, Darius - A Genealogical Account of the Descendants in the Male Line of William Peck of New Haven, CT. Bryan & Goeltz, Hudson, NY, 1877.

Peck, Ira B. - A Genealogical History of the Descendants of Joseph Peck, Alfred Mudge & Son, Boston, MA, 1868.

Hazen, Celeste Pember - John Pember, The History of the Pember Family in America, no printer given, 1939.

Baker, Wesley L. - Study of the Reeve Family, typed, 1970.

Rexford, J. D. - Rexford Genealogy, frontispiece missing.

Hanna, Doreen Potter - Some Descendants of Amos Richardson of Stonington, CT, paperbound, privately printed, 1971.

Vinton, John Adams - Richardson Memorial, Brown Thurston Co., 1876.

Boughton, James - A Genealogy of the Families of John Rockwell and Ralph Keeler, pub. by William F. Jones, NY, 1903.

Sanford, Carleton E. - Thomas Sanford Ancestry, Life and Descendants 1632-4, Tuttle Co., Rutland, VT, 1911.

Sargent, Aaron - Sargent Genealogy (Hugh and William), George Ellis, printer for the author, 1895.

Pearson, Ralph F. - The History of the Scarrit Clan in America, 2 vol., paperback, 1948.

Brainerd, Homer W. - A Survey of the Scovils or Scovills in England and America, printed for private use by the Hartford Co., 1915.

Scranton, Rev. Erastus - A Genealogical Register of the Descendants of John Scranton of Guilford, CT, Case Tiffany Co., 1855.

Sedgwick, Hubert M. - A Sedgwick Genealogy: Descendants of Deacon Benjamin Sedgwick, New Haven Colony Historical Society, 1961.

Seymour, George Dudley - A History of the Seymour Family: Descendants of Richard Seymour, Morehouse and Tuttle, 1939.

Shepard, Gerald Faulkner - The Shepard Families of New England, 2 vols., New Haven Colony Historical Society, 1971.

Sherman, Roy - The New England Shermans, no printer given, 1974.

Carl, Crispin & Shipman - The Shipman Family in America, Shipman Historical Society, 1962.

Shumway, Asahel Adams - Genealogy of the Shumway Family in the United States of America, George Shumway Publisher, 1972.

Fernald, Mrs. Natalie R. - The Skinner Kinsmen: Descendants of Thomas of Malden, Pioneer Press, Washington, DC, no date.

Peck, Thomas B. - William Slade of Windsor, CT, and His Descendants, Sentinel Printing Co., Keene, NH, 1910.

Slafter, Rev. Edmund - Memorial of John Slafter, Henry W. Dutton & Son, Boston, MA, 1869.

Slawson, George C. - The Slason-Slauson-Slawson-Slosson Family, Waverly and Son, Inc., NY, 1946.

Ridlon, G. T., Rev. - A Contribution to the Sole, Solly, Soule, Sowle, Soules, Journal Press, ME, 1926.

Spalding, Charles Warren - The Spaulding Memorial, Am. Publishing Assn., 1897.

Sprague, Warren Vincent - Sprague Families in America, Tuttle Co., Rutland, VT, 1913.

Stanton, William A. - A Record of Thomas Stanton and Descendants of CT, Joel Munsell Sons, Albany, NY, 1892.

Starkweather, Carleton Lee - A Brief Genealogical History of Robert Starkweather and His Son, John Starkweather, Knapp, Peck and Thomson, Auburn, NY, 1904.

Starr, Burgis Pratt - A History of the Starr Family, Case Lockwood Brainerd, 1879.

VanWagenen, Mrs. Avis Stearns - Genealogy and Memoirs of Isaac Stearns and His Descendants., Courier Printing Co., Syracuse, NY, 1901.

Sterling, Albert M. - Sterling Genealogy, Grafton Press, NY, 2 vols., 1909.

Keith, Bertha T. and Montana, Dillon - Stilson-Stillson Family, typed ca. 1954.

Stoddard, Charles - Anthony Stoddard and His Descendants, J. M. Bradstreet & Sons, NY, 1865.

Storrs, Charles - The Storrs Family, privately printed, NY, 1886.

Stowell, Wm. Henry H. - Stowell Genealogy, Tuttle Co., 1922.

Stratton, Harriet Russell - A Book of Strattons, Frederick Hitchcock, NY, 1918.

Dwight, Benjamin W. - The History of the Descendants of Elder John Strong of Northampton, MA, 2 vols., Joel Munsell, 1871.

Tillotson, E. Ward and Sweetser, Edward - The Tillotson Family in America, 2 vols., typed, Pittsburg, PA, 1942.

Tracy, Evert E. - Tracy Genealogy of Lt. Thomas Tracy, Joel Munsell, Albany, NY, 1898.

Trowbridge, Francis Bacon - Trowbridge Genealogy, privately printed for the compiler by Tuttle Morehouse and Taylor, 1908.

Tuttle, George Frederick - Descendants of William and Elizabeth Tuttle, Tuttle Co., 1883.

Brigham, Willard I. Tyler - The Tyler Genealogy: Descendants of Job Tyler of Andover, MA, 1619-1700, printed by Cornelius and Rollin Tyler, 1912.

Upson Family Assoc. of America - The Upson Family in America, Tuttle Morehouse and Taylor, New Haven, CT, 1940.

Lincoln, Waldo - Genealogy of the Waldo Family: Descendants of Cornelius Waldo, Charles Hamilton Press, Worcester, MA, 1902.

Wakeman, Robert P. - Wakeman Genealogy, 1630-1899, Journal Pub. Co., 1900.

Wallbridge, Wm. G. – Descendants of Henry Wallbridge, Who Married Anna Amos, no publisher given, 1898.

Holt, Nellie and Charles E. – Descendants of John Warner, typed 1960.

Assoc. of Des. of Andrew Ward by George Ward – Andrew Warde and His Descendants, A. T. DeLa Mare Printer, 1910.

Jacobus, Donald Lines and Waterman, Edgar – The Waterman Family: Des. of Richard Waterman, 3 vols., Connecticut Historical Society, 1954.

Webster, William and Rev. Melville – History and Genealogy of the Gov. John Webster Family of Connecticut, E. R. Andrews Printing Co., Rochester, NY, 1915.

Coleman, Ruth – Welles-Wells Families of Early Oneida Co., NY, typed, 1978.

Pierce, Frederick – The Descendants of John Whiting, printed for the author by W. B. Conkey Co., Chicago, IL, 1895.

Willard, Joseph and Walker, Charles Wilkes – Willard Genealogy, Willard Fam. Assoc., 1915.

Williamson, Cornelia Barton – Descendants of John Williams, privately printed, Chicago, IL, 1925.

TOWN AND COUNTY REFERENCES STILL AVAILABLE AT THE CONNECTICUT STATE LIBRARY

Adams, Andrew N. – A History of the Town of Fair Haven, VT, Leonard and Phelps Printers 1870.

Aldrich, Lewis C – History of Bennington County, VT, D. Mason & Co., Syracuse, NY. 1889.

Aldrich, Lewis C. – History of Franklin and Grand Isle Counties, VT, D. Mason & Co., Syracuse, NY, 1891.

Aldrich, Lewis C., editor – History of Windsor County, VT, edited for Frank R. Holmes, D. Mason & Co., Syracuse, NY, 1891.

Baldwin, Elmer – History of LaSalle County, IL, Rand McNally & Co., 1877.

Bass, H. Royce – The History of Braintree, VT, Tuttle & Co., 1883

Beers J. B. & Co. – History of Green County, NY, Published by J. B. Beers & Co., NY, 1884

Benton, Everett C. – A History of Guildhall, VT, with brief sketch of Essex County 1886.

Benton, Nathaniel S. – History of Herkimer County, NY, J. Munsell 1856.

Bierce, Lucius – Historical Reminiscences of Summit Co., OH.

Bigelow, Walter J. – History of Stowe, VT, printed by the author 1934.

Blackman, Emily C. – History of Susquehanna Co., PA, Claxton, Remsen and Haffelfinger 1873.

Booker, Warren, Comp. – Historical Notes Jamaica, Windham Co., VT, E.L. Hildreth & Co., Brattleboro, VT, 1940.

Bostwick, Erastus – History and Tales of Hinesburgh, VT, paperback, Essex Pub. Co., VT, 1976.

Bowen, Clarence – Genealogies of Woodstock, CT, Families, Plimpton Press, MA, 1930, 6 volumes.

Boyd, William P. - History of ths Town of Conesus, NY, Boyd's Job Printing 1887.

Brandon, Town of - Brandon, VT, A History of the Town 1761-1961, Pub. by the town 1961.

Briggs, Erasmus - History of the Original Town of Concord, NY, Union Advertizer Co., 1883.

Bronson, Henry, M.D. - History of Waterbury, CT, Bronson Bros. 1858.

Brookfield, Town of - Brookfield, VT, Records Available at the Town Hall.

Butler, L. C., M.D. - Memorial Record of Essex, VT, R.S. Styles Book and Job Printer 1866.

Butterfield, Ernest W. - Early History of Weathersfield, VT, An Address given 1921 at First Congregational Church

Caverly, A. M., M.D. - History of the Town of Pittsford, VT, Tuttle Co. 1872, Pittsford Hist. Soc., 1976

Child, Hamilton - Gazeteer and Business Directory of LaMoille and Orleans Counties, VT, 1883

Gazetteer and Business Directory of Bennington

Gazetteer and Business Directory of Washington Co., 1783-1889

Gazetteer and Business Directory of Chittenden Co.

Gazetteer and Business Directory of Orange Co., VT

Gazetteer and Business Directory of Windham Co. 1724-1884

Gazetteer and Business Directory of Caledonia and Esssx Counties, VT

Gazetteer and Business Directory of Addison Co., VT

All Child Gazeteer and Business Directories published by Syracuse Journal in the 1880's

Child, William H. - History of Cornish, NH, 2 vol., Rumford Press, no date.

Clark, Erwin S. - History of the Town of Addison, VT 1609-1976, paperback, Addison Press, Inc., Middlebury, VT 1978.

Clark, Azariah - Canaan, NY, Church Marriage Records of Azariah Clark 1807-1822, pub. CT State Library 1924 (10 pages)

Cleaver, Mrs. Robert - The History of the Town of Catherine (Schuyler Co., NY), Tuttle Pub. Co., Rutland, VT, 1945.

Connecticut Soc. of Genealogists - Queries in Soc. Quarterly, "The Nutmegger", CT Soc. of Genealogists.

Crockett, Walter - History of Vermont, Centennial Hist. 1923.

D. A. R. - Soldiers of the American Revolution Who At One Time Were Residents of Chautauqua Co., NY, 1925

Connecticut Soldiers Buried in Michigan

D. A. R. Patriot Index by Nat. Soc. 1966

Dana, Henry Swan - History of Woodstock, VT, Houghton Mifflin Co. 1889.

Davis, Gilbert A. - History of Reading, VT, 2 vol., pub. 1903.

Dearborn, John - History of Salisbury, NH, William E. Moore Pub. Co. 1890

Doane, Gilbert H., Ed. - Some Early Records of Fairfield, VT, paperback, Free Press Interstate Printing, 1938.

Douglas, Ben - History of Wayne Co., OH

Dyer, Albion Morris - First Ownership of Ohio Lands, Gen. Pub. Co. 1978.

Edson, Obed - History of Chautauqua Co., NY.

Elwell, Levi H. - Gravestone Records of Shaftsbury, VT.

Farrow, Ella - History of Holland, Vt, Queen City Printers, Burlington, VT, 1979.

Fletcher, Town of - A History of Fletcher, VT, paperback, George Little Press, Burlington, VT, 1976.

Franz, Mrs. Minnie W. - Revolutionary Soldiers of Summit Co., OH. (excerpt in 1972 Spring Issue of Ohio Gen. Soc.)

French, J. H. - 1860 Historical and Statistical Gazeteer of New York State, reprinted The Bookmark Co., Indiana, 1977.

Frost, Mrs. S.K. - Inscriptions from the Old Baptist Cemetery at Carmel, NY, 10 pages.

Galpin, Henry J. - Annals of Oxford, NY, Oxford Book and Job Printing, NY, 1906.

George, W.S. & Co. - Pioneer Collections of Michigan, Lansing, MI.

Goddard, M.E. and Partridge, Henry V. - A History of Norwich, VT, Dartmouth Press, NH, 1905.

Goodrich, George, Editor - The Centennial History of the Town of Dryden, NY, J. Giles Porter, 1898.

Goodwin, H.C. - Pioneer History of Cortland Co., NY, 1859.

Gregory, Hon. John - Early Settlers of Northfield, VT, Argus and Patriot Bk. Co., 1878.

Guilford, Town of - Official History of Guilford, VT, 1678-1961, edited by Broad Brook Grange 1961, Pub. by Town of Guilford and Broad Brook Grange.

Hancock, VT - The Story of Hancock, VT, 1780-1964, with Supplement 1969. Hancock, VT.

Hardin, George A. - History of Herkimer, NY, D. Mason & Co., 1893.

Harris, Dr. C. E. - A Vermont Village, Waterford Booklet, Privately Printed.

Hayden, Chauncey H., Ed. - The History of Jericho, VT, Free Press Printing, Burlington, VT, 1916.

Hayes, Lyman Simpson - History of Rockingham, VT, Pub. by Town of Bellows Falls, VT, 1907.

Hayward, Silvanus - History of the Town of Gilsum, NH, John B. Clark Pub., 1881.

Hemingway, Abby Maria - The Vermont Historical Gazeteer, 4 vol., 1868.

Hill, Ellen C. and Webster, Bob & Lois - Cemeteries of East Montpelier, VT, 1795-1971, Spiral Notebook 1973.

Hill, Ellen C. - Revolutionary War Soldiers of East Montpelier, VT, Bicentennial Committee of E. Montpelier 1975.

Holmes, Beatrice - History of Canaan, VT, 1976.

Howe, Henry - Historical Collection of OH.

Hyde Parke Bicent. Comm. - Hyde Park, VT, Shire Town of LaMoille Co., paperback, Hyde Park Bicentennial Comm., 1976.

Johnson, Cristfield - History of Cuyahoga Co., OH, D.W. Ensign (reprint) 1974.

Jones, Pomroy - Annals and Recollections of Oneida Co., NY, 1951.

Jones, Matt Bushnell – History of the Town of Waitsfield, VT, George E. Littlefield Pub., 1909.

Kinsbury, Frank Burnside – History of the Town of Surry, NH, Town of Surry, NH, 1925.

Kull, Nell M. – History of Dover, VT, paperback, Book Cellar, Brattleboro, VT, 1961.

Lovejoy, Evelyn – History of Royalton, VT, 1769–1911.

McKeen, Rev. Silas – A History of Bradford, VT, J.D. Clark & Son Pub., VT, 1875.

Mansfield, David L. – The History of the Town of Dummerston, VT, Pub. by A.M. Hemenway, 1884.

Mastin, Arthur – History of Cohoes, NY, Joel Munsell, Albany, 1877.

Matthews, Rev. Lyman – History of the Town of Cornwall, VT, Mead and Fuller, 1862.

More, Caroline Evelyn and Griffin, Irma M. – History of the Town of Roxbury, NY, Reporter Co., Inc., NY, 1953.

Munson, George A. – Early Years in Smyrna, NY, Chenango Union Press, 1905.

Newton, Ephraim H. – History of Marlborough, VT, 1787–1864, typed, not published.

Nickerson & Cox – Historical Souvenir of Randolph, VT.

Noble, Winona S. – The History of Cambridge, VT, Pub. Town of Cambridge 1976, soft cover.

Peck, S. L. – History of Ira, VT, Tuttle Co., Rutland, VT, 1926.

Pike, Elizabeth et al. – Pioneer History of Camden, NY, T. J. Griffiths, NY, 1897.

Pitkin, Ozias C. and Pitkin, Fred E. – History of Marshfield, VT, typed and bound 1941.

Pollard, Annie M. – The History of the Town of Baltimore, VT, VT Historical Soc., Montpelier, 1954.

Portage Co. Hist. Soc. – History of Portage Co., OH, 1972, reprint of copy pub. by Warner Beers Co., 1885.

Town of Pompey, NY – Pompey, NY, Our Town in Profile, Pompey Publication Committee, 1976.

Quick, F. N. – Dansville, NY, 1789–1902, ed. by A.O. Bunnell, Instructor Pub. Co., Dansville, NY.

Rann, W. S., Ed. – History of Chittenden, VT, D. Mason & Co., Syracuse, NY, 1886.

Smith, H. P. – History of Rutland, VT.

Rann, W. S. – D. Mason & Co., Syracuse, NY, 1886.

Stiles, Henry R. – The History of Ancient Wethersfield, CT, Grafton Press 1904, Reprint 1974, New Hampshire Pub. Co.

Stocker, Rhamanthur – Centennial History of Susquehanna Co., PA, Regional Pub. Co., Baltimore, MD, 1974.

Streeter, Nellie M. – Town of Lunenberg, VT, 1763–1976, Town of Lunenberg Historical Soc., paperback.

Storke, Elliot G. – History of Cayuga County, NY, D. Mason & Co., 1879.

Sylvester, Nathaniel Bartlett – History of Saratoga Co., NY, Everts & Ensign, Philadelphia, PA, 1878.

Thomas, Arad – Pioneer History of Orleans Co., NY, Orleans American Steam Press, 1871.

Tucker, William H. - History of Hartford, VT, 1761-1889.
U. S. Daughters of 1812 - Residents of CT Who Migrated to Huron Co., OH, typed, Nat. Soc. U. S. Daughters of 1812.
Vail, Henry - History of Pomfret, VT, 2 vols., Cockayne, Boston 1930.
Wager, Daniel, Ed. - Oneida, Our County and Its People, 1896.
Wells, Frederic P. - History of Newbury, VT, Caledonia, St. Johnsbury, VT, 1902.
Wells, Elsie C. - Bakersfield, VT, Bakersfield Bicent. Comm., Phoenix Pub., 1976.
Wheeler, Richard - History of Stonington, CT, Lawrence Verry, Inc., 1966.
White, Pliny H. - History of Coventry, Orleans Co., VT, A.A. Earle, 1859, pamphlet.
Williams, J. C. - History and Map of Danby, VT, McLean and Robbins, 1869.
Williams, H. Z. - History of Trumbull and Mahoning Cos., OH, 1882.
Wood, Grace E. P. - History of the Town of Wells, VT, 1955.
Wright, Ruth - History of the Town of Colchester, VT, Queen City Printers, 1963.
Wyman, Lora M. - History of Athens, VT, with Genealogies, Edwards Bros., Inc., Ann Arbor, MI, 1963, paperback, 1779-1960.

OTHER RESOURCES

1850 Census Records of the various states

Genealogical Quarterlies of VT, OH, MI, etc.

Visits to various cemeteries in VT, CT, and MA.

289

290

BEARDSLEY, Benjamin 234
Deborah 38 Eunice 57 Mrs 33
Nancy 234 Thankful 234
BECK, Roxanna 51
BECKWITH, Charity 179 Hopes-
till 16
BEEBE, Abigail 4 Electa 22
James 22
BEECHER, Elizabeth 105
BEERS, Abigail 206 Daniel 186
Esther 32 Mary 186 Patience
217 Phebe 32
BEESE, Charlotte 154
BELDEN, Elizabeth 123 Jonathan
123 Lydia 182 Mary 123 Sarah
A 164
BELDING, Elizabeth 16 Sarah
Belden 61
BELKNAP, Elizabeth 74 Sarah
100
BELL, Delight 202 Lany 255 Mrs
124 Samuel 202 Sarah 6
BELLAMY, Elizabeth 184
BELLOWS, Daniel 129 Deborah
129 Olive 177 Thankful 129
BEMENT, Phebe 7 8
BEMUS, Farozina 107
BENEDICT, Ann 54 Jonathan 82
Lucy 82 Priscilla 119 Rachel
68 Rebecca 137 Sally 137
Sarah 122
BENHAM, Deborah 104 Elizabeth
14 Hannah 32 Shadrack 14
BENJAMIN, Dolly 256
BENNETT, Abigail 160 Anne 81
Betsey 17 28 137 Catherine
247 Elizabeth 134 Eunice 39
87 228 Frances 245 Hannah 6
Jane 37 Mary 146 Rhoda 205
BENSON, Abbie A 193 Eunice 265
Margaret 193
BENTLEY, Harriet 251
BENTON, Anne 42 Barnabus 11
Dorothy 256 Juliana 53 Lydia
11 Rachel 38
BERRIEN, Catherine 89
BERRY, Eunice 232 Hannah 15
John 100 Kezia 100 Melina 43
BEVINS, Martha 222 Mary 222
Thomas 222
BICKNELL, Charlotte 221
Elizabeth 94 Jerusha 231

BIDLAKE, Sarah 77
BIDWELL, Hannah 88 Jonathan
88 Rachel 88 Sarah 225
Tryphena 152
BIGELOW, Amasa 81 Anne 205
David 139 Jemima 81 Lydia 3
Mercy 139 Rebecca 3
BILL, Abigail 93 Ebenezer 175
Eliphalet 181 Lucretia 175
Mary 20 Mercy 143 144 146
Patience 271 Patty 51
Prudence 240
BILLETT, Sibyl 15
BILLINGLY, Mrs 47
BILLINGS, Betsey 181 Grace 111
John 252 Melinda 124 Olive
252
BINGHAM, Esther 137 Mary 142
BIRCHARD, Elizabeth 114
BIRD, Dorcas 134
BIRDWELL, Abigail 223
BISHOP, Abigail 86 Nancy Ann
177 Rebecca 122 Rhoda 248
Ruth 110 Susan 50
BISSELL, Sybil 175
BIXBEE, Ebenezer 146 Hannah
146 Huldah 146
BLACKLEACH, Elizabeth 38
BLACKLEY, Temperance 170
BLACKMAN, Dolly 72 Jane 158
Lois 119 158 Rebecca 255
Sarah 78
BLACKSLEY, Susannah 169
BLAIR, Mary 203
BLAKE, Angelina 231 Chloe 60
Henry 46 Mehitable 46
BLAKELEY, Sarah 80
BLAKESLEE, Chlorama 6
Minerva 165 Miriam 112 Sarah
Minerva 165 Sina 259 Zophar
165
BLAKESLY, Phoebe 262
BLANCHARD, Minerva 51 Peter
167 Sarah 167
BLANDIN, Parmelia 23
BLINN, Mercy 94
BLISS, David 244 Elizabeth 271
Ellis 178 Lucy 46 Lydia 178
Polly 244 Rebecca 221 Samuel
271 Sarah 244 Tamar 178
BLOORE, Joshua 195 Margaret
195

BLOSS, Richard 177 Zeruah 177
BOARDMAN, Lucy 34 Mary 107
Ruth 202 Sarah 48
BOARN, Rachel 190
BODMAN, Abigail 181
BODWELL, Polly 114
BOGUE, Elizabeth C 174
BOHONON, Andrew 132 Dorcas
132 Susannah 132
BOLAND, Martha 220
BOND, Melinda 129 Sarah 20
BOOTH, Elizabeth 32 Hester 209
Isaac 32 Jemima 173 Lydia 32
Mary 93
BORDEN, Lois 85 Maria 56
BORDMAN, Jerusha 73
BOSS, Martha 40
BOSTWICK, Mary 41
BOSWORTH, Mary 47
BOTSFORD, Dorothy 18
BOUGHTON, Deborah 123
BOUTON, Theodosia Penoyer 202
BOWEN, Abina 144 Clarissa 174
Jerusha 95 Margaret 264
BOWMAN, Harriet 153 Sarah 47
BOYD, Mary 13
BOYNTON, Phoebe 21
BRACKET, Abigail 226
BRADFORD, Anna 52 Edith 32
Hannah 79 242 257
BRADLEY, Abigail 137 Almira
217 Andrew 220 Ann 87
Elizabeth 268 Eunice 137
James 137 Mehitable Alcott 33
Ruth 220 Sarah 156 210 220
BRAINERD, Alice 29 30 Dorcas
105 Elijah 29 70 Lucy 70 Polly
76 Susanna 130 William 130
BRAMAN, Rebecca A 241
BRANCH, Anna 84 Cynthia 167
Elizabeth 84 Samuel 84
BRATTON, Margaret 225
BREED, Mary 33 Mercy 162
Prudence 261
BREESE, Sally 146
BREWSTER, Anna 63 199
Charles Jr 63 Clarissa F 147
Ephraim 227 Hopestill 106
Hulda 54 Huldah 129 Ichabod
54 Jerusha 197 Lydia 54 223
Martha 137 Polly 34 63 227
BRIDGES, Mehitable 51

BRIGGS, Mary 72 Sally 254
BRIGHAM, Betsey 115 Sophia 138
BRINK, Esther 153 Mary 153
Thomas 153
BRINSMADE, Huldah 139
BRINTAL, Margaret 195
BRISCOE, Lucy 44 Molly 44 William 44
BRISTOL, Ann 29 Marion 185
Sarah 100
BROCKETT, Deborah 33 Josiah
33 Sarah 33
BROCKWAY, Naomia 136
BRONSON, Hannah 198 Lois 260
Mary 4 Mercy 213 Rebecca 27
BROOK, Anna 31 32 Mary 31 32
BROOKER, Sarah 146
BROOKS, Benjamin 58 Deborah
135 Elizabeth 164 Mary 58
Sophia 112 Thankful 58
BROOKWAY, Elizabeth 242
BROUGHTON, Marcy 158
BROWN, Abigail 5 101 145 Anna
84 Content 71 Dorothy 145
Elizabeth 3 99 100 117
Elizabeth Starkwether 103
Hannah 188 Henry 145
Humphrey 117 Jemima Gates
226 Kezia 59 Lillis 164 Lucy
186 Lydia 146 Margaret 87
Martha 46 Mercy 53 Nancy 211
Nathaniel 53 Nehemiah 257
Patty 257 Rachel 241 Rebecca
257 Ruth 47 Sarah 8 145 171
189 Sarah Fox 5
BROWNING, Polly 89
BROWNSON, Catherine Jane 83
Harriet 217 Hulda 148
BRUSH, Amy 130 Catherine Esther 66 Frances 4 Nancy 15
Reuben 66
BRYANT, Susan 93
BUCHANAN, Frances 4
BUCK, Anna 13 Daniel 7 Martha
40 Mary 40 261 Nabby 7 Olive
7 Ruth 238 Samuel 40 Zerviah
222
BUCKINGHAM, Anna 134
Jedediah 58 Lucretia 126 Mary
58 Phebe 17
BUCKLEY, Betsey 160 Charles
160 Mary 251

BUEL, Abigail 125 183 Betsey 47
BUELL, Hannah 79 Jesse 205
Lydia 144 Mary 152 Nancy 205
Timothy 79
BUGBEE, Amos 42 Caroline 42
Elizabeth 154 Mehitable 140
Sally 173
BULKELY, Abigail 16
BULL, Esther 85 Mindwell 105
Ursula Gillett 166
BULLARD, Hannah 22 Mehitable
265 Sarah 186
BULLOCK, Levina 193
BUMP, Eleanor 119 Levi 8
Patience 8 Sarah 8
BUNCE, Susan 144
BUNN, Hopa 139 Patty 261
BURDICK, Avis 195 Lydia 33
Mary 260
BURGE, Martha 47
BURGESS, Sarah 126
BURK, Sarah 51 Silas 51
BURKE, Mrs 248
BURNAP, Mary 103
BURNHAM, Abina 144 Betsy 103
Elijah 144 Elizabeth 135 Polly
E 144 Relief 159 Rhoda 66 67
Walter 174
BURR, Anne 210 Beulah 124 Experience 135 Hannah 117 Mary
235
BURRELL, Sarah Maria 130
BURRITT, Anna 81 Anthony 81
Mary Ann 81
BURROUGHS, Abner 192 Margaret
192 Polly 169 Roxalana 192
Sarah 233
BURROWS, Hannah 63 Hannah
Gore 83 Jerusha 215 Julia A
215 Roswell 215
BURT, Rhoda 12
BURTON, Betsey 41 David 79
Polly 79 Ruth 101 164
BUSH, Ebenezer 201 Elizabeth
238 Lurana 201 Phoebe 85
Roxanna T 269 Sarah Mead 85
Tamar 154 Timothy 85
BUSHNELL, Clarissa 131 Matilda
101 Zipporah 21
BUTLER, Abigail 101 Catherine
258 Esther 173 Mary 85 109
187

BUTT, Phebe 39
BUTTERFIELD, Joanna 251
Rebecca 118
BUTTON, Betsey 169 Joseph 169
Matthias 112
BUTTS, Elizabeth 39 Phoebe 39
Sybil 80
BYINGTON, Clarissa 12 Elvira 55
Heman 12 Mary 184
CABLE, Abigail 76
CABLES, Abigail 158
CADWELL, Jerusha 117 Sarah 80
CADY, Amith 168 Mary 260
Mercy 69 Tamasin 177
CALDWELL, Catey 52 Mary 133
CALKINS, Jerusha Brooks 151
CAMP, Hannah 204 Lydia 62
Polly 99
CAMPBELL, Lydia 152 Robert
152 Sarah 83 Sybil 1
CANFIELD, Electa 3 Lee 18
Maria 18 Submission 153
CAPEN, Esther 220
CAREW, Hannah 43
CAREY, Mary 21
CARPENTER, Abigail 46 Achsah
47 Alathea 47 Amos 74 Anna
225 Chloe 119 Dorothy 36 Hannah 19 Huldah 76 Jonah 47
Nancy 76 Polly 73 74
CARR, Nancy 222 Sarah Phillips
266
CARRIER, Abigail 110 Jerusha
242
CARRINGTON, Esther 56
CARTER, Benj 126 Deborah 257
Margery 117 Mercy 207 Phebe
126
CARTWRIGHT, Laura 43
CARVER, Esther 25 Milly 189
Olive 156 Samuel 156 Wealtha
189
CARY, Minerva 81
CASE, Azubah 179 Cynthia 239
Hepzibah 101 Jonah 206
Jonathan 96 Lois 96 Lucy 206
Mary 10 Mercy 263 Ruth 180
Sarah 271
CASS, Lois 197
CASTLE, Aurelia 226 Isaac 124
Mary 123 124 234 Molly 209
Rachel 134

CASWELL, Elizabeth 59
  Jonathan 59 Margery 59
CAULKINS, Polly 22
CAVERLY, Hannah 95
CENTER, Ruth 112
CHADWICK, Hepzibah 2 Jerusha
  242
CHAFFE, Tabitha 42
CHAFFEE, Sophronia 233
CHAMBERLAIN, 10 Abigail 110
  Alice 138 Dorcas 122
  Elizabeth 185 Irene 138 Jane
  233 Mehitable 165 Oliver 55
  Ruth 162 Sabra 56 Sally 55
  Sara 56
CHAMPIN, Mehitable 146
CHAMPION, Elizabeth 191
CHAMPLAIN, Lodowick 8 Mary 8
CHANDLER, Abigail 47 101 An-
  nis Orr 45 Charity 226
  Elizabeth 163 251 Eunice 252
  Jonathan 28 Joseph 226 Josiah
  45 Margaret 45 Mary Bullard
  35 Mehitable 57 Polly 28
  Rebecca 28 Sara 226 Seth 252
CHAPIN, Ebenezer 3 Elizabeth 3
  Maria G 195 Mary 195
CHAPMAN, Abiel 121 Abigail 107
  Anna 13 Benjamin 107 Esther
  193 Lavinia 202 Lydia 29 107
  Philinda 97 Prudence 25 Rhoda
  231 Ruth 167 Sarah 53 Sibyl
  128 Uriah 128 Ursula 99
CHAPPELL, Polly 264
CHASE, Eunice 113 Hannah 12
  Phebe 164 Rachel 63
CHATFIELD, Mary 15
CHEEVER, Lurena 190
CHENEY, Bethia 76
CHESTER, Polly 118
CHICKERLY, Ruth 196
CHIDESTER, Clorinda 139
CHIDSEY, Augustus 30 Ruth 30
CHILD, Alice 252 Charles 165
  Chloe 252 Dorothy 214 217
  Elisha 252 Elizabeth 206 Han-
  nah 44 Jonathan 44 Keziah 165
  206 Lucretia 47 Mary 148
  Nehemiah 47 Samuel 206 Sarah
  154 Sylvia 48
CHILDS, Anna 153 Dorothy 216
  Orinda 56

CHIPMAN, Abigail 166 Handly 16
  Jane 16 Jane Allen 16
CHITTENDEN, Clarinda 120 Lucy
  149 Mary 84 Thankful 128
CHOATE, Annie 14 William 14
CHURCH, Hannah 147 Mary S 159
  Polly 239
CHURCHILL, Melinda 140
CLAPP, Amasa 168 Dolly 168
CLARK, Anna 241 Augustin 142
  Benjamin 51 Charlotte 66 84
  Chauncey 156 Clementine 226
  Climena 37 Deborah 243
  Desire 111 Elizabeth 5 27 28
  51 114 173 Hannah 24 76 77
  115 158 209 243 Jeremiah 77
  Jerusha 259 John 243 255
  Joseph 28 Lucia 98 Lucinda
  127 Lucy 98 Lydia 61 Margery
  124 Martha 34 Mary 126 142
  146 262 Matilda 156 Melina
  241 Miss 91 Nathan 241 Par-
  thena 259 Patience 133 Per-
  melia Strong 247 Philocha 159
  Rebecca 243 257 Relief 255
  Samuel 66 159 Sarah 121
  Stephen 133 Susan 115 Susanna
  51
CLARKE, Sarah Ann 213
CLAUSSON, Mercy 190
CLEVELAND, Abigail 104 111
  269 Benjamin 111 112 Mary 4
  Permelia 266 Rachel 111 112
  Ruth 104 Samuel 104 Sarah 234
  Squire 266 Susan 184 Zurviah
  266
CLINTON, Elizabeth 105 John
  105 Sarah 105
CLOSSON, Mercy 190 191 Nancy
  190
CLOTHIER, Lydia 224
COATES, Mercy 229
COBB, Jemima 58
COBURN, Elizabeth 13 Martha
  145
COCHRAN, Betsey 165
COE, Abigail 67 Hannah 98 Mary
  98 Phoebe 95
COFFIN, Mary Ann 260
COGSDELL, Submit 55 Rebecca
  162
COLBURN, Esther 177

COLE, Abigail 24 Alice 248 Anna 160 Bathsheba 24 Betsey 70 Ebenezer 24 Elizabeth 198 Emily Frances 266 Esther S 265 Margaret 162 Polly 3 140 Rebecca 257
COLEMAN, Hannah 93 Hulda 129 Mary 211 Ozias 129
COLES, Abigail 139
COLLIER, Ann Eliza 88
COLLINS, Elizabeth 203 Mary 92 159 Nancy 143 Roxana 29
COLT, Mary 29
COLTON, Betsey 35 Esther 35 Lucy 36 Mabel 35 Mary 129 Mollie 192 Willard 192
COLVIN, Clarissa 80
COMSTOCK, Deidamia 143 Gideon 22 Hannah 22 Hepzibah 197 Naomi 163 William 197
CONE, Anna 20 Clarissa 161 Eliza 260 Elizabeth 222 Esther 183 Philena 23 Thomas 161
CONGER, Caty 157 Clarinda 201
CONKLIN, Loretta 254 Polly 57 Widow 74
COOK, Anna 204 Chloe 177 Damaris 27 Demaris 26 Dorcas 198 Elizabeth 95 Lucy 71 Melita 47 Nancy 34 Philip 47 Prudence 205 Ruth 170 Sally 36 Samuel 27 Sarah 72 171 Sibyl 128 Susanna 51 Thankful 57 Urzula 151
COOLEY, Eunice 21 Mary 156
COOPER, Sally 270 Zilpah 271
COPP, Lois 16 Mary 267 Samuel 16
CORBETT, Eve 133 Robert 133
CORBIN, Abigail 251 Moses 251 Sarah 251
CORNING, Huldah 30
CORSE, Elizabeth 156
CORWIN, Rebecca 64
COSSITT, Mary 101
COTTER, Esther 98 John 6 Thankful 6
COTTON, Penelope 127
COURTRIGHT, Susan 254
COVEY, Abigail 175
COWDREY, Chloe 7 John 7 Ruth 7

COWDRY, Ruth 115
COWEN, Lucy A 181
COWLES, Amaryllis 159 Martha 111 Statira 269
COWLS, Lois 54
COX, Sarah 124 William 124
COY, Lucinda 80 Mary 1
CRAFTS, Anna 52
CRAM, Susanna 120
CRANDALL, Anna 189
CRANE, John Jr 96 Mary 120 Rebecca 96 Sarah 96
CRAWFORD, Lucretia 236
CRIPPEN, Phoebe 85
CROCKER, Elizabeth 1 191 John 191 Phebe 190 191 192
CROOKS, David 55 Eunice Cone 55 Mary 55
CROPSY, Mary 91
CROSBY, Polly 131 Stata 158
CROSS, Hannah 174 Joseph 149 Mehitable 257 Polly 149
CROSSETT, Archibald 79 Betsey 79
CROUCH, Elizabeth 233
CROWEL, Phebe 113
CROWELL, Rebecca 11
CROXFORD, 116
CULLEN, Susan P 5
CULVER, Eunice 190
CUMINS, Rebecca 172
CUMMINGS, Betsey 181 Lydia 238 Rebecca 129
CUMMINS, Elizabeth 229
CURTIS, Aurelia 226 Benjamin 226 Betsey 169 Elizabeth 71 85 Enoch 135 Eunice 182 Hannah 55 97 Maria Bethiah 5 Marilla 218 Mary 27 85 90 Nancy 71 159 Olive 170 Rachel 200 Rachel P 135 Samuel 85 Sarah 58 100
CURTISS, Abel 67 Eunice 162 Lucy 182 Olive 122 Patricia 121 Rebecca 67 Sarah 59
CUSHING, Elizabeth A 19 Sarah 26
CUSHMAN, Abigail 25 Alcessa 67 Lydia 23 Mary 126 Nabby 105 Priscilla 112 Sarah 51 Thomas 126
CUTLER, Lucinda 129 Rebecca 8

CUTTING, Abigail 174
DAGGETT, Sarah 48
DAILY, Olive 177 178
DAKE, Lucy 113
DAKIN, Sarah 12
DALE, Sarah 156
DANA, Frances 241 Hannah 140
    Isaac 206 James 31 John 140
    Josiah 32 Lois 180 Mary 32
    112 Polly 31 Samuel Jr 112
    Sarah 112 147 206 214
DANIELS, Ann 50 Eleanor 50 Es-
    ther 175 Nathaniel Sr 50
DANIELSON, Mary 69
DANNELLS, Eleanor 133 George
    133
DARBE, Ruth 4 52 104
DARBY, Ruth 52
DARLING, Betsey 36
DARRIN, Lucy 26
DARROW, Grace 232 Lavina Dar-
    rah 100
DART, Daniel 222 Jabish 82
    Jemima 222 Jerusha 82 Lucy
    222 Sarah 22 82
DARTE, Mehitabel 23
DAUCHY, Ruth 268
DAVENPORT, Anne 127
    Elizabeth 255 Emily 258
    Eunice 2 Lois 262 Mary 9
DAVID, Mermelia 84
DAVIDSON, Diedama Morse 54
DAVIS, Abigail 122 Ann 208 Anna
    84 191 257 Clarissa 270 Daniel
    84 Dolly 254 Elizabeth 18 74
    267 Esther 65 213 Hannah 10
    38 Jabez 18 Jacob 113 Jael 44
    45 James 74 Lucy 113 Mary
    122 Mehitabel 74 Noah 191
    Percia 266 Persis 41 Philip
    122 Rebecca 39 Ruth 69 Sarah
    18 109 264
DAVISON, Lydia 50
DAWLEY, Ebenezer 151 Lovina
    151 Mary 151
DAY, Abial Mrs 127 Abiel 121
    Dorcas 121 John 121 Lydia 179
    Mary 42 Sarah 45
DAYTON, Alvira 123 Anna 123
    Sarah A 189 Sybil 34
DEADY, Polly 143

DEAN, Elizabeth 197 Hannah 36
    Mary 36 Ruth 69 Sarah 60 232
    Zephaniah 36
DEARBORN, Hannah 242 Sarah
    127
DeGROFF, Cornelius 169 Sarah
    169
DELANO, Asenath 96 Betsey 61
    Huldah 96 Stephen 96
DEMING, Lucy 28 Ruth 5
DEMMING, Huldah 52 Lucy 85
DENISON, Abigail 158 Elizabeth
    189 Mary 134
DENNISON, Eunice 100 Lois 130
    Susan 174
DENTON, Ann 34 Benjamin 72
    Joanna 72 Mary 72
DERBY, Elizabeth 116 Mary 5
    Ruth 52
DEVOTION, Abigail 192 Edward
    192 Mary 192
DEWEY, Abigail 61 Anna 41
    Lydia 33 Noah 61 Sarah 152
    Tamar 24 Tamasin 257 Tem-
    perance 212
DEWITT, Mary 157
DEXTER, Hannah Swift 99 Phebe
    143
DIBBLE, Anna 101 Aurelia 101
    Daniel 101 Mary 108
DICK, Elizabeth 125
DICKENSON, Lydia 48 Mrs 25
DICKINSON, Ann 66 Dan 268
    Hannah 72 Huldah 92 Lucy 7
    Maria 268 Rachel 268
DICKSON, Marion 207
DIKE, Irena 260
DILLEY, Susannah 190
DIMMICK, Daniel 204 Esther 73
    Hannah 204 Shubael 73 Thank-
    ful 204
DIMMOCK, Mary 115
DIMON, Jane 29
DISBROW, Elizabeth 93
DODGE, Elizabeth Sophia 52
    Eunice 229 Mehitable 255
    Molly 191
DOLP, Ruth 82
DOOLITTLE, Beulah 268 Cynthia
    202 Ebenezer 135 Jerusha 135
    Mary Ann 111 Mary L 217

DORCHESTER, Elizabeth 37
DORR, Mary 134
DORRANCE, Elizabeth 83 Susan 14
DORWIN, Olive 263
DOTEN, Mercy 53
DOTY, Huldah 96
DOUBLEDAY, Anna 192 Nathaniel 192
DOUD, Electa 186 Esther 150 198
DOUGLAS, Asena 49
DOWNER, Elizabeth 134
DOWNING, Lodema 266
DOWNS, David 203 Laura 50 Susan 203
DRAKE, Lovina 87
DRESSER, Sally B 49
DRINKWATER, Mercy 254
DRURY, Abigail 241
DRYER, Huldah 168
DUDLEY, Abigail 135 Elizabeth 49 81 Josiah 81 Sabra 81
DUNBAR, Content 204 Jerusha 267 Joel 201 Mary 201 Olive 73 Sabra 204 Temperance 201
DUNHAM, Deidamia 44 Patience 41
DUNKS, Amelia 88 Millicent 88
DUNLAP, Sally 228 Sarah 203
DUNNING, Abigail 157 Betsey 209
DUNTON, Susan 23
DURGE, Jerusha 145
DURKEE, Andrew 7 190 Bartholomew 109 Electa 7 Elizabeth 102 Eunice 46 252 Jerusha 77 Phoebe 190 Rachel 190 Sarah 145 Susannah 86 Theodosia 109
DUTTON, Abigail 259 Elvira 98 Helen 259 Joseph 98 Mindwell 89 Miranda 259 Sybil 163
DYE, Charlotte 177 Philo 177 Saloma 177
DYER, Abigail 53 John 53
EASTMAN, Sarah 211
EATON, Susan 199
EDDY, Charlotte 253 Lucy 5 Martha 117 Samuel 117 Sarah 45
EDEN, Patience 16
EDGERTON, Abiah 15 Martha 226 Phebe 227 Sarah 144 208

EDSON, Lydia 25 Relief 25 Timothy 25
EDWARDS, Elizabeth 217 Hannah 81 82 Martha 82 Mary 91 94 Sally M 8 Sarah 136 William 82
EGGLESTON, Sabra 133 Sarah 24
ELAITHORPE, Nathaniel 23
ELDERKIN, Elizabeth 132 Judith 25
ELDRED, Thalia 198
ELITHORPE, Esther 23 Jemima 23
ELLINGTON, Joanna 172
ELLINGWOOD, Joanna 172 Johanna 172 Jonathan 172
ELLIOT, Betsey 220
ELLIOTT, Clarissa 230 Elizabeth 45
ELLIS, Rose 17
ELLSWORTH, Aurel 165 Caroline 103 Elizabeth 196 Jemima 101 Samuel 196
ELRED, Elizabeth 196
ELSWORTH, Chloe 258
ELWELL, Mary 91
ELY, Amy 91 Jane 85 Laura 29 Mary 31 Rebecca 91 Wells 91
EMERSON, Ann 62 Dorothy 62 Olive 76 Samuel 62
EMMONS, Hannah 57
ENGLISH, Abigail 222
ENOS, Jerusha Hayden 4 Roger 4
ENSWORTH, Sarah 52
ERSKINE, Content 191
EVARTS, Abner 48 Beulah 48 Damaris 155 Sarah 48 Susannah 48
EVERETT, Daniel 169 Elizabeth 169 170 Mary 96 Sarah 169 170
EVERETTS, Minerva 154
EVERSON, Louisa 88
EVERTS, Mehitable 108
FAIRCHILD, Daniel 180 Eunice 41 Jerusha 180
FANNING, Catherine 69
FANTON, Jane 29
FARGO, Daniel 138 Mary 138 Mary Jeannette 138
FARMAN, Jerusha 241
FARNHAM, John 96 Mary 96 Phebe 117 Rebecca 96

FARNUM, Azubah 13 Elisheba
147 Miriam 117
FARRINGTON, Thyrsa 110
FASCIT, Grace 46
FASSETT, Clara 148 Dr 148
FAY, Esther 87
FELCH, Lucinda 50
FELLOWS, Jonathan 176 Mary
132 176 Mary Ann 224
FELT, Cornelia 113 Harriet 53
FENNER, Sarah 79
FENTON, Dorothy 213 Mary 221
Phebe 136
FIELD, Ann 66 Anna 61 66 Lois
228 Moses 61 66 Roxanna 96
Sally 115
FIELDS, Bennett 266 Hannah 113
Jesse 218 Mary 266 Sally 218
FILER, Abigail 161 Elizabeth 92
FILLEBROWN, Anne 148
FILLEBROWNE, Anna 47
FILLIS, John 8 Mary Roah 8
FINCH, Phebe 101
FINLEY, Esther 63
FISH, Abigail 153 Emma A 228
Huldah 30 Jesse 228 Jonathan
153 Lydia 118 Martha 37
Matilda 153 Miller 30 Rebecca
30
FISHER, Abigail 97 Catherine 187
Cornelius 97 Hannah 97 John
187
FISK, Diana 202 Jonathan 96
Mary 96 Sarah 161
FITCH, Abigail 53 Althea 49
Anna 48 Asenath 49 Elizabeth
5 Hannah 126 200 Lois 244
Lucy 40 96 Mercy 149 Sarah G
70 William 49
FITTS, Hannah 76
FLEMING, Helen 221
FLETCHER, Penuel 237 Rachel
74
FLINT, Abigail 80 Bartholomew
76 Eunice 144 145 Hannah 146
Hannah Tracy 23 James 23
Jerusha 23 25 Lucy 1 Mary 76
144 Mehitabel 167 Philena 76
Polly 236 Sally 1 Samuel 144
FLORENCE, Susan 250
FLOWER, Rhoda 92
FLOYD, Mary 237

FLYNN, Elizabeth 193 Mary H
267 Richard 267
FOBES, Asenath A 205 Lemuel
205
FOLLETT, Mary 268
FOLSOM, Abraham 115 Elizabeth
115
FOOT, Almira Mills 57 Asa 57
Hannah B 241
FOOTE, Anna 7 Betsey 170 Es-
ther 71 Jesse 65 Margaret 62
Mary 7 Mary Shattuck 20
Rosetta 65 Samuel 7 Thankful
182
FORBES, Hannah 240 Mary 84
FORCE, Caroline 87
FORD, Elizabeth 75 Ella 118
Hannah 76 Polly 43 Rachel 45
Zilpah 159
FORMAN, Jonathan 206
FOSTER, Anna 97 Dan 95 Eunice
239 Hannah 46 Harriet B 261
Joseph 22 Nancy 95 Rebecca
200
FOWLER, Jemima 129 Sarah 21
FOX, Allis 132 Caroline 120
Electa 120 Esther 132 133 177
Fannie 13 Moses 120 Ruth 266
Sibbel 24
FRANKLIN, Cynthia 180 Dolly 47
Esther 253
FRASER, Jane 37
FRAZIER, Anna 49 Simon 49
FREEMAN, Anna 73 Annie 20
Harriet 99 Keziah 73 Mary 244
Skiff 73
FRENCH, Charity 174 Elizabeth
15 16 82 Freelove 16 Lois 74
Mary 15 Philena 140 Samuel
15 16 Sarah 4 Sarah E 140
Susannah 229 Theodosia 224
FRISBEE, Rachel 39
FRISBIE, Thankful 182
FRIZZELL, John 63 Lois 63
Martha 63 Patty 152
FROST, Dorcas 3 Sally 147
FULFORD, Ruth 229
FULLER, Abigail 72 Adelia E 43
Catherine 13 Chloe 184 Cyrus
43 Daniel 163 Elijah 184
Elizabeth 4 85 Esther 126 217
Hannah 147 Harriet 43

GRANGER, Aaron 89 Apena 89
Mary 89
GRANNIS, Abigail 222 Patience
51
GRANT, Benjamin 216 Ephraim
53 Esther 13 53 Grace Reed
200 Margaret 9 Sarah 216
Triphena 160
GRAVES, Asenath 221 Fanny 240
Mercy 71 Olive 90 Polly 200
Ruth C 237 Sally 58 Tamson
231
GRAY, Bethiah 104 Betsey 66 209
Elijah 209 Elizabeth 125 Ruth
99 Sally 209
GREEN, Abel 90 Bethany 67
Ebenezer 253 Emily Jane 130
Esther 1 James 61 Jerusha 44
219 Lucretia 146 Mary 61 90
Nancy 113 Pamelia 52 Par-
thenia 61 Permelia 266 267
Phebe 114 Phoebe 239 Polly
90 Vetty 253
GREENE, Jonathan 119 Mary 119
Prudence 261 Sarah 124
GREENSLIT, Sarah 1
GREGORY, Hannah 72 210
Hezekiah 91 Mary 91
GRIDLEY, Martha 206 271
GRIGGS, Harriet 53 Stephen 53
GRIGS, Elizabeth 120
GRISWOLD, 38 Betsey 48
Ebenezer 1 Elias 92 Eunice 1
Grace 253 Hannah 1 64 70
Jemima 64 Lucy 9 Lydia 115
Rhoda 92 Sarah 35 74 Stephen
64
GROSS, Jonah 85 Susanna 85
Susannah 85
GROSVENOR, Ann 50 Joshua 118
Mary 165 Olive 118
GROW, Erepta 42 Hannah 11 John
42 Joseph 56 Persis 213
Phalle 213 Rhoda 18 Timothy
213 Tirza 56
GROWE, Susanna 230
GUERNSEY, Comfort 17
GUILD, Mabel 35
GUNN, Sarah 252
GURDON, Hannah 132 Joseph 132
GUTHRIE, Abbie 209 Ann 129
Eunice 117

HAGER, Nancy 90
HAINES, Abbie Lucinda 266
HAIT, Mary 17
HALE, Abigail 93 Betsey 7 Chloe
105 Elizabeth 238 Hannah 7
Martha 238 Nancy 41 Naomi
108 Patty 240 Rachel 96 Ruth
108 Thomas 108 238
HALEY, Sarah Niles 218
HALL, 236 Benjamin 98 Chloe
268 Dolly 170 Elizabeth 215
Genevieve K 163 Gershom 5
Hannah 170 Hiland 170 James
78 Jennie 268 Jerusha 173
John Henry 163 Katherine 163
Lovica 13 Lydia 31 Mamre 109
Martha 172 Mary 13 76 78 144
Mehitable 170 Nathaniel 204
Phoebe 23 Rachel 5 112 Rhoda
204 Ruth 98 Sarah 176 Tabitha
96
HALLADAY, Anna 71 Cynthia 128
Jesse 128 Sarah 128
HALLOCK, Sarah 150
HALLOWAY, Elsa 227
HALSTEAD, Tamar 209
HAMILTON, Elizabeth 158
HAMLIN, Deborah 138 Mercy 113
HAMMOND, Lucy 227 Mehitable
178
HANCHET, Unice 97
HANCHETT, Mary 208
HANFORD, Ruth 18
HANLON, Johanna 207
HARD, Esther 209 Hester 209
James 41 209 Lois 1 Rachel
30
HARDENBROOK, Lydia A 57
HARDY, Rebecca 59
HARE, Mary 144 Sarah 265
HARLOW, Rhoda 187
HARMAN, Hannah 234 Phineas
234
HARMON, Cellia 213 Mary 6
Sarah 208
HARPER, James 233 John 111
Margaret 111 192 Ruth 233
Sarah 233
HARRIS, Bethia 120 Elizabeth 8
Israel 270 Mary 96 Rachel 117
Sarah 270
HARRISON, Abigail 248 Alma 222

HARRISON (continued)
Lucy 233 Ruth 43
HART, Almira 189 Lucy 95 Mary
37
HARTER, Catherine 92
HARTSHORN, Abigail 7 Clarissa
7 Ebenezer 7
HARTWELL, Amy 201 Laura 161
HARVEY, Deborah 78 Kezia 100
Mary 126 Olive 204 Thomas W
100
HARWOOD, David 35 Elizabeth
35 Hannah 35 36 Lucretia 126
HASKELL, Sarah 222 Susan 174
HASTINGS, Betsey 123 Lydia 22
HATCH, Abigail 45 Elizabeth 157
Honora 248 Mary 23 Patience
15
HATHAWAY, Eunice 265
HAVEN, Abram 46 Relief 46
HAVENS, Lorenza 175 Mary 244
HAWES, Hannah 77
HAWKINS, Mary 100 Sallie 236
Sarah 149
HAWKS, Abigail 21
HAWLEY, Abigail 197 Alice 135
Ann 27 Clarinda 199 Mary 37
HAYES, Eliza C 66 Harriet E 66
Molly 270 Newton 66
HAYNES, Abigail 5 Laura 229
Mary 58
HAYWARD, Azubah 83 Benjamin
219 Betty 111 Hannah 219
HAYWOOD, Elizabeth 13 Rachel
121
HAZEN, Abigail 202 Elizabeth
102 Hannah 117 Joseph 102
159 Joshua 202 Mary 1 159
Mercy 102 202
HEACOCK, Lois 122
HEATH, Amelia 268 Elizabeth 23
Rachel 145
HEATON, Mary 48
HEBARD, Alithea 21 Lydia 199
Nathan 21 Zipporah 21
HEBBARD, Lucy 103 Mary 103
Samuel 103 Sarah 222 Zerviah
103
HEBERT, Prudence 62
HECOCK, Maranah 156
HEDGE, Elutheria 48 Samuel 48
HEDGES, Esther 143 Phebe 4

HELMER, Eva 271
HENDEE, Alma 254 Elizabeth
170 Eunice 170 Joshua 170
HENDERSON, Ann 181
HENRY, Mary 75 77
HERBERT, Sarah 110
HERENDEEN, Lydia 200
HERRICK, Althea 146 Amy 171
Arabella 32 Jerusha 99 Nabby
93 Nathan 171 Phineas 60
Sarah 60 Zipporah 60
HEWITT, Elizabeth 36 Increase
35 36 Martha 20 Mary 35 Sally
69
HIBBARD, Abigail 269 Alithea 21
Elizabeth 12 John Jr 269 Mary
52 Nathan 21 Polly 269 Sarah
52 Zerviah 103 Zipporah 21
HICKCOX, Lucy 203 204
HICKOK, Abigail 116 Amanda 261
Ellen 116 Samuel 116 Thankful
58
HICKOX, Charlotte 89 Ruth 123
HICKS, Israel 61 62 Loretta 61
Lucretia 270 Melinda 240
Phebe 61 62
HICOCK, Eunice 246
HIGLEY, Brewster 93 Esther 65
93 Sally 123
HILDRETH, Asenath 113
HILL, Abigail 106 224 261 Abner
90 Bulah 90 Elizabeth 221 Es-
ther 179 Frances 261 Huldah
188 Jane 180 Lucina 10 Lucy
141 Lydia 22 Mary 192 Sarah
49 William 261
HILLIARD, Jesse 42 Sarah 254
HILLS, Amos 144 Harriet 144
Lucy 268
HINCKLEY, Hannah 138
Mehitable 59 Rhoda 15 Zervia
55
HINE, Millicent 238
HINES, Eunice 164 Kezia 88
HINMAN, Rachel 81 Sarah Maria
123
HINSDALE, Lucy D 33 Lydia 25
Mary 208
HITCHCOCK, Abigail 95 101
Jacob 101 Jotham 95 Margaret
257 Maria 142 Mary 95 Sarah
95 240

HIX, Lillie 72
HOADLEY, Abraham 62 Lucretia
   62 Rachel 107 Samuel 107
   Sibyl 107
HOBBIE, C K 253 Clarina 253
   Tamma 253
HOBBY, Sarah 75
HODGE, Judith 94 Mermelia 84
HODGES, Sarah 178
HOISINGTON, Mary 233
   Theodocia 91
HOLBROOK, Sarah 56 122
HOLCOMB, Lucinda 246 Sarah 97
HOLCOMBE, Esther 105 Martha
   101
HOLDEN, Susanna 128
HOLDRICH, Sarah 112
HOLDRIDGE, Nancy 247 Ruth 258
   Temperance 64
HOLLAND, Sarah 9
HOLLISTER, Abiah 108 Abigail
   111
HOLLY, Adeline E 218 Sarah 198
HOLMAN, Mary 29
HOLMES, Charlotte 108 Emma
   131 Hulday 46 Lucretia 184
   Mary 52 153 Orsamus 144
   Priscilla 34 Ruth 144 Tem-
   perance 245
HOLT, Dinah 80
HOLTON, Lois 26
HOOKER, Elizabeth 92 Horace 92
   Mary 92 Polly Goodwin 233
HOPKINS, Clarissa 199 Dorcas 74
   Duty 100 Harriet 234 Jemima
   170 Nehemiah 170 Olive 100
   Rhoda 250 Tryphena 170
   Wealthy 100
HOPSON, Abiah 69 India 50 John
   50 Sarah 50
HOREY, Lorena 165
HORSFORD, Eunice 64 Joseph 64
   Mindwell 64
HOSFORD, Lucinda 264 Naomi 86
   Susannah 141
HOSMER, Sarah 97 Susan 157
HOTCHKISS, Anna 98 Esther 154
   Rebecca 135 Robert 80 Sarah
   80 Susannah 216 Thankful 51
HOUGH, Abiah 70 Clark 262
   Sophia 262
HOUGHTALING, Lena 168

HOUGHTON, Lucretia 184
HOUSE, Anne 132 Lovica 21
   Marcy 21 Mercy 228
HOVER, Sarah 128
HOVEY, Abigail 6 Benjamin 245
   Edmond 113 Elizabeth 213
   Mary 77 78 113 Molly 76 Pris-
   cilla 213 Ruth 245 Vina 265
HOW, Elizabeth 108
HOWARD, David 217 Diademia
   45 Hannah 36 Keziah 178
   Mabel 191 Martha 217 Mary
   183 Priscilla 174 217 Sally 88
   Saloma 12 Sarah 65
HOWD, Hannah 167
HOWE, Abigail 183 Anne 81
   Elizabeth 1 Hannah 261 Jonas
   261 Mary 142 Ruth 164 Sarah
   261
HOWES, Mary 18
HOWLAND, Jerusha 242 Richard
   242
HOYT, Benjamin 29 Deborah 29
   Hannah 238 Ruth 188 Sarah 110
HUBBARD, Abigail 2 111 Eleazer
   111 Elizabeth 265 266
   Nathaniel 137 Polly 137
   Prudence 235 Rachel 181 Sarah
   36 52 146
HUBBELL, Cecilia 149 David 209
   Elizabeth 209 Eunice 109
   Laura 26 209 Richard 109
HUDSON, Augustus 70 Mary 7
   Mehitable 87 Nellie 70 Polly 7
   Sarah 70 190
HUGGINS, Amy 182
HULBERT, Bethia 230
HULBURD, Patience 148
HULET, Sally 262
HULL, Abigail 6 Elizabeth 37
   Esther 6 Hannah 39 119 Jehiel
   39 Mary 95 133 Ruth 39 Sarah
   29 160
HUMPHREY, Charles 86 Clarissa
   86 Daniel 101 Mary 101 Mary
   Goodrich 101 Naomi 86 Persis
   246 Ruth 240
HUNGERFORD, Benjamin 98
   Eunice 220 Mary 98 Rachel
   Rebecca 105 Sally 194 Samuel
   220 Sarah 247 Zurah 161
HUNT, Amelia 141 Betty 30

HUNT (continued)
Grizzel 11 Hannah 235 Huldah
66 Johanna 172 Margaret Sarah
Ann 200
HUNTER, Anna 130 Eunice 129
Sarah 130 William 130
HUNTINGTON, Abigail 111
Andrew 115 Annis 41 Elizabeth
28 Jabez 25 Judith 25 Julia
Ann 128 Laura 229 Lois 132
Mara 191 Margaret 132 Matilda
173 Nathan 28 Philomela 25
Rebecca 96 Ruth 136 Sarah 21
Theophilus 132 Thomas 173
HUNTLEY, Hannah 141
HURD, Abigail 101 Annis 251
Elizabeth 222 Hester 254 Lois
74 Mary 17 Rachel 141 Ruth
149 Sally 193 Silence 101 254
HURLBURT, 105 134 254 Anna 38
Catherine 168 Clarissa 18
Desire 10 Elizabeth 127
Gideon 38 Jerusha 43
Katherine 113 Mabel 18 Mary 8
Mercy 119 Sarah 212
HUSTED, Fanny Barnum 116
HUSTON, Mary 138
HUTCHINS, Abigail 21 Betsey 21
Clarissa 125 Emily 31 Keziah
165 206 Louisa 190 Lydia 83
Sarah 96
HUTCHINSON, Abigail 235
Hezekiah 68 Jemima 227 John
235 Mary 234 235 Sarah 59
HYDE, Abiah 52 Anna 134 Caleb
172 Clarissa 172 Diadama 38
Jonathan 52 Joseph 244 Lucy
52 Mary 174 Phebe 52 Susan
244 Susannah 252 Zerviah 2
INGALLS, Sibyl 27 Zelinda 19
INGHAM, Mila 259
INGRAHAM, Betsey 42
INGRAM, Hannah 221
INMAN, Malvery 80 Mary 80
ISAACS, Abigail 125 Mary 243
Ralph 243 Sally 243
ISBEL, Mariam 128
ISEFT, Esther 54
ISHAM, Lydia 17 Rose 17
Zebulon 17
IVES, Abigail 222 Joanna 222
Joseph 222 Martha Brooks 151

IVES (continued)
Rebecca 194 Sally 173
JACKSON, Abigail 177 Asa 162
Catherine R 162 Mrs 31
JACOBS, Bedee 114 Hannah 217
Lydia 217 Silas 217 Zerviah 50
JANE, Ann 224
JENNINGS, Betsey 128 Joanna 79
JERALD, Experience 270
JESSUP, Sally 137
JEWETT, Amanda 49 Betsey 54
Deborah 138
JOHNSON, Abigail 97 Amos 146
Anna 21 Clarissa 146 David 51
Dinah 97 Elizabeth 45 Hannah
261 265 Isaac 97 Jemima 26
Lucy 1 Lydia 187 Mary 4 44 45
154 199 244 245 Mary E 70
Penelope 186 Peter 245
Phoebe Lush 220 Rebecca 68
Sarah 36 78 146 Susan 51
JONES, Anna 120 Asa 108 Betsey
8 189 Nancy 148 Polly 108
Rachel T 247 Sally 7 Sibyl 107
JORDAN, Betsey 190 Phoebe 261
JOSLIN, Sally 157
JOY, Lydia 25 70 71 Mollie 192
JUDD, Edward M 43 Elizabeth
112 Laura 43 Lydia A 43
JUDSON, Polly 83 Ruth 230
JUNE, David 103 Hannah 103
KEELER, Elizabeth 194 Rebecca
98 Sarah 272
KELLOGG, Anna 243 Benjamin
143 Clara 25 India 50 Keturah
54 Lois 119 Mary 79 Sarah 265
Sarah Gold 143
KELLS, Harriet 176
KELLUM, Lucinda 237 Luther
237
KELLY, Agnes 207 Timothy G
207
KELSEY, Horace 135 Maria 135
Sally 76 Temperance 105
Thankful 219
KENDALL, Eunice 2
KENDRICK, Abigail 214 Anna 153
Lydia 129
KENNEY, Rachel 104
KENT, Betsey 48 Cath 89 Dan 48
Hannah 19 Katherine Griswold
48 Lydia 37 Rachel 243

KETCHAM, Isabel 246
KETCHUM, Phebe 220
KEYES, Elnathan 68 Polly 76
  Ruth 68
KEYSER, Anna 106 John 106
KIBBE, Sarah 17
KIBBEE, Daniel 17 Mary 17
KIDDER, Nabby 167
KILBORN, Elizabeth 22 Esther 9
  Mary 20
KILBOURNE, Mary 118
KILBURN, Abigail 161 Naomi 108
  Sarah 102
KIMBALL, Bethiah 129 Cynthia
  85 Dolly 154 Hannah 14 167
  Jerusha 64 85 John 64 85 Mar-
  tha 137 Mary 154 Patience 244
  Sarah 225
KIMBERLY, Ann 29 Thomas 29
KIMBLE, Keziah 225
KING, Betsey 75 Desiah 76
  Elizabeth 165 Esther 246 Han-
  nah 219 Lucinda 11 Mindwell
  173 Phebe 6 Sally N 42
  Samantha 183 Samuel 76 77
KINGSBURY, Esther 133 Lucrtia
  111
KINGSLEY, Jane 98
KINNE, Chloe 105 J 133 Mary
  Button 119 Melinda 133
KINNEE, Mariam 54
KINNEY, Jemima 64 Joseph 64
KINSTRY, Lucetta 153
KIRBY, Frances Marvin 218
KIRKHAM, Sarah 62
KIRKLAND, Lucretia 142 Lucy 98
KNAPP, Dolly 185 Hannah 148
  Martha 212 Phoebe A 210
  Prudence 178
KNEELAND, Rachel 139
KNICKERBACKER, Deborah 16
  Elizabeth 197
KNIFFEN, Jane 150
KNOWLES, Ermina 139 Urania
  139
KNOWLTON, Abigail 178
  Mehitable 94 Priscilla 217
  Sally 254
LADD, Achsah 58 Anna 62
  Clarissa 41 Daniel 41 Hannah
  123 Irene 42 Persis 41
LAKE, Mary 157

LAMB, Anna 84 Eleanor 151 Lucy
  60 Mercy 125 136
LAMBERT, Dorothy 91
LAMNER, Francis 249 Lucy 249
LAMOREUX, Elizabeth 187
LAMPHERE, Mary 78
LANCKTON, Sophia 155
LANDON, Hannah 116 Mary 34
LANE, Achsah 82 Charles 82
  Sarah 82 Susan 131
LANGDON, Elizabeth Chauncey
  161 Mary 53 Rachel 55
LAPHAM, Melinda 38
LARABEE, Mary 118
LARIBEE, Beulah 122
LARNES, Albasinda 211
LATHAM, Abigail 92 Jemima 53
  Lucy Harris 125 William Har-
  ris 125
LATHROP, Anne 5 Bethiah 111
  Betsey 5 Caroline 106 Deborah
  8 Elizabeth 234 Lydia 86
  Rachel 190 Samuel 111 Sarah
  12 Seth 5
LATIMER, Rebecca 197
LATTIN, Mattie 6
LAWRENCE, Hannah 45 Mary
  199 Rozina 246 Sarah 10
LEACH, Betsey 251 Jane 251
  Joanna 161 Rebecca 3 Richard
  Jr 3 Samuel 251 Tabitha 3
LEAKE, Lucy 113
LEAVENS, James 60 Laurana 60
LEAVITT, Amelia 23 Arabella 23
  Freegrace 23 Jerusha 23
LEAWORTHY, Elizabeth 245
LEDYARD, Deborah 152
LEE, Abigail 259 Amy 235
  Elizabeth 172 Lucy 269 Lydia
  101 Mary 138 156 Rosanna 103
  Sally 255
LEEDS, Experience 104
LEETE, Anne 126 Gideon 126
  Lucretia 126 Lucy Ann 126
LEFFINGWELL, Hannah 160 255
  Polly 199 Samuel 160
LEONARD, David 6 Hannah 6
  Jerusha 228 Sarah 6 60 Sybil
  185
LESLIE, Hannah 244
LESTER, Mary P 5
LETTE, Lydia 67

MARVIN (continued)
Reynold 16 Sarah 197
MASON, Anna 262 Dorothy 20 143
Elias 154 Eunice 139 Lydia
154 271 Mary 3 Sophia 154
Susannah 185
MATHER, Jane M 123 Lucy 3 106
Lydia 123 Sarah 59 Timothy 3
William 59 Zilpha 262
MATHEWS, Abner 230 Lois 230
MATHEWSON, Roxy 198
MATSON, Anna 71 Hannah 88
Lucy 2
MATTESON, Mary 230
MATTHEWS, Else 123
MATTISON, Mehitable 108
MAY, Anna 47 Asa 47 Ephraim 47
Henrietta 47 Lucy 47 Molly 47
MAYNARD, Ruth 94
MCALLISTER, Margaret 202
Mary 202
MCCAY, Polly 137
MCCLEVELAND, Lydia 32
MCCLURE, Orinda 221
MCCONNELL, Christiana 268
MCCURE, Agnes 233
MCDONALD, Lucretia 106
MCDUFFEE, Jane 24
MCEWEN, Abigail 101 Bertha 34
Phebe 101 Timothy 101
MCFALL, Betsey 251
MCKINSTRY, Paul 69 Sarah 69
MCKNIGHT, Abigail 211
MCLARIN, Rachel 155
MCLEAN, Ann 250
MCMASTERS, Hannah T 47
MCMULLEN, Archibald 236
Lucretia 236 Melissa 236
MCNAUGHTON, Nancy 233
MCNEAL, Sarah 143
MCNITT, Sally 136
MCWHORTER, Janett 237
MEACH, Mehitable 2
MEACHAM, Jerusha 64 Lucia
Ann 92 Sarah 72 Sybel 83 Wil-
liam 72
MEACHUM, Hannah 119
MEAD, Abigail 25 Belinda 79
Dorcas 94 Hannah 48 James 94
Jemima 226 Martha 183 Mary
140 Phebe 45 104 Polly 96
Tammy 217 William 48

MEADE, Ellen 92
MEECH, Betsey 168
MEEKER, Betsey 152 Clarissa
238 Eleanor 29 Ellen 29
Joanna 147 Rebecca 18
MEIGS, Elizabeth 49 Janna 49
Rachel 228
MELINA, Abigail 45 John 45
Sarah 45
MERCHANT, Ann 13 Gurdon 13
MERCY, Lucy 211
MERRELL, Betsey 189
MERRIAM, Abigail 68 Beulah 130
Charlotte 231 James 231
Thankful 204
MERRICK, Abigail 6
MERRILL, Abigail 101 Betsey 40
Hannah 1 29 Martha 126
MERRILLS, Olive 182
MERRIMAN, Electa 223 Lois 143
Phebe 156 Ruth 121 Thankful
247
MERRITT, Eliza 76 Michael 162
Rebecca 162 Truba 185
MERWIN, Hannah 54 Lydia 85
Martha 253
MESSENGER, Daniel 109 Lydia
109 Susanna 109 Susannah 109
METCALF, Lydia 178 Mehitable
178 Sally 258 Samuel 178
MILBER, Ruth 139
MILES, Hannah 40
MILLER, Abigail 263 Almira 9
Bethuel 156 157 Betsey 115
Diadema 244 Drake 263 Esther
9 Hannah 40 Lucy Swift 154
Mary 156 Rachel 268 Roxalana
202 Unice 147 William 9
MILLINGTON, Mary 184
MILLINTON, Martha 103
MILLS, 114 Amelia 150 Augustus
85 Elizabeth 240 Gideon 240
Judith 211 Louisa 85 Peletiah
163 Polly 148 Ruth 33 240
Sarah 57 163
MINER, Dolly 154 John 154 Laura
60 Mary 154
MINOR, Grace 20
MITCHELL, Mary 254
MOBBS, Eunice 119 Pierce 119
Sarah 119
MOFFIT, Anny 6

MONTAGUE, Experience 254
MOON, Electa Ward 226
MOOR, Ruth 256
MOORE, Anna 89 Benjamin 121
Catherine 89 Deborah 258
Eunice 39 157 Eunice W 63
Margaret Nathan 121 Mary 142
225 Richard 89
MOREHOUSE, Molly 171 Trial
245
MOREY, Belinda 152 Lydia 179
Samuel 152
MORGAN, Chloe 71 Edward 66
Enos 71 Grace 66 Gurdin 237
Hannah 7 Lois 71 Lucinda 9
Margaret 269 Maria L 237
Mary 90 189 Nancy 2 Olive 226
Salome 105 Sophia 237
MORRILL, Abraham 110 Rhoda
110 Sarah 110
MORRIS, Darius 28 Fanny
Chandler 28 Letitia 47
Rebecca 28 Sarah 47 William
47
MORSE, Anna 225 Eliza Anna 195
John 35 Joseph 132 Lydia 47
Martha 132 Martha Carpenter
225 Paul 225 Sarah 35 Susan-
nah 35
MOSELEY, Anna 67 68 Increase
67
MOSHER, Jerusha 146 Nicholas
146 Polly 146
MOSLEY, Betsey 145
MOSS, Elizabeth 94 219 John 72
Lydia 72 Martha 216 Rachel 97
Sarah 72
MOULTON, Eunice 77 Samuel 77
Sarah 77
MOWER, Ezra 145 Olive 145
Phebe 145
MOXLEY, Sally 61
MUDGE, Dinah 66
MULFORD, Elizabeth 194
MUMFORD, Lydia 120
MUNGER, Abigail 87
MUNN, James Jr 15 Martha 15
Mary 15 Patience 94 Sarah 245
MUNSELL, Lucinda 242
MUNSON, Abel 182 Esther 161
Eunice 12 Levi 248 Mabel 182
Mary 182 248 Mehitable 182

MUNSON (continued)
Milla 50 Sarah 182
MURDOCK, Abigail 134 Anna 32
Margaret 171 Thomas 32 171
MURRAY, Susanna 98
MYERS, Catherine 92 Michael 92
Nancy 92
MYGATT, Clarissa 117 Comfort
263 Elizabeth 117 Noadiah 117
Polly 263
NAPIER, Anna 184
NASON, Elias 154 Lydia 154
Sophia 154
NATHAN, Margaret 121
NEARING, Henry 119 Lois 119
NEEDHAM, Anna 27 Marcia 126
Ruth 3
NEFF, Abigail 76 Joseph 76
Patience 76
NELSON, Rosamond 69
NESS, Mary Ann 172
NEWCOMB, Abigail 10 Deborah
72 Jemima 64 129
NEWELL, Mehitabel 23 Mercy
232 Sarah 91
NEWMAN, Elizabeth 162
NEWTON, Asahel 33 Bethia 33
Lois 171 Mary 100 Polly 177
NIBLACH, Mary 15
NICHOLS, Comfort 82 Elizabeth
82 Hannah 82 Ruth 160 Sally
99 Samuel 82
NILES, Nancy 252
NIMS, Lucinda 191
NOBLE, Clarissa 202 James 20
Joanna 85 210 Lucretia 102
Olive 20 252 Susan 148
NOBLES, Rebecca 224
NOBLET, Joanna 210
NODDINS, Charlotte 210
NORCROSS, Sarah 198
NORTH, Lucy 28 Samuel 28 Syl-
via 28
NORTHAM, Experience 122 Lydia
137
NORTHROP, Sara 23
NORTHRUP, Caroline 157 Cyrus
157 Rebecca 27
NORTON, Anna 260 Charlotte 170
Huldah 40 Mary 152 Olive 35
Ruth 231 Sarah 78 161
NOYES, David 255 Rebecca 255

NUTTING, Resign M 223
NYE, Lois 163 Peninah 106
  Prudence 178
ODELL, Esther J 218 Peter 218
  Sarah 218
OGDEN, Abigail 140 David 176
  Eunice 176 Jane 176 Phebe 11
OLCOTT, Eunice 120
OLDS, Submit 71
OLIVE, Mary 271
OLIVER, Abigail 261
OLMSTEAD, Eunice 4 Rachel 262
  Susannah 114
OLNEY, Sarah 149
ONDERDONK, Susan 147
OPSON, Erastus 228 Hannah 228
ORCUTT, Daniel 23 Lydia 23
  Mary 71 Solomon 71 Susanna
  25 70 71
ORDWAY, Jacob 86 Mary 86
  Rebecca 86
ORMS, Patience 269
ORMSBEE, Betsey 76
ORMSBY, Gideon 81 Hannah 81
ORVIS, Betsey 76
OSBORN, Mary 131 Prudence 161
OVIATT, Maria 121
OWEN, Amy 30 Electa 46 Irene
  24 25 Joel 46 Joseph 24 Mary
  46 Rachel 271 Ruth 24 Sarah 4
PACKER, Priscilla 162
PADDOCK, Eunice 231
PAGE, Hannah 133 Leah 110 Lois
  259
PAINE, Abigail 183 Elisha 183
  Elizabeth 76
PALMER, Ann 251 Anna 95 Anne
  70 Betsey 77 Elizabeth 197
  244 Hannah 77 166 Hannah
  Rebeckah 134 Huldah 63 199
  Isaac S 70 Lucy 270 Malinda
  105 Martha 152 Mary 25 89
  Parmelia 50 Rachel 47
  Roderick 77 Sabra 225 Susan-
  nah 184
PANGBORN, Hannah 247
PARDEE, Lavinia 16 Martha 114
  Mary 122
PARISH, Sally 75
PARKE, Daniel 179 Esther 179
  Hannah 88 Mary 128 Sally 179

PARKER, Abigail 83 Damarius
  169 David 117 Elizabeth 4 117
  Emma 127 Eunice 41 Hannah
  95 Jane 40 Mary 234 Olive 65
  Peace 65 Phoebe 168 Ruth 147
  Sally 60 Sarah 65 73 Zachariah
  65
PARKHURST, Eunice 105
PARKS, Betsey 39 Clarissa 11
  Daniel 11 Margery 30 Paul 30
  Simeon 39
PARMELE, Temperance 7
PARMELEE, Anne 126 Eunice
  146 Lucy 95 Mabel 102
PARMELY, Mabel 13 Thomas 13
PARMENTER, Sally 108
PARMERLEE, Mary 68
PARMLY, Lydia 115
PARSONS, Abigail 101 Anna 173
  Hannah 103 John 173 Martha
  134
PART, Sarah Kilham 183
PARTRIDGE, Amy 244 245 Han-
  nah 22 97
PATRICK, Jane 40 Mary 72 Sarah
  207
PATTERSON, Hannah 149 Naomi
  129 Rhoda 131
PATTISON, Betsey 271
PATTON, Fanny 267
PAUL, Abigail 114 Elizabeth 105
PAYNE, Elisha 97 Jemima 217
  Mary 80 97
PEABODY, Asa 214 Keziah 129
  Mary 214 Polly 214 Resolved
  35 Sarah 249 Sophie 35
PEACOCK, Hannah 157 158
PEAK, Esther 143 Lois 143
PEAKE, Christopher 36 Ex-
  perience 35 36 Mary 36 Sarah
  35
PEARCE, Keziah 57
PEARL, Elizabeth 104
PEARSALL, Cynthia 272 Daniel
  272 Dwight 272 Erma 272
PEASE, Anna 102 Christopher 102
  Cynthia 36 Eleaba 171
  Elizabeth 3 Hannah 87 90
  Theodora 102
PECK, Abigail 22 91 97 Ann 93
  Augusta M 50 Caty 8 Diana

PECK (continued)
174 Eliza 236 Elizabeth 10 55
100 147 Esther 31 Frances 14
Henry 55 Jeremiah 93 Joanna
72 Lucy 14 Mary 91 Ollie 209
Patience 40 Peleg 174 Rachel
93 Sally 23 Sarah 156 182 223
Taylor 14 Zebulon 91 100
PEIRCE, Melinda 54
PELLET, Caroline E 214
PELLETT, Phebe 2
PELTON, Elizabeth 73 Lucy 138
PENDLETON, Catherine 272
Clarissa 2
PENFIELD, Elizabeth 88
PENNOCK, Elizabeth 3
PENTICE, Mary 214
PERIN, Huldah 45
PERKINS, Charity 132 Elisha 144
Emma 267 Hannah 33 Jacob 96
267 Jerusha 117 Lucy 96 Lydia
223 Susan 144
PERRIN, Asa 177 178 Esther 140
Hannah 177 178 Levina 97
Mehitable 172
PERRY, Abigail 261 Elizabeth
169 Hannah 232 Mary 134 Mary
F 203 Mehitable 236 Merab 69
Ruth 31
PETERS, John 110 John Jr 10
Lydia 10 Margaret 142 Mary
110 123 124 Philena 110 Taph-
ner 257
PETTIS, Elizabeth 1 Joshua 1
Rhoda 1
PHELPS, Abigail 6 7 13 89 266
Arthusa 150 Charles 79 266
Cynthia 62 Dorothy 266 Hep-
zibah 79 Lucy 110 Lydia 179
Mindwell 207 Polly 209 Ruth
39 Ruthven 209 Sarah 180
Susanna 70 180 Susannah 85
Timothy 6
PHILLIPS, Esther 128 John 128
Julia 260 Mary 121 210 Silva
52
PHILLPS, Mary 120
PICKERT, Achsah 87 Bar-
tholomew 87
PICKETT, 109
PIERCE, Esther 73 Eunice 53
Jedediah 199 Lois 9 199

PIERCE (continued)
Lydia 59 Mercy 122 Nathaniel
112 Phebe 112 Philena 166
Priscilla 112 Sarah 89 Susan
199
PIKE, Lydia 217
PINGREE, Beulah 111 Mary 111
Sylvanus 111
PINKHAM, Lydia 145
PINNEY, Isaac 70 Priscilla 215
Sarah 70 Susanna 70 191
PITCHER, Mary 5
PITKIN, Rhoda 20 Thomas 20
PITTEE, Julia Wilder 264
PITTS, Saloma 90
PIXLEY, Polly 109
PLATT, Elizabeth 50 Fanny Bar-
num 116 Laura M 15
PLUMB, Lydia 223 Rachel 135
Rebecca 213 Silvia 203
PLUMLEY, Abigail 61 Sally 214
POMEROY, Abi 21 Rhoda 207
POND, Content 59 Thankful 78
136
POOLA, Thirza 140
POOR, Ezoa 234 Jemima 53
POPE, Hannah 140
PORTER, Abigail 253 Asa 73
Eleanor 140 Esther 219
Jemima 138 John 142 165
Lydia 142 Mabel 30 Mary 73
257 Polly 244 Samuel 140
Sarah 165 219
POST, Abigail 8 Mehitabel 79
Ruth 21
POTTER, Elizabeth 70 Esther
164
POWELL, Elizabeth 191 Lucy 45
Lydia 131 Molly 202
POWERS, Catherine 198
PRATT, Abiah 113 Abigail 110
Elizabeth 263 Isaac 263
Jerusha 76 Justin 110 Mary 17
Sarah 110
PRAY, Abigail 253
PRENTICE, Esther 167
PRENTIS, Rebecca W B 151
PRENTISS, Mary 41 Patty 246
Sarah E 104
PRESCOTT, Elizabeth 42 James
42 Jesse 42 Sarah 42
PRESTON, Almira 168

ROCKWELL, Betsey 148 Beulah
23 Jemima 154 Lois 204 Mary
71 Polly 23
ROGER, Mary 3
ROGERS, Charlotte 209 Ebenezer
6 Elizabeth 51 162 Joseph 51
Rebecca 39 Ruth 6 Sarah 11
Sarah Elizabeth 109
RON, John 264 Julia Ann 264
Rebecca 264
ROOD, Abigail 257 Betsey 248
Eunice 62 Jabez 62 Lydia 233
Mehitable 62 Sarah 75
ROOT, Abigail 44 Abigail L 149
Dorothy 266 Ebenezer 44
Elizabeth 187 Jesse 35 Joanna
58 Lucretia 191 Lydia 75 Mary
206 Ruth E 151 Sallie 33 Sarah
87 Sophia 35 Thankful 176
Wealthy 44 Wm 44
ROOTS, Elizabeth 170
ROPER, Eliza M 203
ROSE, Deborah 84 171 Hannah
128 Harriet 12 Kezia 222
Lurana 143 Sarah 222 229
Zachariah 222
ROSS, Elizabeth 255
ROSSETER, Honor 185
ROSSITER, Clarissa 55
ROWE, Lucy 217
ROWELL, Lois 248
ROWLAND, Azubah 101 Lydia
101 Mary 65 Rebecca 41
Tamor 91 Uriah 101
ROWLEY, Abigail 85 Elizabeth
85 Mary 55 Samuel 85
ROYCE, Abigail 10 Benedict 192
Elizabeth 52 Jerusha 192
Lydia 109 Martha 99 Mehitable
247 Phineas 247 Sarah 134
Thankful 247
RUDE, Rufus 228 Sarah 228
RUGGLES, Catherine 142 Joseph
27 Mercy 27 Rachel 27 Tamar
Ann 33
RUMRILL, Phebe 75
RUMSEY, Sarah 188
RUNDEL, Sarah 194
RUNDLE, Hannah 167
RUSHMORE, Phebe 207
RUSSELL, Amelia 241 Ann 177
Benjamin 241 Dorcas 121

RUSSELL (continued)
Hannah 146 John 101 121 Olive
44 Rebecca 101 Ruhamah 145
Sally 241 Sarah 101
RUST, Anna 191
RYDER, Benjamin 253 Mehitable
253
RYON, Mary 17
SABIN, Anna 114 Jeptha 114
Maria 114 Sarah 78
SACKET, Lorinda 14
SACKETT, Abigail 225 Mary 41
Mehitable 6
SAGE, Jedediah 127 Sarah 127
SALISBURY, Rebecca 79
SALTER, Mary E L 55 Matilda
194
SAMSON, Mercy 117 Olive 62
SANBORN, Dorothy 62
SANDERSON, Elizabeth M 116
SANDFORD, Sylvia 182
SANFORD, Abigail 137 Catherine
116 Charlotte 231 Deborah 85
Lois 50 Lucina 32 Mabel 11
Phebe 43 Samantha 136
SANFRERE, Mary 10 Polly 10
SANGER, Tirza 56
SARGEANT, Dr 26 Esther 242
Sarah 26
SARGENCE, Submit 82
SARGENT, Anna 73 Submit 82
SATERLEE, Electa 179
SAUNDERS, Betsey 109 Harriet
115
SAVAGE, Abigail 25 Lucy 160
Lydia 258
SAWYER, Eunice 119 Lydia 31
Mary 67 111
SAXTON, Polly 65
SAYRE, Abner 147 Anna Nancy
147 Joanna 147
SCARRIT, Anna 107
SCHRIVER, Charlotte 89
SCOFIELD, Joseph 17 Mary 17
SCOTT, Charity 138 Ellen 78
Hannah 194 Huldah 232 James
194 Mercy 124 Oramel 138
Saloma 66 Sylvester 232
SCOVEL, Mary 78 79
SCOVILLE, Chloe 105 Daniel 269
Hannah 255 256 Rebecca 269
Susannah 48

TRAVIS, Elizabeth Ann 175
TREADWAY, Sarah 122 126
TREADWELL, Ann Marie 188
    Hope 143
TREAT, Jane 158
TREGO, Francenia 84
TRIPP, Anna 65
TROWBRIDGE, Hannah 68 Isaac
    31 Rachel 31 Ruth 31
TRUE, Abigail 52
TRUMAN, Annie 195 Jonathan
    195 Joseph 195 Polly 195 Sally
    195
TRUMBULL, Catherine 118 Julia
    269 Julianna 269
TRYON, Honor 162 Huldah 97
TUBBS, Deborah 269 Mary Smith
    98
TUCKER, Clarissa 46 Dorothy 96
    Hulday 46 Lois 37 Mary 37
    Stephen 37 Zephaniah 46
TUCKERMAN, Susanna 136
TULLER, Polly 15
TUNERCLIFF, Amelia 122
TURNER, Anna 63 Betsey 106
    Esther 25 Hannah 94 Lydia 145
    Moses 94 Sarah 34 35
TURRELL, Abel 231 Polly 231
TUTE, Mary 192 Sarah 71
TUTTLE, Abigail 22 Dolly 170
    Lydia 176 Mary 45 Mehitable
    50 Sarah 169 Thomas 45
TYLER, Abigail 5 Elizabeth 36
    Esther 89 Hannah 63 Lucy 87
    Mabel 165 Mary 57 Mehetable
    83 112 Patience 170 Rachel
    242 Rebecca 242 Samuel 242
    Sarah 160 Susanna 130
TYRELL, Thirza 228 Thomas 228
UDALL, Dorothy 143
UNDERWOOOD, Susanna 3
UPHAM, Asa 59 Eunice 59 Lydia
    59 Mary 194 Sophia 249
UPSON, Polly 176
URSLEY, Eunice 44
UTLEY, Olive 187
VALANCE, Huldah 148
VAN BENTHUYSEN, Sarah 227
VAN BURGH, Elizabeth 149 Hex-
    ton 149
VAN CAMPEN, Elsche 205
VAN VALKENBURGH, Alphia 40

VAN VRANKEN, Mary 198 199
VAN WAGENEN, Agnes 177 Ger-
    rit 177
VANDENBURGH, Catherine R 95
VANDERBURG, Margaret 96
VANDERBURGH, Mary 84
VAUGHN, Jonathan 210 Lucy 40
    Mary 210 Sarah 210
VIBBER, Hannah 160
VINANT, Mary 106
VINCENT, Jonathan 130 Loretta
    130 Rebecca 130 Sally 106
    William 106 Zeruiah Sarviah
    106
VINTON, Nancy 75
VOWLES, Phebe 140
WADE, George Jr 3 Hannah 3
    Mary 3
WADHAMS, Abigail 4 Solomon 4
WADSWORTH, Hannah 170
WAID, Eliza Emaline 180 Pem-
    ber 180
WAKEFIELD, Huldah 40
WAKELY, Abner 234 Phebe 234
    Sarah 234
WAKEMAN, Abigail 200
    Ebenezer 224 Eunice 224 Ruth
    29 220 Sarah 29 Wm 29
WALCOTT, Eunice 158 Marcy
    158 Miriam 158 Stephen 158
WALCUTT, Sarah 76
WALDO, Clarissa 265 Daniel 180
    Lois 180 Matilda 143 Ruth 14
    S A 143 Susannah 180
WALKER, Elizabeth 198 269
    Margaret 168 Mary 85 Phebe
    17 Sally 172 Sarah 172 266
WALLACE, Anna 115
WALLER, Sarah 164
WALLEY, Mary 146
WALLIS, Huldah 157
WALTER, Catherine 238 Mary
    240
WANBELTON, Clarissa 192
WANZER, Martha 133
WARD, Abigail 83 Affa 229 Anna
    87 Eunice 113 Fanny 65
    Ichabod 65 Mary 26 89 Olive
    Kingsley 258 Orpha 79 Phebe
    74 Roxanna 247
WARNER, Abraham 17 Azubal 17
    Benjamin 100 101

WHITNEY (continued)
104 Lucy 66 Lydia 25 Mary
224 Sabra 247 Sarah 93 Sarah
Roberts 187 Tamar 234
WHITON, Judith 214 Sarah 58
WHITTAKER, Prudence 70 Sarah
134
WHITTEMORE, Elizabeth 60
Mary 15
WICKHAM, Lucretia 187
WICKWIER, Bridget 267
WIGHT, Dr 133 Jemima 133
WILBER, Marie C 166
WILCOX, Abigail 253 Christiana
Phelps 64 Ebenezer 64
Elizabeth 222 Grace 253 Han-
nah 214 Jemima 225 John 253
Lavina 173 Lydia 264 Martha
64 Mary Ann 98 Sarah 79 Si-
lence 187
WILD, Mary 159
WILDER, Charity Brink 142
David 142 Sarah 63
WILDMAN, Esther 116 Grace 197
Samuel 116
WILEY, Azubah 78 Deborah 78
Judah 78
WILHAM, Esther 9
WILKINSON, Hannah 203
WILLARD, Abigail 14 George 29
Hannah 29 Susan 148
WILLCOCKS, Anne 154
WILLET, Philena 157 Sarah 186
WILLEY, Abel 29 Deborah 29
Grace 99 Mary 29
WILLIAMS, 216 Abigail 94
Adoshe 21 Desire 233 Dorothy
28 Elizabeth 209 259 Emily 34
Eunice 173 Experience 58 Hul-
dah 179 Joseph 254 Loretta
130 Mary 197 228 Mercy 160
Pamelia 175 Phebe 19 Phineas
68 Sally 254 Weltha 66 Zer-
viah 24
WILLIS, Delia 98
WILLOUGHBY, 220 Sarah 18
WILLSON, Diana 175
WILMARTH, Orissa 29
WILSON, Ann 256 Eliza 76
Elizabeth 227 232 267 Huldah
224 Lovica 21 Lucinda 256
Mary 117 230 234 235 248

WILSON (continued)
Olive 181 Polly 146 230 Rhoda
232
WINANS, James 219 Sarah 219
WINCHELL, Lucy 240 Martin 240
WINCHESTER, Sarah 206
WINDHIP, Abigail 12
WINEGAR, Catherine 44 Conradt
44
WING, Lucy 227
WINSLOW, Hannah 131
WINTON, Susanna 81
WISE, Abigail 24 Experience 11
12 Hannah 144 209 Sarah 145
WISHARPT, Catherine 181
WITTER, Esther 160 Polly 9 58
WOLCOTT, Abigail 92 Alexander
92 Betsey 145 Mary 92
WOLF, Ruhama 174
WOOD, Abigail 102 Almira 224
Ann 201 Elizabeth 69 134 Es-
ther 234 Hannah 114 Nancy 4
WOODARD, Phebe 183
WOODBRIDGE, Harriet 234
WOODBURY, Aptha 129
WOODHOUSE, Abigail 85 Mary
85 William 85
WOODIN, Cornelia 222
WOODMANSEE, Sally 155
WOODRUFF, Barnes 111
WOODS, Betsey 62 Lucy 227
Mary 163 Polly 201 Samuel 62
201
WOODSIDE, Mary B 6
WOODWARD, Abigail 80 Abisha
207 Betsey 106 207 Daniel 171
Deborah 221 Hannah 242 Irene
106 Jacob 80 Mehitable 140
Rebecca Smith 87 Ruth 24 171
Sarah 24 Thankful 171 Thomas
140
WOODWORTH, Sarah 206
WOOSTER, Mary 100 Miriam 100
Moses 100
WORCESTER, Naomi 86
WORDEN, Jane 16
WORK, Betty 111 Hannah 111
Joseph 111
WORTHLEY, Betsey 58
WRIGHT, Abial 32 Benjamin 98
Charles 24 Diana 64 Ebenezer
208 Edith 163 Eliza 237